Environmental and Resource Economic

Environmental and Resource Economics: An Introduction

Second Edition

Michael Common

LONGMAN

Addison Wesley Longman Limited
Edinburgh Gate
Harlow, Essex CM20 2JE, England
and Associated Companies throughout the world.

*Published in the United States of America
by Addison Wesley Longman Publishing, New York*

First published 1988
Second Edition 1996

ISBN 0 582 24632-6 PPR

British Library Cataloguing-in-Publication Data

A catalogue record for this book is
available from the British Library

Library of Congress Cataloging-in-Publication Data

Common, Michael S.
    Environmental and resource economics: an introduction/Michael
        Common. – 2nd ed.
    p. cm.
    Includes bibliographical references and index.
    ISBN 0-582-24632-6
    1. Economic development – Environmental aspects.   2. Environmental
        policy. I. Title.
HD75.6.C645 1996
333.7–dc20

                                                            96-24368
                                                            CIP

Set by 32 in 10/12pt Times
Produced by Longman Singapore Publishers (Pte) Ltd
Printed in Singapore

To My Parents

Contents

Preface to Second Edition

Since I wrote the first edition of this book in 1986/7, the world has moved on in a number of, related, ways that affect what an introductory text in environmental and resource economics should cover. In 1987 the publication of the 'Brundtland Report' (World Commission on Environment and Development 1987) put the concept of 'sustainable development' on the agenda for political debate and action. In the 1990s the problems of climate change and biodiversity loss have come to the fore as global environmental problems. The literature on environmental and resource economics has grown enormously, and economists have been prominent in debates about sustainable development, and the means to its attainment. The claims of economists in such debates have been contested, and the usefulness of their methodology has been questioned. There has emerged what claims to be a new sort of economics – 'ecological economics' – that is more relevant to the issues arising in the sustainable development context. And, inevitably, since 1986/7 my own thinking about economics and the natural environment has been modified by these developments.

In preparing this second edition, it seemed natural to reflect all this principally in a new final chapter, Chapter 9, which has the title 'Sustainable development'. In Chapters 1 to 8, the major changes from the first edition are as follows. I have updated the 'Commentary' sections. Chapter 4 now includes a short discussion of the theory of comparative advantage in relation to international trade, which is the background to a new section in Chapter 5 dealing with trade and the environment. In Chapter 8, the discussion of the valuation of non-marketed environmental services is updated, extended and reorganised, and there is a new section on risk and uncertainty. There are many other relatively minor changes to content and organisation. The intended audience, and the motivation for the content and manner of exposition, remain as stated in the Preface to the first edition.

The acknowledgements made in the original Preface need extending as follows. To students at the Australian National University and the University of York, for comments on, and criticisms of, lectures. To Fay Goddard, Edilyn Bajracharya and, especially, Kali Sanyal for help in the preparation of the new manuscript.

Preface

The subject matter of this book is the relationship between economic activity and the natural environment as perceived by economists working in the mainstream of their discipline. It deals with what such economists have to say about the exploitation of natural resources, about environmental pollution, and about the natural environment as a source of enjoyment. I have not, on these topics, tried to say anything new. I have attempted to set out the main parts of the extant corpus of resource and environmental economics in the simplest possible way. In doing this I have focused primarily on analytical rather than empirical material, for reasons to be explained here. The book is intended to be suitable as a course text in two contexts.

It is first addressed to students doing environmental science programmes. All such programmes should involve at least one economics course, and many do. Texts for such courses do exist, but it is my view that they typically concentrate too much on the applications of economics to environmental problems and give insufficient coverage of the conceptual basis of the economic analysis being applied. This is, I think, one of the main reasons why one finds that so many environmental scientists are 'anti-economics' in a rather incoherent and ill-informed way. I do not imagine, nor do I hope, that environmental science students whose economics course is based on this book will be 'pro-economics'. I do hope that they will understand the way economists approach environmental questions, and properly appreciate the insights this approach can offer. For this audience particularly, it is not my intention to 'sell' economics but rather to explain it. No previous knowledge of economics is assumed, and no mathematics beyond simple algebra is used. Apart from the introductory Chapter 1, each chapter comprises the exposition of an analytical story, usually in terms of simple numerical examples, followed by a commentary section which relates the analysis to 'real world' issues and circumstances and provides a guide to additional and further reading. Chapters 2 to 4 and 6 deal with basic economic analysis, Chapters 5, 7 and 8 are where the specifically environmental material is covered. For students doing environmental science programmes the book as a whole should provide the basis for an economics course which can vary in length and depth according to the instructor's assignment of chapters and material dealt with, or referred to, in the commentary sections. For example, a short course could be based on the first five chapters and would be about economics and environmental pollution. A cautionary note to instructors is in order with respect to the final two chapters. Dealing as they do with natural resources and cost benefit analysis, they are obviously of considerable relevance to environmental scientists. However, they cannot be properly understood without the background, which is Chapter 6. Indeed, it is my view that a major source of the communications problems which arise between economists and those concerned with and for the environment on these topics is precisely that neither of the parties is sufficiently clear about the way in which the relevant economic analysis is based on the approach set out in Chapter 6 here.

The book can also be used as a text for an intermediate level course within an economics programme, where it is not possible to assume that the students have any background in mathematics. In this second context Chapters 2 to 4 could be covered rather quickly. I do not think that this material could be entirely dispensed with since although much of the content might have been covered in introductory courses, the approach and emphasis here are likely to be somewhat novel. Chapter 6 includes material on intertemporal efficiency, which is not usually dealt with in introductory economics courses, and which is often overlooked in intermediate courses. This material is, to repeat, essential preparation for the subsequent chapters. Chapters 5, 7 and 8 deal with specifically environmental and resource matters; Chapter 1 deals with the links between economic activity and the environment, and how economists have dealt with such in the past. Again, the use of the book can be adjusted to the length of the course by the extent to which the commentary sections are used. I have, where possible, avoided providing references to journal articles, since such are likely to be technically beyond the audience, of either kind, to which the book is addressed. I have, however, provided directions to the relevant chapters of more advanced texts in the field where instructors requiring such will find references to the original contributions to the literature.

I have used various parts of the book in courses for environmental science and economics students over a number of years. There have been arising comments and criticisms which I have tried to take on board, and I thank the students concerned. I also thank a number of colleagues for their comments and suggestions: Nick Hanley, Peter Bird, and Ron Shone. Anne Cowie did the typing with her usual skill, and displayed great patience through the various revisions. Thanks also to Shirley Hewitt for her help with the drawing of the figures. Branwen, Jane, and Stephanie saw less of me than they might otherwise have done over the periods when I was working intensively on the book. It is usual to express thanks in this respect and I do.

List of figures

List of tables

Acknowledgements

We are grateful to the following for permission to reproduce copyright material:

Ballinger Publishing Company for Table 5.9 from table 2.1, p. 22 of *Environmental Policy: Air Quality*, Volume II by Tolley, Graves and Cohen, Copyright 1982 Ballinger Publishing Company; Organisation for Economic Co-Operation and Development, Paris, for Table 2.12 from table 3.2, p. 55 of *Pollution Charges in Practice*, O.E.C.D. 1980; Penguin Books Ltd. for Table 5.10 from table 16, p. 164 of *Economics and the Environment* by Allen V. Kneese, copyright © Allen V. Kneese, 1977.

We are unable to trace the copyright owner of table 2.11 which appeared on p. 269 of *Economics, Environmental Policy and the Quality of Life* by W. Baumol and W. Oates (1979) and would appreciate any information which would enable us to do so.

Chapter 1

Introduction: economics and the environment

This is a book about economic analysis and its application to questions concerning man's use of the natural environment. It is written primarily for an audience with a small or non-existent previous acquaintance with economics. In the first section of this introductory chapter we look at the historical evolution of economics. In the second we consider the interconnections between economic activity and the natural environment. The final section sets out the objectives of the book and describes its approach and organisation.

1.1 Economics

According to a widely used introductory economics textbook,

> Economics is the study of how people make their living, how they acquire the food, shelter, clothing, and other material necessities and comforts of this world. It is a study of the problems they encounter, and of the ways in which these problems can be reduced.
>
> (Wonnacott and Wonnacott, 1979)

In this section we provide a brief outline of the history of the subject of economics, so defined. The outline is not only brief, but it is also selective, highlighting those developments of particular relevance to the material to follow in later chapters. Readers who are interested in a fuller and more balanced account of the history of economics will find what they require in, for example, Spiegel (1971) or Blaug (1985). Those texts concentrate on the evolution of the mainstream economics which is to be set out and used in this book. An account of the history of the subject which takes a less orthodox perspective, and which emphasises more the critiques of orthodoxy which have always been an important part of the subject, is to be found in Hunt and Sherman (1981).

Classical economics

Concern with the problems people encounter in making their living is as old as human civilisation itself. However, it is usual to regard 1776 as the date when economics, as a separate and systematic study of such problems, came into being. In that year Adam Smith published *The Wealth of Nations*. According to Blaug (1985), this was 'the first full-scale treatise on economics': it contained both historical and theoretical treatments of all aspects of economics as defined above. Smith was concerned with using economic analysis to derive recommendations regarding economic policy. In this respect, his book is widely famous principally on account of the enunciation of the doctrine of the invisible hand:

> But it is only for the sake of profit that any man employs his capital in the support of industry; and he will always, therefore, endeavour to employ it in the support of that industry of which the produce is likely to be of the greatest value, or to exchange for the greatest quantity, either of money or of other goods ... he is in this, as in many other cases, led by an invisible hand to promote an end which was no part of his intention ... By pursuing his own interest he frequently promotes that of society more effectively than when he really intends to promote it.
>
> (Smith, 1776, Book IV, Ch. 2)

Smith perceived that there were circumstances and arrangements in which purely selfish behaviour by individuals could serve the interests of society as a whole. The arrangements were those of an economy organised on the basis of competitive markets. This was a profound insight. Much of the subsequent work of economists has sought to make precise the notion of the interest of society and to establish exactly the conditions under which it could be true that selfish individual behaviour would serve that interest. As we shall see later in this book (Ch. 4 especially), the conditions necessary for Smith's 'invisible hand' of the market to work effectively in the general interest are highly restrictive. The doctrine of the invisible hand is not an adequate guide through the economic problems that a society faces. This is particularly the case with respect to man's exploitation of the natural environment.

Smith lived from 1723 to 1790, and was the first of a group of economists now known as the *classical economists*. Other eminent classical economists were Thomas Malthus (1766–1834), David Ricardo (1772–1823) and John Stuart Mill (1806–73). These classical economists were much concerned with what we would now call environmental questions, in that they were interested in the consequences for the long-run development of the material standard of living of the fact that nature had not seen fit to provide man with limitless amounts of good quality land from which to win the 'necessities and comforts of this world'. Their assessment was a gloomy one. Economic progress was seen as an essentially transient phenomenon, and for a long time economics was known as 'the dismal science'. This now appears somewhat ironical. As we shall see in 1.2, and as the reader is probably aware, in the early 1970s the idea of environmental 'limits to growth' gained some considerable public attention. The proposition advanced was that the experience of increasing levels of material wellbeing (in some countries) in the years 1800 to 1970 could not be the experience to come for all countries for the long-term future, because of the constraints the natural environment set for economic activity. This proposition, essentially that of the classical economists, was in the early 1970s advanced by natural scientists and systems analysts. It was then, with very few exceptions, denied by economists.

For the classical economists, the origin of the pessimism about long-run economic prospects was acceptance of the law of *diminishing returns* in agricultural production. This law can be stated in various ways. The most general version has it that as successively larger amounts of some input to production, say labour, are combined with a fixed amount of some other input, say land, so the additional amount produced for each successive increment of the variable input must eventually decline. In Figure 1.1, we show what this implies for the relationship between total output and total labour input, in the case where the incremental decline starts at labour input level zero. Clearly, output ÷ labour, or output per head, declines as the amount of labour used increases. It is this feature of diminishing returns which gave rise to the classical economists' views on long-run economic prospects.

As told by Malthus (1798), the classical story was that while the living standards of the mass of the population might rise temporarily, the long-run tendency must always be for the wages of workers to be driven down to subsistence level. This arises because Malthus assumed a fixed amount of land to be available. As population grows, the operation of diminishing returns reduces the per-capita food supply. Population growth ceases when the reduction brings the food supply down to subsistence level. Ricardo (1817) addressed a wider range of issues than Malthus and attempted to provide a comprehensive theory of how the whole economic system worked. Ricardo's analysis was also more subtle than that of Malthus. However, the central conclusion was essentially the same as that of Malthus. It was that the economy was 'inevitably on its way to a rendezvous with poverty for most people' (Samuelson and Nordhaus, 1985). The origin of the conclusion was

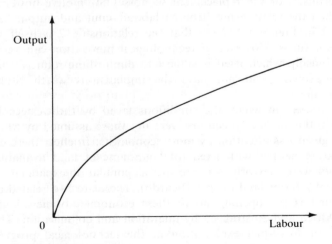

Figure 1.1   Diminishing returns

also essentially the same as with Malthus – the law of diminishing returns. Ricardo did not assume that the total amount of land available was fixed. He did assume that the available land varied in quality, and that the best land would be brought into cultivation first. For Ricardo, the per-capita food supply fell as population grew because successive increments of labour were being applied to inferior grades of land.

For the economies of western Europe, the main features of the nineteenth-century experience were population growth and rising living standards. This experience was not that which the analysis of Malthus and Ricardo appeared to predict. This is one of the reasons why in the latter part of the nineteenth century the interest of economists in those aspects of the work of these classical economists that we have considered greatly diminished – it simply did not square with the observed facts. For these economies, diminishing returns did not arrive during the nineteenth century. Was this because the law of diminishing returns is invalid? The answer which most economists would give now to this question is that the point is not that the law is invalid, but that the conditions in which Malthus and Ricardo envisaged it operating were not the conditions relevant to the nineteenth century. According to Samuelson's widely used introductory economics textbook (Samuelson and Nordhaus, 1985), Ricardo 'bet on the wrong horse of diminishing returns, just when the technological advances of the Industrial Revolution were outpacing that law'. The point is that Malthus and Ricardo assumed an unchanging technology of production, whereas the industrial revolution set in train a progressive process of technological change. Figure 1.2 illustrates what is involved in a simple way. The graph 1 is that from Figure 1.1, and shows the relationship between output and labour input for a fixed amount of land used, and a particular state of technology. Now suppose that some new invention increases the amount that can be produced from the given amount of land, at each level of labour input. This new invention might be artificial fertiliser, or the replacement of horses for motive power by steam engines. Then the relationship between labour input and output becomes as shown by 2 in Figure 1.2. Note that the relationship 2 is itself subject to diminishing returns. However, if technological innovation can keep shifting out a relationship which itself is subject to diminishing returns, then clearly population growth need not have the implications which Malthus and Ricardo envisaged.

Another respect in which the conditions faced by the western European economies in the nineteenth century were not those assumed by Malthus and Ricardo is given less attention by most economists. In effect these economies were operating neither with fixed total amounts of land available (as per Malthus) nor were they bringing into use, as population expanded, successive increments of inferior land (as per Ricardo). There are two related aspects to this. The first is the opening up to these economies of new lands in the America, Africa and Australasia by migration and colonisation. The second is the rôle of fossil-fuel exploitation in the technological progress which followed the industrial revolution. This made the new lands overseas

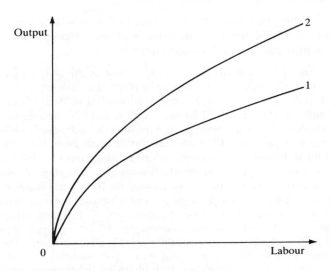

Figure 1.2 Diminishing returns and technical progress

effectively available to the western European economies via its impact on transport systems. It also released land for other uses in those economies themselves, which had formerly been required to provide food for the animals used in transport and agriculture. Cipolla (1962) provides an interesting perspective on population history and economic growth: for detailed investigations of the use of energy in agricultural systems see Leach (1975).

The fourth classical economist mentioned above was J. S. Mill, whose major economics treatise first appeared in 1848. This long book, which went through seven editions, is generally regarded as 'the final synthesis of Ricardian doctrine' (Blaug, 1985) and the full statement of classical economics. Mill stated the law of diminishing returns in agriculture carefully, noting that it held for a 'given state of agricultural skill and knowledge', and declared it to be 'the most important proposition in political economy'. He took the view that 'economic progress must be conceived as a race between technical change and diminishing returns in agriculture', and specifically noted that 'since the 1820s, technical change has outstripped the forces making for rising wheat prices' so that 'the standard of living has risen' (quotations from Blaug, 1985). However, Mill's view was that economic progress must eventually cease, and the economy come to exist in a *stationary state*. Unlike Ricardo and Malthus, Mill did not find this prospect entirely displeasing. In part this is because Mill saw that arrival at the steady state was a distant prospect, and that in the meantime technical progress would have greatly raised the material standard of living at which economic progress would cease. It was also because he took a somewhat broader view of the inputs to material welfare that the natural environment provided than Malthus or Ricardo had done. Mill recognised that land is used for purposes other than agricultural production and resource extraction: it is used for living space and provides satisfaction to man in the form of convenience and beauty. Some of Mill's remarks on these matters strikingly anticipate the present-day sentiments of many conservationists:

> I cannot ... regard the stationary state of capital and wealth with the unaffected aversion so generally manifested towards it by political economists of the old school ... I confess that I am not charmed with the ideal of life held out by those who think that the normal state of human beings is that of struggling to get on; that the trampling, crushing, elbowing, and treading on each other's heels which form the existing type of social life, are the most desirable lot of human kind, or anything but the disagreeable symptoms of one of the phases of industrial progress .... Those who do not accept the present very early stage of human improvement as its ultimate type may be excused for being comparatively indifferent to the kind of economical progress which excites the congratulations of ordinary politicians; the mere increase of production .... It is only in the backward countries of the world that increased production is still an important object: in those most advanced, what is economically needed is a better distribution ....
> There is room in the world, no doubt, and even in old countries, for a great increase in population, supposing the arts of life to go on improving, and capital to increase. But even if innocuous, I confess I see very little reason for desiring it. The density of population necessary to enable mankind to obtain, in the greatest degree, all of the advantages both of cooperation and of social intercourse, has, in all the most populous countries, been attained. A population may be too crowded, though all be amply supplied with food and raiment. It is not good for a man to be kept perforce at all times in the presence of his species ... Nor is there much satisfaction in contemplating the world with nothing left to the spontaneous activity of nature: with every rood of land brought into cultivation, which is capable of growing food for human beings; every flowery waste or natural pasture ploughed up, all quadrupeds or birds which are not domesticated for man's use exterminated as his rivals for food, every hedgerow or superfluous tree rooted out, and scarcely a place left where a wild shrub or flower could grow without being eradicated as a weed in the name of improved agriculture. If the earth must lose that great portion of its pleasantness which it owes to things that the unlimited increase of wealth and population would extirpate from it, for the mere purpose of enabling it to support a larger, but not a happier or a better population, I sincerely hope, for the sake of posterity, that they will be content to be stationary, long before necessity compels them to it.
>
> (Mill, 1857, Book IV)

The classical economists were not, of course, solely concerned with the implications of land scarcity for continuing economic progress. Another major concern was with the determinants of the prices, or values, of the various commodities which comprised the 'material necessities and comforts of this world'. Also, they tried to analyse the distribution of income and wealth within a society. With respect to the former question, the answer that they provided was, essentially, that price was determined by the cost of production. If a pair of gloves sold for twice as much as a pair of shoes, it was because they cost twice as much to produce. Further, the classical economists sought to trace all production costs back to labour costs – they subscribed to the *labour theory of value*. This is also the basis of Marxist economics.

Marx lived from 1818 to 1883, and in his major economics work (Marx, 1867) adopted the labour theory of value from the classical economists. He also shared their view of the future prospects for the bulk of the population. However, for Marx the poor outlook for the working classes derived not from the intrinsic scarcity of natural resources (land in the Malthus/Ricardo terminology) but from the prevailing system of economic organisation. This Marx saw as involving the exploitation of the workers by the owners of capital. He argued that as capitalism developed so exploitation would increase to the point where a workers' revolution would occur. Following the revolution socialism would replace capitalism, and with the end of exploitation the material standards of the workers would dramatically improve. Marx did not, apparently, envisage a socialist society encountering any problems set by environmental limits. Again, Marx is like the classical economists in that most would nowadays say that his 'predictions' have not been borne out by events. Even the workers' revolutions which have occurred have not followed the pattern Marx envisaged. Despite this, Marx and marxism have had, and continue to have, great significance for the state of the world today. However, we shall not in this book be considering any marxist economics. The first reason for this is that it is outside the remit, which is the exposition of conventional mainstream (western) economics, and its application to environmental questions. The second is that marxist economics has very little which is distinctive to say about environmental questions. Marx paid little attention to the influence of the natural environment on economic activity under either capitalism or socialism. The interested reader will find the essentials of Marx's economics set out in Blaug (1985) or Spiegel (1971): they are more sympathetically dealt with in Hunt and Sherman (1981). A brief account of modern marxist economics, written by a Marxist, is Mandell (1968).

Neoclassical economics

Within the development of mainstream economics itself, the labour theory of value was abandoned. Starting around 1870, classical economics began a process of evolution into *neoclassical economics*. This process involved, as well as the abandonment of the labour theory of value, a change in the predominant method of analysis and a change in the substantive issues which were the subject's major concerns. We will look briefly at each of these three developments, and then at some of the more famous neoclassical economists and their contributions.

As noted above, the classical economists thought that prices were determined by the costs of production, all of which costs were ultimately labour costs. Neoclassical economics does not deny that costs influence prices. It does deny that cost is the only determinant of price, and it does deny that labour costs are the only relevant costs of production. In neoclassical economics a commodity's price is a measure of its scarcity, and the more scarce a commodity the higher its price. A commodity may require little labour in its production, yet command a high price either because a large amount of some other input is required in production, or because the demand for the commodity is great. If people are willing to give up large amounts of other commodities to acquire, say, diamonds, then so long as diamonds are rare in nature they will command a high price even if little labour is used in finding them. The point is that scarcity is determined by comparing the amount available with the amount required, by the interaction of supply with demand. The classical economists focused exclusively on supply analysis, and assumed that the amounts of commodities supplied were to be understood solely in terms of the labour costs of production. Neoclassical economics introduced the analysis of demand conditions into the investigation of price determination. We shall discuss the supply and demand analysis of the way commodity prices are determined in Chapter 4 here; it is a distinctively neoclassical analysis.

   The second element involved in the evolution of classical into neoclassical economics is the introduction of a new method of analysis, that of considering *marginal changes*. What is involved can be illustrated by considering diminishing returns again. A graph of a relationship between output and labour input is shown in Figure 1.3(a). The line AB is tangential

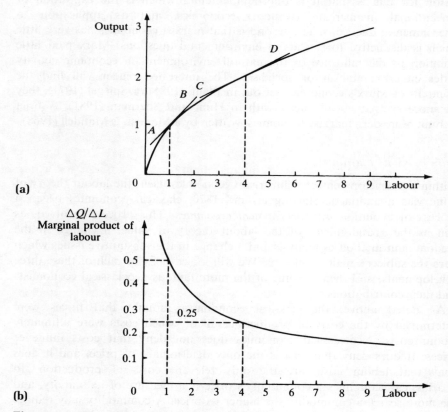

Figure 1.3   Derivation of marginal product of labour

to the graph at the point where labour input is one and the output corresponding is one. The slope of AB is equal to 0.5. Hence, if labour input were increased by a very small amount, output would increase by approximately 0.5 times the amount of that increase in labour input. The line CD is a tangent at the point where labour input is four and has a slope of 0.25, so that a very small increase in labour input would increase output by approximately 0.25 times the increase in labour input. In each case, the approximation would become closer as the increase in labour input considered became smaller, and for infinitesimally small input changes would become exact. Considering all the tangents to points along the graph in Figure 1.3(a) and plotting their slopes against the corresponding labour input levels produces the graph shown in Figure 1.3(b). The vertical axis is labelled $\Delta Q/\Delta L$, where the symbol Δ stands for infinitesimally small change, so that with Q representing output and L representing labour input $\Delta Q/\Delta L$ is the ratio of such a change in output to the associated such change in labour input. We call $\Delta Q/\Delta L$ the *marginal product of labour*; it is shown in Figure 1.3(b) that this falls as labour input increases, and this production relationship exhibits *diminishing marginal returns* to labour. Panels (a) and (b) do not tell different stories; the graph in the latter makes explicit what is implicit in the former, highlighting the fact that what is shown in Figure 1.3(a) involves labour's marginal, as well as its average, product diminishing. This is general, in that the shift to the method of analysing marginal changes is not necessarily a shift to new stories, but is a new way of looking at old stories. This new way of looking at things proved more fruitful. For example, it opened the way for the introduction of the use of the techniques of the differential calculus into economics. We shall use the method of marginal analysis, but not the calculus, extensively in the remainder of this book.[1]

While a shift to the methodology of marginal analysis does not necessarily involve a shift in substantive concerns, it is the case that the methodology is more suited to some problems in economics than others. Certainly, the major substantive concerns of the neoclassical economists were somewhat different from those of the classical economists. We have noted that a major interest of the latter was economic growth, i.e. the prospects for continuing long-term economic progress. This was not so for the neoclassical economists, and this area of inquiry virtually vanished from the writings of mainstream economists between 1870 and 1950. The subject became mainly concerned with the analysis of price determination, and with the associated question of the structure and pattern of economic activity. It concerned itself very much less with the question of whether the total amount of the 'material necessities and comforts' would tend to grow over time, and much more with the question of why a given such total came to be made up in a particular way in terms of the quantities of the various 'material necessities and comforts'. The central question shifted from 'will economic progress continue?' to 'why do we observe the existing pattern of economic activity?'. The latter type of question was more amenable to the marginal analysis. Interest in economic growth re-emerged in the post-Second World War period, for reasons to be examined below. The essence of the neoclassical answer to the question of the determinants of the pattern of economic activity was that the observed pattern was the outcome of an interaction between the technology of production and the preferences of individuals as between the commodities producible with that technology. The pattern of economic activity and the structure of prices are two closely related outcomes from the same process, the interaction of supply (technology) conditions with demand (preference) conditions. We shall explore these issues in Chapters 3 and 4.

The economists primarily responsible for initiating the process by which classical economics was supplanted by neoclassical economics are generally taken to be Jevons (1835–82), Menger (1840–1921) and Walras (1834–1910). Each of these published his major work in the 1870s; for details and references, see Blaug (1985) or Spiegel (1971). Jevons and Menger were particularly associated with the development of the analysis of the demand for commodities, i.e. with the development of the study of preferences over commodities often referred to as *utility theory*, and, in this context, with the introduction of the marginal method of analysis. Walras is principally famous for initiating the formal study of the interdependencies between all of the individuals who comprise an economy, which study is now known as *general equilibrium analysis*. Menger was an Austrian, and the founder of a distinctive 'Austrian school' of economics which, nowadays, is known mainly for its advocacy of minimal state involvement in the economy. Walras was French, and although there is no 'French school' of economics the 'general equilibrium' school has had a major influence on the development of mainstream economics. It is within the general equilibrium framework that the modern analysis of Smith's invisible-hand insight has been conducted: we shall discuss the main results arising in Chapters 3 and 4. In the twentieth century some of the major contributions to this branch of economics have been made by Americans. In the nineteenth century, economists in North America made rather little contribution to the main lines of the subject's development (see Ch. 27 of Spiegel (1971) for details on this). Jevons was English. He cannot be regarded as the founder of any school of economics, despite his major contributions.

There was in effect an 'English school' in economics, but it was actually known as the 'Cambridge school'. Its founding figure was A. Marshall (1842–1924) who was Professor of Economics at Cambridge from 1885 until 1908, and whose best-known work (Marshall, 1890) still appeared as a recommended text for many economics undergraduates in the 1950s. Marshall was especially responsible for developing and spreading the analysis of price determination in terms of the interaction of supply and demand. The most well-known follower of Marshall in the Cambridge school, perhaps the most famous of all economists, was J. M. Keynes (1883–1946). Keynes is generally credited with establishing a new branch of economics, known as *macroeconomics*. As we have noted, neoclassical economics was primarily concerned with the analysis of the pattern of economic activity and prices. This is now known as *microeconomics*. Prior to the so-called 'Keynesian revolution' which followed the publication of Keynes' major work (Keynes, 1936), neoclassical economists took it that economics was all microeconomics, in the sense that there were no economic problems that could not be analysed within the conceptual approach they had developed for the study of price determination. Keynes challenged this, and argued that there were economic problems which required an approach that dealt with broadly defined economic aggregates rather than with the individual households and industries and commodities which were the building blocks of neoclassical economics. Micro means small, macro means large. Keynes' argument was that the economics of the small did not carry over unmodified to the large.

Neoclassical economics took the overall level of economic activity as given. It was not believed that it was fixed, since it was obvious that it was not. During the nineteenth and early twentieth centuries, per capita incomes and the level of economic activity had followed an upward trend, with more or less regular fluctuations about that trend. It was believed that the economy had an inbuilt tendency to operate at an overall level of activity such that all of the available labour force was employed in producing commodities. It was the full employment of labour which fixed the overall level of economic activity. The total quantity of production corresponding would increase over time with a growing population and technical progress: temporary departures from this upward trend were to be expected. The norm was full employment. The basis for this view was the idea that labour was something which could be analysed in the same way as any other commodity. Particularly, it was assumed that in the face of persistent unemployment the price of labour, wages, would fall, so encouraging firms to hire more labour and eliminating the unemployment.

This view of full employment as the norm to which the economy tended was not obviously consistent with the post-First World War experience of most western economies, where mass unemployment persisted for a decade and more. Most economists at the time took the view that the problem arose because wages did not fall in the face of the unemployment. They argued that the only way to solve the unemployment problem was to force wages to fall. Keynes totally rejected this policy. His argument was that it was based on a false analogy between the labour market and the market for, say, shoes. If there is over production of shoes, a cut in their price increases their attractiveness vis-à-vis other commodities and stimulates their sales. On the neoclassical view, the labour market worked the same way, provided wages fell when there was unemployment. Keynes saw that this overlooked a crucial difference between the microrelationship of shoe demand to shoe price and the macrorelationship of labour demand to labour price. A lower price for shoes means lower incomes for the producers of shoes, but this has no significant effect on the demand for shoes since shoe producers are a small part of the total population. Workers are, however, the overwhelming majority of the economically active population. If there is a general wages cut it follows that the general level of income falls with a reduction in the total demand for all commodities, implying a reduction in the demand for the labour to produce those commodities. There may be some increased demand for labour, following the wage cut, in firms where labour can be used instead of other inputs to production. But, there is an offsetting overall reduction in the level of economic activity and the demand for labour. The policy of wage cutting may well, that is, make things worse rather than better.

This very brief sketch of Keynes' argument is designed only to bring out the basic idea that relationships which hold at the microlevel do not necessarily hold at the macrolevel. In making this point, Keynes was responsible for the emergence of macroeconomics and microeconomics as the two main branches of modern mainstream economics, which is sometimes referred to as the *Keynesian-neoclassical synthesis*. In the remainder of this book we shall be concerned with microeconomics rather than macroeconomics. This is because mainstream economics today takes the view that environmental problems arise via the pattern of economic activity rather than from its overall level. Many non-economists take a different view, arguing that environmental problems are caused by economic growth, and can only be solved by the cessation of such. We briefly explore this view, and explain why most economists reject it, in 1.2. To do this we shall not need to go into macroeconomics in any detail. The reader is therefore explicitly advised that while he or she will learn quite a lot of microeconomics in this book, little macroeconomics will be learnt. We shall have nothing to say about such questions as what causes inflation, or how unemployment can be reduced. These are important questions, but they do not, in the conventional view, have any direct connections with environmental questions. Such standard introductory texts as Wonnacott and Wonnacott (1979) or Samuelson and Nordhaus (1985), cited above, contain sections on macroeconomics, as well as microeconomics.

Keynes did not merely seek to demonstrate that wage cutting was an inappropriate response to the problem of persistent mass unemployment. Positively, he argued that the appropriate response was for the government to intervene in the economy so as to maintain the demand for commodities at a level which would produce full employment. This was to be done by striking the appropriate balance between government spending and receipts: in the face of persistent unemployment it would be appropriate for the government to boost the demand for commodities, and thereby for labour, by spending more than it received in tax payments. The neoclassical economists had argued that government deficits were both unnecessary and harmful, and had generally urged minimising the role of the government in economic affairs. In the post-Second World War period, governments took responsibility for the avoidance of unemployment and extended greatly their involvement in the economy. In large part this followed from a widespread acceptance of Keynesian economics, which argued the need for government intervention, and provided the means for it in terms of the concepts and analysis of macroeconomics.

These concepts and the analysis also turned out to be well suited for the study of the phenomenon of economic growth, and this subject returned to the economics agenda in the 1950s. This reawakening of professional interest in the study of the prospects for economic progress was in part also a response to a wider political concern with such issues, which concern was itself part of Keynes' impact. If governments should and could manage the economy so as to avoid the misery and waste of mass unemployment, it was a natural step to think in terms of governments managing the economy so as to ensure continuing economic growth. In the post-Second World War period, the achievement of rapidly rising levels of overall economic activity, of rapid economic growth, became a major objective of government policy. So, in the 1950s and 1960s many economists were using the new tools of macroeconomics to study economic growth. They did not, however, revert in any way to the views of the classical economists. The natural environment (land in the Malthus/Ricardo terminology) did not figure at all in the modern analysis of economic growth, in which the prospects for continuing material progress were seen optimistically. Arndt (1978) provides an account of the way in which economists, and others, promoted the growth objective in this period. Economics was no longer the dismal science. As already noted above, this perspective on economic growth was challenged from outside the economics profession in the early 1970s. The challenge has not caused any very substantial revision of economists' views on the feasibility of continuing economic growth. However, it was one of the stimuli to the emergence of environmental economics as a distinct branch of the subject in the 1970s.

1.2   Economic activity and the environment

In Figure 1.4 we provide a schematic representation of the relationships between economic activity and the natural environment. It shows two classes of economic activity: *production* is making things, *consumption* is using those *commodities*. It is important to be clear that commodities are not solely material objects such as TV sets, newspapers, food, etc., but also include services such as banking, health care, the administration of justice, etc. In Figure 1.4 goods and services, or commodities, flow from production to consumption. We can think of production as done by *firms* and consumption as done by *households*. Households are not only consumers. Their members work in the firms, and Figure 1.4 also shows a flow of labour services from consumption to production. Most of the economics literature is concerned with the analysis of the activities of production and consumption, and the flows between them. Macroeconomics concentrates on the overall levels of the activities and flows; a typical macroeconomics concern is whether the economy contains any mechanism such that the level of productive activity is maintained so as to require all of the available labour services (see the discussion of Keynes above). Microeconomics concentrates on the structure of the production and consumption activities, and the composition of the linking flows. A typical sort of microeconomics question would be: why do

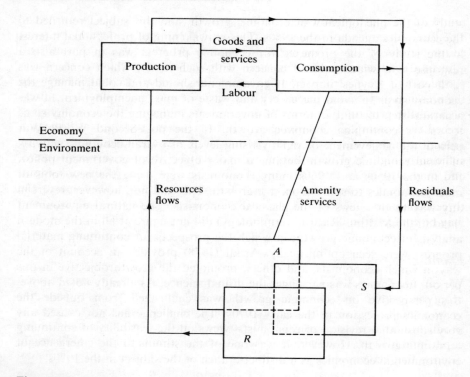

Figure 1.4   Economy environment linkages

we observe the production and consumption of a great deal of commodity x
but little of y?

   In relation to economic activity, Figure 1.4 shows the natural environment
serving three functions: S stands for sink, R for resources, and A for amenity.
Production and consumption both necessarily generate waste products or
residuals, for which the natural environment is the ultimate dumping place or
sink. Examples are discharges into the atmosphere or water courses of
byproducts from production processes, or the discharge of household sewage
into rivers, etc. The natural environment is also the source of inputs to
production, which inputs we call *natural resources*. Examples are mineral
deposits, forests, animal populations. *Amenity services* flow from the
environment directly to consumption, and are living space, natural beauty,
recreation space, etc. In Figure 1.4 we show the three boxes representing
these three functions as intersecting with one another, to reflect the fact that
the three functions interact and may be competitive. To see what is involved
here consider a river and its estuary. There will be discharged into it domestic
sewage and industrial effluent: some firms will draw water for cleaning,
mixing and cooling, and there will be commercial fishing activity: people will
want to swim in, fish from or sail on the river and its estuary. The capacity of
the river system to fulfil any one of these roles is not unlimited, and may be

reduced by the extent to which it is being exploited in the other two respects. The three functions are not necessarily mutually exclusive, but may be so at certain levels of use by the economic system. At low rates of sewage and effluent discharge, the river's natural processes can break down the waste products and there need be no pollution. There will be some conflict between the presence of productive activity along the river and recreational use, purely on aesthetic grounds. If, however, the rates of sewage and effluent discharge exceed the system's assimilative capacity, the resulting pollution will mean a reduction in its ability to provide production inputs and amenity services. A sufficiently high level of pollution will reduce the amenity services to zero, and may also mean that the water cannot be used as a production input. Clearly, this is a particular example of a general class of phenomena: the three economic functions of the natural environment always interact, and may be competitive, or mutually exclusive in the limit.

Economic growth and the environment

We can use Figure 1.4 as the basis for a discussion of the relationship between economic growth and the natural environment. For our purposes economic growth simply means rising levels of economic activity; over time the levels of production and consumption rise, due to population growth and/or higher per capita material living standards. The extreme view is essentially Malthusian, arguing that economic growth cannot go on indefinitely due to environmental constraints. The origin of this view is the observation that natural resources exist in finite amounts, so that the continually increasing flows of natural resources into production implied by continuing economic growth cannot be indefinitely sustained – eventually natural resources are exhausted, and the economic system collapses. A less extreme view sees the eventual problem as less dramatic, but arriving earlier. It notes that rising levels of production and consumption not only imply increasing resources flows, but also increasing discharges of residuals. As these discharges increase so must the natural environment's capacity to successfully assimilate such be approached and exceeded. The resulting pollution impairs the supply of natural resources and/ or the flow of amenity services. On this view, indefinitely prolonged economic growth may be impossible on account of the finite nature of resource stocks. However, this is not the operative problem about economic growth. The problem is rather one of it becoming progressively more difficult to achieve, and progressively more disappointing to the extent realised. It becomes more difficult to achieve because pollution is reducing the ability of the natural environment to deliver useful flows of resources. It becomes more disappointing when realised because pollution and resource extraction are reducing the natural environment's contribution to the quality of life. On this view, the natural environment is not going to put an absolute stop to economic growth some day. It is the case that environmental constraints become more acute as growth goes on, tending to slow it down, and to make the world a less pleasant place to live in (cf. the views of J. S. Mill quoted above).

Now, put this way it would seem difficult not to believe that the process of economic growth must eventually give rise to, and be affected by, environmental problems. Yet, when this sort of argument was advanced in the early 1970s, the reaction of economists was generally dismissive. Many economists took the position that there need be no conflict between economic growth and the environment. It was not argued that there were no environmental problems. It was argued that economic growth did not need to be abandoned as a policy objective as a necessary, or a sufficient, condition for their solution. And, it was argued, economic growth remained both feasible – a growing economic system need not run out of natural resources – and desirable – economic growth need not reduce the quality of life. The basis of this argument was, and is, the idea that a properly functioning price system will accommodate higher levels of production and consumption to the preservation of the natural environment in a satisfactory state.

To explain the economists' position on the economic growth versus the environment issue, we go back to Figure 1.4 and ask: under what conditions would it be true that continually rising levels of economic activity would not imply continually rising rates of resource depletion and residuals generation? What sort of changes in the economy–environment relationships could there be, which if occurring with economic growth would offset its effects, set out above, on the natural environment? An obvious candidate is for more *recycling* to occur as growth proceeds. Recycling involves intercepting residuals after they leave production and consumption and returning them as inputs to production, instead of disposing of them into some environmental medium. This not only cuts down on the load placed upon those media's capacities to absorb wastes, but also cuts down on the amount of resources drawn from the environment for any given level of production. If as production and consumption levels rose, the percentage of residuals recycled increased, the pace of the economy's approach toward environmental constraints, pollution and/or resource exhaustion, would be reduced. Similarly, economic growth accompanied by progressively greater amounts of productive activity being diverted away from production for consumption to activities to pre-treat residuals and/or increase the absorptive capacity of some relevant environmental media would delay the pace of approach toward pollution problems. To the extent that pollution problems are avoided, there are smaller problems arising from its effect on resource availability and amenity.

The second source of an accommodation between economic growth and the natural environment is to be found in the composition of the rising overall level of economic activity. If as economic growth proceeds its composition changes so that per unit of overall economic activity fewer natural resources are used and less residuals generated, the pace at which environmental constraints are approached is, again, reduced. Clearly, some commodities involve greater environmental impact, in terms of resource depletion and/or residuals generation, than others. The suggestion here is that if as material living standards rise, so consumption, and hence production, systematically shifts away from more and in favour of less damaging commodities, economic growth need neither degrade environmental quality nor run into resource exhaustion problems.

Now, in order to take the position that economic growth and environmental preservation are not conflicting objectives it is necessary to argue that these changes in the relationships between the economy and the environment will actually occur as growth proceeds. It is necessary to identify, that is, some feature of the economic system that would induce those changes. The inducement arises, economists typically would argue, from the operation of the price mechanism. The basic feature of this mechanism is the way in which it determines the pattern of economic activity in the light of relative scarcities. As some commodity's price rises, so will the amount of it produced and consumed fall: also, as the cost of an input to production increases, so will less of it be used in production. Conversely, commodities and inputs for which price falls will be consumed and used more. If, as economic growth proceeds natural resources are depleted, their price will rise, and production methods will adapt, using fewer natural resources and more of other inputs. For some commodities, there may be very little possibility for changing the mix of inputs used in production. Where a commodity is intrinsically resource intensive, its price will rise as natural resource prices rise, so reducing the consumption of the commodity. In this way, it is argued, to the extent that resource stocks are run down, the pattern of production and consumption will become less resource intensive, so accommodating economic growth to the environment in this respect.

Further, to the extent that virgin resources become more expensive, recycling will be encouraged by the price mechanism. This mitigates the resource depletion problem further, and reduces the demands per unit of economic activity being made upon the environment's capacity to assimilate wastes. With less resource extraction and less waste generation there is less damage done to the environment's ability to provide amenity services. Thus, with respect to our account given above of the argument that environmental constraints mean either that continuing economic growth is impossible or that it is undesirable, the typical economist's response is that it is invalid because it overlooks the operation of the price mechanism. Ideally, this mechanism ensures that as anything becomes more scarce, less of it is used. This would apply to the environmental functions of waste disposal unit and amenity provider, as well as to the function of providing natural resource inputs. If these functions are impaired by economic growth, waste disposal becomes a more costly activity and the price of amenity services rises. This means that the economic system reduces the demands it makes upon these environmental functions. Given a properly functioning price mechanism as part of the economic system there is, then, no problem. Economic growth as an objective is not ruled out on environmental grounds.

Now, this is in one important respect an over-simplification of the position typically taken by economists. They would argue that if all economy–environment relationships were determined by a properly functioning price mechanism, there would be no problem. They would not argue that all economy–environment relationships are, in fact, determined by a properly functioning price mechanism. The conditions under which the price mechanism, or market system, works 'properly' will be examined in some detail in Chapter 4 below. We will also consider what 'properly' means here. It turns out that it means efficient, but not necessarily fair or just. In Chapter 5 this examination will provide the basis for a discussion of environmental pollution, and in Chapter 7 for a discussion of resource depletion: amenity questions are addressed in Chapter 8. Here we simply assert that one of the conditions necessary for the price mechanism to work 'properly' is that there exist private property rights in those things which the mechanism has to control. The price mechanism works by means of people exchanging things with one another; only things which people own can be so exchanged. This condition is especially pertinent to the question of the price mechanism's ability to properly control the relationships between the economy and the natural environment. With respect to many of the relationships, the condition of ownership by individual participants in economic activity is not satisfied. Some, but not all, mineral deposits are owned, and use rights are thereby tradeable in markets. It is often, that is, necessary to pay a price in order to extract minerals. This is less often the case with those natural resources which are plant and animal populations, many of which are exploited by the economic system on a 'free access' basis – it is not necessary to pay a price in order to exploit the resource. As far as the discharge of residuals into the environment is concerned, ownership of receiving media is almost always absent, and no price is paid in respect of such discharge. The position with the use of the natural environment as a source of amenity services is the same, typically.

So, economists do not argue that environmental problems cannot occur. To do so would be to ignore the fact that such have occurred. They do argue that environmental problems are not the consequence of economic growth as such, but that they are the consequence of inappropriate patterns of economic activity which would not arise, at any level of economic activity, if economy–environment relationships were determined by a properly functioning price mechanism. They accept that we do not have, in this respect, a properly functioning price mechanism. But they argue, and this is the motivation for the sort of environmental economics that this book is principally concerned with, that the functioning of the price mechanism could be greatly improved and/or its job done in some other way. The point is not to abandon the pursuit of economic growth, but to achieve the pattern of economic growth that a properly functioning price mechanism would realise.

In the absence of the required private property rights, achieving such a pattern will require government policies of various kinds to supplement the workings of the price mechanism. Recently, some economists have argued that such policies are more likely to be put in place once people have escaped poverty and are well off in terms of produced commodities. They also argue that as people get richer, so the pattern of their consumption shifts in favour of less environmentally damaging commodities. These arguments lead to the idea that while growth may mean more environmental damage at low levels of income, i.e. total production, once it reaches a certain level, growth is actually good for the environment. On this view the real threat to the environment is poverty rather than affluence. We shall consider the evidence on this in Chapter 9.

Economists and the environment

We noted above the way in which economic growth came back to the forefront of economists' interests in the 1950s, that environmental issues were not greatly of interest to economists until the 1970s, and that the early 1970s saw an attack on the growth objective by a number of non-economists. The anti-economic growth contribution which achieved the most exposure was *The Limits to Growth* (Meadows *et al.*, 1972), which reported the results obtained from a computer model of the world economic system. The study was widely reported as forecasting the collapse of this system sometime around the middle of the next century, the collapse resulting from the system growing exponentially until it hit environmental limits. Certainly, the authors argued for the abandonment of economic growth as a policy objective in the advanced economies. With few exceptions, the book received a hostile and highly critical reception from economists. The basis for this has, in its essentials, been set out above: the main point made was that the computer model made no allowance for the way the price mechanism could accommodate growth to environmental constraints. An extensive literature emerged in the controversy which followed publication of the *The Limits to Growth*: Lecomber (1975) provides an overview of the general and particular issues, and references to the literature. A fairly comprehensive statement of the mainstream economics position was Beckerman (1974). Hirsch (1977) argued that the limits to growth are social rather than the product of physical environmental constraints.

The Limits to Growth did much to promote widespread interest in and concern about environmental problems, which became especially pronounced in the early 1970s. It was not the only source of such interest and concern. Ecologists were prominent in raising questions concerning the compatibility of economic growth with environmental integrity, and their efforts achieved considerable public exposure. Darnell (1973) reports that in 1965 the Ecological Society of America adopted a formal resolution urging members to make their views known. Such views were often such that ecology might well be called the 'dismal science' of the 1960s and 1970s. Addressing the thirteenth National Conference of the United States Commission for UNESCO in 1969, the ecologist Commoner said:

> The ecological facts of life are grim. The survival of all living things – including man – depends on the integrity of the complex web of biological processes which comprise the earth's ecosystem. However, what man is now doing on the earth

violates this fundamental requisite of human existence. For modern technologies act on the ecosystem which supports us in ways that threaten its stability: with tragic perversity we have linked much of our productive economy to precisely those features of technology which are ecologically destructive.

These remarks are quoted by Maddox (1972), who sought to rebut the 'doomsday' message typified in Meadows *et al.* (1972).

Other publications which called into question the feasibility and desirability of economic growth, on environmental grounds, were Commoner (1963) and (1972), Carson (1962), Ehrlich and Ehrlich (1970), and Goldsmith *et al.* (1973). The attack on the growth objective on environmental grounds was one of the reasons why economists began to show renewed interest in environmental problems. Another was simply the growing awareness, based on people's direct experience of pollution and amenity problems in the 1960s. Again, the OPEC-induced oil crisis of 1973/74 undoubtedly helped to focus attention on questions about the availability of natural resources.

It would be wrong to say that with the emergence of neoclassical economics economists completely ignored environmental questions until the 1970s. Jevons, one of the founders of neoclassical economics, himself published a work in 1865 which argued that Britain's economic position would be put in danger by the run-down of her coal reserves (Jevons, 1865). A number of other economists considered the implications of resource depletion (see, for example, Barnett and Morse (1963)), and studied the issues arising in the conservation of natural resources (see, for example, Scott (1955)). With respect to pollution problems, the inability of the market to properly control such is, in technical terms, an example of an *externality* problem (see Chapters 4 and 5 for a full discussion). The existence of such problems was noted by Marshall (1890) in the nineteenth century, and in the early twentieth century Pigou (1920) considered them at some length. However, until the 1970s economists did not pay much attention to externality theory in relation to pollution problems. Kneese, Ayres and D'Arge (1970) drew their fellow economists' attention to the *materials balance principle*. In terms of Figure 1.4, this says that the mass of residuals that flow into the environment must be approximately equal to the mass of the resources flows from the environment. The approximation arises from lags in the circulation of matter round the whole economy/environment system, due, for example, to extracted materials being held up in the economy as material structures which take time to decay and return to the environment. The materials balance view of environmental inputs to and receipts from the economy suggests, given the lack of property rights in the environment as sink for residuals discharge noted above, that excessive pollution generation would be quite common in an unregulated market economy.

For a variety of reasons, economists rediscovered an interest in environmental problems in the early 1970s. They did not, however, find it necessary on account of these problems to abandon the Keynesian-neoclassical synthesis, or the idea that economic growth was feasible and desirable. On the contrary, they took the view that conventional economic analysis could handle environmental problems without any substantial modification. The problems of resource depletion, pollution and environmental amenity had, perhaps, not been given previously as much attention as they warranted. They were recognised as serious substantive problems. But, they were problems which required no new conceptual approaches or analytical techniques. Further, the extant methodology of economics could both identify the origins of the problems, and point to ways in which the problems could be mitigated. The mitigation would involve no major social upheavals, but rather some institutional innovations to enable the price system to function better in respect of economy–environment relationships. Given such innovations, economic growth could be accommodated to environmental preservation.

This is the current position of mainstream economics in regard to the natural environment. It is the exposition of the basis for this position which is the principal subject matter of this book. However, we also consider some dissent from this orthodoxy. Some economists, for example, do take the view that environmental considerations require not just the improvement of the functioning of the price mechanism, but rather the abandonment of the growth objective. This case was argued by Daly (1973), whose case was that the need to operate the economy in a steady-state configuration 'follows immediately from physical first principles'. By a steady-state configuration, Daly means:

> An economy in which the total population and the total stock of physical wealth are maintained constant at some desired levels by a 'minimal' rate of maintenance throughput (i.e. by birth and death rates that are equal at the lowest feasible level, and by physical production and consumption rates that are equal at the lowest feasible level).

Daly explicitly noted the way in which his ideas harked back to those of J.S. Mill noted in the previous section. Daly belongs to a school of economics which calls itself '*ecological economics*', so as to indicate that it takes the interdependence of economic and natural systems seriously, as, it claims, mainstream economics does not. We consider ecological economics in Chapter 9.

1.3 This book

In the preceding two sections we have tried to provide some background to what follows, in terms of the history of economics, and introduced some simple ideas about the relationship between economic activity and the natural environment. In Chapters 2 to 8 we try to set out as clearly and simply as possible the basic approach of modern mainstream economics to environmental problems. Many of those who are concerned with and about the natural environment react negatively to economists' contributions to the debate on the issues involved, taking the position that economics is either irrelevant or wrong. Unfortunately, this position is, in many cases, taken on the basis of a very rudimentary acquaintance with economics. In these chapters the intention is to set out the conceptual and methodological basis for the contributions made by economists to the analysis of, and debate over, environmental issues. Chapter 9 discusses the role for economics in the formulation of environmental policy.

In the remaining chapters of this book the manner of exposition follows from the objective stated above, and from the assumption that the typical reader has a limited prior knowledge of economics. In Chapters 2 to 8 the analysis in all but the final section is abstract, and conducted principally in terms of particular numerical constructions. The purpose is to set out the basic concepts and their use in the most accessible way. The constructions illustrate general arguments. In order to keep these sections of the chapters clear and self-contained, they contain no references to other works or to 'real world' applications. Such matters are dealt with in the final, 'Commentary', section of each of these chapters, where qualifications to the discussion in the preceding sections are also noted. It is not possible in an introductory text to deal fully with all of the caveats which should be borne in mind in applying economic principles to actual environmental and resource use problems, so the reader is urged to follow up some of the references to applied studies which are provided here. The subject matter of Chapter 9 does not readily permit a neat distinction between analysis and application, and it is structured differently from the other chapters. It begins with a discussion of poverty, looks at some recent history, considers some theoretical work on sustainability and some related ideas about national income accounting, looks at two global environmental problems, and finishes with a discussion of policy.

Note

1. The graph in (a) of Figure 1.3 is of $Q = L^{\frac{1}{2}}$ with Q for output and L for labour. That in (b) is, readers with the calculus will realise, that of $\delta Q/\delta L = \frac{1}{2} L^{-\frac{1}{2}}$.

   At many points in the remainder of the book the analysis will involve a similar shift, similarly explained, from a function to its derivative. We shall not at each such point note this, since readers lacking calculus would not be helped, while those with it will realise anyway what is involved, it having been made explicit here.

Chapter 2

Prices, aggregation and decisions

Many of those concerned about the environment appear to misunderstand the rôle of prices in economic analysis. The essential point is that prices are a set of ratios which convert disparate things to a common basis of measurement, such conversion being necessary if decisions involving disparate things are to be made. This chapter uses a simple example of decision making in production to illustrate and amplify this point. It is perhaps the single most important point about economic analysis for environmentalists to understand. In this chapter we do not address the question of how prices are determined – this is dealt with in the next two chapters.

2.1   Prices and aggregation

We consider a fruit grower who has to decide how to operate, in terms of the quantities of outputs to be produced and inputs to be used. We assume that there are just three possibilities for the fruit grower to choose from. These are shown as options I, II and III in Table 2.1, in terms of quantities of apples and pears produced (outputs) using labour, land and pesticide (inputs). Table 2.1 contains all of the technical data relevant to the problem of choosing a particular production plan. It does not, however, contain enough information to enable the choice of a single option to be made. Clearly, the fruit grower will prefer the option which involves the largest excess of outputs over inputs. Equally clearly, this criterion cannot be used to choose either I, II or III on the basis of the data of Table 2.1. While it is true that II involves more apples and pears than I, it is also true that II involves more of every input than does I. The same is true of the comparison of III with II. We have, for example, no way of knowing whether 25 tons of apples and 40 tons of pears from 2.5 man years plus 7.5 acres plus 22.5 tons of pesticide is, according to the stated criterion, better or worse than 20 tons of apples plus 30 tons of pears from 2 man years plus 5 acres plus 20 tons of pesticide.

The problem is that apples, pears, labour, land and pesticides are not

Table 2.1 Technological data for a fruit grower

	Option I	Option II	Option III
Apples, tons	20	25	30
Pears, tons	30	40	45
Labour, man years	2	2.5	3
Land, acres	5	7.5	10
Pesticide, tons	20	22.5	25

commensurable, so that we cannot add and subtract across them to get a measure of the excess of outputs over inputs. That is, we cannot, aggregate across these outputs and inputs, because they have different units of measurement. *Prices* are the means by which we convert all inputs and outputs to a common basis of measurement so that *aggregation* across them is possible. Multiplying a quantity by the appropriate price per unit gives a *value*, and values can be added one to another. To see what is involved we give some prices in Table 2.2. With the price of apples at £100 per ton, the value of the apple output under option I is

20 tons × £100 per ton = £2000

Similarly the value of option I's labour input is

2 man years × £1000 per man year = £2000

Proceeding thus we can convert all of the technical data of Table 2.1 into value data, using the prices of Table 2.2. The results are shown in Table 2.3, where V stands for value so that, for example, the entries for V(PR) give the value of the pear output for each option.

We now have all inputs and outputs measured in the same, value, units. These happen here to be £'s but clearly the point of using prices for valuation so as to make unlike things commensurable would be unaffected if the prices were expressed in $, yen, or whatever. In Table 2.3 are also the symbols B, C and (B–C). B stands for *benefit*, which is the name we give to the total of output values. C stands for *cost*, which is the name we give to the total of input values. (B–C) is the difference between benefit and cost so defined, that is the excess of outputs over inputs measured in value terms. (B–C) is also referred to as *net benefit*, and as *profit*. Clearly, the fruit grower's preference

Table 2.2 Prices facing a fruit grower

Apples	symbol AP	£100 per ton
Pears	symbol PR	£200 per ton
Labour	symbol MY	£1000 per man year
Land	symbol AC	£500 per acre
Pesticide	symbol PT	£100 per ton

Table 2.3 Value data for a fruit grower

		Option I	Option II	Option III
V(AP)	£	2 000	2 500	3 000
V(PR)	£	6 000	8 000	9 000
B	£	8 000	10 500	12 000
V(MY)	£	2 000	2 500	3 000
V(AC)	£	2 500	3 750	5 000
V(PT)	£	2 000	2 250	2 500
C	£	6 500	8 500	10 500
(B–C)	£	1 500	2 000	1 500

for the option which offers the largest excess of outputs over inputs does identify a particular production plan when outputs and inputs are reckoned in value terms. From Table 2.3 we see that the preferred option is II.

Prices, then, are the means by which physically distinct things are converted to a common basis of measurement. It is only via such conversion that we can aggregate, or add up, across outputs and across inputs. It is only when both total output and total input are in value terms that we can directly compare them one with another, so that a decision can be made over available options in terms of the criterion of the largest excess of outputs over inputs. While we have illustrated this here in terms of a simple numerical example, the point is quite general, and absolutely fundamental.

2.2   Absolute and relative prices

We have seen that prices are necessary for decisions which involve choices over physically distinct things. Does it matter what the prices are? That is, do different prices produce different decisions for the same technical, or physically specified, alternatives? The answer to this question is 'yes', though we have to be clear what we mean by 'different prices'. We shall explain what is involved by further consideration of the fruit grower example from the previous section.

Suppose first that all the prices facing the fruit grower were to be doubled. With these new prices the values arising under each option are as shown in Table 2.4, as the reader can readily confirm. In Table 2.4 we see that, in terms of the maximum (B–C) criterion, option II remains the preferred production plan. Comparing the (B–C) entries in Tables 2.3 and 2.4, all that has happened is that each of the three entries has been doubled. It appears that our answer 'yes' to the question 'does it matter what the prices are?' was wrong. This is not so, as the aspects of the prices which matter, their relative sizes as across the various inputs and outputs, have not changed here, although the absolute sizes of all the prices have changed (by the factor of 2 everywhere). There is an important distinction between *absolute* and *relative* prices.

Table 2.4 Consequences of doubling all prices

		Option I	Option II	Option III
V(AP)	£	4 000	5 000	6 000
V(PR)	£	12 000	16 000	18 000
B	£	16 000	21 000	24 000
V(MY)	£	4 000	5 000	6 000
V(AC)	£	5 000	7 500	10 000
V(PT)	£	4 000	4 500	5 000
C	£	13 000	17 000	21 000
(B–C)	£	3 000	4 000	3 000

To show what we mean by relative as opposed to absolute prices we need to select one of the inputs or outputs as a standard of reference, or *numeraire*. We can use the output apples for this purpose initially. In Table 2.2 the absolute prices of apples and pears are £100 and £200 per ton respectively, from which we get the relative price of pears in terms of apples as

$$\frac{P(PR)}{P(AP)} = \frac{£200 \text{ per ton pears}}{£100 \text{ per ton apples}} = \frac{£200/1 \text{ ton pears}}{£100/1 \text{ ton apples}}$$

$$= \frac{£200}{£100} \cdot \frac{1 \text{ ton apples}}{1 \text{ ton pears}}$$

$$= 2. \frac{\text{tons apples}}{\text{tons pears}}$$

What this means is that with the absolute prices for apples and pears of Table 2.2, 1 ton of pears exchanges for 2 tons of apples, so that in terms of the numeraire apples the relative price of pears is 2. Clearly, the absolute price of apples and pears used for Table 2.4 give exactly the same relative price of pears with reference to apples numeraire, since we now have £400 per ton pears divided by £200 per ton apples. This is true for all of the absolute prices of Tables 2.2 and 2.4, as the reader can readily confirm. Clearly, any set of absolute prices which is those of Table 2.2 all multiplied by a common factor will produce the set of relative prices shown in the first column of Table 2.5.

All prices are *exchange ratios*. Absolute prices are exchange ratios with respect to currency units, i.e. money. Thus, the difference between the prices of Tables 2.2 and 2.4 is just that in the latter case twice as many £'s exchange per unit of each input and output. Relative prices are exchange ratios with respect to units of some input or output selected as standard of reference or numeraire. The selection of a particular input or output as standard is arbitrary. In Table 2.5 we show in the first column ratios of absolute prices (expressed as P(MY) for the price of labour, etc.) with that of apples always as denominator, giving the relative prices expressed with apples as numeraire. The absolute prices are those used in Table 2.2 or those used in Table 2.4. In

Table 2.5 Relative prices and exchange ratios

Apples	$\dfrac{P(AP)}{P(AP)} = 1$			1AP exc 0.1MY
Pears	$\dfrac{P(PR)}{P(AP)} = 2$		1PR exc 2AP	1PR exc 0.2MY
Labour	$\dfrac{P(MY)}{P(AP)} = 10$		1MY exc 10AP	
Land	$\dfrac{P(AC)}{P(AP)} = 5$		1AC exc 5AP	1AC exc 0.5MY
Pesticide	$\dfrac{P(PT)}{P(AP)} = 1$		1PT exc 1AP	1PT exc 0.1MY

the second column these relative prices are expressed as exchange ratios: 1MY exc 10 AP means, for example, that to say that the relative price of labour is 10 is just to say that the exchange ratio is 1 labour unit to 10 apples units. Now, in considering the relative prices indicated by the absolute prices of Tables 2.2 and 2.4 we could as well have used labour as apples as the standard of reference. In which case the relative price of pears in terms of man year is

$$
\begin{aligned}
\frac{P(PR)}{P(MY)} &= \frac{£200 \text{ per ton pears}}{£1000 \text{ per man year labour}} = \frac{£400 \text{ per ton pears}}{£2000 \text{ per man year labour}} \\[4pt]
&= \frac{£200/1 \text{ ton pears}}{£1000/1 \text{ man year}} = \frac{£400/1 \text{ ton pears}}{£2000/1 \text{ man year}} \\[4pt]
&= \frac{£200}{£1000} \cdot \frac{1 \text{ man year}}{1 \text{ ton pears}} = \frac{£400}{£2000} \cdot \frac{1 \text{ man year}}{1 \text{ ton pears}} \\[4pt]
&= 0.2 \frac{\text{man years}}{\text{tons pears}} = 0.2 \frac{\text{man years}}{\text{tons pears}}
\end{aligned}
$$

so that the exchange ratio is 1 ton of pears to 0.2 man years. This is shown in the third column of Table 2.5 together with the exchange ratios with respect to man years for the other outputs and inputs. The reader will find it a useful exercise to check the entries in columns two and three of Table 2.5, and to confirm that both columns actually contain exactly the same information about exchange ratios – only the point of reference used differs as between the two columns.

In the previous section we used money as the unit of account when computing values. It should now be apparent that this is not essential. Given that a set of absolute prices implies a set of relative prices we can equally well use any input or output as the unit of account. To do so will make no difference to the decision made by the fruit grower, as Table 2.6 shows. Part (a) there is just the previous exercise, in money terms, reproduced from Table 2.4. In part (b) the £ sign is replaced by AP to indicate that apples are the unit of account. The entries here are obtained using the original technical

Table 2.6 Alternative units of account

| | (a) | | | (b) | | |
	Option I	Option II	Option III	Option I	Option II	Option III
V(AP)	£ 4 000	£ 5 000	£ 6 000	AP20	AP25	AP30
V(PR)	£12 000	£16 000	£18 000	AP60	AP80	AP90
B	£16 000	£21 000	£24 000	AP80	AP105	AP120
V(MY)	£ 4 000	£ 5 000	£ 6 000	AP20	AP25	AP30
V(AC)	£ 5 000	£ 7 500	£10 000	AP25	AP37.5	AP50
V(PT)	£ 4 000	£ 4 500	£ 5 000	AP20	AP22.5	AP25
C	£13 000	£17 000	£21 000	AP65	AP85	AP105
(B–C)	£ 3 000	£ 4 000	£ 3 000	AP15	AP20	AP15

data in physical units, see Table 2.1, and the exchange ratios from the second column of Table 2.5. Thus, for example, V(PR) for option II appears as AP80 because the output of pears is 40 tons and 1 ton of pears converts to 2 tons of apples at the given relative prices. The reader should check from these two sources, Table 2.1 and the second column of Table 2.5, the other entries appearing in part (b) of Table 2.6. We see that using apples, rather than money, as the units of measure for values still leads to the choice of option II, given the criterion of the largest (B–C). It would also be a useful exercise for the reader to confirm that II is the best option using labour as unit of account. To do this, use the physical data from Table 2.1, and the exchange ratio data from the third column of Table 2.5. The result for (B–C) under the three options are: I, MY1·5; II, MY2·0; III, MY1·5.

We have shown that changing absolute prices in such a way as to leave relative prices unchanged does not affect the fruit grower's decision regarding the production plan. We have also shown that with unchanged relative prices it makes no difference to what input or output they are expressed as standard of reference, and that value can be kept account of in terms of the chosen standard of reference. The point of this second demonstration is to make it clear that in using prices for aggregation economists are not, as is sometimes alleged, displaying money fetishism and disregarding the underlying physical and technical realities. Economists work in terms of prices and values expressed in terms of money as unit of account not because they are interested in money as such but because to do so is convenient and accords with everyday practice. Fruit growers, and producers generally, do in fact keep their accounts in money terms. They need not, but they do because it is convenient given that transactions – hiring labour, buying pesticides, selling apples or whatever – are actually effected by exchanging money for things. But, pathological cases apart, this does not, of course, mean that they are interested in money as such, any more than working their analyses in money terms means that economists are concerned about money as such. For producers as for economists, it is the relative prices, not the money or absolute prices, which are of real interest, expressing as they do the terms on

Table 2.7 A changed set of relative prices

	Absolute prices	Relative prices	Exchange ratios
Apples	£100 per ton	$\dfrac{P(AP)}{P(AP)} = 1$	
Pears	£150 per ton	$\dfrac{P(PR)}{P(AP)} = 1.5$	1PR exc 1.5AP
Labour	£750 per man year	$\dfrac{P(MY)}{P(AP)} = 7.5$	1MY exc 7.5AP
Land	£100 per acre	$\dfrac{P(AC)}{P(AP)} = 1$	1AC exc 1AP
Pesticide	£50 per ton	$\dfrac{P(PT)}{P(AP)} = 0.5$	1PT exc 0.5AP

which things of real interest – apples to eat, hours worked, etc. – exchange for one another.

While a change in absolute prices which leaves relative prices unaffected does not lead to a change in the fruit grower's preferred production plan, a change in relative prices does. Given what we have said about the nature of relative prices this should not be surprising – if the terms on which inputs and outputs exchange for one another change we should expect the patterns of outputs and input to change. Tables 2.7 and 2.8 illustrate this. In Table 2.7 we show, in the first column, a set of absolute prices which, compared with those of Tables 2.2 and 2.4, do involve a different set of relative prices from those already considered. This is made explicit in the second and third columns of Table 2.7, to be compared with the first and second columns of Table 2.5. Table 2.8 corresponds to Tables 2.3 and 2.4. It uses the prices from column one of Table 2.7 with the physical data of Table 2.1 to derive the entries shown for the values of inputs and outputs arising under each of the three options. The physical or technical options open to the fruit grower are unchanged. We see, however, that it is now option III rather than option II which yields the largest (B–C). That is to say, that for the same physical opportunities, a change in relative prices will lead the fruit grower to a different choice of production plan. This is an important result, the validity of which is not limited to the particular case for which it has been illustrated here. It is generally true that, for unchanging technical production conditions, a change in relative prices will lead to a change in the chosen production plan.

There is a particular relationship between the pattern of the change in relative prices and the pattern of the consequent change in the chosen production plan. On the input side, the pattern of input mix shifts towards (away from) inputs the relative price of which falls (rises). On the output side, the output mix is moved to involve relatively more of (less of) outputs whose relative price has risen (fallen). We can see these effects at work in the case of the fruit grower here. On the output side, the change from Table 2.2 to Table

Table 2.8 A changed input-output mix

		Option I	Option II	Option III
V(AP)	£	2 000	2 500	3 000
V(PR)	£	4 500	6 000	6 750
B	£	6 500	8 500	9 750
V(MY)	£	1 500	1 875	2 250
V(AC)	£	500	750	1 000
V(PT)	£	1 000	1 125	1 250
C	£	3 000	3 750	4 500
(B–C)	£	3 500	4 750	5 250

2.7 involves a fall in the relative price of pears in terms of apples, or equivalently a rise in the relative price of apples in terms of pears. As a result the production plan chosen shifts from option II to option III. From Table 2.1 we see that this means shifting from producing pears and apples in the ratio $40:25 = 1.6:1$ to producing them in the ratio $45:30 = 1.5:1$. On the input side, the change from Table 2.2 to Table 2.7 involves, for example, a reduction in the relative price of labour in terms of pesticide. From Table 2.1 again we see that the shift from option II to option III involves changing the labour pesticide input ratio from $2.5:22.5 = 0.111:1$ to $3:25 = 0.12:1$ so that the input mix becomes more labour intensive and less pesticide intensive.

These effects induced by changing relative prices are of crucial importance for the way economies work. They are also the basis for the economist's approach to environmental problems, as we shall show in the next section.

2.3 Opportunity cost and pollution reduction

The description of the technically available options open to the fruit grower given in Table 2.1 was actually an incomplete description of the physical inputs to and outputs from his activity. A complete description is given in Table 2.9. Previously we ignored the pollution arising from the use of a pesticide as input. We now assume that this pollution, in the form of runoff

Table 2.9 Complete description of the technological alternatives

	Option I	Option II	Option III
Apples, tons	20	25	30
Pears, tons	30	40	45
Pollution, index	1	8.5	15
Labour, man years	2	2.5	3
Land, acres	5	7.5	10
Pesticide, tons	20	22.5	25

from the land used for fruit growing, can be satisfactorily measured on some physical index. According to Table 2.9 the pollution index increases more rapidly than the pesticide input. Pollution is an output from the fruit-growing activity.

Now, suppose that the fruit grower has, on the basis of the absolute and relative prices of Tables 2.2 and 2.5, chosen to operate option II. As a result there is an amount of runoff occurring which gives rise to a pollution index of 8.5. This pollution is, in contrast to apples and pears, an undesirable output from the fruit-growing operation. Many environmentalists take it as self-evident that all pollution should be eliminated. From Table 2.9 we see that to impose on the fruit grower the condition that his activities give rise to no pollution at all would be to require him to cease fruit growing altogether. While the data of Table 2.9 are hypothetical, this is not untypical of many real world situations – with respect to many productive activities, the call for zero pollution is effectively a call for the cessation of the activity. In the light of this the practical objective sought in pollution control is typically not a level of zero, but some reduction from the existing level.

Let us, then, consider a situation where the fruit grower's chosen production plan is option II, and where, as a result of public concern it is proposed that he be constrained to operate such as to give rise to the smallest amount of pollution consistent with his remaining in the business of growing fruit. From Table 2.9 we see that the proposal is that he should be induced to change from a production plan which is option II to one which is option I. What are the implications of such a proposal? In physical terms they are set out in the first three columns of Table 2.10. Associated with the reduction of 7.5 in the level of the pollution index would be some losses and some gains. On the loss side appear output reductions of 5 and 10 tons for apples and pears. The gains are reductions in input levels, since quantities of input not used in this fruit-growing operation are available for use elsewhere.

How do we compare the gains and losses arising from the reduced level of pollution? As already argued, since the individual gain and loss items are physically distinct and therefore not commensurable, we can only do this by

Table 2.10 Implications of a reduction in pollution

	Option II	Option I	Difference physical	Price	Difference value
Apples	25	20	−5	£100	−£500
Pears	40	30	−10	£200	−£2000
Pollution	8.5	1	−7.5		
Labour	2.5	2	+0.5	£1000	+£500
Land	7.5	5	+2.5	£500	+1250
Pesticide	22.5	20	+2.5	£100	+£250
			Total value change		−£500

using prices to convert everything to value terms. The fourth column of Table 2.10 gives the prices from Table 2.2, which prices give the relative prices subject to which the fruit grower chose option II as his production plan. The fifth column gives the values which result from multiplying together the entries in columns three and four. We see that, at these prices, a switch from option II to option I would mean a reduction in output value of £2500, and a reduction in the value of inputs used of £2000. Benefit less cost for the fruit-growing operation would fall by £500. Another way of putting this is to say that the *opportunity cost* of reducing the pollution index from 8.5 to 1 would be £500.

The idea of opportunity cost is one of the most fundamental concepts in economic analysis. To say that the opportunity cost of some action is £x is to say that the result of the action would be a reduction in the value of all the results of economic activity of £x. In the fruit grower example to arrive at the opportunity cost of the pollution reduction we subtracted from the lost output value of £2500 the reduced cost of inputs, amounting to £2000. This is because, to repeat, inputs released from this fruit-growing activity are available for use elsewhere in the economy, so that the value of such released inputs must be offset against the value of the lost fruit output. A figure for the opportunity cost of an action is, then, a summary of all the effects of the action in one number, which number is a valuation at the ruling prices. The fact that economists express opportunity costs in terms of money does not mean that they are uninterested in the physical realities. It does reflect the fact that only by way of valuation is it possible to aggregate across the many physical consequences of an action, such as pollution reduction, so as to assess the overall impact of that action, and that value is most conveniently expressed in money terms.

It follows from the discussion of the previous section that opportunity cost could be expressed in terms other than money. The opportunity cost of pollution reduction of £500 in Table 2.10 could, for example, be stated in terms of equivalent apples. Thus, given that the price of apples is £100 per ton, £500 is equivalent to 5 tons of apples. Hence, we could perfectly well say that the opportunity cost of reducing this fruit grower's pollution from 8.5 to 1 index unit is 5 tons of apples. By this we would mean that the pollution reduction involves gains and losses with a total net impact equivalent to 5 tons of apple output. In practice, opportunity cost is stated in terms of money rather than apples, or whatever, for reasons of convenience and general intelligibillty. If I am interested in reducing the pollution due to this fruit grower's activities from 8.5 to 1, I will presumably want to know what the implications of so doing are before advocating that the reduction be effected. To tell me only that the physical consequences are as set out in the third column of Table 2.10 is not obviously very helpful – how do I compare, for example, a reduction in pear output of 10 tons with the release for other uses of 2.5 acres of land? Telling me the opportunity cost converts all the items in that third row to the same basis of measurement, and weighs the various physical consequences against one another. This result could be reported to me as being equivalent to the loss of 5 tons of apples. If I have never seen or eaten, or do not like, apples, then stated this way the result gives me little insight as to the opportunity cost involved. However, if the result is given to me in money terms I can, using the appropriate prices, convert from money into whatever real things I find it helpful to think in terms of. If, for example, the price of chocolate is £1 per lb then I can interpret the £500 opportunity cost of the pollution reduction as the equivalent of the loss of 500lb of chocolate.

Our original discussion of the fruit grower's choice of production plan, in sections 2.1 and 2.2 above, was we have now noted based on an incomplete description of the technical opportunities facing him. Implicitly we assumed that the fruit grower was unaware of the pollution arising from his activities. The question which now arises is: would the fruit grower's choice of production plan be different if he were aware of the pollution aspects of each of the options open to him? The answer to this question is: it depends upon whether he calculates costs and benefits with a price attached to pollution or not.

Suppose, first, that for the fruit grower the price to be used in valuing pollution is £0. This is the typical situation for the operators of activities giving rise to pollution. It arises from the fact that the pollution-affected environmental media either have no owners or have owners whose legal rights do not include the ability to extract from polluters compensation for the pollution damage. We can take it that for our fruit grower it is the latter case which is operative. The runoff pollutes nearby streams, which do have owners. However, the owners' property rights are not defined in terms of unpolluted streams so that they cannot extract any compensation from the fruit grower for the pollution his activities cause. Hence, to the fruit grower the pollution generation is a costless activity and he uses the price £0 on pollution in his valuation calculations. The result of this is that knowledge of the polluting consequences of each of the available options makes no difference to his choice of production plan. This the reader can immediately see by considering the use of Table 2.9 with the prices given in Table 2.2 plus a price of £0 per pollution to calculate the (B–C) values under each option.

Now, suppose that there exists an environmental protection agency with the legal power to extract payment from the fruit grower in respect of the pollution he is responsible for. Let the charge so imposed be £70 per index unit of pollution. Then, with the technological options as set out in Table 2.9, and with other input and output prices facing the fruit grower as given in Table 2.2, the reader can easily confirm that we get

	Option I	Option II	Option III
£(B–C)	1430	1405	540

so that the fruit grower will now prefer option I. The imposition of a pollution charge causes the required reduction in the pollution generated. This is a particular illustration of the first of the points made in the previous section – changing the relative prices facing a producer will cause a change in the production plan. Further, the nature of the change here is also as suggested in the previous section – an increase in the relative price of pollution, a cost item, leads to less of it being produced. The nature of the economist's argument for the use of alterations in the relative prices facing pollution generators to secure reductions in pollution levels will be explored in detail in Chapter 5.

We have in this chapter considered the nature of various kinds of prices, and the way they influence the behaviour of an economic agent, the fruit grower. We have assumed that the economic agent's behaviour follows, given the relative prices facing him, from a desire to do as well as he can for himself, to maximise his profits. We have not considered how the relative prices facing the fruit grower are determined. We cannot, therefore, say anything about whether or not the selfish behaviour of this individual economic agent is consistent with the promotion of the general well-being of society as a whole. In the next two chapters we shall be considering the relationship between price determination and the consistency of selfish individual behaviour with the promotion of social interest. We shall, that is, be considering the working, or otherwise, of Adam Smith's 'invisible hand', introduced in 1.1 of the introductory chapter.

2.4   Commentary

The four key issues raised above are:

(i)   the importance of the distinction between relative and absolute prices

(ii)   the relevance of changing relative prices for the use of inputs to production

(iii)   the idea of opportunity cost

(iv)   the rôle of aggregation in decision making.

In this section we show the relevance of our discussion of these issues to real world problems concerning resource use and environmental quality.

Everybody knows that the price of energy rose between the early 1970s and the early 1980s, with marked upward movements in 1973/74 and 1979/80 especially. For the UK there is published annual data on the quantity of energy used, Q_E, and on expenditure on energy, $P_E Q_E$. By dividing expenditure by quantity in any year we can obtain the price per unit paid for energy in that year, i.e. $P_E Q_E \div Q_E = P_E$.[1]

On this basis the price paid for energy by UK consumers (for use in businesses and in homes) rose from 8p per therm in 1968 to 72p per therm in 1989. Figure 2.1 shows how this absolute energy price behaved over the period 1968 to 1989. It also shows the movement of the general price level over the same period, where this is represented as an index number taking the value 1 in 1968. By 1989 this index number stood at 7.24. For any year t the index number for the general price level is calculated as

$$\frac{\sum_{i=1}^{N}(P_i^t Q_i^{68})}{\sum_{i=1}^{N}(P_i^{68} Q_i^{68})} = \frac{(P_1^t Q_1^{68} + P_2^t Q_2^{68} + P_3^t Q_3^{68} + \ldots\ldots + P_N^t Q_N^{68})}{(P_1^{68} Q_1^{68} + P_2^{68} Q_2^{68} + P_3^{68} Q_3^{68} + \ldots + P_N^{68} Q_N^{68})}$$

where P_i^t is the price paid for the ith good in year t
        Q_i^{68} is the quantity of ith good bought in 1968
        P_i^{68} is the price paid for the ith good in 1968

and there are N goods and services bought in the economy of the UK.
The symbol Σ above is a summation sign, with the meaning shown on the
right-hand side. The general price level index in year t is then the cost of
buying the basket of goods and services actually bought in the UK in 1968
at the prices ruling in year t, expressed relative to the cost of the 1968
quantities at 1968 prices. Figure 2.1 shows that over 1968 to 1989 the UK
economy experienced inflation to the extent that the general price level
rose from 1 to 7.24 – at the prices of 1989 for all goods and services total
expenditure on the 1968 basket of goods and services produced and

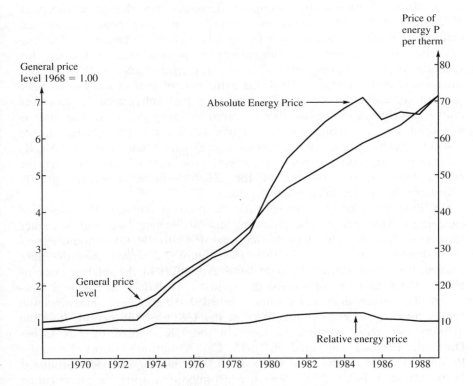

Figure 2.1   The price of energy in the UK 1968–89

consumed in the economy would have been 7.24 times actual 1968 expenditure. This means that absolute prices on average rose by a factor of 7.24. It does not mean that all absolute prices rose by a factor of 7.24 – as Figure 2.1 shows, the absolute price of energy rose by a factor of $9 = 72 \div 8$.

So, over the whole period 1968 to 1989 the price for energy paid by UK energy users rose by more than the price UK citizens paid for goods and services in general. The price of energy relative to prices in general, that is, rose. But clearly the increase in the relative price of energy was a good deal less than the increase in the absolute price of energy. To track the behaviour of the relative price of energy, we just divide its absolute price in year t by the level of the index for the general price level in year t.

Figure 2.1 shows, as Relative energy price, the results so obtained over the period 1968 to 1989. By 1989 the relative, or real as it is sometimes referred to, price of energy was 10p per therm compared with 8p per therm in 1968, which is an increase by a factor of $1.25 = 10 \div 8$. Whereas the absolute price of energy went up ninefold from 1968 to 1989, the relative price increased by just 25%. Both the absolute and relative prices fell back in the latter 1980s, though the former rose again in 1989. Now, the latter price increase is clearly the one which is relevant for decisions about using energy. In production and consumption decisions, it is changes in the price of energy relative to changes in the prices of other commodities that matters. Consider the alternatives facing a household, in terms of allocating available spending over the alternatives of putting fuel in the car for vacation trips or buying beer. The change over 1968 to 1989 in this situation is that whereas in 1968 one extra unit of fuel meant the sacrifice (say) of six units of beer, in 1989 one extra fuel unit meant 7.5 less beer units. The change in the sacrifice involved in using one extra fuel unit is measured by the change in the relative (25%), not the change in the absolute (800%) price. The particular figures here relate only to the UK, but the pattern, and the point, is general – because of inflation over the period 1968–89, the increase in the absolute price of energy greatly overstates the change in its relative price.

UK data for 1968 to 1989 can also be used to illustrate the effects of changing relative prices. The preceding discussion here, and that of earlier sections of this chapter, suggests that over 1968 to 1989 we should expect to find energy use falling in the UK. Figure 2.2 shows that the data confirm this expectation. The right-hand axis refers to the relative price of energy: the time series shown for this is just that derived in Figure 2.1 re-scaled. The other time series shown, labelled 'Energy use', measures the energy intensity of economic activity in the UK over the period. It is the quantity of energy supplied to users in the UK divided by UK Gross Domestic Product measured in 1985 £'s. A nation's Gross Domestic Product, or GDP, is the total value of all the goods and services produced in the nation. It is $\Sigma P_i^t Q_i^t$ for year t, when measured using the prices ruling in year t. In order to eliminate the effects of inflation, year t quantities are aggregated using the prices for some base year.[2] So with 1985 as base year, the time series 'Energy use' in Figure 2.2 is

$$\frac{Q_{Et}}{\sum_{i=1}^{N} P_i^{85} Q_i^t}$$

for t = 1968, 69, ... 1989. It shows energy use falling from 0.248 therms per £1985 of GDP in 1968 to 0.164 therms per £1985 of GDP in 1989, a reduction of some 40%. Note carefully that this is a reduction in energy use per unit of output; production and consumption are becoming less energy intensive.

Now, Figure 2.2 does not prove that the UK economy became less energy intensive over 1968 to 1989 because of the increasing relative price of energy. It is clear that the correlation between energy intensity reductions and energy price increases is not perfect. Even if the correlation were perfect this would not prove the causation. However, we have argued that we should expect that less would be used of something becoming relatively more expensive, and Figure 2.2 certainly does not provide evidence against such hypothesis. We shall put the hypothesis in a slightly more formal way in the Commentary to Chapter 4, where we shall see that this evidence does not lead to rejection of the hypothesis. We can note here that the 1979 upturn in the amount of energy used per unit of output was associated with very low temperatures in

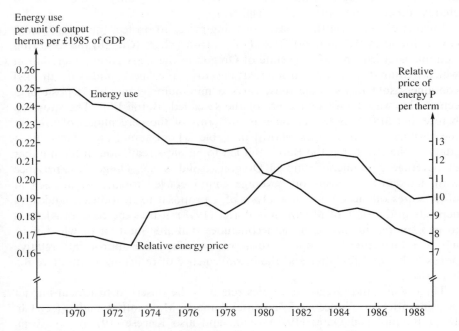

Figure 2.2   Energy use and the price of energy in the UK 1968–89

the UK: 1985 and 1986 were also abnormally cold years. We can also note that while these figures relate to the UK, a similar pattern over 1968–89 – rising relative energy price and falling energy intensity of economic activity – would be found for most advanced economies. The reader will be able to supply for himself numerous particular examples of the motivation to energy conservation consequent upon the higher energy price after 1973/74.

In the hypothetical example considered in the earlier sections of this chapter, we constructed the numbers so that increasing the price the fruit grower paid (from zero) for the damage done to the environment reduced the amount of damage done. For reasons mentioned in 2.3 above and to be considered in Chapter 5, charging a price for environmental damage is in fact not widely observed. However, where environmental damage does carry a price tag there is clear evidence that the damage is less than it would be in the absence of any price tag. Perhaps the longest standing instance of charging for environmental damage is the levying of charges on effluent discharges into the rivers in the Ruhr region of West Germany, which has been going on since the 1930s. While the Ruhr region is the major centre for heavy industry in West Germany, its river system consists of just five relatively small rivers. However, it is now the case that in all but one of these rivers water quality is high enough to permit recreational use, including fishing. A detailed discussion of the Ruhr experience with charging for pollution will be found in Kneese and Bower (1968) or Johnson and Brown (1976). It appears to be a safe conclusion that the charging system has greatly improved water quality in the Ruhr (though perhaps at some cost to air quality – there are no charges on emissions into the atmosphere).

Further evidence on the efficacy of using prices to protect the environment can be found in Baumol and Oates (1979), from where (Ch. 18) the following example is taken. In 1971 the state of Oregon in the USA adopted legislation which required that all carbonated beverage (i.e. beer and soft drinks) containers sold in the state must carry a minimum refundable deposit of 5 cents. This was the major feature of the so-called 'Bottle Bill'. The situation before and after this legislation was, in terms of the percentages of sales in the various container types, shown in Table 2.11. Baumol and Oates cite a study to the effect that the Bottle Bill led to an 88% reduction in the number of beverage containers found in Oregon's solid waste. Oregon's experience with mandatory deposits on beverage containers led to interest in such in other states of the USA. An analysis of a proposal to introduce mandatory deposits in the state of Michigan is Porter (1978): it uses the conceptual basis to be explored in this book, and concludes that the question of whether or not to implement the proposal turns on, in effect, the appropriate relative prices to be used for litter and the inconvenience of returning bottles (see 8.5 here also).

These Ruhr and Oregon examples relate to the observed historical impact of using prices to reduce environmental damage. Many other studies (see Ch. 18 of Baumol and Oates (1979) again, and also Kneese (1977)) have been undertaken to estimate what the effect of introducing charges for pollution

Table 2.11 The effects of introducing mandatory deposits in Oregon

	Before	After
Beer	(%)	(%)
Returnable bottles	36	96
Non-returnable bottles	31	0
Cans	33	4
Soft drinks		
Returnable bottles	53	91
Non-returnable bottles	7	0
Cans	40	9

Source: Baumol and Oates (1979)

would be in various contexts. One such study can illustrate the concept of opportunity cost, in the context of air pollution. A major source of air pollution is the discharge of SO_2 (sulphur) into the atmosphere, which discharge occurs especially in the combustion of fossil fuels. A number of technologies exist by means of which such discharges can be reduced, and a tax on SO_2 emissions has been suggested as a means of encouraging the adoption of such technologies. According to calculations done by the United States Environmental Protection Agency and cited in an OECD report (1980, Ch. 3), the relationship between different tax rates and the consequent reduction in SO_2 emissions in the USA would be as shown in the first two columns of Table 2.12. The third column shows the annual control costs arising, in billions of $US. These are opportunity costs. The tax liabilities arising on the sources of the SO_2 emissions, shown in the fourth column, are not opportunity costs. These tax payments would be costs to the SO_2 generators, but not to the nation as a whole. They would involve only money moving from generators to government. The control costs on the other hand reflect the valuation of the additional inputs to production which would be being used to achieve the indicated reduction in SO_2 emissions. These additional inputs are real costs to the nation as a whole, because they are

Table 2.12 Estimated effects of charges on sulphur emissions in the USA

Tax rate, cents per pound of SO_2 emission	Percentage reduction in emissions	Annual control cost $ billions	Annual tax payment $ billions
5	53	0.9	0.9
10	74	1.7	1.0
15	78	2.1	1.3
20	80	2.4	1.6
25	83	2.8	1.7
30	85	3.0	1.9

Source: OECD (1980)

withdrawn from other productive activities and therefore mean that less is produced elsewhere in the economy. According to these figures, a 53% reduction in SO_2 emissions would require diverting inputs away from producing goods and services and into reducing SO_2 emissions in amount valued at \$0.9 billions. This is the opportunity cost of a 53% reduction. The corresponding £0.9 billions of tax payments is simply a transfer from SO_2 generators to government: the government could, for example, use this revenue to build schools. For a general discussion of the rôle of economic incentives in environmental protection see Anderson *et al.* (1977). We return to this topic in Chapter 5, and also, in relation to carbon dioxide emissions particularly, in Chapter 9.

Finally in this commentary we consider the rôle of aggregation in decision making, and we do this in the context of Environmental Impact Assessment. In the USA the National Environmental Policy Act (NEPA) of 1969 established the requirement that government agencies publish a statement of the environmental impact of proposed major developments. This legislation, and procedures consequent upon it, in the USA has had considerable influence on thinking about controlling the environmental effects of development projects in many countries. Gilpin (1995) outlines the methodologies of EIA and provides a survey of EIA practice around the world: Sardar (1994) is a short EIA textbook. The statement required under NEPA is called an Environmental Impact Statement (EIS), and it is a report based on an Environmental Impact Assessment (EIA) of the proposed development which consists of

(i)   a description of the development
(ii)   a description of the existing environmental conditions in the relevant area
(iii) an assessment of the development's probable environmental impact on the relevant area
(iv)   a review of alternative development projects
(v)   the preparation of a non-technical summary report.

Our concern here is with (iii) and (iv) especially. According to Bisset (1983, p. 169):

> The most commonly used EIA method is the matrix, appearing in a number of guises. The best known, devised by Leopold and his colleagues, is based on a horizontal list of development actions and a vertical list of environmental characteristics. Impacts are identified by relating systematically each development action with all the specified environmental characteristics. When an impact between a project activity and an environmental component is likely the appropriate cell is marked. Although the Leopold matrix has the potential for identifying 8800 impacts, Leopold and his colleagues have estimated that individual projects are likely to result in only 25–50 impacts.
>
> Apart from being used to identify impacts, Leopold and his colleagues devised a scheme to provide an indication of the magnitude and importance of identified impacts. Magnitude refers to the scale of an impact while importance refers to its

significance. It is suggested that both these characteristics be represented by a score on a scale of 1–10 indicating increasing magnitude or importance. For example, a proposed project may reduce the water table over a wide area by a few centimetres. The magnitude score might be 8, but the importance scale might only be 2. Leopold *et al.* suggest that impact cells be bisected and that magnitude scores be placed in the top left-hand corner and importance scores be placed in the opposite corner. When completed, the Leopold matrix provides a useful visual summary of some of the characteristics of impacts.

According to Bisset the Leopold matrix 'cannot be used to evaluate beneficial or harmful impacts *in toto*' or to rank alternative projects, 'because there is no standardised way of assigning the scores nor is there a means of assigning weights to different impacts to determine relative importance'. Similarly, Barbour (1980, p. 192) says that 'No attempt is made to aggregate the numbers to obtain overall ratings.' Rather 'the matrix serves as an initial search list and as a summary' and 'the numbers in the corresponding cells for alternative project options can be directly compared, allowing a point-by-point comparison'.

Now, point-by-point comparisons of alternative projects are of interest of course, but the obvious question which arises is how they can form a basis for a decision between alternatives. If it is revealed that project A has a large important effect on fish and a small unimportant effect on aquatic plants, while project B has a small unimportant fish effect and a large important plant effect, what implications should this have for a decision between A and B? Clearly, the answer must depend on the relative weights the decision maker attaches to fish and plants. According to Bisset and Barbour, EIA avoids imposing such weights, or should so do. But if it does its usefulness to decision makers is clearly somewhat limited. As Wathern notes in a discussion of 'Ecological Modelling in Impact Analysis' (Ch. 3.4 in Roberts and Roberts 1984): 'One of the problems faced by decision makers is the necessity to relate data on a number of different types of impact, some beneficial, some adverse, before arriving at a decision. Several methods have been developed which attempt to express all impacts quantitatively in a form that can then be aggregated.' Also Bisset (1983) notes that: 'There have been repeated attempts to devise methods capable of comparing the relative importance of all impacts. This is accomplished by weighting, standardising and aggregating impacts to produce a composite index for either beneficial or harmful impacts or for alternative project designs.' For present purposes the essential point is the recognition of the need for weighting and aggregation in studying environmental problems. As noted in the earlier sections of this chapter, relative prices are a means of aggregation. The basis for the claim that they are a desirable set of aggregation weights or ratios is examined in subsequent chapters. One problem here is that many environmental impacts do not have prices attached to them: this is discussed in Chapters 5 and 8 especially, though the conceptual basis for the attempt to find surrogate prices is to be found in Chapters 3 and 4.

We refer now to a paper by Effer (Ch. 7.2 in Roberts and Roberts (1984)) reporting experience in preparing environmental assessments for power station siting decisions in Canada. In this exercise potential sites 'were compared on a numerical basis using a number of environmental parameters each of which is assigned a number or weight. Each factor is assigned an environmental factor of concern; 0 – minimal, 1 – slight, 2 – moderate, 3 – significant, 4 – large, 5 – very large, which when multiplied by the factor weight gives a number for that factor and potential site. Summation of values for each site gives a number which allows the site to be rated in order of preference'. Effer notes that in 'criticisms of this study, ecologists and others have objected to the use of numbers in comparing environmental factors'. He reports that: 'We have requested alternative suggestions and to date have had none that could be used in a practical sense to compare and eliminate alternatives.' Economists would argue that cost benefit analysis, using relative prices as weights, is the way to 'compare and eliminate alternatives'. We discuss cost benefit analysis in Chapter 8. Worldwide, a very large number of EIAs and EISs have been conducted since 1970. Views on how useful they have been naturally vary. It would appear that there is fairly wide agreement that they have been useful in raising awareness about environmental impacts generally, and in relation to specific developments. They have done a lot to stimulate research into methods for predicting environmental impacts. On the other hand, many qualified commentators take the view that to date these processes have been somewhat ineffective in providing decision makers with useful information in regard both to yes/no decisions on developments and on the means for impact mitigation in the case of a yes decision. It is noted that: the EIA and EIS procedures are not generally integrated into overall land use planning systems; that they are not suited to dealing with the cumulative effects associated with a series of individual developments in an area; that there is generally, where the development is approved, a lack of any follow-up monitoring to assess the accuracy of the impact predictions.

Notes

1. The data on energy price and quantity are taken from various issues of the annual Digest of United Kingdom Energy Statistics: see, for example, Department of Energy (1984). In the first edition of this book, the empirical analysis of energy demand covered the years 1968 to 1982. The reason why the updating in this second edition only extends the analysis to 1989 is that thereafter the data, required here and in Chapter 5, are not all available on a basis consistent with that for 1968 to 1989.
2. For a further discussion of the concept and measurement of GDP, see for example Samuelson and Nordhaus (1985) or Wonnacott and Wonnacott (1979). The topic is discussed also in 9.3 here. The GDP data used for Figure 2.2 are from Central Statistical Office (1993).

Chapter 3

The economic problem

In Chapter 2 we considered the rôle which prices play in individual decision making, emphasising the way in which the choice from among alternatives depends upon the relative prices facing the decision maker. We did not discuss the question of how the prices involved are determined. We did not look at the question of whether the choices made by individuals added up to a socially desirable outcome. It is to these two, closely related, questions that this and the next chapter are addressed. In this chapter we are concerned with the nature of the economic problem facing a society, with the question of what constitutes a satisfactory solution to that problem, and with conceivable means of realising such a solution. In Chapter 4 we shall focus more narrowly on the rôle of markets in achieving a solution to society's economic problem.

3.1 The nature of the economic problem

It is conventional in economics to call an individual decision-making unit involved in productive activity a *firm*. Firms take as inputs *factors of production* and use them to produce *commodities* as outputs. Factors of production comprise land, labour, natural resources and items of capital equipment (which are buildings, machines, roads, etc.). The decision-making entities which use and consume the commodities produced in firms we shall call *households*. Commodities are, then, things like apples, pears, bread, haircuts, television sets and so on. As well as consuming the output of firms, households supply the labour used in production by firms.

Given a society comprising individual units which are firms and households, it faces an economic problem consisting of three related questions. How much of each commodity should be produced? How shall each commodity be produced? How should the quantity of each commodity which is produced be shared as between the households? These questions have to be answered in the context of the particular circumstances facing the society. The relevant circumstances are: the amounts available of each of the factors of production, the technical opportunities for transforming factors of production into commodities, and the preferences of households as between the various commodities which can be produced.

In order to clarify the nature of this economic problem, we shall set it out in full for a highly simplified society. We assume that there are just two factors of production, land and labour. We assume that there are just two commodities, wheat and cloth, each of which is produced by a single firm. We assume that there are just two households, denoted A and B. We also assume that there is an absolute difference between land which is suitable for wheat growing and land which is suitable for sheep rearing, so that the amounts of land available to wheat and cloth production are fixed. This means that, in terms of the use to be made of factors of production, the only question is how to divide the total amount of labour available as between wheat and cloth production. With L as the total amount of labour available, the constraint on labour use is

$$L_C + L_W = L \qquad [3.1]$$

where L_C is the amount of labour used in cloth production and L_W the amount used in wheat production. Equation [3.1] simply says that the sum of the labour inputs to the two firms must equal the total amount of labour available to the economy. The size of L is the first of the relevant circumstances referred to above. We shall consider an economy for which $L = 100$ units.

The second set of relevant circumstances referred to were the technical opportunities for transforming factors of production into commodities. For our model economy these are the *production functions* for wheat and cloth, which are shown in Figure 3.1. These show, for each commodity, how commodity output varies as the amount of labour input is changed. As

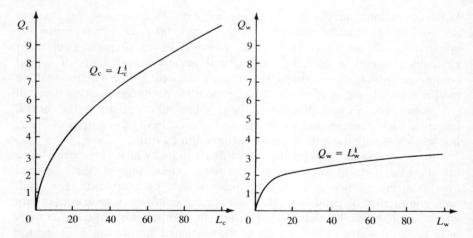

Figure 3.1   Production functions for cloth and wheat

Table 3.1 Some producible cloth and wheat outputs

L_C	Q_C	L_W	Q_W
100	10	0	0
90	9.49	10	1.78
80	8.94	20	2.12
70	8.37	30	2.34
60	7.75	40	2.52
50	7.07	50	2.66
40	6.33	60	2.78
30	5.48	70	2.89
20	4.47	80	2.99
10	3.16	90	3.08
0	0	100	3.16

shown, both production functions have output increasing at a decreasing rate as the input increases. The algebraic equations corresponding to the graphs in Figure 3.1 are

$$Q_C = L_C^{\frac{1}{2}} \tag{3.2}$$

$$Q_W = L_W^{\frac{1}{4}} \tag{3.3}$$

where L_C and L_W are as previously defined, where Q_C stands for the quantity of cloth produced, and Q_W for the quantity of wheat produced. $L_C^{\frac{1}{2}}$ is another way of writing $\sqrt{L_C}$ so that equation [3.2] says that the quantity of cloth produced is equal to the square root of the amount of labour input to cloth production. Similarly, $L_W^{\frac{1}{4}}$ is the same as $\sqrt[4]{L_W}$ so that equation [3.3] says that wheat production is equal to the fourth root of the amount of labour input. Table 3.1 gives the output levels for cloth and wheat corresponding to labour input levels varying from 0 to 100 in steps of 10: the L_C and L_W figures are obtained either by reference to the graphs of Figure 3.1, or by substitution in the equations above. The reason for having the L_C and L_W values run from opposite ends of the range 0 to 100 will become apparent in the next section. Notice that both production functions exhibit diminishing marginal returns (see 1.1 in Chapter 1).

The third set of relevant circumstances are the preferences of households as between the commodities. We describe household preferences across commodities in terms of *utility functions*, and *indifference curves*. A utility function is an algebraic relation which associates a particular pattern of commodity consumption by a household with a particular value of an index of satisfaction or utility for that household. The utility functions for the households A and B in our model economy are

$$U_A = Q_{AC}^{\frac{1}{2}} Q_{AW}^{\frac{1}{2}} \tag{3.4}$$

$$U_B = Q_{BC}^{\frac{1}{2}} Q_{BW}^{\frac{1}{4}} \tag{3.5}$$

Table 3.2 Two household preference systems

Q_{AC}/Q_{BC}	Q_{AW}/Q_{BW}	U_A	U_B
5	0	0	0
4.745	0.890	2.054	2.115
4.470	1.060	2.177	2.146
4.185	1.170	2.214	2.128
3.875	1.260	2.210	2.084
3.535	1.330	2.168	2.019
3.165	1.390	2.097	1.932
2.740	1.445	1.989	1.814
2.235	1.495	1.828	1.653
1.580	1.540	1.560	1.400
0	1.580	0	0

where

U_A is the utility index level for household A
U_B is the utility index level for household B
Q_{AC} is the quantity of cloth consumed by A
Q_{AW} is the quantity of wheat consumed by A
Q_{BC} is the quantity of cloth consumed by B
Q_{BW} is the quantity of wheat consumed by B

Table 3.2 shows how U_A varies with Q_{AC} and Q_{AW}, and how U_B varies with Q_{BC} and Q_{BW} for some illustrative consumption levels. The entries under U_A and U_B are obtained by replacing the symbols on the right-hand sides of equation [3.4] and [3.5] by the appropriate numerical values and calculating the corresponding values for U_A and U_B. Clearly, households A and B have different preferences over the commodities wheat and cloth. Whereas consuming 3.535 units of cloth and 1.33 units of wheat corresponds to a utility index level of 2.168 for A, for B the same consumption levels correspond to a utility index level of 2.019. Further, for household A the utility index reaches its maximum (over the range of variation shown) for $Q_{AC} = 4.185$ and $Q_{AW} = 1.17$ while for household B it is $Q_{BC} = 4.47$ and $Q_{BW} = 1.06$ which produces the maximum for the utility index.

Indifference curves are a convenient way of representing household preferences graphically. They are, in the present context, lines drawn through those wheat/cloth consumption level combinations which produce the same level of the utility index. Table 3.3 shows how such combinations are identified for households A and B having the utility functions [3.4] and [3.5]. If we square both sides of equation [3.4], for example, we get $U_A^2 = Q_{AC} Q_{AW}$, which implies that Q_{AC} is given by U_A^2 divided by Q_{AW}. So, if we set U_A at some particular level and solve $Q_{AC} = U_A^2 \div Q_{AW}$ for Q_{AC} as we vary Q_{AW} we discover those Q_{AC}/Q_{AW} combinations which go with the particular chosen level of U_A. Some results arising for the utility functions for the two households are shown for the utility index levels 2, 3 and 4. These same

Table 3.3 Representative indifference curve coordinates

Household A						Household B					
$U_A = 2$		$U_A = 3$		$U_A = 4$		$U_B = 2$		$U_B = 3$		$U_B = 4$	
Q_{AC}	Q_{AW}	Q_{AC}	Q_{AW}	Q_{AC}	Q_{AW}	Q_{BC}	Q_{BW}	Q_{BC}	Q_{BW}	Q_{BC}	Q_{BW}
4	1	9	1	16	1	4	1	9	1	16	1
2	2	4.50	2	8	2	2.83	2	6.36	2	11.31	2
1.33	3	3	3	5.33	3	2.31	3	5.20	3	9.24	3
1	4	2.25	4	4	4	2	4	4.50	4	8	4
0.80	5	1.80	5	3.20	5	1.79	5	4.03	5	7.6	5

If $U_A = Q^{\frac{1}{2}}_{AC} Q^{\frac{1}{2}}_{AW}$, $U^2_A = Q_{AC}Q_{AW}$ so that $Q_{AC} = U^2_A / Q_{AW}$

If $U_B = Q^{\frac{1}{2}}_{BC} Q^{\frac{1}{4}}_{BW}$, $U^2_B = Q_{BC}Q^{\frac{1}{2}}_{BW}$ so that $Q_{BC} = U^2_B / Q^{\frac{1}{2}}_{BW}$

results are shown graphically, as indifference curves, in Figure 3.2. The terminology arises because the household is 'indifferent' as between all the wheat/cloth consumption bundles lying along such a curve, all such bundles producing the same level of the household's utility index.

Figure 3.2 again shows that households A and B have different preferences as between wheat and cloth. As we move from left to right along an indifference curve the household is reducing its consumption of cloth and receiving increased wheat consumption in sufficient amounts to maintain the level of the utility index constant. From Figure 3.2 it is apparent that, per

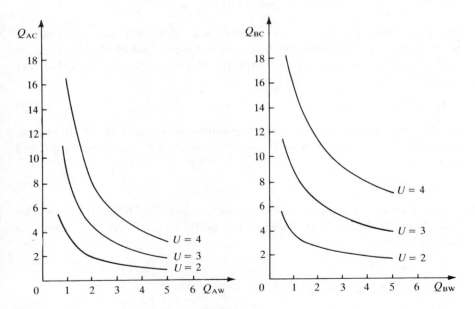

Figure 3.2 Representative indifference curves

unit of cloth consumption given up, the maintenance of a constant level of the utility index requires more wheat compensation for household B than for household A. In this sense, household B has a stronger preference for cloth, as against wheat, than household A.

We have now specified all the relevant circumstances for our simple model economy. We have the data of the economic problem. That problem is, to recapitulate, to fix the output levels for cloth and wheat, to determine how much labour to use in the production of each of these commodities, and to determine how each of these commodities shall be shared between the two households. Now clearly there are many 'solutions' to this problem, in the sense that there are many combinations of Q_C, Q_W, L_C, L_W, Q_{AC}, Q_{AW}, Q_{BC} and Q_{BW} which are feasible, given that there are 100 units of labour available in total. But clearly, when we speak of 'the solution to the economic problem' we do not mean just any old feasible set of output and input levels allocated in any old way between households A and B. What we mean by 'the solution' is a state of affairs which, from among all the many feasible alternatives, is, in some sense, best. This means that in order to discuss the nature of the solution and its realisation we have to specify a performance criterion for the economy, according to which the feasible alternatives can be ranked. We discuss this in the next two sections of this chapter. The essential point is that the measure of economic performance is based on the preferences of the households.

3.2   Production and utility possibilities

We must begin by going back to the availability of labour as input to production and the production functions for wheat and cloth. If we square both sides of equation [3.2] and write the resulting equation the other way around, we get

$$L_C = Q_C^2 \tag{3.6}$$

for the way labour input to cloth production varies with cloth output. Similarly, if we raise both sides of equation [3.3] to the power four and rearrange, we get

$$L_W = Q_W^4 \tag{3.7}$$

for the way labour input to wheat production varies with wheat output. We know that total labour available is 100 units, so if all available labour is being used we have

$$L_C + L_W = 100$$

or, from equations [3.6] and [3.7]

$$Q_C^2 + Q_W^4 = 100$$

which means that

$$Q_C^2 = 100 - Q_W^4$$

or

$$Q_C = (100 - Q_W^4)^{\frac{1}{2}} \qquad\qquad\qquad [3.8]$$
$$= \sqrt{(100 - Q_W^4)}$$

This says that, with all the available labour of 100 units being used, the output of cloth is related to the output of wheat such that Q_C is equal to the square root of 100 minus Q_W raised to the power four. Equation [3.8] is the economy's *production possibility frontier*; it is shown graphically as the curve CW in Figure 3.3. The production possibility frontier shows all the possible combinations of wheat and cloth output available to the economy, given that all of the available labour is being used in one or other productive activity.

We can derive the production possibility frontier shown in Figure 3.3 in a slightly different way, which helps to show exactly what it represents. In Table 3.1 we displayed the wheat and cloth production functions in tabular form. Looking back at it we see that it is so arranged that for every row the sum of L_C and L_W is 100. Thus, the first row corresponds to a situation where all of the available labour is used to produce cloth. Moving to the second row involves shifting 10 units of labour from cloth production to

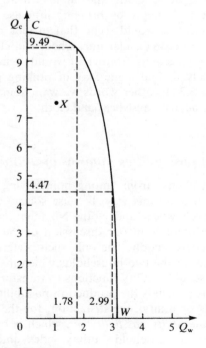

Figure 3.3   Production possibilities

wheat production, resulting in a fall in the former and an increase in the latter. Moving on to the third row, a further 10 units of labour is shifted from cloth to wheat production. And so on down the table until all the available labour is being used in wheat production. Now, the production possibility frontier shown as the curve CW in Figure 3.3 is just the result of proceeding in the same way for very small successive shifts of labour from cloth to wheat production, and graphing the results. That is to say, that what the production possibility frontier shows is how the cloth wheat output mix varies as labour input is shifted between the two production activities, given that all available labour is being used. Two illustrative cloth/wheat combinations are identified in Figure 3.3; the corresponding labour input levels are given in Table 3.1.

It is not, of course, essential in a technical sense to use all of the available labour. The *production possibility set* is, in Figure 3.3, the area bounded by the two axes and the production possibility frontier CW. It is the set of points corresponding to all the possible $Q_C Q_W$ combinations which the economy could produce. While all such output mixes are technically feasible, it is clear that they are not all equally desirable. Starting from any point, such as X, lying inside the production possibility frontier, it is possible to have more cloth and more wheat simply by using some of the available but unused labour in each productive activity. It is only when all the available labour is being used that more cloth means less wheat, or vice versa. There being no virtue in not having more cloth and more wheat, when more of both commodities can be had simply by bringing into use currently unemployed labour, it is pretty clear, it would seem, that in looking for solutions to the economic problem we need consider only wheat and cloth output levels lying along the production possibility frontier. It would seem, that is, that to find a solution we need only to find some way of ranking points lying along the curve CW in Figure 3.3. In other words we want some representation of the society's preferences as between wheat and cloth.

Representation of possibilities in terms of utilities

Actually we cannot choose from among points lying along the production possibility frontier in quite this way, because society as such does not have preferences as between wheat and cloth. No mention of social preferences over commodities was made in our discussion of the data of the economic problem in the previous section. The only such preferences we have to refer to are the preferences of the two households which make up this society. We need to use the households' utility functions to transform the statement about feasible output levels (which is the production possibility set) into a statement about feasible levels of utility, or satisfaction, for the two households. This latter statement is the *utility possibility set*, which is bounded by axes which measure levels of each household's utility index and the *utility possibility frontier*.

To see what is involved here consider Figure 3.4. On the left we show the production possibility set taken from Figure 3.3, along the frontier of which four particular wheat/cloth output combinations are distinguished. The graph to the right has axes labelled U_A and U_B, so that the coordinates of a point are the levels of the utility index for household B and for household A. Take first the point C on the production possibility frontier, representing outputs of 10 for cloth and 0 for wheat. If no wheat is produced, the wheat consumption levels for households A and B must be zero in each case. Reference to the utility function equations [3.4] and [3.5], or to Table 3.2, shows that for both households the utility index level corresponding to zero wheat consumption is zero. Hence the point C on the production possibility frontier maps into the origin of the graph for U_A and U_B. In the same way the point W on the production possibility maps into the origin on the right of Figure 3.4. Consider now the point y on the production possibility frontier, which corresponds to 1.78 units of wheat output and 9.49 units of cloth output. With positive outputs of both commodities, both households could consume both commodities with non-zero levels of the utility index corresponding. The utility index levels actually achieved by each household will depend on how the 1.78 units of wheat and 9.49 units of cloth are shared between the households. Obviously there are a very large number of possible share out patterns, to each one of which will correspond a particular U_A/U_B combination. A small selection of such U_A/U_B combinations, corresponding

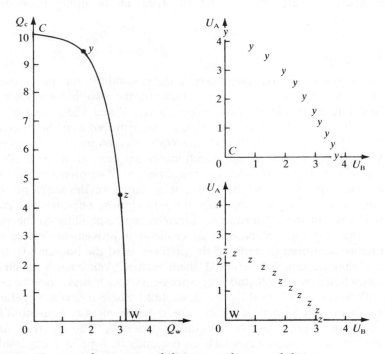

Figure 3.4 From production possibilities to utility possibilities

to y on the production possibility frontier, are shown on the right in Figure 3.4 by the ys. These are obtained by allocating the 1.78 units of wheat and the 9.49 units of cloth to the households A and B in the proportions S and (1-S), for S going from 1 to 0 in steps of 0.1, and computing the corresponding levels of U_A and U_B from equations [3.4] and [3.5]. Thus, for example, for S = 0.8 we get $U_A = 3.288$ and $U_B = 1.064$, and for S = 0.2 we get $U_A = 0.822$ and $U_B = 3.010$. (The reader should check these figures to ensure understanding of the steps involved.) The zs on the right of Figure 3.4 show the U_A and U_B levels arising when we follow the same procedure with respect to the wheat and cloth output levels corresponding to the point z on the production possibility frontier.

Now we have explicitly considered just four of the very many combinations of cloth and wheat output represented by the production possibility frontier. Further, for each of those output combinations we have considered the utility levels arising for just a few of the very many possible ways of splitting the wheat and the cloth between the two households. If we were to consider all of the possible combinations of levels for U_A and U_B corresponding to all the possible output combinations lying along the production possibility frontier, we would get points completely filling the utility possibility set shown as the area AOB in Figure 3.5. The utility possibility set is bounded by the U_A and U_B axes and the utility possibility frontier AB. That is, this economy can produce any of the combinations of levels of satisfaction or utility for the two households, represented by U_A and U_B, lying in the utility possibility set AOB.

Efficient allocations

The significance of this representation of the possibilities for this economy in terms of delivering utility, or satisfaction, to the two households can be discussed in terms of the (illustrative) points 1, 2, 3 and 4 identified in Figure 3.5. If production and output allocation are so arranged that the households' consumption levels give rise to U_A and U_B corresponding to the point 1 in Figure 3.5, then a rearrangement which involves a move to point 2 will make both households better off. This rearrangement may involve a change in the output levels for wheat and cloth and/or a change in the share out of the cloth and wheat outputs as between the households. The essential point is that at the production/allocation arrangement corresponding to the point 1 there exists the possibility for a costless improvement in economic performance measured in terms of the preferences of the households. By this we mean that starting from point 1 there exist rearrangements which make both households better off and rearrangements which make one household better off without making the other household worse off, where 'better off' and 'worse off' are measured against the criterion of each household's own preferences as represented by its utility function. This is true of any arrangement of the economy which corresponds to a point lying inside the utility possibility frontier – for any such point there must exist a move onto the utility possibility frontier which involves an increase in the level of one household's utility index and does not thereby require a reduction in the level of the other household's utility index.

The situation is quite different when we consider points such as 2, 3 and 4 in Figure 3.5 lying on the utility possibility frontier. The economy simply cannot deliver combinations of U_A and U_B levels corresponding to points lying outside this frontier. There is no possible arrangement of labour input levels, output levels, and allocations between households A and B of the outputs which will give rise to a U_A/U_B combination lying outside the utility possibility set. Hence, starting from the point 2 in Figure 3.5 there are only three types of rearrangement of the economy which are possible. A move from 2 to any position inside the utility possibility frontier must make at least one household worse off: a move such as from 2 to 1 makes both households worse off. A move from 2 in a north-west direction along the utility possibility frontier, to 4 for example, makes household A better off, in terms of its own preferences, at the cost of making household B worse off, in terms of its own preferences. A move from 2 in a south-east direction along the frontier, to 3 for example, makes household B better off, as measured by its own utility index, at the cost of making household A worse off, as measured by its own utility index. Given, then, an initial arrangement of the economy such that it corresponds to a point on the utility possibility frontier, there exist no possible rearrangements of output levels for cloth and wheat or of the allocation of these commodities between the households which represent costless improvements. An improvement for one household must be at the expense of the other.

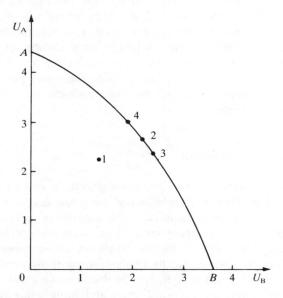

Figure 3.5 The utility possibility set

Arrangements of the economy – in terms of levels for L_C, L_W, Q_C, Q_W, Q_{AC}, Q_{AW}, Q_{BC}, and Q_{BW} – which are such that they give rise to levels of U_A and U_B which lie on the utility possibility frontier are called *efficient allocations*. An efficient allocation is an arrangement of the economy which is such that it is not possible to find a rearrangement which would involve making one household better off, according to its own utility index, while making the other household no worse off, according to its own utility index. It is obviously a 'good thing' to have an efficient allocation in an economy. If a current arrangement of the economy is not an efficient allocation then there exists the possibility for a rearrangement which gives a costless improvement – the possibility, at least, of making one household better off without making the other worse off. To say that an arrangement of the economy is an efficient allocation, or has the property of *allocative efficiency*, is to say that there remain no opportunities for effecting costless improvements.[1] To repeat, the criterion against which 'improvement' and 'cost' are measured here is the preferences of the individual households which constitute the society.

We have now gone some way towards establishing a performance criterion according to which we can compare alternative solutions to the economic problem, so as to be able to identify the 'best' solution. Clearly, solutions which are arrangements of the economy having the property of allocative efficiency are better than solutions lacking this property. To pick a solution not having the property of allocative efficiency is to choose an arrangement of the economy such that there remain unexploited opportunities for making one household feel better off while leaving the other household feeling no worse off. Thus, we know that the best solution must be an arrangement of the economy corresponding to a point lying along the utility possibility frontier. This still leaves us with a large number of potentially best solutions from which to select. But, restriction to this large number of candidate best solutions does at least eliminate the need to consider all of the very many solutions to the economic problem lying inside the utility possibility frontier. The question of choice over the set of efficient allocations is taken up in the next section of the chapter.

3.3   The command economy

To proceed we can suppose that the economy is to be run by an all-knowing and all-powerful planner. By 'all-knowing' we mean that the planner knows all the data of the economic problem – the amount of available labour, the production functions for wheat and cloth, and the preferences of the households over wheat and cloth. By 'all-powerful' we mean that once the planner has decided upon some particular arrangement of the economy as being the best solution to the economic problem, he can realise that solution in the economy simply by ordering firms and households to produce and consume at the levels decided upon. An economy so endowed with a planner who can decide upon and enforce the best solution to the economic problem we shall call a *command economy*. The point of considering such an economy is not to suggest that this is how any actual economies do, or should, operate. It is to bring out further the nature of the problem that any economy faces, and to provide a background to further discussion, especially that of the market economy in the next chapter.

In our command economy, then, the planner knows that $L = 100$, that labour input and output levels in cloth and wheat production are related as given by equations [3.2] and [3.3] graphed in Figure 3.1, and that household preferences are as given by equations [3.4] and [3.5] graphed in Figure 3.2. His problem is to use these data to decide upon the best solution levels of L_C, L_W, Q_C, Q_W, Q_{AC}, Q_{AW}, Q_{BC}, and Q_{BW}. For this he needs a criterion against which to rank alternatives. This criterion is the *welfare function* which transforms levels of the utility indices for A and B into a single welfare index. An illustrative welfare function is

$$W = 0.5U_A + 0.5U_B \qquad [3.9]$$

where W stands for welfare. Equation [3.9] says that welfare is the weighted sum of the levels of the utility index for the two households, with the weights in each case equal to 0.5. Figure 3.6 shows equation [3.9] graphically, for some illustrative U_A U_B level combinations. Thus, for example, $W = 1$ for $U_A = 2$ and $U_B = 0$, for $U_A = 0$ and $U_B = 2$, and for all combinations of U_A and U_B lying along the straight line joining these two points. As W gets bigger so the straight line shifts out to the north east, remaining parallel. Clearly, although Figure 3.6 shows W varying in steps of 1, W can vary

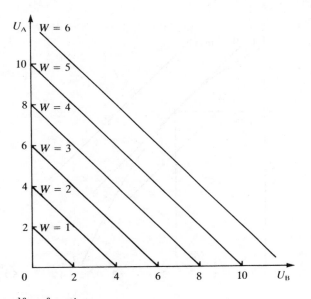

Figure 3.6   A welfare function

continuously, and the six straight lines shown are only an illustrative selection of the very straight lines, joining U_A U_B combinations, corresponding to all possible W levels. It is important to note that this welfare function, or performance criterion, is based on the individual preferences, or utility functions, of the households which comprise the society.

The planner ranks possible arrangements of the economy according to the levels they produce for welfare, measured according to equation [3.9]. His preferred arrangement is that which corresponds to the maximum attainable level for W. Given the way W depends on U_A and U_B, we already have, from the previous section of this chapter, a description of the attainable levels of W in the utility possibility set, bounded by the utility possibility frontier. From among all the points in the utility possibility set, the planner will choose that which produces the maximum level for W. Figure 3.7 brings together the utility possibility set and the welfare function. In terms of maximising W, we want to move as far out from the origin, in a north-easterly direction, as is possible. The limits of what is possible are given by the utility possibility frontier, and clearly the maximum attainable W value is where a W straight line is tangential to the utility possibility frontier. This point of tangency identifies the maximum attainable level for the welfare index. More important, it also identifies for the planner the U_A and U_B levels for his best solution to the economic problem, and thereby the levels for Q_{AC}, Q_{AW}, Q_{BC}, Q_{BW}, Q_C, Q_W, L_C and L_W, to be obtained by working through the utility and production functions. In the command economy, the planner having thus identified the best solution to the economic problem, brings

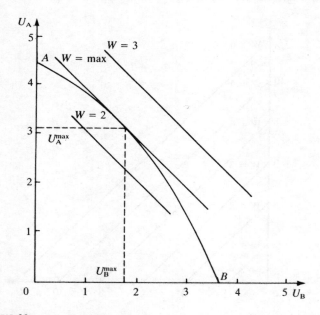

Figure 3.7   Welfare maximisation

about its realisation by simply telling firms and households how much to produce and consume.

Now the welfare function [3.9] weights the utility index levels for the two households equally. This is not the only possibility open to the planner. More generally the welfare function is

$$W = wU_A + (1 - w)U_B \qquad [3.10]$$

where w is a number in the range 0 to 1. As w varies, so will the planner's best solution vary. Figure 3.8 illustrates for three arbitrarily chosen values for w. As w decreases, so the best solution selected by the planner will move more towards a pattern of wheat and cloth production which is determined by the preferences of household B rather than household A. In the limit with $w = 0$, $W = U_B$ and the pattern of wheat and cloth production in the planner's best solution to the economic problem will be that which, given available labour and the production possibilities, maximises the utility index level for household B. Household A will have a utility index level of zero, implying that consumption by it of wheat and/or cloth is zero. At the other extreme, for $w = 1$, the production of wheat and cloth will be determined entirely by the preferences of household A, and B's utility index level will be zero.

What is of particular interest here is that whatever the value taken by w, the best solution to the economic problem always corresponds to a point on the utility possibility frontier. The planner will never, that is, be interested in arrangements corresponding to points inside the utility possibility frontier, whatever the relative weights he attaches to the two households' utility

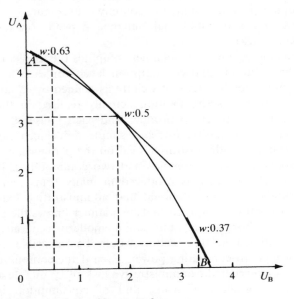

Figure 3.8 Variations in the welfare weights

indices. In the terminology introduced at the end of the previous section, we are saying that, for any value taken by w in the performance criterion (equation [3.10]), the planner will always pick an efficient allocation as his solution. We call w and $(1 - w)$ the planner's *distributional weights*, and we are saying that whatever these are, the set of economic arrangements of interest to the planner is the set of efficient allocations for the economy.

With this in mind, the economic problem can be thought of as two separate problems. The *allocation problem* is the problem of so arranging things that an efficient allocation obtains, in the sense that it corresponds to a point on the utility possibility frontier. The *distribution problem* is the problem of choosing one particular arrangement from among the many arrangements which are solutions to the allocation problem. In the command economy the separation of these problems is essentially a conceptual matter. The actual computation of the best arrangement for the economy would not necessarily proceed sequentially from solutions to the allocation problem to a solution for the distribution problem. However, the distinction is crucial, as we shall see, for appreciating the rôle of markets. To anticipate, it can be claimed for a market economy that, under certain conditions, it solves the allocation problem. It cannot be claimed for a market economy that it will, without some government interference, produce a distributional outcome which would be widely regarded as fair. In terms of Figure 3.5, that is, it can be claimed that a totally unplanned and uncontrolled market economy will end up at a point on the utility possibility frontier rather than inside it. It cannot be claimed that the point arrived at will have any particularly desirable properties in terms of fairness as between households A and B. This should not be taken to imply that we are claiming that fairness as between A and B will obtain in our command economy – as Figure 3.8 illustrates, the command economy's distributional outcome depends on the value for w which the planner uses.

In the command economy the planner computes the levels of labour inputs, cloth and wheat outputs and consumption levels for each household which give the maximum possible level of welfare as defined by equation [3.10], and then ensures that this is the solution actually realised in the economy by telling each firm how much to produce and each household how much to consume of each commodity. For our simple model economy neither the computational nor the administrative load on the planner is very great, there being but two firms, two households and two commodities. But with many commodities, each of which is produced in many firms and consumed by many households, the computational and administrative loads do become great. Note also that it is required that the planner knows the production and utility functions. For a real but small modern economy the sort of computation outlined in this section would be infeasible even given the availability of modern computing power. Even if the computational problem could be solved, consider the administrative task of issuing detailed operating instructions to thousands of firms, and of consumption instructions to millions of households. As already noted, our discussion of the command economy was motivated not by its attraction as a story about how things might actually be done, but by virtue of the way it brings out the nature of the economic problem. Further, it is precisely by reflecting on the enormity of the computational and administrative tasks which would face the planner of a command economy that we can appreciate the remarkable properties of systems of economic organisation which avoid facing a planner with such tasks.

The market system of economic organisation will be discussed at some length in the next chapter. It involves, ideally, no planning functions at all – a set of markets both computes and realises an arrangement of the economy which represents an efficient allocation. However, before discussing the operation of a market economy, it will be useful to consider what we shall call the *planned economy*. In terms of the discussion of the previous paragraph, the essential point about the planned economy is that, by means of the responses of firms and households to prices, the planner can avoid the administrative task of telling firms and households exactly how to behave so that his computed best solution is realised. In the planned economy, that is, the planner identifies and computes the best solution to the economic problem in exactly the manner described in the previous section. To bring about the realisation of this solution he simply declares the prices of all commodities and inputs, and then allows households and firms to make their own decisions about consumption levels and production plans given these fixed prices. It is possible to show that provided that the planner promulgates the correct set of prices, and that firms and households have certain kinds of motivation, such decentralisation works in the sense that all the separate decisions taken actually produce the arrangement of the economy which is the planner's computed solution. The correct set of prices the planner needs to declare require no additional calculation – they are part of the already computed solution. The motivation required of firms and households is the pursuit of self interest.

We will illustrate these remarks concerning the planned economy in section 3.5 below. Prior to doing that we need to develop a methodology for analysing the behaviour arising in the pursuit of self interest. This we do, for firms, in the next section. The methodology is that of marginal analysis, introduced in Chapter 1 in our discussion of neoclassical economics.

3.4   Marginal analysis and net benefit maximisation

Recall that in Chapter 2 we showed the rôle of prices in decision making as being the means by which physically different inputs and outputs were converted to a common basis of measurement. We called the value of all inputs 'cost', and the value of all outputs 'benefit', and we explored the consequences of the firm (i.e. fruit grower) choosing that production plan which offered the greatest excess of benefit over cost. We now note that this is exactly the behaviour which would follow from the pursuit of self interest.

The difference between benefit and cost is just the return, widely known as profit, which accrues to the firm itself. The standard assumption in economic analysis is that firms seek to maximise profit, the difference between benefit and cost. The observed behaviour of firms is to be interpreted as the result of their choosing from among the alternative production plans available to them that one which offers maximum profit. In our discussion in Chapter 2 the firm faced just three alternatives. We now wish to consider the more general case where possible input and output levels vary continuously, and to derive an alternative version of the decision rule 'operate where profit is maximised'. We do this by utilising the marginal analysis approach.

Let us use the symbol Q to represent the output level of a firm, B for benefit, and C for cost. A plausible general assumption is that B and C vary with Q as shown in panel (a) of Figure 3.9; B increases with the output level at a decreasing rate, C at an increasing rate. $B-C$ for any level of Q is clearly just the difference between the height of the two curves at that level of Q. Thus (profit equals) $B-C$ first increases with Q, reaches a maximum, and then declines with Q. It should be clear that the level of Q for which profit is at its maximum is where the curves for B and C have the same slope, shown as Q^* in (a) of Figure 3.9. Panel (b) of Figure 3.9 shows the graph of $B-C$, read off from the difference between the curves in panel (a), reaching a maximum at Q^*. This is labelled NB for *net benefit*, which is an alternative name for profit. We shall prefer to use the term net benefit in what follows for reasons which will become apparent, especially in Chapter 5.

In Figure 3.10, panel (a) is a reproduction of panel (a) from Figure 3.9. In panel (b) of Figure 3.10 we show the benefit function and tangents to it at points corresponding to the output levels, Q_1 and Q_2. Consider a small increase in output from Q_1, denoted ΔQ_1. Then reading off the tangent we find the corresponding small benefit increase as ΔB_1, with $\Delta B_1/\Delta Q_1$ as the slope of the tangent. Now, ΔB_1 is an approximation to the true benefit change associated with the output change ΔQ_1, and clearly the

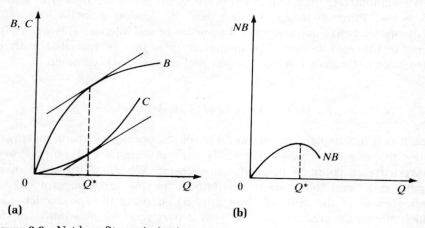

(a)   (b)

Figure 3.9   Net benefit maximisation

approximation will get better as the ΔQ_1 considered gets smaller. If we make ΔQ_1 infinitesimally small there will be no approximation. For such a ΔQ_1 the ratio of the corresponding ΔB_1 to ΔQ_1 is known as *marginal benefit*, evaluated at Q_1. Marginal benefit is a number which tells us by how much benefit increases for an infinitesimally small increase in output: the number, generally, varies with the level of output. This can be seen in (b) of Figure 3.10 by looking at Q_2 and a ΔQ_2, equal to the ΔQ_1 depicted there, and the corresponding ΔB_2. Marginal benefit is just the slope of the benefit curve. *Marginal cost* stands in the same relation to cost as marginal benefit does to benefit: panel (c) of Figure 3.10 illustrates this.

Now, in (d) of Figure 3.10 we show two straight lines, labelled *MC* for marginal cost and *MB* for marginal benefit, the former showing marginal cost increasing with Q, the latter showing marginal benefit decreasing with Q. These lines are just the plots of the slopes of the B and C curves in panel (a) against Q. They intersect at the output level Q^*, necessarily the same as the output level for which B and C have equal slopes in panel (a). Thus, if the firm follows the rule 'operate at that output level for which marginal cost equals marginal benefit', it will thereby operate at the output level which maximises net benefit equals benefit loss cost. We have shown that $MC = MB$ must occur at that level of Q for which $B–C$ is greatest. An alternative way to see why the marginal equality rule identifies a net benefit

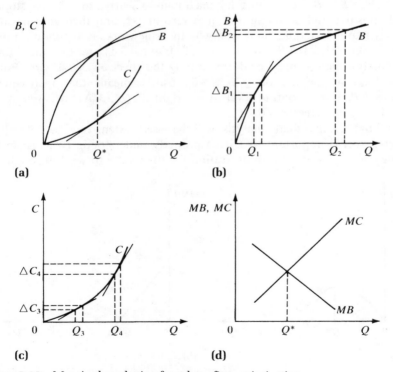

Figure 3.10   Marginal analysis of net benefit maximisation

maximising output level is based on consideration of panel (d) alone, in the light of the definitions of marginal cost and benefit. At the output level Q^*, since marginal cost $\Delta C/\Delta Q$ (for Δ vanishingly small) equals marginal benefit $\Delta B/\Delta Q$ (for the same vanishingly small ΔQ) it follows that moving from Q^* to $Q^* + \Delta Q$ or to $Q^* - \Delta Q$ will leave $B\text{–}C$ unchanged in size. Now consider some Q to the left of Q^* where MB is larger than MC. In this case, increasing output by a vanishingly small amount will increase B by more than C; that is, will increase $B\text{–}C$. Clearly, this must be true for any output level below Q^*. On the other hand, for output levels greater than Q^*, MC is larger than MB, so that moving towards Q^* (cutting output) will have the effect of reducing costs by more than benefits, so increasing $B\text{–}C$. Again, this must be the situation for any output level greater than Q^*. If $B\text{–}C$ increases as Q moves towards Q^* from above or below, then Q^* is the output level for which $B\text{–}C$, net benefit, is maximised.

An alternative marginal rule for identifying the net benefit maximising output level is 'operate where marginal net benefit is zero'. This is shown in Figure 3.11, with the $NB = B\text{–}C$ relationship in panel (a) being that shown in (b) of Figure 3.9. *Marginal net benefit* is just the slope of the net benefit function: it stands in the same relation to net benefit as does marginal cost to cost and marginal benefit to benefit. The graph for marginal net benefit is shown in (b) of Figure 3.11. It cuts the Q axis at the same output level as that for which $NB = B - C$ attains its maximum. Clearly, in (a) the slope is initially positive and declining, becomes zero at Q^*, and then goes negative. In purely marginal terms, the reason why this rule works is as follows. For an output level Q^*, $MNB = 0$ in (b) of Figure 3.11 means that for a (vanishingly) small increase or decrease in Q the effect on NB is zero. For an output level to the left of Q^*, MNB positive means that increasing Q increases NB. For an output level to the right of Q^*, MNB negative means that reducing Q increases NB.

This kind of marginal analysis will be used extensively in subsequent chapters, so it is important that it be properly understood. To assist in this we now consider a numerical illustration for the reader to work through. We

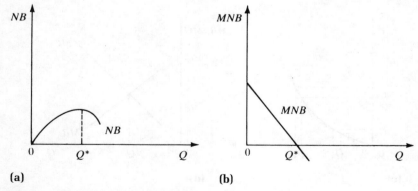

Figure 3.11   An alternative marginal analysis

consider a firm which can sell its output at a price of £12 per unit, whatever the amount produced, so that its benefit function is

$$B = 12Q \qquad\qquad [3.11]$$

shown as the straight line B in (a) of Figure 3.12. Since B is a straight line with a constant slope of 12, MB for marginal benefit is shown in (c) of Figure 3.12 as a horizontal line at height 12. That MB is horizontal, rather than downward sloping as above, does not affect the working of the marginal rule.[2] The firm's cost function is

$$C = Q^2 \qquad\qquad [3.12]$$

shown as the curve labelled C in (a) of Figure 3.12. Reading off the slope of this curve as Q varies and plotting it against Q gives the behaviour of marginal cost as Q rises shown as MC in (c) of the figure. In (a) the output level for which B and C have the same slope is $Q = 6$, which is, in (c), the output level for which $MB = MC$. Consider the implications, in (a) and (c) of Figure 3.12, for the firm of operating with $Q = 5$ or with $Q = 7$.

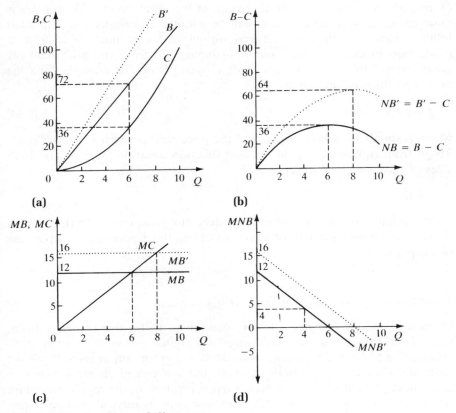

Figure 3.12 A numerical illustration

From equation [3.11] and [3.12], $NB = B - C$ is given by

$$NB = 12Q - Q^2 \qquad\qquad [3.13]$$

the graph for which is shown in (b) of Figure 3.12. It attains its maximum where $Q = 6$, and the corresponding level for $B - C$ is read off the vertical axis as £36. In (d) we show how the slope of the NB graph in (b) varies with Q: MNB is equal to zero at $Q = 6$. Given the meaning for MNB set out above, consider the implications for the firm, in terms of net benefit and using (d), of operating where $Q = 4$, for example.

In Chapter 3 we used the example of the fruit grower to show how a change in the prices facing a firm would, working through the pursuit of self-interest, lead to changes in input and/or output levels. The same point can be illustrated in the present context. Suppose that the price this firm receives per unit of output increases from £12 to £16. Then, in (a) of Figure 3.12, the new benefit function is shown by the dotted line labelled B', and correspondingly for marginal benefit in (c), for net benefit in (b) and for marginal net benefit in (d). The new net benefit maximising output level is $Q = 8$.

In this example we have related costs incurred directly to the level of output, neglecting any explicit discussion of the inputs used. This practice is quite common in economics, and will be adopted at various stages in what follows. However, the link between output and cost must arise from a production function relating output to input, and from the price paid for input, even if this is not always made explicit. Thus, for example, here the firms's production function is

$$Q = L^{\frac{1}{2}} \qquad\qquad [3.14]$$

where L stands for labour input, and the price paid per unit of labour is £1. To go from equation [3.14] to the cost function equation [3.12] square both sides of equation [3.14] to get

$$L = Q^2$$

for the quantity of labour needed to produce any given output level, and then simply use the price per unit of labour to obtain the dependence of input cost on output level.

Working from marginal relationships to totals

Often in economic analysis it is very convenient to be able to derive from, say, information about the relationship of marginal cost to the output level, information about the total cost incurred at any given output level. While we shall not want to do this until the next and subsequent chapters, this is a convenient place at which to explain what is involved in the simple procedure necessary for this purpose. We can use the numerical example just considered.

Consider first the question of by how much total costs increase if output increases from $Q = 1.0$ to $Q = 1.5$, given that marginal cost varies with output as shown in (c) of Figure 3.12, which relationship is also shown in Figure 3.13. The representation in (b) there uses larger scales on each axis to make the exposition clearer. Recall our discussion of what marginal cost is, based on Figure 3.10 above: $MC = \Delta C / \Delta Q$, where ΔQ is an infinitesimally small change, so that $\Delta C = \Delta Q . MC$. For ΔQ small, but not infinitesimally so, this will hold approximately, i.e. $\Delta C \backsimeq \Delta Q . MC$. Let 0.1 be a small change in Q, and in (b) of Figure 3.13 consider Q going from 1.0 to 1.5 in steps of 0.1. When reading up from the horizontal axis to the MC line and then across to the vertical axis we have

Q	MC
1	2.0
1.1	2.2
1.2	2.4
1.3	2.6
1.4	2.8

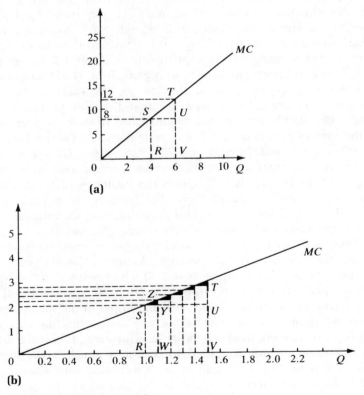

Figure 3.13 From marginal to total cost

so that using $\Delta C \simeq \Delta Q.MC$ we have

for ΔQ from 1.0 to 1.1, ΔC as $0.1 \times 2.0 = 0.2$
for ΔQ from 1.1 to 1.2, ΔC as $0.1 \times 2.2 = 0.22$
for ΔQ from 1.2 to 1.3, ΔC as $0.1 \times 2.4 = 0.24$
for ΔQ from 1.3 to 1.4, ΔC as $0.1 \times 2.6 = 0.26$
for ΔQ from 1.4 to 1.5, ΔC as $0.1 \times 2.8 = 0.28$

so that by summing these ΔCs the approximate increase in total cost going from $Q = 1.0$ to $Q = 1.5$ is 1.2.

This is an approximation because we have used ΔQs of size 0.1 rather than vanishingly small ΔQs. As we made the ΔQs get smaller and smaller so repetitions of the above calculation would produce answers closer and closer to the exactly correct answer. However, we do not need to proceed thus, since it is clear from (b) in Figure 3.13, what the nature and size of the approximation error at each step is. Consider the first step from $Q = 1$ to $Q = 1.1$, for which above we calculated the area of the rectangle $RSYW$, i.e. 0.1×2.0. Clearly, if we went from R to W not in one step of 0.1 for ΔQ but in very many steps of infinitesimally small ΔQ, and at each step calculated $\Delta C = \Delta Q.MC$ and added up all the results what we would calculate would be the area $RSZW$, equal to $RSYW$ plus SYZ, rather than just $RSYW$. That is, the approximation error in working in a single step from $Q = 1$ to $Q = 1.1$ is given by the area of the shaded little triangle SYZ. As shown, this is the case each time we take a step of $\Delta Q = 0.1$. If we add the sum of the areas of the five shaded triangles to the approximate result of 1.2 we get the exact result for the cost increase associated with going from $Q = 1.0$ to $Q = 1.5$.

It is not necessary to proceed thus to get the exact answer required. Inspection of Figure 3.13 (b) indicates that the area formed by the five rectangles like $RSYW$ plus the five small shaded triangles is given by $RSTV$, itself the sum of rectangle $RSUV$ and triangle SUT. The area of $RSUV$ is $(1.5 - 1.0) \times 2 = 1$, and the area of SUT is $0.5 \times SU \times UT = 0.5 \times 0.5 \times 1 = 0.25^3$. Hence, the exact amount of the cost increase associated with going from $Q = 1.0$ to $Q = 1.5$ is 1.25. Given the small size of (a) in Figure 3.12 this is not very easily checked there, but from equation [3.12] $C = 1$ for $Q = 1$ and $C = 2.25$ for $Q = 1.5$. This procedure and the rationale for it are quite general: areas under marginal cost graphs give the corresponding total costs. Thus, in (a) of Figure 3.13 consider the output increase from $Q = 4$ to $Q = 6$ and the associated increase in costs. As above, this is given by the area $RSUV$ plus the area SUT, which is $(6 - 4) \times 8$ plus $0.5 \times (6 - 4) \times 4$ equals 16 plus 4 equals 20. Check this using $C = Q^2$ from equation [3.12]. To find the total cost of producing some level of output from the marginal cost function, we again proceed in the same way considering the change to the output level of interest from an initial level of zero. In Figure 3.13(a) for $Q = 6$, for example, the associated total cost is equal to the area of the triangle $0VT$ equal to $0.5 \times 6 \times 12$ or 36. This checks with what is shown in Figure 3.12(a), and with equation [3.12].

This method of deriving information about total quantities from information on marginal relationships is quite general in the further sense that it is not restricted to the case of costs, but applies to any situation where the marginal relationship is known. To find the total over some interval, find the area under the marginal relationship over the same interval. In terms of Figure 3.12, total benefit can be calculated from the area under the MB line in (c), and total net benefit from the area under the MNB line in (d). As an exercise the reader could use (d) there to find the net benefit levels corresponding to $Q = 2$, 4, 6 and 8, checking the results using $NB = 12Q - Q^2$ from equation [3.13] above.

3.5   The planned economy

We can now return to the discussion of the use of prices to secure an optimal solution to the economic problem, i.e. an efficient allocation, which was introduced at the end of section 3.3 above. We called an economy in which a planner computed the required solution but brought about the realisation of such by allowing firms and households to respond self-interestedly to planner-declared prices, rather than telling them what to do, a 'planned' economy.

Suppose now that the planner has computed a welfare-maximising solution to the economic problem and that it involves the requirement that there be produced 6 units of cloth and 2.828 units of wheat. This is the point X on the production possibility frontier shown in Figure 3.14. The tangent to this point, AB, identifies the slope of the production possibility frontier at X as $0A/0B = 27.14/3.6 = 7.543$. This means that, starting from X, the increase in cloth output obtainable for a very small reduction, ΔQ_W, in wheat output is $\Delta Q_C = 7.543 \Delta Q_W$. With the slope of the production possibility frontier changing continuously, this relation holds exactly only for vanishingly small changes in Q_W. This is exactly analogous to our discussion above of marginal changes. At X, this is the ratio at which the production possibilities of the economy (i.e. the production functions for wheat and cloth) mean that it is possible to exchange wheat for cloth output at the margin. Now, in the previous chapter we considered relative prices as exchange ratios. So, our planner knowing that wheat exchanges technically, i.e. in production terms, for cloth at this ratio at the solution he wishes to see realised, would naturally think of this ratio as a relative price for wheat and cloth. That is, for the planner, the relative price for wheat and cloth involved in the solution to the economic problem is 7.543. In money terms, an absolute price of £12 per unit for cloth and of £90.516 for wheat gives this relative price for wheat in terms of cloth.

We now wish to show that given these wheat and cloth prices, the firms producing wheat and cloth will produce exactly 6 units of cloth and 2.828 units of wheat as a result of their net benefit-maximising decisions. We also need the planner to state the price to be paid for labour. This he sets at £1 per unit, for reasons to be explained shortly. Then, for the cloth-producing

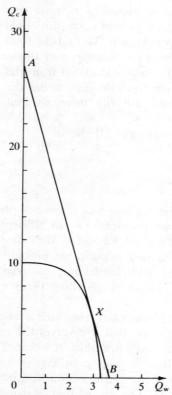

Figure 3.14 The production exchange ratio

firm we have

Benefit = £12Q_C

and for the wheat-producing firm we have

Benefit = £90.516Q_W

From equations [3.6] and [3.7] (which themselves follow directly from the production functions [3.2] and [3.3]) we recall that labour inputs to cloth and wheat production are given by $L_C = Q_C^2$ and $L_W = Q_W^4$, so that with labour costing £1 per unit we have

Cost = £Q_C^2

for cloth production, and

Cost = £Q_W^4

for wheat production. For cloth production we have, then,

Net Benefit = £$(12Q_C - Q_C^2)$ [3.15] and for wheat production

$$\text{Net Benefit} = £(90.516Q_\text{W} - Q_\text{W}^4) \qquad\qquad [3.16]$$

These net benefit relationships are graphed in Figure 3.15. If the cloth firm operates where its net benefit is greatest it will produce exactly the 6 units of cloth the planner requires. Similarly, the self-interested wheat firm will produce as the plan requires. The planner does not need to tell the firms how much to produce, to have his best solution realised as the way production is organised. He needs only to tell the firms the prices at which to buy and sell inputs and outputs. Further, the relative price for the outputs which he needs to establish is nothing but the production exchange ratio for the commodities at the output levels he calculated when finding the best solution to the economic problem.

It remains to see why £1 per unit is the appropriate price to set for labour. The important points involved will be covered by looking just at cloth production. With the price of cloth at £12 per unit, the planner needs to know what price for labour will result in net benefit being maximised when 6 units are produced using 36 units of labour (since $L_\text{C} = Q_\text{C}^2$). Figure 3.16 shows what this calculation involves. Panel (a) shows how benefit varies with output, and panel (c) shows how cost varies with output for different prices per unit of labour – £2, £1, and £0.5. Panels (b) and (d) show the corresponding marginal benefits and marginal costs. From our discussion above we know that the output level at which net benefit is maximised is the output level at which marginal benefit equals marginal cost. Thus, the problem of finding the required price for labour is just the problem of finding the labour price which gives a marginal cost curve which intersects the marginal benefit line at a point for which $Q_\text{C} = 6$. As panel (d) shows, the required price is £1 per unit of labour.

The reader will recall that in Chapter 2 we emphasised the distinction

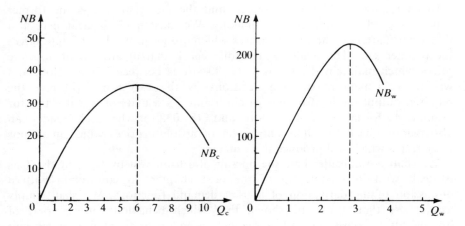

Figure 3.15   Net benefits in cloth and wheat production

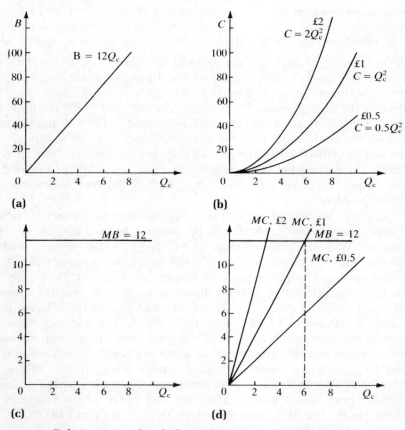

Figure 3.16 Relative prices for cloth and labour

between relative and absolute prices, and the fact that it was the former which were relevant for decision making. We must make it clear here also that what matters is the relative prices which are given by the absolute prices the planner sets. The reader can readily check that at any set of absolute prices which maintain the ratios $1:12:90.516$ as between labour, cloth and wheat, net benefit maximising decisions by the two firms will give the required output levels of 6 units of cloth and 2.828 units of wheat – try, for example, £2 for labour, £24 for cloth, and £181.032 for wheat. The reader can also readily check that it is only a set of absolute prices which maintains these ratios which will produce this outcome.

We shall not consider here the pursuit of self-interest by households. This is dealt with in section 4.3 of the next chapter, in connection with a discussion of the derivation of market demand functions. We shall simply assert here that it can be shown that selfish behaviour on the part of households is consistent with a planner using prices to realise an efficient allocation.

So in the planned economy, efficiency in allocation can be realised by self-interested responses to a set of prices declared by the planner. The planner's view of the appropriate solution to the distribution problem cannot be so realised. The appropriate prices declared by the planner will cause the economy to move to a point on the utility possibility frontier. Where the point lies on the frontier depends upon the relative wealth and incomes of the households A and B. If A is rich relative to B, then the efficient outcome will be one which favours A against B, and vice versa. The planner can guide the economy to the point on the utility possibility frontier indicated by his welfare weights by using taxes on wealth and/or income together with payments to households. Thus, if A is rich relative to B while the planner weights the utilities of A and B equally, he would tax A and give to B, redistributing wealth and/or income as between them. Notwithstanding this requirement to operate a redistributive tax/gift system, it is clear that using prices instead of commands to realise efficiency in allocation greatly reduces the administrative burden placed upon the planner. In the command economy the planner must instruct each household on consumption quantities and each firm on input quantities and output delivery destinations. In the planned economy, given the appropriate redistribution of wealth and income, it is necessary only to declare prices for each commodity and input. The economy of effort in our model economy is not great – 3 prices to declare instead of 4 sets of instructions. But consider an economy with 1000 commodities each produced, using 3 inputs, by 100 firms, and where there are 5 million households. In this case there are 1003 prices as against 5 100 000 sets of instructions, each of some length.

However, while the transition from the command economy to the planned economy greatly reduces the planner's administrative workload, it remains true that the planner has to compute the solution to the economic problem and the prices necessary for its realisation. The computation requires as inputs the production functions for all the firms and the utility functions for all the households. Clearly for an economy with many firms and many households, this is a very large information requirement. The really significant change is that which arises if the planner as information gatherer and computational agent can be entirely eliminated. This is exactly what a system of markets, ideally, makes possible. Such a system of markets in all inputs and commodities itself computes the set of relative prices required for efficiency in allocation. With respect to the goal of efficiency in allocation the planner becomes entirely redundant, being needed for neither information gathering nor computation. This will be discussed in the next chapter. We should note here however that all that can be claimed for an ideal market system is that it will bring about the realisation of an efficient allocation. The efficient allocation realised may or may not be one which could be regarded as fair as between households. There remains, that is, a rôle for central intervention in the economy to promote fairness in distribution. Also, we should note here, as will be discussed more fully in the next chapter, that the conditions necessary for it to be true that a system of markets could, un-aided, realise an efficient allocation are such that it is not possible to believe that they describe any actual economy.

3.6   Commentary

Production and utility functions are the fundamental concepts in economic analysis, describing respectively the terms on which technology permits commodities to be exchanged for one another and preferences across different commodities. They are discussed in detail in all standard microeconomics texts: see, for example, Hirshleifer (1980) (Ch. 3 on utility functions and Ch. 9 on production functions) or Layard and Walters (1978) (Chs 5 and 7). We shall consider some of the implications derivable from the existence of production and utility functions in the next chapter.

According to Hirshleifer (1980, p. 270), 'The production function shows, as a matter of technology, how output produced depends upon the amounts of input factors employed.' In general, there is no presumption as to the particular form of the technological relationship between output level and input levels. Production functions for different commodities are expected to differ. Note also that the idea of the production function in no way requires the existence of just one variable input. We assumed in equations [3.2] and [3.3] that labour was the only variable input to wheat and cloth production solely for the sake of simplifying the discussion of the essential features of the economic problem. In wheat production, for example, we would expect output to depend upon fertiliser input as well as labour input. In such cases, the diagrammatic representation of the wheat production function is as shown in Figure 3.17. The axes measure quantities of the inputs of labour and fertiliser. The curved lines are known as *isoquants*, and each such corresponds to a particular level of wheat output which can be produced by any of the labour/fertiliser input level combinations lying along it. Thus, for example, the output level Q_W^1 can be produced using the input combinations $L_W' F_W'$, $L_W'' F''$ or $L_W''' F'''$, or any of the combinations lying along $Q_W^1 Q_W^1$. Note that the output level represented by an isoquant increases as we move out in a north-east direction in Figure 3.17, so that $Q_W^3 > Q_W^2 > Q_W^1$.

Now, there is one empirical generalisation about the form taken by production functions which is taken to be universally valid. This is the law of diminishing marginal returns, which says that if inputs of one factor are increased while other inputs are held constant then eventually the marginal return to that factor must decrease. By the marginal return to the factor we mean the increase in output associated with a small (strictly a vanishingly small) increase in the factor input. Both Figure 3.1 (for equations [3.2] and [3.3]) and Figure 3.17 illustrate the law of diminishing marginal returns. This is most obvious in Figure 3.1, where there is only one input allowed to vary. It can be seen in Figure 3.17 by noting that it is drawn for $Q_W^1 = 20$, $Q_W^2 = 30$, and $Q_W^3 = 40$, and looking at the fertiliser input increases required

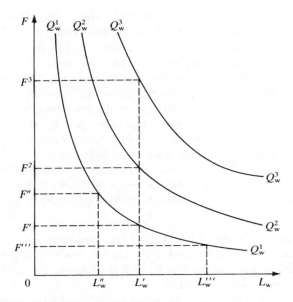

Figure 3.17   Isoquants for wheat production

to move from Q_W^1 to Q_W^2, F^2–F', and then to Q_W^3, F^3–F^2, for labour input constant at L_W'. Both Figures 3.1 and 3.17 show diminishing returns operative over the entire range of variable input levels. The law of diminishing marginal returns does not require this, but only that marginal returns diminish eventually. It must be emphasised strongly that the context of the law of diminishing marginal returns is one where one input level is being increased while at least one other input level is being held constant. It is not taken to be a valid empirical generalisation that marginal returns to factors eventually decrease if all factor input levels are being increased, though of course this may be true in some circumstances.

The law of diminishing returns was an important feature of the ideas of Malthus and Ricardo, mentioned in Chapter 1 here. It is a physical law rather than a proposition of economics itself. Economists, that is, take it as given that diminishing marginal returns apply in all productive activity, and concern themselves with working out the implications thereof. It is of some interest that in stating 'the principles of environmental science', Watt (1973) gives as principle four, the following: 'For all categories of resources, when resource availability is already high, the effect of a unit increase in resource availability often decreases with increasing availability, up to some maximum.' Watt does not note the fact that this is a version of the law of diminishing returns widely recognised in economics. He does note that 'it is primarily an empirical generalisation'. Watt does not explicitly state that his principle is to be taken as applying only in situations where the availability of one resource is being increased while that of, at least, one other is being held constant. It is, however, clear from the examples he cites that this is the case.

The production function relates physical output quantities to physical input quantities, and can be regarded as a mathematical or graphical model of some physical reality. Presumably, for this reason, the concept usually gives little trouble to beginning students in economics, who do, however, often find the concept of the utility function difficult. Clearly, a utility function is not a model of physical reality. It is, rather, an analytical construct which economists find useful in modelling people's preferences and deriving the implications arising. We stated in section 3.1 above that a utility function is that which 'associates a particular pattern of commodity consumption ... with a particular value of an index of satisfaction or utility'. The existence of such a function, associating each combination of commodity consumption levels with a particular value for the utility index, can be shown (see, for example, Hirshleifer (1980) Ch. 9) to be equivalent to a situation in which

(i)   the consumer or household knows for all possible pairs of alternative combinations of commodity consumption levels, indicated as A and B, whether A is preferred to B, or B is preferred to A, or that it is indifferent between A and B;

(ii) it is the case that if combination A is preferred to combination B, and B is preferred to combination C, then A is preferred to C.

Condition (i) here is the *complete ordering condition*, and (ii) is the *transitivity condition*. It will be apparent that these are not very strong conditions, in the sense that they are not implausible assumptions to make about the preferences of an idealised consuming unit. They are simply the requirement that all possible commodity consumption bundles can be ranked in order of preference.

A utility function is simply the mathematical representation of such a *preference ordering*, in that it associates particular values of the utility index with particular consumption bundles. Table 3.2 illustrated this. Two points must be noted here. The first is that since the utility function is merely representing an ordering, the values for the utility index that it produces have only *ordinal* significance, and do not have *cardinal* significance. Thus, from Table 3.3, we know that for the utility function $U_A = Q_{AC}^{\frac{1}{2}} Q_A^{\frac{1}{2}}$, $Q_{AC} = 4$ and $Q_{AW} = 1$ gives $U_A = 2$ while $Q_{AC} = 16$ and $Q_{AW} = 1$ gives $U_A = 4$. This does not mean that the bundle (16, 1) is liked twice as much, or delivers twice as many utility units, as the bundle (4,1). It simply means that (16,1) is preferred to (4, 1). Another way of seeing that the numbers output by the utility function have no cardinal significance is to note that $U_A = K Q_{AC}^{\frac{1}{2}} Q_{AW}^{\frac{1}{2}}$, where K is any number, produces exactly the ranking by U_A values for all possible (Q_{AC}, Q_{AW}) bundles as does $U_A = Q_{AC}^{\frac{1}{2}} Q_{AW}^{\frac{1}{2}}$. The second point to be noted is that while the conditions (i) and (ii) above are equivalent to the existence of a mathematical relationship attaching ordinal values to all possible commodity consumption bundles, they do not guarantee that the relationship is of the form of equation [3.2] or [3.3], or that the corresponding indifference curves are as shown (i.e. smoothly continuous and bending in toward the origin) in Figure 3.2. To get utility functions which have this type of indifference map corresponding, some further conditions on preferences have to be satisfied. One of these, the continuity condition, turns out to be important in practical applications of the principles of cost benefit analysis. This is discussed briefly in Chapter 8 in relation to the valuation of environmental services for the cost benefit analysis of projects which impact on those services. Hirshleifer (1980) and Layard and Walters (1978) discuss preference orderings and utility functions in the context of produced commodities.

At one time economists assumed that preferences could be, and needed to be, represented by utility functions with cardinal significance. It was assumed, for example, that $U_A = Q_{AC}^{\frac{1}{2}} Q_{AW}^{\frac{1}{2}}$ meant that the bundle (16,1) did deliver twice as many utility units as the bundle (4,1). This, in turn, meant that it was being assumed that there existed utility units for measurement of similar status to units for physical measurement, and hence that the utility or satisfaction levels of different individuals or households could be directly compared. This is no longer the case. Clearly, if the absolute magnitudes produced by A and B's utility indices are arbitrary, it makes no sense to say that $U_A = 500$ while $U_B = 250$ means that A is twice as happy or satisfied as B. Now, clearly the assumption that utility functions have only ordinal significance is weaker than the assumption that they have cardinal significance. It has been established that a number of testable propositions about the responses of consumption units to changes in their environment can be derived from the weak assumption of ordinal utility functions: one such class of proposition is derived in 4.3 of the next chapter. Formerly it was thought that such propositions depended upon the stronger assumption of utility functions with cardinal significance. The fact that it has been shown that the same testable propositions can be derived from weaker assumptions is regarded as scientific progress by economists.

However, it will no doubt have occurred to the reader that the use of utility functions with only ordinal significance gives rise to some difficulties with the analysis of the economic problem set out in this chapter. If the choice of K in $U_A = KQ_{AC}^{\frac{1}{2}} Q_{AW}^{\frac{1}{2}}$, and by extension of T in $U_B = TQ_{BC}^{\frac{1}{2}} Q_{BW}^{\frac{1}{2}}$, is entirely arbitrary, then clearly the welfare function $W = wU_A + (1 - w) U_B$ is itself arbitrary. If we are not, that is, prepared to admit of a meaningful cardinal scale of measurement for utility, it makes no sense, it seems, to look for a solution to the economic problem by way of searching for the maximum of a weighted sum of individual utility levels. If utility functions have only ordinal significance, then interpersonal comparisons based upon them have no meaning. It is now generally accepted by economists that if individual utility functions are to be taken as having purely ordinal significance, then it is not possible to construct a welfare function which would be acceptable for use in a democratic society. This does not mean that the analysis set out above is of no use. First, it did serve to explain the nature of the economic problem and responses to it, albeit on the basis of an implicit assumption stronger than most economists would now want to adopt.

Second, the concept of efficiency in allocation does not require the assumption that utility indices have cardinal significance. It involves only the requirement that one individual cannot be made better off except by making another individual(s) worse off. The allocation problem can, that is, be handled with the weak assumption of ordinal utility functions. This is one of the reasons why economists have in the main felt on firmer ground in analysing policy with respect to the achievement of allocative efficiency than discussing distributional issues. A useful introduction to the problems arising in the concept of a welfare function is to be found in Chapter 1 of Layard and Walters (1978), which also discusses the economic problem generally along lines similar to those followed here.

In 3.2 we used the concepts of production and utility functions to set out the opportunities open to our simple model economy, given the input resources available to it. The essential ideas emerging are trade offs, first as between the production and consumption of different commodities, and second as between the delivery of satisfaction to different households. These same types of trade off are very much real features of real economies. In real economies they are multi rather than two dimensional and hence cannot be represented in simple diagrammatic form. Their statement in real economies is complex. However, it can, and has been, done for the commodity production and consumption trade offs, by the construction of large models of the production relationships in real economies using historical data, and some special assumptions. The most widely used approach is *input-output analysis*, a technique originated by the economics Nobel Laureate W. Leontief. A good introductory account of input-output analysis, with examples of its uses, is O'Connor and Henry (1975). Leontief (1966) is a useful collection of articles on the principles and applications of input-output analysis by its originator, a number of which are written in non-technical terms. One of the more interesting applications reviewed is an analysis of the effects of disarmament on the economy of the USA. These input-output techniques can also be used to explore the trade offs between the patterns of production of commodities in the economy and dimensions of environmental quality. We shall briefly discuss this, and provide some references, in the commentary section of Chapter 5.

In 3.3 we discussed the 'command economy', and in 3.5 the 'planned economy'. In neither case were we attempting to describe, even in idealised terms, what went on in any actual economy anywhere. The purpose was rather to set our discussion of the market economy, to follow in Chapter 4, in context. It is difficult to appreciate the attractions of the market economy fully without some understanding of the difficulties attendant on alternative approaches to the solution of the economic problem, even under idealised conditions. Our discussion of the command and planned economies does, however, have some relevance to actual economic systems. The economy of the Soviet Union had some of the features of what we called a command economy: it was centrally planned and plan realisation was 'primarily by means of bureaucratic commands, couched primarily in physical magnitudes'

(Neuberger and Duffy, 1976, p. 168). As we shall note in the next chapter, just as our command and planned economies are idealisations without exact real world equivalents, so it is that there is no economy anywhere that corresponds very closely to the idealised market economy. Even the economy of the USA is much affected by government intervention (beyond the operation of a redistributive tax/welfare system). There are a number of books on comparative economic systems, i.e. the description of actual economies and their functioning: three examples, which do not require much by way of previous background in economics, are Halm (1968), Leeman (1977) and Neuberger and Duffy (1976).

Notes

1. An alternative terminology is used in some of the economics literature, an efficient allocation being referred to as a *Pareto optimal* allocation, allocative efficiency as *Pareto optimality* and a move from a non-efficient to an efficient allocation as a *Pareto improvement*. This alternative terminology refers to Wilfred Pareto (1848–1923), an Italian economist who is credited with introducing the concept into economic analysis: for further details see Blaug (1985).
2. Of course, if it were the case that both B and C were straight lines so that MB and MC were both horizontal, then the rule $MB = MC$ would not identify a net benefit maximum. This would be because no such maximum exists, as consideration of a variant of (a) in Figure 3.12 with B and C as straight lines will indicate.
3. The area of a right-angled triangle is equal to one half of the length of the base times the height.

Chapter 4

The Market Economy

In the previous chapter we distinguished between efficiency in allocation and fairness in distribution as elements of the economic problem. We noted that, in some circumstances, the task of achieving efficiency in allocation can be left entirely to a system of markets. In this chapter we shall show how markets can do this. We shall see that the circumstances in which they can do it are not circumstances that we would expect to be operative in actual economies. We shall, however, argue that this does not mean that the analysis of ideal market systems is of no practical use. Economists study such ideal systems with the purpose of providing a yardstick against which to assess, and to suggest policies for improving, the performance of actual, imperfect, market systems. This aspect of matters is considered generally in 4.5 below, and with particular respect to environmental problems in subsequent chapters. It is not possible to understand the economist's approach to environmental policy without the background of the analysis of how markets work ideally.

4.1 Market equilibrium

In this section we consider how markets work to fix prices and quantities. We are not initially concerned about whether the prices and quantities so fixed are in any sense desirable. This is dealt with in the remaining sections of this chapter, where we also look more closely at the origins and significance of the demand and supply functions to be introduced here.

Figure 4.1 lays out the essentials of the standard demand and supply analysis of market functioning, where P stands for the price of some commodity and Q stands for the quantity of that commodity. In part (a) we show the *supply function* for the commodity, with Q^S, the quantity supplied, increasing as P increases.[1] It is important to be clear that this supply function is a statement about what sellers of the commodity would plan to do, given that price is at a certain level. Thus, with a price of P_1 the amount sellers would plan to sell during the relevant period is Q_1^S, and with a price P_2 they would plan to sell Q_2^S. We mean by this that the supply function is a statement about the response of sellers' planned quantities offered for sale as price varies – it is a statement of the conditional, on price, intentions of sellers. That the amount it is planned to offer for sale should increase with price is intuitively reasonable, and we shall defer until 4.2 further enquiry into the upward slope of the supply function. Two points need to be made here before proceeding. First, that in setting out a graph of quantity planned to sell against price in part (a) of Figure 4.1, we are definitely not suggesting that the only thing which influences selling plans is the price of the commodity. We are holding other influences, the wage rate for example, constant for the purpose of seeing clearly what the relationship between sales plans and price implies. Second, in drawing the supply function graph as a straight line we are not suggesting that all supply functions are, in fact, of this form. We are merely illustrating the essentials in the simplest possible way.

Consider now Figure 4.1(b), where we show the *demand function* for the commodity, with Q^D, the quantity demanded, falling as price rises. Again, the demand function is not a graph of what is actually bought at various prices, but it is a graph showing how planned purchases vary with price. Thus, what

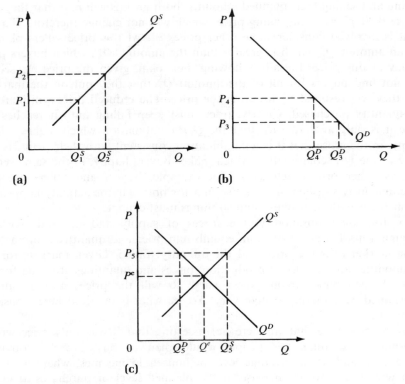

(a)

(b)

(c)

Figure 4.1   Market equilibrium

part (b) says is that if the price of this commodity were P_3 planned purchases during the relevant period would be Q_3^D and that if price rose to P_4 the quantity people would plan or wish to buy would fall to Q_4^D, for example. Again for the moment we simply note that a downward sloping demand function is intuitively plausible, with planned purchases increasing as price falls, and that the straight line form of the graph is used for convenience only. Finally we again draw attention to the fact that in drawing the graph in Figure 4.1(b), we are not saying that it is only a commodity's price which determines how much of it people plan to buy. We are concentrating on the quantity price relationship in order to derive its implications.

This we do in part (c) of Figure 4.1, which represents the market for this commodity, where sellers and buyers interact. To represent this interaction we put the demand and supply functions together, and we see that they intersect to determine a price, P^e, and a corresponding quantity, Q^e. Here the superscript e stands for *equilibrium*. The point is that at the intersection of the demand and supply functions the plans of buyers and sellers are mutually consistent, so that the market is in equilibrium in the sense that there are no forces tending to change quantity and price. With an actual price P^e, the amount buyers plan to purchase is Q^e: with an actual price P^e, the amount sellers plan to sell is Q^e. If both buyers and sellers respond to the price P^e by buying and selling their planned amounts, both groups will find that they can realise their plans at the ruling price, which will not change therefore. To see what is involved consider some other price, P_5. At this price sellers plan to sell an amount Q_5^S which is greater than the amount, Q_5^D, which buyers plan to buy at this price. Initially following their plan, given the price P_5, sellers will not find buyers for all of the amount Q_5^S that they put on the market, and they will respond by lowering the price. The reduced price will increase the quantity purchased. Clearly, price must keep falling until it reaches P^e since it is only at that price that the Q/P combination which makes sellers happy, in the sense that it is a combination consistent with their plans, is the same as the Q/P combination which makes buyers happy, in the same sense. At any other price, such as P_5 for example, buyers and sellers are not simultaneously satisfied in the sense that for both what is actually happening is consistent with their plans, and so things must change.

So, for some commodity, the forces of supply and demand working through a market give rise to an equilibrium price and quantity combination – the market fixes the price and the quantity traded. Given markets for all commodities and factors of production, prices and quantities are fixed for all such. As economic circumstances vary, so will the prices and quantities determined by a market system vary. To see what is involved here, consider Figure 4.2.

We noted above that we were not asserting that it was only price which determined the quantities people would plan to buy. Another obvious influence would be the average level of household incomes, where a rise in such would lead to an increase in the planned level of purchases at every price for the commodity. This outward shift in the demand function is

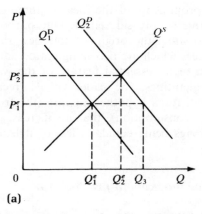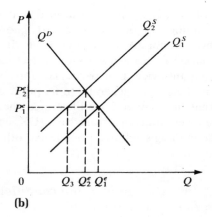

Figure 4.2 Demand and supply shifts

illustrated in Figure 4.2(a). At the original equilibrium price, the quantity demanded following the income increase is Q_3, whereas the quantity supplied is Q_1^e. Purchasers will find that they cannot get their hands on as much of the commodity as they plan at this price, and will bid the price up. A new market equilibrium will be established with a higher price, P_2^e, and a higher quantity, Q_2^e.

In Figure 4.2(b) we consider the effects of a shift in the supply function. We consider a case where the commodity in question is produced using some factor of production which becomes scarcer, so that its price rises, increasing production costs and so reducing at every price for the commodity the amount producers would plan to sell. The supply function shifts from Q_1^S to Q_2^S, so that if price remained at P_1^e, the quantity of the commodity offered for sale would fall to Q_3. But this Q_3/P_1^e combination cannot persist, since at P_1^e, buyers will plan to buy an amount Q_1^e. The price will be bid up and a new equilibrium will emerge with price at P_2^e and quantity at Q_2^e – it is only at this combination of price and quantity that, following the change in supply conditions, the plans of sellers and buyers are mutually consistent.

We noted in Chapter 1 that in the early 1970s the idea that if economic growth continued the world would run out of some natural resources in the foreseeable future was forcefully advanced, and attracted wide popular interest. Economists generally responded to the effect that those advancing this idea simply did not understand how markets worked. The idea itself is really an elaboration of Figure 4.2(a): economic growth means higher incomes, so that the quantities of commodities consumed rises. Where the commodities in question are scarce natural resources of which there is just so much in existence (oil), or use such scarce natural resources (cars use oil), this must imply the eventual exhaustion of the resource. The typical economist's response derives from Figure 4.2(b). As the resource gets scarcer, so its supply function will shift upwards, raising its price and reducing the quantity consumed. Economists argued that the proponents of the idea of imminent running out of resources had ignored this supply side effect. Our purpose here is not to decide this issue. It is to show the origin of the view that market forces will work to protect resources which are becoming scarcer, and that this view is a particular application of an essential feature of the way markets work generally to fix prices and quantities. The reader will also recall that in Chapter 2 we illustrated the point, for a hypothetical case (the fruit grower) and an actual case (UK energy consumption), that an increase in something's relative price leads, other things being equal, to less of it being used.

A first statement of the conditions for markets to produce an efficient allocation

In the next three sections of this chapter we are going to consider the way in which the set of prices and quantities which are a set of market equilibria may be those corresponding to efficiency in allocation. The use of 'may' rather than 'will' here is deliberate and important. In order to demonstrate that market outcomes correspond to efficiency in allocation, it is necessary to assume that certain 'ideal' conditions hold with respect to the circumstances in which the markets are to operate. In the next three sections we shall be assuming that those conditions are satisfied. The conditions are:

  (i)   the absence of *external effects*;
 (ii)   the absence of *public goods/bads*;
(iii)   all households and firms have *complete information*;
 (iv)   all households and firms act as *price takers*.

We now provide a very brief statement of the nature of each of these conditions. They will be discussed more fully in section 4.5 below, where we shall also consider how non-satisfaction of the conditions affects the outcomes that markets produce. We must also note that there are some additional necessary conditions, concerning the nature of firms' production functions and households' utility functions, that we shall not be considering, since to do so would involve exposition well beyond the technical level permissible here. The interested reader will find such matters dealt with in works referenced in the final commentary section of this chapter.

An external effect, or *externality*, exists when the activity of a firm or a household gives rise to consequences for other firms or households, which consequences are not intentional and do not figure in the costs or benefits associated with the activity as perceived by the originating firm or household. A good example of an externality is the release by a firm of polluting waste products into some environmental media.

A public good is a commodity which is consumed in equal amounts by everybody in a society. Examples are the services provided by the defence forces, or the criminal justice system. Clean air is a public good; polluted air is a public bad. An alternative approach to the concept of a public good or bad is in terms of the fact that it is non-rival in consumption – more consumed by one individual does not mean less available for others. Ice cream is rival in consumption; air pollution is not.

Households and firms have complete information when with respect to any prospective exchange or market transaction they are fully aware of its implications for their profits (in the case of firms) or utility (in the case of households).

A price taker is a participant in a market transaction who acts in the belief that he is unable by his own behaviour to influence the terms on which the transaction takes place. Essentially, the requirement is that everybody is for any potential market transaction confronted with a single fixed price at which they must decide how much to buy or sell – nobody is allowed to manipulate a price in his own interest.

This is a very terse account of these conditions. It is unlikely that the reader will have much appreciation now of what they mean. Things should become clearer in the next three sections, where it is assumed that these conditions hold, and in 4.5, where we discuss the nature of the conditions again.

4.2   The supply function

In this section we consider the origin of the supply function, and its significance. We do this assuming that all of the ideal conditions set out above hold. The origin of the supply function lies in the net benefit, or profit, maximising activities of firms. We discussed the analysis of such at some length in 3.4 of the previous chapter, and our point of departure now is that discussion.

Recall that we showed that the output level which maximises net benefit is that for which marginal benefit equals marginal cost. In Figure 3.12 we illustrated this for a particular numerical example, and showed how the net benefit maximising output level varied as the price per unit of output varied. In Figure 4.3(a) here we reproduce the marginal cost function, MC, for this firm from (c) of Figure 3.12. We also show the marginal benefit function, labelled MB and horizontal at a level given by the output price, as price varies in steps of £2 from £10 to £20, and, as Q^*_{10}, Q^*_{12}, etc., the corresponding net benefit maximising output levels. This firm's supply function, shown in Figure 4.3(b), is simply what we get when we plot net benefit maximising outputs against the corresponding output prices. While we have considered explicitly only a few of the output prices that the firm might face it is clear that this is simply for expositional purposes, and that the procedure applies for very small price changes giving the continuous supply function actually shown. The firm's supply function is nothing but its marginal cost function.

Now, while this account of the deviation of the firm's supply function is

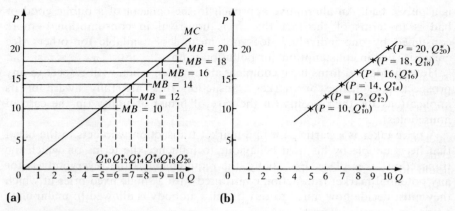

Figure 4.3   The supply function for a price taker firm

in terms of a particular numerical example, it should be clear that the logic involved is general. We obtain a firm's supply function by considering how its profit maximising output responds to changes in the price that its output sells for. It is in this sense that a firm's supply function shows how the quantity that it plans to sell varies with price. Note also that in so deriving the firm's supply function we have made use of one of the assumptions that comprise the 'ideal' conditions set out at the end of the previous section, i.e. the price taker assumption. We have said: given that the output price facing the firm is fixed with respect to its own behaviour at £x, what output level will it produce in order to maximise its net benefit. The firm is not, that is, allowed any control over the price at which it can sell its output. Consequently, given that net benefit is maximised where $MC = MB = P$, varying P traces out a supply function which is the MC function.

Unless there is just one firm producing the commodity, the firm's supply function is not the same thing as the market supply function for the commodity. However, given the supply functions for all of the firms producing a commodity we can easily derive the market supply function, and see what its significance is. Figure 4.4 shows what is involved. There are N firms producing the commodity, and these N firms in the standard terminology comprise an *industry*. Each of the N firms has its own supply function relating as described above its planned net benefit maximising output to the prices it might face. The industry, or market, supply function is just the horizontal summation of the supply functions of the individual firms. To see how this works, consider some particular price, P_1, which will be the price facing all firms in the industry. From each firm's supply function we read off its corresponding planned output, Q_1^*, for the first firm and so on, with Q_i^* for the ith firm. The total industry supply at this price is just

$$\sum_{i=1}^{N} Q_i^* (= Q_1^* + Q_2^* + \ldots + Q_N^*), \text{ and the combination } P_1 \text{ and } Q^* = \sum_{i=1}^{N} Q_1^*,$$

fixes a point on the industry supply function. Proceeding in the same way for the various price levels and plotting each price against the corresponding $Q^* = \sum_{i=1}^{N} Q_1^*$ traces at the industry supply function.

We have now shown where the upward sloping supply functions which we used in 4.1 come from. Price and quantity increase together as a result of the supplying firms planning to produce and sell at some given price that quantity which maximises their net benefit. Under the ideal conditions which we have assumed in deriving the supply function for a commodity, the way in which this arises from the behaviour of firms gives it a special significance in terms of our discussion of the economic problem and solutions thereto. It should now be clear that the supply function for a commodity is also a graph of the marginal cost of that commodity against its output level. Thus, on the right of Figure 4.4 we can read the supply function as showing how marginal cost increases with output. With output at Q^*, for example, we read off that marginal cost is P_1. What this means is that a very small increase in output from Q^*, for example, would require the use of resources, to be drawn away from other uses elsewhere in the economy, which would raise the costs of production in this industry by an amount equal to P_1. The upward slope of the supply function shows that this marginal cost increases as the industry's output increases, indicating that as this industry's output increases so the value of the resources it needs to transfer from elsewhere in the economy to its use in order to increase its output by a very small amount increases.

For the illustrative numerical example that we have used here the firm's marginal cost function, and hence the firm's supply function, turned out to be an upward sloping straight line. We also used upward sloping straight lines in deriving the industry supply function in Figure 4.4. While it would be generally thought to be appropriate to assume that marginal cost increases with output, at least over relevant ranges of output, the linear form of the relationship has been imposed here for expositional convenience only. A more appropriate general assumption would probably be that marginal cost first falls then increases with output at an increasing rate. We must emphasise here, however, that the interpretation of the supply function as a marginal cost function is in no way conditional upon the linearity of the latter. Clearly, if in Figures 4.3 and 4.4 the marginal cost functions had been drawn as curves with slope increasing as output increased, the derivation of the supply

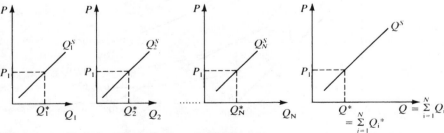

Figure 4.4 Deriving the industry supply function

functions would have been the same, though the result would have looked different – non-linear supply functions.

4.3   The demand function

In this section we consider the origin and significance of market demand functions, given that the ideal conditions hold. We begin with a numerical example, illustrating a general approach and general results, for a household consuming just two commodities, wheat and cloth. Let W and C represent wheat and cloth quantities, and P_W and P_C the corresponding prices. Initially the household's income is £100, and $P_W = £2$ and $P_C = £2$. Thus, the consumption opportunities facing the household are represented by all of the C/W combinations lying in the triangle $0AB$ in Figure 4.5. If all income is spent on wheat, 50 units are consumed: all income spent on cloth gets 50 units. The straight line joining these two extremes is the *budget line*, or *budget constraint*, the equation for which is

$$100 = 2W + 2C \qquad\qquad [4.1]$$

and which joins all those C/W combinations available to the household given that it spends all of its income. Points lying inside AB correspond to situations where not all of the household's income is spent: points lying outside AB represent C/W combinations which the household cannot consume, given its income and the prices for wheat and cloth.

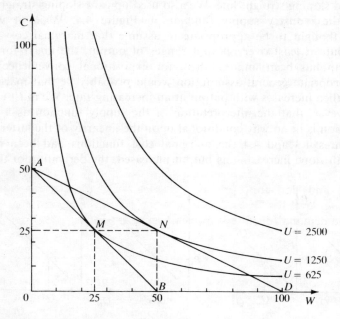

Figure 4.5   Household utility maximisation

We have now described the opportunities open to the household. In order to discuss choice from among these opportunities we need also to describe the household's preferences. This we do with utility function, which concept was introduced in 3.2 of the previous chapter, to which it might now be useful to refer. We assume here that the household's utility function is

$$U = CW \qquad\qquad [4.2]$$

for which some indifference curves are shown in Figure 4.5. We assume that the household seeks to attain the highest level of satisfaction or utility that it can, given the opportunities open to it. That is to say that it seeks, in terms of Figure 4.5, to get onto the highest indifference curve possible, given that it has an income of £100 and faces $P_C = £2$ and $P_W = £2$. As shown there, the outcome of such constrained utility maximisation involves $C = 25$ and $W = 25$, corresponding to the point M on $U = 625$. M is also on the budget line AB. This must be the case, as were it otherwise the household could consume more of both commodities, so increasing utility. M is the point of tangency for AB and the indifference curve $U = 625$. To see the significance of this, note that the indifference curves actually shown in Figure 4.5 are a very small sample from the very many such which could be drawn for the utility function, see [4.2]. In the neighbourhood of $U = 625$ we could, for example, draw indifference curves for $U = 625.00001$ and $U = 624.99999$, $U = 625.00002$ and $U = 624.99998$ and so on. We did not do so for the obvious reason that it would make the diagram unintelligible. However, it is clear that constrained utility maximisation must be represented by a point of tangency between the budget line and an indifference curve. Starting from M in Figure 4.5, for example, consider a small move along AB in either direction. Such must represent a move to a point on an indifference curve for which U is lower, say $U = 624.99999$.

So, a household maximising its utility subject to given income and prices consumes quantities of wheat and cloth identified by the point at which the budget line is tangential to the highest attainable indifference curve. We now consider the implications of this for household behaviour in the face of a varying price for wheat, with income and the price of cloth constant. Suppose that P_W drops to £1, so that the budget line shifts to AD. Then, as shown in Figure 4.5, the household is able to attain a higher level of utility, and consumes more wheat, as indicated by the point of tangency N^2. If we consider P_W varying over the range 0.5 to 5.0. for P_C and household income constant, and find for each P_W, in this way, the corresponding utility maximising, level for W, and then plot the W results against P_W, we get the household demand function shown in Figure 4.6.

The demand function and willingness to pay

This derivation of the household's demand function from constrained utility maximising behaviour is crucial to an understanding of the rôle of demand functions in the interpretation of the properties of a market solution to the economic problem. The point is that the household's demand function tells us how its willingness to pay for the commodity, in terms of forgone consumption of other commodities, varies with the level at which it consumes the commodity. What is involved can be brought out by considering M and N in Figures 4.5 and 4.6.

At M in Figure 4.5 the slope of the indifference curve, for $U = 625$, is equal to the slope of the budget line AB. With $P_C = P_W = £2$, this is one, since $0A = 0B$. Now consider a marginal increase in wheat consumption from the level corresponding to M (recall that the concept of a marginal change was introduced in section 1.1, and discussed again in section 3.4 in connection with the analysis of net benefit maximisation). Ask: what is the maximum amount of cloth consumption that the household would willingly forgo to secure such a marginal increase in wheat consumption? We know that the slope of the indifference curve is one, so that for marginal changes which involve movements along it in the neighbourhood of M, $\Delta C / \Delta W = 1$, or $\Delta C = \Delta W$. With the utility level held constant, and considering marginal changes, wheat and cloth exchange on a one-for-one basis. Offered the prospect of a marginal increase in wheat consumption from starting point M, the household would be willing to sacrifice for it, at the most, an equal amount of cloth consumption. Any larger sacrifice would mean moving to a lower indifference curve and a lower level of utility. Note now that in Figure 4.6, corresponding to M with $W = 25$ we read off $P_W = £2$. With $P_C = £2$, this means that if we regard P_W as the amount of money per unit of W that the household is willing to pay for a small increase in W consumption, this translates into a willingness to sacrifice cloth for wheat at the margin on a one-for-one basis.

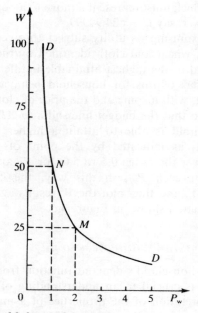

Figure 4.6 A household demand function

Now consider N, where in Figure 4.5 the utility maximising wheat consumption level is 50 and the slope of the indifference curve for $U = 1250$ is, by virtue of the tangency of AD, $\frac{1}{2}$. Here $\Delta C/\Delta W = \frac{1}{2}$ implies $\Delta C = \Delta W/2$ so that for a marginal increase in W, maximum willingness to sacrifice cloth consumption would be an amount $\Delta C = \Delta W/2$. As compared with M, wheat consumption is higher, and willingness to pay, in terms of forgone cloth consumption, for marginal increases in such is lower. Looking at N in Figure 4.6, for $W = 50$ we read off $P_W = £1$. If we take this to mean that £1 is the amount of money the household would be, at the most, willing to pay per unit for a marginal increase in wheat consumption, then with $P_C = £2$ this translates into a willingness to sacrifice $\frac{1}{2}$ a unit of cloth per unit of wheat. Again, if we read the demand function as giving willingness to pay for marginal increases in wheat consumption, P_W, as wheat consumption varies, we see that what Figure 4.6 is saying is, for the given cloth price, exactly what Figure 4.5 is saying.

The point, then, is a two-part-one. First, we can interpret a household's demand function either as giving the amount that it would wish to consume as price varies, or as giving its *marginal willingness to pay* as the amount consumed varies. The way Figure 4.6 is drawn, with quantity on the vertical and price on the horizontal axis, lends itself to the former interpretation. In future we shall show price on the vertical and quantity on the horizontal axis, as goes naturally with the latter interpretation. Second, while the representation of marginal willingness to pay as dependent on the level of consumption expresses such in terms of money, this does not mean that it is being assumed that households are concerned with money as such. Given the existence of a budget constraint and prices for commodities, willingness to pay money corresponds to willingness to sacrifice the consumption of other commodities. It is the willingness to forgo other consumption, as a function of the level of consumption of the commodity in question, that is actually what we are interested in when we consider demand functions in this way. For P_C fixed, we could in Figure 4.6 very simply rename and rescale the horizontal axis to show cloth sacrifice, or willingness to pay, rather than money as such. In this illustrative example, such a way of representing things would be simple to do and to interpret because there is only one alternative commodity which could be consumed. Where there are many alternative commodities to the one to which the demand function relates, expressing marginal willingness to pay in monetary terms is obviously convenient. We could, of course, re-express it in terms of any of the alternative commodities, given fixed money prices for all those alternative commodities.

Consumer's surplus

In Figure 4.7 we show the demand function for some commodity, with price, P, on the vertical axis and quantity, Q, on the horizontal axis. The demand function is one which is graphically represented by a straight line, i.e. it is a

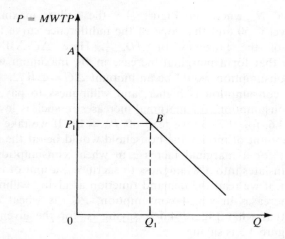

Figure 4.7 Consumer's surplus and total willingness to pay

linear demand function. This simply makes the exposition easier to follow. We shall comment below on how the discussion relates to non-linear demand functions, such as that shown in Figure 4.6. The vertical axis is labelled $P = MWTP$, where $MWTP$ stands for marginal willingness to pay, following our discussion above. In 3.4 of the previous chapter we explained how a total could be obtained from a corresponding marginal relationship by taking the area under the latter. If in Figure 4.7 the household faces the price P_1 at which it purchases the quantity Q_1, its total expenditure is price times quantity given by the area $0P_1BQ_1$. Its *total willingness to pay* for the quantity Q_1 is given by the area $0ABQ_1$. The difference between total willingness to pay and total expenditure is the area P_1AB, known as the household's *consumer's surplus*.

To see what consumer's surplus represents and how it arises, consider a particular example. Suppose that the household demand function is

$$P = 10 - Q \qquad [4.3]$$

shown in Figure 4.8. Suppose initially that the commodity can only be bought in discrete units – the household can buy 1 unit, 2 units, 3 units, etc., but not 1.1 units or 3.75 units. Suppose also that the price per unit facing the household is £6, so that it buys 4 units, with an expenditure of £24. Does this £24 reflect the household's willingness to pay for a consumption of 4 units? No. With consumption at 4 units, marginal willingness to pay is £6, as considered above. But marginal willingness to pay varies with consumption. Suppose the household is, instead of being able to buy as much as it wants at a single price per unit, offered a separate deal for each unit of the commodity. Offered just one it will, we read off from the demand function in Figure 4.8, be willing to pay £9 for it. Offered an additional unit it will be willing to pay £8 for it. From Figure 4.8 we have for such sequential purchasing of units that at each extra unit available, willingness to pay for

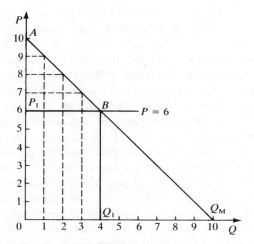

Figure 4.8   The origin of consumer's surplus

such goes £9, £8, £7, £6, £5, £4, etc. If the household actually ended up buying 4 units under this sort of purchasing arrangement, its total expenditure would be £9 + £8 + £7 + £6 = £30. This is the household's total willingness to pay for 4 units of this commodity. For downward sloping demand functions, total willingness to pay exceeds total expenditure with normal purchasing arrangements because with such arrangements the household pays for all units purchased only its marginal willingness to pay at the overall level of consumption.

Consumer's surplus is just the difference between total willingness to pay and total expenditure. In the example of Figure 4.8, with price set at £6 and the household buying 4 units, consumer's surplus is £6. On the first of the 4 units bought the household buying all units at £6 per unit gets for £6 something for which it would be willing to pay, if offered it for nothing, £9. With respect to this unit, when bought under normal arrangements, the household has realised a surplus equivalent to £3. By 'normal arrangements' we mean simply that sellers normally proceed by asking for order quantities at a fixed price per unit, not by asking for price offers for 1 unit only, then having sold that by asking for price offers for another unit, and so on. Normal arrangements, in this sense, are those that are operative where buyers and sellers are price takers. With respect to the second of the four units bought at £6 the household's surplus is £2, for the third it is £1, and for the fourth it is £0. The total consumer's surplus is £6 = £3 + £2 + £1 + £0. It is, of course, necessarily the case that on the last of the units bought the consumer's surplus is £0.

We have thus far assumed that the commodity can only be traded in discrete units. Clearly the argument to the existence of consumer's surplus would still apply if it could be purchased in amounts which were 0.01 of a unit, or 0.001 of a unit, or 0.0000001 of a unit. Imagine that in our discussions above the units were 100's of lbs, or 1,000's of oranges, or millions of screws, with price defined with respect to such units. Now imagine that trade is done in units which are lbs, oranges and screws respectively, with prices defined per lb, per orange, per screw. In the new circumstances we can see that total willingness to pay would still exceed total expenditure in the way described above, and that consumer's surplus as the difference between these two would arise as described above. Calculating total willingness to pay and consumer's surplus in the above manner would, however, in each of these cases, be extremely tedious. However, it is clear that if we calculated the area of the triangle AP_1B in Figure 4.8, this would represent an approximation to the true size of the consumer's surplus, and that the approximation would improve as the steps in which Q and P are allowed to vary got smaller. In the limit, if we imagine Q and P varying continuously rather than in discrete steps, calculating consumer's surplus as the area of triangle AP_1B is not an approximation at all, but gives the exact result, as stated in the discussion of Figure 4.7 above. This exactly parallels our discussion of working from areas under marginal relationships to totals in 3.4, as noted above, where Figure 3.13 and the discussion thereof are especially relevant – the reader may find it useful to refer back.

It was stated above that though conducted in terms of a linear demand function, our discussion of total willingness to pay and consumer's surplus would not be of relevance only to such. It should now be clear that so long as the demand function is downward sloping, consumer's surplus will exist and is measured, for Q and P varying continuously, by the relevant area under the demand function. The reader can check this by considering the argument above in the context of Figure 4.6. What is true is that the area under a non-linear demand function is not calculable by the simple formulae of elementary geometry, but requires the use of advanced mathematical techniques. This is one of the reasons why elementary economics texts generally show demand functions as linear. We shall follow this practice here in what follows. It provides a simple way of making some important, general, points.

From the consumer's point of view, consumer's surplus is clearly a 'good thing'. Suppose in Figure 4.8 that P and Q can vary continuously, and that the commodity is supplied to the household free of charge. Then consumer's surplus is given by the area of the triangle $0AQ_M$, equal to 50. We can regard this as the benefit accruing to the household from free availability of this commodity. Equally, the benefit accruing if a price of £6 is charged and four units are consumed is given by total expenditure equal to the area $0ABQ_1$. This is a gross benefit, against which is to be set the cost incurred equal to expenditure given by the area $0P_1BQ_1$, so that the net benefit is just consumer's surplus P_1AB. Given our account of the derivation of a household demand function, it should be clear that expenditure, as the area under a demand curve over 0 to the consumption level, is a measure of the gross benefit associated with a particular level of consumption.

Correspondingly, the demand function is the relationship between marginal gross benefit and the consumption level. To say that at the consumption level Q_1 the household's marginal willingness to pay is P_1 is just to say that its perception of the marginal benefit of consumption at this level is P_1 in the sense that this measures the most that it would willingly give up to secure a marginal increase in consumption.

From household demand functions to the market demand

So far we have been considering the demand function for a single household. What about market demand functions? As shown in Figure 4.9, aggregation over the household demand functions for some commodity is exactly analogous to aggregation over the supply functions of individual firms to get the market supply function. For any price, say P_1, we sum the arising quantities demanded by households to get $Q^* = \sum_{j=1}^{M} Q_j^*$, where there are M households indexed by the subscript j and where Q_j^* is the utility maximising consumption level for the jth household given the price, P_1, facing all M households. Proceeding similarly for other prices for the commodity we map out the market demand function. Note carefully that there is no presumption that all households have the same preferences, so that for any given price it is not true that all households consume equal quantities. Clearly the interpretation of the demand function for a commodity as relating the marginal benefit of its consumption to the consumption level carries over from the individual demand function to the market demand function. The latter is telling us about the behaviour of marginal benefit for all households. Similarly, the concepts of total willingness to pay and consumer surplus apply in the same way with respect to the market demand function. It will be apparent to the reader on a little reflection that the use of the areas under the demand function is likely to be more appropriate with market than with individual demand functions. Finally we note that the identification of total willingness to pay with total benefit from consumption of the commodity also applies for the market demand function.

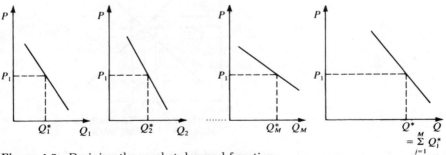

Figure 4.9 Deriving the market demand function

4.4   Efficient allocation by markets

We have shown that, given the ideal conditions, the supply function for a commodity is just the marginal cost function for that commodity, and the demand function is just the marginal benefit function for that commodity. We shall now show that this means that the market equilibrium, where the supply and demand functions intersect (see 4.1), gives the price and quantity for the commodity required for an efficient allocation.

Consider first Figure 4.10. The two upper panels translate from supply and demand curves into the marginal cost and marginal benefit terminology. The market equilibrium is where marginal cost equals marginal benefit. In 3.4 we showed that net benefit is maximised where marginal cost equals marginal benefit. We did this there in the context of a firm's net benefit (profit), and marginal cost and benefit functions. But clearly the result holds for any marginal cost and marginal benefit functions and the corresponding net benefit as total benefit minus total cost. Thus, we know that producing a commodity at the output level where society's marginal cost arising, with the marginal cost schedule given by the market supply function, is equal to

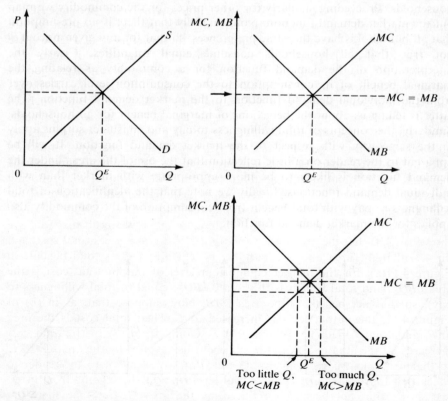

Figure 4.10   Market equilibrium in terms of marginal costs and benefits

society's marginal benefit arising, with the marginal benefit schedule given by the market demand function, is to produce at the output level which maximises society's net benefit from the production of this commodity. And we see that this is exactly the market equilibrium outcome. With all commodities being produced in the amounts indicated by the corresponding market equilibria, efficiency in allocation is achieved in that for every commodity society's net benefit associated with its production is being maximised. Hence it is not possible to find an alternative set of output levels which would make any household better off, except at the cost of making at least one other household worse off.

To see what is involved consider the situation for any one commodity as illustrated in the lower panel of Figure 4.10. If output is fixed at a level higher than Q^E, marginal cost exceeds marginal benefit. This means that a small reduction in the output level would reduce costs by more than benefits. It would release, that is, inputs which are of greater value than the benefits of the output they are generating in this line of production. The released inputs can be used elsewhere in the economy to produce additional units of the output of some other commodities, which additional units are valued (in terms of willingness to pay) more highly than the last output units of the commodity we are looking at. Were this not so, the price per unit of the input would be lower than it is to give the marginal cost function we are considering for this commodity. Suppose, in the lower part of Figure 4.10, that output were fixed at some level below Q^E. This would mean that marginal cost was below marginal benefit. Consequently an expansion of output would bring into use in the production of this commodity inputs valued at less than the value of the output they would give rise to. Such an output expansion would, that is, increase the net benefit arising in the production of this commodity, making it possible to make somebody better off without making anybody worse off. In sum, because the supply function gives the marginal social valuation of inputs to, and the demand function the marginal social valuation of outputs from, commodity production, producing every commodity at the level where 'supply equals demand' maximises net benefit in the production of every commodity.

We can look at this from a slightly different angle if we recall that we have shown (in 3.4) that the area under a marginal cost graph gives total cost, and (in 4.3) that the area under a marginal benefit graph gives total benefit. In Figure 4.11(a), for the market equilibrium level of output total cost is the area $0BQ^E$, and total benefit is the area $0ABQ^E$ (equal to total willingness to pay), so that net benefit is the area $0AB$. Now suppose that, as in (b) of Figure 4.11, the output level is increased to F. Then total cost is the area $0EF$, and total benefit is the area $0ACF$. Going from (a) to (b) total cost increases by the area Q^EBEF, and total benefit increases by the area Q^EBCF, so that net benefit is reduced by the area BEC. We leave it to the reader to check that for a reduction in the output level from Q^E to I, going from (a) to (c), shows that net benefit is reduced by the area GBH. Since there are reductions in net benefit for a move of any size to either side of Q^E, it follows

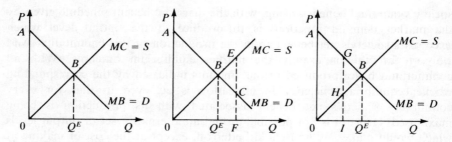

Figure 4.11   Market equilibrium in terms of costs and benefits

that the output level Q^E is that which maximises net benefit. And this argument about the net benefit maximising property of the market equilibrium clearly applies for all commodities, where the ideal conditions hold.

It is in this way that a system of markets solves the economic problem. With net benefit maximised in the production of every commodity there exists no alternative pattern of commodity output levels which offers greater total net benefit so that it would be possible to make one household better off without making any other household worse off. The system of markets gives rise, that is, to efficiency in allocation.

In saying this, we are assuming that the ideal conditions briefly introduced at the end of 4.1 above, and to be considered more fully in 4.5 below, are operative. The statement that markets give rise to efficiency in allocation is a conditional statement. If certain conditions are not met, it will not be true. It is also important to be clear that even if the conditions are satisfied, all that can be claimed for markets is that they produce efficiency. It cannot be claimed that they produce social justice. This point was made in the previous chapter, and is illustrated in the sub-section below. Also we now make explicit something implicit in our discussion of market outcomes and efficiency in this chapter.

We have said that, given ideal conditions, market demand and supply functions are social marginal benefit and marginal cost functions, so that demand equals supply implies net social benefit maximisation. If the reader recalls our discussion of the demand function's origins and derivation, he will realise that in describing the market demand function as a 'social' marginal benefit function, the word social is being used in a way that implies a particular view of society. Since the market demand function is derived by aggregating household demand functions, which reflect the preference systems of individual households, it follows that the market demand function values marginal benefits as perceived by individual households taken all together. That is, there is no rôle in marginal benefit evaluation for a conception of society as anything other than the aggregation of the households which comprise it. Individual household preferences and only individual household preferences, determine social benefit assessment. Actually this is equally true on the cost side, though this is not readily apparent from our discussion. To accept the claim that markets produce social efficiency, it is necessary to accept that social efficiency is appropriately measured using criteria based only on the preferences of individual households. This most economists do without much real thought about the matter, and without being explicit about it.

Market outcomes and fairness

The reader will recall from our discussion of the nature of the economic problem, in the previous chapter, the distinction we made between efficiency in allocation and fairness in distribution. We noted there that there are a (very) large number of efficient allocations which represent solutions to the economic problem, and that these efficient allocations differ in their distributional implications. The distributional implications of the efficient allocation realised by a market system depend upon the distribution of incomes across households. To see what is involved we can consider a simple example for the market for a particular commodity. We will assume that there are just two households, A and B, and that the household demand functions are

$$Q_A^D = Y_A - 6P \qquad\qquad [4.4]$$

and

$$Q_B^D = Y_B - 6P \qquad\qquad [4.5]$$

where Y stands for household income, Q^D for quantity demanded, and P for price (the same for both households however much they buy). These two demand functions are graphed on the left in top half of Figure 4.12 for $Y_A = Y_B = 100$. Summing these two horizontally as discussed above in section 4.3 gives the market demand function shown at the right of the top half of Figure 4.12, which has the equation:

$$Q^D = 200 - 12P \qquad\qquad [4.6]$$

The intersection of this with the supply function for this commodity gives an equilibrium price of £6 and total quantity sold of 128. Going back to the household demand functions with this price we find that each household consumes 64 units. In the lower part of Figure 4.12 the situation is different in that $Y_A = 140$ and $Y_B = 60$. Proceeding as in the upper half we get the market demand function, equation [4.6], again, so that market equilibrium price and total quantity sold are unchanged. However, going back to the household demand functions with $P = £6$ we now get $Q_A = 104$ and $Q_B = 24$.

In this example, changing the distribution of income does not change the market demand function. It is a special case set up to provide a simple illustration of the general point that the efficient allocation produced by the market depends upon the distribution of income. Special cases apart, we

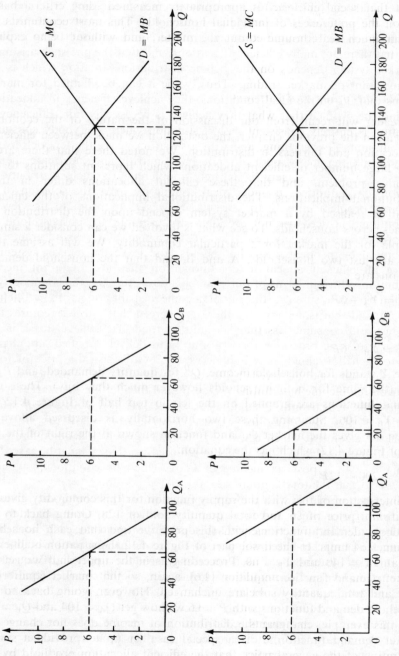

Figure 4.12 Market outcome and income distribution

would expect distributional changes to change market demand functions, so that the market clearing prices and the associated quantities would change, as well as the allocation of the total quantity across households.

Now, the point of the example in Figure 4.12 is not to suggest that all households should consume equal amounts of commodities. It is to make it clear that there are many efficient allocations, and that the one such arising in a market system depends on the income distribution situation which is the starting point of market trading. Thus, while it can be claimed for market systems that, given the ideal conditions, they achieve efficiency in allocation, it cannot be claimed that what they achieve is necessarily fair. Efficiency in allocation is entirely consistent with a situation where everybody consumes equal amounts of everything, and with a situation where the few rich live in luxury while the many poor do not have nutritionally adequate dietary intakes. So, unless society is entirely indifferent to such distributional questions, it cannot, even under ideal conditions, leave the solution of its economic problem entirely to markets. However, to promote its view of distributional justice, it is not necessary, for example, to subsidise food for the poor. What the society needs to do is to change, by taxes and grants, the distribution of incomes across households, and leave the market system to achieve an efficient allocation conditional on the post tax/grant income distribution. Thus, in terms of our example above, suppose the commodity in question is food, suppose the initial income distribution is $Y_A = 140$ and $Y_B = 60$, and that, somehow or other, it is agreed that fairness requires that no household consume less than 50 units of food. To achieve this it is not necessary to issue orders to food producers to deliver specified amounts of food to each household. Nor is it necessary to subsidise the price of food. The result can be achieved by taxing away £26 of A's income and redistributing income by granting this to B, and then letting the market work. We get this redistributive requirement by setting $Q_B^D = 50$ and $P = 6$ in equation [4.5] and solving for Y_B as $Y_B = Q_B^D + 6P = 50 + (6 \times 6) = £86$. This is the income at which B will buy 50 units of food. If B's actual income is £60 this means that a grant of £26 is required, so that A must be taxed £26 leaving A with a post-tax income of £114, which by equation [4.4], gives $Q_A^D = 78$ so that the total amount of food sold is 128 units.

This very simple example illustrates the thinking behind the standard approach of economists to economic policy, which is to treat separately the questions of allocative efficiency and distributional justice. No economist arguing for a market-based solution to the economic problem would claim that a market system would itself necessarily produce a pattern of household consumption levels of commodities which society would consider fair. In fact there are good reasons for believing that it would not. What an economist would claim is that the correct approach is to operate a system of redistributive taxes and grants to produce whatever society believes is a fair, post-tax post-grant, income distribution, and then to let the market system work to produce the particular efficient allocation conditioned by the modified income distribution. In terms of economic policy, that is, the standard approach is to treat the allocation and distribution problems separately. If the ideal conditions are operative, the only sort of policy needed is a redistributive policy. If they are not then, as well as a redistributive policy, it is necessary to have policies for intervention in markets so as to achieve efficiency in allocation. As we showed in the previous chapter, whatever the distributional outcome society may wish to see, it will never make sense to tolerate allocations which are not efficient. If a situation of inefficient allocation exists, then it is possible to make somebody better off without making anybody worse off. If this is the case then the distribution problem does not immediately arise – the lot of the worst off can be improved without taking away from the best off.

4.5   Market failure

In this section we discuss how violations of the conditions stated at the end of 4.1 as 'ideal' conditions prevent markets achieving efficiency in allocation. We also briefly discuss some policy implications arising. Where markets do not produce allocative efficiency, we have *market failure*. When economists discuss market failure and policy with respect to it, they have in mind only the efficiency objective – they are not referring to distributional problems.

The condition of *complete information* is quite quickly dealt with. If households are misinformed about the properties of some commodity they buy, for example, as these affect their satisfaction or utility levels, then the demand function for the commodity will not accurately reflect the variation of marginal benefit with consumption. Accordingly, the market equilibrium will not involve the maximisation of true net benefit, and it cannot be the case that the overall allocation is efficient. The general policy implications of this are obvious. Where incomplete information exists it should be corrected. There is a clear rôle for social intervention in a market system to correct information deficiencies. It is, of course, much harder to identify particular instances of information deficiency, and to devise effective means of correcting such. Apart from anything else, it will in practice be difficult to separate out information deficiencies from 'misguided' preferences. The term misguided appears in quotes because in economics we can properly take no view on whether household preferences are good or bad for the household. Preferences are just what they are, and it is the job of the economic system to do the best that can be done (to produce, that is, an efficient allocation) according to the yardstick of the given household preferences. If in a situation of complete information households generally like things which would generally be agreed to be bad for them – alcohol, say – an efficient allocation will reflect that. It is not the job of economists to provide the mix of commodities which is good for households. It is their job to provide the mix of commodities which households, on the basis of full information, want. From the viewpoint of economic analysis all that matters is properly informed willingness to pay. The properly informed qualification is crucial.

But, given it, economic analysis takes as the ultimate measure of everything households' willingness to pay on the basis of existing preferences.

External effects and public goods

We now turn to the no *external effects* condition. External effects are the consequences of unintended interdependencies between economic decision making units. They may be, from the perspective of the affected party, beneficial or harmful. A good example of a beneficial, or positive, external effect arises with the training of workers by firms. If a worker is trained at the expense of firm A and after completion of the training moves to firm B where he receives the same wage and where his training is of use, then firm A generates a positive external effect on firm B. The standard examples of harmful, or negative, external effects are pollution generation. A firm which releases waste products into the air or a river reduces the quality of the air or water available to other firms and households. In neither of these examples is the effect concerned produced intentionally. Firms do not train workers with the object of making them useful to other firms, nor do they release waste products with the object of causing harm. Both of these examples illustrate the origin of the externality problem in the absence of property rights, with the consequence that markets do not exist through which the benefits (of training) can be captured by the externality generator, or the costs (of pollution) can be imposed on the externality generator. It is by virtue of the non-existence of a market in the externality that the generator of such takes no account of it in decision making.

What is involved can be explored further by considering some commodity in the production of which smoke is released into the atmosphere, polluting it and causing increased cleaning costs for everybody. The full costs of production attributable to the commodity include these increased cleaning costs. But, in the absence of anybody owning the atmosphere, these increased costs will not be borne by the producers of the commodity in question, since there is nobody who can charge the producers for the use they make of the atmosphere as a waste disposal unit. The increased cleaning costs for everybody are not the intention of the commodity producers, they are a side effect of their intended activity, which they are able to ignore because they are not charged for it. The pollution is an external effect, and the increased cleaning costs arising are *external costs*. As Figure 4.13 illustrates, the neglect by the producers of the external costs they cause means that their output level is not that required for efficiency in allocation. We show the marginal cost (supply) function and the marginal benefit (demand) function intersecting to give the output level Q^*, at which net benefit is maximised. However, this marginal cost function is not the marginal cost function which the producers perceive, since the external costs do not accrue to them. The costs and marginal costs facing the producers are everywhere below true costs and true marginal costs. In Figure 4.13 we show as *private marginal cost* the marginal cost schedule which actually faces the producers. The term 'private'

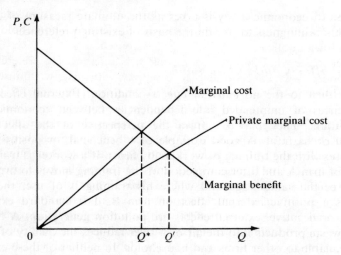

Figure 4.13   External costs and allocative efficiency

arises because of the distinction between the true costs arising for society as a whole and the costs facing the producers, which reflect only the charges they face where private property rights exist. The producers' equation of private marginal cost with marginal benefit, in order to maximise their private net benefit or profit, leads to the output level Q'. They produce, with respect to the efficient allocation levels, too much of the commodity and too much smoke. This is the situation which applies generally with harmful external effects arising in production – too much of the commodity and too much of the external effect. In general terms the response to this kind of market failure is pretty obvious. It is to intervene in the market situation so that the private marginal cost schedule coincides with the marginal cost schedule, so that the producers face as private costs all of the costs they impose on society. We shall elaborate on this general statement in the next chapter, where we shall also discuss the nature of the external effect problem, in relation to environmental pollution, more fully.

In 4.1 we said that commodities which were non-rival in consumption were called *public goods*. We gave as examples the commodities which are the services of defence and police forces. While we did state that all households necessarily consumed equal amounts of a public good, we did not say that all households would have the same demand functions for the public good. It is definitely not the case that all households have identical relationships between household marginal benefit from, or willingness to pay for, a public good and quantities of that public good. Just consider, for example, the situations of two households with respect to police services where one household is a family owning a house in an exclusive suburb which contains valuable antiques and family heirlooms and the other is an individual living in a rented room and owning no personal property. Or, with respect to the policing of streets and public areas, consider the situations, in terms of willingness to pay for such, of a rich recluse who has everything delivered to his home and a rich man about town. So clearly, household demand functions for a public good do differ across households.

In order to see what the implications of such differences in preferences for a public good are we can consider an economy with just two households. In Figure 4.14 panel (a) shows household A's demand function for the public good, panel (b) shows household B's. Suppose we consider the situation where 2 units of the public good is supplied. Then this is the amount consumed by each household. For household A we read off marginal benefit at this consumption level as £4 from panel (a) and for household B marginal benefit is £1.50 from panel (b). Hence, with 2 units of the public good provided, the marginal benefit for all households is £5.5. This is shown in Figure 4.14(c). The demand, or marginal benefit, function shown in panel (c) is derived by considering all possible levels of supply of the public good in the same way – it shows how collective willingness to pay varies with the amount provided.

The question now is, how much of the public good should be provided? The answer is the amount consistent with efficient allocation, the amount which maximises the collective or social net benefit of the consumption of the public good. As before we can identify this level of provision by finding the value of Q for which marginal benefit equals marginal cost. For the marginal cost schedule shown Figure 4.14(c), the required level of provision is 4 units. We can now see why the provision of a public good cannot be handled by a market. With 4 units supplied, household A's marginal benefit or willingness to pay is £3 while that of household B is £1. Thus, household A should face a price of £3 per unit and household B a price of £1 per unit. It is unusual, but not unknown, for different purchasers to pay different prices for the same commodity. This can occur where the seller can identify consumers with different demand functions, and can prevent such consumers trading the bought commodity amongst themselves. But this is precisely what the supplier of a public good cannot do. He cannot get individual consumers to reveal their willingness to pay for varying quantities supplied to them individually, precisely because all consumers necessarily consume the same quantity. The supplier of, for example, railway journeys may believe that the retired have a different demand function from the non-retired. He can check this belief by offering different prices for the same journey to the two groups, and by observing the effect on ticket sales to each group. The public good supplier cannot so do. Indeed, some consumers of a public good may have a positive incentive to misrepresent their willingness to pay. In the example of Figure 4.14, A might well, if asked about, and expecting to be charged according to, willingness to pay, understate its willingness to pay for various levels of supply, knowing that it will get whatever level of supply is eventually forthcoming. With non-public goods this problem does not arise, as the household which is willing to pay more will reveal this by paying more in order to move consumption from other households to itself. With non-rival consumption, consumption cannot shift between households in this way and so they have no incentive to reveal willingness to pay by bidding.

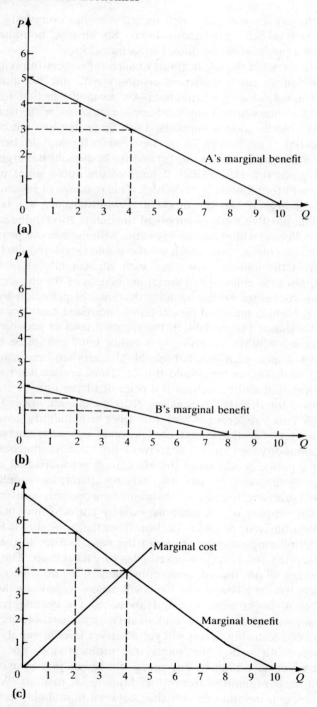

Figure 4.14   The public good problem

So, non-rival consumption means that a public good cannot be supplied by the market system. It has to be provided by some public non-market agency, at a common level to all consumers. Of course, this public provision does not itself entirely solve the problem, for the public agency still has to figure out the level of supply required for efficient allocation, and the related question of the appropriate way of covering the costs of supply. Looking briefly at the first problem, we can see that what the agency needs is information on willingness to pay by individual households. In principle it could simply ask households. But depending on what households think is the way costs are going to be met, there is likely to be a systematic bias in the responses. If it is assumed that households will be charged according to their willingness to pay, we have already noted the incentive to understate such willingness. If it is assumed that the public good will be supplied at no charge, with costs being covered by the revenue from an income tax say, respondents will have an incentive to overstate their willingness to pay. Thus, to say that public goods must be publicly supplied is to specify one type of market failure, but is not in itself a solution to the problem of arranging for the optimal amounts of public goods to be provided.

Actually the two conditions of no external effects and no public goods can effectively be stated as the single condition that there exist private property rights in all of the inputs to and outputs from productive activity, and in all those things which affect the utility indices of households. The existence of private property rights is necessary for trade. Markets work properly only with respect to those things which can be traded. Trading, whether via the intermediation of money or not, is just the exchange of property rights. One can offer in exchange for something only that which one owns. This is not to say that decisions about the use of things not privately owned would not get made in a market economy. They would, but the point is that the decisions would not be informed by the relative prices emerging from market trading, but would be side effects of market trading in privately owned things. There would then be no reason to suppose that these unaccounted for side effects would be consistent with efficiency in allocation.

Reference back to our two examples of external effects indicates that in each case the generating party took no account of the effect because of the absence of private property rights. Firms do not own their workers, so they cannot trade in trained workers, which means that they take no account of the implications of the training they provide for the economy as a whole. Neither firms nor households own units of the air over a city, so those who discharge pollution into it have to pay nobody for the use they make of it, so they give no attention to the lower air quality they cause. It is the absence of private property rights which gives rise to external effects. It needs to be noted, however, that the non-existence of property rights as the origin of external effects does not necessarily reflect the technical impossibility of such rights existing. It may merely reflect the prevailing institutional conditions and legal framework. The recorded existence of slavery indicates that it is not technically impossible for workers to be owned. It is, however, as a purely technical matter impossible for individual firms and households to own quantities of the air.

As already noted, clean air is a public good. In the case of public goods, private property rights are absent by reason of the technical impossibility of their existence. Non-rivalness in consumption means that individual ownership of units of the public good is absolutely impossible, and cannot be legislated for. To see this, and to illustrate the connection between market exchange and individual ownership, consider beer and policing services. The production of, and allocation to households, of beer can be left to markets, but the provision of policing services cannot. Markets work for beer because it is possible to isolate a unit of beer for the exclusive enjoyment of which something (usually money) can be offered in exchange. If an innkeeper accepts what I offer in exchange, I consume the beer and thereby exclude others from the consumption of that particular pint of beer. I acquire exclusive private property rights in beer, up to an amount determined by what I part with. In principle I need not consume the beer immediately – I could keep it in a container for later consumption, or for later sale or exchange for something else. The point is that I can, by exchange and trade, acquire a private property right which gives me exclusive disposal rights over an identifiable particular unit of beer. With policing services the situation is obviously quite different. There is, and can be, no identifiable unit of such to which I can gain exclusive disposal rights. If a community is well policed all its members enjoy the service and it cannot be parcelled out between them in units for each member's exclusive benefit. Hence, markets cannot provide policing. They can provide personal security, of course. I can buy better doorlocks, bullet-proof vests, the services of a bodyguard. But a high degree of personal security is not the same thing as the enjoyment of living in a well-policed community.

Price taker and non-price taker firms

Finally, we look at the consequences of violation of the condition that every household and firm acts as a price taker. That is the requirement that no participant in any market transaction should be able to influence the terms on which the transaction takes place. We concentrate on this condition in the context of firms, since it is obvious that many firms are not price takers, while most households in most situations appear to be reasonably described as price takers. The price taker firm can sell as much or as little as it likes at the ruling price – variations in the quantity it offers for sale do not affect the price per unit which it receives. Thus, the price taker firm cannot force up the price it can get by holding supplies back from the market. Recall that in 4.2 we showed that for such a firm its supply function is just its marginal cost function. We now wish to show that where a firm is not a price taker, its supply function is not its marginal cost function. This being the case our argument above to the effect that the market outcome is an efficient allocation outcome breaks down, since where the industry consists of non-price taker firms the market supply function is not the marginal cost function for the commodity. We can show that where a commodity is produced in an industry which is not composed of price taker firms, the market equilibrium output of the commodity will be smaller than the output required for efficiency in allocation.

In Figure 4.15 we contrast the situations of the price taker and the non-price taker firm. As shown in the upper part of the figure, the price taker firm faces a horizontal demand function indicating that any amount can be sold at a constant price. This implies that revenue, equals benefit, increases steadily with output, which in turn gives marginal benefit as constant and equal to price. For a firm which is not a price taker, the demand function slopes downwards, indicating that as more output is put on to the market the price it will fetch falls. If price falls with increased sales, revenue increases with sales but at a decreasing rate. Thus, the second graph along the bottom of Figure 4.15 shows the non-price taker firm's benefit increasing at a decreasing rate as output increases. Marginal benefit is the slope of the benefit graph, so marginal benefit falls with output increasing. The final diagram along the bottom of Figure 4.15 shows price and marginal benefit graphed against output. We see, and this is generally true for non-price taker firms, that marginal benefit is everywhere less than price, and that as output increases marginal benefit falls more rapidly than price.

Now consider Figure 4.16 where we derive the implications of these contrasting situations for the competitive market outcome. The top two diagrams refer to the price taker firm, and are just a restatement of the

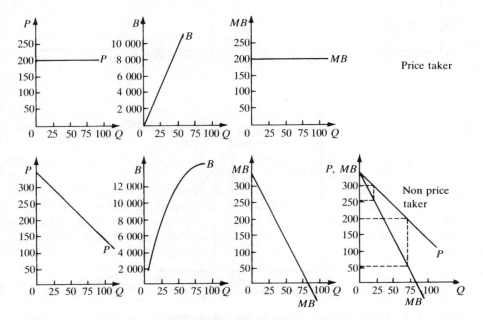

Figure 4.15　Marginal benefit functions for two types of firms

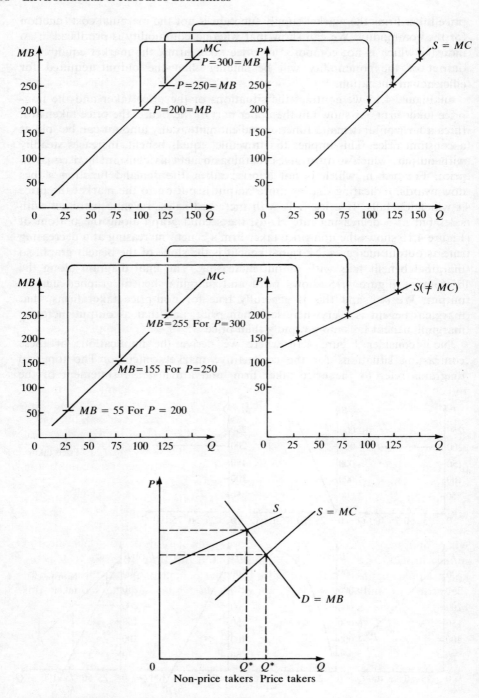

Figure 4.16 Non-price taker firms do not supply enough

analysis of Figure 4.3. The firm's net benefit maximising output is where marginal cost equals marginal benefit, which here is equal to price. Hence, to derive the graph of the firm's net benefit maximising outputs related to various prices, i.e. the firm's supply function, we simply read off points along the marginal cost graph. For example, with price at £300 the firm would plan to sell, would maximise profit by producing and selling, 150 units.

The middle two diagrams in Figure 4.16 refer to the non-price taking firm, which to clarify matters has the same marginal cost function as the price taker firm. The non-price taker firm also maximises net benefit where marginal cost equals marginal benefit, and it also will wish to supply quantities which maximise benefit. However, for it marginal benefit is not the same as price. Take price equal to £300, and the lower right graph of Figure 4.15 gives the corresponding marginal benefit as £255. To get the amount the non-price taker firm would supply at marginal benefit equal to £255 we just use the marginal cost function and read off the output corresponding to marginal cost equal to £255. This is 127.5 units. So, for this firm with price £300, the corresponding net benefit maximising output, or planned supply, is 127.5 units. This gives us one point on the non-price taker firm's supply function. We obtain others by proceeding in the same way for different levels of price, as shown in Figure 4.16. We see that for the non-price taker firm, the supply function is not the marginal cost function, but lies above it.

The implications of this are shown at the bottom of Figure 4.16, where we consider market demand and supply. Where the industry consists of price taker firms we have a supply function which is the marginal cost function, and so we get a market equilibrium corresponding to an efficient allocation of resources. Where the industry consists of non-price taker firms, the market supply function will, as discussed above, for the same cost conditions be displaced upwards. Hence, in this case, the market equilibrium quantity will be smaller, and the price higher, than efficiency in allocation requires. Non-price taker behaviour destroys the ability of markets to generate equilibrium outcomes which are efficient allocations of resources.

The policy implications which follow from the existence of non-price taking firms are easy to state but difficult to put into practice. It is easy to state that what is required for efficiency in allocation is that all firms produce where marginal cost equals price. The problems arise in devising measures to induce firms facing downward sloping demand functions so to do, this being against their inclination to maximise their net benefit or profit. Discussion of the problems and suggested responses would be beyond the scope of this book.

Microeconomic objectives and government intervention

So, if an economy existed in which all of the ideal conditions were operative, then in that economy governmental intervention could be restricted to the running of the system of taxes and grants required to achieve a fair distribution of income. The achievement of allocative efficiency could be left to the pursuit of self interest via market activity. However, nobody believes that there exist economies where all of the ideal conditions are operative. In practice governmental intervention is required to secure allocative efficiency. The point of the analysis of the ideal conditions model economy is to provide the basis for effective governmental intervention, in that it identifies potential sources of market failure in terms of informational deficiencies, external effects, public goods and non-price taker behaviour. If any of these are in fact operative, the analysis of the ideal conditions model economy establishes the case for intervention and indicates the nature of the required intervention for the attainment of allocative efficiency.

We must be clear, however, that it is not implied that government intervention will necessarily be successful in the sense of securing a fair distribution of income and allocative efficiency. First, there are legitimate disagreements about what might constitute a fair distribution of income. Second, successful intervention would require that the government have information which might in fact be difficult or impossible to acquire. This point arose clearly in the discussion above of the supply of a public good in the amount required for allocative efficiency. It will come up again in our discussion of methods for pollution control in the next chapter.

4.6   International trade theory

The dominant idea concerning international trade in economics is the *theory of comparative advantage*. This theory is used both to explain why trade between nations occurs, and to show that free trade is beneficial to all participating nations. In both respects, the core idea is specialisation based on different comparative advantages in the production of commodities.

In Figure 4.17 we consider two nations, A and B, and two commodities, X and Y. We assume that both nations have the same population sizes, but differ in their endowments of natural resources and capital equipment. B has a relatively large endowment of natural resources per capita, and a relatively small amount of capital per capita, but has more of both than A. The production of X is relatively resource intensive, that of Y relatively capital intensive. The lines $X_A Y_A$ and $X_B Y_B$ show the production and consumption possibilities in each country in the absence of trade between them, when they operate as *closed economies*. In A, $0X_A$ is production with all inputs used in the production of X, and $0Y_A$ is production with all inputs used in the production of Y, and similarly for B. Any output combination lying along $X_A Y_A$ is producible and consumable, and similarly for $X_B Y_B$. Given the assumed production possibilities, the relative prices of X and Y in each country are given by the slopes of these lines. In A one unit of X exchanges for $(0Y_A/0X_A)$ units of Y, in B one unit of X exchanges for $(0Y_B/0X_B)$ units of Y. The actual pattern of production and consumption in each country depends on preferences in relation to the price ratio as determined by the resource and capital endowments.

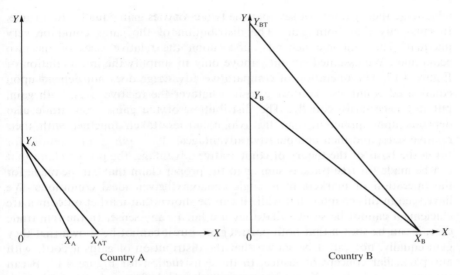

Figure 4.17 Trade and consumption opportunities

Now, assume that the two countries completely open their borders to trade. Assume also that transport costs between the two are zero. Then, the same relative price as between X and Y must hold in both countries. If it did not there would be un-exploited opportunities for profits to be made by importing/exporting according to the direction of the price differential. Exactly what the common relative price will turn out to be depends on production possibilities and consumer preferences in the two countries. In Figure 4.17 the parallel lines $X_{AT}Y_A$ and X_BY_{BT} show the common relative price after the opening up to trade. The reason for drawing the price lines as shown is as follows. $0Y_A$ is the amount of Y that A produces if it specialises completely in that line of production. If it does this and buys X from B, selling Y to B, the terms on which it can exchange Y for X in consumption are shown by Y_AX_{AT} which has the slope corresponding to the world relative price for X and Y. Similarly, $0X_B$ is B's production of X given complete specialisation, and it can then consume, by exchanging X for Y at the common relative price, along X_BY_{BT}. By specialising in production of the commodity in which they have comparative advantage and engaging in trade, both countries improve their consumption opportunities. As *open economies*, both can consume more of both commodities. Just what larger quantities of both commodities each nation will consume depends upon the world price ratio established after opening up to trade, and on preferences.

This is the principal intellectual basis for the economists' presumption in favour of free trade. Even where one country is absolutely more productive, both can gain from trade by specialising to exploit their comparative advantage. For trade to be beneficial to both, all that is necessary is that the two countries have different relative productivities. The comparative advantage theory does not say that the two countries gain equally from trade. It says only that both gain. The distribution of the gains could be very unequal. The outcome depends, first, upon the relative sizes of the two economies. We assumed equality above only to simplify the interpretation of Figure 4.17. The operation of comparative advantage does not depend upon equal sized countries. According to it, whatever the relative sizes, both gain, but not necessarily equally. The distribution of the gains from trade also depends upon preferences in the two countries, taken together with their relative sizes, and their comparative advantages.

On the basis of the theory of comparative advantage, the proper claim that can be made for free trade is similar to the proper claim that can be made for the operation of markets in a single economy, given ideal conditions. We have seen in this chapter that while it can be shown that market outcomes are efficient, it cannot be shown that they are fair in any sense. In the free trade case, it can be shown that both parties gain, but it cannot be shown that they gain equally, nor can it be shown that the distribution of gains accords with any particular concept of justice. In the construction for Figure 4.17, B can consume more of both X and Y per capita than A before and after trade.

The construction of Figure 4.17 involves a number of special assumptions which are not necessary to establish the result that both nations gain from trade. It is assumed there that the rates at which X exchanges for Y in production in both countries are constant over all output levels. This is implausible. As inputs are progressively moved from one line of production to the other, one would expect the successive increments in output in the latter line of production would decrease. In this case, instead of being straight lines, $X_A Y_A$ and $X_B Y_B$ would be curves bowed out away from the origin, as in the manner of the production possibility frontier shown in Figure 3.3. In this case, it can still be shown that both countries will gain from trade and specialisation, but they will not completely specialise as in Figure 4.17. Each will continue to produce some of both commodities, but each will be a net exporter for one commodity and a net importer for the other. We also assumed zero transport costs for the purposes of Figure 4.17. This is a fairly standard assumption in international trade theory. Dropping it does not seriously affect the arguments. Positive transport costs work to reduce the extent of specialisation and trade, but they do not alter the case to be made for it on the basis of comparative advantage. That case for free trade does not depend on the assumption of just two countries, or upon the assumption of just two commodities. With many countries and many commodities, the story becomes more complicated, but the essential ideas carry through.

The theory of comparative advantage is developed for situations where both (all) countries can produce both (all) commodities. This is not generally the case. If A has no oil deposits, it cannot produce oil. Less limiting cases arise where production is technically feasible, but would be prohibitively expensive so that it would not be possible to sell the output – Iceland could grow oranges in hot houses, but the domestic market for the output at a price to cover the costs would be non-existent. In such circumstances the argument for trade is that it extends the range of choice open to a country's consumers. Icelanders can consume oranges grown overseas by exporting fish: inhabitants of countries without oil deposits can drive cars by exporting some cars in exchange for oil. Mention should also be made of the view that international trade is desirable because, as compared with a situation of autarchy, it promotes peace and harmony between nations. If A has no oil but B has and will not trade then A may be motivated to invade B to gain access to oil. Trade reduces the potential for international conflict, on this view.

4.7 Commentary

The story told in sections 4.1 to 4.4 is essentially the modern version of Adam Smith's invisible-hand story (see 1.1). Smith claimed that the uncoordinated pursuit of self interest by firms and households would promote the general interest. Since 1776 economists have put a great deal of intellectual effort into making precise the notion of the 'general interest' and specifying the conditions under which it would be true that selfish behaviour could lead to its attainment. The results of these efforts are summarised in the two fundamental theorems of welfare economics, which are proofs that:

(a) Given certain conditions, if a general competitive market equilibrium exists, it corresponds to an efficient allocation.

(b) Given certain conditions, any efficient allocation can be realised as a general competitive market equilibrium with the appropriate set of taxes and transfers between individuals.

The 'certain conditions' for both theorems are very restrictive. The discussion in the chapter here focussed on those most relevant to the way economists approach environmental problems. If the conditions held for any actual economy, which very few economists would accept to be the case, then the rôle of government could be restricted to running a tax/transfer system so as to achieve some version of equity, and then leaving the problem of achieving allocative efficiency entirely to markets. For this separation of the problems of efficiency and equity to hold, even given the 'certain conditions' being satisfied, the taxes and transfers that the government uses have to be of a special kind – they have to be 'lump sum' in nature. Taxes and transfers are of this kind when they do not themselves affect any of the incentives facing individuals. In principle, government could figure out such a set of taxes and transfers which would promote equity, but the information requirements and administration costs render this infeasible. Feasible lump sum taxes would be uniform across individuals, and not being related to ability to pay, would be seen as unfair. Layard and Walters (1978) discuss these matters in more detail: see also Hirshleifer (1980). Böhm (1974) provides a concise overview of the rôle of markets in the attainment of economic efficiency and provides further references in this area.

The use of supply and demand analysis, as outlined in 4.1 above, is widespread in economics. Ch. 2 of Hirshleifer (1980) goes through the basic analysis and provides numerous examples of its application. The conditions necessary for a market system to be capable of realising an efficient allocation are discussed in Ch. 1 of Layard and Walters (1978), in Ch. 17 of Hirshleifer (1980) and in Ch. 2 of Böhm (1974). On the derivation of the industry supply function, 4.2 above, see Ch. 7 of Layard and Walters (1978) and Ch. 10 of Hirshleifer (1980), for example. The derivation of the demand function for a commodity from the assumed utility maximising behaviour of households, 4.3 above, is considered in Ch. 5 of Layard and Walters (1978) and Chs 3, 4 and 5 of Hirshleifer (1980). In 4.4 we showed how, under ideal conditions, market equilibria correspond to allocative efficiency. Alternative demonstrations can be found in Ch. 1 of Layard and Walters (1978) or in Ch. 1 and/or Appendix 1 of Böhm (1974). The sources of market failure (4.5) are discussed in Ch. 2 of Böhm (1974). For discussion of the allocative implications of non-price taker behaviour in markets, see Ch. 8 of Layard and Walters (1978) or Ch. 11 of Hirshleifer (1980). We shall be considering external effects and public goods issues at some length in the next chapter.

The theory of comparative advantage in relation to international trade was formulated in 1817, by the classical economist David Ricardo (see Blaug 1985). It is discussed in introductory economics texts such as Samuelson and Nordhaus (1985) and Wonnacott and Wonnacott (1979). In such treatments, the theory usually makes two assumptions about the conditions of production for all commodities in all countries. First, that it occurs under *constant returns to scale*, so that if all input levels are increased by $x\%$ output increases by $x\%$. Second, that within each country it takes place under competitive conditions, so that all firms act as price takers and cannot exercise market power, as would be the case with a monopolistic producer. Most economists take the view that dropping these assumptions strengthens, rather than weakens, the case for free trade. First, to the extent that there are potential *economies of scale*, such that for an $x\%$ increase in output input requirements go up by less than $x\%$ so that unit costs fall, free trade will promote the realisation of such, by increasing the size of the markets for specialised producers. Suppose that both A and B produce widgets. Widget production is such that automation is cost effective only if the market is x units per annum, but once adopted it halves the cost of production. A and B have populations such that their domestic widget markets are $0.7x$. In the absence of trade, often referred to as autarchy, both produce high cost widgets. With free trade, one will specialise in the production of low cost widgets to the benefit of consumers in both countries. The competitive argument in favour of free trade is that opening the domestic economy to imports increases the competition faced by domestic firms, reducing their market power.

The comparative advantage story assumes that opening up to trade allows only produced commodities to cross national frontiers. The basic inputs to production – labour, capital, natural resources – are assumed to be immobile after opening up to trade. This is a standard assumption. In the case of natural resources, immobility follows, generally, from purely physical considerations – oil deposits are necessarily fixed in location, for example. In the case of capital and labour, immobility arises rather from institutional arrangements adopted by sovereign nation states. Suppose that such arrangements did not exist, so that labour and capital could move freely across national frontiers. Then, there would be a tendency to equality across nations in the earnings of these factors. Just as free trade in a commodity leads to a single international price, transport costs aside, so free movement of factors of production would tend to produce *factor price equalisation*. Without factor mobility, free trade in commodities can act as a surrogate means to factor price equalising tendencies. A low wage country moving into the export of labour intensive products would see the domestic demand for labour increase, tending to increase wage rates, for example.

Views on the desirability of factor price equalisation differ. The argument that it can involve increased wage rates in low income countries are matched by arguments that it can also involve reduced wage rates in high income countries. The latter problem is made more pressing by the fact that in the world today capital is actually highly mobile across national boundaries, whereas labour is generally immobile. The international mobility of capital means that there is a tendency toward the equalisation of rates of return on it in different countries. To the extent that a country has high labour costs, on account of high wages and/or low labour productivity, the rate of return on capital employed in it will be low. Capital will flow from such a country to others where labour costs are lower, implying a higher rate of return on capital. For a country suffering a capital drain on this basis, there will be unemployment, unless labour costs are reduced. Some economists now argue that international capital mobility undermines the standard arguments, based on comparative advantage, for trade, and that there is case for some restrictions on trade: see, for example, Ch. 11 of Daly and Cobb (1989).

The *infant industry argument* is of longer standing, and is considered in most introductory text discussions of international trade. Here the argument, which assumes capital immobility, is that temporary protection of a domestic industry may be justifiable in order that it can make a potential comparative advantage actual. Essentially this argument derives from recognition that whereas the theory takes comparative advantage patterns as given and fixed, they are in fact the product, to some extent, of historical experience. Thus, for example, at a point in time A may have an existing timber products industry which can produce more cheaply than the same industry in B, notwithstanding the fact that B is better endowed with forests. This arises because prior to trade A developed timber processing capacity, whereas B did not. Then, the infant industry argument would allow B to restrict the import of timber products from A so that its domestic firms could put in place the processing capacity to realise their underlying comparative advantage. Import restrictions may also be justified on a strategic importance argument. Trade involves specialisation. The theory of comparative advantage focuses on the gains from this, but it is recognised that it can also involve some costs. A country that gives up producing some commodity faces the prospect that it will become unavailable if foreigners refuse to supply it. This may happen in times of international conflict. Hence, economists see a role for restricting trade and specialisation on strategic grounds. Certain commodities may be identified as of special strategic importance, and a decision made to maintain domestic production despite some cost penalty.

There are three basic ways in which a nation can restrict its external trade. It can place physical restrictions on flows of commodities across its borders. These usually take the form of import/export quotas, where a government issued permit or quota is required to engage in trade; such permits may be tradeable. It can levy charges on commodity flows across its borders, such as tariffs on imports, or, less commonly, levies on exports. These charges are a source of government revenue, and tariffs particularly have been important in this rôle in some countries at some points in history. Finally, it can subsidise domestic producers. Economists generally take the view that if restrictions on trade are going to be used, price type interventions are superior to physical controls. Recently arguments have been made for the use of trade restrictions to secure environmental objectives. Economists, generally, have opposed such arguments. These issues are considered in Chapter 5.

The UK demand for energy

We now illustrate the application of the approach developed in this chapter to a 'real world' problem by considering the analysis of energy use. In the commentary section of Chapter 2 we looked at movements, over 1968 to 1989, in the energy intensity of UK economic activity and the price of energy. We saw that over the whole period the relative (or real) price of energy increased by some 25%, while the energy intensity of economic activity, measured by therms used per unit of Gross Domestic Product, declined by some 30%. We can now look at this again using the concept of the demand function. The data to be used are given in Table 4.1. For Q, Y and P this is the same data as was analysed in section 2.4: in Fig. 2.2 the right-hand vertical axis measures P from Table 4.1, and the left-hand vertical axis measures $Q \div Y$. The new information in Table 4.1 is that for W. These data are constructed from figures for annual mean temperatures for England and Wales, Scotland and Northern Ireland given in the *Annual Abstract of Statistics* for the UK (Central Statistical Office 1991). The sources, and derivation, of the data series for Q, Y and P were given in section 2.4.

Now Q is energy delivered to all final energy users, i.e. to households for consumption and to firms for use in production. We consider in turn the analysis of the demand for energy by households and firms.

In section 4.3, we saw that the standard analysis of utility maximising behaviour by a household indicates that if the price of a commodity falls, its consumption rises. Actually, the theory does not state that this is necessarily

Table 4.1 Data for the analysis of UK energy use

	Q	Y	P	W
1968	55 169	222 181	8.01	9.8
1969	56 768	227 670	8.14	9.7
1970	57 953	232 301	7.86	9.9
1971	57 002	236 227	7.88	10.3
1972	58 041	242 826	7.60	9.6
1973	61 034	260 907	7.37	10.0
1974	58 284	256 994	9.16	9.9
1975	55 876	254 961	9.30	10.3
1976	57 327	261 693	9.49	10.3
1977	58 533	268 410	9.68	9.8
1978	59 208	276 252	9.10	9.7
1979	61 695	283 955	9.67	9.2
1980	56 537	278 160	10.78	9.8
1981	54 921	274 964	11.66	9.6
1982	54 279	279 738	12.02	10.2
1983	54 043	290 148	12.26	10.4
1984	53 890	296 001	12.24	9.8
1985	56 319	307 901	12.13	9.0
1986	57 845	319 730	10.89	9.0
1987	58 010	334 407	10.60	9.4
1988	58 982	349 404	9.90	10.1
1989	58 508	356 698	10.00	10.7

Q UK energy consumption by final users, millions of therms.
Y UK Gross Domestic Product (at factor cost), millions of 1985 £s.
P Relative (or real) price of energy to UK final users, pence per therm.
W UK mean temperature, degrees centigrade.

the case for all commodities, but it is what we would expect on the basis of the theory for most commodities, and we shall take it that it is our expectation in the case of household energy consumption. (See the references given to Layard and Walters (1978) or Hirshleifer (1980) in connection with demand functions for an explanation of how a commodity's consumption might fall as its price falls.) What would we expect to happen to household energy consumption as household income increases? Panel (a) of Figure 4.18 uses the same utility maximising analysis as in Figure 4.5, to show that we would then expect energy consumption to rise. An increase in household income, with the relative prices of the two commodities (which are energy and all other commodities treated as a single alternative in Figure 4.18 (a)) remaining unchanged, means that the budget constraint shifts outwards while retaining the same slope. The utility maximising consumption levels of both commodities increase. Again, preferences can be such that as income increases, a commodity's consumption falls. However, such cases are rare and we shall take it that energy is not such a case.

So, for the consumption of energy by households, the analysis of utility maximising behaviour leads us to expect that it will fall/rise as household

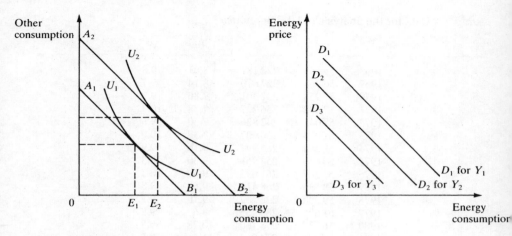

Figure 4.18   Household energy demand and income variation

income decreases/increases. For income constant, the household demand for energy increases/decreases as the relative price of energy falls/rises. Panel (b) of Figure 4.18 brings together these two relationships, showing a demand function for energy which slopes downwards to give quantity demanded falling as price rises, and which shifts as income varies. With $Y_1 > Y_2 > Y_3$, this figure shows the household demand for energy increasing with household income, for the relative price of energy constant.

The theoretical analysis of the demand for energy by firms is based on the production function concept. In 3.5 we considered a production function where two inputs were involved; see Figure 3.17 for the diagrammatic representation. Let us now take the two inputs to production to be energy and labour, and consider the choice of input mix by a firm whose objective is to minimise the cost of producing a fixed level of output. In Figure 4.19 (a) we show the isoquant for the fixed output level, and a family of isocost lines AB, $A'B'$, etc. At every point along an *isocost line* the firm's total expenditure on inputs, its total cost of production, is the same. As we move outwards from the origin to the north east successive isocost lines represent larger total cost. Given the production of the amount of output represented by the isoquant QQ and the relative prices for inputs represented by the slope of these isocost lines, the firm minimises cost by using $0L$ units of labour and $0E$ units of energy. Clearly, a move along QQ, in either direction, away from X would involve moving on to a higher isocost line.

Now, if the relative price of energy to labour changes, the slope of the isocost lines changes: recall that the endpoints of an isocost line give the amounts of each input purchased if all of expenditure on inputs goes to purchase just one type of input. If energy becomes more expensive, the isocost lines get steeper. As shown in Figure 4.19 (b), this means a change in the input mix such that more labour and less energy is used. It also means that the minimum cost of producing the output level corresponding to QQ is

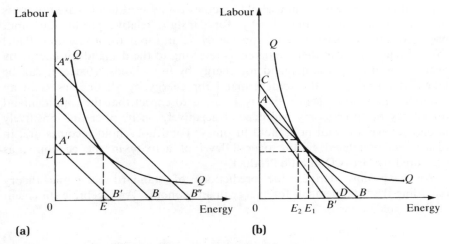

Figure 4.19   Energy use and energy price in production

increased. For constant total expenditure on inputs, the energy price increase shifts AB to AB' which will be tangential to an isoquant for an output level lower than that for QQ. CD is drawn parallel to AB' and corresponds to a greater expenditure on inputs. Clearly, on the basis of this analysis we would predict that for cost minimising firms the demand for the input energy will fall/rise as the relative price of energy rises/falls. We would expect, that is, that firms' demand function for energy would, like households' demand function for energy, be downward sloping. This follows from the assumption that firms seek to minimise the cost of producing given output levels, whereas we have previously assumed that firms seek to maximise net benefit, equals profit. The prediction carries over to the profit-maximising case. To maximise profit a firm selects its output level and its input mix with which to produce the chosen output level. Now clearly, whatever the chosen output level, the profit arising at that output level will be maximised only if the cost of producing it is minimised. Hence, if the relative input prices facing profit-maximising firms change, the theory would predict a change in the output level and a shift in the input mix such that relatively more/less of the cheaper/dearer input is used. We would expect, that is, that there would be a negative relationship between changes in firms' use of an input and changes in the relative price of the input, given the assumption that firms maximise profits. We have seen, however, that this expectation also arises on the weaker assumption that firms seek to minimise the total cost of producing any output level, however that level might be chosen.

So, we expect a downward sloping demand function for energy as an input to production. Also, it is clear from Figure 4.19 that we would expect the production input demand for energy to increase as the quantity of output produced increases. We know that, for most commodities anyway, household demand increases as household incomes increase. It follows that we would expect that an increase in household incomes would lead to increased outputs of most commodities, and thereby, for constant relative production input prices, to an increased demand for energy as an input to production. Panel (b) of Figure 4.18 can then be taken as referring to the demand for energy by firms, as well as to the demand for energy by households. Hence, it can be taken as referring to the total demand for energy by all final users in an economy. Economic theory, that is, leads us to expect that the total demand for energy in an economy will depend negatively on its price and positively upon the level of total household incomes. Total household incomes are, in turn, directly related to the overall level of activity in the economy, as measured by Gross Domestic Product.

We have now derived the predictions of standard economic theory regarding the total demand for energy in an economy. An algebraic statement of these predictions is

$$Q = a + bY - cP \qquad [4.7]$$

where Q is the quantity of energy demanded, Y is the level of economic activity, P is the relative price of energy, and a, b and c are the parameters of the demand function. The parameter c in equation [4.7] gives the slope of the demand function; the parameter b gives the amount by which it shifts upwards for a unit increase in Y. We now wish to see whether the predictions of economic theory are realised in the data for the UK given in Table 4.1. To do this we use the techniques of *econometrics*, and particularly we estimate the values of the parameters a, b and c by *least squares regression*. For a discussion of least squares regression and econometrics see, for example, Gujarati (1995) or Thomas (1993). In order to properly estimate the way energy demand responds to variations in P and Y we have to allow for the effect of temperature variations, so we actually estimate a, b, c and w for

$$Q = a + bY - cP + wW$$

with Q, Y, P and W as defined and given in Table 4.1. The result obtained is

$$Q = 73513.63 + 0.0389Y - 1300.04P - 1452.10W \qquad [4.8]$$

and we see that the theoretical predictions hold – the Y coefficient is positive and the P coefficient is negative. We also find that with this numerical relationship 70% of the actual variation in energy use shown in Table 4.1 is explained by the variation in Y, P and W.

Now clearly equation [4.8] should be useful for analysing the history of UK energy demand over 1968 to 1989, and for forecasting how future energy demand will respond to future income and price developments. We will not, however, use it for these purposes; we will use a different algebraic representation of the energy demand function. Equation [4.7] is a *linear demand function*. We have already noted that the theory does not require demand functions that can be drawn as straight lines, and that such are used in diagrammatic exposition principally for simplicity and convenience.

Actually, when we come to use historical data to estimate demand functions as immediately above, the linear form has some disadvantages. One of these is that the estimated values for the parameters giving the response of quantity demanded to a change in price or income depend on the units in which price and income are measured. This can give to rise to confusion, especially when comparing different demand functions. If, for example, we had measured Y in Table 4.1 in units of thousands of millions of 1985 £'s, instead of equation [4.8] we would have obtained as the least squares regression estimate for the energy demand equation

$$Q = 73513.63 + 38.90Y - 1300.04P - 1452.10W$$

A second, and related, disadvantage attaching to the linear form concerns the measurement of the price and income elasticities of demand. These elasticities are measures of the sensitivity of quantity demanded to changes in price and income, to be used in comparing and classifying commodities. The *price elasticity of demand* is the ratio of the proportional change in quantity demanded to the associated proportional change in price. The *income elasticity of demand* is the ratio of the proportional change in quantity demanded to the associated proportional change in income. That is, if we represent price elasticity as ε_p and income elasticity as ε_y, we have

$$\varepsilon_p = (\Delta Q/Q)/(\Delta P/P) \text{ and } \varepsilon_y = (\Delta Q/Q)/(\Delta Y/Y)$$

where Δ means very small change in, as usual. To see the problem with linear demand functions, consider ε_p and a unit change of price. By virtue of linearity the ΔQ corresponding to a unit price change is the same, and given by the slope parameter c in equation [4.7], whatever the initial level of P and Q. It follows that ε_p varies in value according to the levels of P and Q from which the change occurs. Similarly for ε_y. This means, for example, that if linear demand functions for energy are used, simple comparisons of the characteristics of energy demand in different countries in terms of elasticities of price and income are impossible.

These problems are avoided if the demand function is given, instead of the algebraic form [4.7], the form

$$Q = aY^b P^{-c} \qquad\qquad [4.9]$$

which, by taking logarithms on both sides, is the same as

$$\log Q = \log a + b \log Y - c \log P \qquad\qquad [4.10]$$

With this *double logarithmic demand function*, the price and income elasticities are constants for all values of Y and P, and we have

$$\varepsilon_p = -c, \, \varepsilon_y = b$$

so that estimating the values of c and b gives directly the elasticities of interest. Figure 4.20 shows the graphical representation of equations [4.9]/[4.10], where $Y_1 > Y_2 > Y_3$. This constant elasticity feature of the double

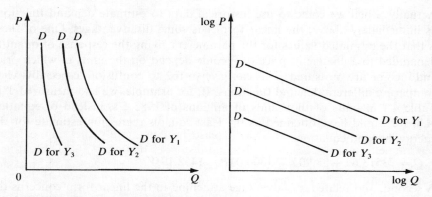

Figure 4.20   The double logarithmic demand function

logarithmic demand function is clearly very convenient, as is the property that the values taken by estimates for b and c are unaffected by the units in which Y and P are measured. Hence, the form of equation [4.9]/[4.10] is used in applied work in commodity demand. Using this form with the data of Table 4.1, by inputing the (natural) logarithms of the Q, Y, P and W figures to the calculations for the least squares regression, gives the result

$$\log Q = 9.3305 + 0.2163 \log Y - 0.2369 \log P - 0.2393 \log W \qquad [4.11]$$

corresponding to which we have 71% of the observed Q variation accounted for by the observed variation in Y, P and W. The predictions of the theory, in terms of the directions of effect on Q produced by changes in Y and P, are again confirmed. The income elasticity of energy demand is 0.2163; the price elasticity is −0.2369.

We can now use these elasticities to (i) compare the characteristics of energy demand with the demand for other commodities, (ii) do some conditional forecasting, and (iii) look again at the history of UK energy use over 1968 to 1989. Commodities are said to be *necessities* if they have $\varepsilon_y < 1$ and *luxuries* if $\varepsilon_y > 1$: in the former case expenditure on the commodity grows less fast than income as income increases; in the latter case it grows more rapidly. Over 1968 to 1989 energy was a necessity in the UK, and this is what is found for energy in most economies, at most times. When the effect on demand of energy price variation is allowed for, the demand for energy does not, contrary to many views, grow at the same rate as the level of economic activity. In terms of price elasticity, we say that a commodity's demand is *elastic* if ε_p is less than −1 (−1.5 eg) and *inelastic* if $\varepsilon_p > -1$ (−0.5 eg). The demand for energy in the UK is inelastic. Actually −0.2369 is rather a small (absolute) value to find for a price elasticity – as commodities generally go, energy has a demand which is relatively insensitive to price variations. But note that it is not completely insensitive to price, which is what is implied in some of the more extreme positions taken on the 'energy crisis', and the rôle of economic growth in creating natural resource scarcity.

Given equation [4.11], conditional forecasting of the UK's demand for energy is straightforward. One approach simply applies the price and income elasticity definitions to any postulated changes in Y and P. If, for example, it is assumed that the level of economic activity in the UK will increase by 50% while the relative price of energy remains constant, an income elasticity of 0.2163 gives an 11% increase in UK energy demand. Alternatively, a constant level of Y together with a 50% increase in P would give a forecast decrease, via $\varepsilon_p = -0.2369$, of 11.9% in UK energy demand. The combined effect of a 50% increase in Y and a 50% increase in P is simply the sum of these separate effects, i.e. UK energy demand decreases by 0.9%. These conditional forecasts ignore any temperature-induced variations. An alternative approach is to use equation [4.11] directly, assuming that temperature in the year being forecast for will be at the average taken by W over 1968 to 1989. From Table 4.1 this average is found to be 9.8, for which the (natural) logarithm is 2.2866. Inserting this value for log W in equation [4.11] and rearranging gives

$$\log Q = 8.7843 + 0.2163 \log Y - 0.2369 \log P \qquad [4.12]$$

as an equation which gives log Q, and hence Q, for given values for Y and P. Suppose, for example, we are told that in 1990 the UK's Gross Domestic Product (at factor cost) is going to be 360,000 (in millions of 1985 £'s). We are also told that the UK price of energy in 1990 is currently expected to be 15% up on the 1989 price, i.e. $10.00 \times 1.15 = 11.5$ p per therm. These figures in equation [4.12] give $Q = 58,279$ million therms as the 1990 conditional (on $Y = 360,000$ and $P = 11.5$) forecast for UK demand for energy by final users.

This account of forecasting glosses over many of the difficulties that attend the exercise in practice. We have tried to emphasise the fact that any forecast of commodity demand is conditional upon assumptions, or forecasts, of the commodity's price and the level of economic activity or income. Over and above this there remain inherent uncertainties, arising from the fact that income and price elasticities are not known but are estimated from historical data.[3] Our account is intended only to show the general nature and usefulness of procedures based on economic theory and econometric techniques. For a discussion of the inherent problems generally associated with econometric techniques and their application, see the texts cited above.

In 2.4 we looked at the data of Table 4.1 on Q, Y and P, noted the falling energy intensity of UK economic activity and the rising relative price of energy in the UK. We can now look at this again, using equations [4.11] and [4.12]. In Figure 4.21 the solid line shows the evolution of UK final energy consumption over 1968 to 1989 given by equation [4.12] using the historical values for Y and P shown in Table 4.1. The energy consumption levels it shows for each year are, that is, not the actual levels of Table 4.1, but those obtained by plugging the actual Y and P levels into equation [4.12] and solving it for Q. The solid line of Figure 4.21 shows what would have happened to UK energy demand over 1968 to 1982 if in each year UK temperature had been at its average over the whole period, and if demand had been exactly determined by equation [4.11] given historical levels for Y

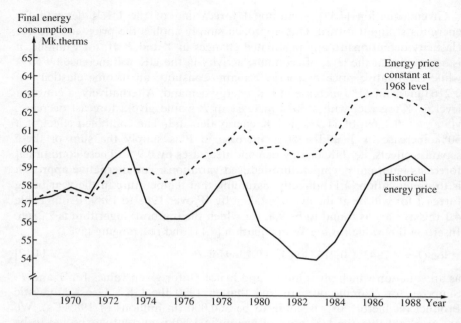

Figure 4.21   UK energy consumption for constant and historical prices

and P. It is a reference point for the study of UK energy demand which abstracts from the vagaries of the weather and random effects on energy demand. The broken line in Figure 4.21 joins up levels for Q which are obtained from equation [4.12] when we plug in the actual historical levels for Y in each year together with $P = 8.01$ for every year. That is, the broken line shows what would have happened to UK energy demand if Y had evolved as it in fact did, but P had remained constant at its 1968 level of 8.01 p per therm. The difference between the solid and broken lines is, then, measuring the effect on UK energy demand of deviations in the price of energy away from its 1968 level. Clearly, after 1973 the price of energy was such as to reduce the use of energy on average. UK energy users did respond to the relative price of energy as economic theory predicts.

Notes

1. The discussion here implies that P is to be regarded as the independent and Q as the dependent variable, while in Figure 4.1 the vertical axis is for P and the horizontal is for Q, violating the normal convention. In economics it is usual to proceed in this way in diagrammatic expositions.
2. As shown in Figure 4.5, the change in P_W does not alter cloth consumption. This is not the general case, but arises because of the particular utility function, equation [4.2], used to construct this example. Generally, we would expect C and W to change for a change in P_w. The

argument to follow concerning the significance of a demand function is general, and is not conditional on the special form taken by equation [4.2].

3. This can be illustrated as follows. In the first edition of this book the period for which the data for this exercise were available was from 1968 to 1982 only. Using that data the equation corresponding to [4.11] was estimated as

$$\log Q = 6.1094 + 0.5215 \log Y - 0.2982 \log P - 0.3548 \log W$$

so that the estimated income and price elasticities were 0.5215 and 0.2982 respectively. Using data for 1968 to 1982, rather than 1968 to 1989, roughly doubles the size of the income elasticity, and reduces the estimated price elasticity by about 20%.

Chapter 5

The Economics of Pollution

Having considered the nature of the economic problem and the rôle of markets in solving that problem, we are now in a position to discuss one aspect of the relationship between economic activity and the natural environment. In the terminology introduced in Chapter 4, pollution is a problem of market failure. Possible responses to the problem follow from an analysis of the particular type of market failure involved. It turns out that the most obvious response is available only for a very limited class of pollution problems. Further, it appears to be the case that there is no feasible response which can be expected to fully correct the market failure involved. However, with respect to more limited goals economic analysis offers some useful policy implications.

5.1 Pollution as an externality problem

A price-taking firm produces some commodity Q, and its cost function is

$$C_F = Q^2 \qquad\qquad [5.1]$$

graphed in Figure 5.1 (a). Also shown is the graph of the firm's receipts against its output level, labelled B for benefit. With the price of the commodity at £12, this is just the graph of:

$$B = 12Q. \qquad\qquad [5.2]$$

The firm will wish to operate at the output level for which the excess of benefit over cost is greatest. This output level is $Q = 6$, where in Figure 5.1(a) the slopes of the graphs for B and C_F are the same. As discussed in section 3.4, the rule 'operate where the excess of benefit over cost is greatest' can also be expressed as 'operate where marginal cost equals marginal benefit'. This version of the rule is illustrated in Figure 5.1(b), where MC_F is the graph of marginal cost against output for the firm, and where MB is marginal benefit, here constant and equal to the selling price. Recall that marginal cost at any output level is just the slope of the cost curve at that output level, and that

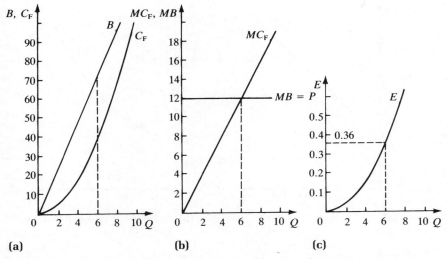

Figure 5.1   A polluting firm's costs benefits and effluent discharge

marginal benefit is the slope of the benefit function. Now, this firm is located next to a lake into which it discharges the effluent arising in production. With E standing for effluent, the relationship between effluent discharge and quantity of the commodity produced is as shown by the graph Figure 5.1(c), for which graph the corresponding equation is:

$$E = 0.01Q^2 \qquad\qquad [5.3]$$

We see that the firm will, when producing Q at the net benefit maximising level of six units, discharge 0.36 units of effluent into the lake.

Thus, given that its use of the lake as a waste-receptable imposes no costs on the firm, it will produce at the output level six and discharge 0.36 units of effluent. This is the best situation for the firm in the circumstances it faces. Is it also the best, in the sense of corresponding to efficiency in allocation, situation for society? We assume that the lake is the source of water for a nearby town, and that the costs of supplying the town with clean water are shown by the graph in Figure 5.2(a), for which the equation is:

$$C_W = 20 + 50E \qquad\qquad [5.4]$$

Thus, with zero effluent discharge water supply costs are £20, and as the amount of effluent increases so do water supply costs. Using the graph in Figure 5.1(c), or equation [5.3], the relationship between water supply costs and effluent discharge can be transformed into the relationship between water supply costs and the firm's output level shown in Figure 5.2(b). Water supply costs increase with the firm's output level at an increasing rate.

Now, the increased water supply costs do not appear in the firm's calculations, but they are real costs to be borne by society as a whole. If we

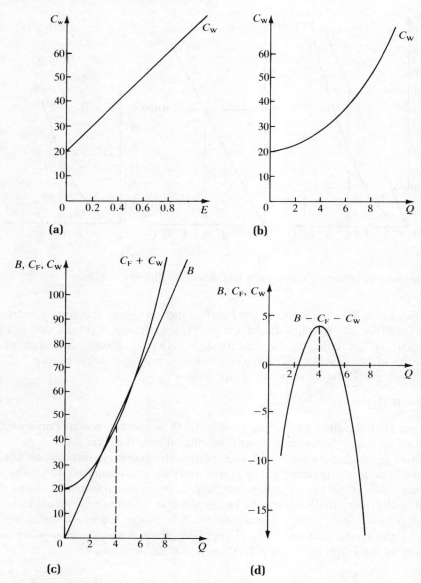

Figure 5.2   Deriving the socially optimal pollution level

add the firm's cost to the water supply cost at each output level, using the graph of C_F in Figure 5.1(a) and the graph of C_W in Figure 5.2(b), we get the graph of $C_F + C_W$ shown in Figure 5.2(c). This shows how the costs of interest to society – those associated with resources used as inputs by the firm (C_F) and those imposed on the water supply undertaking by the firm (C_W) – vary with the firm's output level. From society's viewpoint on costs it is the behaviour of $C_F + C_W$ as Q varies that matters. The benefits to society as the firm's output level varies are measured by the benefits as seen by the firm, since the social value of the production of the firm is price times quantity. Hence, from society's viewpoint the relevant question is: at what output level for the firm is the excess of B over $C_F + C_W$ at its maximum attainable size? In Figure 5.2(c) the graphs of B and $C_F + C_W$ are plotted, and they have the same slope for $Q = 4$. In Figure 5.2(d) the same information is shown in a slightly different way with the graph of $B - C_F - C_W$ attaining a maximum at the output level for the firm where $Q = 4$. Thus, whereas the firm wants to produce 6 units of output, the interests of society as a whole require it to produce 4 units of output. Reading off the graph in Figure 5.1(c) (or using equation [5.3]), this implies that whereas the firm's interests imply 0.36 units of effluent discharge, society's interests require only 0.16 units of effluent discharge. Given that we are assuming ideal conditions obtaining in the economy except in relation to this particular firm, we can say that efficiency in allocation requires that the firm produce 4 units of output and 0.16 units of effluent, whereas the firm is in fact going to produce 6 units of output and 0.36 units of effluent.

This is an example of 'market failure'. Because the ideal conditions are not satisfied, the market outcome does not coincide with an efficient allocation. The source of market failure in this case is the absence of private property rights in the lake, which means that the firm is not charged for its use of the lake as a waste disposal unit. In the terminology introduced in the previous chapter, see especially 4.1 and 4.5, the firm's effluent discharge is an external effect (or externality), and the costs arising from the discharge are *external costs*. The external costs are the costs of supplying water which are additional to what such costs would have been had effluent discharge been zero. In Figure 5.3(a), EC is the graph of external costs against the firm's output level: note that EC in Figure 5.3(a) is just C_W from Figure 5.2(b) shifted downwards by 20 at every level of Q, since water supply costs are £20 when effluent discharge, and hence output

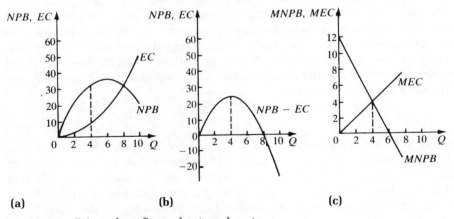

(a)   (b)   (c)

Figure 5.3   Private benefits and external costs

Q is zero. In Figure 5.3(a), NPB stands for *net private benefit* which is net benefit as perceived by the firm, or profit. In Figure 5.3(a), the EC and NPB graphs have the same slope where Q equals 4, so that at this output level the excess of NPB over EC is maximised. This is shown explicitly in Figure 5.3(b), where NPB–EC is graphed. Note that NPB–EC is equal to $B - C_F - C_W + 20$, and compare Figure 5.3(b) with Figure 5.2(d). The story of Figure 5.3(a) and (b) is not a new one, it merely tells the previous story with some new terminology. Figure 5.3(c) shows for this new terminology the general correspondence between the output level identified by the rule maximise the excess of benefit over cost (here NPB over EC) and that identified by the rule set marginal benefit equal to marginal cost (here $MNPB$ and MEC). $MNPB$ is *marginal net private benefit*, the slope of NPB in part (a): MEC is *marginal external cost* the slope of EC in part (a). That the output level for which $MNPB = MEC$ is the socially desirable output level can readily be seen by considering small movements away from $Q = 4$ in Figure 5.3(c). If the firm's output level is set at, say, 4.1 then MEC exceeds $MNPB$ – the move from $Q = 4$ increases the external cost, the additional cost of water supply, by more than the excess of value of the extra output over its extra cost in terms of direct inputs as reflected by the firm's net private benefit. If the firm's output level is set at, say, 3.9 then $MNPB$ exceeds MEC so that the move involves forgoing output from the firm which has a larger net value to society than the extra water supply costs avoided.

External costs borne by a household

Since it is important to be clear that external costs do not arise only when a firm's activities affect production costs, we will now modify the example just discussed such that the effluent discharge into the lake affects a household rather than a water supply undertaking. The characteristics of the polluting firm remain exactly as previously described. However, we now have as the sole user of the lake an individual household which uses it for recreational purposes such as swimming, boating, fishing, etc. We can imagine that the household owns the land around the lake, except that on which the firm has its plant, but has no property rights in the water itself. The household prefers, other things being equal, the lake to be unpolluted. For simplicity, we can represent its preferences by

$$U = Y^{\frac{1}{2}} - E^{\frac{1}{2}} \qquad\qquad [5.5]$$

where U is utility or satisfaction, Y is household income and E is effluent discharge into the lake. What equation [5.5] says is that, for a given level of income and hence consumption of commodities, the utility or satisfaction that the household derives from that income decreases as the effluent discharge of the firm increases, diminishing the quality of the recreational facilities afforded to the household by the lake. As E increases, so the level of income required to maintain a constant level of utility increases. The household has a preference system according to which extra pollution reduces the satisfaction yielded by a given level of income. Suppose the household has an income of £100 so that when $E = 0$, U takes the value 10. Now compute the extra income required to maintain the utility index at the level 10 as pollution of the lake occurs and increases, with E taking values 0.1, 0.2 etc. The graph in Figure 5.4(a) plots the required income increases against E. The graph in Figure 5.4(b) plots the same increases against the firm's output level, Q. We go from (a) to (b) by using the relationship between E and Q given as equation [5.3] and shown in Figure 5.1(c). The label EC is for external cost, since Figure 5.4(b) shows how the costs incidentally imposed on the household by the firm vary with the firm's output. These costs are measured as the income compensation required to maintain the level of the household's utility index constant, at the no pollution level, as Q varies.

We can now proceed as we did in the previous example to find the level at which the firm should operate when society's interests, as opposed to just its own interests, are taken into account. Since the household is the only party affected by the firm's effluent discharge, the difference between society's interest and the firm's interest is fully accounted for by the external costs imposed on the household by the firm. In Figure 5.5, we show how $NPB - EC$ varies with the firm's output level in this case, with NPB (as $B - C_F$) coming from Figure 5.3(a), and with EC coming from Figure 5.4(b). The excess of NPB over EC is maximised at $Q = 4.95$. Note that this is not the same socially desirable output level as that which obtained in the previous example, though it is, again, below the output level the firm chooses. The difference between this outcome for efficiency in allocation and that in the case where the only lake user (other than the

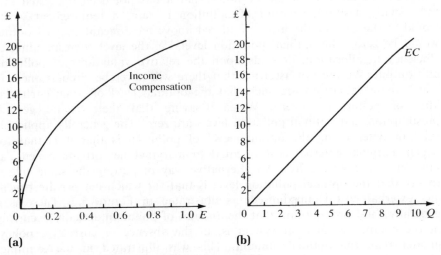

Figure 5.4   External costs borne by a household

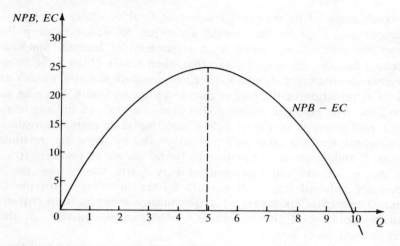

Figure 5.5 Socially optimal output level for firm imposing external costs on a household

polluting firm) was a water supply undertaking arises, we must note, because of the difference in the way variations in the firm's behaviour generates levels of external cost. The relationship between effluent discharge levels and output levels does not vary as between the two cases. The valuation of the damage done by any given effluent level does differ as between the two cases.

With these two very simple examples the basic idea in economics about environmental pollution has been set out. Pollution arises as an external effect so that there is in a market system more of it than efficiency in allocation requires. It should be noted that it has not been suggested that the socially desirable amount of pollution is zero, a requirement which would in the case of the firm considered above have meant that its output would be zero. The optimal pollution level, i.e. the level corresponding to efficiency in allocation, depends upon the relative valuations of pollution and output. We are not asserting that there will never be circumstances in which these valuations are such that the optimal level of some particular kind of pollution is zero. We are saying that there is no general presumption that optimal pollution levels are zero. The generally applicable rule for determining the optimal level of pollution is that it is that for which marginal external cost is equal to marginal net private benefit, as illustrated in Figure 5.3(c). An alternative way of putting the same rule is to say that the optimal pollution level is that for which net private benefit less external cost is maximised, as illustrated in Figure 5.5. There is a generally valid presumption that the amount of pollution actually occurring in the competitive market system is, in the absence of corrective policy, greater than the optimal amount. This was illustrated in the examples above.

5.2   Bargaining solutions to the externality problem

Having explained why we would expect a system of competitive markets to result in polluting activities being conducted at a higher level than is socially desirable, it is now natural to look at what economists have to say about how pollution levels can be reduced. In this section we discuss an approach which seeks to go to the origin of the problem and to create conditions in which private and selfish behaviour will produce pollution levels consistent with allocative efficiency. This approach says essentially that since the problem arises from the absence of private property rights, the solution is the simple one of establishing private property rights within which the pursuit of self interest will be compatible with socially desirable outcomes. It needs to be explicitly stated at the outset that, for reasons to be explained, this approach is simply not available as a practical proposal for the significant problems of environmental pollution. It will work only where the problem is, though possibly important to affected individuals, socially and environmentally a small order problem. Despite this, we shall spend some time on it. The reason for this is primarily that consideration of the arguments involved is highly instructive in revealing the nature of the externality problem, and particularly in clarifying the way in which what has been referred to as a 'socially desirable outcome' is indeed an outcome which represents an efficient allocation.

External costs imposed on a firm

We can begin by going back to the first example considered in the previous section, where the lake into which the firm discharges effluent is used by a water supply undertaking. We saw in the previous analysis of this example that efficiency in allocation requires the firm to produce less output and discharge less effluent than it actually does – whereas the firm's self interest indicates output at 6 units and effluent discharge at 0.36 units, the social interest indicates output at 4 units with discharge at 0.16 units. From the overall social viewpoint, it is worth giving up 2 units of the firm's output to secure a reduction in effluent discharge of 0.20 units. The question which arises is: how to secure this reduction in output and effluent discharge? One answer is to give the water supply undertaking legal entitlement to the use of the lake in an unpolluted state. Surprisingly perhaps, another answer is to give the firm an absolute legal right to pollute the lake as it sees fit.

To see how these answers arise, consider first a situation where the firm giving rise to the pollution of the lake is required to compensate fully the water supply undertaking for the additional costs pollution imposes on it. Table 5.1 shows what is involved. In the first five columns the symbols (Q for output, etc.) are as in our previous discussion of this example, as are the numbers appearing. Thus, for example, column 4 shows that $P.Q - C_F$ (i.e. the excess of private benefit over private cost) is greatest for $Q = 6$, when, in column 5, E (effluent discharge) is 0.36. In column 6 the numbers give the

Table 5.1 Compensation of pollution sufferer by pollution generator

Q	P.Q	C_F	P.Q $-C_F$	E	COMP	P.Q $-C_F$ $-$COMP	C_W	C_W $-$COMP
0	0	0	0	0	0	0	20	20
1	12	1	11	0.01	0.5	10.5	20.5	20
2	24	4	20	0.04	2.0	18.0	22.0	20
3	36	9	27	0.09	4.5	22.5	24.5	20
4	48	16	32	0.16	8.0	24.0	28.0	20
5	60	25	35	0.25	12.5	22.5	32.5	20
6	72	36	36	0.36	18.0	18.0	38.0	20
7	84	49	35	0.49	24.5	10.5	44.5	20
8	96	64	32	0.64	32.0	0	52.0	20
9	108	81	27	0.81	40.5	−13.5	60.5	20
10	120	100	20	1.00	50	−30.0	70	20
1	2	3	4	5	6	7	8	9

sums of money the firm would need to pay the water supply undertaking to offset its increased costs arising from the level of effluent discharge. '*COMP*' stands for compensation, which is calculated from the graph in Figure 5.2(b) by reading off C_W for each Q and subtracting 20. The figures in column 7 of Table 5.1 relate to the firm's net private benefit after payment of the required compensation. It is seen in column 7, by finding the largest figure, that, given that it pays compensation, the firm's preferred output level is $Q = 4$, with $E = 0.16$. This what is required for efficiency in allocation, as we know from the previous section. With compensation payments entering its calculations, the firm itself will wish to operate at $Q = 4$. Columns 8 and 9 relate to the position of the water supply undertaking and show that, given the receipt of the compensation, it will be indifferent as between the possible output levels at which the firm could operate.

How would the payment of the compensation actually arise? Suppose that the water supply undertaking were to be legally invested with a property right to a clean lake. Equivalently, suppose that the firm was made legally liable for the damage done by its effluent discharge. Then, the two parties interested in the lake would bargain with each other against the legal background. And, such bargaining would lead to an outcome with the firm operating at $Q = 4$, for with such legal background this is where the firm maximises its gains, and the water supply undertaking has no incentive to seek any different outcome. The outcome $Q = 6$ and $E = 0.36$ of the previous section arose because of the lack of clearly defined property rights in the lake, so that the firm's activities gave rise to external costs. What is now being said is that the efficient allocation outcome, $Q = 4$ and $E = 0.16$, will emerge as the result of self-interested bargaining once clearly defined property rights, in favour of the water supply undertaking, are established, so 'internalising' the external costs. The solution

Table 5.2 Payment by pollution sufferer to pollution generator

Q	E	C_W	BRIBE	C_W + BRIBE	P.Q	C_F	P.Q $-C_F$	P.Q $-C_F+$ BRIBE
10	1.00	70	16	86.0	120	100	20	36
9	0.81	60.5	9	69.5	108	81	27	36
8	0.64	52.0	4	56.0	96	64	32	36
7	0.49	44.5	1	45.5	84	49	35	36
6	0.36	38.0	0	38.0	72	36	36	36
5	0.25	32.5	1	33.5	60	25	35	36
4	0.16	28.0	4	32.0	48	16	32	36
3	0.09	24.5	9	33.5	36	9	27	36
2	0.04	22.0	16	38.0	24	4	20	36
1	0.01	20.5	25	45.5	12	1	11	36
0	0	20	36	56.0	0	0	0	36
1	2	3	4	5	6	7	8	9

to the external cost problem is to pass a law establishing property rights, i.e. making the firm liable for all the costs its activities give rise to.

This is not, perhaps, a surprising conclusion to reach. As already noted, however, there exists an alternative way of arranging the property rights situation which will also lead, via bargaining, to an efficient allocation outcome. This involves establishing for the polluting firm an absolute and clearly defined right to discharge into the lake as much effluent as it wishes. In such circumstances the water supply undertaking will have an incentive to offer to the firm compensation for not exercising such right to the full. In Table 5.2 such compensation is referred to as 'BRIBE', it being difficult to think of a more suitable, less pejorative, term for a payment not to do something harmful. The figures in the first three columns of Table 5.2 come from Figure 5.2(a) and (b). The bribe figures in column 4 are calculated, from the figures in columns 6, 7, 8 and 9, as the levels of payment from the water supply undertaking to the firm which would be necessary to make the firm indifferent between the output level in question and the output level, $Q = 6$, at which its private net benefit is maximised. What the bribe payments shown do is to compensate the firm for operating at an output level other than that which maximises private net benefit. In column 5 is shown the water supply undertaking's potential outlays at each output level for the firm, i.e. the sum of costs, C_W, plus the bribe. It is seen that such take a minimum value of £32.0 at $Q = 4$. Given, from column 9, that the firm is indifferent across output levels, we can see that, with the firm having the clear legal right to pollute at will, bargaining between the water supply undertaking and the firm will lead to a situation with $Q = 4$ and $E = 0.16$, as required for efficiency in allocation. For example, consider an initial situation where $Q = 6$ and $E = 0.36$. The water supply undertaking offers the firm payment of £1 to reduce output to 5. In terms of overall net benefit as total receipts less costs, the firm has no reason to refuse, and its acceptance reduces the water supply undertaking's total outlays. From a position of $Q = 5$, it pays the water supply undertaking to increase the bribe to £4, and again by accepting the firm incurs no loss. However, at the resulting position where $Q = 4$ and $E = 0.16$, there is no incentive for the water supply undertaking to offer any further increase in the bribe.

So, starting from a position where property rights are not clearly defined there are two routes to an outcome which represents an efficient allocation – define property rights in favour of either the firm or the water supply undertaking. It is important to be clear that while the two routes are equivalent in terms of achieving efficiency in allocation, they are not equivalent in all respects. Notice particularly from Tables 5.1 and 5.2 that they have entirely different distributional implications. Starting from a position where $Q = 6$, the Table 5.1 route to the achievement of $Q = 4$ involves a reduction in net benefit retained by the firm of £12 and a reduction in costs borne by the water supply undertaking of £18. The Table 5.2 route on the other hand means that the firm's net benefit position is unaltered while total costs to the water supply undertaking decrease by £6. Which assignment of property rights is to be preferred is not something which it is possible to generalise about. The choice would depend upon a view of what represents justice in distribution and on the circumstances of the particular case. No doubt many readers would in the present example consider it obviously 'fair' that the property rights should be assigned as in Table 5.1, i.e. with the firm made fully liable for the damage caused by its activities. However, it is not inconceivable that the situation is one where the water is to be supplied to, and hence the costs of so doing met by, a small number of rich households, while the firm is a cooperative venture by a number of low income individuals. The point is that even if a bias in favour of the poor is an agreed matter, the particular circumstances of a given case need to be known before such a bias can decide which way the property rights should be assigned. What is generally true is that where the conditions of this simple example hold, a matter to be discussed shortly, property rights assigned either way will produce an outcome which is an efficient allocation.

Now, this discussion of the solution to the external cost problem by way of assigning property rights will no doubt have prompted some questions in the reader's mind about the nature of the problem. Before turning to these it will be useful to present a second numerical example to illustrate what is involved in the bargaining solution, and then to restate the argument in a general and diagrammatic way.

External costs imposed on a household

The second example to be considered is based on the second example of the previous section, where the sole user of the lake into which the firm discharges effluent is a household with preferences as represented by equation

[5.5], and illustrated in Figure 5.4(a). Our discussion of this case in the previous section showed that efficiency in allocation requires an output for the firm of $Q = 4.95$ with effluent discharge at $E = 0.245$. Tables 5.3 and 5.4 show how bargaining with clearly defined property rights will achieve this outcome. Table 5.3 relates to a situation where the household has property rights in clean water, so that the firm is liable for the damage it inflicts upon the household. This damage is measured by the additional income, over $Y = 100$, necessary to hold the household's utility level at $U = 10$ (the level for $E = 0$ with $Y = £100$) as the effluent discharge increases. The compensation payments for which the firm will be liable in this way are shown in column 6 of Table 5.3; they can be read off the graph in Figure 5.4(b). The net benefit position of the firm, after the payment of this compensation, is shown in column 7 of Table 5.3, where it is seen that net benefit after such payment attains a maximum where $Q = 4.95$. Columns 8, 9 and 10 make it explicit that with such compensation being paid the household is indifferent as to the firm's output level and consequent effluent discharge level. Again, the point is that given the household's clear property right in clean water, bargaining between it and the polluting firm will mean that the outcome corresponding to an efficient allocation is realised. For, the firm's self interest is best served by an offer to operate where $Q = 4.95$ and $E = 0.245$ accompanied by the payment of £10.145 to the household, and the household has no reason to reject such an offer in favour of any other which the firm might make.

Table 5.4 relates to a situation where property rights are assigned in the firm's favour, so that it has the clear legal right to pollute as it wishes. It is now up to the household to offer the firm payment for reducing its output and effluent discharge below the levels $Q = 6$ and $E = 0.36$ which maximise the firm's net private benefit. The bribes necessary are shown in column 4 of Table 5.4, being calculated as the difference between the figure for $P.Q - C_F$ at a particular output level and the value of 36 for $P.Q - C_F$ obtaining at $Q = 6$. In column 5 we show the household's income remaining after payment of the bribe. The figures in column 6 are the household utility levels arising, via equation [5.5], for the pollution levels shown in column 2 and the income net of bribe figures shown in column 5. We see that the household utility level is highest where $Q = 4.95$ and $E = 0.245$. Columns 7, 8, 9 and 10 relate to the position of the firm, and show that, given receipt of the bribe, it is indifferent as between different output levels. Again, we conclude that with property rights assigned to the firm, bargaining will lead to a situation where there is an efficient allocation with $Q = 4.95$ and $E = 0.245$. The offer which does most for the household is 'if you operate where $Q = 4.95$ and $E = 0.245$, I will pay you £1.103', and the firm has no incentive to reject this offer for any other which might be forthcoming.

Comparing Tables 5.3 and 5.4 we see, again, that while either assignment of property rights leads to a situation where there is efficiency in allocation, with $Q = 4.95$ and $E = 0.245$, the two assignments have different distributional implications. At $Q = 4.95$, Table 5.3 (where the household has

Table 5.3 Compensation of a pollution affected household

Q	$P.Q$	C_F	$P.Q - C_F$	E	COMP	$P.Q - C_F -$COMP	Y	$Y+$ COMP	U
0	0	0	0	0	0	0	100	100	10
1	12	1	11	0.01	2.01	8.99	100	102.01	10
2	24	4	20	0.04	4.04	15.96	100	104.04	10
3	36	9	27	0.09	6.09	20.91	100	106.09	10
4	48	16	32	0.16	8.16	23.84	100	108.06	10
4.95	59.4	24.503	34.897	0.245	10.145	24.752	100	110.145	10
6	72	36	36	0.36	12.36	23.64	100	112.36	10
7	84	49	35	0.49	14.49	20.51	100	114.49	10
8	96	64	32	0.64	16.64	15.36	100	116.64	10
9	108	81	27	0.81	18.81	8.19	100	118.81	10
10	120	100	20	1.00	21.00	−1.00	100	121.00	10
1	2	3	4	5	6	7	8	9	10

the property rights) has $U = 10$ and $(P.Q - C_F - COMP) = £24.752$, whereas Table 5.4 (where the firm has the property rights) has $U = 9.450$ and $(P.Q - C_F + BRIBE) = £36$. Unless one has some kind of ethical view to the effect that households should always be favoured over firms, it is not clear which property rights assignment is to be preferred. A bias in favour of the poor and against the rich does not solve the problem unless we know who is poor and who is rich. To repeat, it is not always the case that generators of pollution are rich compared with those who suffer its effects.

Table 5.4 Payment by a pollution affected household

Q	E	Y	BRIBE	$Y -$BRIBE	U	$P.Q$	C_F	$P.Q - C_F$	$P.Q. - C_F +$BRIBE
10	1.00	100	16	84	8.165	120	100	20	36
9	0.81	100	9	91	8.639	108	81	27	36
8	0.64	100	4	96	8.998	96	64	32	36
7	0.49	100	1	99	9.250	84	49	35	36
6	0.36	100	0	100	9.400	72	36	36	36
4.95	0.245	100	1.103	98.897	9.450	59.4	24.503	34.897	36
4	0.16	100	4	96	9.398	48	16	32	36
3	0.09	100	9	91	9.239	36	9	27	36
2	0.04	100	16	84	8.965	24	4	20	36
1	0.01	100	25	75	8.560	12	1	11	36
0	0	100	36	64	8.000	0	0	0	36
1	2	3	4	5	6	7	8	9	10

A general statement of the bargaining solution

In Figure 5.6 we provide a general graphical approach to the bargaining solution to externality problems. As in the previous discussion, $MNPB$ stands for marginal net private benefit and MEC for marginal external cost. We have already seen that efficiency in allocation requires Q to be at Q_E^* where $MNPB = MEC$. On the other hand, in the uncorrected externality situation the firm will operate at Q_P^* where $MNPB = 0$ and net private benefit is maximised. We assume that there is just one firm generating pollution, and just one party suffering from such. Starting from the position Q_P^*, suppose that the sufferer is assigned property rights in the polluted environmental media. It can then extract from the firm compensation for its suffering, which suffering is measured by the area under the MEC graph between the origin and the point along the horizontal axis at which the firm is operating. Thus, for example, with the firm operating at Q_P^* total external costs are given by the sum of the triangle areas 2, 3 and 4. Similarly, areas under the $MNPB$ graph correspond to total net private benefit levels, so that for Q_P^* total net private benefit is given by $1 + 2 + 3$. This correspondence between areas under marginal curves and totals is general, and was discussed in Chapter 3 for the costs and benefits of a firm. Also the reader can check the point in this context by referring to Figure 5.3, especially panels (a) and (c), and the discussion thereof. At $Q = 4$, for example, the area under MEC in (c) is $1/2 \times 4 \times 4 = 8$ which is the height of the EC curve over $Q = 4$ in (a), and the area under $MNPB$ is $16 + (1/2 \times 4 \times 8) = 32$ which is the height of the NBB curve over $Q = 4$.

In Figure 5.6, it follows that a reduction in Q from Q_P^* towards Q_E^* reduces the firm's liability for compensation by more than it reduces its net private benefit before payment of compensation. A reduction from Q_E^* toward zero,

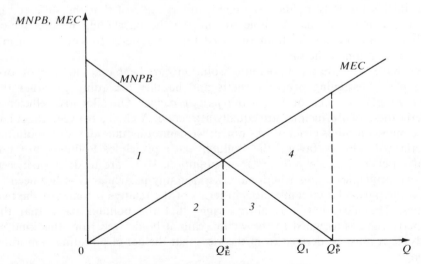

Figure 5.6 Bargaining solutions to the externality problem

however, reduces net private benefit before compensation payment by more than it reduces compensation liability. In fact, it is clear that considering its position net of compensation payments, the firm would choose Q_E^* where net private benefit less compensation payment is the area 1, which is the best the firm can do. By the assumption of full compensation the sufferer, at this position, receives compensation in amount given by the area 2. The bargaining process will result in this outcome being realised, since with MEC greater than $MNPB$ it pays the firm to reduce output, and with $MNPB$ greater than MEC it pays the firm to increase output. It is not necessary that the firm knows what MEC is at every level of Q at the outset, since the bargaining process will itself reveal this information. At Q_P^*, for example, the firm will find that it has to offer an amount of money equal to the sum of the areas 2, 3 and 4 to induce the sufferer to accept the resulting pollution situation. It will find that this sum is such that after paying it out it is left with an amount equal to the area 1 less the area 4. It then tries the output level Q_1, computing its corresponding net private benefit and ascertaining how much it would have to pay out in compensation to induce the sufferer to accept the corresponding pollution situation. And so on and so on. The bargaining process will converge on the output level Q_E^*, where the firm is doing the best that it can for itself, given its liability for compensation.

We have already seen that the alternative assignment of property rights, with the firm having the right to pollute, will lead to an efficient allocation outcome also. In this case, the output level Q_E^* will involve the firm forgoing, compared with Q_P^*, net private benefit equal to the area 3. For this it is compensated by payment, bribe, from the sufferer. The move from Q_P^* to Q_E^* is worthwhile to the sufferer since for the payment of an amount given by the area 3, damage valued at an amount given by the sum of the areas 3 and 4 is avoided. A little experimentation with alternatives will convince the reader that, in this property rights assignment, this is the best that the sufferer can do. The reader will also be able to imagine the bargaining process which leads to this outcome, without the need for the sufferer to know the firm's $MNPB$ situation at the outset.

We have seen that a bargaining solution can be based on one of two principles – assigning property rights and liability according to either the *polluter pays principle* or the *victim pays principle*. On allocative efficiency criteria these two principles are equally attractive. A choice between them has to be made on other grounds. As noted, we cannot assume that distributional criteria will always favour the polluter pays principle. Polluters are not always richer than the sufferers from pollution. If we are to decide between the two principles on distributional criteria in any particular case, we need to know the particular circumstances in terms of the relative incomes of the two parties. The idea that it is always right that the polluter pays, that the property right is assigned to the victim, cannot be derived from this kind of analysis. It must be derived from the view that the act of polluting is morally wrong.

We should also note here that the illustrative examples used above were somewhat special, in that either principle leads to exactly the same pollution level. While it is generally true that either principle will lead to an outcome which is allocatively efficient, it is not generally true that both will lead to the same allocatively efficient outcome. Recall that there are, for any given set of circumstances, a very large number of allocatively efficient outcomes. The special feature of the examples used here was that the distributional consequences of the property rights assignment had no effect on the MEC and $MNPB$ functions. More generally, one might expect, for example, that as the household was better or worse off as it received or paid compensation, so its preferences as between income and pollution might vary. We do not go into the more complex analysis required to deal with such situations. The essential ideas are brought out in the special cases considered here.

Bargaining costs

Now, it will perhaps have struck the reader in following this discussion through that there was in our original account of the externality problem, in the previous section, an implicit assignment of property rights in the lake in favour of the polluting firm. It was, after all, allowed to discharge effluent into the lake as it wished in order to pursue its self interest. Is it not the case, generally, that to say that an externality problem exists is just to say that property right lie *de facto* with the pollution generator? Fairly obviously, the answer to this question is 'yes'. But why then do the sufferers not bribe the externality generators, the polluters, to reduce the level of the external costs they impose, as described in this section? Another way of putting this is as follows. Given that we have seen that self interested bargaining where polluters have the legal right to pollute will lead to situations where polluters are bribed to produce the optimal, in the sense of corresponding to efficiency in allocation, amount of pollution, surely it is not possible to argue that there will ever exist situations where the amount of pollution is, in this sense, excessive. If in the situation which is supposed to be the origin of the problem, *de facto* property rights exist, what is the point of proposing a solution by way of creating property rights?

The answer to this apparent paradox lies in the fact that, thus far, we have assumed *bargaining costs*, alternatively known as *transactions costs*, to be zero. What we mean by this, in terms of the resolution of the paradox, is as follows. With our lake example, the outcome $Q = 6$ and $E = 0.36$ arose where property rights were *de facto* assigned to the polluting firm. The argument was that with property rights explicitly assigned *de jure*, the outcome would be $Q = 4$ and $E = 0.16$ (in the case where the lake was used by a water supply undertaking). The basic idea behind this is that the *de jure* assignment of the property rights would, ideally, reduce the costs of bargaining such that it would occur where formerly it did not. With the legal system silent on property rights, the water supply undertaking could take the firm to a court where it might win compensation for some existing level of damage inflicted on it. With an explicit declaration of property rights in favour of the firm or of the user of the lake, both parties can bargain in the certain knowledge that legal action would produce certain consequences. Hence, the legal action will become unnecessary. Ideally it will not occur and, against a clear and unambiguous explicit declaration of property rights, one way or the other, costless bargaining will result in the outcome required for efficiency in allocation.

As a practical matter the upshot of all this is as follows. Where excessive pollution is observed it exists because bargaining costs are perceived by the parties to be so high as to preclude the possibility of bargaining leading to mutual gains. This situation arises because property rights are not explicitly defined. It follows that the solution to problems of excessive pollution is to explicitly define property rights. It does not matter, from the efficiency in allocation standpoint, which way the explicit property rights are assigned. Either way, the explicit property rights will enable bargaining to occur leading to the desired outcome.

The reader may well, and rightly, remain sceptical about the practical significance of this for the problems of environmental pollution of concern in the real world. A fairly obvious problem is, in many cases, the difficulty of just measuring pollution as a prior requirement to assessing external costs and hence compensation liability, if property rights are to be assigned to the sufferer. However, within the framework of this type of analysis this is not actually a problem. This is because what matters for determining the socially desirable level of pollution is not the physically measured amount of such, but the affected party's perception of the damage they suffer. It is clearly also the latter which is relevant to bargaining. It will no doubt have been noticed by the reader that our examples have been such that there is just one pollution generator and just one pollution sufferer. This was done in order to simplify the discussion. It is not the case that the argument for bargaining solutions, based on explicit property rights, to excessive pollution problems rests on there being just one party on each side. However, it is the case that there are good grounds for believing that bargaining solutions are viable only when the number of parties on each side is small. This is because, obviously, the costs of actually bargaining must rise steeply as the number of parties involved increases, even when explicit property rights exist. To see what is involved imagine that our lake still receives effluent discharge from just one firm, but that instead of having just one user it is used for water supply and recreational purposes by the inhabitants of a nearby city of 1 million people. Clearly, in such a case the costs of having the firm bargain with each of the sufferers from its effluent discharge would be such that bargaining simply would not occur even with clear and explicit property rights in existence. It is presumably because the problems of environmental pollution so typically involve very large numbers of affected parties that one so rarely observes a response to such problems by way of legislation to establish *de jure* property rights.

A further difficulty attending the practical usefulness of bargaining solutions to pollution problems was obscured by the nature of the examples which we have considered. This is the fact that if two parties are to bargain with one another, it must be clear to both that there is something to bargain about. If, for example, a pollution sufferer is to offer the source of the pollution a 'bribe', he must be able to identify the source, and it must be the case that the source acknowledges itself as such. Clearly, in most circumstances the pathway linking a particular sufferer with a particular source is not readily identifiable. Equally clearly, such identification problems are likely to increase with the number of sources of some pollutant and with the number of affected parties.

Non-rivalness in pollution suffering

While large numbers of generators and/or sufferers, and hence high bargaining costs, are an important impediment to the practical usefulness of bargaining solutions, based on explicit property rights, there is another which arises even in small numbers situations. This is the fact that, in the case of significant problems of environmental pollution, the pollution has to be regarded as public in nature, i.e. is non-rival in consumption. We saw in 4.5 that markets simply cannot provide public goods in the way required for efficiency in allocation. Analogously, the bargaining approach cannot work with respect to the proper level of provision of public bads. This is actually a matter which is logically quite distinct from the question of the number of pollution-affected parties. As a matter of fact, in the case of most significant problems of environmental pollution, the pollution is in the nature of a public bad which affects many people, so that there are two reasons why the bargaining solution is not applicable. That the large numbers and the public bad aspects are distinct is something we shall make explicit by considering an example where just two parties consume the public bad.

We look at an example where we have the same firm discharging effluent into the same lake as previously. However, there are now two other users of the lake. These are the water supply undertaking and the household, previously considered as separate users of the lake. To recapitulate, there is the private cost function

$$C_F = Q^2 \tag{5.1}$$

and the private benefit function is

$$B = 12Q. \tag{5.2}$$

The cost function for the water supply undertaking is

$$C_W = 20 + 50E \tag{5.3}$$

and the utility function for the household is

$$U = Y^{\frac{1}{2}} - E^{\frac{1}{2}} \tag{5.4}$$

Table 5.5 External costs when pollution suffering is non-rival

Q	$P.Q - C_F$	E	EC_W	EC_H	EC	$\dfrac{P.Q - C_F}{-EC}$
1	11	0.01	0.5	2.01	2.51	8.49
2	20	0.04	2.0	4.04	6.04	13.96
3	27	0.09	4.5	6.09	10.59	16.41
3.311	28.769	0.110	5.5	6.743	12.243	16.526
4	32	0.16	8.0	8.16	16.16	15.84
4.95	34.897	0.245	12.25	10.145	22.395	12.502
5	35	0.25	12.5	10.25	22.75	12.25
6	36	0.36	18.0	12.36	30.36	5.64
7	35	0.49	24.5	14.49	38.99	−3.99
8	32	0.64	32.0	16.64	48.64	−16.64
9	27	0.81	40.5	18.81	59.31	−32.31
10	20	1.00	50.0	21.00	71.00	−51.0

Here E is the level of effluent discharge by the firm, which is related to its output level according to

$$E = 0.01Q^2 \qquad\qquad [5.5]$$

Notice carefully that the pollution level experienced by both the water supply undertaking and the household is given by E. The pollution is a public bad in the sense that any given quantity of E is not shared between water supply undertaking and household. Rather, both experience the same level of pollution in the lake, the level being measured by E, the level of the firm's effluent discharge. As the reader will appreciate, this is the natural way to think about pollution problems – a given level of pollution is, typically, experienced by all those affected, rather than shared out between them. As we shall see, it is this non-rivalness in consumption which renders bargaining solutions non-operative.

We have already seen how the external costs imposed by the firm on the water supply undertaking and the household, as separate lake users, vary with E: see Figure 5.3 and Figure 5.4 respectively. This information is brought together in Table 5.5, where EC_W are external costs imposed on the water supply undertaking, EC_H are external costs imposed on the household, and where $EC = EC_W + EC_H$. The level of E required for efficiency in allocation is $E = 0.11$, with a corresponding output level of $Q = 3.311$. In Table 5.5 it is seen that this is where the excess of net private benefit $(P.Q - C_F)$ over external cost (EC) is greatest. In Figure 5.7 we explicitly show that it is for $Q = 3.311$ that marginal net private benefit $(MNPB)$ equals marginal external cost (MEC). Recall that with just the water supply undertaking using the polluted lake, efficiency in allocation required $Q = 4$, and that with just the household using the polluted lake the requirement was $Q = 4.95$. Notice also in Table 5.5 that is still the case that the firm will want, in the absence of explicit property rights and bargaining, to operate where $Q = 6$ and $E = 0.36$, in order to maximise net private benefit $(P.Q - C_F)$.

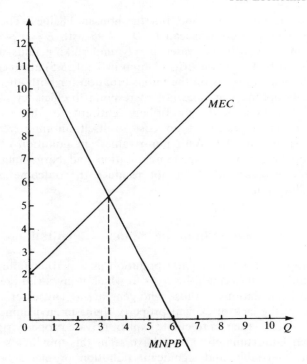

Figure 5.7   Marginal external cost for non-rival pollution suffering

The problem for a bargaining solution in this context is that the outcome to which polluter–water supply bargaining would lead, $E = 0.16$, does not coincide with that to which polluter–household bargaining would lead, $E = 0.245$. And neither of these outcomes coincides with that required for social optimality, $E = 0.11$, where the pollution is non-rival in consumption so that this is the pollution level that both are optimally required to experience. In Table 5.5 we see that if the polluting firm were fully compensating each affected party, it would be paying each different amounts of money for experiencing the same level of pollution. In such a circumstance, the affected party receiving the smaller amount of money would seek to have its compensation increased to the level received by the other. To the extent that it succeeded, the bargaining process would not converge on the socially optimal situation, since $Q = 0.11$ would not be the polluting firm's preferred position given its compensation liability.

Alternatively, suppose that the property right in favour of the polluting firm were made *de jure* and explicit and consider the position of the two affected parties with respect to the offering of bribes. The initial position with zero bribes on offer is $Q = 6$, $E = 0.36$. Both affected parties have an incentive to offer zero by way of bribe, signalling zero willingness to pay for less pollution, believing that the other party will make an offer on which they can *free-ride* to a lower pollution level. Suppose that the water supply undertaking offers no initial bribe, but the household does. Then we know that the bargaining process will lead to $Q = 4.95$ with $E = 0.245$ (see Table 5.4), as a result of which the water supply undertaking finds its pollution imposed costs cut by £5.75 (see EC_W column in Table 5.5) at no cost to itself. While this outcome improves on the initial situation for both affected parties, it is not socially optimal, i.e. does not correspond to efficiency in allocation. Similarly, if the household left bribery entirely to the water supply undertaking, it could realise at no cost to itself an improvement in its situation equivalent to £4.2. With non-rivalness in pollution consumption, there are strong incentives to misrepresentation and bargaining, even with small numbers on each side, will not produce the outcome required for efficiency in allocation.

5.3   Feasible goals and optimal instruments in pollution control

Economists approach environmental pollution as a market failure problem. There is too much of it because the costs to which it gives rise are external to the benefit–cost calculations of those who generate it. This externality in turn arises because of the lack of explicit property rights in environmental media. The obvious solution, then, is to create explicit private property rights in such affected media. Unfortunately, as we have seen, this 'obvious solution' will not work for interesting and significant pollution problems because such involve large numbers and/or publicness in pollution suffering. This does not mean that economists think that they have nothing to say about significant pollution problems. On the contrary, they have a great deal to say about public policy to correct market failure generally, and excessive environmental pollution particularly.

We will look at the question of the means by which the socially optimal level of pollution can be realised in the context of the example considered in the previous section where both the water supply undertaking and the household experience the same level of pollution of the lake. In this case, we know that the socially optimal pollution level is 0.11, corresponding to an output level for the polluting firm of $Q = 3.311$. We assume that society has created an Environmental Protection Agency, an EPA, in which it has vested complete legal power in respect of the control of effluent discharges into lakes – in effect, the EPA has, on behalf of society, an explicit property right in clean lakes. The question then is, in what particular ways can the EPA exercise its powers so as to achieve, for the lake we are considering by way of example, $E = 0.11$? The instruments of control to be considered are *regulation*, *subsidisation*, and *taxation*.

The regulatory approach simply involves telling the polluting firm what to do: the EPA acts in a manner analogous to the planner in the command economy considered in section 3.3. The EPA, that is, orders the firm to produce $Q = 3.311$ with $E = 0.11$. This involves telling the firm to do something which goes against its self-interest. As Table 5.5 shows, in

Table 5.6 Subsidisation and taxation for socially optimal pollution control

E	NPB $= P.Q - C_F$	S $= 81.2(0.36 - E)$	$NPB + S$	T $= 81.2E$	$NPB - T$
0.01	11	28.420	39.420	0.812	10.188
0.04	20	25.984	45.984	3.248	16.752
0.09	27	21.924	48.924	7.308	19.692
0.11	28.769	20.300	49.069	8.932	19.837
0.16	32	16.240	48.240	12.992	19.008
0.245	34.897	9.338	44.235	19.894	15.003
0.25	35	8.932	43.932	20.300	14.700
0.36	36	0	36.000	29.232	6.768

complying with the order the firm would be forgoing net private benefits in amount £7.231, the difference between £36 for $Q = 6$ and £28.769 for $Q = 3.311$. There would then be incentives for the polluting firm to attempt to avoid compliance with the regulations, implying the need for monitoring by the EPA and the availability to it of sanctions to be imposed on the firm for non-compliance. The incentive for non-compliance would be eliminated if the EPA were to compensate the firm for the profit losses incurred in complying with the regulations. There are, however, some obvious difficulties here. First, the EPA would require to receive the necessary funds from government and this would imply higher taxation. Second, many people (voters) would object to public expenditure being used to compensate a firm for not doing what the law says it should not do anyway. Many people believe that 'the polluter should pay'.

Actually, if these objections are set aside, the EPA could realise the socially optimal level of pollution by subsidising the firm in respect of effluent discharge reduction, and not issuing any orders at all. Table 5.6 shows what is involved. In the second column are shown the polluting firm's net private benefit levels corresponding to various levels of effluent discharge. At the head of the third column S stands for subsidy payment, by the EPA to the firm. This payment is £81.2 for each unit of effluent that the firm cuts back by from the level of discharge that it would be producing when maximising its profit with no controls on its activities, i.e. $S = 81.2 (0.36 - E)$. As shown in the fourth column of Table 5.6, if the firm opts for that level of effluent discharge that maximises its profit inclusive of subsidy, it will choose to operate at that output level which produces the socially optimal pollution level. The EPA does not, that is, need to tell it what to do: it simply fixes the appropriate rate of subsidy.

While the subsidisation approach can do the job, it is open to the same objections as the compensated–regulation approach, notably that involves using public expenditure to pay polluters. Note in Table 5.6 that for every E level below 0.36, the polluting firm would make larger profits with subsidisation than it did before the EPA sought to modify its behaviour. The taxation approach, on the other hand, makes the polluter pay. Suppose that the EPA says to the firm, 'You can discharge as much effluent into the lake as you wish, but on each unit discharged a tax of £81.2 is to be paid to us'. The last two columns of Table 5.6 show that in this case, the polluting firm's self-interest would also lead it to discharge the socially optimal effluent quantity. In this case the EPA is the recipient of funds from the polluting firm, which suffers reductions in profit at all levels of output and effluent discharge.

So, either subsidisation or taxation can realise the goal of inducing the firm, acting in pursuit of its own self interest and with no direct regulation bearing upon it, to behave as required for efficiency in allocation. The two instruments differ only in their distributional implications. This can be seen even more clearly if we note that $S = 81.2 (0.36 - E)$ is the same as $S = (81.2 \times 0.36) - 81.2E$ or $S = 29.232 - 81.2E$. A per unit subsidy on effluent not sent out of £81.2 is equivalent, that is, to giving the firm a lump sum of £29.232 and then taxing it on effluent discharged at a unit rate of £81.2.

There remains the question of where the tax/subsidy rate of £81.2 comes from. How does the EPA know the tax rate to use to induce socially optimal behaviour by the polluting firm? As the reader can easily check, if a tax/subsidy rate different from £81.2 is set, net private benefit maximisation by the firm will not lead to $E = 0.11$. The EPA should set the tax/subsidy rate at the level of marginal external cost corresponding to the socially optimal pollution level. Figure 5.8 shows what is involved for the taxation approach. The objective is to have the polluting firm's net of tax marginal net private benefit function cut the horizontal axis at E_S^*, the level of effluent discharge

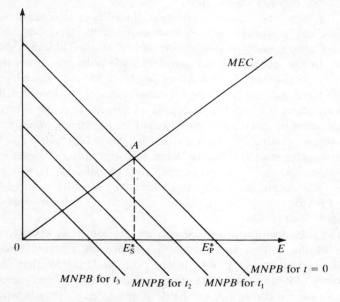

Figure 5.8   The tax rate for socially optimal pollution control

corresponding to efficiency in allocation. As the tax rate is increased from zero, so as shown the net of tax $MNPB$ function shifts downwards; $t_3 > t_2 > t_1$, where t is the unit effluent tax rate. Clearly, the required shift will be realised when t is equal to E_s^*A, the level of marginal external cost when effluent discharge is socially optimal. In the case of our illustrative example, marginal external cost for $E = 0.11$ is just £81.2.[1]

It is very important to note here that what the EPA needs to know is not the value of MEC at $E = E_P^*$, the pre-intervention situation, but the value of MEC at $E = E_s^*$, the socially optimal effluent discharge level. The EPA cannot, that is, simply measure the existing level of marginal external cost. It has rather to know the MEC function and the $MNPB$ function, and to use this information to find what E_s^* is, then read off from the MEC function the corresponding MEC level. In the case of the example considered above, the EPA would need to know how the polluting firm's profits varied with E, how the water supply undertaking's costs varied with E and how the household's utility index varied with E. And this in a situation where none of the parties has any incentive to reveal to the EPA accurate information about its costs or preferences.

If we move outside the realm of examples constructed for expositional convenience, it is not difficult to appreciate that the goal of the socially optimal level of pollution is an infeasible one for an EPA to pursue, on informational grounds. In a situation of many generators and sufferers, to find the required tax/subsidy rate, the EPA would need to know for every generator how profit varies with emissions and for every sufferer how costs arising varies with total emissions. Only if it had this information, could it find the common tax/subsidy rate to apply to all generators. But clearly, acquiring this information with (say) thousands of generators and millions of sufferers would represent such a massive research effort as to be, practically, impossible. This is not to say that some information on pollution reduction costs and benefits cannot be obtained: these matters are discussed in the commentary section at the end of the chapter. It is to say that such information as can reasonably be expected to be made available will necessarily be sketchy and uncertain, and incapable of forming the basis for the precise calculation of the socially optimal pollution level and, therefore, of the tax/subsidy rate required to realise it. It should also be explicitly mentioned that the same informational impediment attends the use of the regulatory approach to the socially optimal pollution level.

Instruments for the attainment of arbitrary pollution standards

As a practical matter, then, the control of pollution to the levels required for efficiency in allocation is not a realistic objective of policy. This is because private bargaining on the basis of private property rights will not work on account of large numbers and/or non-rivalness in consumption, and, in the absence of such, the information which an EPA would need to identify the goal would be impossible to obtain. In this situation, economists have given their attention to the question of which are the best means to adopt for attaining *arbitrary standards* in respect of pollution levels. The term 'arbitrary' here means only that the target level of pollution sought is not, except by chance, that set by the requirements of efficiency in allocation. It is, rather, a standard adopted on the basis of scientific and public health considerations. With respect to the means of realising such a standard, economists mean by 'best' the instrument which does the job at the least cost. The policy instruments to be considered are regulation, taxation and the creation of a market in *pollution licences* or *permits*.

As usual, we discuss the basic issues involved in the context of a simple numerical example. We can again consider the discharge of effluent into a lake, this time by two firms identified as 1 and 2. Both firms are price-takers, both produce the same commodity, and both face the same price of £12. Also, both firms have private costs behaving according to $C = Q^2$, so that net private benefits are given by

$$NPB_1 = P.Q_1 - C_1 = 12Q_1 - Q_1^2 \qquad [5.6]$$

and

$$NPB_2 = P.Q_2 - C_2 = 12Q_2 - Q_2^2 \qquad [5.7]$$

The reader will recognise that both of these firms have private cost and benefit structures identical to those of the firm considered previously in this chapter. Having both of the firms with the same relationship between net private benefits and output is in no way essential to the arguments to follow here. The upper part of Figure 5.9 shows the way in which marginal net private benefits vary with output, with $Q_1 = Q_2 = 6$ for net private benefit maximisation. For these two firms, effluent discharge varies with output according to

$$E_1 = 0.1Q_1 \qquad [5.8]$$

and

$$E_2 = 0.2Q_2 \qquad [5.9]$$

These relationships are shown in the lower part of Figure 5.9, where we see that corresponding to net private benefit maximisation we have $E_1 = 0.6$ and $E_2 = 1.2$, so that total pollution, E, is 1.8 units.

Now, suppose that the EPA responsible for this lake adopts the arbitrary standard of $E = 0.9$. It wishes, that is, to reduce total effluent discharge into the lake by 50%. One way the EPA could proceed is by telling each of the firms to cut back on discharges by 50%. We shall call this the *uniform regulation* approach. If firm 1 cuts E_1 to $0.6 \times 0.5 = 0.3$, Q_1 corresponding is 3. If firm 2 cuts E_2 to $1.2 \times 0.5 = 0.6$, Q_2 corresponding is 3. This is shown in the lower part of Figure 5.9. We use the upper part of the figure to calculate the costs of attaining the required standard using this instrument. Costs are the social valuation of the losses incurred in realising the standard. This

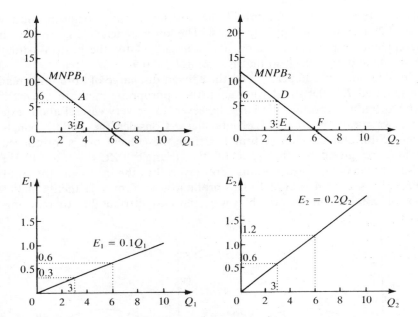

Figure 5.9 Uniform regulation of effluent discharges

social valuation is not simply the output loss, $3 + 3 = 6$, times the price per unit, 12, giving 72. Such a measurement would overstate costs in as much as the lower output levels mean that less inputs are used, the released inputs being available for use elsewhere in the economy. The costs are properly measured in terms of the sum of the reductions in profit, or net private benefit, in each firm. Recall that given the ideal conditions for a market economy which are, except in respect of the externality phenomenon, being assumed here, profit is a measure of social value – it is the difference between the social value of the inputs to and the output from productive activity. So, the social valuation of the costs of cutting $E = E_1 + E_2$ is the sum of the consequent profit reductions in the two firms. Recall further that we can measure total net private benefit, or profit, as the area under the marginal net private benefit line (see 3.4 and 5.1 especially). Hence, the costs of attaining the arbitrary standard of $E = 0.9$ by means of the uniform regulation instrument are, in the upper part of Figure 5.9, given by the sum of the areas of the triangles ABC and DEF. Now area $ABC = \frac{1}{2} \times 3 \times 6 = 0.9$ and area $DEF = \frac{1}{2} \times 3 \times 6 = 9$, so that the cost here is £18.

We now consider the use of the *uniform effluent tax* instrument for the attainment of the same standard of $E = E_1 + E_2 = 0.9$. Figure 5.10 refers. We assume the imposition of a tax on effluent discharge at the rate of £36 per unit, applicable to both firms. The upper two panels of Figure 5.10 show what such a tax does to the net private benefit functions for each firm, with *NPBT* standing for net private benefit after tax payments. The middle panels show how the corresponding marginal functions respond to the imposition of this tax. It is seen that for firm 1 the post-tax profit maximising output is $Q_1 = 4.2$, and for firm 2 it is $Q_2 = 2.4$. The lower panels of Figure 5.10 show the effluent–output relationships, and we read off for the post-tax situation $E_1 = 0.42$ and $E_2 = 0.48$, so that $E = E_1 + E_2 = 0.9$.

So, a tax rate of £36 per unit on the effluent discharge of both firms realises the required $E = 0.9$ standard. Again, the appropriate measure of cost is in terms of reduced profits. We have, however, to be very careful about exactly what we mean by 'reduced profits' here. Consider the middle panels of Figure 5.10, and the case of firm 1. Before the effluent tax is introduced its profits are given by the area of the triangle $0ZC = \frac{1}{2} \times 6 \times 12 = £36$. With the tax in place, profits are given by the area of the triangle $0YB = \frac{1}{2} \times 4.2 \times 8.4 = £17.64$. The profit loss to firm 1 is then £18.36, the area of $YZCB$. This is not, however, the cost attributable to reducing E_1

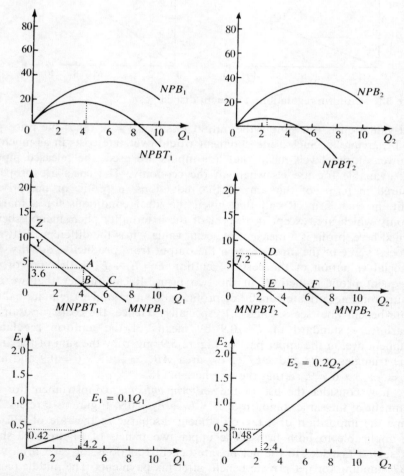

Figure 5.10 Uniform effluent discharge taxation

from 0.6 to 0.42 which is relevant from society's viewpoint. This is because part of the profit loss so measured is a *transfer payment* from the firm to the EPA, rather than a real loss of social value to society as a whole. Given $Q_1 = 4.2$ and $E_1 = 0.42$, firm 1 pays over to the EPA an amount $0.42 \times 36 = £15.12$. The real loss to society involved in cutting $Q1$ from 6 to 4.2 is the firm's profit loss of £18.36 net of this transfer payment of £15.12, i.e. $18.36 - 15.12 = £3.24$. This is also, the reader can check, the area of the triangle ABC, which is the profit loss which firm 1 would suffer in cutting Q_1 from 6 to 4.2, and hence E_1 from 0.6 to 0.42, in the absence of any tax on effluent discharges. This area ABC is the proper measure of the social cost of reducing E_1 from 0.6 to 0.42, with the area $YZAB$ measuring that part of the tax-induced total profit loss, i.e. area $YZCB$, which is simply a transfer payment. The point is that transfer payments of this kind do not represent reductions in the net value of social production – what no longer accrues to firm 1 as profit, accrues to the EPA and can be disposed of by it. The proper measure, in respect of firm 1, of the cost of effluent discharge reduction is the consequent reduction in its profit computed ignoring any tax liability, and this is just the area ABC.

A similar argument establishes that for firm 2 the relevant cost of the uniform effluent tax induced reduction of E_2 from 1.2 to 0.48 is given by the area $DEF = \frac{1}{2} \times 3.6 \times 7.2 = £12.96$. The sum, in the middle panels of Figure 5.10, of areas ABC and DEF is $3.24 + 12.96 = £16.2$. This is the cost of reducing E from $E_1 + E_2 = 0.6 + 1.2 = 1.8$ to $E_1 + E_2 = 0.42 + 0.48 = 0.9$ arising when the reduction is induced by the imposition of an effluent discharge tax at the rate £36. It is less than the cost of the same reduction in E achieved by the uniform regulation instrument, which was found to be (see Figure 5.9) £18. In fact, £16.2 is the least cost at which the 50% reduction in E can be achieved! In order to demonstrate why the tax instrument has the property of realising the desired standard at the least possible cost, it will be convenient to describe its operation in a slightly different way. This will also introduce some terminology common in the pollution economics literature, and demonstrate the origin of the real superiority of effluent taxation over regulation.

Control costs and abatement levels

The relationship between effluent discharge levels and output levels for each firm is given above as equations [5.8] and [5.9]. These equations can be rearranged and written as

$$Q_1 = 10.E_1 \qquad\qquad [5.8']$$

and

$$Q_2 = 5.E_2 \qquad\qquad [5.9']$$

We can now use equations [5.8'] and [5.9'] to write the net private benefit functions with E_s instead of Qs on the right hand side, by substituting for Q_1 and Q_2. The results are:

$$NPB_1 = 120E_1 - 100E_1^2 \qquad\qquad\qquad [5.10]$$

$$NPB_2 = 60E_2 - 25E_2^2 \qquad\qquad\qquad [5.11]$$

These equations describe how net private benefit varies with effluent discharge. Note that if $E_1 = 0.6$, equation [5.10] gives $NPB_1 = 36$, and if $E_2 = 1.2$, equation [5.11] gives $NPB_2 = 36$. From Figure 5.9, upper panels, it can be checked, by calculating the areas under the lines for the marginal net private benefit functions over the interval from the origin to $Q = 6$, that these are the initial profit levels for the two firms.

Now, we define as *control costs* for a firm the difference between profits when the firm is allowed to maximise profit with no attempt by the EPA to influence its effluent discharge level and profits for any level of effluent discharge below that corresponding to such unconstrained profit maximisation. In computing control costs we ignore any transfer payments arising from the method of control adopted. We know that for each firm unconstrained maximised profits are 36. We also have equations [5.10] and [5.11] giving profits, or net private benefits, as they depend on the level of effluent discharge. It follows that control costs in each firm are given by

$$CC_1 = 36 - 120E_1 + 100E_1^2 \qquad\qquad\qquad [5.12]$$

and

$$CC_2 = 36 - 60E_2 + 25E_2^2 \qquad\qquad\qquad [5.13]$$

where CC represents control costs. These relationships are graphed in the upper panels of Figure 5.11. Note that $CC_1 = 0$ for $E_1 = 0.6$ and $CC_1 = 36$ for $E_1 = 0$: and that $CC_2 = 0$ for $E_2 = 1.2$ and $CC_2 = 36$ for $E_2 = 0$. For both firms, control costs fall at a decreasing rate as E increases.

The lower panels of Figure 5.11 show how *marginal control costs* vary with effluent discharge levels: these marginal graphs are derived from the corresponding total graphs in the usual way. We know that with effluent discharges taxed at the uniform rate of £36 per unit, net private benefit maximisation will lead to $E_1 = 0.42$ and $E_2 = 0.48$. If in the lower panels of Figure 5.11 we read off MCC_1 corresponding to $E_1 = 0.42$ and MCC_2 corresponding to $E_2 = 0.48$, we find $MCC_1 = MCC_2 = -36$. We leave for the moment the question of why both firms end up with the same marginal control costs. Here we are concerned with the fact that it is such equality that makes $E_1 = 0.42$ and $E_2 = 0.48$ the least cost allocation of effluent discharge between the two firms given that $E = E_1 + E_2$ is to be 0.9. To see what is involved, suppose that, maintaining $E = E_1 + E_2 = 0.9$, a small reallocation from the situation shown in Figure 5.11 is effected such that E_1 goes up and E_2 goes down by an equal amount. Then MCC_1 will be, say, -35 and MCC_2 will be, say, -37. But, if marginal control costs are not equal in the two

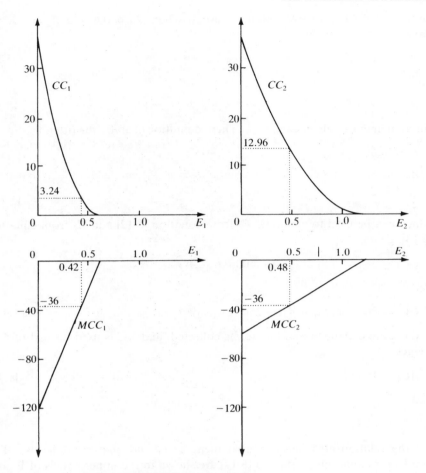

Figure 5.11 Control costs and effluent taxation

firms, then clearly the total of control costs across both firms can be reduced, holding $E = E_1 + E_2$ constant, by allowing effluent discharge to increase where marginal control costs are higher and reducing it where they are lower. The same point can be seen by considering movements away from $E_1 = 0.42$ and $E_2 = 0.48$, holding $E = E_1 + E_2 + 0.9$, in the upper panels of Figure 5.11. It is only when marginal control costs are equal that total control costs are minimised.

In much of the literature the issues which we are dealing with here are discussed in terms of *abatement* and *abatement costs*. Figure 5.12 is Figure 5.11 translated into use of these concepts: *A* stands for abatement, *AC* for abatement cost and *MAC* for marginal abatement cost. The level of abatement for a firm is the difference between the amount of effluent it would discharge in order to maximise profit in the absence of any EPA action to effect its discharge and the amount actually discharged given EPA action.

With an initial, no-EPA action, situation where $E_1 = 0.6$ and $E_2 = 1.2$, we have

$$A_1 = 0.6 - E_1 \qquad\qquad [5.14]$$

and

$$A_2 = 1.2 - E_2 \qquad\qquad [5.15]$$

for abatement levels in each firm. These definitions can be rewritten as

$$E_1 = 0.6 - A_1 \qquad\qquad [5.14']$$

and

$$E_2 = 1.2 - A_2 \qquad\qquad [5.15']$$

which can be used to eliminate E_1 from equation [5.12] and E_2 from equation [5.13], giving

$$CC_1 = 36 - 120(0.6 - A_1) + 100(0.6 - A_1)^2$$

and

$$CC_2 = 36 - 60(1.2 - A_2) + 25(1.2 - A_2)^2$$

If these are expanded and like terms collected, and AC is used instead of CC, we get

$$AC_1 = 100A_1^2 \qquad\qquad [5.16]$$

and

$$AC_2 = 25A_2^2 \qquad\qquad [5.17]$$

for the relationships between abatement costs and abatement levels.[2] The graphs for equations [5.16] and [5.17] are shown in the upper panels of Figure 5.12.

So, abatement costs are just control costs related to effluent discharge not sent out rather than to effluent discharge sent out. The upper panels of Figure 5.12 show, in each firm, abatement costs increasing with the level of abatement at an increasing rate. The lower panels show marginal abatement costs, derived from the abatement cost graphs in the usual way, i.e. by reading off the slopes of the latter as abatement varies. Note that marginal abatement costs increase as abatement increases, but at different rates in each firm. Now, recall that we found that for an effluent discharge tax rate of £36, $E_1 = 0.42$ and $E_2 = 0.48$, and we argued above that this was the E_1/E_2 combination which realised $E = E_1 + E_2 = 0.9$ at the least, control, cost. From equation [5.14] above $E_1 = 0.42$ implies $A_1 = 0.18$, and from equation [5.15] $E_2 = 0.48$ implies $A_2 = 0.72$. If, in the lower panels of Figure 5.12, we read off MAC_1 for A_1 at 0.18 and MAC_2 for A_2 at 0.72, we find $MAC_1 = MAC_2 = 36$. And we recall that 36 is the effluent tax rate applicable to both firms.

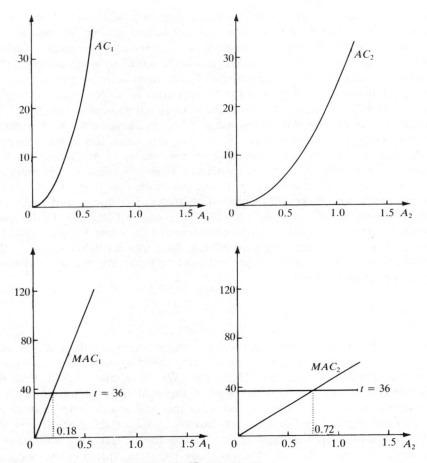

Figure 5.12   Abatement costs and effluent taxation

Two points arise here. The first is that $MAC_1 = MAC_2$ is necessary for the A_1/A_2 combination to be that which realises the total abatement involved at least cost. The argument here is the same as that above concerning the equality of marginal control costs. Simply consider some situation for which $A = A_1 + A_2 = 0.9$ but where A_1 and A_2 are not such that $MAC_1 = MAC_2 = 36$, and it is clear that there is possible some rearrangement, in terms of A_1 and A_2, which gives $A = A_1 + A_2 = 0.9$ at lower total, across the two firms, abatement cost.

The second point concerns the question of why it is that both firms, seeking to maximise their net private benefit, given the existence of a uniform effluent discharge tax, end up with the same marginal abatement cost. The answer to this question is really quite straightforward. Effluent discharge abatement for the firm is an activity which has costs and benefits associated with it. The costs are the abatement costs shown in Figure 5.12. The benefits are avoided tax liability. A profit-maximising firm will conduct any of its activities at that level for which the excess of benefit arising over cost arising is greatest. We have seen, in a number of contexts, that the level for which the excess of benefit over cost is greatest is the level for which marginal cost equals marginal benefit. In the context of abatement activity, marginal cost is marginal abatement cost, shown for the two firms in the lower part of Figure 5.12 as MAC_1 and MAC_2. In this context, marginal abatement benefit, MAB, is just the tax rate on effluent discharge, which is the same for both firms so that $MAB_1 = MAB_2 = 36$. MAB is the tax rate since this is the marginal reduction in tax payment associated with increases in abatement. A firm considering whether to vary its abatement level will compare the marginal abatement cost with the tax rate on effluent discharge. If the former is the larger, profits net of tax will increase if abatement is reduced, and vice versa. So, with both firms facing the same tax rate, both will abate up to the levels at which they have equal marginal abatement costs. Table 5.7 shows what is involved, with T representing total effluent discharge tax liability, and $NPBT$ representing private benefit, or profit, net of such liability: the other symbols are as previously defined.

Calculating the uniform tax rate

We have shown that an EPA can realise some arbitrary standard of pollution control by imposing upon firms discharging the relevant effluent a uniform tax rate per unit of effluent discharge. We have also shown that the appropriate uniform tax rate will lead to the attainment of the standard at the least possible cost to society, and is for this reason a preferred instrument to uniform regulation. We have not, however, said anything about how the EPA would calculate the 'appropriate' tax rate for the least cost realisation of its chosen standard. It is to this obviously important question that we now turn, again using our simple numerical example to show what is, generally, involved.

We derived above

$$NPB_1 = 120E_1 - 100E_1^2 \tag{5.10}$$

and

$$NPB_2 = 60E_2 - 25E_2^2 \tag{5.11}$$

as equations describing how net private benefits in each firm would vary with the level of effluent discharge. Since our purpose there was to find how control costs varied with effluent discharge levels, we did not allow for tax payments in finding net private benefits. Recall that the tax payments are a transfer from firms to the EPA, not a real cost borne by society as a whole. However, the firms will consider their profits after tax when deciding how much effluent to discharge, as discussed immediately above in connection with Table 5.7. Hence, when considering how the firms' behaviour will

Table 5.7 Abatement costs and benefits

A_1	E_1	T_1	$NPBT_1$	MAC_1	$MAB_1 = t$
0	0.6	21.60	14.40	0	36
0.1	0.5	18.00	17.00	20	36
0.18	0.42	15.12	17.64	36	36
0.2	0.4	14.40	17.60	40	36
0.3	0.3	10.80	16.20	60	36
0.4	0.2	7.20	12.80	80	36
0.5	0.1	3.60	7.40	100	36
0.6	0.0	0.00	0.00	120	36

A_2	E_2	T_2	$NPBT_2$	MAC_2	$MAB_2 = t$
0	1.2	43.20	−7.20	0	36
0.2	1.0	36.00	−1.00	10	36
0.4	0.8	28.80	3.20	20	36
0.6	0.6	21.60	5.40	30	36
0.72	0.48	17.28	5.76	36	36
0.8	0.4	14.40	5.60	40	36
1.0	0.2	7.20	3.80	50	36
1.2	0.0	0.00	0.00	60	36

respond to effluent taxation, the EPA must work with net of tax profit functions. These are easily derived from equations [5.10] and [5.11] as

$$NPBT_1 = 120E_1 - 100E_1^2 - tE_1 = (120 - t)E_1 - 100E_1^2 \qquad [5.18]$$

and

$$NPBT_2 = 60E_2 - 25E_2^2 - tE_2 = (60 - t)E_2 - 25E_2^2 \qquad [5.19]$$

where t is the uniform effluent tax rate, and we write $NPBT$ to emphasise, with the T, that it is net of effluent tax profits that are being considered.

These relationships are graphed in the upper part of Figure 5.13, for various possible values for t. In the lower part we show the graphs of the corresponding marginal relationships, where $MNPBT$ stands for marginal net private benefit after payment of effluent taxation. The equations for these marginal relationships are:

$$MNPBT_1 = (120 - t) - 200E_1 \qquad [5.20]$$

$$MNPBT_2 = (60 - t) - 50E_2 \qquad [5.21]$$

Now, the EPA knows that profit-maximising firms will operate where $MNPBT = 0$, and it wants to realise $E = E_1 + E_2 = 0.9$. If we write

(i) $MNPBT_1 = (120 - t) - 200E_1 = 0$
(ii) $MNPBT_2 = (60 - t) - 50E_2 \;\; = 0$
(iii) $E_1 + E_2 \;\; = 0.9$

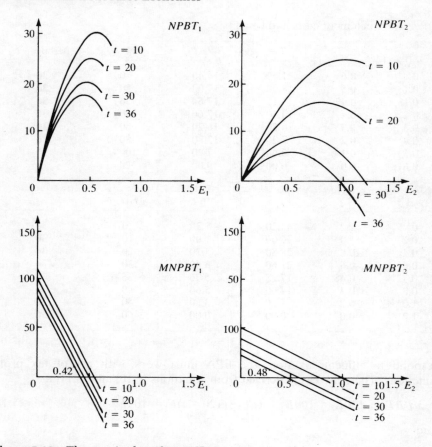

Figure 5.13   The required uniform effluent tax rate

we see that we have three equations in three unknowns E_1, E_2 and t. To solve, write (i) as

$$120 - 200E_1 = t$$

and (ii) as

$$60 - 50E_2 = t$$

where setting the left-hand sides equal gives

$$120 - 200E_1 = 60 - 50E_2$$

or

(iv) $60 = 200E_1 - 50E_2$

Now, from (iii) we get

(v) $E_1 = 0.9 - E_2$

which we can use to eliminate E_1 from (iv), getting

$$60 = 200(0.9 - E_2) - 50E_2$$
$$60 = 180 - 250E_2$$
$$250E_2 = 120$$
$$E_2 = 120/250$$
$$(vi) \quad E_2 = 0.48$$

Substituting from (vi) into (v) gives

$$E_1 = 0.9 - 0.48$$
$$(vii) \quad E_1 = 0.42$$

Now we use either (i) with $E_1 = 0.42$ or (ii) with $E_2 = 0.48$, to solve for t as 36.

So, given knowledge of each firm's profit function, in terms of the dependence of such on the effluent discharge level as in equations [5.10] and [5.11], the EPA can calculate the rate of uniform taxation which will lead to the attainment of the arbitrary standard of least cost. Two important points arise. First, it will be clear that the information which the EPA has to have to calculate the tax rate is also the information which enables it to calculate the E_1 and E_2 levels which represent the least cost realisation of the overall $E = E_1 + E_2$ standard for which it is aiming. That is to say that if the EPA had enough information to calculate the required tax rate, it could also calculate the instructions about E_1 and E_2 levels which it could issue to the firms for the realisation of the least cost attainment of the standard by non-uniform regulation. It is not, given the required information, impossible to attain an arbitrary standard at least cost using the regulatory instrument. It is merely impossible to attain the standard at least cost by using uniform regulations, i.e. telling both firms to reduce discharges by 50%.

The advantage of uniform effluent taxation over effluent regulation is not, then, that the former can hit the target at least cost but the latter cannot. Nonetheless, economists recommend effluent taxation over regulation. Why? The answer to this question is our second point, and concerns the availability of information to the EPA. We have shown above that if the EPA knows how firms' profits vary with effluent discharge levels, then it can precisely attain some target standard either by uniform taxation or by non-uniform regulation. That is, either by saying to both, You pay £36 per unit effluent discharge, or by saying to 1, You will discharge $E_1 = 0.42$ and to 2, You will discharge $E_2 = 0.48$. It is not, however, realistic to suppose that an EPA would know the profit functions for the firms discharging effluent. Given that prior to EPA activity firms had no interest in effluent, firms themselves would not really know the implications for their profits of varying discharge levels. Suppose, more realistically then, that the EPA does not know the equations like [5.10] and [5.11] and so cannot do the calculations set out above. What then are the instruments available to it, and how do they compare?

The instruments are uniform regulation and uniform effluent taxation. We know that uniform regulation will realise the desired arbitrary standard, but that it will not do so at least cost. Uniform effluent taxation, on the other hand, will not necessarily now realise the target standard, but whatever pollution reduction it does bring about will have been realised at least cost. The first of these statements follows obviously from our earlier discussion. Desiring an $x\%$ reduction in E, having all firms cut back by $x\%$ takes no account of the differing abatement costs in different firms, and so is unnecessarily costly. But it does mean that an overall cut of $x\%$ is achieved. The second statement also follows from our earlier discussion, but perhaps less obviously so. In discussing, for example, Figure 5.12, we argued that since both firms would operate with $MAC = MAB = 36$, the standard $E = E_1 + E_2 = 0.9$ would be realised at least cost due to $MAC_1 = MAC_2$. Now, suppose that the uniform effluent tax rate had been something other than £36. Then clearly the same argument would still yield a situation in which $MAC_1 = MAC_2$. But it would not be true that the corresponding E_1 and E_2 would sum to 0.9. That is, with the tax rate set 'incorrectly' the target standard of pollution would not be realised. But some pollution reduction below $E = E_1 + E_2 = 0.6 + 1.2 = 1.8$ would be achieved, and whatever the reduction achieved was, it would have been achieved at least cost.

Further, suppose in the absence of the information necessary to figure out that a target of $E = 0.9$ requires a tax rate of £36, the EPA 'arbitrarily' sets a rate of, say, £10. Then, see the lower part of Figure 5.13, this would give $E = E_1 + E_2 = 0.55 + 1.00 = 1.55$ for a pollution reduction of $1.8 - 1.55 = 0.25$. And, no less costly way of getting $E = 1.55$ than $E_1 = 0.55$ and $E_2 = 1.00$ exists. After observing the firms' adjustments to $t = £10$, the EPA would realise that its target of $E = 0.9$ had not been realised. So it would raise the rate to $t = £20$, which again would achieve some reduction, again at least cost. And so on, and so on. While unable to go directly to the desired least cost solution by virtue of lack of information, the EPA could hope to get to it in successive steps, each of which would itself be a least cost reduction.

This is the real reason for preferring uniform effluent taxation to regulation. In a world where the EPA had complete information on every firm's abatement costs, the least cost criterion would not discriminate between non-uniform regulation and uniform taxation.[3] The point is that such a world is nothing remotely like the real world.

Marketable pollution permits

We now consider an instrument which enables the EPA to realise the standard it aims for directly and at least cost, even in the absence of information on firms' abatement costs. This is the creation of a market in pollution permits or licences. As is now usual, we present generally relevant ideas in the context of our simple numerical example. Actually, once stated the ideas themselves turn out to be rather simple, but powerful, and to have considerable intuitive appeal.

In the upper panels of Figure 5.14 we show for each of the two firms how profits vary with the level of effluent discharge, when there is no tax on effluent discharge. The middle panels show the corresponding marginal relationships, as *MNPB* for marginal net private benefit. Suppose now that a firm can discharge effluent only to the extent that it holds permits so to do. Suppose also that there exists a market in which such permits can be bought, and sold. How much would a firm be willing to pay for a permit? Clearly, the answer to this question is to be found in the relationship between profits and effluent discharge levels – given the possibility of acquiring an additional permit, the amount the firm would be willing to pay for it will depend on the effect acquisition of it will have on profits.

To see what is involved consider firm 1, and suppose that it currently owns permits allowing $E_1 = 0.3$, and is offered a permit allowing further effluent

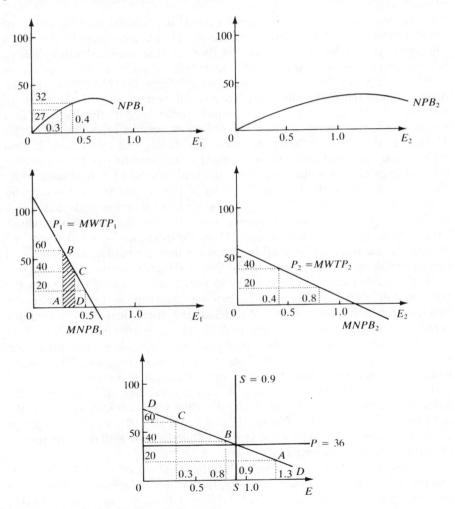

Figure 5.14 A market in pollution permits

discharge in amount 0.1. Acquisition of this additional permit would increase its profits as shown in the upper left panel of Figure 5.14, and as also shown by the shaded area $ABCD$ in the middle left panel. Looked at either way the profit increase consequent upon acquisition of this permit is £5, and this is clearly the most that the firm would be willing to pay for it. Now suppose that the permit on offer is in respect of an amount of effluent discharge of 0.001 units. Then maximum willingness to pay by firm 1 will be given by an area like $ABCD$, which is $ABC'D'$ where $C'D'$ is a vertical line up from $E_1 = 0.301$. The area $ABC'D'$ is too small to draw, but clearly a close approximation to it will be given by the height of the line AB. As the size of the permit on offer gets even smaller, so will AB become a better approximation to its value to the firm in terms of the effect of its acquisition on profits.

If we consider a strictly marginal permit acquisition, starting from an initial holding of 0.3 of permits, the height of AB gives exactly the firm's willingness to pay for it, as £60 in fact. We say that marginal willingness to pay for permits, at $E_1 = 0.3$, is $AB = £60$. Now, clearly, we can consider as initial holding any level of E_1, and read off from the $MNPB_1$ graph the corresponding marginal willingness to pay for permits in just this way. In fact, the $MNPB_1$ graph can be alternatively understood as the graph of firm 1's marginal willingness to pay for pollution permits, showing how this declines as the permit holding increases. The reader will recall from section 4.3 that the relationship between marginal willingness to pay for something and holdings of that something is the demand function for that something. The graph shown in the left middle panel of Figure 5.14 is just the demand function, for firm 1, for pollution permits. It shows how the price that firm 1 is willing to pay for a marginal permit, read off from the vertical axis, varies with its holding of pollution permits. Thus, for example, for a holding of 0.5 of permits, the price we read off is £20: when firm 1's holding is 0.6 units of permits, its demand goes to zero because $E_1 = 0.6$ gives maximum profits.

Exactly similar considerations apply to firm 2, and the graph shown at the right middle panel of Figure 5.14 can be regarded as firm 2's demand function for pollution permits. We derive the total demand function for permits in the usual way (see section 4.3). At any permit price, read off E_1 and E_2 corresponding on the horizontal axis and sum: the price and $E = E_1 + E_2$ give a point on the aggregate demand function. The middle panels of Figure 5.14 show explicitly, for example, that for $P = 20$, $E_1 = 0.5$ and $E_2 = 0.8$ giving $E = 1.3$, giving A on the total demand function in the lower panel: for $P = 40$, $E_1 = 0.4$ and $E_2 = 0.4$ so $E = 0.8$, giving B on the total demand function: for $P = 60$, $E_1 = 0.3$ and $E_2 = 0.0$ so $E = 0.3$, giving C in the lower panel. The total demand function for pollution permits is shown as DD in the lower panel of Figure 5.14.[4]

Now the EPA's objective is the arbitrary standard of $E = 0.9$. So it just creates permits in this amount. The supply function for permits is then SS in the lower panel of Figure 5.14, a vertical line at $E = 0.9$. The market clearing price is read off from the vertical axis as $P = £36$. If we go back into the middle panels we can read off that at this price firm 1 will buy an amount 0.42 of permits and firm 2 an amount 0.48. That is, we get $E_1 = 0.42$ and $E_2 = 0.48$, which we know to be that E_1/E_2 combination which gives $E = E_1 + E_2 = 0.9$ at the least possible cost. The EPA can realise its standard at least cost if it simply creates permits in amount equal to that standard, and then lets the market allocate this fixed supply as between the polluting firms. It requires no information about the polluting firms. Note further that we have not had to say anything about the way in which the permits are initially introduced, so that it does not matter for the result how they are introduced. The EPA could initially give permits to each firm in equal amounts (of 0.45) or it could give permits to each firm in amounts proportional to their initial discharge levels (0.3 to 1 and 0.6 to 2), or it could auction the permits initially. In each of these cases, the permit price would emerge as £36 and the standard would be realised at least cost. As between the three cases, the distributional implications would, of course, differ.

While this is a remarkable result of general applicability which we cannot actually prove here, given our mathematical limitations, the intuition of it is really fairly simple and follows from our earlier discussion of the uniform tax instrument. The first point is that there can be only one market price for the permits, so that all firms face the same price. Given that, our earlier discussion of profit maximising firms' decisions about the optimal levels of abatement applies to show that all firms will operate where marginal abatement costs are equal. This means that total abatement, or control, costs are minimised. The standard realised at least cost must be that desired by the EPA, since the total quantity of permits available is fixed at the standard by the EPA.

Overview

We have covered quite a lot of ground in this section, so it will be useful to summarise where we have got to in relation to the properties of the alternative instruments that an EPA might use for the control of pollution to an arbitrary standard. Assume that:

(a) all the polluting firms are competitive profit maximisers
(b) the EPA can costlessly monitor emissions, can costlessly collect any tax revenues, and can costlessly enforce compliance with its regulations, or permit allocations, regarding allowable emissions levels
(c) the EPA knows the abatement cost functions for all the polluting firms

Now consider the properties of the following instruments available to the EPA: emissions regulation; uniform emissions taxation; tradeable emissions permits. Call an instrument 'efficient' if it achieves whatever reduction in emissions that its use brings about at the least cost, and 'dependable' if the reduction that it brings about is that actually desired by the EPA. Then:

(1)   emissions regulation is efficient and dependable
(2)   emissions taxation is efficient and dependable
(3)   tradeable emissions permits are efficient and dependable

On the stated assumptions, the three instruments are exactly equivalent on these two criteria. In this respect the key assumption is c. Given that knowledge, the EPA can calculate the emissions levels for each firm that will secure the overall reduction required at the least cost, as well as the uniform tax rate required to secure the overall emissions reduction required. It is the dropping of this, implausible, assumption that differentiates between the three instruments. If we are only prepared to make assumptions 1 and 2, then:

(1)   emissions regulation is not efficient, but is dependable
(2)   emissions taxation is efficient, but not dependable
(3)   tradeable emissions permits are dependable and efficient

These are the standard results in the literature. If the EPA does now know all the abatement cost functions it cannot calculate the differentiated regulations that will realise its target at least cost. Requiring an $x\%$ overall emissions reduction, it can tell every firm to cut by $x\%$, getting what it wants, but not at least cost. Equally, the EPA cannot calculate the uniform tax that will mean hitting the overall target. Any tax rate will bring about some overall reduction at the smallest possible cost, but it will not be the required reduction. In the case of tradeable permits, the EPA issues a total amount of permits equal to its target, so achieving it is assured. And, given many competitive firms maximising their profits, the reduction will be achieved at the smallest possible total abatement cost.

5.4   Pollution and international trade

Thus far we have considered the problem of environmental pollution for a closed and isolated economy, ignoring the fact that economies trade with one another. In recent years it has become clear that environmental problems and trade are linked, so that environmental considerations may have implications for trade policy, and vice versa. We now briefly consider some of the issues arising.

The first step is to distinguish the various types of environmental linkages that can arise. Figure 5.15 provides a simple categorisation of the situations that can arise in relation to trade and environmental pollution. Just two countries, A and B, are considered here, but the basic ideas carry over to many country situations. In all three cases trade flows both ways; A exports goods and services to B and imports them from B, and vice versa. The cases are differentiated on the basis of the pollution flows arising. In Type I situations any pollution damage arising from each nation's economic activity is confined within its own frontiers. In Type II situations, there are *unidirectional environmental spillovers* such that economic activity in one

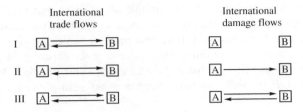

Figure 5.15   Trade and the environment: a typology

country gives rise to pollution damage in the other country. In Type III situations there are *reciprocal spillovers*. Both countries' economic activity gives rise to damage in the other country. In Type II and III situations there is *trans-boundary pollution*, whereas in a Type I situation there is not.

No spillovers

In Type I situations pollution damage does not cross national frontiers, there are no spillovers. We are dealing with problems of domestic pollution arising from domestic production. This is the simplest and clearest context in which to consider the most basic question arising: does pollution damage undermine the case for free trade? That case was set out in 4.6 in terms of the comparative advantage argument. Here, we present it in a slightly different way, in terms of consumer's surplus and *producer's surplus*. The concept of consumer's surplus was discussed in 4.3, and see especially Figure 4.7 and Figure 4.8. Recall that it is the area under the demand function over the horizontal line for the market price, and arises because there are consumers who would pay more than the market price for non-marginal units. Producer's surplus is the analogous concept on the production side of the market. It is measured as the area over the supply function under the horizontal line for the market price. In the upper part of Figure 5.16, for example, the producer's surplus with the supply function $0S$ and the price P is the area of the triangle $0aP$. The rationale here is exactly analogous to that for consumer's surplus. While all units are actually sold at the market price P, for all except the marginal unit, supply would be forthcoming at lower prices. There is a surplus to producers on all non-marginal units sold at the price P. The sum of these surpluses is the area $0aP$.

The upper part of Figure 5.16 refers to a country that becomes an importer of the commodity X after the opening to trade. The demand function is dD and the supply function is $0S$, so that in the absence of international trade X_O is produced and consumed at the price P. The world price for this commodity is P_W, so that with trade domestic production is X_s and domestic consumption is X_D. The opening to trade affects both producer's and consumer's surplus in regard to the commodity X. Consumer's surplus increases from Pda to $P_W dc$, and producer's surplus is reduced from $0aP$ to $0bP_W$. The former increase is clearly larger than the latter decrease, and there is a net gain given by the area of the triangle *abc*. Given that ideal conditions hold everywhere in the economy, this is the alternative version of the argument for trade for a country that becomes an importer. The lower part of Figure 5.16 refers to a country that becomes an exporter. In this case, consumer's surplus is reduced from Pda to P_Wdc, and producer's surplus is increased from $0aP$ to $0bP_W$. Again, there is a net gain given by the area of triangle *abc*.

We now suppose that the production of the commodity X gives rise to pollution that is confined within the borders of the producing country, and consider whether this undermines the case for trade. We assume that this pollution problem is the only source of market failure. In the case of a country which becomes an importer, the opening to trade means a lower level of domestic production, X_s rather than X_O in the upper part of Figure 5.16, and hence reduces the pollution arising. Trade reduces the external costs associated with the production of X, and so reinforces, rather than undermines, the case for trade. In the case of a country which becomes an exporter, production increases, from X_O to X_s in the lower part of Figure 5.16, so that pollution and the associated external costs increase. Consumers pay a higher price, get less surplus, and experience an increase in external costs. The increase in external costs associated with the opening to trade may be greater than the excess of the producer's surplus gain over the consumer's

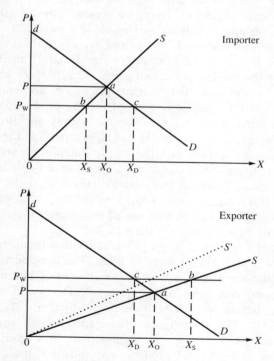

Figure 5.16   Domestic pollution and the gains from trade

surplus loss, area *abc*, so undermining the case for trade. This, however, ignores the possibility of introducing some policy to reduce the pollution at the same time as opening to trade.

Suppose that the opening is accompanied by, for example, uniform taxation of the emissions arising in the production of X. In that case, the supply function will shift to a position such as that of $0S'$. As compared with the trade but no pollution policy situation, there will be a reduction in the external cost of pollution and in producer's surplus, with no change in consumer's surplus $P_W dc$ given that the world price is not affected by the adoption of a pollution control policy in one country. The question of whether pollution undermines the case for trade, then turns on the size of the external cost reduction achieved by the pollution policy in relation to the associated loss to producers. This is an empirical question, the answer to which will vary from case to case according to the nature of the supply function, the rate of emissions tax, and the way external costs depend upon output and pollution levels. There is, however, one circumstance in which we can be sure that the reduction in external costs will be greater than the loss to producers, so that opening to trade and introducing a pollution control policy will be a net welfare gain. That is where the tax is set at the optimal rate. The simplest way to see why this is so is to revert to our earlier discussion of the optimal level of pollution as that at which the marginal costs and benefits of pollution reduction are equal. Consider Figure 5.6 again. It was originally developed in the bargaining context, but it has subsequently become clear that in terms of demonstrating the nature of the optimal, in the sense of allocatively efficient, outcome, it is generally applicable. For present purposes, Q_P^* there corresponds to the situation with trade but no pollution policy, and Q_E^* to that with trade and taxation at the optimal rate. The gain to consumers in terms of avoided external costs when the tax is introduced is given by the area 3 plus 4. The loss to producers by the area 3. There is a net gain.

If the opening to trade is accompanied by the introduction of a policy – it does not have to be emissions taxation, tradeable permits or regulation could do the same job – that optimally controls pollution, then pollution arising in domestic production does not undermine the case for trade, even for an exporting country. We have already noted the difficulties involved in empirically identifying the optimal level of pollution, or equivalently, of determining the optimal rate for uniform emissions taxation.

Unidirectional spillovers

We have actually discussed unidirectional damage flow situations already, in 5.1 and 5.2 above. There we considered a situation, within an economy, where a firm's activities gave rise to costs for a water supply undertaking. In the absence of clearly defined property rights, those costs were external to the firm, and there was excessive pollution of the lake used by it and the water supply undertaking. We considered a solution to this problem arising from bargaining based on well-defined property rights. The analysis developed can be applied to two nations, with country A taking the place of the firm, and country B taking the place of the water supply undertaking. Figure 5.17 is just Figure 5.6 with new labels on the two lines representing the interests of the two actors. In Figure 5.17, MNB_A shows how the marginal net benefits of the relevant activity conducted in A vary with the level of that activity, X_A. If X_A gives rise to damage in A, this is accounted for by MNB_A, which is for benefits net of any costs. MEC_B shows how the marginal damage arising in B varies with the level of X_A. In B, X_A gives rise only to damage. All the benefits associated with X_A arise in A.

In Figure 5.17, X_{AO} identifies the optimal level of X_A, on the basis of the same arguments as used with Figure 5.6. Similarly, X_{AI} gives the level at which the activity X_A will actually occur, in the absence of policy intervention. If there was a world government, the discussion of policy which went with Figure 5.6 would apply here. The world government could assign a property right to either A or B, and bargaining between them would lead to the outcome X_{AO}. Alternatively, the world government could tax the activity X_A at a rate which would bring about X_{AO}.

However, the point is precisely that there is not a world government which can assign property rights as between nations, or impose taxes on them. Note that country A itself has no reason to impose on its citizens the tax, or use any other policy instrument, that would lead to the outcome X_{AO} rather than X_{AI}. Given that MNB_A refers to net benefits, X_{AI} is optimal from the perspective of country A. In this situation, the victim pays principle applies. The activity level will be reduced from X_{AI} only if country B pays country A so to do. The arguments used with Figure 5.6 apply here in the same way to show that with B paying A in respect of reductions in X_A, the outcome will be X_{AO}. In discussing the usefulness of the property rights solution in terms of Figure 5.6, we noted a number of limitation on its applicability. That discussion applies here as well in its essentials.

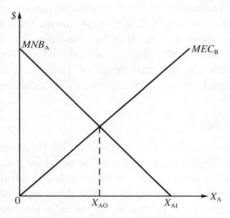

Figure 5.17 Bargaining over a unidirectional spillover

Reciprocal spillovers

The Type III category covers a number of variations on the theme of reciprocal spillovers, but here we shall discuss just the polar case in which waste emissions occur in all countries, and in which all emissions contribute to global pollution which is non-rival in consumption as between all countries. To keep matters simple, we shall assume that there are just two countries, A and B: economic activity in A generates pollution in B as well as A, and vice versa.

We considered the case of pollution non-rival in consumption within the boundaries of a nation state in previous sections of this chapter. In 5.3, we had two firms emitting wastes in amounts S_1 and S_2. Individuals experienced pollution Z, where $Z = S_1 + S_2$. We discussed the nature of the optimal level of pollution in such circumstances, and argued that such a level represented an infeasible policy goal, by virtue of the difficulties of identifying it. We saw that the operative policy goal would be an arbitrary standard, and discussed alternative policy instruments for the attainment of such a standard. If nation states did not exist, and there was a single world government, that discussion would apply here. But, the point of departure for international trade is the existence of nation states which pursue their individual interests. There is not a world government, so that there cannot be a world EPA established by it. The relevant actors here are nation states. The question to be considered is whether they will act to control pollution. This question itself has two parts. First, will they act individually? Second, will they act collectively? The answers are almost certainly not, and it all depends, respectively.

The analytical basis for these answers is widely known as the *prisoners' dilemma game*. This gets its name because the basic structure involved was originally developed for a context where two individuals are arrested for a crime. If both confess, both receive reduced sentences. If neither confesses, both receive the standard sentence, as they are guilty and can be proved so at some trouble to the police. If only A confesses, for both, he gets a much reduced sentence, and correspondingly for B. Table 5.8 uses illustrative numbers for the application of this structure to reciprocal spillovers involving two trading nations.

Table 5.8 shows the pay-offs to each country, given its action and that of the other. SQ stands for status quo, and EPA for environmental protection agency. Each country can be in one of two states, following recognition of the existence of the global pollution problem. It can do nothing, and remain in the status quo making no attempt to do anything about the control of its domestic emissions. It can set up an EPA mandated to control domestic emissions to some arbitrary standard. In Table 5.8 we are assuming that the arbitrary standard would be the same in each country, that the two economies are of the same size, and have the same costs of emissions abatement. These assumptions are not essential to the argument, but do simplify it.

Table 5.8 The incentive structure with reciprocal spillovers

		B	
		SQ	EPA
	SQ	1/1	2/0.8
A			
	EPA	0.8/2	1.5/1.5

Given two states for each nation, there are four possible outcomes, each represented by a cell in Table 5.8. In each cell, the number to the left of / refers to country A, that to the right to country B. The numbers are for the welfare of the representative individual in each nation, taking account of pollution damage. The numbers are normalised so that when both countries do nothing to control emissions, welfare in each is unity. This serves to emphasise that these are purely imaginary numbers, made up to illustrate the essential nature of the problem. The numbers in the other cells arise as follows. In the top right cell, A does nothing while B sets up an EPA. As compared with the full status quo, A gains while B losses. B incurs the domestic costs involved in emissions abatement, and suffers a loss of competitiveness in international trade, while gaining some benefit from the reduced pollution due to its own emissions, but not those of A, being reduced. A gains exactly the same pollution reduction benefit, benefits from B's loss of competitiveness, and incurs no abatement costs. The bottom left cell shows the numbers reversed, as it refers to the reciprocal situation. Comparing the, top left, cell for the full status quo with these two cells, it is clear that for neither country is there an incentive to act alone. So to do would confer gains on the other country, and involve domestic losses.

The bottom right cell is for a situation where both countries set up EPAs. In this situation, the reduction in the common level of pollution experienced by each is twice that if either acts unilaterally. Both incur domestic abatement costs, but neither suffers from any loss of competitiveness. Both countries are better off than in the full status quo. But neither is as well off as it would be if it did not act and the other did. Each country has an incentive to free ride on the emissions abatement of the other, if it can. Given that each has this incentive not to act on domestic emissions, in the absence of some kind of agreement between the nation states, there will be no emissions abatement anywhere. However, if each could be assured that the other would act if it did, there would be incentives to act as both would be better off than in the full status quo. This is the nub of the matter in reciprocal spillover situations. All parties are better off as participants in an effective international agreement that each acts to reduce emissions, but none has an incentive to act unilaterally. Indeed, each has an incentive to try to free ride on the efforts of the other. The operative problem is the negotiation of international agreements on emissions abatement.

5.5   Commentary

We have shown, in 5.1, that economists see environmental pollution as a market failure problem, originating in the lack of clearly defined private property rights in environmental media. And, in 5.2, that the obvious solution to the problem, of establishing private property rights and then leaving things to private bargaining, is not available with respect to other than trivial pollution problems. Further, in 5.3, we argued that while instruments for the attainment of socially optimal pollution levels (i.e. those consistent with efficiency in allocation) can be envisaged, that goal is not a realistic one on account of the lack of the information necessary for identifying it. As a practical matter, we are interested in 'arbitrary' standards in respect of pollution levels. In this context, we argued, in section 5.3, for a reliance on incentive based instruments (effluent taxation, or tradeable pollution permits) over regulatory control. The basis for this argument was that incentive based instruments minimised the informational requirements placed upon an EPA in seeking to realise some arbitrary standard at least cost.

The first systematic treatment of the idea that not all of the costs borne by society show up in market transactions was provided in the 1920s. Pigou (1920) made the distinction between private and social costs, and advocated a system of corrective taxes to bring private and social costs into equality. In our terminology, the difference between private and social cost is external cost: a tax on residuals discharge set so as to secure allocative efficiency is often called a *Pigouvian tax*. With a few exceptions (see Kapp (1950) for example) economists did not until the early 1970s regard the existence of external costs, and the question of eliminating them, as important policy issues. There were a variety of reasons for this. Undoubtedly one was an implicit view that external costs were exceptional and rare blemishes on the market system. The early 1970s saw a reassessment of this position, at least in respect of environmental pollution. This was in part a response to the observed incidence of pollution problems, which was widely believed to have increased dramatically during the 1950s and 1960s (see, for an influential statement of this position, Commoner (1972)). Kneese, Ayres and D'Arge (1970) drew the attention of economists to the materials balance principle, introduced in 1.2. Clearly, if an economy necessarily returns to the natural environment a quantity of materials equal to the amount of raw materials extracted, then residuals discharges to the environment must be seen as routine and pervasive rather than exceptional. In itself, such pervasiveness of residuals discharge does not necessarily imply that external costs are pervasive. However, given the observed lack of private property rights in airsheds, watercourses, etc., the pervasiveness of residuals discharges does establish a presumption that external cost problems are also far from being rare or exceptional.

We have seen that the calculation of a Pigouvian tax rate requires knowledge of marginal external costs not at the initial situation but as they would be at the allocatively efficient target level of pollution. This, in turn, requires knowledge of household preference systems and of the production technologies of firms. It is precisely the attraction of bargaining and markets that, where they can work, they reveal the information that identifies allocatively efficient outcomes. This is what makes the mediation of self-interested behaviour through bargaining and markets such an attractive solution to economic problems, and explains the attraction for some economists of the property rights approach to pollution problems set out in 5.2 above. That approach derives from Coase (1960), and the demonstration that, in certain circumstances, private bargaining against a background of explicit property rights in favour of either a pollution sufferer or a pollution generator will lead to an efficient outcome is often referred to as the *Coase Theorem*. There is no question that this theorem is wrong. The results do follow from the assumptions. The point is rather that the assumptions are such that the theorem is irrelevant to any pollution problem of significance. The Coase Theorem is discussed in most intermediate microeconomics texts: see, for example, Ch. 17 of Hirshleifer (1980). In our treatment of the theorem in 5.2 we noted that the illustration used was special in that the outcome was the same whichever way the property right was assigned. A treatment which illustrates the general result that whichever way the property right assigned the outcome is allocatively efficient is provided in Ch. 13 of Hartwick and Olewiler (1986).

The demonstration that uniform effluent changes across sources of such will realise a given reduction in total effluent discharge in the cheapest possible way is known as the *Least Cost Theorem*. It appears to have first been set out formally and generally in Baumol and Oates (1971). Our illustration of this theorem in 5.3 above assumed just two firms discharging into a lake: it applies however large the number of firms and whatever the affected environmental media. The idea of marketable pollution permits appears to have been first expounded in Dales (1968), but the first rigorous proof of the least cost property of such a system is Montgomery (1972). The Appendix to Common (1989) provides a reasonably transparent mathematical demonstration of the equality of the equilibrium price for emissions permits and the uniform tax rate required to achieve a given arbitrary reduction in total emissions. The relative merits of effluent taxation and marketable pollution permits are considered in Ch. 6 of Fisher (1981). Cropper and Oates (1992) is a recent survey of the environmental economics literature, which provides references to journal articles dealing with the issues covered in this chapter. There, as in much of the literature, the instrument that we have referred to as 'regulation' is referred to as *command and control*.

On simplifying assumptions and their relevance

In setting out the analysis in the previous sections of this chapter we have used numerical examples embodying some rather special assumptions. We did this to bring out the essentials in the clearest possible way. We now briefly consider, primarily with respect to the attainment of an arbitrary standard, the implications of relaxing some of those assumptions. We also note here some additional matters, the proper treatment of which is beyond the scope of an introductory text.

The numerical examples involved a very rigid production technology, in which the level of effluent discharge is determined solely and uniquely by the level of output. There is not, that is, any possibility for a firm to reduce its effluent discharge while holding output constant by using more inputs and/or changing the input mix. Clearly, in practice it would be a very unusual firm which could not for a fixed output level reduce its effluent discharge by changing its inputs to production. Most obviously, it could use more labour and/or machinery to clean residuals from productive activity before releasing such to the environment. Given this, it is comforting to know that none of the results presented above, depend upon the rigid technology assumption, which was adopted solely for expositional convenience. In the original demonstrations of the least cost property of uniform effluent taxation (Baumol and Oates (1971)) and of marketable pollution permits (Montgomery (1972)) the rigid technology assumption was not used, but rather it was assumed that discharges could be reduced with output held constant by using extra inputs. Nor is the rigid technology assumption necessary to establish, conceptually, the existence of a Pigouvian tax at a rate equal to marginal external cost at the social optimum which can realise that social optimum level of pollution. This is made explicit in Baumol and Oates (1988) or Fisher (1981), for example. These are both relatively advanced texts in terms of economics and mathematics. In fact, flexible technologies are quite difficult to analyse without the use of mathematics, and many less advanced texts use the rigid technology assumption. An exception is Burrows (1979) where a flexible technology is modelled and analysed by means of diagrams. We can note here that it should be obvious that where firms have flexible technologies, the information requirements for implementing Pigouvian taxes will be greater than suggested in our discussion in 5.3 above.

Our numerical examples not only assumed a rigid technology, but also assumed, in effect, that such a technology was immutable and unchanging in the face of any EPA activity. Again, technological innovation in production is widely observed and the assumption of an immutable technology therefore inappropriate. This, most economists argue, strengthens the case for incentive type instruments (effluent taxation, marketable pollution permits) as against regulatory control. The reasons are fairly obvious, and are emphasised in, for example, Mills (1978) and Baumol and Oates (1979). Basically the point is that a firm told that it can discharge effluent up to amount x, has no incentive to look for ways of reducing discharges below x. On the other hand, a firm which must pay for each unit of discharge balances payments so arising against the costs of reducing discharges. This balancing was discussed at some length in 5.3 above where the firm's technology was rigid and unchangeable, with, for example, $E_1 = 0.1Q_1$. But suppose that the firm thought that it might be possible for it to devise and adopt a new technology with $E_1 = 0.05Q_1$. Then, clearly, it would weigh the costs of the switch to this new technology against the benefits of the reduced effluent tax liability in the usual way. Clearly if firms have to pay, via taxation or permit acquisition, to discharge effluent, they will have an incentive to, at least, consider new, less polluting, technologies.

We assumed throughout our discussion that polluting firms were motivated by profit maximisation. In fact, the results we obtained do not require this assumption. They require only the weaker assumption that firms seek to minimise their costs. By 'weaker assumption' we mean that, as discussed in the commentary section to Chapter 4, cost minimisation is necessary for profit maximisation. The fact that incentive-based pollution control instruments work given only the weak assumption of cost minimisation is seen by many as reassuring, since it is often argued that the profit maximisation assumption is not descriptively accurate for many productive activities.

While effluent discharge taxes and marketable pollution permits have many attractive features, we must also be clear about their limitations. We note, first, that what can be claimed for them is that they can lead to the realisation of some arbitrary standard at least cost. It cannot, generally, be claimed that the least cost involved is either small or worth incurring. Once made, this point is obvious, but appears quite often to be effectively overlooked in the advocacy of such incentive-based instruments for pollution control. We shall discuss some aspects of the assessment of the costs and benefits of pollution abatement below. A second point concerns the question of whether the cost which is minimised is the true social cost of achieving the standard. It is such if, as we assumed in the previous sections of this chapter, the externality problem which is the origin of the excessive pollution being tackled is the only departure from the ideal conditions affecting the economy we are concerned with. If the ideal conditions, discussed in Chapter 4, are not satisfied in other respects, then the market prices used to derive the control costs we are minimising will not accurately reflect relative social valuations, so that what is being minimised is not the socially appropriate minimand.

In the case of marketable, or tradeable, emissions permits, the claim that they are efficient and dependable requires the assumption that the demand side of the market for the permits is competitive so that the emissions sources act as price-takers. Where there are just a small number of firms, and/or some of the firms are very large, the possibility exists that they may act so as to manipulate the price of permits for strategic reasons such as damaging other firms in the industry. The ability to buy permits need not, in principle, be restricted to emissions sources. Those suffering pollution could buy permits and 'sterilise' them, so as to reduce the amount of pollution. If such behaviour occurred it would increase competition on the demand side of the market, and would reduce emissions below the arbitrary standard set by the EPA. In principle, this kind of behaviour could bring about the realisation of the optimal level of emissions reduction. In practice, this kind of behaviour would be expected to be unlikely, and there does not appear to be any evidence that it has actually taken place.

The analysis in the preceding sections of this chapter has assumed that the EPA could monitor the emissions behaviour of firms at no cost, and that it could enforce compliance with regulations/permit holdings at no cost. The costs of monitoring and enforcement are sometimes referred to as *compliance costs*. The assumption that compliance costs are zero is fairly standard in the environmental economics literature. In a strict sense it is clearly not valid in any pollution context. The interesting questions concern how relaxing these assumptions affects the relative merits of the different instruments, and how monitoring and enforcement costs differ across particular pollution problems. Regulation of emissions levels requires that the EPA knows how much each source emits and that each source emits only the permitted amount. Taxation requires knowledge of amounts and payment of the tax liability arising. A permit system has the same requirements as regulation, plus the requirement that the EPA knows at every point in time the actual permit holding of each source. There is a presumption that compliance costs would be higher with a tradeable permit system.

Clearly, for all instruments, compliance costs would be expected to be lower the smaller the number of sources of emissions. *Stationary sources* are things like factories and power plants, while the prime examples of *non-stationary* sources are motor vehicles. For the standard instruments, compliance costs are lower with stationary than non-stationary sources. Both factories and motor vehicles are what are known as *point sources*. The term 'non-point' is used to refer to pollution which has its origin in the run-off from agricultural land (due to the use of fertilisers and pesticides), or in the contamination of urban storm water run-off due to motor vehicle depositions on roads, for examples. *Non-point source pollution* presents obvious monitoring and enforcement problems. There are two instruments available to an EPA which can address monitoring and enforcement costs, and which are especially relevant for mobile and non-point source problems. The first is a variant on the regulation/command and control theme, where rather than specify the allowable quantities of emission, the EPA specifies allowable processes, equipment or inputs. Thus, for example, it could regulate the fuel to be burned by motor vehicles and/or the emissions control equipment that they must incorporate. This type of regulation has historically been by far the most common type of pollution control actually used. The second is the taxation of the input that is the material source of the emission of concern. Thus, for example, motor vehicle emissions could be controlled by taxing fuels at rates reflecting the arising emissions according to fuel type. Similarly, the problem of agricultural run-off could be addressed by taxing purchases of fertilisers and pesticides. In both of these cases a system of tradeable permits in inputs is an alternative to input taxation in principle, but would be expected to involve higher compliance costs.

Common (1977) showed that if the EPA knows the production function linking inputs to output and emissions, it can use input taxation to achieve an arbitrary standard at least cost. Input taxation and tradeable permits in inputs have recently attracted a lot of attention in the context of the rôle of carbon dioxide emissions in the enhanced greenhouse effect. This is because the emissions themselves would be expensive to monitor, but, where they arise in fossil fuel combustion, are known from the quantity of fossil fuel burned: see 9.7. Chapter 11 of Hanley and Spash (1993) discusses the nitrate pollution of rivers and streams and groundwater arising from the use of nitrogen fertilisers, and some attempts to control it. Chapter 17 of Tietenberg (1992) provides a useful introduction to mobile source air pollution, and an account of policies adopted to deal with it from motor vehicles in the USA.

The pollution problems addressed by the analysis considered in this chapter have no time dimension – what polluters, sufferers and any EPA do today has no implications for the situation that any of them face tomorrow. This assumption is not appropriate for many actual pollution problems, where effects over time are important, due to the fact that what is relevant to the perceived current damage is not the current flow of emissions but the accumulated stock. In such a case, we have

$$P_{t+1} = P_t + E_t - D_t$$

where P_t is the stock of pollution at the start of period t, E_t is the flow of emissions into the environment during period t, D_t is the amount by which the initial stock depreciates, or decays, during period t, and P_{t+1} is the stock at the end of period t. Often, the amount of depreciation may be assumed to be proportional to the initial stock, so that

$$P_{t+1} = P_t + E_t - d_t P_t$$

where d_t is the factor of proportionality, which has a time subscript to indicate that it may vary over time. The stock of this pollution grows or declines as E_t is greater or less than D_t. D_t may be on account of processes in the environment that transform the pollutant into something not regarded as a pollutant, or on account of physical processes which transfer the pollution out of the environment of concern. For some pollutants, such processes may be totally non-existent (heavy metals) or so slow as to be effectively non-existent (long-lived nuclear wastes). In such cases, D_t is zero and P_{t+1} is just $P_t + E_t$. Note that where D_t is not zero, setting E_t below D_t means that P_{t+1} is less than P_t. The accumulation of pollution is then a reversible process, so long as D_t is never driven to zero. For some emissions and some receiving media, depreciation may be such that there is no accumulation over time. Then, with d_t equal to one, we have:

$$P_t = E_t$$

which is the situation considered previously in this chapter.

If d_t is not equal to unity, how does this affect the analysis presented previously? It completely changes the analysis of the optimal level of pollution, but leaves un-affected the discussion of the choice between alternative instruments of policy. If account is taken of future welfare and the level of emissions now affects the future level of pollution, then clearly the optimal level of current emissions will be different from that which would be considered optimal if we did not care about the future and/or if the current level of emissions did not affect future pollution levels ($d_t = 1$). On the other hand, given that we know what we want the current level of emissions to be, the previous discussion of the means to realising that level stands. So, where there is a time dimension to a pollution problem, consideration of the optimal target for policy is different from that set out here, but consideration of policy instruments is not. We shall not here discuss the analysis of the optimal target where pollution accumulates as a stock. To do so would require some background in the role of time in economics which we will not provide until later chapters. It turns out that the analysis of stock pollution problems, in terms of optimal levels over time, is very similar to the analysis of renewable resource management problems, to be considered in Chapter 7. We shall there, in the commentary section, say a little about this similarity, and provide references to the literature. Here we can note that the relevance for policy of this literature is not very great. We have argued that in the case where pollution is a problem without a time dimension, what is policy relevant is the pursuit of arbitrary, rather than optimal, standards of control. The considerations that lead to this conclusion, essentially that the acquisition of the knowledge required for the identification of optimality is infeasible, clearly apply with greater force where there is a time dimension.

Finally here we consider the relationship between emissions from the various sources and the level of pollution as it affects sufferers and is of concern to an EPA. In our discussion in the previous sections of this chapter we made a major special assumption in this regard. If we let P_j represent the ambient pollution level in the jth sub-area of the overall area of interest, and E_i represent effluent discharges by the ith source, we assumed that

$$P_j = P = \sum_{i=1}^{N} E_i \quad \text{for } j = 1, 2, \ldots M$$

where there are M sub-areas and N sources. We assumed, that is, that effluent discharges mix perfectly in the relevant environmental media and then affect all parts of it equally. Clearly, in making such an assumption we entirely overlook many factors (topography, streamflow, prevailing winds, source locations, etc.) which are determinants of pollution dispersion processes. The study and modelling of pollution dispersion processes, as they relate ambient conditions to source discharge rates, is an important and extensive special area of study, which we cannot even begin to go into here. For our purposes, the important point to note is that the arbitrary standard of concern (or the notion of pollution levels corresponding to allocative efficiency) will refer to ambient conditions rather than to total discharges. Our special assumption made these the same, but while this simplifies it is clearly not generally appropriate. The question which then arises is: how does the analysis based on the special assumption relate to the practically relevant situations where there is not a single ambient level which is the sum of amounts discharged?

The answer to this question is basically reassuring. It is that while allowing for more complex and realistic dispersion processes complicates the story, it does not change its essentials. This is why it was legitimate to use the simple special dispersion assumption for expositional purposes. If that assumption is dropped in favour of, say,

$$P_j = P = \sum_{i=1}^{N} \alpha_i E_i \quad \text{for } j = 1, 2, \ldots M$$

where α_i is some parameter depending on the location of the ith source, then it is still true that arbitrary standards in each sub-area can be realised at least cost by emissions taxation or a system of marketable pollution permits with the advantages over the regulatory approach already discussed. It is no longer true that the tax rate is to be the same across all sources: it would have to vary with α_i. For marketable pollution permits, these would now have to be defined in terms of contributions to P rather than in terms of amounts of emissions. Also, it is clear that the information requirement placed upon the EPA is now different – it needs to know the α_i, it needs to know the pollution dispersion process.

There is now quite a substantial literature, both theoretical and empirical, dealing with pollution control policy where the target is specified in terms of ambient standards and where there is not perfect mixing and uniform dispersion. Most of this literature is quite demanding in terms of the mathematics. In Tietenberg (1992), Ch. 14 provides a relatively simple introduction to the theory, and Ch. 15 reviews some empirical work from the USA. References to the literature will be found there, and in Cropper and Oates (1992). In the next sub section we look at an empirical study which illustrates some of the issues.

Notwithstanding some recognition of the mismatch between the circumstances of the real world and the assumptions usually made in the core theoretical literature, environmental economists remain strongly committed to a presumption in favour of price incentive type instruments – taxes and tradeable permits – over regulatory instruments. As we shall consider below, their arguments to this effect have had rather little effect on the actual choice of instrument in practice, to date, though recent years have seen some changes in this respect.

On the costs and benefits of pollution abatement

We have argued that in the field of pollution control, the goal of allocative efficiency has effectively to be abandoned, in favour of the pursuit of arbitrary standards. This does not mean that there is no interest in attempting to assess the costs and benefits of pollution abatement programmes. It does mean that economists generally recognise that such cannot be measured in the way that identifying a pollution level consistent with allocative efficiency requires. But, in respect of any proposed or implemented standard, the question of the size of its benefits in relation to its costs must remain of importance. Presumably, society would not want to adopt a standard the least cost of realising which was demonstrably greatly in excess of the benefits arising. Economists recognising the difficulties and uncertainties involved, see themselves as having a rôle in providing cost and benefit estimates as inputs to the policy formation process which determines the 'arbitrary' standards adopted.

In introducing their survey of environmental economics, Cropper and Oates (1992) note that:

> The economist's view had – to the dismay of the profession – little impact on the initial surge of legislation for the control of pollution. In fact, the cornerstones of federal environmental policy in the United States, the Amendments to the Clean Air Act in 1970, and to the Clean Water Act in 1972, *explicitly* prohibited the weighing of benefits against costs in the setting of environmental standards (italics in the original).

They note some improvement in the situation in the 1980s:

> Under Executive Order 12291 issued in 1981, many proposed environmental measures have been subjected to a benefit-cost test. In addition, some more recent pieces of environmental legislation ... call for weighing benefits against costs in the setting of standards.

However, it turns out that there were legal restrictions which limited the applicability of the Executive Order, and Cropper and Oates conclude that:

> benefit cost analysis has not been entirely ignored in setting environmental standards, but its use has been selective ... EPA was allowed to weigh benefits against costs for only 5 of the 18 major regulations that it issued between 1981 and 1986.

The situation is broadly similar in other industrial economies.

Assessing the benefits of pollution reduction programmes involves practical and conceptual difficulties. It involves determining the effects of the programme and then valuing and aggregating those effects: in the case of pollution abatement benefits, market prices are often either non-existent or inappropriate for valuation purposes. Methods for non-market valuation are discussed in Chapter 8. A more comprehensive discussion, but still at an introductory level, is Hanley and Spash (1993). More advanced treatments are found in, for examples, Freeman (1979), Freeman (1985), Cropper and Oates (1992). To see what benefit assessment involves we can look at the categories of damage due to air pollution. It is usual to distinguish the following categories: human health effects, vegetation effects, material damage effects, aesthetic effects.

Human health effects associated with reduced pollution levels can be broken down into reductions in mortality and reductions in morbidity (ill health). The quantitative relationship between a reduction in the ambient level of some particular pollutant type and mortality and morbidity rates is, in all cases, uncertain, despite a great deal of research effort. On the basis of ten different statistical studies of USA data, for example, 'a decrease in sulphur and particulate pollution of, say, 50 percent would be expected to lead to a reduction in mortality of between 0.5 percent and 5 percent' (Freeman, 1982). This is a wide range of uncertainty. It arises from a variety of sources and may well be irreducible: for discussion of the issues see Lave and Seskin (1977). The range of uncertainty with respect to morbidity is perhaps even greater; for a 20% reduction in average levels of sulphate compounds and particulates, US studies give reductions in morbidity ranging from 0.2% to 8% (quoted in Freeman (1982)). The valuation of these health effects is highly contentious. With respect to mortality some argue that it is either wrong or impossible to value a human life. However, there is evidence that people are willing to pay to avoid increased risks of death, and that extra compensation is required in occupations with higher than average risks. On this basis, estimates of the value of a single avoided mortality range from $1.6 million to $9 million (Cropper and Oates 1992). With respect to morbidity, very little is known about people's willingness to pay to avoid ill-health: see Cropper and Oates (1992).

In principle the assessment of the benefits from pollution reduction associated with vegetation should be more straightforward and certain. The effects of various levels of pollution on growth should be observable, and market prices are acceptable social valuations in the case of commercial crops. However, even with attention restricted to commercial crops, there is in practice considerable uncertainty about the quantitative relationship between a given reduction in pollution of a given kind and the consequent value of increased crop yield. It is, for example, difficult to reliably extrapolate results obtained in controlled laboratory experiments on dose-response relationships to field conditions.

With respect to material damage effects matters could be expected to be even more straightforward, since the costs of coping with corrosion are well-known. While this is true, there remains, as will be illustrated below, a range of uncertainty about the reduced material damage benefits to be attributed to a given programme for improved air quality.

People may feel worse off when exposed to lower air quality even in the absence of health effects. Many people apparently do feel worse off in the presence of air pollution, over and above any allowance for the impacts already considered. The effects of pollution which are not linked to tangible physical effects are usually referred to as aesthetic, or amenity, effects. Clearly, in respect of aesthetic effects, the evaluation of the benefits of reductions in pollution levels is not a two-stage process. There are no physical effects to be measured for the attachment of per unit valuations. The usual approach to a direct valuation of aesthetic effects in urban areas is via house price differentials across locations differing in the degree of environmental pollution. A well developed statistical methodology, hedonic pricing, exists for disentangling the effect of air pollution on property values from that of other influences such as house size, proximity to job opportunities, etc. One problem which arises here is the possibility for double counting. To the extent that higher levels of air pollution reduce house prices, it cannot be assumed that the reductions reflect only aesthetic effects. Thus, if people generally are aware of the effects of air pollution on health, it has to be assumed that some part of the observed pollution reduction in house prices is attributable to people's disinclination to live in less healthy locations. Unfortunately, there is no completely reliable way of separating out the contributions from health effects, vegetation effects, materials damage effects and aesthetic effects to the overall impact of air pollution on property values.

In order to provide a quantitative perspective on the significance of the uncertainties in the assessment of air pollution damages, Table 5.9 here is reproduced from a paper by Freeman (1982), which reviewed a number of sources for estimates of physical impacts and valuations. The figures given are annual benefit estimates. Note first that for total benefits the range is from $4.6 to 51.2 billions – in round figures the range is a factor of 10. This degree of uncertainty is not untypical in studies of pollution abatement benefits. Second, note that, looking at the point estimates, some 80% of the total benefit arises in respect of health effects. In calculating, health benefits Freeman used $1 million for the value of an avoided fatality: recall that much smaller and much larger estimates can be found in the literature.

Cropper and Oates (1992) survey the literature on the benefits of pollution control in the USA. In addition to the categories of benefit discussed above, they look at recreation benefits, especially water quality improvements. We consider the valuation of non-marketed recreational facilities in Chapter 8.

We begin a discussion of the costs of pollution abatement by looking at a study which illuminates some of the previous discussion of the properties of alternative instruments that an EPA might use, in the context of a situation where it is necessary to explicitly consider the dispersion processes involved in the determination of ambient environmental quality.

In discussing this, the term *effluent charge* is used instead of 'emissions tax' for consistency with usage in the source of the study report. Kneese (1977) discusses the results of a number of studies of the economics of water quality management in a variety of geographical locations. What follows is a summary of his reporting of the results of a study of the Delaware river basin, which is a densely populated and industrial area on the eastern seaboard of the USA. The study proceeded by first constructing a mathematical model of the watercourse, concerned especially with the determination of the dissolved oxygen (DO) levels at various points according to streamflow conditions and discharges into the watercourse at a number of identified outflows. This dispersion model was used, together with information on the costs of effluent treatment at the various outflows, to determine the total costs of meeting some selected water quality standards, set in DO terms, by four different methods. Table 5.10 here gives some of the results arising in this study. The figures in the body of the table are the model estimated costs of achieving the standard indicated in the left-hand margin,

Table 5.9 Estimated air quality improvement benefits in the USA

Benefits for a 20% air quality improvement, $billions, 1978 Category	Range	Most likely point estimate
Mortality	2.8–27.8	13.9
Morbidity	0.29–11.9	3.1
Total health	3.1–39.7	17.0
Vegetation	0.2–2.4	0.7
Materials, soiling and cleaning	1.0–7.4	2.9
Property values*	1.1–8.9	2.7
Grand total[†]	4.6–51.2	21.4

* Because of overlap, property value benefits are not strictly additive with the categories.
[†] Sum of other categories and 30% of property value benefits to reflect aesthetic benefits to homeowners.
Source: Freeman (1982)

Table 5.10 Results on cost savings using effluent charges

DO objective (parts per million)	Cost of treatment under alternative programmes: Millions of dollars per year			
	FILC	UT	SECh	ZECh
2	1.6	5.0	2.4	2.4
3.4	7.0	20.0	12.0	8.6

Source: Kneese (1977)

by one of the four methods considered. FILC stands for full information least cost. This is the cost calculated by the model, in the light of the information available to it regarding treatment costs at each outflow, as the least which could be incurred in order to meet the indicated standard. The implementation of the pattern of discharges from the various outflows identified by the model as corresponding to these cost figures would require the river basin authority to tell each outflow operator how much to discharge. This FILC solution does not require equal treatment levels at all outflow points.

UT stands for uniform treatment. 'In this solution each waste discharger is required to remove a given percentage of the wastes previously discharged. The percentage is the minimum needed to achieve the DO standard in the stream and is the same at each point of discharge. This solution may be considered typical of the conventional administrative effluent standards approach to the problem of achieving a stream quality standard' (Kneese, p. 163, 1977). The total treatment costs are, for both standards, much greater with this conventional uniform standards programme than the computed least cost.

SECh stands for single effluent charge. Under this scheme the model computes the cost of achieving the specified standard if each outflow operator independently minimises his overall costs given that he faces a charge per unit discharge. The charge is the same for all outflows: the model computes the uniform charge required for achieving the standard. This method of achieving the required standard is an application to a particular case of the approach of the least cost theorem as set out in 5.3 above. The cost reductions over the uniform treatment approach are very large. The reader will notice, however, that costs are not reduced to those identified by the model as least. This appears to mean that the least cost theorem has not worked! Not so, because the conditions in the Delaware river basin model are not those for which the least cost theorem was considered in 5.3. The point is that in the model used in this study, achievement of the specified standard is required in a particular stretch of the Delaware river. The contribution of the various outflows to river quality in that stretch depends not only upon discharge levels at the various outflows, but also on where in the river basin the outflows are located. The further an outflow is from the river stretch where the standard is set, the less its impact, per unit of discharge, on quality in the river stretch of concern. The conditions we assumed for the least cost theorem in 5.3 abstract from this sort of phenomenon, as noted above. The simplification we made in 5.3 in no way affects the real operational content of the theorem: at the cost of some complication in specification and proof, it can readily be modified to handle differential contributions across sources according to location. The result then obtained is that the tax rate or effluent charge should vary according to source location, in a manner fixed by the physical process which relates discharges by site to the pollution level.

This is shown, for the Delaware study, in the last column of Table 5.10. This is headed ZECh, which stands for zone effluent charge. In this solution the model imposes a uniform effluent charge on all of the outflows in each of the zones distinguished: within each zone, every outflow faces the same charge per unit of effluent. The model computes the zone effluent charges which give the lowest cost of achieving the standard. Charges differ across zones because discharges in different zones contribute differently to standard realisation, as discussed above. With zone differentiated effluent charging, the cost of meeting the higher standard is reduced below that with uniform charging across zones, and approaches the absolute minimum identified by the model in the light of all of the relevant information. The reason why the ZECh minimised cost is greater than the least cost identified by the model is because of the relatively small number of zones – 3 – according to which charge differentiation is allowed. As more zones were distinguished so the ZECh figure would approach more closely the FILC figure. However, this would increase the administrative complexity of the system. The important points are, first, that the information required to go from SECh to ZECh is contained in the streamflow or dispersion model. A river basin authority implementing such a system would not need detailed information on treatment costs at each outflow to operate either SECh or ZECh. The model used such information to identify the FILC solution in terms of permitted discharges at each outflow. Second, the relevant comparison is between SECh or ZECh and UT, the latter being, as noted above, the conventional approach. The effluent charging system, of either variety, is demonstrated to be more cost effective than the conventional approach.

This study of pollution abatement costs is based on empirical modelling, rather than on actual experience, as are many of the studies reported in the literature. That literature addresses two main questions. First, what have the costs of actually adopted pollution abatement programmes been? Second, how large are the cost savings associated with the use of more efficient instruments, such as price incentives, rather than less efficient instruments, such as regulation? The Delaware study just discussed addressed this second question: more recent studies will be considered below.

Jorgenson and Wilcoxen (1990) used a model of the USA economy to examine the costs of environmental regulation there. They begin by noting that whereas over the period 1947 to 1973 the average annual growth rate for national income, Gross National Product (to be discussed in 9.4) was 3.7%, over the period 1973 to 1985 it was only 2.5%. Two events coincided with this slowdown – the oil price increase of 1973/4 and 'the advent of environmental regulation'. The model of the economy is used to separate out the effect of the latter. Jorgenson and Wilcoxen find that, given their model, a reduction of 0.191% in the growth rate for 1973 to 1985 can be attributed to environmental regulation. They consider this a large effect: 'we show that pollution abatement has emerged as a major claimant on the resources of the US economy'. The use of the adjective 'major' here is, of course, a matter of judgement. Others have taken these results to show that pollution control costs were relatively minor, and, for example, cited them as evidence for the argument that high pollution control costs could not have been responsible for industry leaving the USA, since the costs were not high (Esty 1994).

How large are the cost savings offered by price incentive instruments? This question has been addressed in a number of studies, including the Delaware study discussed above. Hahn and Hester (1989b), and see also Hahn (1993), look at experience in the USA with the introduction of emissions trading in relation to atmospheric emissions over the period 1974 to 1986. Most of this trading was in the form of 'netting', whereby a firm that creates a new source of emissions in a plant can avoid the emissions limits that would otherwise apply by reducing emissions from another source in the plant. Hahn and Hester estimate the number of such 'trades' as between 5000 and 12 000, and the cost savings arising as between US$500 million and US$12 billion. This is a wide range! Basically, the problem is that the 'trades' are internal to firms, so that neither the number of such nor the cost savings involved in each case are part of the public record. In 1979 the EPA allowed 'bubbles', by means of which emissions standards apply to a whole plant, rather than to individual sources within the plant. Hahn and Hester estimate that 'bubbles' saved US$435 million in compliance costs over the period. It should be noted that 'netting' and 'bubbles' are not really examples of tradeable permits as envisaged in the theoretical literature. They are, rather, in the nature of more flexible systems of regulation.

Most studies of the cost savings attributable to price incentives as envisaged by economists are based on models rather than actual experience, since as discussed below, there is little actual experience to draw upon. Hahn and Hester (1989a) report savings of some US$230 million for an actual tradeable permits scheme in the USA for the use of lead additives in gasoline. However, it turns out that this is an EPA estimate made before the scheme started. Hahn and Hester offer the opinion that, as trading activity was higher than expected, the actual savings are likely to have been greater. They also report on an actual trading system, that is one involving permit trades between different firms, started in 1981 in Wisconsin for discharges into the Fox River. Modelling studies, similar to that for the Delaware described above, prior to the introduction of the system indicated annual savings of the order of US$7 million. In fact, actual cost savings have been 'minimal', and there have been very few actual trades between firms.

Pollution control instruments in practice

The position on the correspondence between what is argued in the economics literature regarding the choice of pollution control instrument and what happens in legislative choice from among the range of alternative instruments is neatly summarised as follows:

> With few exceptions, the economics literature ... is strongly in favour of using incentive-based instruments for environmental policy, in particular effluent taxes, but also corresponding subsidies or tradeable pollution certificates. The regulatory approach on the other hand ... is with few exceptions rejected. However, there are but few cases in which incentive-based instruments have been applied in practical environmental policy, regulation is the dominating approach.

This quotation dates from 1985 (Frey *et al.* 1985). Another from that year is:

> Over the long sweep of history direct regulations (prohibitions, specifications of behaviour, nonmarketable permits to discharge) have been the instruments of actual choice for dealing with pollution, whether from geese in village brooks or petroleum refineries on major rivers. Unlike commodity prices and markets, which existed before economists began analysing them, administratively set prices or legislatively created markets do not appear to have sprung up as intuitive responses to externality problems. Quite the reverse: even after sustained intellectual development of these concepts in the period since 1960, we can find few examples of their application.
>
> (Bohm and Russell 1985).

The situation has not materially changed since 1985. While economists' advocacy of price incentive instruments has continued, there have been but few instances of governments actually introducing them. For the OECD countries, the situation is reviewed in OECD (1989). Some cases of pollution charges in use in OECD countries are reported, but in many cases the objective is the recovery of the regulatory agency's costs rather then to affect behaviour via price incentives. Hahn (1995) considers the situation in Europe.

In the UK environmental protection has long been predominantly by way of regulation: see Lowe and Lewis (1980) or Sandbach (1982). In the report of the Royal Commission on Environmental Pollution (1984) past experience and future prospects for pollution control were discussed – nowhere in the report was there any mention of the use of taxation or tradeable permits. While these instruments are still not used at all widely, there has recently been an upsurge of interest in them as alternatives to regulation, among politicians and the business community as well as academic economists: see Jacobs (1995). Much the same situation applies in Australia: see Christoff (1995).

As suggested in the previous subsection, the situation in the USA is somewhat different. While the principal approach historically has been regulatory, Mills (1978) and Baumol and Oates (1979), in recent years policy makers have shown interest in combining that approach with price incentives, particularly in the context of stationary source atmospheric pollution. Moves toward something approximating to a tradeable permit system were discussed above: see also Blackman and Baumol (1980), McGartland and Oates (1985), and Tietenberg (1992). It is interesting that whereas most of the interest in the OECD countries has been in emissions taxation, in the USA this has received relatively little attention, and it is tradeable permits that have been advocated and experimented with: see Nelson (1987).

The question arises as to why legislators have been so slow to heed the advice of economists in this area. A number of possible answers, not mutually exclusive, are reviewed in Common (1989). One is that the standard economic analysis overlooks important aspects of the problem that politicians and their advisers are more aware of. There are two dimensions to this. The first concerns the criteria against which alternative instruments are evaluated. Economists focus almost exclusively on abatement costs and, to a lesser extent, dependability. Bohm and Russell (1985) and Baumol and Oates (1979) consider a wider range of criteria, some of which, such as voter acceptability and perceived equity, are likely to be of at least as much interest to policy makers as efficiency. It may be that one of the factors behind the increasing interest in price incentive type instruments for environmental protection in the last decade has been the overall political tendency in industrial countries toward placing greater weight on efficiency considerations generally, and restraining government expenditure, and less on equity considerations. In this light, one point of difference between emissions taxation and tradeable emissions permit systems is of interest. The former raises revenue for the government, whereas the latter does not. Economists are showing increasing interest in the revenue potential of environmental taxation.

The second dimension concerns the characteristics of pollution problems.

We have already noted, for example, that the economics literature largely ignores the costs of monitoring and enforcement. Baumol and Oates (1979) note that 'there are some very important circumstances in which direct controls seem distinctly superior to fees', where by 'fees' they mean emissions taxation. They distinguish three considerations that can favour regulation over 'fees': metering, i.e. monitoring, problems; uncertainty; extremely hazardous pollutants.

Clearly, in order to levy a charge per unit of effluent discharged or to ensure that effluent is discharged only up to the extent that permits are held, an EPA must measure effluent discharged. As Baumol and Oates (1979, p. 308) put it: 'Economists have often been somewhat cavalier in their single minded advocacy of pricing techniques without much consideration of the metering issue.' It also has to be noted that if metering is impossible or very costly, the ensuing difficulty for control via effluent charges or permits also applies to systems which seek to impose direct controls on the amount of effluent discharged by firms. An approach which avoids this problem is that which specifies treatment procedures or the use of only approved types of process and/or equipment. This does not require continuous metering. It requires periodic inspection to ensure that the prescribed procedures and equipment are being followed and used. As documented in, for example, Mills (1978) and Lowe and Lewis (1980), such an approach to environmental protection is widely followed.

The environmental uncertainty problem for emissions fees arises from the fact that the implications of a given level of emissions for environmental quality depend upon environmental conditions. Baumol and Oates (1979, p. 310) cite as an example the case of auto emissions, where modest levels which 'may pose a negligible threat to human health and well-being during normal weather conditions ... may have grave consequences during an atmospheric 'inversion' which prevents the escape of the pollutants'. The problem is that the environmental conditions which create the environmental pollution problem are typically not predictable much in advance of their occurrence. Should effluent charges be set so as to achieve the required pollution standard in the face of the adverse environmental conditions? This would mean high fees, high costs, and over achievement with respect to the standard for most of the time when environmental conditions are normal. On the other hand, while it is not infeasible to vary the effluent charge according to environmental conditions, it is the case that a higher fee level during critical periods can be expected to have only minimal effects on the quantity of emissions as there is insufficient time for adjustment to the higher fee level. However, it is, of course, precisely during such critical periods that a reduction in the quantity of emissions is required. In such circumstances there is a clear rôle for direct controls, such as simply banning temporarily any emissions at the onset of the adverse environmental conditions. Such a use of direct controls at times of crisis does not preclude the use of emissions charges as well 'in order to bring basic pollution-abatement procedures into line with normal environmental conditions' (Baumol and Oates, p. 311, 1979).

With extremely hazardous pollutants, a simple prohibition on the emission of such may well be appropriate. In this limiting case, the prohibition is formally equivalent to setting the effluent discharge tax at an infinite rate, i.e. at a rate so high that there are no conceivable circumstances under which anybody would pay it. The simplest way to impose such a charge is to prohibit the discharge of the pollutants.

There is, in fact, a class of instrument for pollution control that we have not yet considered, which has been very popular in practice with governments. We have not considered *moral suasion* previously because it does not figure much in the economics literature. Moral suasion involves the manipulation of the preferences of and information available to individuals, and of the information available to firms. Particular forms include:

- product labelling regulations
- publicity campaigns and the exhortation of 'environmentally friendly' behaviour
- financing research on pollution prevention and the dissemination of the arising results
- facilitating the activities of environmental pressure groups

Given that such instruments do not have specified quantitative targets, evaluation of their effectiveness is difficult. This may be one reason for their popularity. Economists are typically sceptical about the efficacy of moral suasion.

Economy-wide analysis of pollution reduction possibilities

In the commentary section of Chapter 4 we noted the existence of the methodology of input–output analysis, and indicated that it could be used to explore trade-offs between commodity production and environmental quality. The point of departure for input–output analysis is the observation that the various industries in an economy are interdependent, in as much as any one industry uses as inputs to its production the outputs of other industries. In much of economic analysis it is convenient and legitimate, as we have done in this chapter, to ignore these inter-industry flows. However, for some purposes it is illuminating to trace out their implications. This task is in input–output analysis made feasible by assuming that in the production of a given commodity there are no possibilities for substitution as between different inputs – to produce one unit of the commodity 'cars' requires exactly a units of steel, b units of energy, c units of plastic, d units of labour and so on. Clearly, the assumption of fixed coefficients in production processes is a strong one. It means, for example, that input mixes cannot respond to changing relative prices. However, the assumption greatly facilitates the analysis and is generally regarded as acceptable for the purposes for which it is used.

The basic exposition of how the input–output methodology can be used to explore trade-offs between commodity production and levels of pollution is given in Leontief (1970), where a simple numerical example is used. More general expositions are accessible only to those familiar with matrix algebra:

examples are Stone (1972) and Kneese (1977). Given data on inter-industry commodity flows and discharges into the environment, the mathematical technique of linear programming can be used to explore the way in which social choices as between commodity consumption mixes and available production technologies would respond to different social valuations of commodities and environmental quality. O'Connor and Henry (1975) provide an introduction to the use of linear programming with input–output data, Kneese (1977) discusses some applications to environmental issues, and Nijkamp (1980) provides an exhaustive (and heavily mathematical) account of the current state of the art in respect of environmental analysis using input–output techniques and their extensions.

Examples of the application of these techniques to data for actual economies are Leontief and Ford (1972), Ridker (1972) and Victor (1972). We briefly discuss some of the Leontief and Ford results to indicate the nature of the insights that input–output analysis can provide. This study is concerned with exploring the relationship between air pollution and patterns of economic activity in the USA. They consider discharges of five pollutants arising in the production of 90 commodities. In the production of the commodity 'household furniture' there are no pollutant discharges at all. However, considering an increase in the output of this commodity worth $1 million Leontief and Ford find that total USA residuals discharges would increase by:

11.75 tons for particulates
31.14 tons for sulphur oxides
3.6 tons for hydrocarbons
46.02 tons for carbon monoxide
4.97 tons for nitrogen oxides

Although furniture production itself is non-polluting, it uses inputs, the production of which is polluting. Thus, for example, electric lathes used in furniture factories create no airborne residual discharges, but the generation of the electricity they consume does, and in fairly large amounts. This is exactly the kind of hidden environmental impact that input–output methods can reveal.

As a second example from the Leontief and Ford study, consider their analysis of the implications of meeting the requirements, in 20 industries, of the 1967 Clean Air Act. They express their results in terms of price increases. They find that the price of the commodity household furniture would rise by 0.4%, notwithstanding the fact that the standard imposed in no way directly affects furniture production as no air pollution arises in such production itself. One of the reasons the price of furniture rises is because electricity costs rise: Leontief and Ford find a 7% increase in the price of electricity. The largest price increase they identify is 17% for non-ferrous metals: the smallest is 0.08% for tobacco products. The increase in the price of the output of the petroleum refining industry is just 0.2%, which indicates that in terms of its own activities and the production of the inputs it uses petroleum refining is a (surprisingly?) low ranking generator of atmospheric pollution.

In 7.5 we shall consider the use of input-methods to study the ways in which an economy uses energy, and especially the fossil fuels. The relevance of these methods is that some productive activities use little energy directly, but use inputs which have been produced using energy. Modern agriculture, for example, uses lots of fertiliser, the production of which involves large inputs of energy: see Leach (1975). As noted in 7.5, fossil fuel combustion is a major source of, especially atmospheric, pollution of several kinds. Among the atmospheric emissions involved is carbon dioxide. As discussed in Chapter 9, increasing atmospheric concentrations of this gas play a major rôle in the enhanced greenhouse effect, which is expected to change the global climate. Input–output methods have been used to study the important question of the relationship between the consumption mix and an economy's total carbon dioxide emissions: see, for examples, Proops *et al.* (1993), Common and Salma (1992).

So, input–output methods are of considerable value in understanding the less obvious aspects of the relationship between economic activity and environmental quality. A major lesson is that changes in the consumption mix can have large, and sometimes unexpected, effects on the amounts of pollution generated in the economy. Even with input mixes fixed and pollution generation coefficients fixed in each line of production, less pollution does not necessarily mean less economic activity but can be realised by changes in the mix of consumption across different commodities. The assumption made in input–output analysis that input mixes and pollution coefficients with respect to output levels are fixed is a simplifying assumption which permits the analysis of very large amounts of data. It is, we have noted earlier in this commentary, and elsewhere, an assumption that we would not generally expect to be valid in circumstances of changing relative prices. To the extent that input mixes and pollution coefficients change as we would expect them to in the face of changing relative prices, so input–output analysis would, for example, understate the leverage that a system of effluent charges would exert on environmental quality. None the less it remains a useful tool for exploring the quantitative dimensions of the relationship between the level and pattern of economic activity and environmental quality.

Trade and the environment

Economists generally believe that environmental considerations do not undermine the case for free trade:

> trade *per se* is not a direct cause of environmental problems. Some distortion must be present – most obviously, the absence of an appropriate environmental policy – in order for there to be a possibility that international trade will create or worsen environmental problems.

This quotation is from Anderson (1992a), where there is a more extended account of the analysis considered here in 5.4: see also Runge (1995). The conclusion here is that there is no environmental case for policies to restrict trade, provided that, optimal, policies to address environmental problems directly are in place. The absence of distortions condition, equivalently the existence of optimal environmental policies condition, greatly limits the relevance of the conclusion. Such environmental policies are not generally in place.

In 5.4 we showed that, on standard assumptions, where an opening to trade meant that a country became an importer of a good the production of which involved polluting emissions, there would definitely be a welfare gain. If a country becomes an exporter, there is definitely a gain only if there is simultaneously introduced optimal, in the sense of fully internalising the external costs arising, pollution control. We have argued that the informational requirements for optimal pollution control are such that it is, generally, an infeasible policy objective. The analysis in 5.4 also incorporates a number of other special assumptions. It assumes, for example, that the country is a price-taker on the world market, so that shifting the domestic supply function has no effect on the world price: see Anderson (1992a) for discussion of the consequences of dropping this assumption.

Whatever the welfare implications, the analysis of the exporter case in 5.4 indicates that controlling domestic pollution will reduce domestic producer's surplus. The loss of international competitiveness argument frequently arises in debates over domestic environmental policy. The basic argument is that unless all nations introduce environmental protection policy, those that do will suffer at the expense of those that do not – that production will move to *pollution havens*. According to Esty (1994):

> Politically, no trade and environment issue commands more attention than the potential loss of jobs to overseas producers that can achieve lower production costs because of the low environmental standards ... in which they operate.

This is a source of both opposition to domestic policy to protect the environment, and of calls for trade measures to protect domestic industry against low overseas environmental standards. Esty notes that most economists 'see the competitiveness argument as a nonissue and potentially protectionist contrivance' and consequently 'argue against trade measures aimed at addressing environmentally derived competitiveness concerns'. Economists treat these arguments as nonissues because 'study after study has concluded that differences in environmental compliance costs are rarely a serious competitiveness factor' (Esty 1994). Porter (1990) argues that domestic environmental policies may actually enhance an industry's competitive position by encouraging technological innovation; see also Cairncross (1992). In any event, the intersection of domestic environmental concerns and policies with trade issues is the subject of much political debate: Esty (1994) describes how such issues have been handled by, and influenced, the main international organisation responsible for overseeing trade arrangements and practices.

Competitiveness concerns arise in, but are not confined to Type I situations as distinguished in 5.4. They are also a major issue in deliberations over responses to the enhanced greenhouse effect. This is an example of a Type III situation, which will be discussed at length in 9.7. An example of a Type II situation is the *acid rain problem*. While there is disagreement about some of the dimensions of this problem, it appears to be agreed that a major element is the long distance transport in the atmosphere of sulphur emissions arising in fossil fuel, especially coal, combustion: see Pearce (1987). Often the emissions cross national frontiers so that some of the damaging depositions take place in a country different to that where the fossil fuel combustion occurs. The damage is mainly in the form of the corrosion of buildings and other man-made structures, the loss of biotic populations in rivers and lakes, and harm to forests which reduces timber productivity and the amenity services provided. In regard to the damage to the natural environment, the extent of the damage for a given level of deposition varies with geological and soil conditions in the deposition area.

The problem of acid rain is seen as serious in Europe and North America. In the latter case, the situation approximates to that shown in Figure 5.17, in that while emissions get transported both ways across the border, the balance of cross border damage imposition is dominantly from the US to Canada. In Europe the situation in regard to trans-frontier damage flows is obviously much more complex. However, some countries such as the UK are clearly net damage exporters, while others such as Norway are clearly damage importers. Mäler (1990) discusses how the principles discussed using Figure 5.17 could work in the context of the acid rain situation in Europe, using the analytical framework of game theory, which is discussed in 8.4.

Finally here there are two points that can usefully be made. The first is that it makes little sense to be for or against international trade in general on environmental grounds. Arguments can be made in some cases that free trade promotes environmental objectives, while in others contrary arguments can be made. The matter is essentially empirical and to be considered on a case by case basis: Anderson (1992b) reports the results of a study of the environmental implications of increased world trade in agricultural products, and provides reference to other studies. The second is that the current world situation is not one of general free trade. Restrictions on trade are in fact ubiquitous. Most economists deplore this.

Government failure

Restrictions on free trade in goods and services are maintained by national governments. Economists see some government behaviour as preventing the realisation of the benefits from the operation of free markets. Given that we have discussed environmental pollution as a market failure problem, it is necessary to make the point that while this is the way that economists mainly approach the problem, this does not imply that they see governmental action as always being welfare improving, either generally or in the particular context of the natural environment.

Some economists have argued that the democratic political process is to be understood by applying to it the assumption of self-interested behaviour used for the analysis of markets processes; see, for example, Buchanan and Tullock (1980). The basic argument is that the result of the pursuit of self-interest by actors in the political process does not lead to it adopting policy objectives, or using policy instruments, which are consistent with efficiency, or with social justice. Rather, the outcomes reflect the relative strengths, and the interests, of the actors within the process. Frey *et al.* (1985), for example, propose that the explanation for the limited extent to which price incentive instruments have actually been used in pollution control lies in the self-interest of the public servants who advise politicians and run pollution control systems. Their argument is that, as compared with price incentive systems, the regulatory approach involves more jobs, and power, for public servants.

Pollution problems have not been solely a problem in societies with democratic political systems and economies run, mainly, on the basis of markets. Since the breakup of the former Soviet Union, the full extent of the environmental damage that occurred in that version of a command and control economy has become clear – widespread and severe atmospheric, soil and water pollution, deforestation and desertification. Many would argue that environmental damage in the former Soviet Union and its satellites was much worse than in the western industrial economies: see, for example, Bernstam (1991).

Notes

1. The required tax rate here was actually calculated as follows. $E = 0.01Q^2$ implies $Q = 10E^{\frac{1}{2}}$, so that $NPB = 12Q - Q^2$ and $EC = 2Q + 0.51Q^2$ can be written as $NPB = 120E^{\frac{1}{2}} - 100E$ and $EC = 20E^{\frac{1}{2}} + 51E$ giving $MNPB = 60E^{-\frac{1}{2}} - 100$ and $MEC = 10E^{-\frac{1}{2}} + 51$. Setting $MNPB = MEC$ and solving for E gives $E_s^* = 0.11$. With effluent taxation at the per unit rate of t, $MNPB = 60E^{-\frac{1}{2}} - 100 - t$ and setting this equal to zero with $E = 0.11$ and solving for t gives $t = 81.2$.

2. For CC_1, for example, the algebra goes as follows:

$$
\begin{aligned}
CC_1 &= 36 - 120(0.6 - A_1) + 100(0.6 - A_1)^2 \\
&= 36 - 72 + 120A_1 + 100(0.36 + A_1^2 - 1.2A_1) \\
&= -36 + 120A_1 + 36 + 100A_1^2 - 120A_1 \\
\therefore AC_1 &= 100A_1^2
\end{aligned}
$$

3. This statement is actually somewhat over-strong. It would probably be the case that it would be more costly to the EPA to issue many regulations to many firms than to declare a single uniform effluent tax rate. However, EPA administration costs are ignored in the analysis here as they are in much of the literature. Some other considerations favouring taxation over regulation will be mentioned in the commentary section at the end of the chapter.

4. Some, attentive, readers may think that something has gone wrong when

they look at DD together with the demand functions for the two firms shown in the middle panels of Figure 5.14. DD shows the demand for permits as zero at $P = 72$, whereas the left middle panel shows 1 having a positive permit demand for P up to £120. Nothing has, in fact, gone wrong. At P in excess of £60, 2's demand for permits is negative. It would, for $P > 60$, be a net supplier of permits, its supply offsetting some of firm 1's demand.

Chapter 6

Time in Economic Analysis

Thus far we have considered the economic problem and responses to it in a timeless context. We have been able to look at the economics of environmental pollution within this context. The next environmental question to be considered is the exploitation of natural resources. This question cannot be looked at in a timeless context, since the essential issues which arise are about allocation over competing uses at different points in time. Hence, before looking at natural resources we must extend our economic analysis to encompass allocation over time. This we do in this chapter. The next chapter uses the concepts and results discussed here to look at natural resources and their exploitation over time.

6.1 Consumption and saving

In this section we discuss the analysis of household decisions which involve choice over time. We shall see that this analysis is not essentially different from the analysis of household decisions concerning commodity consumption levels at a point in time, which we discussed in Chapters 3 and 4. We need here some new terminology, but the basic elements of the analysis are the same – a statement of the opportunities which are open to the household, and a preference system for selection from among such opportunities.

We shall, to simplify, consider just two periods of time, to be labelled 0 and 1. The household receives on the first day of each period some income, Y_0 and Y_1. The household's problem is to decide how much to spend on commodities in each period: we shall call its total expenditure on commodities in each period *consumption*, and use the symbols, C_0 and C_1 for consumption in each period. The household has to decide upon C_0 and C_1 on the first day of the first period, when it knows with certainty what Y_0 is and what Y_1 will be. We shall call the difference between Y_0 and C_0 *saving*, denoted S_0. On the first day of the first period the household, given Y_0 and Y_1, chooses C_0, and thus S_0, and C_1, and contracts to buy the commodities which comprise C_0 and C_1, for delivery on the first day of each period. Given that C_0 is not necessarily equal to Y_0, it must also consider contracts concerning *bonds*, which contracts are the means by which it takes care of the difference between C_0 and Y_0, and shifts consumption over time.

The buyer of a bond gives up something now in exchange for the entitlement to something in the future: the seller of a bond acquires something now in exchange for the commitment to provide something in the future. It is convenient, and corresponds with standard practice, to think of the 'something' here as money, and this we shall do. We must, however, emphasise yet again that money is just a proxy for real, physical, things. While we shall discuss contracts in bonds in terms of money units, we could do so in terms of units of apples, pears or whatever. To put this another way, we are saying that while the buyer of a bond exchanges money now for money in the future, this does not represent an interest in money units as such, but is a convenient way of exchanging command over (i.e. the ability to consume) real physical commodities now for command over real physical commodities in the future. With this in mind, a bond is, physically, a piece of paper which says 'the owner of this bond will receive £x on date y from the person named here on return of this bond to such person'. To proceed we shall assume that the household must, on the first day of the first period, consider buying or selling bonds for which £x is £1.05, for which the date y is the first day of period 1, and for which the market price is £1. In this situation, the household faces an *interest rate* which is 5%, or 0.05 as it is more usually expressed in economics. We shall use the symbol r for the interest rate. Generally, we have

$$r = (x - P_B)/P_B \qquad [6.1]$$

where x is the sum to be received one period hence and P_B is the price paid for the bond now. For the household we have considered above $x = £1.05$ and $P_B = £1$.

In Figure 6.1 we set out the opportunities open to the household, in (a), and its preferences over such, in (b). If the reader refers back to Figure 4.5, and the discussion thereof, he will see the essential correspondence between the analysis there and what follows here. In Figure 6.1(a), the feasible consumption set, the opportunities open to the household, is given by the triangle $0AA'$. The *budget line AA'* gives all those combinations of C_0 and C_1, which are such that all of the income arising in the two periods is spent on consumption in one or other of the periods. The point E corresponds to $C_0 = Y_0$ and $C_1 = Y_1$, with zero saving in period 0. Moving upwards along AA' from E, C_0 is less than Y_0 so that saving is positive and so C_1 is greater than Y_1. Moving down AA' from E, C_0 is greater than Y_0 so that saving is negative giving C_1 less than Y_1. Positive saving would involve the household in buying bonds, negative saving would mean selling bonds. In the former case the household gets C_1 greater than Y_1 by virtue of saving and the interest it has earned: in the latter case C_1 is less than Y_1 by virtue of the

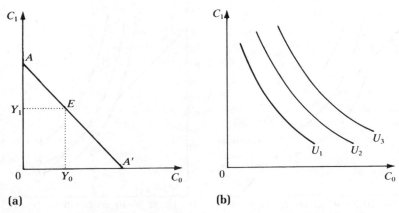

Figure 6.1 Opportunities and preferences for consumption shifting by borrowing/lending

need to repay what has been borrowed plus interest. The equation for AA' in Figure 6.1(a) is

$$C_1 = Y_1 + (Y_0 - C_0)(1 + r) = Y_1 + S_0(1 + r) \qquad [6.2]$$

and we see that as S_0 is positive or negative so C_1 exceeds or is less than Y_1 to an extent dependent on the size of r. With S_0 positive the household buys bonds in amount $B_0 = S_0$, and so receives £$S_0(1 + r)$ on the first day of period 1. With S_0 negative it sells $B_0 = S_0$ on the first day of period 0, and so from Y_1 it has an obligation pay out £$S_0(1 + r)$ on the first day of period 1 to those who purchased the bonds it sold.

Now, the household has preferences as between consumption in the two periods, which we describe in the same way as we described preferences over commodities at a point in time (see 3.1 and 4.3 especially). Figure 6.1(b) shows some indifference curves representing the household's preferences over C_0 and C_1, derived from the household's utility function. All combinations of C_0 and C_1 lying along U_1 give rise to the same level of the utility index, and in this sense the household is indifferent as between all such combinations. All combinations lying along U_2 are equivalent in terms of satisfaction, and all such combinations are preferred to, give rise to more satisfaction than, combinations lying along U_1. Similarly the level of the utility index U_3 is greater than U_2, with the same interpretation for C_0/C_1 combinations lying along U_3 and U_2. The indifference curves shown in Figure 6.1(b) are just a selection of the very many such which could be drawn representing small differences in the level taken by the utility index.

The analysis proceeds, as in the consideration of choice over commodities in Figure 4.5 (for example), by bringing together opportunities and preferences to find that available C_0/C_1 combination which gives the greatest

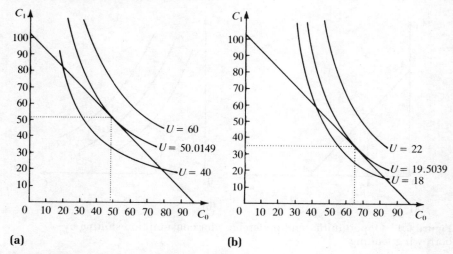

Figure 6.2 Intertemporal utility maximisation

satisfaction as measured by the utility index. Figure 6.2 shows what is involved using two numerical examples. In both cases we have $Y_0 = Y_1 = £50$ and $r = 0.05$ so that the budget line is exactly the same in parts (a) and (b), and is

$$C_1 = 50 + \{1.05(50 - C_0)\} \qquad [6.3]$$

from equation [6.2] above. An alternative derivation of this budget line, which perhaps indicates more clearly how consumption is shifted over time by buying and selling bonds, is given in Table 6.1. The first column identifies period 0 consumption levels, and the second translates these into period 0 savings and bond purchases/sales: a minus sign indicates dis-saving to be financed by the sale of bonds. Where the second column entry is positive, $1.05B_0$, shown in the third column, gives receipts from bond redemption available, in addition to income, for consumption expenditure in period 1. Where the entry in the second column is negative, the third column entry is also negative, indicating the expenditure required, out of period 1 income, to redeem in period 1 bonds sold in period 0, thereby reducing consumption in period 1. The slope of the budget line in Figure 6.2 is 1.05, so that, as shown in Table 6.1, increasing C_0 by £1 always reduces C_1 by £1.05. The opportunity cost of £1 of C_0 is, that is, £1.05 of C_1. Put the other way round, and reading up Table 6.1, we see that forgoing £1 of C_0 increases C_1 by £1.05.

From our discussion of choice over commodities, in section 4.3, we know that utility is maximised where the budget line is tangential to an indifference curve. In Figure 6.2(a) the household's utility function is

$$U = C_0^{\frac{1}{2}} C_1^{\frac{1}{2}} \qquad [6.4]$$

Table 6.1 Shifting consumption over time

C_0	$S_0 = 50 - C_0 = B_0$	$1.05B_0$	$C_1 = 50 + 1.05B_0$
0	50	52.5	102.5
1	49	51.45	101.45
2	48	50.40	100.40
3	47	49.35	99.35
.	.	.	.
.	.	.	.
47	3	3.15	53.15
48	2	2.10	52.10
49	1	1.05	51.05
50	0	0	50
51	−1	−1.05	48.95
52	−2	−2.10	47.90
.	.	.	.
.	.	.	.
95	−45	−47.25	2.75
96	−46	−48.30	1.70
97	−47	−49.35	0.65
97.62	−47.62	−50	0

and the utility maximising position is $C_0 = £48.81$ and $C_1 = £51.25$, so that the household saves and buys bonds in period 0. As Figure 6.2(b) shows, households do not necessarily choose positive saving. The outcome depends on the interaction between preferences and opportunities. For (b) household preferences are given by

$$U = C_0^{\frac{1}{2}} C_1^{\frac{1}{4}} \tag{6.5}$$

and utility maximisation leads to $C_0 = £65.08$ and $C_1 = £34.17$. In this case, $S_0 = £(50 - 65.08) = -£15.08$, so that the household dis-saves in period 0 financing consumption over income by the sale of £15.08 worth of bonds to be redeemed for $£(15.08 \times 1.05) = £15.83$ in period 1, leaving $C_1 = £(50 - 15.83) = £34.17$.

We noted above that the slope of the budget line in Figure 6.2, where the interest rate is 0.05, is 1.05. Generally, the slope of the budget line giving the terms on which C_0 and C_1 can be exchanged, by saving/dis-saving effected by buying/selling bonds, is $1 + r$. This is simply because £1 not consumed in period 0 but used to buy a bond, makes $£(1 + r)$ available in period 1. It will be obvious from Figure 6.2 that changes in the interest rate facing a household will, for given preferences, change its utility maximising choice of C_0 and C_1, as such changes alter the slope of the budget line. This is directly analogous to the effects of changing relative prices in the analysis of the choice of commodity consumption levels discussed in 4.3. Indeed, it will be apparent that one plus the interest rate is just the price of period 0

Table 6.2 The effects of interest rate variation

(a) $U = C_0^{\frac{1}{2}} C_1^{\frac{1}{2}}$

r	C_0	S_0	$C_1 = Y_1 + (1 + r)S_0$
0.01	49.7525	0.2475	$50.25 = 50 + (1.01 \times 0.2475)$
0.05	48.8095	1.1905	$51.25 = 50 + (1.05 \times 1.1905)$
0.10	47.7272	2.2728	$52.50 = 50 + (1.10 \times 2.2728)$
0.15	46.7391	3.2609	$53.75 = 50 + (1.15 \times 3.2609)$
0.20	45.8333	4.1667	$55.00 = 50 + (1.20 \times 4.1667)$

(b) $U = C_0^{\frac{1}{2}} C_1^{\frac{1}{4}}$

r	C_0	S_0	$C_1 = Y_1 + (1 + r)S_0$
0.01	66.3366	−16.3366	$33.50 = 50 - (1.01 \times 16.3366)$
0.05	65.0794	−15.0794	$34.1667 = 50 - (1.05 \times 15.0794)$
0.10	63.6364	−13.6364	$35.00 = 50 - (1.10 \times 13.6364)$
0.15	62.3188	−12.3188	$35.8333 = 50 - (1.15 \times 12.3188)$
0.20	61.1111	−11.1111	$36.6667 = 50 - (1.20 \times 11.1111)$

consumption in terms of period 1 consumption – a unit increase in C_0 is at the cost of a $(1 + r)$ decrease in C_1. Table 6.2 shows how variations in r affect the utility maximising choice of C_0 and C_1, for the two preference systems of Figure 6.2. In Table 6.2(a) we see that as r increases so C_0 falls and S_0 rises. And this is exactly what we would expect from the interpretation above of $(1 + r)$ as the price of C_0 in terms of C_1. As r increases so more is saved by the household because the pay-off to saving, in terms of C_1, goes up with r. In Table 6.2(b) we see that dis-saving decreases as r increases, so that C_0 falls and C_1 rises. Again, given the price interpretation of the interest rate, this is what we would expect. In Table 6.2 the household with preferences given by [6.4] is for all r a saver, and the household with preferences given by [6.5] is for all r a dis-saver. This categorisation of households into savers and dis-savers is useful for illustrative purposes, but should not be taken to be general. It is quite possible for a household to have preferences and an income stream such that as the interest rate increases it goes from being a dis-saver to being a saver.

6.2   Production and investment

In the previous section the household's problem was to decide upon a pattern of consumption over time, given its pattern of income receipts over time. We now wish to discuss the situation where the pattern of income receipts can itself be chosen by decisions about how much to *invest* in the initial period. We do this in two stages. First, we consider a situation where the household's consumption levels are directly tied to its income levels, there being no possibility for lending or borrowing via bond market dealings. In this case the analysis is concerned solely with the decision about how much to invest. Second, we consider situations where the household can invest and deal in the bond market, in which case its consumption levels are not directly tied to its chosen income levels.

As usual we shall illustrate the basic general ideas by means of a simple numerical example. We consider a household which owns and operates with its own labour a firm in the wheat growing business. Again we restrict the analysis to just two time periods, the present period 0 and the future period 1. On the first day of period 0 there exists 100 units of harvested wheat. The problem facing the household-firm is to decide how much of this wheat to sell to get period 0 income, and how much to plant as seed for the crop to be harvested at the end of period 0 so as to be saleable on the first day of period 1 to provide period 1 income. The quantity of wheat sold at the beginning of period 0 we shall denote by Q_0, the amount sold at the beginning of period 1 by Q_1. The amount of seed planted, the amount invested, in period 0 is then $100 - Q_0$. With I standing for investment, the quantity of wheat used as seed in period 0, we have

$$I = 100 - Q_0$$

and with the relationship between harvest size, H, and seed planting given by

$$H = 20I^{\frac{1}{2}} = 20\sqrt{I}$$

we get

$$Q_1 = 20(100 - Q_0)^{\frac{1}{2}} = 20\sqrt{(100 - Q_0)} \qquad [6.6]$$

for the relationship between period 1 wheat sales and period 0 wheat sales. This relationship is shown graphically in Figure 6.3. As wheat available on the first day of period 0 is shifted from sale to seed, so the amount available for sale on the first day of period 1 increases at a decreasing rate. Whereas reducing Q_0 from 100 to 90 increases Q_1 from 0 to 63.2456, reducing Q_0 from 60 to 50 increases Q_1 by 14.9302, for example.

Table 6.3 shows, in the first two columns, some of the Q_0/Q_1 combinations lying along the curve shown in Figure 6.3. The figures under i in the third column give values for the *rate of return* which measures the return to marginal increases in the level of investment. We denote such as ΔI, and since $\Delta I = -\Delta Q_0$, with ΔQ_1 for the corresponding increase in Q_1, the rate of return is defined as:

$$i = (\Delta Q_1/\Delta I) - 1 = (\Delta Q_1 - \Delta I)/\Delta I = (\Delta Q_1 + \Delta Q_0)/ - \Delta Q_0 \qquad [6.7]$$

In Table 6.3 we show, in the fourth column, the level of investment at which i in the corresponding row is evaluated. We see that as I increases so the payoff to an increase in investment declines steadily. The rate of return is just

Table 6.3 The rate of return and the level of investment

Q_0	Q_1	i	I
99	20	30.6228	1
90	63.2456	2.1623	10
80	89.4428	1.2361	20
70	109.5446	0.8257	30
60	126.4912	0.5811	40
50	141.4214	0.4142	50
40	154.9194	0.2910	60
30	167.3320	0.1952	70
20	178.8854	0.1180	80
10	189.7366	0.0541	90
1	198.9975	0.0005	99

the slope of the Q_1/Q_0 curve from Figure 6.3 less one. The slope of the curve is

$$s = -\Delta Q_1/\Delta Q_0$$

and so

$$s - 1 = -(\Delta Q_1/\Delta Q_0) - 1$$
$$= (\Delta Q_1/\Delta I) - 1$$
$$= i.$$

Hence we have

$$1 + i = s. \qquad\qquad [6.8]$$

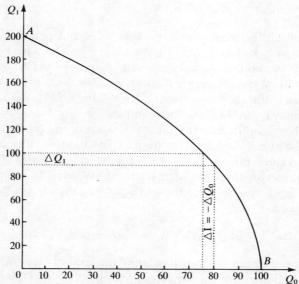

Figure 6.3 Intertemporal production possibilities

If we assume for simplicity that wheat growing is, apart from the labour input, a costless activity, then the consumption possibilities open to the household-firm follow directly from its chosen Q_0 and Q_1 and the price of wheat in each period. If we assume the price of wheat to be constant at £1, then income in each period is just $£Y_0 = £Q_0$ and $£Y_1 = £Q_1$. With, as we are currently taking to be the case, no possibilities for rearranging consumption over time, given income over time, by way of trading in bonds, the household's consumption possibilities are exactly the same as its income possibilities. We have, that is, $C_0 = Y_1 = Q_0$ and $C_1 = Y_1 = Q_1$. It follows that the consumption opportunities open to the household are given by the curve of Figure 6.3 with the axes relabelled C_0 and C_1, or equivalently by

$$C_1 = 20(100 - C_0)^{\frac{1}{2}} = 20\sqrt{(100 - C_0)} \tag{6.9}$$

which is just equation [6.6] with C_0 and C_1 substituted for Q_0 and Q_1. The household's problem is to choose the amount of investment, which by virtue of $I = 100 - Q_0$ is a choice of Q_0, that gives rise to the C_0/C_1 combination which yields the greatest utility or satisfaction.

This problem differs from that considered in the previous section only in that the consumption opportunities open to the household are given by equation [6.9] above, reflecting the consequences of different amounts of investment, rather than by the budget line, equation [6.2], reflecting the consequences of dealing in bonds given the income stream. Figure 6.4 shows what is involved in the present case. In part (a) the household's preferences are given by equation [6.4], and in part (b) by equation [6.5]: in both (a) and (b) the consumption shifting opportunities are the same, and are given by equation [6.9] above. We see that the optimum C_0/C_1 combination is that for which the graph of equation [6.9] is tangential to an indifference curve. Such a point of tangency corresponds to the highest attainable level of the utility index for moving away from it in either direction would mean moving to a lower indifference curve. In Figure 6.4(a) $C_0 = £66.67$ and $C_1 = £115.4642$, and the amount invested is $100 - 66.67 = 33.33$. In (b) $C_0 = £80$ and $C_1 = £89.4427$ so that the amount invested is 20. Households with preferences given by equation [6.5] invest, for the same technical opportunities, less than households with preferences given by equation [6.4]. Recall that in the previous section we found that, for the same interest rate, equation [6.5] led to less saving than equation [6.4]. It will be clear that if we altered the technical opportunities facing a household with given preferences, by changing the relationship between harvest size and seed, we would change the chosen C_0/C_1 levels and the amount invested. This is analogous to the effects, discussed in the previous section, of varying interest rates on savings decisions.

Investment with borrowing or lending

We now move on to the second stage of the discussion, to consider a situation where the household-firm can deal in the bond market as well as invest in wheat production. There are then two ways in which consumption

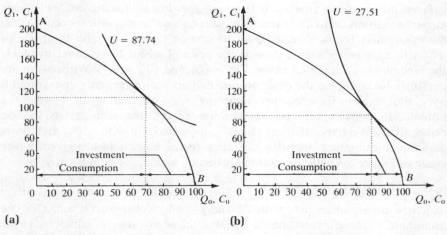

Figure 6.4 Investment opportunities and consumption preferences

can be shifted over time, by investment and by borrowing or lending via bond sales or purchases, and the consumption opportunities available will reflect both of these options. Consider Figure 6.5 where the curve AB is just that from Figures 6.3 and 6.4, so that we are considering a situation where the production and investment based opportunities open to the household-firm are as discussed above. Additionally now bonds can be bought or sold at a price which gives an interest rate of 10% or 0.10. Suppose first that we ignore the possibility of investment (by keeping back some of the 100 units of wheat available for seed) so that the household has an income of £100 on day one of period 0 and zero on day one of period 1. Then the consumption possibilities open to the

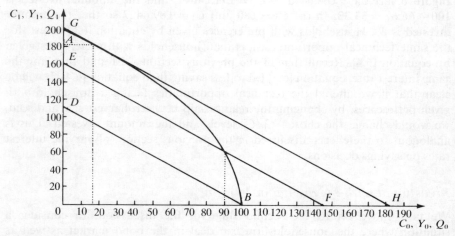

Figure 6.5 Consumption possibilities with investment and borrowing/lending

household are given by the budget line BD, which has slope equal to 1.10. If the household sets $C_0 = £100$ then $S_0 = £0$ and so $C_1 = £0$ for $Y_1 = £0$. If the household chooses $C_0 = £0$ then $S_0 = £100$ and $C_1 = £110$, at D for $Y_1 = £0$. The line BD traces out intermediate C_0/C_1 combinations available by means of saving and lending in period 0. Clearly, the opportunities available by way of saving and buying bonds are inferior to those available by way of investing in wheat production.

Now we allow the household-firm both to invest and deal in bonds. Suppose it invests 10 so that $Q_0 = 90$, and, reading off from the AB graph in Figure 6.5, $Q_1 = 63.2456$. This gives $Y_0 = £90$ and $Y_1 = £63.2456$, for which income stream the consumption possibilities arising from buying or selling bonds are given by the line EF, slope 1.10. If the household-firm uses all of Y_0 to buy bonds it will receive, in addition to the wheat sale proceeds of £63.2456, a sum of £99 ($= 1.10 \times 90$) on the first day of period 1. Hence, the maximum value C_1 can take is £162.2456 ($= 99 + 63.2456$) with $C_0 = £0$ corresponding: this gives the point E in Figure 6.5. If, at the other extreme, C_1 is set at zero this makes all of the receipts from wheat sales in period 1 available for the redemption of bonds sold at the start of period 0. The maximum amount that can be borrowed is then £57.4960 ($= 63.2456 \div 1.1$), so that the maximum for C_0 is £147.4960 ($= 90 + 57.4960$), corresponding to $C_1 = £0$: this gives point F. Given that Q_0 is set at 90, the C_0/C_1 combinations available as a result of the possibility of buying or selling bonds for which the rate of interest is 0.10 are given by the line EF; to the left of $Q_0 = 90$ bonds are bought, to the right of $Q_0 = 90$ they are sold. If no bonds are bought or sold, $C_0 = Q_0 = £90$ and $C_1 = Q_1 = £63.2456$.

Clearly for $Q_0 = 90$ the consumption possibilities arising from the possibility of trading in bonds, given by EF, are everywhere superior to those arising for $Q_0 = 100$, given by BD. For investment set at 10, investment plus borrowing or lending gives, for any C_0, a larger attainable C_1 than does just borrowing or lending alone. The comparison of investment equal to 10 plus borrowing or lending with the possibilities which arise when only investment is allowed is ambiguous. For given C_0, the C_1 read off from EF is below that read off from AB to the left of $Q_0 = 90$, but above it to the right. The ambiguity arises because the level of investment is fixed. If the level of investment chosen by the household is allowed to vary, then investment plus lending/borrowing gives better opportunities than does either investment alone or borrowing or lending alone. To see this in Figure 6.5 we just imagine drawing straight lines of slope 1.10 through the point on the curve AB lying above $Q_0 = 90$, $Q_0 = 89$, $Q_0 = 88$, ... $Q_0 = 60$, $Q_0 = 59$, ... and so on. Clearly, as Q_0 is reduced so this exercise will produce a series of straight lines parallel to EF successively shifting outwards. The line GH arises when $Q_0 = 17.3554$, for which the corresponding Q_1 read off from AB is 181.8181. It is tangential to AB. If Q_0 is reduced to 17 the straight line parallel to EF and BD drawn through the corresponding point along AB will lie below GH. And so will the straight line parallel to EF lie below GH for any Q_0 above or below $Q_0 = 17.3554$.

Given that Q_0 and Q_1 are related according to equation [6.6] so that feasible combinations of Q_0 and Q_1 lie along AB, the feasible combination which produces the line parallel to EF lying the furthest out to the north east is $Q_0 = 17.3554$ and $Q_1 = 181.8181$. If the household-firm sets Q_0 at 17.3554 and invests $100 - Q_0 = 82.6446$ so that $Q_1 = 181.8181$, the consumption possibilities open to it by means of borrowing or lending on the basis of the income stream $Y_0 = 17.3554$ and $Y_1 = 181.8181$ are given by the line GH. Given that the income streams it can choose are determined by the seed harvest relationship, i.e. must line along AB, this is the best set of consumption possibilities it can achieve. Further, the possibilities given by GH are everywhere as good as or better than those given by AB, and everywhere better than those given by BD. That is to say that the consumption possibilities made available by being able to invest in wheat production and borrow or lend are better than those which would be available if only investment or only borrowing or lending were possible. To see this we simply observe that for any C_0 we read off from GH a larger corresponding C_1 than from DB, and that the same is true regarding AB except for $C_0 = £17.3554$ where the C's are the same. Along GH, $C_1 = £0$ implies $C_0 = £182.6446$ at H and $C_0 = £0$ implies $C_1 = £200.9090$ at G.

So, by choosing the appropriate level of investment, given that opportunities for borrowing and lending exist, consumption possibilities are maximised. The particular levels of consumption in each period chosen will depend upon preferences as between consumption in each period. Before looking at this, several points need to be made about the discussion thus far. The first is that the maximisation of the possibilities for consumption by choice of investment level is independent of preferences. Clearly, in Figure 6.5 the household-firm will want to get to the situation represented by GH whatever its preferences as between C_0 and C_1. This must be so as for any C_0, GH gives the maximum C_1 corresponding. Not to move to $Q_0 = 17.3554$ would mean that for any level of C_0 available C_1 was being foregone.

The second point involves the introduction of the concept of *present value*. Given the income stream Y_0 and Y_1 arising on the first days of periods 0 and 1, we define the present value of that income stream as

$$PV = Y_0 + (Y_1/(1 + r)) \qquad [6.10]$$

In this terminology the preceding discussion has been a demonstration of the proposition that, whatever its preferences over consumption at different dates, the household-firm will pick as its optimum level of investment that which gives the income stream with the largest present value. Generally, investment is undertaken up to the level which maximises the present value of current and future income. In the case of the household-firm discussed above we have for $Y_0 = £17.3554$, $Y_1 = £181.8181$ and $r = 0.10$ a maximised present value of £182.6446. We note that this is just C_0 for $C_1 = £0$. Again this is general, the present value of an income stream being just the maximum amount that could be consumed now by borrowing against it. Thus, for

Table 6.4 Interest rate variations investment and present value

r	Y_0	I	Y_1	PV
0.01	1.9704	98.0296	198.0198	198.0296
0.05	9.2971	90.7029	190.4761	190.7029
0.10	17.3554	82.6446	181.8181	182.6446
0.15	24.3856	75.6144	173.9131	175.6144
0.20	30.5556	69.4444	166.6666	169.4444

$Q_0 = 90$, the *EF* line gives, for $C_1 = £0$, $C_0 = £147.4960$ and this is the present value of $Y_0 = £90$ and $Y_1 = £63.2456$, for $r = 0.10$.

For given technical opportunities for shifting income over time by means of investment, as represented by *AB* in Figure 6.5 for example, the maximum present value, and hence the corresponding income and investment levels, depends upon the rate of interest. We have already noted that the slope of the lines *BD*, *EF* and *GH* in Figure 6.5 is equal to $1 + r$, where r is the interest rate, equal there to 0.10. If r is increased/reduced the slope of these lines is increased/reduced. For *AB* fixed, then, a larger value of r will move the point of tangency for *GH* and *AB* to the right, implying less investment, with Y_0 higher and Y_1 lower. Table 6.4 gives some numerical values for various levels of the interest rate for the case considered above where *AB* of Figure 6.5 describes the way in which investment shifts income over time. Again we should note that higher interest rates meaning lower investment levels, and vice versa, is generally true.

The fourth and final point to be made concerns the relationship between the interest rate and the rate of return to investment. In terms of Figure 6.5, we have previously noted that the slope of the lines *GH*, *EF* and *BD* is $1 + r$ and that the slope of *AB* is $1 + i$, where r is the interest rate and i is the rate of return to investment. Clearly, at the point of tangency the slopes of *GH* and *AB* are equal so that $r = i$. The optimum level of investment, the level which maximises the present value of the income stream, is that for which the rate of return is equal to the rate of interest. If we look back at Table 6.3 we see how the rate of return falls as investment gets larger, and that it will take the value 0.10 for I somewhere between $I = 80$ and $I = 90$. In Figure 6.5 we have identified, by finding where $i = r = 0.10$, 'somewhere' as $I = 100 - Q_0 = 82.6446$, for $Q_0 = 17.3554$. This equality of i and r for the present value maximising investment level is no accident arising for this particular example – it is necessary and general.

To see what is involved consider that $Q_0 = 90$ so that $I = 10$ and from Table 6.3 we read the corresponding rate of return, i, as 2.1623. In equation [6.7] i was defined as

$$i = (\Delta Q_1 - \Delta I)/\Delta I$$

which on rearrangement gives

$$\Delta Q_1 = (1 + i)\Delta I$$

for the Q_1 increase corresponding to a marginal increase in investment of ΔI. With $Y_1 = Q_1$ this means that for $I = 10$, a marginal investment increase yields $\Delta Y_1 = 3.1623\Delta I$. And, if $r = 0.10$, this means that this ΔI improves consumption possibilities since Y_1 up by £$3.1623\Delta I$ means that the extra amount that can be borrowed in period 0 is $3.1623\Delta I \div 1.1 = 2.87248\Delta I$, which is greater than the $\Delta C_0 = \Delta Y_0 = \Delta I$ foregone in period 0. Again, consider an initial situation with $I = 50$ for which, see Table 6.3, $i = 0.4142$. Then $\Delta Y_1 = \Delta Q_1 = 1.4142\Delta I$, so that an extra amount equal to $1.4142\Delta I \div 1.1 = 1.2856\Delta I > \Delta I$ can be borrowed. Clearly, for all I such that i is greater than r it will be true that a marginal increase in investment improves the consumption possibilities open to the household-firm. For $i = r$ increasing investment leaves consumption possibilities unchanged, since $1.1\Delta I \div 1.1 = \Delta I$ and the increase in the amount that can be borrowed is exactly equal to what is to be foregone. For i less than r, increasing investment worsens the consumption possibilities. Clearly this argument applies whatever the value of r, the interest rate.

We now bring the preferences of the household-firm into the picture to consider the choice from among the C_0 and C_1 levels made available by investment plus borrowing or lending. This is done in Figure 6.6, for a situation where preferences over C_0 and C_1 are given by the utility function

$$U = C_0^{\frac{1}{2}} C_1^{\frac{1}{2}}$$

which is equation [6.4] as used in the previous section and earlier in this section (when considering the situation where consumption could be shifted over time only by the choice of the investment level). In Figure 6.6 AB and GH are exactly as in Figure 6.5. We are, that is, considering a household-firm which faces the production/investment situation previously discussed, and which can borrow or lend at $r = 0.10$. We already know that the household-firm will invest 82.6446 with $Q_0 = 17.3554$ and $Q_1 = 181.8181$ so as to maximise present value, and that the consumption opportunities open to it thereby are given by GH. The household-firm chooses the C_0/C_1 combination which offers the maximum utility or satisfaction attainable given that its opportunities are described by GH. This means that the discussion of the first section of this chapter is applicable to this stage in the choice process. The point of maximum attainable utility is identified by the tangency of GH to an indifference curve, and in Figure 6.6 gives $C_0 = £91.3223$ and $C_1 = £100.4545$, with the corresponding level of U at 95.78. If we refer back to Figure 6.4(a) we see that there the maximum attainable level for U is 87.74. By virtue of being able to borrow or lend as well as choose the level of investment the household-firm is able to attain a higher level of utility than when its only choice is over the level of investment. To realise this improvement the household-firm invests 82.6446 so that $Y_0 = Q_0 = £17.3554$. With $C_0 = £91.3223$ this means that it borrows, by selling bonds, $91.3223 - 17.3554 = £73.9669$. Given that $r = 0.10$ the amount it needs to pay out in period 1 by way of bond redemption is $73.9669 \times 1.10 = £81.3636$.

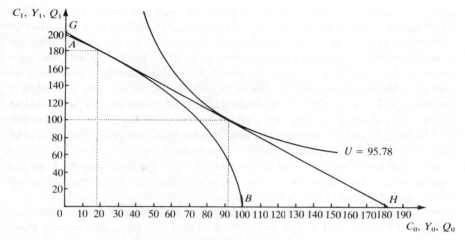

Figure 6.6   Two stage intertemporal optimisation

Period 1 income is equal to Q_1 at £181.8181, so that after bond redemption it has an amount which is $181.8181 - 81.3636 = £100.4545$ available for consumption. This is exactly the amount already identified above as its chosen level for C_1.

We see, then, that for the household-firm which can both invest and lend or borrow by operating in the bond market, attaining its preferred pattern of consumption over time is a two-stage process. Whatever its preferences as between C_0 and C_1 it will invest up to the level for which $i = r$, thus maximising present value and giving itself the best attainable consumption opportunities. Given this optimised consumption opportunity set, it attains its preferred C_0/C_1 combination by borrowing and lending on the basis of the Y_0/Y_1 income stream associated with the present value maximising investment decision. The final outcome depends upon: (i) the opportunities for shifting income over time by investment, (ii) the interest rate, and (iii) preferences over consumption at different dates.

6.3   Interest rate determination

We have thus far considered a single household-firm facing a given interest rate. We now wish to consider the determination of the interest rate in an economy where income, and hence consumption, can be shifted over time by investment. To do this we note from our discussion of the household-firm that its two rôles – deciding how much to invest and deciding how much to currently consume – are separable. Whatever its preferences over C_0 and C_1, it invests that amount which maximises present value, i.e. that amount such that $i = r$. The consumption-saving choice is then made on the basis of the Y_0 and Y_1 stream which results from the investment decision, and does not affect that decision.

This means that we can treat investment decisions as being taken by firms, and consumption-saving decisions as being taken by households. Firms are concerned with production and do not have preferences over production at different points in time. The households who receive income from firms do have preferences concerning consumption over time. But, what we have seen above is that whatever the preferences of the households who own and control firms, the investment decisions of firms are in no way affected by such preferences. The firm always serves the interest of its owners by investing up to the point which maximises the present value of the firm. The owners then use the bond market to achieve the best consumption pattern available on the basis of the maximised present value of the firm.

Before considering the implications of this for the determination of the interest rate, it is necessary to say something further about the nature of bonds, and the market for them.

Recall that for expositional convenience, we are considering just two periods of time, 0 and 1. On day one of period 0 trading in bonds occurs. Bonds are created and sold by would-be borrowers and bought by would-be lenders. They are a commodity, physically pieces of paper, by means of trade in which borrowing and lending is fixed. There will be market trading in bonds which fixes their price, just as with any other commodity. The supply schedule for bonds reflects the plans of borrowers, the demand schedule reflects the plans of lenders. The intersection of the supply and demand functions gives the equilibrium price of bonds and the equilibrium quantity.

Now, in equation [6.1] above we defined the interest rate as

$$r = (x - P_B)/P_B$$

which can be written as

$$r = (x/P_B) - 1$$

where x is the sum, indicated on the piece of paper which is the bond, to be paid to the bond holder on day one of period 1, and P_B is the price paid for the bond. To simplify, suppose that bonds can only be issued with $x = £1.05$. Then, as the market clearing bond price varies, with the demand and supply for bonds, so will the interest rate vary. As the bond price increases so will the interest rate decrease, and vice versa. Thus, from either of the formulae given above, we see that for $x = £1.05$, so:

$P_B = £1.0396$ is equivalent to $r = 0.01$
$P_B = £1.0000$ is equivalent to $r = 0.05$
$P_B = £0.9836$ is equivalent to $r = 0.0675$
$P_B = £0.9546$ is equivalent to $r = 0.10$
$P_B = £0.9130$ is equivalent to $r = 0.15$
$P_B = £0.8750$ is equivalent to $r = 0.20$

To proceed we suppose that for all the firms in the economy taken together, sales receipts on day one of period 0, R_0, and sales receipts on day one of period 1, R_1, are related as shown by AB in Figure 6.7(a). This relationship arises from all firms being able to transfer sales receipts between the two periods by means

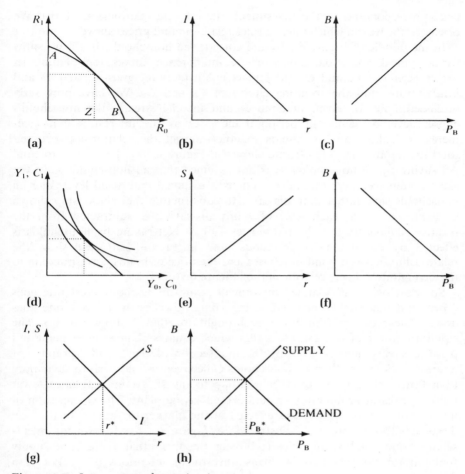

Figure 6.7   Interest rate determination

of investment, in the manner discussed above for the wheat-growing example. Since the firms produce different commodities we measure investment in value terms, and we assume that all prices are the same in both periods. We also assume that on day one of period 0 the firms must pay to households all of the costs incurred in producing the output then available for allocation as between sales and investment. This payout is given by OB in Figure 6.7(a). This means that firms must finance investment by selling bonds. We know that firms invest up to the point where the rate of return equals the rate of interest, and in Figure 6.7(a) we show as BZ the present value maximising level of investment for some particular level for the interest rate. As the rate of interest increases/decreases so will the amount of investment firms will wish to do decrease/increase. In Figure 6.7(b) we plot the desired level of investment against the rate of interest. As investment varies so must the quantity of bonds firms wish to sell vary. In Figure 6.7(c) we show the relationship between planned bonds sales and bond price corresponding to the investment interest rate relationship of (b). We discussed the way in which interest rates relate to bond prices above.

In the middle of Figure 6.7 we are considering households. In (d) we show for a typical household some of the indifference curves representing its preferences over C_0 and C_1, the budget line it faces for given Y_0 and Y_1 and interest rate, and the resulting choice of C_0 and C_1. We have previously discussed how for given preferences and income stream, the household's chosen level of saving in period 0 increases as the interest rate it faces increases. Taking all households together we get the relationship between total saving and the interest rate shown in Figure 6.7(e). This refers to total net saving by all households. It is not assumed that all households have the same preferences over C_0 and C_1, nor is it assumed that at all levels of r all households save rather than dis-save. In constructing the relationship shown in Figure 6.7(e) at each level of r any dis-saving is subtracted from the positive savings to give the plotted level of S. Net saving by households is effected by net purchases of bonds, and in Figure 6.7(f) we show the relationship between bond purchases and the price of bonds corresponding to the saving interest rate relationship of Figure 6.7(e).

So, we have firms' planned investment going up as the interest rate goes down, and households' planned saving going down as the interest rate goes down. These two relationships are brought together in Figure 6.7(g). The equilibrium rate of interest, r^*, is that which equates planned investment and planned saving, and is given by the intersection of the S and I graphs. At interest rates higher than r^* households collectively would wish to save more than firms collectively would be wanting to invest. At interest rates lower than r^* investment intentions would exceed saving plans. The equalisation of investment and saving plans is effected in the market for bonds, in the way discussed above and now illustrated in Figure 6.7(h). Investment means selling bonds and saving means buying them, so that there is a supply function for bonds based on firms' investment intentions (see (c)) and a demand function based on households' saving intentions (see (f)). Trading in bonds fixes the market equilibrium price for bonds, P_B^*, and thereby the equilibrium interest rate. At P_B^*, the supply of bonds exactly matches the demand so it is necessarily the case that at P_B^*, to which r^* corresponds, planned investment and saving are exactly equal.

We can now see what it is that determines the interest rate in an economy. It is the interaction between investment opportunities and preferences over consumption at different dates. For given preferences, the interest rate will be higher the more productive is investment. For given investment productivity, the interest rate will be higher the more households, typically, prefer consumption now to consumption in the future. If the reader works through the discussion of this and the preceding section carefully, he will see that the following two propositions hold. First, that if at every level of investment the rate of return increases, the equilibrium interest rate will rise. Second, that if preferences over C_0 and C_1 change so that C_0 is preferred relatively more, the equilibrium rate of interest will rise. Note also that in the former case the higher $r*$ goes with more investment and saving – the I line in Figure 6.7(g) shifts up and to the right – while in the latter case it goes with less investment and saving – the S line in (g) shifts down and to the right.

6.4 Project appraisal

In the previous sections of this chapter we have been concerned with some basic ideas about the way time enters into economic analysis. For the purpose of explaining these we made a number of simplifying assumptions. Particularly, we considered just two periods of time, we assumed that firms could vary continuously the level of investment, and we concerned ourselves with the determination of the equilibrium rate of interest. In this section we discuss *project appraisal*, which is the method by which firms can actually make decisions toward the maximisation of their present values.

In practice investment opportunities present themselves in the form of discrete lumps which are called *projects*. Thus, for example, decisions are made not about whether to invest an extra £1 but about whether to acquire a new machine, an extension to a factory, or a whole new factory. In addition to the characteristic of arising in discrete lumps, actual investment projects typically have consequences stretching over many periods. Acquiring a new machine or building is a decision which will affect a firm's expenditures and receipts for a long period of time. The analysis of such decisions amounts to an extension – over time – and a modification – in respect of lumpiness – of the discussion of the previous section. No fundamentally new concepts are required.

Extension over time is straightforward, though we can usefully introduce some new terminology. First we consider *compounding*, or lending at *compound interest*. If the interest rate is r then a bond bought now for £1 can be redeemed for £$(1 + r)$ one period hence, i.e. £1 lent for one period at r becomes £$(1 + r)$ after one period. Suppose that instead of spending the £$(1 + r)$ one period hence I use it to buy bonds to the value of £$(1 + r)$. Then two periods hence, I will realise £$\{(1 + r)(1 + r)\} = $ £$(1 + r)^2$ for consumption, i.e. £1 lent at r for two periods becomes £$(1 + r)^2$. By the same reasoning £1 lent at r for 3 periods becomes £$(1 + r)^3$, and so on. Generally, the sum PV lent for t periods at the interest rate r becomes

$$V_t = PV(1 + r)^t \qquad\qquad [6.11]$$

by virtue of compounding, effected by the repurchase of bonds each period. Alternatively, we can think of bonds with redemption dates t periods, rather than one period, hence. Then equation [6.11] fixes any one of V_t as redemption value, PV as purchase price and r as the interest rate, given the other two. Thus, for example, if a two period bond can be bought for £1 to be redeemed for £1.21, the interest rate is 0.10 from

$$1.21 = 1(1 + r)^2$$

solved for r.

Discounting is just compounding in reverse. The present value of £1 available today is £1. The present value of £1 available one period hence is £$\{1 \div (1 + r)\}$ because if I actually had £$\{1 \div (1 + r)\}$ now I could transform it into £1 = £$\{1 \div (1 + r)\}(1 + r)$ one period hence by lending at r. It follows that a promise of £1 to be available one period hence is worth exactly £$\{1 \div (1 + r)\}$ now. Discounting is the process of transforming future money sums into their equivalent present values. How much is £1 two periods ahead now worth? What, that is, is the present value of £1 two periods ahead? Clearly the answer is £$\{1 \div (1 + r)^2\}$, as £$\{1 \div (1 + r)^2\}(1 + r)^2 =$ £1. Generally, the discounting formula is just equation [6.11] rearranged as

$$PV = V_t/(1 + r)^t \qquad\qquad\qquad [6.12]$$

The reason for using the symbol *PV* for the initial sum in the discussion of compounding is now apparent. Also, the reader will now appreciate that in our discussion of investment choice in the preceding section what we called the present value of the firm, to be maximised by the choice of Y_0 and Y_1, via investment, was just the result of discounting Y_0 and Y_1. We had, that is,

$$PV = Y_0 + Y_1/(1 + r)$$

where the present value of Y_0 now is Y_0 (see above), and of Y_1 one period hence is $Y_1 \div (1 + r)$ (also see above). The firm's present value was the sum of the present values of its receipts at the two dates. More generally, we have

$$PV = V_0 + V_1/(1 + r) + V_2/(1 + r)^2 + \ldots + V_t/(1 + r)^t + \ldots$$
$$+ V_T/(1 + r)^T \qquad\qquad\qquad [6.13]$$

for the present value of the income stream V_0 today, V_1 one period hence, ... V_T T periods hence. To find the present value of an income stream we discount each element in it and sum the resulting present values.

The net present value criterion

Now let us consider project appraisal.[1] Associated with undertaking an investment project there will be an arising time stream of costs and benefits, as

Period	Costs	Benefits
0	C_0	B_0
1	C_1	B_1
2	C_2	B_2
.	.	.
.	.	.
.	.	.
T	C_T	B_T

Costs associated with the project will be, typically, the expenses involved in acquiring and operating the machine or building. Benefits will be, typically, the sales receipts arising from the use of the machine or building. Applying equation [6.13] to the cost and benefit streams we have

$$PV_{\text{COST}} = C_0 + \frac{C_1}{1+r} + \frac{C_2}{(1+r)^2} + \ldots + \frac{C_\text{T}}{(1+r)^T} = \sum_{t=0}^{T} \frac{C_t}{(1+r)^t}$$

$$PV_{\text{BENEFIT}} = B_0 + \frac{B_1}{1+r} + \frac{B_2}{(1+r)^2} + \ldots + \frac{B_\text{T}}{(1+r)^T} = \sum_{t=0}^{T} \frac{B_t}{(1+r)^t}$$

and we define the project's *net present value* as

$$NPV = PV_{\text{BENEFIT}} - PV_{\text{COST}} = \sum_{t=0}^{T} \frac{B_t}{(1+r)^t} - \sum_{t=0}^{T} \frac{C_t}{(1+r)^t}$$

$$= \sum_{t=0}^{T} \frac{B_t - C_t}{(1+r)^t} \qquad [6.14]$$

When considering a single project, the decision rule is to adopt or go ahead with the project only if its net present value is positive. As we shall illustrate below, undertaking a project with a positive NPV will increase the firm's present value. On the other hand, undertaking a project with a negative NPV would, we shall show, reduce the firm's present value. In fact, if the firm undertakes all those projects available to it which have positive NPVs. it maximises its present value. This last point is not a new idea, it is just an extension in time, and a modification for lumpiness of the demonstration in 6.2 of the firm maximising present value by expanding investment up to the level at which the rate of return equals the rate of interest. We shall illustrate this shortly also. We shall also see that the analysis of the previous section carries over to the present, in that we find here that higher/lower interest rates mean less/more investment.

Table 6.5 provides some calculations which illustrate the rationale of the decision rule 'undertake only projects with a positive net present value'. We consider a single project for which the consequences of adoption are set out at the head of the table. Let us suppose the project is the acquisition of a machine. The machine costs £100 and must be paid for on day one of period 0. The machine has a life of 4 periods, and its use gives rise to costs of £10 arising on the first day of each of periods 1, 2 and 3. Its use results in sales receipts, B, of £50 on the first day of periods 1 and 2 and of £45.005 on the first day of period 3. So, if the machine is acquired the cash flow resulting is −£100, +£40, +£40, +£35.005.

Consider first a situation where the interest rate is 5% or 0.05, set out in Table 6.5(i). Applying the formula [6.14] to the B and C figures shown at the top of Table 6.5 gives an NPV of £4.6151, as the reader should check. We now look at the financing implications of the cash flow. We assume, for clarity, that the firm is to finance the project by dealing in one period bonds.

Table 6.5 Net present value and interest rate variations

t	C	B	Cashflow
0	100	0	−100
1	10	50	+40
2	10	50	+40
3	10	45.005	+35.005

(i) $r = 0.05$ NPV = £4.6151*

t
0   Sell £100 of bonds
1   Redeem bonds at £105.0, so sell £65 of bonds $(105 - 40)$
2   Redeem bonds at £68.25, so sell £28.25 of bonds $(68.25 - 40)$
3   Redeem bonds at £29.6625, surplus of £5.3425[†] $(35.005 - 29.6625)$

*$4.6151 \times 1.05^3 = 5.3425$[†]

(ii) $r = 0.075$ NPV = £0*

t
0   Sell £100 of bonds
1   Redeem bonds at £107.5, so sell £67.5 of bonds $(107.5 - 40)$
2   Redeem bonds at £72.5625, so sell £32.5625 of bonds $(72.5625 - 40)$
3   Redeem bonds at £35.005, surplus of £0[†] $(35.005 - 35.005)$

*$0 \times 1.075^3 = 0$[†]

(iii) $r = 0.10$ NPV = −£4.27874*
0   Sell £100 worth of bonds
1   Redeem bonds at £110, so sell £70 of bonds $(110 - 40)$
2   Redeem bonds at £77.0, so sell £37.0 of bonds $(77 - 40)$
3   Redeem bonds at £40.7, surplus of −£5.695[†] $(35.005 - 40.7)$

*$4.2787 \times 1.1^3 = 5.695$[†]

So, on day one of period 0 the firm sells bonds to the value of £100 to raise the money to buy the machine. This means that on day one of period 1 it needs to pay out, given $r = 0.05$, £105 $(= 1.05 \times 100)$ to redeem these bonds. Given net cash receipts of £40 this means issuing £65 worth of new bonds. On day one of period 2 the redemption payment amounts to £68.25 $(= 65 \times 1.05)$, so that with the net cash receipts of £40 a further £28.25 of bonds must be issued. This gives a bond redemption requirement of £29.6625 $(= 28.25 \times 1.05)$ on day one of period 3, so that with net cash receipts of £35.005 the firm ends up with a surplus of £5.3425.

In Table 6.5 (ii) we carry through the same calculations for the case where $r = 0.075$, and in (iii) for $r = 0.10$. We see that $r = 0.075$ gives NPV = 0 and a final surplus of zero, that $r = 0.10$ gives a negative NPV and a final deficit. So, we can see that a positive NPV indicates that a project yields a firm a surplus, and a negative NPV that a project gives rise to a deficit, while a zero NPV means that the firm just breaks even. Further, the value computed for the NPV can be seen in Table 6.5 to give a precise numerical indication of what the corresponding project offers the firm. In (i), (ii) and (iii) we see that the NPV is exactly the final surplus divided by $(1 + r)^3$. NPV is, that is, just the present value of the eventual surplus arising from the project. Put the other way round, a calculated positive value for NPV gives the amount that the firm would have to lend at compound interest at the ruling rate to end up with the final surplus arising from the project. Put yet another way, a positive NPV is the additional, over the period for project financing, amount that the firm could borrow on day one of period 0 and be able to repay on day one of period 3 from the project surplus. A project's NPV is the amount by which it increases the firm's present value. A negative NPV indicates that the corresponding project would reduce the firm's present value.

The rationale of the positive NPV criterion for project acceptance is now clear – projects with positive NPVs make the firm better off, increase its present value, while projects with negative NPVs make it worse off, reduce its present value. We have explained this by considering a particular project against a varying interest rate. But clearly the same considerations regarding the implications of positive and negative NPVs apply if we consider projects with differing cost and benefit streams against a single interest rate. Equally, it is clear that a firm with a set of possible projects open to it can rank them according to their NPVs. It will maximise its present value by adopting all projects down to, but not including, the first one with a negative NPV. Now suppose the interest rate falls. It is clear from our discussion of Table 6.5 that some projects which initially had a negative NPV will, at the lower interest rate, have a positive NPV. The cut-off point on the project rank list will move downward and the total number of projects suitable for adoption increase. The firm's planned amount of investment will increase. This will be true for all firms. So, our analysis of project appraisal confirms that the level of planned investment will be inversely related to the rate of interest, as discussed in 6.2 above.

The rate of return criterion

In the course of that discussion we noted that a firm which sought to maximise its present value would set the level of investment where the rate of return was equal to the rate of interest. Where, as in this section, investment opportunities arise in discrete lumps which are projects, it is also true that present value maximisation requires undertaking all of those projects for which the rate of return exceeds the rate of interest. Equivalently, for a single project considered alone the decision rule is 'go ahead with the project if its rate of return exceeds the rate of interest'. To see what is involved we need first to provide a definition of the rate of return suitable for a project which has consequences extending over many periods. Our previous definition, equation [6.7], was for situations where the level of investment was continuously variable by marginal amounts, and covered only two periods.

To provide a definition for the project appraisal situation we first go back to our definition of net present value as

$$\text{NPV} = \sum_{t=0}^{T} \frac{B_t - C_t}{(1+r)^t} = (B_0 - C_0) + \frac{(B_1 - C_1)}{(1+r)} + \frac{(B_2 - C_2)}{(1+r)^2}$$
$$+ \dots + \frac{(B_T - C_T)}{(1+r)^T}$$

which is equation [6.14]. What we are doing here is for given Bs and Cs, fixing the interest rate and solving for the NPV. We could, alternatively, for given Bs and Cs, fix the NPV figure at some value and then find the interest rate corresponding. The rate of return on a project is defined as that rate of interest in equation [6.14] which makes the NPV solution on the left-hand side equal to zero. We define the rate of return, i, according to

$$0 = \sum_{t=0}^{T} \frac{B_t - C_t}{(1+i)^t} = (B_0 - C_0) + \frac{(B_1 - C_1)}{(1+i)} + \frac{(B_2 - C_2)}{(1+i)^2} + \dots$$
$$+ \frac{(B_T - C_T)}{(1+i)^T} \qquad\qquad [6.15]$$

The first thing to note about this definition is that it is in no way inconsistent with our earlier definition, equation [6.7]. Indeed equation [6.7] is just a special case of equation [6.15]. To see this we first write equation [6.15] for just two periods, 0 and 1, as

$$0 = (B_0 - C_0) + \frac{(B_1 - C_1)}{1+i}$$

We next recall that equation [6.7] involved ΔQ_1 an output increase in period 1 and ΔI an investment increase in period 0, giving rise to ΔQ_1. In the project appraisal format of equation [6.15] ΔI is C_0 and ΔQ_1 is B_1, with B_0 and C_1 both equal to zero. If we make these substitutions in our truncated equation [6.15] above, we have

$$0 = -\Delta I + (\Delta Q_1/1 + i)$$
$$\Delta I = (\Delta Q_1/1 + i)$$
$$(1+i)\Delta I = \Delta Q_1$$
$$1 + i = \Delta Q_1/\Delta I$$
$$\text{i.e. } i = (\Delta Q_1/\Delta I) - 1$$

which is just equation [6.7]. The definition [6.15] is a generalisation of our earlier definition of i, and uses the benefit cost terminology rather than referring directly to output gains and losses.

The second thing to note about equation [6.15] is that given a set of values for the Bs and Cs, it is actually going to be difficult to calculate the corresponding value of i. Unless, that is, the Bs and Cs extend over only two or three periods. This is one of the reasons why, as a practical matter, the net present value decision rule 'go ahead with a project if its NPV is positive' is preferred to the rate of return decision rule 'go ahead with a project if it has i greater than r'. As we have already indicated, the two rules are equivalent, in that a project which passes/fails the NPV test will pass/fail the i test, and vice versa. Also, it is the case that undertaking all projects with positive NPVs will lead to the same selection of projects as will undertaking all projects for which i exceeds r. Whichever way arrived at, it is this selection of projects the adoption of which will maximise the firm's present value.

We can illustrate these ideas for the project previously considered in Table 6.5. We do not need to do any calculations to find the rate of return for this project, as Table 6.5 (ii) tells us that it has $i = 0.075$, as the definition equation [6.15] indicates. What we need to do is to explain why this means that the project should be undertaken if the rate of interest is less than 0.075 and should not be undertaken if the rate of interest is greater than 0.075. The explanation is actually already laid out in Table 6.5. In the case (i) there the project increases the firm's present value because by virtue of going ahead with it the firm can borrow £100 and end up with a surplus, the rate of return on money tied up in the project being greater than the rate of return on money tied up in bonds, which rate of return is the interest rate. In case (iii) the project decreases the firm's present value because the rate of return on money tied up in the project is less than the rate of return on bonds. Clearly, with $i = 0.075$ and $r = 0.10$ the firm would do better than the project if it used the initially borrowed £100 to buy bonds – it would then leave its present value unchanged.

We have here discussed project appraisal by firms. One purpose of so doing has been to illustrate the relevance of the basic ideas of 6.2 above to the practical problems faced by firms. In this connection we should make explicit also the point that firms can do project appraisal solely on the basis of the net present value or the rate of return criteria precisely because, as demonstrated in 6.2, this serves the interest of their owners whatever the preferences for consumption over time of such owners. Were such separation not possible, the appraisal of projects by firms would be greatly complicated. A second purpose in discussing project appraisal by firms has been to provide some background for our discussion, in Chapter 8, of project appraisal by government agencies. Such project appraisal is frequently referred to as *cost benefit analysis*, and is of considerable importance to environmental management theory and practice. Finally, we note that the ideas considered in this and the previous sections of this chapter are of central relevance to the subject matter of the next, the exploitation of natural resources. Before discussing that, however, we need to develop some more basic ideas in the next section of this chapter.

6.5   Efficiency in intertemporal allocation

Thus far in this chapter we have been discussing the way in which markets, including a market in bonds, allocate inputs to production and consumption over time. A major focus has been the determination of the interest rate, or equivalently the price of bonds. We have also looked closely at the way the investment decisions of firms are related to the interest rate they face. We have not considered whether the intertemporal, i.e. between time periods, allocations produced by markets have any desirable features. It is to this question that we now turn. The reader will recall that in Chapter 4 we showed that, given ideal conditions, a market equilibrium allocation at a point in time would be an efficient allocation. We noted, however, that for a given economy – in terms of quantities of factors of production, production functions and utility functions – there existed a very large number of efficient allocations, and that there could be no presumption that the particular efficient allocation realised by a market system would be desirable in terms of its implications for the distribution of material well-being across households. We shall now see that the situation is essentially the same when we consider market allocation over time – under ideal conditions it will be efficient, but there is no presumption of fairness.

To begin we need to specify the nature of an efficient intertemporal allocation. The basic idea is the same as in the static context of Chapters 3 and 4, in that efficiency is a situation where something cannot be increased except by reducing something else. We could, in fact, define an efficient intertemporal allocation as one such that it is not possible to increase the utility of a particular household in a particular period except at the cost of decreasing the utility of that household in some other period or periods and/ or decreasing the utility of some other household or households in any period. This is a straightforward extension of the definition for a single period. However, it is for our purposes a definition which would be unnecessarily complicated and which would raise extraneous issues. We shall instead work with a concept of intertemporal efficiency which is less comprehensive, but which brings out the main issues. We shall state the concept after describing the technological setting.

We revert to a two-period analysis, as in sections 6.1 and 6.2. We assume that there is a single commodity food, which exists in the form of wheat or maize – in consumption households find wheat indistinguishable from maize. However, the terms on which wheat output can be shifted over time are different from those on which maize output can be so shifted. If W represents wheat and M represents maize we have

$$W_1 = 20(100 - W_0)^{\frac{1}{2}} = 20\sqrt{(100 - W_0)} \qquad [6.16]$$

and

$$M_1 = 15(50 - M_0)^{\frac{1}{2}} = 15\sqrt{(50 - M_0)} \qquad [6.17]$$

for the relationship between harvests on day one of period 1, W_1 and M_1, and the amounts made available for consumption, W_0 and M_0, on day one of period 0. Wheat investment is $(100 - W_0)$ and corn investment is $(50 - M_0)$. The reader will recall our discussion of wheat sales and investment in section 6.2 above, and notice that equation [6.17] here is just equation [6.6] from there with W_1 and W_0 replacing Q_1 and Q_0. Consumption in each period is $C_0 = W_0 + M_0$ and $C_1 = W_1 + M_1$. The relationships of equations [6.16] and [6.17] are shown graphically as AB and DE in Figure 6.8(a) and (b).

In this context we shall say that an intertemporal allocation is efficient if for some fixed level of C_0 it makes C_1 as large as is possible. An intertemporal allocation is efficient, that is, when C_1 cannot be increased except by making C_0 smaller. If there were only one way of producing food this would not be a very interesting concept, as then any C_0 and C_1 combination would be efficient. Suppose, for example, that food is just wheat and that maize does not exist. Then the possibilities for shifting food consumption over time are given by equation [6.16] and AB in Figure 6.8(a) only, with $C_0 = W_0$ and $C_1 = W_1$. Clearly, in this case fixing a value for $W_0 = C_0$ immediately fixes a single unique value for $W_1 = C_1$. Thus, with C_0 fixed, C_1 immediately follows; any level for C_1 along AB has the property that it cannot be increased except by making C_0 smaller. This is not the situation when there are two ways of producing food. Then, there are many W_0/M_0 combinations consistent with a given level for C_0, and because the W_0 into W_1 and M_0 into M_1 relationships differ so differing W_0/M_0 combinations imply different levels for C_1. An efficient allocation involves a W_0/M_0 combination which is such that, for the corresponding C_0, C_1 cannot be increased.

Table 6.6 illustrates what is involved, for C_0 set at 25 and 50. The first two columns give a few of the many W_0/M_0 combinations consistent with the fixed C_0 level specified. The third and fourth columns give the W_1/M_1 combinations corresponding, obtained by substitution in equations [6.16] and

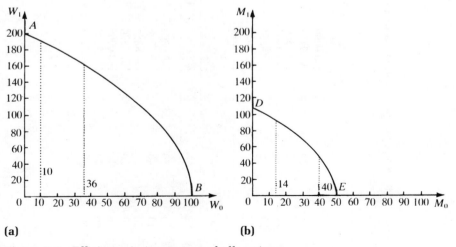

(a)   (b)

Figure 6.8   Efficiency in intertemporal allocation

Table 6.6 Intertemporal consumption shifting with two types of production

(i) $C_0 = 25$

W_0	M_0	$W_1 = 20(100 - W_0)^{\frac{1}{2}}$	$M_1 = 15(50 - M_0)^{\frac{1}{2}}$	$C_1 = W_1 + M_1$	i_w	i_m
0	25	200.0000	75	275.0000	0.0005	0.5000
5	20	194.9359	82.1584	277.0943	0.0260	0.3693
10	15	189.7366	88.7412	278.4778	0.0541	0.2677
15	10	184.3909	94.8683	279.2592	0.0847	0.1859
20	5	178.8854	100.6231	279.5085	0.1180	0.1180
25	0	173.2051	106.0660	279.2711	0.1547	0.0607

(ii) $C_0 = 50$

W_0	M_0	$W_1 = 20(100 - W_0)^{\frac{1}{2}}$	$M_1 = 15(50 - M_0)^{\frac{1}{2}}$	$C_1 = W_1 + M_1$	i_w	i_m
0	50	200.0000	0	200.0000	0.0005	22.7171
10	40	189.7366	47.4342	237.1708	0.0541	1.3717
20	30	178.8854	67.0820	245.9674	0.1180	0.6771
30	20	167.3320	82.1584	249.4904	0.1952	0.3693
36	14	160.0000	90.0000	250.0000	0.2500	0.2500
40	10	154.9194	94.8683	249.7877	0.2910	0.1859
50	0	141.4214	106.0660	247.4874	0.4142	0.0607

[6.17] or by using AB and DE in Figure 6.8. The fifth column gives the sum of W_1 and M_1 which is C_1, the amount of food available for consumption in period 1. We see, for both $C_0 = 25$ and $C_0 = 50$, that C_1 varies as the W_0/M_0 mix yielding the fixed C_0 varies. For $C_0 = 25$, C_1 is maximised with $W_0 = 20$ and $M_0 = 5$: for $C_0 = 50$, C_1 is maximised with $W_0 = 36$ and $M_0 = 14$. The latter case is identified in Figure 6.8. In the final two columns of Table 6.6 we give, as i_w and i_m the rates of return on wheat and maize investment for the investment levels, $100 - W_0$ and $50 - M_0$, corresponding to the W_0/M_0 combinations shown. We see that, for both $C_0 = 25$ and $C_0 = 50$, $i_w = i_m$ at the investment levels which give the maximum for C_1.

This outcome is not a coincidence. An efficient allocation is necessarily an arrangement such that $i_w = i_m$. It is precisely the equality of the rates of return on the two types of investment which makes it impossible to reallocate a fixed total of investment between the two types so as to increase C_1. From our definition of the rate of return [6.7], we have on rearrangement

$$\Delta Q_1 = (1 + i)\Delta I$$

so that for wheat and maize here

$$\Delta W_1 = (1 + i_w)\Delta I_w$$
$$\Delta M_1 = (1 + i_m)\Delta I_M$$

Now consider a sacrifice of period 0 consumption ΔC_0, and the question of whether it should be wheat consumption which is foregone and invested, so that $\Delta I_W = \Delta I$ and $\Delta I_M = 0$, or maize consumption which is forgone and invested, so that $\Delta I_M = \Delta I$ and $\Delta I_W = 0$. Clearly if i_w is larger than i_m putting the investment into wheat production yields a larger ΔC_1 than does putting it into maize production, and vice versa. With $i_w = i_m$ it makes no difference whether ΔI is used to increase investment in wheat or maize. The same point can be seen in terms of the graphs of Figure 6.8. At $W_0 = 36$ and $M_0 = 14$, AB and DE have the same slopes, $1 + i_w = 1 + i_m = 1.25$. At $W_0 = 10$ and $M_0 = 40$, so that $C_0 = 50$ again, the slope of AB is less than that of DE: see Table 6.6 for i_w and i_m. Starting from this latter point, consider increasing W_0, i.e. reducing wheat investment, and decreasing M_0, i.e. increasing maize investment, so as to hold $C_0 = 50$. Clearly, for a given switch of investment from wheat to maize the lost C_1 via less W_1 is less than the gained C_1 via more M_1. It is only when we reach $W_0 = 36$ and $M_0 = 14$ that there is no C_1 pay off to reallocating investment between wheat and maize. Clearly, a similar argument applies if we start from a point such as $W_0 = 40$ and $M_0 = 10$, and again we end up at $W_0 = 36$ and $M_0 = 14$ where C_1 is maximised for C_0 fixed at 50.

So, an efficient intertemporal allocation has the property that the rates of return on the different forms of investment are equal. Intertemporal efficiency requires, that is, the equalisation of the rates of return on different forms of investment. We have already noted that our concept of efficiency in allocation, that C_1 cannot be increased except by decreasing C_0, is a narrow one. However, it is the case that all notions of intertemporal efficiency which might be adopted require this condition of equality of rates of return. It is not difficult to see why, in general terms. Suppose we assume that households only live for one period. Then we could define intertemporal efficiency as a state such that the utility of one household in period 1 could not be increased except at the cost of reducing the utility of some other household or households in periods 0 or 1. Clearly, whatever other conditions this might require, it will require that C_1 is such that it cannot be increased except by decreasing C_0. The equality of rates of return across different types of investment is the most important of the conditions for intertemporal efficiency, and the only one which we shall consider.

Once noted the condition of equal rates of return across different types of investment is intuitively obvious and appealing – if rates of return differ, more next period output can be had without any sacrifice of current consumption by shifting some of total investment from the type with the lower rate of return to the type with the higher rate of return. Clearly the condition applies however many ways there are of producing consumption goods. Also, the appeal of the condition does not depend on the assumption that there is just one commodity which can be produced in different ways. Using relative prices for aggregation across commodities we can work in terms of the values of consumption, of investment in different lines of production, and of total investment. It will still be the case that £'s of C_1 are maximised for a given £'s level of C_0 when all rates of return, calculated in value terms, are equal. Finally, here we can note that although we have explicitly considered just two periods of time, it is obvious that however many periods may be of interest, the equality of rates of return across alternative investment opportunities must hold in every period if allocation over the whole sequence of periods is to be efficient.

When discussing the concept of efficiency in allocation in the one period context, in Chapters 3 and 4, we emphasised that corresponding to any particular specification of the economic problem – in terms of quantities of factors of production, production functions and utility functions – there exist a very large number of efficient allocations. It will be apparent from our discussion above that the same is true in the intertemporal context. There are for the wheat/maize problem considered as many efficient intertemporal allocations as there are levels at which C_0 can be held constant while maximising C_1 by equalising rates of return. As in the static context, so here it is the case that to realise an efficient allocation is not, necessarily, to achieve a fair or just allocation. This point will assume some importance in our discussion of natural resource exploitation in the next chapter.

With respect to efficiency itself, it is obviously a 'good thing' whatever ethical criteria might be adopted regarding justice in intertemporal allocation. Whatever the relative weights a planner might place on C_0 and C_1, there will never be any point in seeking situations in which C_1 is less than the maximum possible for a given C_0. With suitable changes of terminology our discussion of the relation between the allocation and distribution problems in

Chapter 3 applies to the two period intertemporal economic problem. In the static context we saw, in Chapter 4, that under certain conditions the task of achieving an efficient allocation could be left to competitive markets. The same is true in the intertemporal context. Indeed, we have already implicitly demonstrated that competitive markets can, ideally, achieve an efficient intertemporal allocation. We have shown, in this section, that such obtains when the rates of return to different types of investment are equalised. We have also shown, in sections 6.2 and 6.4, that a competitive firm seeking to maximise its present value will invest up to the point where the rate of return equals the rate of interest. Given that, via a competitive bond market, all firms face the same rate of interest it follows that all firms will be investing up to points such that all have equal rates of return. Specifically, in the wheat/maize economy considered above suppose that one competitive firm handles wheat production and another maize production. Both seek to maximise their present value, in order to do which both invest up to the level such that the rate of return is equal to the rate of interest. Hence, the competitive firms ensure that $i_w = i_m$ and hence that an efficient intertemporal allocation is realised.

Two points need to be kept in mind here, both analogous to points made in our discussion of the rôle of markets in the static context, in Chapter 4. First, the claim that can be made is that markets produce efficient intertemporal allocations, and we have noted above that efficiency does not necessarily imply fairness. If we refer back to Table 6.6, for example, it is not immediately apparent that either of the efficient allocations – (i) has $C_0 = 25$ and $C_1 = 279.5085$ and (ii) has $C_0 = 50$ and $C_1 = 250$ – could be regarded as fair between the two periods. The second point is that markets produce efficient intertemporal allocations only given that certain conditions are operative. A full discussion of these conditions is beyond the scope of this book, and the interested reader is referred to the next section for guidance to further reading on this matter. What we can note here is that the conditions required are essentially those discussed in the static case (see Chapter 4), reinterpreted to cover a situation where identical physical commodities available at different dates are treated as different commodities. That is, apples on day one of period 0 are treated as a different commodity from apples on day one period 1. So, if we have n commodities in the usual sense and are considering two periods, the conditions for efficiency in allocation via markets are to apply over $2n$ 'commodities'. We should also note that for this purpose bonds are commodities.

Even these brief remarks should suggest that the conditions required for markets to allocate efficiently over time are even more restrictive than those required for markets to achieve an efficient allocation at a point in time. Thus, for example, in the first two sections of this chapter we considered a situation where there were markets in bonds and wheat. We had market participants taking all decisions on the first day of period 0 under conditions of absolute certainty about the implications of such decisions for utility and production outcomes on day one of period 1. Under such conditions, we have subsequently argued, the competitive market outcome would represent an efficient allocation. However, such conditions clearly have rather little connection with those operative in real economies, where the future implications for utility and production of current decisions are highly uncertain. The intertemporal analogue of the complete information condition introduced in Chapter 4 is, that is, not a very convincing description of the situation faced by actual economic decision makers.

Putting matters rather bluntly, few people would believe that as a matter of fact we can rely on unregulated competitive markets to allocate efficiently over time. As in the static case, the real point about the consideration of the conditions under which, and the manner in which, market systems might allocate efficiently over time is that it provides a standard of reference against which to look at actual market operation and to design policies to correct market failure. This will become apparent in our discussion of the economics of natural resource exploitation in the next chapter. We shall see there, for example, that in many cases such exploitation occurs under regimes in which the private property rights condition (see Chapter 4) is not satisfied. It follows that we would expect, in such cases, an inefficient pattern of use over time, and that we might hope to improve matters by implementing policies to establish, or provide a surrogate for, private property rights. Equally, given that we know from our examination of markets and efficiency that efficient market outcomes are not necessarily fair, we also know that policy with respect to such resources has to consider matters other than solely the correction of market failure.

6.6   Commentary

We have in this chapter discussed in a very simple way some of the basic ideas in the economics specialisation known as *capital theory*. As noted by Samuelson and Nordhaus (1985, p. 650) in their widely used introductory economics text: 'Capital theory is one of the deeper subjects in microeconomics.' As well as being quite difficult, capital theory is controversial. According to Bliss (1975, p. vii): 'When economists reach agreement on the theory of capital they will shortly reach agreement on everything else ... there is very little danger of this outcome.' In view of its difficulty and its uncertain status, it might well be thought desirable to entirely avoid capital theory in an introductory text. In fact, many introductory texts do not attempt any systematic discussion of capital theory. This option is not available in a text on environmental and resource economics, for two reasons. First, the economics of natural resources literature is itself a subset of capital theory and its applications. It is impossible to appreciate the economist's approach to natural resources issues without understanding this, and having some acquaintance with capital theory. Natural resource economics is the subject matter of the next chapter. Second, capital theoretic ideas are the basis for the techniques of project appraisal, discussed in 6.4 above, which techniques are themselves fundamental to the cost benefit analysis of projects with environmental impacts, to be discussed in Chapter 8.

In this commentary section we shall not discuss applications of the ideas developed in preceding sections. As indicated, this sort of material is provided in the next two chapters. Instead we shall simply try to guide the interested reader to sources for further reading, for purposes of clarification and amplification, or to pursue matters further.

Sections 6.1 and 6.2 dealt with intertemporal choice by individual economic agents facing given interest rates. The extent to which introductory and intermediate economics texts discuss this analysis varies widely. At the intermediate level, useful accounts can be found in Hirshleifer (1980, Ch. 16) and Gravelle and Rees (1981, Ch. 15). In section 6.3 we considered how the interactions among the behaviours of individual economic agents determine the interest rate. (On this again see Hirshleifer and Gravelle and Rees for brief accounts, and also Herfindahl and Kneese (1974, Ch. 3).) A more extended account is part III of Poindexter and Jones (1980), where the existence of different types of bonds, and of other financial instruments for consumption and income shifting, is explicitly treated, so that the existence of many 'interest rates' can be explained and analysed. Poindexter and Jones also introduce risk and uncertainty into the analysis of interest rate structures.

In this chapter we ignored risk and uncertainty and the related existence of many types of financial asset in order to set out basic ideas in a simple way. For the same reason, we made no attempt to describe the institutional frameworks of capital markets, where interest rates and other rates of return are determined. For the USA, part IV of Poindexter and Jones (1980) describes such 'real world' phenomenon; and for the UK, Midgley and Burns (1977) is a useful short introductory description of actual capital markets and their functioning.

There is now a very extensive literature on project appraisal, the subject matter of section 6.4. A useful brief introduction is Hawkins and Pearce (1971), while longer and more exhaustive treatments are Merrett and Sykes (1973) and Bussey (1978). The last of these, particularly, deals with modifications to the techniques called for by risk and uncertainty, i.e. by the fact that the cost and benefit streams are not, as we assumed, known but are estimates at best. The reader who follows up any of these references will find that the account which we gave above of the rate of return criterion for project appraisal was over-simplified, though not for our purposes misleading.

The main purpose in 6.5 was to develop the idea of efficiency in intertemporal allocation, and to indicate how a market system could realise such given certain conditions. As will become apparent in the next chapter, the idea of intertemporal efficiency is the most fundamental idea in natural resource economics. Unfortunately, it is not possible to refer the reader to alternative discussions of it which do not assume either a good background in economics or reasonable mathematical training. The idea is typically ignored in non-mathematical economics texts, and most resource economics texts take it as already familiar to the reader. An early, and not too heavily mathematical, treatment is Dorfman, Samuelson and Solow (1958, Chs 11 and 12). It is discussed, in a mathematical fashion, in Burmeister (1980, Ch. 1) which is a capital theory text and rather advanced. One natural resource economics text which does provide some discussion of the basic issues is Dasgupta and Heal (1979, Ch. 4). Again, the discussion assumes that the reader knows a reasonable amount of mathematics. However, Dasgupta and Heal do make very clear their view on the likelihood that a system of competitive markets will, un-aided, realise intertemporal efficiency:

> One does not need to be particularly perceptive to recognize that chances are slight that, as a descriptive device, the notion of an intertemporal competitive equilibrium of a private ownership economy will be adequate for the world as we know it.
>
> (Dasgupta and Heal, 1979, p. 107)

Or, as we put it 'bluntly' above, it is difficult to believe that we can rely on competitive markets to allocate efficiently over time.

Note

1. A notational problem becomes especially acute here. We have used the symbol C for consumption in this chapter, whereas in previous chapters, and here in this chapter, it is used for cost. The usage in both cases is so natural, and so widespread, that it is impossible to avoid it. The context should always make it clear in which use the C symbol is being employed.

Chapter 7

Natural Resource Exploitation

Our discussion of natural resource exploitation appears immediately after a chapter on time in economics because the principal economic problems associated with natural resource use are concerned with allocation over time. In this chapter we shall first distinguish between the two major classes of natural resources. We shall then discuss, for each resource class in turn, the characteristics of allocations over time which are efficient, and the problems associated with the achievement of such allocations. Finally in this chapter we shall consider some aspects of the question of fairness, as between time periods, in natural resource exploitation.

7.1 Taxonomy of natural resources

On the broadest definition, natural resources are all those things available to man as 'gifts of nature'. In terms of the discussion in Chapter 1, all of the links between economic activity and the natural environment involve the use of natural resources, on this broad definition. However, in this chapter we shall follow popular, and the standard economics, usage and mean by natural resources the living and non-living endowments of the earth which are exploited by man as sources of food, raw materials and energy. Thus, what we refer to here as natural resources are the environmental inputs to economic activity which come from the box R in the lower half of the schematic diagram which is Figure 1.4 (p. 14).

So conceived, natural resources exist in the environment as *stocks* from which economic activity draws *flows* of input. The major distinction drawn in economic analysis is between living and non-living stocks, with the former known as *renewable* and the latter as *non-renewable natural resources*. Thus renewable resources reproduce over time, while non-renewable resources do not. Renewable resources are animal and plant populations: non-renewable resources are mineral deposits. Mineral deposits are, necessarily, exhaustible in the sense that for any particular deposit there is no constant rate of extraction, other than the rate zero, which can be maintained indefinitely –

continued use must mean eventual exhaustion. Non-renewable resources are, for this reason, often referred to by economists as *exhaustible resources*. It is, of course, true that if the initial size of a mineral deposit is large and the rate of extraction small the deposit may be exploited over a very long time. However, the situation with mineral deposits is fundamentally different from that with animal and plant populations. Because renewable resources are subject to biological reproduction there are, for such, constant rates of use which are indefinitely sustainable. This is not to say that exploited animal and plant populations are never used in such a way as to involve their extinction. There are numerous historical examples of over-exploitation to the point of extinction. However, the point is that with renewable resources such exhaustion is not, as it is with non-renewable resources, a physical necessity. Rather it is a consequence of the particular pattern of exploitation adopted, in a situation where alternative, non-exhausting, patterns could have been adopted.

We have defined non-renewable natural resources by virtue of the absence of reproduction, and identified them as mineral deposits. Examples of non-renewable resources are, then, deposits of coal, oil, iron ore, gold, bauxite, tin, etc. Within the class of non-renewable resources a further distinction can be made between the fossil fuels and the others. The point of this distinction is primarily that burning fossil fuels uses such up in a way that, say, smelting and using iron ore do not. To a degree, the non-fuel minerals can be recycled, whereas combustion is a physically irreversible process. In what follows we shall, without further comment, use the term 'oil' as a proxy for 'non-renewable resource', since it will be more convenient to talk in terms of such a concrete example of the general category of non-renewable resources, and to do so will involve no loss of generality.

Renewable resources have been defined by virtue of biological reproduction, and identified with plant and animal populations. Actually as used by economists the term requires a further qualification, in that it refers to a plant or animal population exploited by the techniques of hunting or gathering. Agriculture is not part of the subject matter of renewable resource economics. The distinction between agricultural and hunting or gathering techniques is not always absolutely clear-cut. The essential point of the distinction is, however, clear enough. It refers to whether or not the technique for exploitation of the animal or plant population involves deliberate manipulation of the population's reproductive systems. The technology of commercial ocean fishing ranges from the very simple to the highly sophisticated, but always takes the reproductive behaviour of the target species as given. Even the most primitive agricultural practices, on the other hand, involve the modification of reproductive behaviour. So, the economics of renewable resources is the economics of hunting and gathering activity. The principal examples studied by economists have been commercial ocean fisheries. So much is this the case that it would be reasonable to use the terms 'renewable resource economics' and 'fisheries economics' interchangeably. In saying this we are classifying whales as fish, as economists have always done on the grounds that the economic circumstances of whale exploitation are not essentially different from those of, say, herring exploitation. In what follows we shall, in fact, use the terms 'renewable resource economics' and 'fisheries economics' interchangeably.

7.2   Non-renewable resources

We shall discuss the economics of non-renewable exploitation in three stages. First, we wish to discover the characteristics of an efficient intertemporal allocation of a non-renewable resource stock. Second, we shall consider the question of whether there are circumstances in which the realisation of such an allocation can be left to market forces. Third, we look at the possibilities for and consequences of market failure in non-renewable resource exploitation in order to address the question of whether market forces are, in fact, likely to realise efficient allocations. We shall leave discussion of the question of fairness in the allocation of non-renewable resource use over time to the final section of this chapter.

An efficient depletion programme

To discuss the characteristics of an efficient programme of non-renewable resource depletion we consider an economy with a stock of oil under the ground, that stock to be used up over two periods of time, 0 and 1. In order to enable us to focus on the question of the way the oil should be extracted and used over time, we shall assume that it is the only natural resource the economy exploits. We shall also assume that within each period the ideal conditions discussed in Chapter 4 are operative and that a system of competitive markets is securing an efficient allocation within each period. This means that within each period relative prices accurately reflect relative social valuations according to willingness to pay. This in turn means that we can legitimately use market prices to aggregate across quantities to obtain value totals which give social benefits and costs. We also assume the existence of a bond market and the equalisation of the rates of return on all types of investment with the rate of interest, as discussed in the previous chapter. This means that r, the interest rate, indicates the rate of return on any type of investment, and that, apart from the question of oil to be considered, we know that intertemporal allocation is efficient.

We let X represent the size of the oil stock on the first day of a period and Q the amount of oil extracted in a period. Then

$$Q_0 = X_0 - X_1 \qquad\qquad [7.1]$$

and, with all the oil being used up in both periods,

$$Q_1 = X_1. \qquad\qquad [7.2]$$

It follows that the amounts of oil extracted in each period are related by

$$Q_1 = X_0 - Q_0 \qquad\qquad [7.3]$$

shown in Figure 7.1(a), for $X_0 = 200$. We note that the slope of this relationship between Q_1 and Q_0 is unity, so that reducing Q_0 by 1 unit increases Q_1 by exactly 1 unit, and vice versa. Now, we can regard available oil not extracted in period 0 as oil invested in period 0 – oil investment is $(X_0 - Q_0)$. On this basis it would appear, from equation [7.3] and Figure 7.1(a), that i_0, the rate of return to oil investment, is zero for any level of oil investment. For recall that in the previous chapter we initially defined (see equation [6.7]) the rate of return to investment as

$$i = \frac{\Delta Q_1 - \Delta I}{\Delta I}$$

with ΔQ_1 as the increase in period 1 availability resulting from a small reduction, $\Delta I = -\Delta Q_0$, in period 0 use. Since for oil $\Delta Q_1 = \Delta I$ this definition gives $i_0 = 0$.

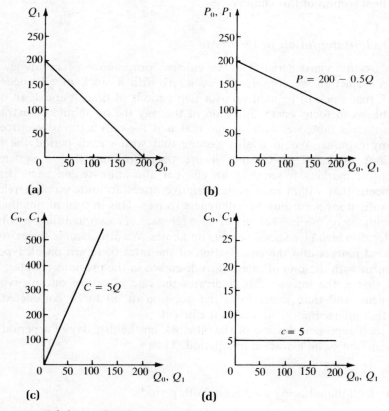

Figure 7.1   Oil demand and costs

However, this definition is in terms of physical quantities and assumes that social value is solely given by physical quantity. In the contexts in which we used this definition in the previous chapter this assumption was appropriate. It is not appropriate in the context of non-renewable resources such as oil. Clearly, given an initial oil stock of fixed size and physical transfer between periods on a one-for-one basis (unlike wheat in the previous chapter where ΔQ_1 was greater than ΔI corresponding), any use of oil in period 0 means that oil is scarcer in period 1 than it was in period 0. We would expect increased scarcity to mean increased social valuation and price, and in the oil context we need a definition of the rate of return which allows for this type of effect. What we want is the definition above with ΔI replaced by the social value of a small reduction in oil use in period 0 and ΔQ_1 replaced by the social value of the consequent small increase in oil availability in period 1. We define the rate of return to oil investment as

$$i_0 = \frac{(P_1 - c_1)\Delta Q_1 - (P_0 - c_0)\Delta I}{(P_0 - c_0)\Delta I} \qquad [7.4]$$

where P is the price of extracted oil and c is the marginal cost of extracting oil. Actually this is not a new definition. Recall in our discussion of project appraisal that we provided, as equation [6.15], a definition of the rate of return, i, on a project which was, for two periods,

$$0 = (B_0 - C_0) + \frac{(B_1 - C_1)}{1 + i}$$

with B and C representing benefit and cost. For the 'project' which is forgoing ΔI of oil to get ΔQ_1, we have

$$B_0 - C_0 = -(P_0 - c_0)\Delta I$$
$$B_1 - C_1 = (P_1 - c_1)\Delta Q_1$$

so that

$$0 = -(P_0 - c_0)\Delta I + \frac{(P_1 - c_1)\Delta Q_1}{1 + i}$$

i.e. $(1 + i)(P_0 - c_0)\Delta I = (P_1 - c_1)\Delta Q_1$

i.e. $(P_0 - c_0)\Delta I + i(P_0 - c_0)\Delta I = (P_1 - c_1)\Delta Q_1$

i.e. $i(P_0 - c_0)\Delta I = (P_1 - c_1)\Delta Q_1 - (P_0 - c_0)\Delta I$

or $i = \dfrac{(P_1 - c_1)\Delta Q_1 - (P_0 - c_0)\Delta I}{(P_0 - c_0)\Delta I}$

as in equation [7.4] above.

With the rate of return on oil investment properly defined, by equation [7.4], it is straightforward to see what a programme of oil extraction corresponding to efficiency in intertemporal allocation involves. We established in the previous chapter that efficiency in intertemporal allocation requires that the rates of return on all types of investment be equal. It follows immediately that efficiency requires that the rate of return on oil investment be equal to that on other investments. Further, we have assumed that elsewhere in the economy rates of return have been equalised and are all equal to r, the rate of interest, which equality we know to be a characteristic of the outcome when present value maximising firms are managing non-oil investment. So the condition which describes an oil depletion programme corresponding to efficiency in the intertemporal allocation of the oil stock is

$$i_0 = r = i_N \qquad [7.5]$$

where i_N is the rate of return on non-oil investments, and where i_0 is given by equation [7.4].

Let us now look at the implications of this condition in the context of a simple numerical example. The demand function for oil is

$$P = 200 - 0.5Q \qquad [7.6]$$

which is shown in Figure 7.1(b). We recall, from 4.3, that this can be interpreted as a statement about the marginal social value of, i.e. marginal willingness to pay for, oil as its consumption varies. The total cost of extracting oil depends upon the quantity extracted according to

$$C = 5Q \qquad [7.7]$$

shown in Figure 7.1(c). This means that the average and marginal costs of oil extraction are constant so that

$$c = 5 \qquad [7.8]$$

as shown in Figure 7.1(d). If we write equation [7.4] as

$$i_0 = \frac{(P_1 - c_1)\Delta Q_1}{(P_0 - c_0)\Delta I} - 1$$

and set $\Delta Q_1 = \Delta I$ and use equations [7.6] and [7.8] to substitute for the P's and c's, we get for the rate of return on oil investment

$$i_0 = \frac{(200 - 0.5Q_1) - 5}{(200 - 0.5Q_0) - 5} - 1$$

and we eliminate Q_1 here by using $Q_1 = 200 - Q_0$ from equation [7.3], so that

$$
\begin{aligned}
i_0 &= \frac{(200 - 0.5(200 - Q_0)) - 5}{(200 - 0.5Q_0) - 5} - 1 \\
&= \frac{200 - 100 + 0.5Q_0 - 5}{195 - 0.5Q_0} - 1 \\
&= \frac{95 + 0.5Q_0}{195 - 0.5Q_0} - 1 \\
&= \frac{95 + 0.5Q_0 - (195 - 0.5Q_0)}{195 - 0.5Q_0} \\
&= \frac{-100 + Q_0}{195 - 0.5Q_0}
\end{aligned}
$$

We now suppose that $r = i_N = 0.05$, so that the condition for efficiency in oil allocation, equation [7.5], gives

$$\frac{-100 + Q_0}{195 - 0.5Q_0} = 0.05$$

i.e. $-100 + Q_0 = 0.05(195 - 0.5Q_0)$

i.e. $-100 + Q_0 = 9.75 - 0.025Q_0$

i.e. $1.025Q_0 = 109.75$

i.e. $Q_0 = 107.0732.$

We have found, that is, that an oil depletion programme which is such that oil is allocated efficiently between the two periods involves extracting 107.0732 units of oil in period 0 and 92.9268 (= 200 − 107.0732) units in period 1. From equation [7.6] we get the corresponding prices as $P_0 = £146.4634$ and $P_1 = £153.5366$.

In this particular example we have found that efficiency involves the quantity of oil extracted falling over time, and the price of oil rising over time. In fact, it is generally true that, where all other markets are functioning properly and where the marginal cost of oil extraction is constant, efficiency requires the quantity of oil extracted to fall over time and its price to rise over time. This result does not depend upon the particular numbers used here, nor does it depend on considering a depletion programme stretching over just two periods. To see this we note that for $c_0 = c_1 = c$ and $\Delta Q_1 = \Delta I$, equations [7.4] and [7.5] imply

$$\frac{(P_1 - c) - (P_0 - c)}{(P_0 - c)} = r \qquad\qquad [7.9]$$

i.e. $\dfrac{P_1 - c - P_0 + c}{P_0 - c} = r$

so that

$$P_1 - P_0 = r(P_0 - c) \qquad\qquad [7.10]$$

so that for r greater than zero and $(P_0 - c)$ greater than zero, $(P_1 - P_0)$ is greater than zero. This means that P_1 is greater than P_0, which in turn means that, for a downward sloping demand function, Q_1 will be less than Q_0. Also, this argument holds for any pair of adjacent time periods, so that if we consider oil depletion over many periods we can see that efficiency requires the oil price rising continuously over time and the quantity extracted falling continuously over time.

Two more points which apply generally to efficient oil depletion programmes can usefully be illustrated here. The first is that the higher is the rate of interest, and thus the rate of return on non-oil investments, the faster the price of oil increases and the quantity extracted decreases. To see this we simply note that equation [7.10] indicates that for $(P_0 - c)$ fixed, $(P_1 - P_0)$ increases with r. For the numerical example we have used, Table 7.1 shows

Table 7.1 Interest rate variation and efficient depletion programmes

$i_N = r$	Q_0	Q_1	P_0	P_1	$\dfrac{(P_1 - c_1) - (P_0 - c_0)}{(P_0 - c_0)}$
0.01	101.4428	98.5572	149.2786	150.7214	0.01
0.05	107.0732	92.9268	146.4634	153.5366	0.05
0.10	113.8095	86.1905	143.0953	156.9048	0.10
0.15	120.2326	79.7674	139.8837	160.1163	0.15
0.20	126.3636	73.6364	136.8182	163.1818	0.20

how oil prices and quantities change as r changes: the figures shown are calculated by obtaining Q_0 and Q_1 as above, and then getting the P's corresponding from the demand function.

The second point concerns the rate at which the value of oil in the ground changes. In using equation [7.10] above to show that P, the price of extracted oil, will generally be increasing over time we assumed $(P_0 - c)$ to be greater than zero. We assumed, that is, that the price of extracted oil initially, and therefore always, exceeds the marginal cost of extracting oil. This implies that oil in the ground itself has social value. And, of course, it does precisely because by being left in the ground its use can be shifted from one period to another without physical loss, and because the total amount of oil available for use over both periods is fixed. That is, oil in the ground is scarce and intertemporally shiftable, and therefore has value. If the amount of oil in the ground were of unlimited size, oil in the ground would not have value, though of course extracted oil would. Equally, if oil not extracted in one period were somehow to vanish anyway and not be available for future extraction, oil in the ground would not itself be valuable. But because oil in the ground is, in fact, both scarce and shiftable over time, oil in the ground itself has social value. In each period the value of a unit of oil in the ground is simply the difference between the price of extracted oil and the marginal cost of extracting oil. Equation [7.9] then tells us how the value of oil in the ground changes between periods 0 and 1, when oil is being depleted as required for efficiency in allocation. We see that its proportional increase is exactly equal to the rate of interest, which is in turn equal to the rate of return on non-oil investment. This is illustrated for the above numerical example in Table 7.1. Again this is a proposition which is true however many periods of time the depletion programme stretches over – when oil is being depleted efficiently its value, as oil in the ground, is increasing at a proportionate rate equal to the interest rate.

Market realisation of an efficient depletion programme

Having examined the characteristics of an efficient programme of oil depletion, we now turn to the question of whether such can be realised by market forces. The answer to this question is 'yes' in certain circumstances, and in general terms the reason why this answer can be given follows fairly obviously from the preceding discussion. We have assumed that the conditions for efficiency in allocation by competitive markets are known to be satisfied in every respect save that pertaining to oil depletion. Now assume that oil depletion is in the hands of competitive firms. We know (i) that competitive firms select their investment levels so as to maximise their present values, (ii) that to maximise present value a firm invests up to the level at which $i = r$, and (iii) that an efficient oil depletion programme is one for which $i_0 = r$. So the competitive oil firms will invest in oil, keep it in the ground, to the extent that $i_0 = r$ and so will deplete the oil stock efficiently.

We can usefully look into this general argument a little more closely. For this purpose it is convenient to assume that two different classes of firms exist in the oil business. One class of firms own the separate oil deposits which comprise the economy's oil stock, the other class of firms extract and sell oil. We assume that in each class all firms are price takers, and that oil can be extracted under the same cost conditions from any oil deposit. There are then two sorts of oil-related markets, one in which permits to extract oil are traded, and one in which extracted oil is traded. We continue to assume that these and all other markets in the economy operate under ideal conditions (discussed in Chapter 4), that there exists a properly functioning bond market, and that rates of return on all non-oil investments are equal to the interest rate. As above, we confine our attention to the two periods 0 and 1, and we assume that trading in permits to extract oil in both periods and in obligations to deliver extracted oil in both periods takes place, together with trading in bonds, on the first day of period 0.

A firm which owns an oil deposit has to decide how many permits for extraction in each period to sell, and this decision fixes its investment in oil. We call the price of a permit to extract a unit of oil the *rent* per unit of oil: this price is alternatively known as the *royalty* per unit. We use R_0 for rent in period 0, R_1 for rent in period 1. The sale of a permit to extract in period 0 gets the firm R_0, the sale (on day one of period 0) of a period 1 extraction permit yields R_1. The proportionate increase in the rent from 0 to 1 is

$$\dot{R} = \frac{R_1 - R_0}{R_0} \qquad [7.11]$$

and $\dot{R}$ gives the rate of return associated with selling one less period 0 permit so as to sell one more period 1 permit. Now, if $\dot{R} = r$ the oil deposit-owning firm will have no incentive to alter the quantities of period 0 and period 1 permits it sells as the rate of return it is getting from oil in the ground is equal to the interest rate, so that it is maximising its present value. Given our assumptions this will be true of all such firms. If $\dot{R}$ is less than r, there is for all such firms an incentive to reduce investment in oil in the ground by selling more period 0 extraction permits, and hence fewer period 1 permits. This will reduce R_0 and increase R_1, so increasing $\dot{R}$ and moving it toward r. Conversely, if $\dot{R}$ is greater than r, oil deposit-owning firms will increase investment, selling fewer 0 permits and more 1 permits, thus increasing R_0 and reducing R_1. It is only when $\dot{R} = r$ that owners of oil deposits have no incentive to alter the depletion programme implied by their sales of extraction permits, since $\dot{R} = r$ means that each such owner is maximising present value by investing in oil up to the level at which the rate of return so achieved is equal to the interest rate.

Now consider the firms in the extraction business, which are the buyers of oil extraction permits. How much will they be willing to pay for such permits? We recall that such firms are price-takers, and (from Chapter 4) that such firms operate to maximise their current net benefits where price is equal to marginal cost. For the oil-extracting firms price is P the price of extracted oil, and marginal cost is the marginal cost of extraction c, plus what they pay, say, x, for an extraction permit. In the $P = c + x$ equation each extracting firm works with, P, is given by the market in extracted oil and c is, on our assumptions, fixed. So this net benefit maximisation condition fixes x, the price such firms are willing to pay for extraction permits, as $x = P - c$.

Considering oil-owning and oil-extracting firms together as they deal in extraction permits, we see that the former are in equilibrium when $\dot{R} = r$, and the latter when $x_0 = P_0 - c$ and $x_1 = P_1 - c$, where R is the rent per unit acceptable to permit sellers and x the price buyers are willing to pay. It follows that the markets in period 0 and period 1 permits are in equilibrium when

$$R_0 = x_0 = P_0 - c$$
$$R_1 = x_1 = P_1 - c$$

and

$$r = \dot{R} = \frac{R_1 - R_0}{R_0}$$

so that

$$r = \frac{(P_1 - c) - (P_0 - c)}{(P_0 - c)}$$

which is just equation [7.9], the condition describing an oil depletion programme which is intertemporally efficient. We have shown how competitive markets in extracted oil and oil extraction permits do achieve, under the assumed conditions, efficiency in oil depletion.

The separation of the activity of oil extraction from the ownership of oil deposits is convenient for the purpose of explaining how markets can realise efficient oil depletion programmes, but is not essential for that purpose. To see this suppose now that oil-extracting firms own oil deposits themselves, and are price takers in the market for extracted oil, where prices are P_1 and P_0. Suppose also, as previously, that all oil deposits are identical and that marginal extraction costs are constant and the same for all oil deposits. Each oil company arrives at its depletion programme by investing in its oil in the ground up to the point where $i_0 = r$. For each oil company we have

$$i_0 = \frac{(P_1 - c)\Delta Q_1 - (P_0 - c)\Delta I}{(P_0 - c)\Delta I}$$

and $\Delta Q_1 = \Delta I$, so that $i_0 = r$ implies

$$\frac{(P_1 - c) - (P_0 - c)}{(P_0 - c)} = r$$

If we now define R as the valuation of a unit of oil in the ground which is implicit in an oil-owning and extracting firm's behaviour, this is both the efficiency condition, equation [7.9], and $\dot{R} = r$. Without the separation of oil ownership from oil extraction there is no market, in extraction permits, in which the behaviour of R, rent, can be directly observed. But, the level of R at 0 and 1 is implicit in, and can be inferred from, the observed behaviour of the unified oil firms. If that behaviour is such that $\dot{R} = r$, the oil depletion programme is efficient.

Now, whether we think of extraction and ownership as separate activities or not, we see that the owners of oil deposits actually receive, in each period, an amount $R = P - c$ on each unit of oil extracted. We have also seen that R is the social value of oil in the ground, arising from its scarcity and shiftability over time. Oil deposit ownership entails the receipts of payments, rent, which arise from pure scarcity and which do not represent compensation for any effort expended in oil extraction. It is not obviously fair that oil deposit owners should capture all of the scarcity value arising from the fact that society has found ways of using oil, and that the users of the oil should get none of it. This consideration has lead to much interest in taxing the rents arising in oil, and other non-renewable resource, depletion. However, we must emphasise that, if it is granted that markets are operating under ideal conditions, this taxing of resource rents is not required for the purpose of securing efficiency in allocation and has to be argued for on the grounds of securing a fairer distribution of income as between resource owners and users. Indeed, care has to be taken to ensure that the system of taxation used does not distort the competitive depletion programme, for if it does, the improved distributional situation is achieved only at the cost of inefficiency in intertemporal allocation.

Market failure and depletion programmes

We have argued that it is possible to achieve an efficient oil depletion programme via market outcomes. We have definitely not argued that actual market outcomes for oil depletion are always efficient. Market outcomes are, with respect to oil depletion as elsewhere, efficient only if there are no sources of market failure. We now briefly look at two types of market failure of relevance to oil, and non-renewable resources in general, depletion. These two are not the only conceivable sources of divergence between the market outcome and the efficient programme, but space does not permit of an exhaustive discussion, and these examples do illustrate some of the issues. The discussion of these examples will, it must be hoped, suffice to impress upon the reader that it is not being claimed that as a matter of fact markets deplete efficiently.

The first example concerns the assumption made thus far that the firms owning and extracting oil are price takers. Given that the price taker condition is essentially the condition of a very large number of firms in an industry (see Chapter 4), it will be apparent to the reader that it is not an obviously appropriate assumption with which to consider the workings of oil industries. We will now consider a situation where the economy's entire oil stock is owned, extracted and sold by a single firm, a *monopoly*. While it is not clear that it will be true under all conceivable circumstances (regarding extraction costs and the slope of the demand function), it is the case that we would generally expect such a monopolist to deplete more slowly than is required for efficiency. We shall consider a case, the numerical example already looked at, where monopoly does involve slower depletion. We will look at the monopoly outcome together with an alternative approach to the efficient/competitive price taker outcome. This will not only indicate what is involved in the monopoly case, but will give further insight into the nature of the efficient allocation programme.

Consider Figure 7.2, which brings together the demand and marginal, equals average, cost functions from Figure 7.1. For the output level Q^*, the corresponding price for extracted oil is P^*. At this output level total willingness to pay (see 4.3) for extracted oil is given by the area of the triangle AP^*B, which is consumers' surplus (again see section 4.3), plus the area of the rectangle P^*BQ^*0. The total costs of oil extraction are given by the area of the rectangle $0EDQ^*$. Given the assumptions that we make, to the

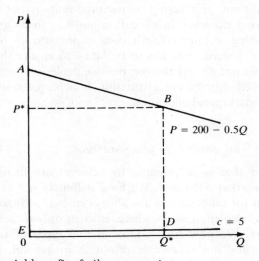

Figure 7.2 Net social benefit of oil consumption

effect that ideal conditions hold everywhere in the economy, market prices reflect social valuations so that the benefit to society of the amount of extracted oil Q^* is given by total willingness to pay and the cost is given by the total costs of extraction. The social net benefit, or SNB, of an amount Q^* of extracted oil is, that is, $AP^*B + P^*BQ^*0 - 0EDQ^* = AP^*B + P^*BDE$.

Now suppose that a national oil agency is charged with the responsibility for drawing up an oil depletion programme and implementing it. The agency adopts as its objective the maximisation of the present value of social net benefit from oil use over the periods 0 and 1. It wants, that is, to pick Q_0 and Q_1 so as to maximise

$$TSNB = SNB_0 + (1/1 + r))SNB_1 \qquad\qquad [7.12]$$

Why is this an appropriate objective? By our assumptions we know that the rate of interest r measures the rate of return on all, non-oil, types of investment in the economy. It follows that in all non-oil sectors of the economy a unit of social net benefit forgone in period 0 gets transformed into $(1 + r)$ units of social net benefit in period 1. From

$$r = (\Delta SNB_1 - \Delta SNB_0)/\Delta SNB_0$$

we get

$$r = (\Delta SNB_1/\Delta SNB_0) - 1$$

so that

$$(1 + r)\Delta SNB_0 = \Delta SNB_1$$

or

$$\Delta SNB_0 = (1/1 + r)\Delta SNB_1$$

This says that in the economy as a whole a period 0 unit of social net benefit is equivalent to $(1/1 + r)$ units of period 1 social net benefit. Hence 1 and $(1/1 + r)$ are the appropriate weights to use in adding together period 0 and period 1 social net benefits arising from oil use, as in equation [7.12]. Given these weights the agency's objective is the largest possible total of social net benefit, $TSNB$, from oil use over both periods.

Table 7.2, part (ii), shows the numbers arising for three illustrative depletion programmes considered by the agency when $r = 0.05$. The numbers are obtained by taking a pair of numbers for Q_0 and Q_1 which sum to 200, the initial national oil stock. The associated figures for P_0 and P_1 then come from the demand function $P = 200 - 0.5Q$. We then find the areas for AP^*B and P^*BDE (see Figure 7.2) in each period, and get

$$TSNB = (AP^*B)_0 + (P^*BDE)_0 + (AP^*B)_1/(1 + r) + (P^*BDE)/(1 + r)$$

We see that of the three programmes considered, that which gives the largest figure for $TSNB$ is $Q_0 = 107.0732$ and $Q_1 = 92.9268$. This programme is, in fact, that which from among all programmes such that $Q_0 + Q_1 = 200$ gives

Table 7.2 Monopoly depletion programme compared with efficient programme

	Q_0	Q_1	P_0	P_1	$(AP*B)_0$	$(AP*B)_1$ $1+r$	$(P*BDE)_0$	$(P*BDE)_1$ $1+r$	$TSNB$	$TMNB$
(i)										
	100.00	100.00	150.00	150.00	2500.00	2380.95	14500.00	13809.52	33190.48	28309.5
	102.3171	97.6829	148.8415	151.1585	2617.20	2271.90	14717.45	13597.32	33203.85	28314.7
	104.00	96.00	148.00	152.00	2704.00	2194.29	14872.00	13440.00	33210.29	28312.0
(ii)										
	106.00	94.00	147.00	153.00	2809.00	2103.81	15052.00	13249.52	33214.33	28301.5
	107.0732	92.9268	146.4634	153.5366	2866.17	2056.05	15146.94	13145.74	33214.89	28292.6
	108.00	92.00	146.00	154.00	2916.00	2015.24	15228.00	13055.24	33214.48	28283.2

the largest values for $TSNB$. Reference back to our original discussion of the characteristics of an efficient oil depletion programme, and see Table 7.1, shows that $Q_0 = 107.0732$ with $Q_1 = 92.9268$ is the efficient programme for $r = i_N = 0.05$. The programme which maximises $TSNB$ is, generally, the efficient depletion programme. Indeed, now that the point has been made for a particular example, a little reflection should convince the reader that picking Q_0 and Q_1 to maximise $TSNB$ defined by equation [7.12] is just the same as picking Q_0 to give a rate of return on oil investment equal to $r = i_N$. The answer to the question of how the oil planning agency can realise this depletion programme should be readily apparent. It simply needs to declare that extracted oil will be traded at $P_0 = £146.4634$ and $P_1 = £153.5366$ and that permits to extract oil will be traded at $R_0 = (P_0 - c) = £141.4634$ and $R_1 = (P_1 - c) = £148.5366$. Reference back to our discussion of the rôle of markets in securing efficiency in oil allocation will indicate that with such prices fixed, the self-interested behaviour of oil-extracting and oil-owning firms will produce $Q_0 = 107.0732$ and $Q_1 = 92.9268$. Such reference will also indicate that the oil planning agency is, in the assumed conditions, totally redundant, as markets in extracted oil and permits to extract oil would themselves generate the required prices and quantities.

We now turn to the case where a single firm owns and operates all of the oil deposits. The objective of such a firm will be to maximise its present value, which is

$$TMNB = MNB_0 + (1/1 + r)MNB_1 \qquad [7.13]$$

where $TMNB$ stands for total monopoly net benefits, and MNB for monopoly net benefits in a period. In terms of Figure 7.2, MNB is given by the area of the rectangle $P*BDE$, which is total receipts less total costs accruing to the firm. The firm chooses Q_0 and Q_1 so as to maximise equation [7.13] and to satisfy $Q_0 + Q_1 = 200$: not being a price taker, it does so in the light of the implications of the demand function. Table 7.2(i) shows under $TMNB$ the numbers arising for three illustrative programmes as considered by the monopolist, and the corresponding figures for $TSNB$. Of the programmes considered, that with $Q_0 = 102.3171$ and $Q_1 = 97.6829$ maximises the firm's present value. In fact, of all programmes such that $Q_0 + Q_1 = 200$ this is the programme which gives the largest present value; Table 7.2(ii) shows $TMNB$ for the three programmes considered when discussing the oil planning agency. We see that the monopolist selects Q_0 as less than required for an efficient allocation of the oil stock over time, and Q_1 as more than so required. The monopoly, that is, depletes more slowly than efficiency requires. The reason for this is essentially as follows. Starting from, for example, the efficient allocation it pays the monopolist to reduce Q_0 and increase Q_1 because the slope of the demand function is such that the increase in net revenue in period 1, after discounting, exceeds the reduction in net revenue in period 0. Thus, looking at the middle rows of Table 7.2(i) and (ii), we see that going from the latter to the former increases $(P*DBE_1)/(1 + r)$ by £451.58 and reduces $P*BDE_0$ by £429.49. We have already noted that while it cannot be claimed with complete generality that monopolists always deplete more slowly than efficiency requires, it does appear to be the case that this is what we should expect to be the usual situation. In this sense there is some justification for the contention that insofar as conservationists wish to see depletion proceed more slowly than efficiency requires, as some apparently do, they should favour monopolistic exploitation.

We now turn to a brief look at another type of market failure which might well be operative in the non-renewable resource depletion context. We have thus far assumed that market prices fully reflect social valuations, thus ruling out the existence of any external costs associated with oil extraction and use. On the basis of, for example, widely reported concern over marine oil spills and the clean-up costs of such, and of the problems arising from the atmospheric emissions of internal combustion engines, we can say, at the least, that this is not an assumption to which we should be strongly committed. We discussed external costs associated with environmental pollution in Chapter 5, and the reader will recall that the problem arising is, essentially, that market prices do not reflect social valuations. Let us suppose, in the context of our numerical example, that due to external costs arising in the use of oil the marginal social valuation of extracted oil varies with the quantity of oil used according to

$$MSV = 200 - 0.8Q \qquad [7.14]$$

rather than according to the demand function

$$P = 200 - 0.5Q$$

If we rework the above exercise for the oil planning agency, based on Figure 7.2, using equation [7.14] rather than the demand function to calculate total willingness to pay for extracted oil, we find, for $r = 0.05$ again, that the efficient depletion programme has $Q_0 = 105.4878$ and $Q_1 = 94.5122$. As compared with the original case where there were no external costs arising in oil use, this means extracting and using less oil in period 0. Since the competitive market outcome will be based on the market demand function for oil rather than the true marginal social valuation function, equation [7.14], we know and have previously shown that it will give $Q_0 = 107.0732$ and $Q_1 = 92.9268$. We know, that is, that where there are external costs associated with oil use the market will deplete the oil stock more quickly than is required for efficiency in allocation. In saying this we are, of course, assuming that oil use is not subject to a Pigouvian tax (see Chapter 5) at the rate required for externality correction.

Now suppose we concentrate on period 0, and consider both of these types of market failure together. Suppose, that is, that we know that all depletion is in the hands of a monopolist and that oil use gives rise to external costs. Can we then say anything about the relationship of the Q_0 to which market forces will give rise to the Q_0 required for efficiency in allocation? At the level of general statements the answer to this question is 'no'. We do know that generally we would expect a monopolist to set Q_0 lower than required. We also know generally that external costs in oil use will mean that Q_0 is larger than required. So, we can say that on account of monopoly considerations Q_0 is too low, while on account of pollution externality considerations Q_0 is too large. But we do not, in general, know which of these considerations dominates. We do not know whether we should wish to see the monopolist increase or reduce Q_0. As the reader will appreciate, since oil depletion is typically not in the hands of firms which are price takers and oil use does typically gives rise to uncorrected externalities, this means that in fact we have very little basis on which to believe that oil is being depleted either too slowly or too rapidly in actual market situations.

In our numerical example we do know which way things work out. We know that in the light of the external costs arising in oil use, efficient allocation requires $Q_0 = 105.4878$. We also know that, on the basis of the market demand function, the monopolist has $Q_0 = 102.3171$. Hence, the external cost considerations do not outweigh the monopoly considerations in this case – the monopolist's depletion programme is too slow even taking account of the externality. However, we must be clear that we are able to say this for this particular case only because we had an oil planning agency do the computation of the efficient depletion programme, given the presence of the external cost, on the basis of all the relevant quantitative information. What this means is that, in practice, in order to decide whether market forces were depleting too rapidly or too slowly, we would need to know: (i) the cost conditions for oil extraction, (ii) the market demand function for extracted oil, and (iii) how external costs varied with oil use. This is, as a practical matter, a stringent information requirement (as we emphasised in respect of (iii) in Chapter 5). Given that these two types of market failure are not the only possible such relevant to oil depletion, it seems safe to conclude that a statement to the effect that the oil depletion programme emerging in an actual market system is that required for efficient allocation – or is more rapid or more slow than so required – should be treated with some scepticism, unless properly supported by a great deal of empirical evidence about the particular circumstances of the case.

The problem we have discussed here is a particular example of the general class of *second best problems*. Generally such problems arise where we have two or more sources of market failure. We will discuss the case of just two. The point is that given two types of market failure we have two departures from efficiency in allocation, and that action to correct either alone may move us toward or away from the efficient allocation. Without detailed calculations based on all of the relevant information we have no way of knowing which will be the case. Thus, given oil depletion by a monopolist and external costs arising in oil use, we know that we have two sources of market failure. The second best problem is that we do not generally know whether either (i) making the monopolist behave as a price taker or (ii) taxing the external effect at the rate required for efficiency in allocation will alone move things toward or away from an efficient allocation. Whether tackling either market failure singly will make things better or worse can only be ascertained on the basis of detailed numerical information on all of the circumstances of the particular case. In the numerical example considered above we can see that since we have

$Q_0 = 105.4878$ required for efficiency
$Q_0 = 102.3171$ for the monopolist outcome
$Q_0 = 107.0732$ for the price taker outcome

to make the monopolist behave as a price taker, leaving the externality uncorrected, would involve overcorrection, in the sense that the resulting Q_0 would be greater than that required for efficiency. We can say this because we have all of the relevant information. Where such is not available we cannot be sure whether correcting one market failure, while leaving another (or others) uncorrected, will improve matters or make them worse.

7.3 Renewable resources

As noted in the first section of this chapter, the characteristic that distinguishes renewable from non-renewable resources is that the former reproduce biologically but the latter do not. One unit of oil not extracted now means exactly one extra unit available for future extraction; one unit of fish not caught now does not mean exactly one unit extra available for future catching. The economic principles of renewable resource use are not different from those of non-renewable resource use – in both cases the essential question is how much to use now and how much to leave for future use, and, for efficient allocation over time, in both cases the answer depends on the rate of return to use foregone now. However, while the principles are the same they are being applied to different physical circumstances in each case – with oil there can be no future physical return to forgone current use; with fish there can be.

If we use i_F to represent the rate of return in fishing, then the condition for intertemporal efficiency in fishing is:

$$i_F = r = i_N \qquad [7.15]$$

Here i_N and r are as defined in the previous section. Also, the rationale for this condition is exactly the same as that developed in the previous section. Further, we can argue that, given certain conditions, this requirement will be the competitive outcome in fishing in exactly the same way as we did for oil extraction in the previous section. If we assume many identical fishing grounds each exclusively owned by an economic agent acting as a price taker, then we know that in pursuit of present value maximisation each will operate such that $i_F = r$. But, by assumption, $i_N = r$, so that equation [7.15] is satisfied.

Hence, in this section our concern is not to demonstrate that a competitive outcome can realise intertemporal efficiency in respect of renewable resource exploitation. Rather, it is, first, to see what intertemporal efficiency looks like in this context. To do this we need to discuss the way in which fish consumption can be shifted over time, i.e. to discuss the population dynamics of fish stocks. Our second concern will be to consider the pattern of exploitation of renewable resources to be expected where the stocks of such are not owned by economic agents. This is the state where such resources are exploited on a free access basis, which state is that generally considered actually operative with respect to ocean fisheries.

Density dependent growth

It is standard in the fisheries economics literature to assume *density dependent growth*, with population growth in any period varying with population size at the start of the period. Figure 7.3 illustrates, with X_t representing the stock size at the start of period t, and G_t the absolute amount of growth corresponding. With X_{t+1} for stock size at the start of period $t + 1$, we have:

$$G_t = X_{t+1} - X_t \qquad [7.16]$$

In both panels of Figure 7.3, growth increases with stock size up to some stock size X^*, then declines and reaches zero at X_m. This general form for density dependent growth is that typically assumed in the fisheries economics literature. The stock size X_m corresponds to the fish-carrying capacity of the environment the fish population is exploiting. The stock size X^* is that for which G_t attains its maximum. In Figure 7.3(a), G_t is positive for all X_t below X_m, whereas in (b) G_t is negative for X_t below X_c. In the latter case the subscript c stands for critical, since if the stock size falls below X_c there is negative growth and the stock is doomed to extinction. This sort of phenomenon may arise due to the difficulty of finding mates at low population densities.

For our purposes it will be convenient to work with the particular form of density dependent growth which is *logistic growth*. This is illustrated in Figure 7.4. Panel (a) provides the same form of representation for logistic

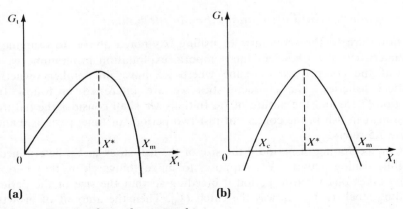

(a)   **(b)**

Figure 7.3   Density dependent growth

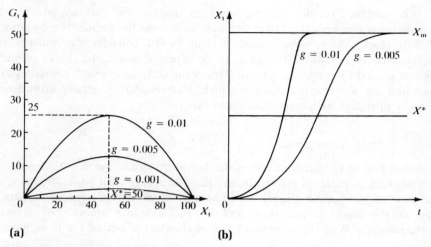

Figure 7.4   Logistic growth

growth as in Figure 7.3, showing how G_t varies with X_t. Note that the curves are symmetric about X^*. Panel (b) shows the plot of X_t against time, i.e. it shows how a population with logistic growth would vary over time on introduction to a new environment. The equation for logistic growth is

$$G_t = gX_m X_t - gX_t^2 \qquad\qquad\qquad [7.17]$$

where g is a parameter the effects of variations in which are shown in Figure 7.4 as determining the rate at which the population size approaches X_m. For larger g, the approach is more rapid (see Figure 7.4(b)), so that for any X_t (except $X_t = 0$ and $X_t = X_m$) G_t is greater the larger is g, as shown in Figure 7.4(a).[1] It is true for any logistic growth function, as illustrated in Figure 7.4(a), that $X^* = X_m/2$.

Sole ownership and efficiency: the simplest case

We now turn to the economics of fishing. As noted above, to examine the characteristics of an efficient intertemporal exploitation programme we can look at the competitive outcome where we have price taker owners of identical fisheries. The characteristics we are interested in follow from equation [7.15] and the nature of i_F. Initially we shall consider the nature of investment in fish in the context of just two periods of time, periods 0 and 1. Figure 7.5 refers.

At the beginning of period 0 the size of the fish stock is $\bar{X}_0$, determined by previous fishing activity. We suppose, to make things clear, that period 0 fishing takes place before period 0 breeding so that the size of the period 0 breeding stock is X'_0, $\bar{X}_0$ less the catch Q'_0. Then the amount of growth is read off the growth curve as $X'_0 G'$ and fixes the stock at the start of period 1,

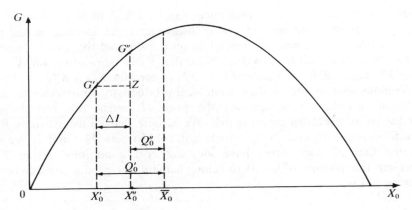

Figure 7.5 Investment in a fishery

X'_1; from equation [7.16] $X_{t+1} = X_t + G_t$. Now suppose that a smaller catch, Q''_0, is considered. Catching Q''_0 instead of Q'_0 means leaving more fish in the water in amount ΔI, i.e. increasing investment in fish in the water. With catch size Q''_0, the breeding stock is X''_0 and growth is $X''_0 G''$ for an opening stock of X''_1 for period 1. So, considering the consequences of a reduced catch size, of an increase in investment in fish in the water, we have

$$X'_1 = \bar{X}_0 - Q'_0 + (X'_0 G')$$
$$X''_1 = \bar{X}_0 - Q''_0 + (X''_0 G'')$$

and subtracting gives

$$X''_1 - X'_1 = (\bar{X}_0 - \bar{X}_0) - (Q''_0 - Q'_0) + (X''_0 G'' - X'_0 G')$$
$$= 0 + (Q'_0 - Q''_0) + (X''_0 G'' - X'_0 G')$$

and from Figure 7.5 we see that this is

$$X''_1 - X'_1 = \Delta I + Z G''$$

Now, if ΔI is sufficiently small that $G'G''$ is approximately a straight line, we have s as the slope of $G'G''$ equal to $ZG''/\Delta I$, or ZG'' equal to $s\Delta I$. In which case

$$X''_1 - X'_1 \simeq \Delta I + s\Delta I$$

where $\simeq$ stands for approximately equal to. As we make ΔI smaller so this approximation will improve, and if we consider a marginal change in the catch size we have

$$\Delta X_1 = \Delta I + s\Delta I$$

exactly, with ΔI as a marginal investment increase and ΔX_1 as the corresponding increase in stock size at the start of period 1. We have, that is,

$$\Delta X_1 = \Delta I(1 + s) \tag{7.18}$$

where s is the slope of the growth curve for $X_0 = X'_0$. In physical terms, the pay-off to extra investment in fish in the water is an increase in the next period's stock size in amount dependent on the slope of the growth function at the relevant period 0 stock size. Note that s can be positive, for X'_0 less than X^*, negative, for X'_0 greater than X^*, or zero for $X'_0 = X^*$.

We now need to add to these biological productivity considerations some economic assumptions concerning the price of caught fish and the cost conditions in respect of catching fish. We assume that all fish-catching firms face fixed prices P_0 and P_1 for caught fish sold in periods 0 and 1. We also assume that all such firms have identical cost conditions. Using E to represent the quantity of inputs to fishing activity, the production function in each period is:

$$Q = E^{\frac{1}{2}} \tag{7.19}$$

E stands for 'effort', and in the fisheries economics literature this is often measured in terms of numbers of boats. Rearranging [7.19] gives

$$E = Q^2$$

so that if the price per unit of effort is W, the cost function is

$$C = WE = WQ^2 \tag{7.20}$$

giving the dependence of total fishing costs on the quantity of fish caught. This cost function is graphed in Figure 7.6(b), where (a) displays the production function corresponding, i.e. equation [7.19]. If we let c represent marginal cost, the slope of the total cost function, the relationship between c and catch size is shown in Figure 7.6(c), and is described by

$$c = 2WQ \tag{7.21}$$

Now consider a marginal reduction in the period 0 catch size, so that there is a marginal increase in investment in fish in the water ΔI. Then, we have

$$i_F = \frac{(P_1 - c_1)\Delta Q_1 - (P_0 - c_0)\Delta I}{(P_0 - c_0)\Delta I}$$

for the rate of return to fish investment. This is just equation [7.4] from the previous section save for i_F replacing i_0 on the left-hand side. Here ΔQ_1 is the increase in the period 1 catch made possible by ΔI in period 0. Clearly $\Delta Q_1 = \Delta X_1$, where ΔX_1 is the period 1 stock size increase consequent upon ΔI. We discussed the relationship between ΔX_1 and ΔI above, and found it to be given by equation [7.18]. If we replace ΔQ_1 by ΔX_1 in the above expression for i_F we get

$$i_F = \frac{(P_1 - c_1)\Delta X_1 - (P_0 - c_0)\Delta I}{(P_0 - c_0)\Delta I}$$

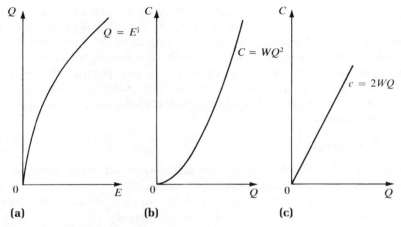

Figure 7.6   Fishing production and cost functions

where using equation [7.18] to eliminate ΔX_1 gives

$$i_F = \frac{(P_1 - c_1)\Delta I(1 + s) - (P_0 - c_0)\Delta I}{(P_0 - c_0)\Delta I}$$

$$= \frac{(P_1 - c_1) + s(P_1 - c_1) - (P_0 - c_0)}{(P_0 - c_0)}$$

$$= \frac{(P_1 - c_1) - (P_0 - c_0)}{(P_0 - c_0)} + \frac{s(P_1 - c_1)}{(P_0 - c_0)}$$

Recall now that in discussing oil depletion we introduced the idea of rent, R, as the price of a permit to extract oil, showing that R would equal the difference between the price of extracted oil and the marginal cost of oil extraction. We showed also that in the absence of a market in extraction permits, with unified oil deposit ownership and operation, $R = P - c$ would be implicit in the behaviour of the unified oil firms. Fish in the water share with oil in the ground the characteristics of scarcity and shiftability over time, so that rent arises in the same way in fish exploitation as in oil depletion. Accordingly, we can here use $R = P - c$ for the rent attaching to fish in the water, this valuation either being manifest in a catch permit market or implicit in the behaviour of firms owning and operating fishing grounds. Substituting $R = P - c$ in the above expression for i_F gives

$$i_F = ((R_1 - R_0)/R_0) + (R_1/R_0)s \qquad [7.22]$$

The content of this result for i_F is just a simple and natural extension of that giving

$$i_0 = (R_1 - R_0)/R_0$$

for oil. Recall that R is the value to the firm of oil/fish in the unextracted condition. With oil there is no reproduction so that a unit of oil not extracted currently is just one unit for extraction in the future, and the payoff to not extracting currently is just the rate of change in the value of oil in the ground. In the case of fish the same payoff obtains, insofar as R_1 is not equal to R_0. But additionally there is the possibility of physical return, reflected by s, to be allowed for, and, as indicated in equation [7.22], such physical change is to be valued allowing for any change in per unit valuation. The condition characterising competitive, and efficient fish exploitation programmes is, for the assumed conditions,

$$i_F = \dot{R} + (R_1/R_0)s = r \qquad [7.23]$$

with fishing firms so arranging catches as to make fish in the water of equal attractiveness to other possible lines of investment.

We have derived equation [7.23] by considering just two adjacent periods, 0 and 1. But clearly if we consider many periods 0, 1, 2, ... t, $t+1$, $t+2$, ... T, then equation [7.23] will apply for any pair of adjacent periods in this sequence. Hence, we have generally

$$i_F = \dot{R}_t + (R_{t+1}/R_t)s = r \qquad [7.24]$$

where $\dot{R}_t = (R_{t+1} - R_t)/R_t$ and where t and $t+1$ identify any adjacent periods. In the fisheries literature much interest focuses on the idea of a *sustainable yield catch*, which is a catch which maintains the stock size constant from one period to the next. With catching, the stock size evolves over time according to

$$X_{t+1} = X_t + G_t - Q_t$$

so that for $X_{t+1} = X_t$ we have

$$Q_t = G_t \qquad [7.25]$$

showing that a sustainable yield catch is one which is equal in size to natural growth. It follows that the graphs in Figure 7.3, and in Figure 7.4(a), can be interpreted as graphs of sustainable yield catches, showing how such vary with the stock size X. The *maximum sustainable yield catch* is the sustainable yield catch corresponding to $X = X^*$ in those figures. X^* is, that is, the stock size which gives the largest sustainable yield catch. A sustainable yield catch is one that can be maintained at constant size over time, and the maximum sustainable yield catch is the largest from among the class of such. Catches, for a given stock size, larger than the corresponding natural growth decrease stock size and cannot be maintained over time. To many interested in fisheries exploitation it appears self-evident that what is required is maximum sustainable yield catching, with the stock size maintained at X^* over time. We are now in a position to consider whether this is what intertemporal efficiency requires.

It is intuitive, and can be shown to be the case for most circumstances, that competitive fishing firms will adopt catch programmes which are sustainable yield programmes. They will, that is, adopt programmes which, apart from transitional effects, involve catching so as to maintain a constant stock size and have a constant catch size. Since we know that equation [7.24] must hold throughout the exploitation programmes adopted, we can use it to see whether the sustainable yield will be maximum sustainable yield. We note first that if the stock size is being held constant, it must be true that R, the value of fish in the water, is constant. Were it not the case that $R_{t+1} = R_t$ it clearly would not be optimal, in the sense of maximising the present value of the fishery, to have $X_{t+1} = X_t$. With $R_{t+1} = R_t$ we have $\dot{R} = 0$ and $R_{t+1}/R_t = 1$ so that equation [7.24] becomes

$$s = r \qquad\qquad\qquad [7.26]$$

which is a simple result with strong implications for the constant stock size corresponding to intertemporal efficiency.

Recall that s is the slope of the relationship between G, natural growth equals sustainable yield catch, and X, stock size. For density dependent growth, see Figures 7.3, 7.4 and 7.5, s is positive for X below X^*, zero for $X = X^*$, and negative for X greater than X^*, where X^* is the stock size corresponding to maximum sustainable yield. Now, r positive in equation [7.26] means s positive, so that the corresponding stock size is less than X^*. We have found, that is, that if the interest rate is positive, reflecting positive rates of return to increases in non-fish investment, then intertemporal efficiency requires that fish stock sizes are held below those corresponding to maximum sustainable yield. To put this in the other way round, maximum sustainable yield catch programmes are consistent with intertemporal efficiency only if it is the case that the interest rate, and hence non-fish rate of return, is zero. Note further that equation [7.26], with density-dependent growth as shown in Figures 7.3, 7.4 and 7.5, implies that the higher is r the lower are intertemporally efficient fish stock sizes.

Why is this? Why is it the case the maximum sustainable yield programmes are not, with the interest rate positive, intertemporally efficient? The answer here is really rather simple, and follows directly from the notion of intertemporal efficiency, as set out in 6.5, together with what we have assumed about the population dynamics of fish stocks. If X is at X^*, the return to a marginal increase in investment in fish in the water is zero. If returns elsewhere in the economy are positive, the economy should, in the interests of efficiency, reduce fish investment, so increasing i_F, and increase non-fish investment, reducing i_N. If such a reallocation of overall investment is not made, then the economy remains in a situation where a future gain is available at no current cost.

Sole ownership and efficiency: stock size influences catch costs

The cost conditions assumed in deriving equation [7.26] were rather special inasmuch as the costs of a given catch size did not depend upon the size of the fish stock. This is not a very plausible general assumption. Generally it would be more appropriate to assume that the costs of catching a given quantity of fish would be greater the smaller the amount of fish in the fishing ground, it being more difficult to find and net fish at low density. Taking this consideration on board complicates the analysis and modifies the results, but does not affect the principles involved.

We now assume that the production function, instead of equation [7.19], is

$$Q = AE^{\frac{1}{2}}X \qquad\qquad [7.27]$$

where A is a parameter variations in which reflect variations in the effectiveness per unit of effort. This production function is shown in Figure 7.7(a) for $A = 0.1$ and selected levels of X. The total cost function corresponding to equation [7.27] is

$$C = WQ^2/A^2X^2 \qquad\qquad [7.28]$$

shown in Figure 7.7(b), where reading off how the slope varies with Q gives the graph for marginal cost against catch size shown in Figure 7.7(c). We see that the rate at which marginal catching costs increase as catch size increases depends on stock size, being greater the smaller the stock size.

In order to consider the implications of this sort of cost behaviour, it will be useful first to go back to i_F where costs do not depend on stock size, which from equation [7.24] is

$$i_F = \dot{R}_t + (R_{t+1}/R_t)s$$

The rationale here is quite straightforward. The return to an increase in investment in fish in the water has two components. The first, $\dot{R}_t$, arises from any change in the unit value of fish in the water. Also, investment affects the future size of the stock of fish in the water according to s. The second component of i_F values this physical change, allowing for any variation in the unit valuation of fish in the water.

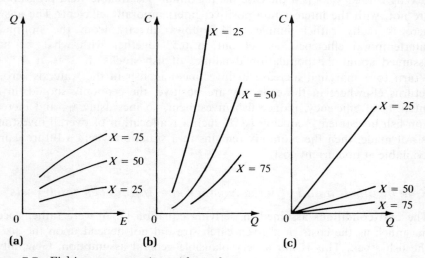

Figure 7.7 Fishing costs varying with stock size

Now, when the terms on which catching takes place are given by equations [7.27] and [7.28], this is not the end of the story. In so far as increasing investment now varies next period's stock size, it also varies the terms on which catching takes place next period. The simplest way to approach this is to note that equation [7.27] and Figure 7.7(a) show that an increase in X means that more fish are caught for constant effort. Denote the marginal increase in catch size at $t+1$ consequent upon ΔI in t as $\Delta Q'_{t+1}$. This must now be taken account of in the assessment of i_F. Two effects arise. First, there is the increase in the value of the landed catch. Second, the stock size increase is smaller than it would otherwise have been.

Taking both of these effects into account we write now

$$i_F = \dot{R}_t + (R_{t+1}/R_t)s + (P_{t+1}/R_t)\Delta Q'_{t+1} - (R_{t+1}/R_t)\Delta Q'_{t+1} \qquad [7.29]$$

noting that valuation of the stock size decrease, the fourth term, allows for changes in the unit valuation of fish in the water, and that valuation of the catch size increase, the third term, values allowing for the relative price of caught fish vis-a-vis fish in the water.

Proceeding as before and confining attention to sustainable yield catch programmes for which R is constant over time, we get from equation [7.29]

$$i_F = s + (P/R)\Delta Q' - \Delta Q'$$
$$= s + ((P/R) - 1)\Delta Q'$$
$$= s + ((P - R)/R)\Delta Q'$$
$$i_F = s + (c/(P - c))\Delta Q'$$

where at the last stage we are using $R = P - c$. The efficiency condition is $r = i_F$, so that for an efficient programme we have

$$r = s + (c/(P - c))\Delta Q'$$

or

$$s = r - (c/(P - c))\Delta Q' \qquad [7.30]$$

to be compared with equation [7.26] above arising for the case where catch costs do not vary with stock size.

To interpret the result, equation [7.30], recall that for X less than X^* (the maximum sustainable yield stock size) s is positive, for X equal to X^* s is zero and for X greater than X^* s is negative. We see first that it is not now the case that $s = 0$ requires $r = 0$, since s is equal to r minus a positive item. It is possible now to have r positive and $s = 0$. It is possible, that is, to have a situation where positive rates of return on non-fish investments co-exist with an intertemporally efficient fishing programme of maximum sustainable yield management. Note that we say only that this is possible. Clearly there is no reason to suppose that it will generally be true that

$$r = (c/(P - c))\Delta Q'$$

giving $s = 0$. Indeed, what equation [7.30] indicates is that for a positive rate

Table 7.3 Intertemporally efficient constant fish stocks

$$G = gX_m X - gX^2 = Q$$
$$C = WQ^2/A^2X^2$$

For $r = 0.05$, $g = 0.005$, $X_m = 100$, $W = 10$, $P = 12.5$, $A = 0.1$: $X = 50$

(i) *Interest rate variations*	r	0.05	0.10	0.20
	X	50	39.1	27.0
(ii) *Growth rate variations*	g	0.005	0.003	0.001
	X	50	29.3	3.4
(iii) *Cost variations*	W	10	8	6
	X	50	48.6	47.3
(iv) *Price variations*	P	12.5	15	17.5
	X	50	51.1	51.7
(v) *Productivity variations*	A	0.1	0.2	0.5
	X	50	45.4	44.9

of interest, s may be positive, zero, or negative, depending on the relative sizes of r and the second term on the right-hand side. The intertemporally efficient constant stock size may be greater than, equal to, or less than X^*. The outcome depends upon the size of r (reflecting rates of return elsewhere in the economy) and upon the precise nature of the production function and the population dynamics of the fish species in question.

We can illustrate this last point by considering the results arising in a constructed numerical example. We use the cost function equation [7.28] and the particular form of density dependent growth which is logistic growth, given by equation [7.17] above with $X_m = 100^2$. Table 7.3 shows the results obtained for a base case where the constant X size turns out to be the maximum sustainable yield stock size (50 for $X_m = 100$, see the discussion of logistic growth above) and for variations in the several parameters of the problem. We comment on these results as follows:

(i)   No significance should be attached to the base case having $X = 50$. This is merely a convenient way of presenting the results. It is definitely not meant to imply that this is the 'usual' or 'normal' outcome.

(ii)   As one parameter is varied as indicated, the others remain at their base case values.

(iii) Other things being equal, higher interest rates mean lower constant fish stock levels.

(iv)   Other things equal, a species which grows more slowly will be maintained at a lower constant stock size.

(v)   Other things equal, lower costs per unit of effort mean lower stock sizes.

(vi)   Other things equal, higher fish prices mean larger stock sizes.

(vii)   Other things equal, the more productive is a unit of effort, the smaller the constant stock size.

So, the determination of the sustainable yield stock size corresponding to intertemporal efficiency involves the interaction of a number of considerations. This is the single most important lesson to be derived from this kind of analysis. There is no one management rule, such as maximum sustainable yield, which is appropriate in all circumstances. A second important point is that intertemporal efficiency may require that some species of fish be maintained at low stock levels. The results in Table 7.3 suggest that if the interest rate is high, this will be the case for species which grow slowly and are easily and cheaply caught. In some circumstances it may be consistent with efficiency to maintain a stock size at a level so low that it is vulnerable to extinction if adverse environmental conditions arise.

Now, we have found it convenient to discuss the nature of an intertemporally efficient fishing programme in terms of the behaviour of competitive firms operating fisheries. It was convenient so to do because we saw, in the previous section on non-renewable resources, that given certain conditions competitive firms will behave as required for intertemporal efficiency in a way (by investing such that $i = r$) which relates intuitively to the notion of such efficiency. We must emphasise that we did not proceed in this way out of a belief that fisheries are, in fact, exploited by competitive firms as required by intertemporal efficiency considerations. To say that under certain conditions the competitive outcome will be socially optimal is definitely not to say that the actual competitive outcome is socially optimal. This point should by now be familiar to the reader, in general terms. We shall not work through, or even list, all of the sources of market failure pertinent to renewable resources. We shall rather look at just one in some detail. The source of market failure to be examined is much discussed in the fisheries economics literature, being characteristic of the conditions under which most ocean fisheries are, in fact, exploited.

Free access fishing

In discussing fishing under ideal conditions we assumed a number of firms each working a particular fish stock, with the implication that each such firm could deny any other fishing firm access to its stock, except on payment for permits to catch fish. We assumed that each firm had private property rights in a fish stock. As is well known this is not, in fact, the way things work, especially in ocean fishing. Rather, fishing grounds have no owners and are exploited by boats who have, effectively, *free access* to the grounds. Fishing grounds and fish stocks are typically *common*, not private, *property*. Consider, then, the situation as it affects fishing firms which own no fish stocks but which can exploit many on a free access basis. Such a firm will not decide its current catch size on the basis of the rate of return to fish left in the water since it has no reason to suppose that it will capture all, or any, of the future benefits arising from currently catching less than the maximum that it possibly can. The discussion above of fishing under ideal conditions considered sole owners of fish stocks would could capture the future benefits and who, accordingly, sought to maximise such by investing in their stocks up to the point where $i_F = r$. Under a free access regime rates of return on fish investment are of no interest to any fishing firm.

With fishing grounds available to fishing firms on a free access basis, it is assumed that new firms will enter the exploitation of any particular fishery so long as it is possible for them to earn positive profits by so doing. The level of fishing effort for a free access fishery is determined by this zero profit condition. To find the implications of free access, then, we need to find the implications of the zero profit condition taken together with the population dynamics of the exploited stock. To see what is involved we assume that costs of fishing are given by equation [7.28] above, from which, on dividing both sides by Q, we get average costs as

$$ac = WQ/A^2X^2 \tag{7.31}$$

where ac stands for the average cost of catching a unit of fish. Clearly, profits are zero when this average cost is equal to the price for which a unit of caught fish sells, so that the zero profit condition is:

$$P = WQ/A^2X^2 \tag{7.32}$$

We assume that population growth in the exploited species is according to the logistic growth equation [7.17] above, so that sustainable catches are given by

$$Q = G = gX_mX - gX^2 \tag{7.33}$$

In equations [7.32] and [7.33] we have two equations in two unknowns, X and Q. If we solve for X and Q we find the constant stock size and corresponding sustainable yield catch size for long run bioeconomic equilibrium under a free access regime. If we do this for $g = 0.005$, $X_m = 100$, $W = 10$, $P = 12.5$ and $A = 0.1$, we find that the solution for X is $X = 28.57$. Reference back to Table 7.3 indicates that for the same parameter values we found $X = 50$ required for efficiency and arising under sole owner exploitation. It is generally true that sustainable yield stock sizes emerging under free access are smaller than efficiency requires. In this sense free access leads to overfishing. Note, however, that we do not find X to be very small. It is not generally true that free access leads to catching to extinction, though it may do in some circumstances. It should be fairly obvious that it is the fact that average cost rises as stock size falls that tends to prevent free access extinction. By using alternative values for g, W, P and A in equations [7.32] and [7.33] and solving for X, the following propositions can be confirmed:

(i)   For larger g, the constant stock size is larger.

(ii)   For larger P, the constant stock size is smaller.
(iii)   For larger W, the constant stock size is larger.
(iv)   For larger A, the constant stock size is smaller.

Figure 7.8 illustrates. In each part, with the same scales, we show the graphs corresponding to equations [7.32] and [7.33], and the point of intersection identifies the solution, the eventual free access outcome, in terms of X and Q.

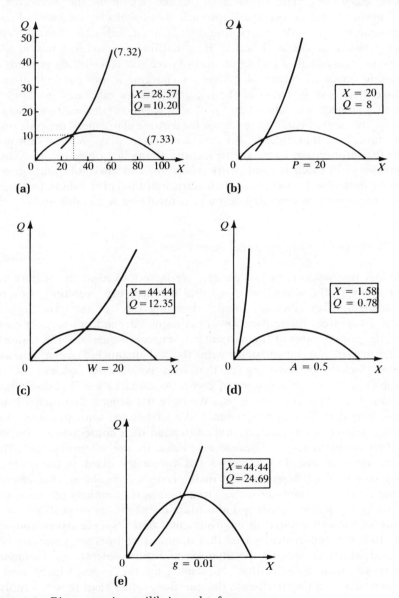

Figure 7.8 Bioeconomic equilibria under free access

Environmental & Resource Economics

In Figure 7.8(a) we have the case referred to above where $g = 0.005$, $W = 10$, $P = 12.5$ and $A = 0.1$. In the other parts these are the parameter values except for the indicated change in a single parameter value.

With reference to the standard set by the requirement of efficiency in allocation, free access means overfishing, though it does not necessarily lead to fishing to extinction. This is one of the main lessons to be learnt from fisheries economics. The implication of the lesson is the need for the modification of free access situations such that fishermen are induced to act in the same way as sole owners would. It is not feasible to envisage private property rights in ocean fisheries. It is feasible to envisage nation states establishing individual or collective control over access to fishing grounds and controlling access by means of quotas, or charging a levy per unit of catch. We have identified, in terms of the requirements for efficiency in allocation, the policy objectives. These are not simply maximum sustainable yield catching; the desired catch programme for a particular fishery depends on the circumstances of that fishery. We can see that it may well be difficult to obtain the information necessary to identify the policy objective, in terms of sustainable yield catch size, in many cases. We can also note that observed moves by nation states to extend their territorial limits for fishing jurisdiction are consistent with an emerging desire to control free access fishing.

7.4 Fairness in intertemporal allocation

In the last two sections of this chapter we have looked at the requirements for efficiency in the allocation of natural resource use over time. For non-renewable resources efficiency implies declining rates of use over time. For renewable resources the implications of efficiency depend upon, among other things, the growth rates of the particular resources in question: the realisation of efficiency is not inconsistent with the exhaustion of some renewable resource stocks. We have argued that it is possible to conceive of ideal conditions given which a system of competitive markets will realise efficient programmes of natural resource use. We have not argued that actual market systems do realise efficient programmes. We have noted some possible sources of market failure in this context, and considered their consequences. We must now discuss questions of fairness or justice in the allocation of natural resource use over time. In Chapters 3 and 4 we emphasised, in the context of the discussion of a timeless variant of the economic problem, that efficiency does not necessarily imply fairness. The situation is essentially the same when we consider natural resources and allocation over time, as we shall see.

Many of those interested in environmental and resource issues appear to believe that it is self-evidently true that natural resources are currently being over used with reference to the interests of future generations. Economists typically see their rôle as that of identifying the issues which must be addressed in attempting to discuss the question, rather than that of supplying an answer to it. We shall proceed here in this spirit. We shall make no attempt to decide whether some or all natural resources are currently being over used. We shall try to set out a sensible framework for the analysis of the question, and to clear up some apparently widespread misconceptions. As a first step in this direction we can note that from the economist's perspective much of the discussion about actual rates of resource use and the future implications of such confuses two distinct questions. The first question is: are the use rates observed as the outcome of the operations of markets as they actually exist those required for efficiency in intertemporal allocation? The second question is: from among the many available efficient intertemporal allocations which should we now choose having regard to the interests of future generations?

It is the discussion of the issues attending the second of these questions that this section is primarily concerned with. On the first question we should note here that while economists would agree that in fact natural resource exploitation by market forces does not occur under ideal conditions, there would not be much general agreement about the direction of the divergence of the actual outcomes from the efficiency requirements. Most economists would, it seems, be reluctant to assent to the proposition that with respect to the standard of efficiency, natural resources are now being over used, or under invested in. This is because natural resource exploitation is agreed, in fact, to be subject to a number of different types of market failure which do not all point to the same direction of departure from the efficiency standard. We have seen, for example, that where the firms exploiting natural resource stocks are not price takers, the competitive outcome will involve less current use than the efficiency standard requires. On the other hand, we have seen that where there are external costs attaching to resource extraction and/or use, or where private property rights in resource stocks are absent (i.e. the free access situation), the competitive outcome will involve current over use with respect to the efficiency standard. In general we can have no firm view on the actual net result of competitively realised departures in different directions from the efficiency standard. We should also note that, in fact, governments commonly intervene in the operation of markets in natural resources, and that it would be incorrect to assume that such interventions are always well conceived.

Intertemporal planning: basic ideas

We now turn to the question of fairness in intertemporal allocation. To establish the framework we begin by leaving aside natural resources issues and considering just two periods of time, the present and the future, labelled 0 and 1. We look at the economy as a whole, and we suppose that the levels of total consumption in each period, C_0 and C_1, are to be chosen, at the start of period 0, by a planning authority with complete information. This procedure, for the purpose of highlighting the essential issues, is analogous to our discussion of the command planned, timeless, economies in Chapter 3. The analysis is not intended as descriptive. It is intended to bring out the underlying issues in thinking about fairness over time. We assume allocative efficiency holds in each period, and between periods. We assume that the population size is the same in both periods. The planning authority's problem involves bringing together the possibilities for shifting consumption over time and a means of ranking the various combinations of C_0 and C_1 which are possible.

Taking the latter input to the problem first, the planning authority works with

$$V = V_0 + (1/1 - \rho)V_1 \qquad [7.34]$$

where V_0 is the planning valuation of C_0, V_1 the planning valuation of C_1, and ρ is the *social discount rate* the planning authority uses. As ρ varies so the relative weights attached to V_0 and V_1 in the ranking system vary. For $\rho = 0$, V weights V_0 and V_1 equally: for ρ greater than 0, a unit of V_0 contributes more to V than does a unit of V_1. We can note here that many would regard it as self-evident that fairness as between those alive now and those alive in the future requires that the planning authority set $\rho = 0$. We shall see that it is not self-evident that $\rho = 0$ is fair. The parameter ρ is also sometimes referred to as the planning authority's *rate of time preference*, for obvious reasons. To use equation [7.34] we need to say how consumption is valued by the planning authority. We assume

$$V_0 = 2C_0^{\frac{1}{2}}, V_1 = 2C_1^{\frac{1}{2}} \qquad [7.35]$$

so that in each period the valuation of an extra unit of consumption declines as the level of consumption increases. Put another way, equation [7.35] says that the planning authority works on the assumption that, within a period, the social satisfaction attached to consumption increases with consumption at a declining rate. Figure 7.9 illustrates.

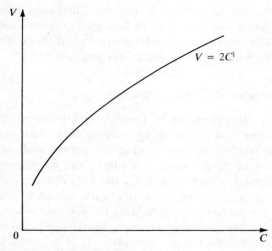

Figure 7.9 Contemporary consumption valuation

Using equation [7.35] to substitute in equation [7.34] we get

$$V = 2C_0^{\frac{1}{2}} + 2(1/1 + \rho)C_1^{\frac{1}{2}} \qquad [7.36]$$

for the planning authority's ranking, or preference, system in terms of levels of C_0 and C_1. Figure 7.10 illustrates the effects of variations in ρ on this system. Each of the three curves shown joins up the C_0/C_1 combinations which, for the indicated value for ρ, produce a particular constant level for V. The curve labelled $\rho = 0.1$, for example, traces out combinations of C_0 and C_1 which when used in equation [7.36] with $\rho = 0.1$ give $V = 40$. These curves in Figure 7.10 play the same rôle with respect to the valuation index, equation [7.36], as did the indifference curves with respect to a household utility index (see section 4.3, for example) and we shall refer to them as *social valuation indifference curves*. If we look at the points at which these curves cut the line OA in Figure 7.10, drawn at 45° to the horizontal, we see that as ρ increases so they get more steeply sloped. This means that the larger is ρ the greater is the increase in C_1 required to maintain the level of V constant in the face of a small reduction in C_0. Larger values for ρ mean, that is, a stronger planning preference for current over future consumption.

Now, the problem is to select values for C_0 and C_1 such that, for a given value for ρ reflecting social preferences as between current and future consumption, V defined by equation [7.36] takes the largest value possible in the light of the opportunities for shifting consumption over time. To make things simple we shall assume that consumption is just food consumption,

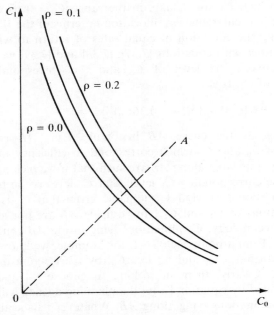

Figure 7.10 Intertemporal social valuation indifference curves

and that food consists of the two commodities, wheat and maize, which two commodities are perfect substitutes for one another so that households are totally indifferent as to whether the food they eat is actually wheat or maize. Then

$$C_0 = W_0 + M_0, \quad C_1 = W_1 + M_1 \qquad [7.37]$$

and the combinations of C_0 and C_1 over which the planning authority can choose depends upon the relationships between W_0 and W_1 and M_0 and M_1, and upon the wheat/maize mix which is C_0. With respect to the possibilities for shifting wheat and maize over time we assume

$$W_1 = 20(100 - W_0)^{\frac{1}{2}} \qquad [7.38]$$

and

$$M_1 = 15(50 - M_0)^{\frac{1}{2}} \qquad [7.39]$$

where $(100 - W_0)$ is current wheat investment and $(50 - M_0)$ is current maize investment. The reader should recognise equations [7.38] and [7.39]: they previously appeared as equations [6.16] and [6.17] in our discussion of efficiency in intertemporal allocation in section 6.5. We saw there that for any given level for C_0 the corresponding level for C_1 varied with the W_0/M_0 mix which comprised C_0. We saw that for given C_0, C_1 took its maximum possible value when the W_0/M_0 mix was such that the rates of return on wheat and maize investment were equalised. We identified such a W_0/M_0 mix as that corresponding to efficiency in intertemporal allocation, and noted that for each level which C_0 could take, in the range $C_0 = 0$ to $C_0 = 150$, there corresponded a particular efficient allocation in terms of the W_0/M_0 mix.

Now, by using the condition of equal rates of return to wheat and maize investment together with equations [7.37], [7.38] and [7.39] we can derive the relationship between the level of C_0 and the corresponding maximum attainable level of C_1. It is

$$C_1 = 20(96 - 0.64C_0)^{\frac{1}{2}} + 15(54 - 0.36C_0)^{\frac{1}{2}} \qquad [7.40]$$

which is shown as the curve AB in Figure 7.11. AB is the locus of combinations of C_0 and C_1 which correspond to efficiency in intertemporal allocation. All points lying along AB are such that if we pick any C_0 and read off from AB the corresponding C_1 level, that C_1 level is the highest possible level of consumption in period 1 attainable given that C_0 is at the chosen level. Combinations of C_0 and C_1 lying outside AB are not attainable given the economy's technology. Combinations lying inside AB could be costlessly improved upon: from a point such as Z, for example, we know that we could move to Z', with more C_1 and no less C_0, by rearranging the wheat/maize investment mix. Clearly, then, in seeking to choose C_0 and C_1 so as to maximise V defined by equation [7.36] the planning agency will consider only those C_0/C_1 combinations lying along AB. Whatever its social discount rate, reflecting preferences as between current and future consumption, it will not

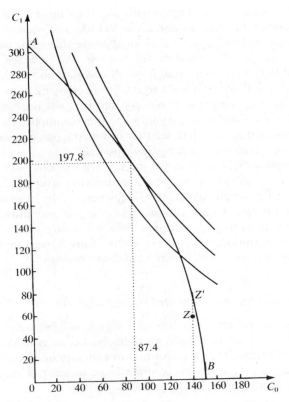

Figure 7.11   An optimal intertemporal allocation of consumption

select a C_0/C_1 combination lying inside AB. Whatever else it wants, the planning agency certainly wants efficiency in intertemporal allocation.

In Figure 7.11 we also show some of the valuation indifference curves for the planning agency's preference system, equation [7.36], for the case where the social discount rate, ρ, is 0.05. As should now be familiar, the optimum solution to the planning problem – which is to find the C_0/C_1 values which make V defined as equation [7.36] attain its maximum possible value given that C_0 and C_1 must be related according to equation [7.40] (i.e. lie along AB) – is identified by the tangency of a valuation indifference curve with AB, the boundary of the set over which choice is possible. We see in Figure 7.11 that for $\rho = 0.05$, the chosen level of C_0 is 87.4 and of C_1 is 197.8. Given that we have seen that the slopes of the planning indifference curves vary as ρ varies, it will be obvious that the chosen C_0 and C_1 must vary with ρ. If the Figure 7.11 exercise is repeated for $\rho = 0.00$ we find that the planning agency chooses $C_0 = 84.8$ and $C_1 = 201.87$. This result illustrates two general points of importance. First, that lower values for ρ mean lower values for C_0 and higher values for C_1, given the same possibilities for shifting consumption over time. Conversely, if the planning agency raises ρ it will select a higher C_0

and a lower C_1. Thus, for example, with $\rho = 0.10$ the Figure 7.11 exercise produces the choice $C_0 = 90.00$ and $C_1 = 193.65$. The second point is that $\rho = 0.00$ does not lead to $C_0 = C_1$. We noted above that some would regard it as self-evident that $\rho = 0$ is required for fairness. We now see that it is not necessarily true that it leads to equal levels of consumption in the present and the future. Indeed in this case it leads to the future enjoying more than twice as much consumption as the present! We say that it is not necessarily true that $\rho = 0$ implies $C_0 = C_1$: we do not say that $\rho = 0$ never implies $C_0 = C_1$. This is an important distinction. We shall see that just as the outcome of this kind of planning exercise varies with ρ for given possibilities in terms of (efficiently) shifting consumption over time, so for given ρ the outcome will depend upon the particular possibilities for shifting consumption over time. Hence, one cannot simply and generally take a view on fairness on the basis of the value of the social discount rate. Conservationists who argue that justice as between generations requires us to plan with $\rho = 0$ are not, as we shall see, necessarily wrong in their prescription, but they are guilty of gross oversimplification of a complex problem, and may well be wrong in their prescription.

An optimal programme of capital accumulation

Before bringing natural resources into the story it will be useful to generalise the above analysis by dividing time more finely. Let us consider planning at the beginning of period 0 for a consumption programme stretching out over periods $0, 1, 2, \ldots, T$, where T is some large number. Corresponding to equation [7.40] we now have

$$V = \sum_{t=0}^{T} \left(\frac{1}{1+\rho}\right)^t V_t = V_0 + \left(\frac{1}{1+\rho}\right) V_1 + \left(\frac{1}{1+\rho}\right)^2 V_2 + \ldots$$
$$+ \left(\frac{1}{1+\rho}\right)^T V_T \qquad\qquad [7.41]$$

with

$$V_t = 2C_t^{\frac{1}{2}} \quad \text{for } t = 0, 1, 2, \ldots T. \qquad\qquad [7.42]$$

The planning problem is to pick from among all the feasible sequences of consumption levels $C_0, C_1, C_2, \ldots C_T$ that one which gives the maximum value possible for V defined by equation [7.41]. To focus on the essential issues we shall assume that there is just one commodity in the economy. We assume that this commodity can, in any period, either be consumed or added to the accumulated stock, which we call the *capital stock*. With just one commodity and one type of investment we do not have to worry about the equalisation of rates of return across different types of investment, and the possibilities for shifting consumption over time are given by

$$C_t = Y_t - I_t = Y_t - (K_{t+1} - K_t) \quad \text{for } t = 0, 1, 2, \ldots T \qquad [7.43]$$

and

$$Y_t = K_t^\alpha \quad \text{for } t = 0, 1, 2, \dots T \tag{7.44}$$

where Y_t represents the output of the commodity in period t, I_t the amount not consumed but invested, and K_t the size of the capital stock at the beginning of period t. The equation [7.44] is the production function for the commodity: we are assuming for simplicity that capital is the only input to production. Figure 7.12 shows the relationship [7.44] for three different values taken by the parameter α: Y increases with K at a decreasing rate for any value of α, but as α gets smaller so, for given K, Y gets smaller and the rate of increase of Y with K gets smaller. Equation [7.43] says that in any period output is either consumed or invested. The implications of this can be seen by writing it as

$$K_{t+1} - K_t = Y_t - C_t$$

and looking at the production function [7.44] – for given K_t and Y_t, less C_t means larger K_{t+1} and therefore a larger Y_{t+1} with the possibility for larger C_{t+1}. Consumption is shifted over time by means of investment and capital accumulation: the problem is to find the programme of capital accumulation which gives a consumption sequence which is optimal in the light of the valuation of consumption at different dates.

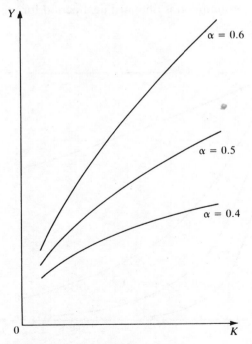

Figure 7.12   Capital input and output as α varies

So, the planning problem, is, for some given initial capital stock size K_0, to find from among the C_0, C_1, ... C_T sequences that are feasible by virtue of equations [7.43] and [7.44] that one which maximises V defined by equations [7.41] and [7.42]. Our interest is especially in how this choice of consumption programme will be affected by variations in ρ in equation [7.41] and α in equation [7.44]. If we denote the weights which equation [7.41] attaches to V in different periods as w_t so that $w_t = (1/1 + \rho)^t$ (i.e. $w_0 = 1$, $w_2 = (1/1 + \rho)^2$, $w_{10} = (1/1 + \rho)^{10}$ etc.) then Figure 7.13 shows how these weights decline over time for different values of ρ. The general nature of the time path of consumption the planning agency will choose is shown in Figure 7.14: consumption increases at a decreasing rate over time and eventually stabilizes at a constant level C^*. While consumption is increasing, investment is positive and the capital stock is growing: once consumption is constant investment is zero and capital accumulation ceases.

Table 7.4(i) illustrates how the level of C^* varies with variations in the parameters ρ and α, the former reflecting the social discount rate or rate of time preference, the latter reflecting the productivity of capital. Table 7.4(ii) shows how the level of K corresponding to C^* behaves.

Considering first variations in α, we see that for any ρ, C^* and K^* increase with α. This is the first illustration of the point made above that the outcome of the planning exercise varies with changes in the consumption shifting opportunities, for a constant time preference rate. Basically the interpretation of these results is straightforward. The more productive is capital, i.e. the larger is α, then the more consumption is obtained next period for a given sacrifice of

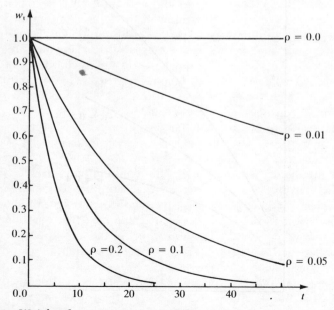

Figure 7.13 Weights for consumption at different dates

Table 7.4 Stationary levels for optimal programmes
          (i) C* values

	$\rho = 0.01$	0.03	0.05	0.10	0.15
α					
0.2	2.12	1.61	1.41	1.19	1.07
0.4	11.70	5.62	4.00	2.52	1.92
0.6	50.00	16.67	10.00	5.00	3.33
0.8	464.76	89.44	41.57	14.70	8.00

(ii) K* values

	$\rho = 0.01$	0.03	0.05	0.10	0.15
α					
0.2	42.30	10.71	5.66	2.38	1.43
0.4	467.84	74.97	32.00	10.08	5.13
0.6	2 500.00	277.78	100.00	25.00	11.11
0.8	27 885.48	1788.85	498.83	88.18	32.00

consumption in the current period. Hence, for given time preference, the more productive is capital, the more it will be accumulated. The process of accumulation does not go on indefinitely, however, because as Figure 7.12 shows the productivity of capital declines as it is accumulated. Now holding α constant and looking across rows in Table 7.4, we see that C^* and K^* fall as ρ increases. Again the interpretation of this is not difficult. The higher the social discount rate the less weight is attached to the future consumption payoff to consumption foregone currently, so that less consumption is currently foregone and less capital accumulated. Table 7.4 suggests that where they are planned in the manner we have assumed, economies with low social discount rates and highly productive capital eventually become very rich ($\alpha = 0.8$, $\rho = 0.01$), while economies with high social discount rates and less productive capital never escape from low consumption levels ($\alpha = 0.2$, $\rho = 0.15$).

What has this got to do with fairness in allocation over time? Capital accumulation benefits the future at the expense of the present. As equation [7.43] makes plain, K_{t+1} is greater than K_t only when C_t is less than its maximum attainable value $C_t = Y_t$. So consumption growth via capital accumulation involves sacrifices by early generations to realise benefits for later generations. Deciding how large the sacrifices and benefits should be is a question of deciding what is fair between generations. The question cannot be approached, let alone settled, solely in terms of the appropriate level for the social discount rate. As Table 7.4 makes clear, the implications of variations in ρ are not independent of the technological circumstances. For example, consider the situation where planning is currently being done with $\rho = 0.05$ and it is suggested that fairness requires that $\rho = 0.01$ should be used. If $\alpha = 0.2$ the consequent increase in C^* is from 1.41 to 2.12, while if $\alpha = 0.8$ it is from 41.57 to 464.76. Presumably our attitude to increasing the sacrifices made by current and early generations, as going from $\rho = 0.05$ to $\rho = 0.01$ means, cannot be independent of the size of the improvement this confers on later generations and the size of the base for such improvement.

We have previously noted that $\rho = 0$ is frequently advanced as constituting fairness. There are no entries for $\rho = 0$ in Table 7.4. This is because for $\rho = 0$, whatever value α takes in the range 0 to 1, C^* and K^* do not exist. For $\rho = 0$, that is, capital accumulation continues throughout the planning sequence however large T may be, and so consumption grows without limit, rather than behaving as shown in Figure 7.14. It is not obvious that it is fair that successive generations should go on getting richer than their predecessors for ever. In saying this we are, of course, assuming that ever growing consumption levels can be maintained. The assumption is valid given the assumptions that we started with, as represented in equations [7.43] and [7.44]. But, of course, it is precisely this assumption that conservationists would argue is invalid in the world we live in, arguing that however desirable continually rising consumption levels might be they are not feasible in the light of the availability of natural resources. It is to this sort of argument that we can now turn, asking what difference would natural resource constraints make to the issues that arise in planning exercises of the type considered above?

Non-renewable resources: the role of technology

We consider first the case of non-renewable resources, which presumably give rise to the most serious concern, as they are in a technical sense exhaustible. Also, we have seen that efficient intertemporal allocation involves use rates for non-renewable resources which decline over time, which may itself appear

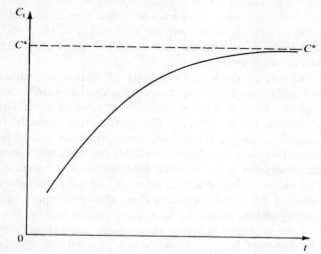

Figure 7.14 An optimal path for consumption

unfair to future generations. This appearance results from the implicit assumption that resource use itself matters. In the case of non-renewable resources this is not an obviously appropriate assumption, generally. Presumably what people care about is the quantity and quality of the goods and services they consume, and the availability and use of non-renewable resources is of interest only insofar as it affects this consumption. I certainly derive no satisfaction from oil in the ground as such, though I do derive satisfaction from being kept warm, from being able to make long journeys quickly and conveniently, from using plastics and so on and so on. If I could continue to do these things in the absence of any oil left in the world, I would feel no loss on account of the disappearance of the last drop of oil. I seem to be a representative individual in this respect.

So, to address the problem of fairness in the intertemporal allocation of, say, oil use we must consider the way such use affects consumption levels. We need, that is, to look at the technology which converts oil into goods and services for household consumption. We do this in a very broad brush way to bring out the key issues, as simply as possible. We assume that we can still think in terms of a single commodity which can be either consumed or added to the capital stock in any period. However, we now assume that the production of this commodity uses oil as well as capital. The production function is, that is

$$Y_t = Y_t(K_t, Q_t) \tag{7.45}$$

where Q_t represents oil use in period t and where the $Y_t = Y_t (K_t, Q_t)$ symbolisation simply means that particular pairs of values for K_t and Q_t give particular values for Y_t in a definite, but currently unspecified, way. Production functions with two inputs can be represented graphically by means of *isoquants* (see also 3.5). An isoquant is a line joining up those combinations of levels of the two inputs which give rise to a particular constant output level. Figure 7.15(a) illustrates the general idea. The output level Y_1 can be produced by all those input combinations lying along the isoquant labelled $Y_1 Y_1$: Q' with K' and Q'' with K'', for example, both produce Y_1 units of output. Y_2 is some higher output level, producible by all those input combinations lying along $Y_2 Y_2$.

Let us now consider three particular production function types, according to which oil and capital can be combined to produce output, and the corresponding isoquant shapes. We consider

$$Y_t = aK_t + bQ_t \tag{7.46}$$

to which the isoquant shapes in Figure 7.15(b) correspond,

$$Y_t = \min(aK_t, bQ_t) \tag{7.47}$$

with Figure 7.15(c) corresponding, and

$$Y_t = AK_t^\alpha Q_t^{1-\alpha} \tag{7.48}$$

to which the isoquants in Figure 7.15(d) correspond.

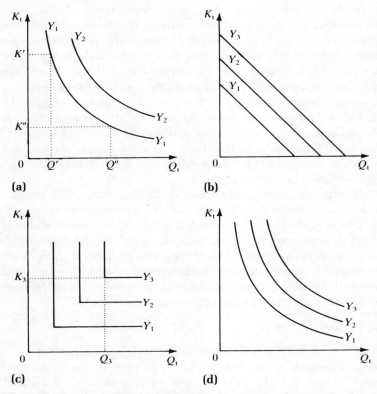

Figure 7.15   Production technologies using capital and oil inputs

Our interest is in the possibilities for substitution as between oil and capital in each of these cases. For equation [7.46] and Figure 7.15(b) it is not difficult to see that oil is not essential in production. Setting $Q_t = 0$ in equation [7.46] does not necessarily mean that $Y_t = 0$, since $Y_t = aK_t + 0 = aK_t$. In the diagram also we can see that any given output level can be produced without using any oil given enough capital. For the production function equation [7.47] oil is essential to production in the sense that zero oil input means zero output. Equation [7.47] is to be read as saying that Y_t is equal to the minimum of aK_t and bQ_t; if aK_t is smaller than bQ_t then $Y_t = aK_t$, if bQ_t is smaller than aK_t then $Y_t = bQ_t$. Hence, $Q_t = 0$ implies $Y_t = 0$. In terms of the illustration in Figure 7.15(c), the output level Y_3 requires, as minima, input levels K_3 and Q_3. If either one of these levels is not available, the output level Y_3 cannot be produced. With the production functions [7.46] and [7.47] the possibilities for substitution between oil and capital in production are unambiguous and do not depend upon the particular values of the parameters. With equation [7.48] the essentialness of oil in production is a less clearcut issue and the value of the parameter α is crucial. We shall defer discussion of this case until we have looked at the implications of the cases equations [7.46] and [7.47] for the intertemporal planning problem.

We deal first with the planning problem which is to choose the consumption programme which maximises

$$V = \sum_{t=0}^{T} \left(\frac{1}{1+p}\right)^t V_t$$

which is equation [7.41], where in each period consumption is valued according to equation [7.42] so that

$$V_t = 2C_t^{\frac{1}{2}}$$

given that the feasible consumption programmes to be selected from among are described by

$$K_{t+1} - K_t = Y_t - C_t$$

which is equation [7.43] rearranged, and the production function [7.46], i.e.

$$Y_t = aK_t + bQ_t$$

In this problem, output can be produced without using oil. It follows that the problem is not in its essentials any different from the one we considered above in which natural resource use did not feature. If, to take the limiting case, the stock of oil were zero at the start of period 0, then it is clear that (apart from a change in the particular algebraic form of the production function) with $Q_t = 0$ for all t, the planning problem immediately above is the same as that considered previously. Put very simply, the point is that if oil is not essential in production, then future generations will have no cause for complaint if we bequeath them no oil, provided we also bequeath them capital.

We now consider the planning problem when oil is essential in production, so that we wish to find the consumption programme which maximises V from equations [7.41] and [7.42] given feasible programmes described by equation [7.43] and

$$Y_t = \min(aK_t, bQ_t)$$

which is equation [7.47]. Now this problem is very different from that previously looked at. With a production function like equation [7.47] the amount of oil use in period t sets an upper limit to the amount of output produced – if $Q_t = 10$, for example, then the output level is b times 10, however much capital is available. In terms of Figure 7.15(c), if Q_3 is the amount of oil to be used no more than Y_3 can be produced, however much capital is available. What this means is that we can look at the planning problem where oil is essential in production as if oil were the only input to production, since no amount of capital accumulation can overcome any problems associated with low, or zero, rates of oil input to production. In this case, ignoring capital in production and the rôle of capital accumulation, the feasible consumption paths for the economy are described by

$$Y_t = C_t \tag{7.49}$$

and

$$Y_t = bQ_t \tag{7.50}$$

instead of equations [7.43] and [7.44] as they were in our original formulation of the planning problem. With X_t representing the stock of oil at the beginning of period t we also have

$$X_t - X_{t+1} = Q_t \tag{7.51}$$

describing how the size of the remaining oil stock changes over time: for Q_t positive, X_{t+1} is less than X_t.

If we use $\bar{X}_0$ to represent the given size of the oil stock existing at the beginning of period 0 when the planning exercise takes place, then since total use over all T periods cannot exceed the total amount available, we know that

$$\sum_{t=0}^{T} Q_t = \bar{X}_0 \tag{7.52}$$

and given $C_t = bQ_t$ from equations [7.49] and [7.50] this means that only consumption paths such that

$$\sum_{t=0}^{T} C_t / b = \bar{X}_0 \tag{7.53}$$

are feasible. The consumption paths from among which the planning agency can select are, that is, limited by the condition that they must satisfy equation [7.53]. Clearly the planning problem has been reduced to sharing out the initial stock of oil, $\bar{X}_0$ over T periods in such manner as to maximise

$$V = \sum_{t=0}^{T} (1/1 + p)^t C_t^{\frac{1}{2}}$$

as the choice of an oil share, Q_t, for any period immediately fixes the consumption level for that period. Put another way, what we are saying here is that given the assumed production conditions, the initial oil stock implies that there is a fixed total amount of consumption

$$\sum_{t=0}^{T} C_t = b\bar{X}_0$$

to be shared out between the T periods, by choosing a C_t sequence that maximises V.

Given that there is a fixed total amount of consumption to be allocated over time, many would say that fairness obviously requires equal shares for each period, so that the planning agency should choose the consumption programme

$$C_t = b\bar{X}_0/T \quad \text{for } t = 0, 1, 2, \ldots T \tag{7.54}$$

It will be clear that this programme will give the maximum for V if and only if the social discount rate being used is zero. The planning agency's chosen programme will involve equal shares if it uses $\rho = 0$, so that consumption in each of the T periods is weighted equally. For ρ greater than zero the weights attached to consumption at different dates decline steadily as t increases (see Figure 7.13), and it is clear that using a positive social discount rate would lead to the choice, for maximum V, of a consumption programme in which C_t declines with increasing t, the rate of decline increasing with ρ.

It appears that we have here identified a situation where the simple equation of a zero social discount rate with the requirement of fairness in intertemporal allocation is valid. Unfortunately, even here things are not quite that simple. The problem arises from the observation that if all of $\bar{X}_0$ is shared equally (or in any way) between the T periods, then there is no oil available for use in periods $T+1$, $T+2$, ... By assumption this means zero consumption in periods $T+1$, $T+2$, ... , and, unless it is known that the economy will anyway cease to exist at the end of period T, this is not obviously fair to those alive after the period T. So, presumably the planning agency should plan subject to the requirement to leave some oil in existence at the end of period T. But how much? In order to answer this question the planning horizon must be extended from T to $T+1$. But then exactly the same problem arises with respect to periods $T+2$, $T+3$, ... And so on and so on. If oil is essential to production and consumption, and if it is not known when the economy will anyway cease to exist, it is difficult to avoid the conclusion that the planning horizon must be indefinitely far into the future – the planning agency should operate with T equal to infinity. But, if it does so the equal shares choice is simply not open to it, for there is no way that the finite amount of $\bar{X}_0$, can be divided up into an infinite number of equal shares. Unless, that is, the equal shares are of size zero. The problem pick a sequence of C_t levels stretching out to $T = \infty$ (infinity) so as to maximise

$$V = \sum_{t=0}^{\infty} (1/1 + \rho)^t C_t^{\frac{1}{2}}$$

given that

$$\sum_{t=0}^{\infty} C_t = b\bar{X}_0$$

where $\bar{X}_0$ is a finite number and ρ is zero has the solution $C_t = 0$ for all t. Solutions for selected positive values of the social discount rate, for $b = 1$, are illustrated in Figure 7.16. Here the initial period's consumption level is set arbitrarily at 100 so as to give some indication of how variations in the value of ρ affect the length of time taken for C_t to fall to 1% of its initial level. It should be noted that C_t approaches the level zero *asymptotically* – this means that for no value of ρ does C_t actually become zero during a finite number of periods, though the difference between C_t and zero may be extremely small.

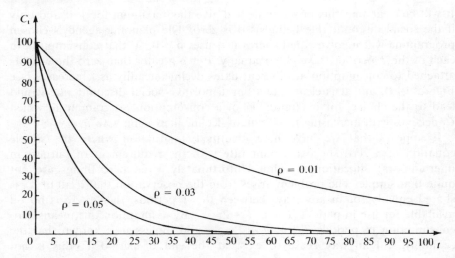

Figure 7.16 Consumption paths with oil essential in production

We now turn to the case where the production function is equation [7.48], for which case the isoquants are illustrated in Figure 7.15(d). Comparison of (d) there with (b) and (c) suggests that for equation [7.48] the possibilities for substitution between oil and capital in production are intermediate between the extreme cases whose implications we have just examined. However, if we set $Q_t = 0$ in equation $Y_t = AK_t^\alpha Q_t^{1-\alpha}$ we apparently get $Y_t = 0$: with $A = 1$ and $\alpha = 0.5$, for example, $Y_t = K_t^{\frac{1}{2}} Q_t^{\frac{1}{2}}$ and with the square root of 0 as 0 this gives $Y_t = 0$ for $Q_t = 0$. This would seem to imply that with equation [7.48] oil is essential in production, with implications the same as those discussed immediately above for the production function [7.47]. It turns out, in effect, that this is true for some values of A and α, but not for others. By this we mean that if the rôle of oil in production is sufficiently small then there exists some positive constant level of consumption which can be maintained for ever, while if the rôle of oil in production is greater than this the only constant level of consumption maintainable for ever is the level zero.

The proper analysis of this situation requires some advanced mathematics, but we can see what is involved by way of some simple numerical experiments. We consider a 1,000 period time horizon, i.e. $T = 1,000$. We assume that in period 0, $Y_0 = 100$, $K_0 = 100$ and $Q_0 = 10$. We impose declining oil use such that

$$Q_{t+1} = 0.95Q_t \quad \text{for } t = 0, 1, 2, \ldots T \tag{7.55}$$

which means that oil use in every period is just 95% of oil use in the previous period. This means that very little oil is used in later periods: part (i) of Table 7.5 shows the oil use levels which follow from equation [7.55] and $Q_0 = 10$ at 100-period intervals. The numbers are written in such a way as to avoid writing lots of zeros: 10^{-x} is $1/10^x$, so that 0.123×10^{-7}, for example, is

Table 7.5 Declining oil use and the sustainability of constant consumption

(i)	t	Q_t
	100	0.592×10^{-1}
	200	0.351×10^{-3}
	300	0.208×10^{-5}
	400	0.123×10^{-7}
	500	0.728×10^{-10}
	600	0.431×10^{-12}
	700	0.255×10^{-14}
	800	0.151×10^{-16}
	900	0.894×10^{-19}
	1000	0.529×10^{-21}

(ii)	α	t^*	Y_t
	0.5	33	2.41×10^2
	0.6	51	1.045×10^3
	0.7	84	1.036×10^4
	0.8	161	1.007×10^6
	0.9	452	1.407×10^{12}
	0.91	525	3.428×10^{13}
	0.92	619	1.883×10^{15}
	0.93	744	3.309×10^{17}
	0.94	917	3.337×10^{20}
	0.95	—	4.923×10^{24}

$0.123 \times 1/10^7 = 0.0000000123$. Given the level of oil use fixed for every period, we have output produced according to equation [7.48] for varying values of α and for A so fixed as to make $Y_0 = 100$ given the value taken by α. The level of capital input in each period is calculated as part of the experiment, as follows. We pick some level for consumption which is to hold constant over time starting at $t = 0$, and then the capital stock evolves over time according to

$$K_{t+1} - K_t = Y_t - C = I_t \quad \text{for } t = 0, 1, 2, \ldots T$$

where C is the constant consumption level, and I_t is investment. If we write

(i) $C = Y_t - I_t$
(ii) $C = Y_{t+1} - I_{t+1}$

and subtract (i) from (ii) we get

$$0 = Y_{t+1} - Y_t - I_{t+1} + I_t$$

or

$$I_{t+1} - I_t = Y_{t+1} - Y_t$$

so that Y_{t+1} greater than Y_t implies I_{t+1} greater than I_t, and Y_{t+1} less than

Table 7.6 Time paths for capital and output

t	K_t	Y_t
0	100	100
100	67 232	639
200	88 331	97
300	83 454	12
400	74 959	1.5
500	66 020	0.17
600	57 027	0.02
700	48 028	0.002
800	39 028	0.0003
900	30 028	0.00003
1000	21 028	0.000003

Y_t implies I_{t+1} less than I_t. Clearly this means that if in an experiment we find that Y reaches a maximum and then starts to decline, then investment must also start to decline. But declining investment must mean a more slowly growing capital stock, which must, in turn, given declining resource use, mean that the downturn in income is not reversible. Once Y and I start going down they must keep going down. This means that if Y ever turns down, then eventually the size of the capital stock must start to decline. Given declining resource use rates this must mean that eventually it is no longer possible to produce enough output to provide the chosen constant consumption level.

In Table 7.5(ii) we show some results from the experiment just described for $C = 90$, so that in period 0 10% of income is invested. For each value of α, under t^* we give the date at which Y reaches its maximum before starting downwards, and under Y_{t^*} we give the maximum level attained by Y ($1.007 \times 10^6 = 1,007,000$, for example). According to the test 'does Y attain a maximum within 1,000 periods?', we see that $\alpha = 0.95$ implies that the constant consumption level $C = 90$ is indefinitely sustainable while for smaller values of α it is not. Note that the value shown under Y_{t^*} for $\alpha = 0.95$ is not the maximum Y can attain, but the level reached at $t = 1,000$, at which date Y is still growing. Table 7.6 shows the history of K_t and Y_t for $\alpha = 0.6$: somewhere between $t = 200$ and $t = 300$ the level of Y_t falls below 90, and thereafter the consumption level is maintained by using up the capital stock. This cannot go on forever, but as Table 7.6 indicates it can go on for a long time – at $t = 1,000$ consumption can be maintained at the level 90 in this way for approximately another $21,000 \div 90 = 233$ periods. For $\alpha = 0.95$, the capital stock at $t = 1,000$ is 1.082×10^{27}!

The results of these experiments make three points very clearly. First, that quite a modest level of investment initially can, even with declining oil use rates, lead to the accumulation of a very large capital stock. Second, that with a large capital stock large amounts of output are producible, notwithstanding low levels of oil use. Third, see Table 7.5(ii) especially, that the implications of these considerations for the sustainability of constant consumption in the face of declining oil use depend crucially on the value taken by α in equation [7.48]. To further emphasise this last, and most important, point we can note the results of two further experiments. First, for $\alpha = 0.95$ we can raise the constant consumption level to $C = 99.5$ and still find Y growing at $t = 1,000$. Second, for $\alpha = 0.5$ we can cut C to 30 and still find that Y reaches a maximum within the first 50 periods.

So, it is clear that if it is appropriate to assume a production function of the type [7.48], the implications, in terms of fairness over time, of declining oil use depend crucially on the precise numerical value of the parameter α. The point of this, and of our earlier consideration of equations [7.46] and [7.47], is that in order to take a view on whether what we are currently doing, in terms of non-renewable resource use, is or is not fair to future generations we have to know rather precisely the rôle resources play in production, as well as what the social discount rate is. In principle, the rôle of resources in production is an empirical matter. It is, however, a complicated one. It seems unlikely that it is appropriate to assume that non-renewable resources are absolutely essential in production as equation [7.47] implies, or that they are as inessential as equation [7.46] implies. But, even if we agree that equation [7.48] is the appropriate form to assume that the production function takes, we see that this agreement in itself does not solve the problem, in that we still need to know rather precisely what value of α it is appropriate to assume. In the judgement of this author, we do not have much idea whether we should assume something like $\alpha = 0.5$ or something like $\alpha = 0.95$.

In order to bring out the essential issues here we have ignored many complicating factors present in reality. We have assumed just one type of non-renewable resource input, 'oil': we ignored possibilities for recycling: we have ignored technical progress in resource use: we have ignored population growth: we have ignored external costs arising in resource use and extraction. We shall not go into these issues here. We simply note that while they complicate they do not alter the nature of the essential basic arguments. These are, first, the idea of efficiency in allocation as defining a basic goal the achievement of which delineates the frontier over which distributional choices are to be made (see Figure 7.11). Second, the idea that what matters is the distribution of consumption over time, not the availability per se of natural resources at different points in time. Third, the fact that fairness over time is not just a question of the social discount rate used. The implications of adopting a particular value for the social discount rate depend crucially on the technological circumstances, about which it is probably appropriate to assume that we know, to the degree required, rather little: see Chapter 9.

Renewable resources: the role of preferences

We conclude this section with a brief look at questions of intertemporal fairness in the context of renewable resources. The two main reasons for so doing are, first, to show again in a different context the interaction between the social discount rate and the technological conditions, and second to consider the implications of having the size of the resource stock itself contribute to social valuation. While it is difficult to believe that it is appropriate to assume that people typically derive satisfaction simply from knowing that there is more rather than less oil under the ground, it may well be that it is appropriate to assume *conservationist preferences* with respect to renewable resource stocks. By 'conservationist preferences' we mean that people derive satisfaction from knowing that renewable resources exist, quite independently from any of the implications of such existence for production and consumption levels. To explore these issues in the simplest possible context we assume that renewable resources are the only input to production and ignore the rôle of capital.

The first planning problem to look at is that of finding the sequence of consumption levels, C_0, C_1, C_2, ... such that

$$V = \sum_{t=0}^{\infty} (1/1 + \rho)^t 2C_t^{\frac{1}{2}}$$

attains the maximum value possible given that the feasible consumption sequences are defined by

$$X_0 = \bar{X}_0$$

and

$$X_{t+1} - X_t = G_t - C_t = (gX_m X_t - gX_t^2) - C_t. \qquad [7.56]$$

Here X_t is the size of the fish, equals renewable resource, stock size at the beginning of period t, $\bar{X}_0$ is the given stock size at the beginning of the planning exercise. G_t is natural growth, and C_t is consumption. Note that in formulating the problem we have defined V over a sequence stretching out to infinity. The relationship [7.56] says that the stock size evolves over time such that if C_t is greater than G_t it falls, if C_t is less than G_t it increases, and if $C_t = G_t$ it is constant from t to $t + 1$. For the purposes of illustration we have assumed that natural growth is logistic and the reader will recall our discussion of logistic growth in the preceding section of this chapter, and particularly the graphs of sustainable yield catches against stock size, for various values of g, in Figure 7.4.

It can be shown that the solution to a planning problem like this will, for any values of ρ and g, involve a sequence of consumption levels which may rise or fall over time, depending on the initial level of $\bar{X}_0$, but which converges on a constant consumption level. Correspondingly the solution will involve eventually catching and consuming fish so as to hold the stock size constant at some level X^s. The optimal consumption programme will, that is, be such that eventually it involves sustainable yield catching. We look just at this sustainable yield catch on which the programme eventually converges in terms of the associated level for X^s, for variations in the parameters g, for the growth rate of the fish species, and ρ, the social discount rate. We fix X_m at 100, so that the fish stock size corresponding to the maximum sustainable yield is 50. In Figure 7.17 we show how X^s varies with ρ for three selected values of g. The first point to note is that for any value of g, the optimal plan's eventually sustainable yield consumption is the maximum sustainable yield only if $\rho = 0$ – for any g positive ρ implies X^s less than 50. The second point to note is that for any g, X^s declines as ρ increases, but that the rate of decline increases as g gets smaller. Whereas for $g = 0.01$, $\rho = 0.1$ gives $X^s = 45$, for $g = 0.001$ $\rho = 0.1$ gives $X^s = 0$. Generally the point is that the extent to which a high social discount rate implies dangerously low fish stock sizes depends upon the growth rate of the fish species.

Now, in setting up this planning problem we have followed the format of the non-renewable resource problem in assuming that planning proceeds on the basis that it is only consumption that yields satisfaction. As noted above, for renewable resources it is not unreasonable to argue that planning should be based on the assumption that households care directly about the stock size, so that for any given level of consumption satisfaction is the greater the larger is the size of the renewable resource stock. It is the implications of such planning that we now consider. We now assume that

$$V_t = 2C_t^{\frac{1}{2}} + 2ZX_t^{\frac{1}{2}} \tag{7.57}$$

so that for a given period the planning valuation depends on the consumption of fish and the size of the fish stock. Figure 7.18 illustrates equation [7.57] in terms of valuation indifference curves for the period t. In part (a) Z is set at 0.1, and we show those combinations of C_t and X_t which

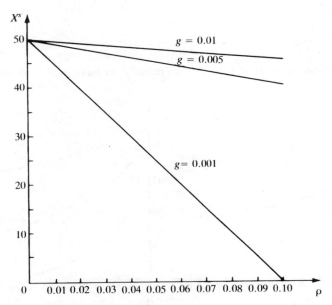

Figure 7.17 Planning with renewable resources: variations in the growth and discount rates

give V_t levels of 6, 8 and 10. In part (b) we hold V_t constant at 10, and show how the combinations of C_t and X_t corresponding depend upon the value taken by the parameter Z. Larger values of Z indicate a stronger preference for stock size as against consumption, as shown by the way the slope of the valuation indifference curves increases with Z in Figure 7.18(b) (so that for a given reduction in X_t it requires more extra C_t to hold V_t constant).

The planning problem now is to find the consumption sequence which maximises

$$V = \sum_{t=0}^{\infty} (1/1 + \rho)^t V_t$$

where V_t is given by equation [7.57], subject to the feasible alternatives being given by equation [7.56]. Again it turns out that solutions to this problem are sequences which eventually converge on a sustainable yield catch and a constant stock size X^s, and again we look at how X^s responds to variations in parameter values for X_m fixed at 100. Figure 7.19 illustrates some results in the same way as did Figure 7.18: in part (a) Z takes the value 0.1, in part (b) the value 0.25. We see, first, that it is still true that X^s falls as ρ increases for given g, for any value of Z. We also see that it is not now true that the rate at which X^s falls with increasing ρ increases as g decreases everywhere. It is true that for $\rho = 0.1$, X^s falls with decreasing g for any value of Z. The principal difference made introducing the conservation motive, that is by using

$$V_t = 2C_t^{\frac{1}{2}} + 2ZX_t^{\frac{1}{2}}$$

rather than

$$V_t = 2C_t^{\frac{1}{2}}$$

is that it is not now true that it is necessary to have $\rho = 0$ in order to get

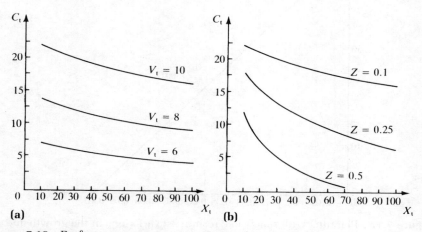

Figure 7.18   Preferences over consumption and stock size

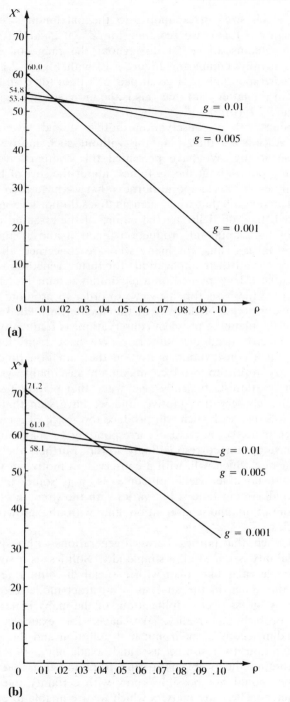

Figure 7.19   Planning with renewable resources: stock size has value

$X^s = 50$, the stock size corresponding to the maximum sustainable yield. Indeed, in Figure 7.19(b), we see that for $Z = 0.25$ and for $g = 0.01$ or $g = 0.005$, X^s remains above 50 throughout the range of variation in ρ considered. Generally, comparing Figure 7.19 with Figure 7.17, we see that the X^s value corresponding to a given pair of values for g and ρ is larger in the former than the latter, and that this is the more so for the larger value of Z used in Figure 7.19(b).

That planning with a conservation motive should give rise to larger planned fish stock sizes than planning without such motive is reassuring rather than surprising. We have presented this comparison principally in order to make a point about the usefulness about the sort of highly abstract (unreal ?) analyses of intertemporal fairness that we have been considering in this section. The point is that while such analyses do not give us firm rules on how to proceed, they do delineate the nature of the essential issues (as with the analysis of the capital–oil production function above) and can help us avoid some mistakes. Thus, for many who are concerned about renewable resource use rates and their implications for future generations it is a moral imperative that such be exploited on a maximum sustainable yield basis. It is not difficult to see the basis for this view. In order to promote the realisation of this objective in terms of the way of thinking encapsulated in our general formulation of the planning problem conservationists frequently argue for the adoption of a zero social discount rate. We have seen that if planning proceeds without a conservation motive in the valuation function, $\rho = 0$ is indeed necessary for it to produce maximum sustainable yield outcomes. However, conservationists typically also argue that planning should involve valuation with a conservation motive, and we have seen that a zero social discount rate together with such will produce too much of a good thing – X^s will be greater than the stock size corresponding to maximum sustainable yield, and consumption correspondingly lower. Further, the value for the social discount rate which will, with a conservation motive in valuation, give a maximum sustainable yield outcome is not some unique number appropriate to all circumstances, but varies with the strength of preference as between consumption and conservation and with the growth rate of the exploited species.

It turns out, then, that fairness between generations with respect to natural resource availability is not at all a simple idea. Still less is it something to be realised by simple rules like 'plan with a social discount rate of zero'. We have learned this much in the analysis of abstract model economies which are, undoubtedly, gross over-simplifications of the many issues which attend the fairness problem in reality. We have, for example, ignored the intertemporal dimensions of environmental pollution and the relationship of pollution generation to resource use and availability. We have avoided directly confronting the problems arising from the fact that our notional planning agency could not possibly know with certainty the values of the critical parameters. These are matters which we are unable to explore fully in a book of this length and written at an introductory level, and we refer the reader to the further reading discussed in the next section. Some of the issues arising are discussed further in Chapter 9.

7.5   Commentary

In the preceding sections of this chapter we have tried to set out as simply as is possible some of the basic ideas from the economic theory of natural resource exploitation. We begin this commentary section by providing some guidance to the literature, where the topics we have considered are dealt with at greater length and with more rigour. We then look briefly at energy economics, which is a distinct specialisation within the resource economics field. That is followed by a sub section on measuring resource scarcity. The section finishes with a discussion of the question of the optimal level of pollution where there is a time dimension to the problem.

There are a number of texts on resource economics, most of which assume of the reader some previous economics and some mathematical ability. In some cases the mathematics is quite advanced. Texts which deal with renewable and non-renewable resources are: Dasgupta and Heal (1979), Howe (1979), Fisher (1981), Hartwick and Olewiler (1986), Conrad and Clark (1987), Perman *et al.* (1996). Dasgupta and Heal is particularly comprehensive and thorough, but difficult. Clark (1976) is also thorough, but deals only with renewable resources. Dasgupta (1982) is also principally about renewable resources, and pollution, but is less demanding mathematically. Hartwick (1989) is a short advanced treatment of non-renewable resources only. Satisfactory non-technical expositions of the theory of natural resource economics are rare: attempts in this direction are McInerny (1976) and Norton (1984). The proposition that competitive non-renewable resource extracting firms will behave so that the proportional change in the rent is equal to the rate of interest, see [7.9] and [7.11], is known as the *Hotelling Rule*, or principle. Berck (1995), which is quite difficult, surveys attempts to confirm the hypothesis that resource extraction firms do in fact follow this rule: if they do, it is not compellingly obvious.

We have here said nothing about what might be called the 'geography' or the 'applied economics', of natural resources, by which we mean such questions as where and in what quantities resources are located, actual patterns and practices in exploitation, trade in resources, etc. Such issues are covered in, for example, Rees (1985), Fernie and Pitkethly (1985) and Simmons (1984). These books are descriptive rather than analytical in character. Anderson (1985) deals only with Canada, which, however, is a country well-endowed with, and heavily dependent on the exploitation of, both renewable and non-renewable resources. Anderson provides descriptive material, surveys the relevant economic theory, and uses it to explore the policy issues in respect of resource exploitation that have arisen in Canada.

In this, and the previous, chapter we have been considering decisions taken now on the basis of assessments concerning future flows of costs and benefits.

We have implicitly assumed that these assessments are correct, that the future is known to the decision maker. This is, of course, an inappropriate assumption. As a matter of fact, decision makers, whether they be individual economic agents (households or firms) or planners, do not know the future with certainty. And clearly the analysis of intertemporal decision making should be conducted so as to consider the implications of such lack of certain knowledge about the future. Economists have done quite a lot of work in this direction, both regarding general problems of intertemporal allocation and with respect to the particular circumstances attending natural resource exploitation. Fisher (1981) provides (in Ch. 2) a short overview of the results arising in the non-renewable resources context, and references to the literature: see also Hartwick (1989), and Conrad and Clark (1987), which deals also with renewable resources. Norton (1984) deals with some aspects at an introductory level, and Webb and Ricketts (1980) apply the basic ideas to some issues arising in the energy context. We briefly consider risk as it affects cost benefit analysis in 8.4.

In discussing the question of the attainment of intertemporal efficiency in the non-renewable resource context, in 7.2, we considered the polar cases in which there were, on the one hand, many price-taking competitive firms, or, on the other hand, a single monopolist firm. In each of these cases we assumed that the 'ideal' conditions were satisfied elsewhere in the economy. We also assumed that there was no uncertainty (see above), that the total size of the oil stock was fixed, and that the oil stock was homogeneous. Now, clearly, in fact non-renewable resources are typically exploited through market structures which are intermediate between our polar cases. Also, it is typically the case that the total size of the stock believed to exist changes over time as the result of exploration activity, and that the various deposits which comprise the total stock vary in respect of quality and extraction cost conditions. All of these considerations have been addressed in the literature, particularly with respect to the oil industry. Fisher (1981, Ch. 2) surveys some of this literature and provides references: see also Hartwick (1989). Griffin and Steele (1980, Ch. 4) use the sort of economic analysis set out in this book to look at the international oil market, and especially the role of OPEC.

We did not, in 7.2 and 7.3, discuss market failure in resource exploitation in a systematic way. We did discuss monopoly and external costs with respect to non-renewable resources, and the lack of private property rights in the renewable resources context. Also, we have above noted the existence of literature dealing with some other relevant issues. The two sources of market failure attending natural resource exploitation which have received most attention from economists are non-price taker behaviour in the non-renewable context, and free access in the renewable context. This should not be taken to imply that free access problems never attend non-renewable resource exploitation, or that market structure considerations are irrelevant with respect to renewable resources. Rather, this reflects economists' judgement that the dominant issues in each context are market structure and free access respectively.

While these are matters of judgement, rather than results emerging from exhaustive empirical analysis, it shall be noted that the judgements appear to be, at least implicitly, endorsed by non-economists. Thus, for example, much of the general anxiety about renewable resource depletion has gone under the heading of the *tragedy of the commons*. This terminology in connection with what we called, in 7.3, exploitation under a free access regime appears to have been introduced by Hardin (1968), and has gained wide currency; see also Hardin and Baden (1977) and Hardin (1993). The wide currency of the 'commons', or common property, terminology is unfortunate as it is inaccurate and misleading. Common property is not necessarily subject to free access. In principle, it may be managed consistently with the requirements for allocative efficiency, as would be the case if the resource were state property and the government adopted such a management goal, and had the necessary information. In practice, throughout history there have been many examples of common property resources so managed as to persist for very long periods. It appears to be widely believed by those concerned about such things that exploitation on a free access basis necessarily implies 'tragedy' in the sense of exploitation to extinction, or at least to very low stock size levels. We saw, in 7.3, that this is as a general proposition a mistaken belief. The free access outcome will depend upon the interplay of many factors. Equally, we saw that even where exploitation is not on a free access basis, and does conform to intertemporal efficiency, it will not necessarily involve maximum sustainable yield harvesting and may imply very low stock size. What is generally true is that, for a given renewable resource, the free access outcome will involve overuse with respect to the level required for efficiency in allocation – the stock size will be too small.

Discussing results from Henderson and Tugwell (1979) regarding a Canadian lobster fishery, Dasgupta comments that they

> show that free entry does not lead to the fisheries' ruin. Indeed, the stationary stock under free entry exceeds the MSY stock. The fishery is thus well preserved. However, there is excessive fishing at the unregulated solution, in the sense that the optimum stock is still larger. The catch is certainly greater than the optimum, but then so is the effort applied. The latter costs more than the gains obtained from larger harvests.
>
> (Dasgupta, 1982, p. 140)

The optimum to which Dasgupta refers here is the intertemporal efficiency requirement. Economists advocate interference in free access renewable resource exploitation so as to move toward this optimum, and prefer price incentive type intervention to the regulatory approach.

Many of the issues arising with respect to the choice of instrument here parallel those arising in the pollution context: see Chapter 5 above. In the case of fisheries, as in the pollution case, there has been a recent upsurge of interest in the use of price incentive instruments for management by governments. This has followed a period in which, primarily by the extension of their coastal jurisdictions, nation states converted free access ocean fisheries into managed common property resources: see Rettig (1995). In the fisheries context, the interest has been mainly in tradeable permits to catch fish, often referred to as *individual transferable quotas*, or ITQs. These have actually been brought into use in several fisheries. Anderson (1995) discusses the theory of ITQs and some of the practical difficulties of implementing such systems: Moran *et al.* (1991) report on an example of their use, in the paua fishery of the Chatham Islands (New Zealand). For a discussion, in the Canadian context, see Anderson (1985) Chapter 8.

In stating the distinction between renewable and non-renewable resources, in 7.1, we noted that as the former term is used by economists it denotes not only biological reproduction but also that such is not managed as part of the exploitation strategy. The economics of renewable resources is, that is, the economics of hunting and gathering. Where man manipulates biological reproduction it is agriculture that it is involved. The exploitation of trees sometimes involves felling virgin timber stands, sometimes the harvesting of un-managed subsequent growth, and sometimes it involves managed reproduction and subsequent harvesting. *Forestry economics*, then, straddles what is usually meant by renewable resource economics and agricultural economics. It is sometimes argued that in many cases the felling of virgin stands should be regarded as a form of mining, of non-renewable resource exploitation, given the dubious prospects for regrowth of the felled species. Forestry economics is, then, a distinct specialisation. The subject is dealt with, in terms of theory and application, in Anderson (1985) and Dasgupta (1982), and at a more advanced level in Johansson and Löfgren (1985) and Montgomery and Adams (1995). Forests differ also from ocean fisheries in that they can provide, in terms of the schema of Figure 1.4 above, amenity services in a fairly direct and obvious way. We look at some of the issues arising in this connection in the next chapter: see also Chapter 7 of Anderson (1985), or Bowes and Krutilla (1989) for an extended treatment.

We saw, in 7.2 and 7.3, that because natural resources are scarce and shiftable over time, they have value in the un-extracted state. This rent accrues to the owners of the resources, where such exist. Where exploitation is within an unregulated free access regime, no rent attaches to the resource. With respect to the realisation of intertemporal efficiency the existence of rent is necessary. However, to the extent that it accrues to private resource owners and corresponds to the mere fact of ownership rather than to the expenditure of any effort, rent is widely regarded as unfair. There is much interest in measures to transfer rent from individual private owners to society at large, in the form of government, which is the source of rent-creating scarcity. There is, that is, much interest in resource rent taxation. Systems to effect rent transfer have to be carefully designed so that they do not distort the incentives facing resource owners in such a way as to cause them to adopt depletion/harvesting programmes which are not consistent with intertemporal efficiency. A useful introduction to the basic issues and some approaches, in the context of non-renewable resources, is Webb and Ricketts (1980, Ch. 6). The issue of governmental *rent capture* is also discussed in Anderson (1985).

As discussed in these references, taxation is not the only conceivable approach to rent capture: governments have also shown interest in the public ownership and exploitation of resource stocks, and in systems of competitive bidding for extraction licences.

Rent capture is not the only source of an interest in the taxation of resource exploitation activities. Taxes may be considered as a means to the social control of exploitation under free access conditions; see above. Nor is it the case that in the absence of free access it can be generally presumed that the market outcome is intertemporally efficient. We have noted that there are other potential sources of market failure which may in some cases lead to current overuse. Further, it may be argued that even in the absence of market failure, fairness as between those alive now and future generations requires that some resources be used less now than the market outcome would be. There are, then, many who are prepared to advocate the taxation of resource exploitation activities, rather than of resource rents, in the interests of resource conservation. A good example is Page (1977) where it is argued that such taxation would not only act directly on resource extraction, but would also promote conservation by encouraging *recycling*. Recycling policy is considered in Pearce and Walter (1977). The case for resource extraction taxation, as set out by Page, is based upon market failure considerations, on the effects of some existing governmental interventions, and on intertemporal fairness considerations. Daly (1973) argues for resource depletion quotas, rather than taxes, as part of his programme for a steady state economy. Daly's arguments are based on intertemporal fairness, rather than market failure, considerations. See also Daly and Cobb (1989). Given the recent emergence of concern about the enhanced greenhouse effect, see 9.5 and 9.7 here, there is now interest in taxing the use or production of fossil fuels, since their combustion is the major source of emissions of carbon dioxide, which is the most important of the greenhouse gases: see, for examples, Pearce (1991), Carraro and Siniscalco (1993), Common (1995) Ch. 9.

Energy economics

Energy economics is now a recognised specialisation within economics. There exist associations of energy economists, conferences are held, journals published, many universities run courses, and a number of textbooks have appeared. Examples of the latter are Webb and Ricketts (1980), Eden *et al.* (1981), Griffin and Steele (1980), Peirce (1986) and Weyman-Jones (1986). Why should energy economics exist, where, say, copper or iron-ore economics does not? There are a number of considerations attaching to energy which taken together make it distinct and important enough to have its own specialisation within economics. It is not the case that energy economics involves different principles and methods from other economics. Rather, it is the case that the principles and methods of resource and environmental economics, especially, come into exceptionally sharp focus in the energy context, and that energy-related issues are major policy concerns in modern economics.

All of the following considerations apply to energy:

(i)   The currently important energy resources are non-renewable resources which, when used as energy sources, cannot be recycled.
(ii)   Energy use is pervasive in modern economies – it is an input to every commodity produced.
(iii) The extraction and use of the currently important energy resources is a major source of environmental pollution.
(iv)   It is widely believed that in the case of energy allocative efficiency requirements conflict with equity objectives.
(v)   Energy supply projects are typically large, with consequently long lead times, and have long lives.

Before looking at these considerations in a little detail, it will be useful to provide some background and perspective.

Energy is actually a somewhat elusive concept, but here it will suffice to say that is the capacity to do work. Energy comes in a variety of forms and is measured in a variety of units. A widely used unit is the British thermal unit, Btu, which is the amount of energy required to raise the temperature of one pound of water from $39.2°F$ to $40.2°F$. Where large quantities are involved, the Quad, Q, is used, it being one quadrillion Btu, i.e. one Q is 10^{15} Btu. We now use some figures taken from Georgescu-Roegen (1976). The sun radiates annually 10^{16} Q of energy, of which some 5×10^6 Q reaches the earth's atmosphere, about 25% of which is of the wavelengths that stimulate *photosynthesis*. Photosynthesis captures annually some 1,000 Q of *solar radiation*, of which between 1 and 5% (depending on plant type) is converted into the chemical energy stored in plant tissue. Man uses incoming solar radiation by eating plants and animals that eat plants, by using wind and water movements powered by it, by burning plants, and by using domesticated animals to supplement human muscle power. Man also uses stored past receipts of solar radiation by burning *fossil fuels* (coal, oil, gas) which are organic materials transformed by geological processes. The amount of fossil fuel initially in existence is estimated as some 2×10^5 Q, which is roughly equivalent to just two weeks solar radiation arriving at the earth's atmosphere, or to 180 years of worldwide photosynthetic capture. It is thought that the sun will continue to supply solar radiation at roughly the current level for another 5 billion years or so. Total world energy consumption by man is now of the order of 300 Q per annum.

Cipolla (1962) distinguishes two energetic revolutions in human history. The Agricultural Revolution began *c*. 8000 BC. Prior to it man was a hunter-gatherer 'incapable of doing anything better than dashing all over the place trying to capture or to collect any edible plant or animal in sight' (Cipolla, 1962, page 37). In this state an economy could expand only up to the point where the annual destruction of plants and animals equalled natural growth. In the Agricultural Revolution man learned how to control and increase his food base: 'The total amount of energy that the human species could dispose of – chemical energy from plants and animals, heat from plants, power from draught animals – increased in proportions inconceivable in the old Paleolithic societies' (Cipolla, 1962, page 40). The energy resource exploitation did not remain static during the ten millennia separating the beginning of the Agricultural Revolution from the next energetic revolution, the Industrial Revolution. Man increased the efficiency of plant and animal energy convertors, and developed the watermill, the windmill and the sailing boat to utilise the energy in water and wind. Some limited use of fossil fuels occurred. However, 'eighty to eighty-five percent of the total energy income at any time before the Industrial Revolution must have been derived from plants, animals and man' (Cipolla, 1962, p. 46). This meant that land was the key resource.

The Industrial Revolution was, essentially, about the systematic exploitation of the energy stored in fossil fuels by means of inanimate convertors, of which the steam engine, using coal, was the first. The way in which such exploitation changes the energetic basis of human existence can be appreciated by looking at its impact on agriculture. A detailed account of the energetics of food production is given in Leach (1975), and see also Bayliss-Smith (1982). Here we simply note the three key features of the transition to industrialised agriculture. First, fossil fuel-based agricultural machinery and transport systems mean the elimination of draught animals, so that land formerly used to feed such animals becomes available for feeding man. Second, the use of fossil fuels to produce and apply fertilisers in large quantities raises photosynthetic efficiency and effectively increases available land. Available land is also increased by improved transport systems and the increased ability to clear, drain, irrigate, etc. Third, the use of machinery raises output per man, releasing labour to the industrial and service sectors of the economy.

Leaving aside energy resources as food, and human muscle power, industrialised economies use little animate energy, and inanimate energy consumption is predominantly based on the fossil fuels – coal, oil and gas. In the long view of human history 'man's reliance on fossil fuels for his supply of energy can be but a short episode' (Thirring, 1958, quoted in Cipolla, 1962, page 54). This follows from the fact, noted as (i) above, that the fossil fuels are non-renewable resources. We must also note that the basis of the nuclear fission process, uranium, is also a non-renewable resource. The obvious question arising is, how long a 'short episode' is it likely to be?

This question cannot be answered definitively, but we can look at some data which indicates the orders of magnitudes involved. Table 7.7 shows, in the second column, the 1991 world production levels for the three fossil fuels, and for nuclear and hydroelectricity. The column heading is PJ for PetaJoule, the unit of measurement. One PJ is approximately 1000th of a Quad. The third column gives the shares of the fuels shown in the total at the bottom of the second column. The fourth column gives the proportion of world output that is consumed by the industrialised economies, which are the OECD economies plus central Europe and the former Soviet Union.

Table 7.8 shows, in the second column, figures for the world's proven

Table 7.7 Energy production in 1991

	PJ	Fuel share %	Industrialised share of consumption %
Oil	132 992	39.7	72.2
Gas	76 275	22.8	84.3
Coal	93 689	28.0	60.0
Nuclear	22 669[a]	6.8	94.5
Hydro	9 311[b]	2.8	65.1
Total	334 890		

[a] The figure relates to the amount of fossil fuel that would have been burned to generate the amount of electricity actually sent out by nuclear plants.
[b] The figure is for the amount of electricity actually sent out from hydroelectric plants.
Source: WRI (1994)

commercial reserves of the three fossil fuels in 1990. These figures are for deposits that are known to exist in specific locations, for which extraction would be commercially viable at current prices for the extracted fuel, using existing technology. The third column figures are for these reserves divided by the production levels – they give the lifetime of the reserves assuming the continuation of current production levels. Two points arise here. First, annual production levels are expected to increase as the world economy grows. This would mean that these figures overstate the reserve lifetimes. Second, and meaning that these figures understate how long fossil fuels are likely to last, there are much larger quantities of the fuels under the ground than indicated in the second column. There are additional reserves that are known to exist, but which it would not be commercial to utilise at current prices and with current technology. As stocks are depleted so prices will rise, and new technology developed. Also, geologists can infer the existence of deposits that have not been positively identified. The size of these inferred reserves is, of course, speculative, and changes over time.

The fourth column shows the proportion of total world fossil fuel proven commercial reserves accounted for by each of the three fuels. Note that although Table 7.7 shows coal to be considerably less important than oil in terms of current production, Table 7.8 shows that it accounts for some 70% of these reserves and on the basis of these reserves will last much longer than oil. This general picture would carry over to the situation expressed in terms of non-commercial and inferred reserves. Table 7.8 also shows, in the fifth column, the share of world proven commercial reserves located in the industrialised economies. Note that from Table 7.7 these countries consume over 70% of world output of oil, but have only 10% of oil reserves. This is why oil figures so largely in international politics. The share of world proven oil reserves located in the OPEC countries is 78%.

Table 7.8 Proven commercial fossil fuel reserves 1990

	PJ	Years	Share %	Industrialised share %
Oil	5 639 794	42	16.1	10.1
Gas	5 004 802	66	14.3	52.9
Coal	24 423 986	261	69.6	69.5
Total	35 068 582			

Source: WRI (1994)

In the 1970s and 1980s, following the oil price increases of 1973/4 engineered by OPEC, the world's energy problem was seen in terms of scarcity of the fossil fuels, and especially of oil. This prompted a great deal of interest in nuclear power (see Eden *et al*. 1981, Patterson 1976), and in the so-called 'alternative' energy sources, such as geothermal energy, wind energy, solar power and tidal energy. Basically the idea was that coal would be a 'bridge' to a future in which there was much greater reliance on nuclear power and these alternatives, and non-conventional fossil fuel sources such as oil shales and tar sands: see Stobaugh (1983), CONEAS (1980), Leach *et al*. (1977), Lovins (1975), Nordhaus (1973). At that time, with the exception of the nuclear fuel cycle, rather little attention was generally paid to the environmental impacts of the use of the various energy sources. This has now changed, especially in respect to the fossil fuels, on account of the emissions of sulphur and carbon dioxide arising when they are burned. The former is seen as a major factor in the acid rain problem (see 5.5), and the latter in the enhanced greenhouse effect (see 9.5 and 9.7). In both cases, coal is the fossil fuel that gives rise to the worst problems.

The second of the considerations attaching to energy which we cited above was the pervasiveness of its use in a modern economy. We have now suggested that it is the pervasive use of inanimate energy sources that is the essential characteristic of modern industrial economies. From the use end we must add to the fossil fuels electricity, which is itself generated either by burning fossil fuels, or by nuclear fission, or from the movement of wind and water, or (currently to a very limited extent) from solar radiation. Any interruption in the supply of any one of coal, gas, oil or electricity is a major problem for an industrial economy. There is not in such an economy a household or a firm that does not, in normal circumstances, use one or more of these fuels each and every day of the year. Once made the point is obvious, but its significance is apt to be overlooked, except in times of supply interruption.

Also frequently overlooked is the fact that production processes use these fuels indirectly as well as directly. The extent to which the production of various commodities is more or less 'energy intensive' is not adequately reflected in the direct inputs of the various fuels to the production processes for the commodities. Production uses fuels indirectly, via the use of inputs which have themselves been produced using fuels as inputs. Building houses does not directly use large amounts of energy, but built houses are relatively energy intensive commodites as cement and brick production are highly energy intensive activities. In the UK in 1968, for example, the construction industry's direct use of electricity accounted for only 18% of its total electricity use.

One way to investigate the pattern of fuels use in production, to take account of indirect as well as direct use, is by means of input–output analysis; see 3.6 and 5.5. Common and McPherson (1982) present results so obtained for the UK in 1968 and 1974. These are of interest not only for what they reveal about relative *energy intensities* at a point in time, but also for how such change over time. Chapman (1975) also examines in some detail the way energy is used in production, both directly and indirectly. Dovers (1994) reports data on the direct and indirect use of energy in the Australian economy.

The extraction and use of fossil fuels and uranium typically involves significant adverse effects on the environment, as noted at consideration (iii) above. There is a presumption that such effects are excessive in relation to the requirements of allocative efficiency. Typically such effects are in the nature of public bads, so that private bargaining cannot be expected, and governmental regulation is widely believed to be inadequate in terms of the abatement resulting (see Chapter 5 on public bads and bargaining, and for references concerning the costs and benefits of abatement). It is not possible here to work systematically through the specifics of the environmental effects of the various fuel cycles: a useful summary is Ch. 9 of Eden *et al.* (1981), and see also Wilson and Jones (1974), Ashley, Rudman and Whipple (1976), SCEP (1970) and CONEAS (1980), for example.

All fossil fuel combustion converts chemical energy into heat, some of which is used to do work. In electricity production some 60% of the energy content of the input fuel appears as waste heat, and is not converted into electricity. This is true of fossil fuel inputs and uranium input. The result is sometimes called *thermal pollution*: see Chapman (1975). Concern over thermal pollution, mainly seen as a localised problem, has now largely given way to concern about global warming on account of the enhanced greenhouse effect: see 9.5 and 9.7.

While relatively abundant, coal is inherently dirty. On the other hand, given routine operations and effective waste disposal, the nuclear fuel cycle through to electricity gives rise to relatively little environmental damage. In saying this, it must be noted that the costs of ensuring 'routine operations and effective waste disposal' are not now fully reflected in the costings attributed to the nuclear fuel cycle. The renewable energy sources are widely regarded as environmentally benign. However, they are often users of lots of space, and involve visual intrusion and loss of environmental amenity, and local climatic and ecological impacts may be expected. The point being made here is that all energy supply systems have some adverse environmental impacts. The problem is to compare the environmental costs across alternative systems, not to wish them away with respect to some system which finds favour.

It is, however, very difficult to do this at all satisfactorily. We shall, in the next chapter, look at some of the problems arising, in connection with the evaluation of a hydroelectric facility by cost benefit analysis. Ideally, what is required for a comparison of alternative energy systems is, for delivery of a given quantity of energy suitable for a given purpose, a comparison of the sum of all of the costs arising in each case. Inhaber (1979) approaches a number of energy sources on a consistent basis, but costs them in a restricted way in that he looks only at the risks to humans per unit of energy delivered. The measure of risk used is man-days lost per MW (Megawatt) per year of energy output: a death is equated to 6,000 man-days lost. Lost man-days considered are both occupational and public health originating, i.e. pollution effects are in principle accounted for (at least insofar as they affect human health). Further, the whole energy delivery system is accounted for – risks are assessed in the construction of extraction and use facilities, as well as those arising in the activities of extraction, transport, conversion and use. Accidents are allowed for, but risks associated with terrorism or nuclear weapons proliferation are not included in the analysis. Inhaber's conclusions include the following:

(a) Coal carries the highest risk, and this arises mainly from atmospheric pollution (3,000 man-days per MW year).

(b) Natural gas is the lowest risk energy source (6 man-days per MW year).

(c) Nuclear energy is second lowest to gas in risk terms (10 man-days per MW year).

(d) The renewable sources are intermediate between coal and natural gas (30–1,000 man-days per MW year).

Inhaber's results and methods have been criticised. For example, for renewables he assumes a coal-fired back-up system. The costs associated with the role of carbon dioxide emissions from fossil fuel combustion were not considered.

The fourth consideration attaching to energy, cited above at (iv) (p. 292), was the widely believed existence of a conflict between the energy price requirements of allocative efficiency and the goal of distributional equity. We have seen that intemporal efficiency requires non-renewable resource-based energy prices to rise over time (7.2), and we have suggested that energy is generally now under-priced since its suppliers and users do not bear the external costs they generate (7.2 and above). On the other hand, according to Webb and Ricketts (1980, p. 3):

> Energy is often viewed as a 'necessity' in the same way as housing and health, and is of considerable concern to designers of social security systems. Energy is certainly a 'necessity' in the technical sense that the income elasticity of demand is less than unity. It is this aspect of the demand for energy which makes energy pricing so sensitive from a distributional point of view.

Table 7.9 UK budget shares 1980

Weekly income (£)	Food	Housing	Fuel and light	Cumulative percentage of households
< 30	1.48	1.34	2.01	3
30–40	1.49	1.82	2.23	11
40–50	1.43	1.51	1.94	17
50–60	1.40	1.53	1.72	22
60–70	1.32	1.36	1.43	26
70–80	1.28	1.25	1.53	29
80–100	1.21	1.16	1.35	37
100–120	1.17	1.00	1.19	44
120–140	1.07	1.03	1.02	53
140–160	1.05	0.94	0.99	62
160–180	1.01	0.94	0.91	70
180–200	0.98	0.89	0.85	76
200–250	0.87	0.95	0.80	87
250–300	0.83	0.84	0.71	94
300–350	0.77	0.83	0.64	96
> 350	0.66	0.80	0.62	100
All households budget share	0.1783	0.1441	0.0535	

Clearly, if rising energy prices are required for efficiency in allocation, and if rising energy prices hurt the poor more than the rich, efficiency and equity are in conflict with respect to energy. Accepting the need for higher energy prices on allocative grounds, in UK the Supplementary Benefits Commission (1979) in its 1978 Report urged consideration of a comprehensive fuel rebate or bonus scheme for low income households in the UK. Many other UK commentators argued for the emergence of *fuel poverty* as a serious social problem in the 1970s. Table 7.9 illustrates the basis for the belief in the regressive impact of higher energy prices. Under 'Fuel and light' the figures for each income band are the ratio of the fuel and light budget share for that income band to the fuel and light budget share for all households taken together, which is shown at the bottom of the table. For comparative purposes the same information is given for expenditures on Food and Housing.

The figures shown in Table 7.9 are based on data from Department of Employment (1982), which reports the results of a family expenditure survey. They show that poorer households spend a larger proportion of their income on fuel and light than do richer households. This is what would be expected with an income elasticity of demand less than unity (see 4.6 for a definition of the income elasticity of demand, and of a necessity). It implies that an increase in energy prices would hurt the poor more than the better off: it implies, that is, that higher energy prices would be regressive in their impact. The extent to which this holds in the UK is investigated in Common (1985) on which the following discussion is based. The methodology involves using input–output data to compute the commodity price increases which would be consequent upon a given set of increases in the prices of the fuels used in production, accounting for both direct and indirect use. It is described in Common (1985): see also National Economic Development Office (1975).

Table 7.10 reports some results from a simulation exercise which computes the cost of living increase, as measured by the Laspeyres price index, for households, of various types and at various income levels, due to a doubling in the prices of the four primary fuels input to the UK economy (coal, oil, natural gas, and nuclear and hydro electricity) as it affects the fuel and light commodities purchased by households. A Laspeyres price index uses the expenditure pattern obtaining before the price increases to get the overall effect of the price increases: the formula used is given at the beginning of 2.4, with 1968 referring to 'before the price increases'. The results are based on the household expenditure patterns reported in Department of Employment (1982). Column I gives the post energy price rise index number for all households of the indicated composition: prior to the energy price rise, index numbers are everywhere unity. Whereas for old age pensioners the cost of living increase is 8%, for two adults plus children households the increase is 3%. Column II gives, for each household composition type, the ratio of the Laspeyres index for the worst affected income band to the Laspeyres index for the least affected income band. Thus, for example, for single adult non-retired households the cost of living increase for the worst affected income band was 4% greater than that for the least affected income band. In almost

Table 7.10 Cost of living impacts of higher fuel and light prices

	I Laspeyres Index, all households	II Ratio of highest to lowest index number
1 OAP	1.08	1.02
1 RTD	1.07	1.02
1 Non-RTD	1.04	1.04
2 OAPs	1.08	1.02
2 RTD	1.05	1.03
2 Non-RTD	1.03	1.03
2 Adults + 1 Child	1.03	1.02
2 Adults + 2 Children	1.03	1.03
2 Adults + 3 Children	1.03	1.01
All households	1.04	1.06

OAP: Retired, and mainly dependent on state pension
RTD: Retired, not mainly dependent on state pension
Non-RTD: Non-retired adult.

Table 7.11 Cost of living impacts of all commodity prices responding to higher energy prices

	I Laspeyres Index, all households	II Ratio of highest to lowest index number
1 OAP	1.11	1.02
1 RTD	1.09	1.02
1 Non-RTD	1.08	1.03
2 OAPs	1.11	1.01
2 RTD	1.09	1.01
2 Non-RTD	1.08	1.02
2 Adults + 1 Child	1.08	1.01
2 Adults + 2 Children	1.08	1.02
2 Adults + 3 Children	1.08	1.01
All households	1.08	1.04

OAP: Retired, and mainly dependent on state pension
RTD: Retired, not mainly dependent on state pension
Non-RTD: Non-retired adult.

every case the worst affected income band was the lowest, and the least affected was the highest income band. The evidence of Table 7.10 is consistent with the hypothesis that higher energy prices are regressive in impact. However, in view of the large increases in primary energy prices simulated, the cost of living effects are, perhaps, smaller than might have been expected by many commentators.

Actually with respect to the equity aspects of higher energy prices, the analysis of Table 7.10 is rather less than half the story. There are two missing elements: accounting for indirect as well as direct energy consumption by households; allowing for substitution responses in production and consumption. The first point is that, as noted above, higher energy prices affect all commodity prices. This may be important for the assessment of their regressive impact. For example, while the poor spend proportionately more on fuel and light, one imagines that the rich spend proportionately more on private motoring and air travel, for both of which prices will go up with energy prices. Table 7.11 gives the results, obtained using the input–output analysis methodology, directly comparable to those of Table 7.10, which arise when energy prices are allowed to affect all commodity prices and when households' entire expenditure patterns across all commodities are considered. The package of primary fuel price increases is the same as for Table 7.10. In Table 7.11 as compared with Table 7.10 the increase in the levels of the cost of living increase is everywhere greater. Also, the degree of regressivity, as measured in column II, never gets worse going from Table 7.10 to Table 7.11, and generally gets less.

These results show that allowing for indirect as well as direct effects does not affect the proposition that higher energy prices hurt the poor more than the rich. However, they also indicate that the impacts are quite small. It needs to be noted in this context that the results in Tables 7.10 and 7.11 are in the nature of upper limits on the cost of living impacts. This is because the methodology assumes that household consumption patterns and production input mixes remain constant in the face of the changing relative prices. To the extent that, as we would expect, consumption and production input mixes change, with less energy intensive being substituted for more energy intensive commodities and inputs, the impact on the cost of living of the higher energy prices would be reduced. Some evidence bearing on the consumption part of this is given in Common (1985).

As we have noted, and will discuss further in 9.7, fossil fuel combustion releases carbon dioxide into the atmosphere where it plays a major role in the enhanced greenhouse effect. It has been proposed by a number of economists that *carbon taxation* be introduced in order to reduce these emissions. The effect of carbon taxation would be to increase the prices of the fossil fuels to their users, both firms and households. Objections to carbon taxation have consequently been raised on the grounds that they would be regressive in their impact: see Smith (1993). The methodology by means of which the regressive impact of higher energy prices is examined as above, can be easily extended to look at the impact of carbon taxation. The results parallel those above. Carbon taxation is regressive in impact, but the assessed regressivity is less when indirect as well as direct effects are accounted for. Common (1995) reports, in Ch. 9, results for Australia. Symons *et al.* (1991) report results for the UK, and show how the, substantial, revenue arising from such taxation could be used to offset the regressive impact.

As noted in consideration (v) (p. 292), energy supply projects are typically large, and have long lives and long lead times. This means that there is a need for planning in the energy supply industries, and in most industrial economies governments are actively involved in such, and in supporting energy research and development. In the next chapter we shall consider a – hypothetical – energy supply project to bring out some of the issues arising from the long project lives involved, as they affect project appraisal, especially with respect to environmental impacts. Webb and Ricketts (1980), Weyman-Jones (1986) and Peirce (1986) discuss energy supply planning. Private investors are expected to underinvest in research and development on account of their inability to capture all of the benefits which may arise. Given finite budgets and competing claims, governments face a very difficult problem in deciding which energy research and development programmes to support at what level. For further discussion, see the CONEAS (1980) report intended to assist US policy formulation in this respect.

It is certainly the case that careful economic analysis can contribute greatly to the discussion of energy questions, and to the formulation of sensible energy policies. However, it would be facile not to recognise explicitly that the formulation of energy policy involves many issues not amenable to economic analysis alone. The point will only be illustrated here by reference to just two examples. The first concerns the linkage between the widespread development of nuclear power generation systems and the proliferation of the capability to manufacture nuclear weapons. The existence and strength of this linkage are matters of dispute, but it seems difficult to be sure that the risk of nuclear conflict does not increase with the spread of nuclear electricity generation. An interesting discussion, in the UK context, of how consideration of this and other essentially political issues might be incorporated into a coherent framework for energy policy formulation is Pearce, Edwards and Beuret (1979). The second is the question of national security, and the ramifications of the views taken on this, in relation to energy supplies, by nation states for international relations. Some of these issues are addressed in Willrich (1975). It is also the case that national security considerations, which are difficult (at best) to bring within the range of standard welfare economics application, frequently exert a strong direct influence on domestic energy policy. Many economists argue that energy is just a commodity like any other. Many governments, by their actions, simply do not believe this.

Scarcity and growth

Does economic growth mean increasing resource scarcity? While many argue that where non-renewable resources are concerned at least, it must, economists have been sceptical about this proposition. In considering future prospects, they argue that the best guide is past performance. The work of Barnett and Morse (1963), from which this sub section takes its title, was the first systematic study of the historical data across a number of renewable and non-renewable resources. It analysed data for the USA for the period 1870 to 1957. It found that the unit costs of production in the extractive industries considered fell over this period. Barnett and Morse argued that this was to be explained in terms of economies of scale in production, technical progress, substitutions as between resources as inputs to manufacturing, discoveries of new deposits, and imports. Papers in Smith (1979) sought to update the work of Barnett and Morse, and a number of similar studies are reviewed in Fisher (1981). According to Fisher, only tentative conclusions are warranted, but the studies may indicate that the period of diminishing resource scarcity has come to an end.

It has been noted that the unit cost of production in an extractive industry is not the only possible measure of scarcity: see Brown and Field (1978). Other candidates are the prices of the products produced using the output from the extractive industry, and the *in situ* price, or rent, of the resource itself. The idea that increasing scarcity would show up in increasing extraction costs reflects the assumption of extraction starting with the most accessible and highest quality deposits, and moving to less accessible and lower quality deposits as the better ones are exhausted. This need not be the case. New discoveries may turn out to be lower cost than existing known deposits. And, where extraction does track a decreasing quality gradient as depletion proceeds, technical progress may work to offset increasing costs. Non-increasing unit extraction costs do not necessarily imply that scarcity is not increasing.

Similar problems attend the use of product price as a measure of scarcity. There is an additional consideration with this indicator. Price depends upon demand as well as the costs of supply. A resource may be being depleted, with no technical change working to reduce extraction and production costs, yet the price of the product not be rising on account of the increasing use of substitutes for that product depressing demand for it. Economists typically do not see this as a problem. On the contrary they see it as a virtue of this indicator. If we consider oil, for example, the point that is made is that nobody is interested in oil in the ground *per se*. What is of interest is the services that extracted and refined oil can perform. To the extent that an increasing use of other means of performing the services of interest keeps the price of oil based products down, it is argued, the relevant scarcity is not increasing.

In principle, economists see the proper measure of scarcity as the price of the resource *in situ*. The basis for this view is the assumption that there exist markets in which rights to extract now and at future dates are traded. Traders in such markets are assumed to be well informed. Then, if scarcity does increase, taking account of demand as well as supply, the price of rights to extract now and in the future will increase. In practice problems with this measure are recognised. First, where markets for rights to extract in the future do exist, typically the futurity that they cover is not very great. For some non-renewable resources there are no futures markets at all. Second, traders are often not well informed. Third, in many cases, markets in even current extraction rights do not exist, or are of limited coverage. Fourth, in many cases the market in extraction rights is characterised by having relatively few participants, so that strategic behaviour can distort the market signals. Such distortions affect in turn the price of products based on the resource. The most famous examples of this kind of problem are the oil price increases of 1973/4 and 1979.

For these reasons, economists find it difficult to use in practice the measure that is, in principle, the correct one. Another follow-up study to Barnett and Morse used both unit costs and product prices to test the hypothesis of increasing scarcity for some resources in the USA for the 1960s and 1970s. It concluded that:

> No single index of scarcity is without practical or theoretical flaws ... taken together, the two indexes of scarcity analysed here confirm the hypothesis that scarcity increased in the 1970s for nonrenewable energy resources and for some renewables.

> (Hall and Hall 1984)

Some analysts have tried to avoid the complexities in the interpretation of the economic data relating to resource scarcities by considering physical indicators, such as the amount of energy required to make a resource available for use: see Cleveland (1993), Hall *et al.* (1992).

Many economists claim that the historical record shows that growth to date has not been accompanied by increasing resource scarcity, and that this invalidates the idea that resource scarcity is a threat to future growth prospects. To oversimplify somewhat, the argument here is that Barnett and Morse shows that *The Limits to Growth* is wrong. Quite apart from the ambiguity of the historical record, there are some problems with this argument. The first is the validity of extrapolating from these studies to derive future global prospects. The original Barnett and Morse study, for example, just looked at costs in the USA, and explicitly noted that these, in some cases, may have been held down by imports. Clearly, the world as a whole cannot import extracted natural resources. Second, *The Limits to Growth* was not solely concerned with the implications of resource depletion. Its argument is about material growth in a materially closed system, and concerns flows of emissions as well as the flows of resource extraction. The prospects for growth are, on this view, constrained by the limited assimilative capacities for wastes of the natural environment, as much as by resource availability. We return to the global situation in these respects in Chapter 9.

Stock pollutants

In 5.5 we noted that for some pollutants the question of the optimal level of pollution would involve a time dimension, because the source of damage is the accumulated stock of pollution, rather than the current flow of emissions. We can, again, think of a lake as the environmental media into which emissions are discharged and which is of interest. The level of pollution evolves over time according to

$$P_{t+1} = P_t + E_t - A_t \qquad [7.57]$$

where P stands for pollution, E for emissions and A is the lake's *assimilative capacity*, the amount by which the stock of pollution in it declines in a period by biological processes in the lake which transform the pollutant into something not perceived as causing any damage. The standard assumption is that the size of A_t depends on P_t, as in

$$P_{t+1} = P_t + E_t - d_t P_t$$

which is the way we wrote this model in 5.5. This model of the pollution accumulation process has been examined in several contributions to the environmental economics literature, such as Plourde (1972) and Forster (1975): see also Perman *et al.* (1996). The mathematics for the proper analysis of this model is quite difficult. However, note that [7.57] is essentially the same as the equation for the evolution of a fish stock, where P is the equivalent of the stock size, A is the equivalent of the natural growth, and E is the equivalent of the harvest size. In this case the natural growth term is actually for a reduction in the stock, and the harvest term is actually for an addition to it.

This analogy, given the changed roles of natural and human activities, suggests what one important result from the analysis here will be. Recall that in the case of the competitive sole owner fishery we showed that while the outcome satisfies the requirements for allocative efficiency, it does not guarantee that the fishery will not be harvested to extinction. In this stock pollution case, suppose that there is an EPA which knows that [7.57] is the way pollution behaves over time, and which controls the level of E over time by some policy instrument. Suppose further that the EPA sets the target standard for E in each period so that over time the levels for E are as required by intertemporal efficiency. It would do this by calculating the time path for E which maximises the discounted sum over time of the benefits arising in the production which is responsible for E net of the external costs arising from the consequent levels of P. This is exactly analogous to the competitive fishery owner maximising the discounted sum of future profits. In this case, the EPA's optimal programme may involve allowing E to evolve such that the lake eventually becomes biologically dead, with A equal to zero. This will be the more likely the higher is the rate at which future benefits and costs are discounted, and the slower the natural processes of cleansing in the lake. Even assuming, that is, that externalities are fully internalised, and that intertemporal efficiency conditions are satisfied, it may be optimal to allow pollution to proceed to the extent that it renders the receiving environment biologically dead.

Pearce (1976) considered a somewhat different assumption about the way pollution effects are transmitted over time. In this model there is no pollution so long as the emissions flow does not exceed the lake's assimilative capacity, ie $P_t = 0$ for E_t less than or equal to A_t. If there is no pollution, then the lake's assimilative capacity is unchanged, but if in a period pollution occurs, then in the next period assimilative capacity is lower:

$$A_{t+1} = A_t \text{ for } P_t = 0$$
$$A_{t+1} < A_t \text{ for } P_t > 0 \qquad\qquad [7.58]$$

This set of assumptions about how pollution effects are transmitted over time appears to accord more closely with the way natural scientists think about such matters at an abstract level. Given these assumptions, Pearce showed that if the EPA behaved myopically, controlling E in every period such that current MEC equals current MNPB but taking no account of the future, then assimilative capacity would fall over time and eventually reach zero, and the level of production responsible for the emissions would fall over time toward some constant level. Again, the result is a biologically dead lake. Pearce noted that if instead the EPA controlled E so that pollution never occurred, there would be no fall in the level of production.

The two outcomes are shown in Figure 7.20. The line P^M shows how the level of pollution damage cost evolves when the EPA exercises myopic control, ie controls E for current allocative efficiency but not for intertemporal efficiency. The Line Q^M shows the corresponding evaluation of the value of the production responsible for E. The line Q^B shows how this value evolves given that no pollution is ever allowed. There is no line shown for pollution corresponding to Q^B, as there never is any – the line for P^B would coincide with the horizontal axis. Pearce claims that this shows that the no pollution ever rule is superior to the EPA's myopic balancing of the costs and benefits involved. Actually, this is true only if we look at things over an indefinitely long time horizon and do not discount future gains and losses. In Figure 7.20, the horizontal hatching shows the production gains to following the myopic economic optimality rule rather than the no pollution rule. The vertical hatching identifies the losses. Clearly, the relative sizes of the gains and losses will vary with the circumstances of particular cases, in terms of the value of production, the pollution damage costs, and the date at which Q^B crosses Q^M. Only if we consider t out to infinity, and treat £s at all dates as of equal value when considered from time t equals zero, can we be sure that the losses are greater than the gains. Only in those circumstances can we be sure that the no pollution rule is better than the myopic balancing of the costs and benefits of allowing some pollution.

This can be looked at the other way round. Suppose that in the case of [7.58] the EPA were told that P^M and Q^M in Figure 7.20 would be the result of its myopia, and that it could follow the no pollution rule and achieve Q^B. Under what circumstances would it be likely to go for P^M and Q^M? If it adopted a short time horizon and/or a high discount rate. Then the short term production gains would weigh more heavily against the long term production losses and pollution damage. The outcome here is effectively very like that in the standard analysis considered above, based on [7.57]. Particularly, using a high rate at which to discount the future means that the prospects of the biological death of the receiving environment are increased.

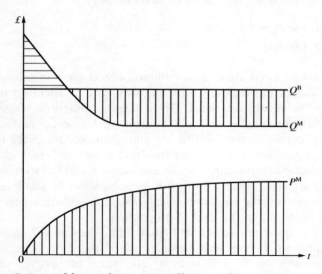

Figure 7.20   Gains and losses from a no-pollution rule

This is a matter which worries many who are concerned for the natural environment, to which we shall return in the next chapter.

Notes

1. The logistic equation is often put in a slightly different form as

$$G_t = rX_t - (r/K)X_t^2$$

where r is the innate capacity for increase and K is the maximum population size (see, for example, Krebs (1972, Ch. 11)). This is the same as equation [7.17]

$$G_t = gX_m X_t - gX_t^2$$

where $g = r/K$ and $K = X_m$.

2. To reinforce the point made at the end of the preceding paragraph, it can be noted that in order to determine, for example, the effect on X of variations in W, the unit cost of effort, it is necessary to give the production function and the growth function particular forms. If we were only prepared to assume density dependent growth (instead of the special logistic version) and a production function such that Q increased with E and X (instead of the special [7.27]), then we could not say in which direction X would change for a change in W.

Chapter 8

Cost Benefit Analysis

The title of this chapter may strike the reader as somewhat odd in that we have thus far in the book done little that was not looking at costs and benefits. There is a sense in which economics is cost benefit analysis, and vice versa. However, here we are using the term *cost benefit analysis* in the specialised way economists have come to use it to refer to the appraisal of projects from the perspective of society as a whole rather than from the perspective of those responsible for the decisions on projects. We do this here because it draws together many of the ideas discussed in the preceding chapters. We first set out the methodology of cost benefit analysis as social project appraisal. We then discuss, in 8.2, some of the issues arising in the analysis of a proposal to build a hydroelectric power facility. In 8.3 we review the question of the appropriate choice of discount rate in the social analysis of projects and in 8.4 we consider risk and uncertainty.

8.1   The methodology of cost benefit analysis

As usually understood, the term cost benefit analysis refers to the social appraisal of projects. We discussed project appraisal by firms in section 6.4. The essential difference between project appraisal by firms and cost benefit analysis is that the former values, and thereby aggregates over, the consequences of project adoption at market prices whereas the latter does so at the prices corresponding to relative social valuations. As we have been at some pains to argue, in an economy characterised by ideal conditions everywhere, market prices would be identical to relative social valuations, so that in no case would there be any difference between the outcome of an appraisal of a given project conducted by a firm or conducted by an agency concerned with the interests of society as a whole. In saying this we are assuming that the interests of society as a whole are adequately served by securing the objective of efficiency in allocation. We are, that is, assuming the markets work in the context of a socially acceptable distribution of income. This assumption is implicit in the methodology of cost benefit analysis[1].

However, the fact that there exists a methodology for cost benefit analysis itself implies that it is not widely accepted that the ideal conditions, under which social project appraisal would be redundant, are operative in actual economies. We have also been at some pains to argue in earlier chapters that actual economies are characterised by market failure – there are public goods (and bads), not all economic agents act as price takers, not all economic agents have complete information, there are not well defined private property rights in all inputs to and outputs from production and consumption activities. Hence, the prices emerging in markets cannot generally be taken to be those corresponding to the relative social valuations required for efficiency in allocation, and there is a rôle for cost benefit analysis.

This is not to say that project appraisal can never proceed on the basis of valuation and aggregation at market prices. The point is not, that is, that in an actual economy every conceivable project requires to be subjected to a cost benefit analysis by some governmental agency. For many projects it will be appropriate to proceed on the basis that all of their consequences can be valued and aggregated at actual market prices. This will be the case where none of the consequences are in the nature of public goods, where there are no external costs or benefits arising, and where the markets in which the prices emerge are dominated by price taker behaviour on the basis of complete information. Equally, where a project is appropriately to be subjected to a cost benefit analysis, it is not necessarily the case that market prices cannot be used with respect to some of its consequences. Where market prices are regarded as inappropriate, the agency doing the cost benefit analysis has necessarily to determine the appropriate prices for itself: we discussed in Chapter 2 the essential rôle of relative prices in aggregation. The principle involved in such determination is clear and simple – what matters is willingness to pay. As we shall see, actually putting this principle into practice raises difficult issues.

There are five basic elements to a cost benefit analysis exercise:

(i)   Project definition and identification.
(ii) Complete enumeration of the consequences of going ahead with the project.
(iii) Aggregation over consequences at each time period in the project's life to get time series for project costs and benefits.
(iv) Aggregation of the cost and benefit streams over time to get a figure for the project's net present value.
(v)   Sensitivity analysis.

We now discuss each of these in turn briefly. Further discussion of matters of principle and practice will arise when we look at an application in the next section and in 6.3 when we consider (iv) here especially.

A *project* is an item of investment which can be analysed as an independent unit. If two items of investment are so closely linked that neither can fulfil its purpose without the other, then they comprise a single project. Thus, for example, in the context of electricity supply a new power station and the transmission lines connecting it to the national grid would clearly be a single project for analysis. On the other hand, a new power station connected to the national grid and a new retail outlet for electrical appliances are clearly separate projects. Or again, it is clear that the project which is the electrification of a railway system must include the new electric locomotives required, while electrification and improved station facilities for passengers are distinct projects. The proper identification of the project is clearly a necessary first step in its appraisal. Without such identification it is impossible to consider properly the consequences of going ahead.

Taking together (ii) and (iii) above produces two sets of numbers:

$$B_0, B_1, B_2, \ldots B_T$$
$$C_0, C_1, C_2, \ldots C_T$$

for the benefit and cost streams associated with the project. While these numbers are of primary concern in economic analysis, it is important to be clear that arriving at them involves two conceptually distinct stages in the analysis. The *enumeration* stage (ii) involves the physical consequences of the project, so that its output is in terms of man hours of labour inputs, tons of cement used, tons of apples produced, tons of sulphur emitted into the atmosphere, and so on and so on at each date from 0 through to T. The *aggregation* stage (iii) involves using prices to aggregate over the desirable consequences (more apples available, etc.) to get the B_0, B_1, $B_2, \ldots B_T$ series, and over the undesirable consequences (less labour available for alternative uses, more sulphur in the atmosphere, etc.) to get the C_0, C_1, $C_2 \ldots C_T$ series. The distinction between physical enumeration and valuation and aggregation is not always very apparent in actual cost benefit studies, but it is important to keep it in mind for several reasons. The first of these is that, as we have previously emphasised (see Chapter 2 especially), economic analysis in general and cost benefit analysis in particular is not concerned with money totals as such. It is the case that monetary aggregation is a convenient way of describing the implications of adopting a project giving rise to a variety of physical consequences. The second point concerns the problems which necessarily arise in doing a cost benefit analysis and the reliability of such as a guide to social decision making. It is often argued that cost benefit analysis is especially vulnerable where it involves attaching prices to things which are not marketable. It is difficult to know how to value, for example, the loss of wildlife habitat involved in, or the human deaths which will be avoided as, the result of road improvement schemes. But those who make this point against cost benefit analysis often appear to overlook the fact that it is also very difficult to know how many human lives will be saved, or how much wildlife will be affected, by a given road improvement scheme. Valuation and aggregation presupposes physical enumeration, and at both stages cost benefit analysis must involve uncertainty.

At stage (iv) we compute:

$$\text{NPV} = \sum_{t=0}^{T} \frac{B_t - C_t}{(1 + r)^t} = (B_0 - C_0) + \frac{(B_1 - C_1)}{(1 + r)} + \frac{(B_2 - C_2)}{(1 + r)^2}$$
$$+ \ldots \frac{(B_T - C_T)}{(1 + r)^T} \qquad\qquad [8.1]$$

The reader will recognise this expression – it first appeared as equation [6.14] in 6.4, where we discussed project appraisal by firms. The reader will recall that we showed there that the firm should adopt all projects for which the net present value, *NPV*, was positive, in order to maximise its present value. In Chapter 6 we also showed that, given a properly functioning bond market and ideal conditions everywhere in the economy, firms so acting to maximise their present value lead to the realisation of efficiency in intertemporal allocation. In cost benefit analysis the decision rule is that projects which have positive net present values are socially desirable, while those that do not are not. The rationale for this cost benefit analysis decision rule is also that following it promotes the attainment of the goal of efficiency in intertemporal allocation.

In writing equation [8.1] as an exact reproduction of equation [6.14] we emphasise the sense in which we are not now introducing any fundamentally new ideas. We also risk some misunderstanding, which we can hope to avoid by noting explicitly what is involved. While the same symbols *B*, *C* and *r* appear in equations [6.14] and [8.1], they have somewhat different connotations. In project appraisal by a firm *B* and *C* refer to the results of using market prices to aggregate over those consequences which affect the firm's revenues and expenditures. Hence, for a given project, the *B* and *C* series appearing in equations [6.14] and [8.1] would be the same only if ideal conditions held everywhere in the economy, in which case cost benefit analysis as such would be redundant. In discussing equation [6.14] and the implications of following the decision rule based on it, *r* represented the rate of interest determined in a properly functioning bond market set in an economy where ideal conditions held everywhere. The discussion of cost benefit analysis implies other circumstances and one of the ongoing questions in the development of cost benefit analysis as a technique for use in such 'other circumstances' is the way *r* in equation [8.1] should be given its value. We shall leave discussion of this question until the third section of this chapter.

The final stage of a cost benefit analysis exercise is *sensitivity analysis*. This involves reworking the exercise through to the computation of the NPV according to equation [8.1] for alternative values for some of the inputs. We have in the preceding paragraphs noted the difficulties and uncertainties that attend providing the inputs required at the stages (ii) (physical enumeration of consequences) and (iii) (valuation and aggregation at each period in the project's life). We have also noted that the appropriate way to fix the value of *r* to be used in equation [8.1] is not a settled matter. It follows that it would be inappropriate to proceed with a cost benefit exercise on the basis that it can provide, even within its own efficiency in allocation terms of reference, a uniquely correct answer on whether a project should go ahead or not. Rather, it seems appropriate to regard the exercise as one in assembling, organising, and analysing information on a project so as to inform social debate and decision-making. This will be especially appropriate where the project will be undertaken, if adopted, by some governmental agency. Reworking the cost benefit analysis for different values for inputs can identify areas of input to which the positive NPV rule is especially sensitive, and thus identify those areas where either more information has to be collected or where an essentially political decision has to be made.

This discussion of the methodology of cost benefit analysis has been rather brief. The discussion of the use of this methodology in the next section is designed to illuminate the points made here.

8.2   Cost benefit analysis of a hydroelectric facility

In this section we look at the cost benefit analysis of a project which is the construction of a hydroelectric plant. The project data are not taken from any actual proposal, but have been invented in order to form the basis for a discussion of the main issues which arise in this sort of context. Actual hydroelectric plant proposals have been the subject of cost benefit analyses, especially in the USA. The reader interested in examining the issues raised here as they have in fact been handled in cost benefit analyses of actual projects will find references to the literature in the commentary section at the end of the chapter. The objective in looking here at an invented example is to reveal the nature of the issues arising in a simplified context, so as to bring them out more clearly. The issues we identify here are those which arise in practice: the particular numbers we use to illustrate the issues are hypothetical and should not be taken as referring to any actual hydroelectric scheme.

The project is to build a dam, which will result in the flooding of a river valley behind the dam site, together with the installation of the necessary turbines, etc., for electricity generation and the transmission lines to feed the electricity generated into the grid. The river valley is in a remote area which is uninhabited and is not farmed, but which is used for wilderness type recreational activities (walking, camping, etc.) and which is the habitat for a number of rare species of plant and animal. In respect of one of the plant species the river valley in question is the only known place where the plant grows wild. The flooding of the valley behind the dam will destroy the habitat for the rare plant and animal species. The hydroelectric plant will take five years to construct and bring on line, and will thereafter deliver electricity to the national grid for 45 years. This project lifetime is dictated by safety considerations. The project includes the controlled destruction of the dam after 50 years and the removal of the transmission lines, etc.

The project consequences are then:

(i)   The use of inputs of labour, machinery and raw materials for the construction of the entire hydroelectric facility, for its running and maintenance, and for its eventual removal.

(ii)   The supply of electricity to the national grid for a period of 45 years.

(iii) The loss, for a period of 50 years, of a wilderness recreation facility.

(iv)   The destruction of wildlife habitat.

We now discuss each of these in turn.

Construction, operating and removal costs

The engineering specifications for the entire facility give construction input requirements and scheduling which when valued at market prices total £200 million for each of the five years of the construction phase. The running and maintenance inputs at market prices come to £500 000 per annum for years 6 through to 50. The removal of the dam and its associated facilities is scheduled for year 50, when the cost of the shut down and removal operation will be £100 million, again valuing the various inputs required at their market prices. It should be noted that all of these figures are necessarily in the nature of estimates at the point in time when the project is to be subjected to a cost benefit analysis. In large civil engineering works there is an observed tendency to underestimate, at the planning stage, the quantities of inputs which will be required during construction. The input quantities at all stages are, we have noted, aggregated using market prices for the purposes of our cost benefit analysis. We are assuming, that is, that in terms of the inputs for construction, maintenance and shutdown, market prices are appropriate for social valuation. This assumption would not necessarily be appropriate in all conceivable circumstances. If, for example, it were known that the construction stage labour inputs would be drawn largely from the ranks of the otherwise unemployed, the market wage would overstate the social valuation of labour inputs. We are assuming here that this is not the case.

Electricity output valuation

The size of the dam in relation to the riverflow is such that, given average rainfall, the annual electrical output will be 6,570 GWh.[2] Less rainfall in a year would mean less electricity sent out, more rainfall more electricity. The planning assumption is 6,570 GWh for each of the 45 years. How should this electrical output be valued per unit? In terms of the value of the resource input savings it realises for the electricity supply system. The principle involved here is clear. By building a hydroelectric plant the electricity supply system reduces its fuel costs for meeting any given demand for electricity to the extent that output from the hydroelectric plant, fuel cost zero, displaces output from plant (coal, oil or gas fired or nuclear plant) with non-zero fuel costs. The valuation of the hydroelectric plant's output therefore depends on the fuel(s) which would have been used in the absence of the plant. In practice determining the quantities of savings of the various fuels attributable to the hydroelectric plant is an exercise which involves modelling the entire electricity supply system. To focus on the essential issues we shall assume that we are considering an electricity supply system in which, in the absence of the projected hydroelectric scheme, the only fuel which can be burned is coal. Then the output from the proposed plant displaces coal, and is to be valued in terms of such resource input savings. The quantity of coal input saved by virtue of 6,570 GWh of hydro plant output depends on the thermal efficiency of coal-burning power stations. A widely used 'ready reckoner' conversion factor is 500 tons of coal to generate 1 GWh of electricity. On this basis the planning assumption electrical output of the hydro plant means a reduction in the coal burn of 3,285,000 tons per year. We shall assume that the market price for coal is £10 per ton, in the year in which work on the project is to commence.

We shall not assume that this price is the appropriate social valuation per ton of coal input saved in every year of the project's life, however. There are two reasons for this. First, coal is a non-renewable resource. Second, burning coal to generate electricity gives rise to external costs. In 7.2 we saw that efficiency in intertemporal allocation requires that the price of a non-renewable resource rises over time at a proportional rate equal to the interest rate, assuming constant marginal extraction costs. Since cost benefit analysis is concerned with efficiency in allocation, we should in each year of the project's life value the coal saving at the price corresponding to efficient intertemporal allocation. We cannot know that price. During the life of the project the interest rate may change, marginal extraction costs for coal may change, and/or vast new coal deposits may be discovered. All that we can do is to take for our central evaluation the assumption that the price of coal rises at a proportional rate equal to the interest rate.

External benefits

It is well known that burning coal to generate electricity gives rise to pollution problems, especially atmospheric pollution. The external costs avoided by the substitution of non-polluting hydroelectricity for coal-fired electricity are benefits to be attributed to the project as are the coal resource savings. Quantification of the project benefits so arising is difficult. The atmospheric pollution from coal combustion has adverse effects on material structures, giving rise to corrosion, and to cleaning costs. It also has adverse effects on plants and animals, including man. In quantitative terms most research attention has focused on the effects on human health, and we shall explicitly consider only such here. This is not to be taken to imply that the other effects of atmospheric pollution due to coal combustion are trivial. In terms of their physical dimensions they clearly are not, though there is much uncertainty involved; see 5.5, 9.5, and 9.7.

If we consider just human health effects then estimating the costs attributable to the burning of coal to produce electricity is a two-stage process. First, we have to quantify the health effects, and second we have to value them. At both stages there is much uncertainty, despite, in the former case especially, a great deal of research effort. The health effects are increased morbidity (disease incidence) and mortality due to coal combustion. Relatively little is known about the former. Regarding increased mortality, based on central estimates for the mortality effects of the various pollutants emitted in coal combustion and considering the emissions from a typical 1 GW plant operating at a 75% load factor (i.e. running 75% of the year), one estimate is of 80 extra deaths per year attributable to plant operation. However, the range of estimates for the excess mortality, attributable to such a plant, which can be found in the literature is from 10 to 100! Since there are 365 days in the year and 24 hours in a day, a 1 GW plant operating at a 75% load factor sends out 6,570 GWh per year ($365 \times 24 \times 0.75$). This is the estimated average yearly output of the hydro plant, and we shall take for our central case the assumption that its operation would mean 80 fewer premature deaths per year.[3]

We now turn to the social valuation of a reduction in mortality. Putting a value on human life is a difficult and contentious area. The basic principle here is, as elsewhere, that social valuation should reflect willingness to pay. Now clearly if an individual is asked what he would be willing to pay to prevent his own certain death on the morrow, his answer will be the largest sum of money on which he can lay his hands. Conversely, if an individual were asked how much he would require to compensate him for the certain prospect of death tomorrow, the answer would be, in most cases, an indefinitely large sum of money. But, projects do not give rise to the prospects of certain life or death for specific individuals. Rather they give rise to decreases or increases in mortality rates for whole populations, and hence to changes in the probability of death for individual members of that population. Individuals can and do make choices which involve changes in the probability of death, as, for example, when they travel by car rather than walk in urban areas, demonstrating that they value the time saved more than the increased probability of death. In principle, then, one can infer willingness to pay for changes in the probability of death from observed behaviour. The implementation of this principle is difficult. One approach which has been adopted is to look at wage rate differentials across occupations of varying degrees of riskiness. Other things equal, it is an observable fact that wage rates are higher for riskier jobs. To see how such information might be used, suppose it were the case that across occupations (after adjusting for skill requirements, unpleasant working conditions, etc.) an increase in the risk of premature death of 0.001 were associated with an increase in the annual wage of £100. It is assumed that this £100 is the compensation required by a typical individual for an increase of 0.001 in the probability of premature death. So for 1,000 people the total willingness to pay for a 0.001 reduction in the probability of death would be £100,000. But for a population of 1,000 a reduction in probability of 0.001 means one less premature death, and so £100,000 would be taken as the social valuation of the saving of one life.

We shall use the illustrative figure of £100,000 in our cost benefit analysis. The range of variation in the values for a human life that can be found in the literature is rather large. As we noted above, this is a difficult and contentious area. It is, however, a problem which it is impossible to avoid. If a project does involve changes in the probability of premature death for members of a population, such consequences have to be weighed against the project's other consequences. One way to do this is by explicitly valuing human life and including such consequences in the cost benefit arithmetic. There are those who argue that this is immoral. If those who take such a view are nonetheless willing to take a decision on the project, presumably on the basis of the valuation of the project's other consequences, then they are implicitly valuing human life. Suppose, for example, that it is known that a particular course of action will result in 100 premature deaths, and that in respect of all its other consequences it offers an excess of total social benefit over total social cost of £x. Then, those who would reject this course of action on the basis of this information are saying that society should be willing to pay at least £$(x \div 100)$ to avoid one premature death. Further, if the argument is that premature deaths cannot be traded off against benefits to society under any circumstances, then what is being said is that this course of action should be rejected however large £x is.

External costs

We now consider the project consequence which is the loss of the wilderness recreation facility to walkers, campers, etc. Since use of this facility has not been the subject of market transactions we have no market price or quantity data to quantify and value this consequence. The *travel cost method*, TCM, involves using data on the costs incurred by visitors in getting to the valley to infer their willingness to pay for the recreation facilities that it offers. This method is sometimes referred to as the *Clawson method*, after the economist who is credited with the original idea.

The first step is to ascertain the number of visitors and where they come from. This is done by counting, and by interviewing a sample of them over an appropriate period – say, a full week in the summer. We suppose that by such means it is estimated that the numbers of visits from five zones defined by distance from the valley is as shown in Table 8.1. The population sizes of the zones are used to get figures for visits per thousand of population from each zone. The cost of a visit is the cost of travel, which is assumed to be directly related to distance, principally via fuel and other running costs for cars. An alternative source of information on travel costs is asking interviewed visitors how much they spent on their visit. The data from the last two columns of Table 8.1 are plotted in Figure 8.1: the equation for the line joining up the crosses is

$$v = 10.5 - 0.3c \hfill [8.2]$$

Table 8.1 Visits data from survey of visitors

Zone	Population	Visits	Visits Per Thousand	Cost of Visit
1	2 000 000	15 000	7.5	£10
2	8 000 000	48 000	6.0	£15
3	2 500 000	11 250	4.5	£20
4	15 000 000	45 000	3.0	£25
5	22 666 000	34 000	1.5	£30
		153 250		

where v represents visits per thousand of population and c represents travel costs per visit.[4]

Now, access to the valley is not charged for, but by using equation [8.2] it is possible to simulate the effect of charging at different levels and thus to ascertain willingness to pay. To do this we have to assume that all users of the valley as a wilderness recreation facility react in the same way to all cost changes associated with use, i.e. they regard £s spent on travel to the valley as exactly equivalent to £s spent to pay a charge for access to the valley. On this assumption, we can proceed, as shown in Table 8.2, to derive the hypothetical demand schedule ABCDEF shown in Figure 8.2. With zero admission charge we know from Table 8.1 that there are 153,250 visitors per year in total: this gives point A in Figure 8.2. Now, if an admission charge of £5 were imposed then the total cost of a visit from each zone would rise by £5 to the levels shown against 'Cost' in Table 8.2(i). We now use equation [8.2] to get the number of visits per thousand of population from each zone corresponding to these costs. Thus, for example, for zone

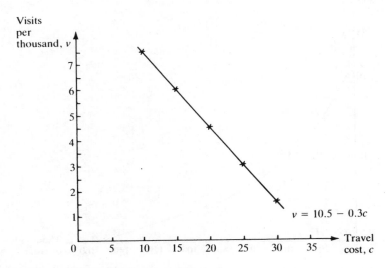

Figure 8.1 Visits dependent on travel costs

Table 8.2 Simulating the effects of various admission price levels
(i) Admission Price = £5

Zone	1	2	3	4	5	Total
Cost	£15	£20	£25	£30	£35	
Visits	12 000	36 000	7 500	22 500	0	78 000

(ii) Admission Price = £10

Zone	1	2	3	4	5	Total
Cost	£20	£25	£30	£35	£40	
Visits	9 000	24 000	3 750	0	0	36 750

(iii) Admission Price = £15

Zone	1	2	3	4	5	Total
Cost	£25	£30	£35	£40	£45	
Visits	6 000	12 000	0	0	0	18 000

(iv) Admission Price = £20

Zone	1	2	3	4	5	Total
Cost	£30	£35	£40	£45	£50	
Visits	3 000	0	0	0	0	3 000

1 $v = 10.5 - (0.3 \times 15) = 10.5 - 4.5 = 6.0$. Using the zone population data from Table 8.1 these per thousand of population figures are transformed into the 'Visits' figures in Table 8.2(i): Six visits per thousand from zone 1 with a population of 2 million gives 12,000 visits, for example. Note that since the survey revealed nobody incurring travel costs in excess of £30, it is assumed

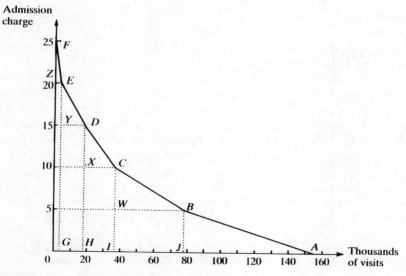

Figure 8.2   A surrogate demand function for wilderness recreation

Table 8.3 Calculating total willingness to pay for wilderness recreation

Area *ABJ* = $1/2 \times AJ \times BJ = 1/2 \times (153\,250 - 78\,000) \times 5 = £188\,125$
Area *BCIJ* = Area *BCW* + Area *WIJB*
= $[1/2 \times (78\,000 - 36\,750) \times 5] + [5 \times (78\,000 - 36\,750)]$
= $[1/2 \times 41\,250 \times 5] + [5 \times 41\,250]$
= $103\,125 + 206\,250$
= £309\,375
Area *CDHI* = Area *CDX* + Area *XHIC* = £234\,375
Area *DEGH* = Area *DEY* + Area *YGHD* = £262\,500
Area *EFOG* = Area *EFZ* + Area *ZOGE* = £67\,500

that with an admission charge of £5 there will be no visitors from zone 5. Adding across the visits row under (i) in Table 8.2 we get a total of 78,000 visits from all zones for an admission charge of £5. This identifies point *B* in Figure 8.2, and *C*, *D*, *E* and *F* are similarly identified by the calculations from Table 8.2(ii), (iii) and (iv).

We have now obtained a *surrogate demand function* for the wilderness recreation facility which will become unavailable if the project goes ahead. Our valuation of the annual cost to be assigned to the project on this count is the total willingness to pay for the availability of the facility, because it will be entirely lost if the project goes ahead. We want, that is, the area under *ABCDEF* in Figure 8.2. We find this in a piecemeal way, by calculating separately the areas *ABJ*, *BCIJ*, *CDHI*, *DEGH* and *EFOG*, and then summing them. Table 8.3 shows the calculations. We find that the annual total willingness to pay for the wilderness recreation facility is £1,061,875. We shall use the round figure of £1 million per year for the cost to be charged to the project on this count. We can note that with no admission charge, total willingness to pay is the same as consumers' surplus.

Finally we come to the destruction of wildlife habitat which would be involved in going ahead with the project. If visitors to the valley which is to be flooded were the only people whose utility were affected by the destruction of this wildlife habitat, such destruction would not be an additional cost to charge against the project. This is because in counting their willingness to pay for the recreation facility we have counted the loss they suffer from not being able to see the wildlife. However, it is not reasonable to suppose that visitors to the valley are the only people who derive satisfaction from the existence of the animal and plant populations affected. We noted that in respect of one of the plant species, this valley was the only known place where it grows. It appears to be the case that people derive satisfaction from the knowledge that rare plant and animal species exist in natural habitats quite independently of their own prospects of ever visiting such habitats. Also, the extinction of species means the loss of material for scientific study, and of possible future sources of things to direct use to man (such as inputs to the manufacture of medicinal drugs). The problem involved in including these considerations in a cost benefit analysis is apparent. What we can fairly easily do, and shall do here, is to proceed with the cost benefit analysis, leaving out the habitat destruction cost. If the project does not then pass the positive net present value test, the habitat destruction cost is irrelevant to the decision on the project. If the project does, on this basis, have a positive net present value, its size tells us what willingness to pay for habitat preservation would have to be in order for it not to be socially desirable to proceed with the project. It is then possible to consider whether willingness to pay for the habitat preservation is plausibly sufficiently large to stop the project. Such a procedure can inform public debate on the project and stimulate efforts to infer the size of willingness to pay for habitat preservation.

In the last couple of decades economists have developed methods for estimating habitat loss type values. It has become conventional to regard the amenity value of an environmental public good, such as the unflooded valley in our illustration, as comprising four components. With TEV for *total environmental value*, we have

$$TEV = UV + EV + OV + QOV \qquad [8.3]$$

where

1.   UV, *use value*, arises from visiting and using the area for recreation.
2.   EV, *existence value*, arises from the knowledge that the area exists and will continue to exist in its present state, and is independent of any actual or prospective use of the area.
3.   OV, *option value*, relates to willingness to pay to ensure that the area is available for future use, should the desire for use arise.
4.   QOV, *quasi-option value*, relates to willingness to pay to avoid an irreversible commitment to development of the area now, given that there is the expectation of future growth in the knowledge relevant to the implications of the proposed development.

It turns out that it is typically very difficult to put numbers to EV, OV and QOV separately. These three components together are sometimes referred to as *non-use values*, NUV, or *passive use values*, PUV.

The travel cost method can only be used to estimate use values. It is an indirect method which seeks to infer information about willingness to pay for the use of the area from observed behaviour in regard to visiting the area. Clearly, non-use values cannot be inferred in this way. There is no behaviour to which the indirect method can be applied. To estimate such values economists have developed the *contingent valuation method*, CVM. It gets name from the fact that the willingness to pay that it reveals information on is contingent on a hypothetical scenario presented to a sample of individuals. In the illustrative example being considered here, a sample of individuals would be told about the valley and its rôle as habitat, and asked what they would be willing to pay to preserve the habitat from destruction. Averaging across the individual hypothetical valuations in the sample, gives a per capita willingness to pay, which is multiplied by the size of the relevant population to give total willingness to pay in respect of non-use values. The idea is that this number is to be compared with the positive net present value, if it is positive. If this number is smaller than the net present value, then on allocative efficiency criteria the hydroelectric project should go ahead, otherwise not.

Total annual willingness to pay for the valley's non-use values could be included in the cost benefit analysis, as an annual cost attributable to the project just like any other cost. The test for allowing the project to proceed would then be whether the calculated net present value was equal to or greater than zero. In the workings below, we follow the former procedure, leaving PUV out of the arithmetic for the net present value.

Calculating the project's NPV

So, in terms of our central assumptions, the project involves the following cost and benefit streams:

(i) £200 millions per year for years 1 to 5 inclusive for construction costs, £100 millions in year 50 for shut-down costs, and £500 000 per year in years 6 to 50 for running and maintenance costs.

(ii) A reduction in the coal burn of 3 285 000 tons per year for years 6 to 50 inclusive: coal is valued at £10 per ton in year one, and its value grows at an annual rate equal to the interest rate.

(iii) A reduction in excess mortality of 80 per year in years 6 to 50 inclusive: an avoided premature death is valued at £100 000.

(iv) A loss of wilderness recreation facility with services valued at £1 million per year. This loss takes effect in year 1. It is not apparent that there is a uniquely correct date at which it would be appropriate to assume the cessation of this annual loss. Clearly the loss continues beyond year 50, as removing the dam, etc., does not immediately restore the valley to its former state. It might be argued that, say, 50 years after the removal of the dam natural processes will have effectively reinstated the wilderness recreation facility. But strictly speaking the valley will never revert to exactly its former state: clearly there is no reason to suppose that the rare species will re-establish themselves in the valley. We shall evaluate the project on two assumptions: first that the wilderness recreation facility is lost for 100 years, and second that it is lost forever.

(v) As noted, the destruction of the wildlife habitat is permanent. Insofar then as this destruction gives rise to costs over and above those counted at (iv), such costs accrue in all future years.

Table 8.4 sets out the flows of costs and benefits associated with the project, leaving aside the loss of habitat costs, over a period of 100 years. The figures shown under coal savings arise as follows. The quantity of coal saved in years 6 through to 50 is 3 285000 tons. In year 1 the price of coal is £10 per ton. The price of coal, as explained, is assumed to grow at the rate of interest, which is 5%. Hence in year 2 the price of coal is

Table 8.4 Cost and benefit streams over project lifetime

| | Costs | | Benefits | |
| | £ millions | | | |
Year	Construction running removal	Wilderness recreation	Coal savings	Mortality reduction
1	200	1	0	0
2	200	1	0	0
3	200	1	0	0
4	200	1	0	0
5	200	1	0	0
6	0.5	1	41.9	8
7	0.5	1	44.0	8
.	.	.	.	.
.	.	.	.	.
48	0.5	1	325.4	8
49	0.5	1	341.7	8
50	100.5	1	358.8	8
51	0	1	0	0
52	0	1	0	0
.	.	.	.	.
.	.	.	.	.
98	0	1	0	0
99	0	1	0	0
100	0	1	0	0

$£10(1 + r) = £10(1.05) = £10.5$, in year 3 $£10(1 + r)^2 = £10(1.05^2) = £11.025$, and so on. In general we have

Coal Saving at $t = 3\,285\,000 \times 10 \times 1.05^{t-1}$

where t indicates the year. The remaining entries in Table 8.4 follow directly from our earlier discussion.

Two points can usefully be made here. The first concerns the project lifetime. This is not fixed by the date at which the project ceases to do that for which it was intended, in this case the generation of electricity. It is fixed by the date at which it is true that all of the consequences attributable to the project have ceased to exist. In this case the latter date is a matter of some uncertainty, as noted, but it is at least 100 years after project initiation. What is clear is that considering only the period over which electricity is sent out as the project lifetime, and so abbreviating Table 8.4 at $t = 50$, could lead to serious mistakes in social project appraisal. The second point concerns the relevance of the distinction between absolute and relative prices emphasised in Chapter 2 here. It is the latter which are of concern in cost benefit analysis. We have in constructing Table 8.4 assumed that the general price level is constant, so that absolute and relative prices are the same. In cost benefit

Table 8.5 Discount factors for $r = 0.05$

$$d_t = \left(\frac{1}{1+r}\right)^{t-1} = \left(\frac{1}{1.05}\right)^{t-1}$$

Year	d_t
1	1.0000
2	0.9524
3	0.9070
4	0.8638
5	0.8227
6	0.7835
7	0.7462
8	0.7107
.	.
.	.
.	.
46	0.1113
47	0.1060
48	0.1010
49	0.0961
50	0.0916
51	0.0872
52	0.0831
.	.
.	.
.	.
98	0.0088
99	0.0084
100	0.0080

analysis, any anticipated movements in the general price level, but not in relative prices, should be ignored. The analysis should, that is, be conducted as if it were known that there would in future be zero inflation.

The next step in the cost benefit analysis is to aggregate these benefit and cost streams over time to obtain their present values. To do this we discount each figure appearing in Table 8.4 by multiplying it by the appropriate discount factor: the process of calculating present values was explained in 6.3. Table 8.5 shows the discount factors for an interest rate of 0.05, on the assumption that the sums to be discounted arise on the first day of each year.[5] We see, for example, that the present value of £1 at $t = 50$ is just £0.09 with $r = 0.05$. Using these discount factors on the data of Table 8.4 we get the discounted cost and benefit streams shown in Table 8.6. Note that the discounted benefit stream arising from coal savings is constant from $t = 6$ to $t = 50$ because the price of coal is increasing at a proportional rate equal to the rate of interest. Summing down the columns in Table 8.6 we get:

Present value construction, etc., costs	925.7
Present value wilderness recreation costs	20.8
Present value cost	946.5

Table 8.6 Discounted costs and benefits

	£ millions			
	Costs		Benefits	
Year	Construction running removal	Wilderness recreation	Coal savings	Mortality reduction
1	200	1	0	0
2	190.48	0.95	0	0
3	181.41	0.91	0	0
4	172.77	0.86	0	0
5	164.54	0.82	0	0
6	0.39	0.78	32.85	6.3
7	0.37	0.75	32.85	6.0
.	.	.	.	.
.	.	.	.	.
.	.	.	.	.
48	0.005	0.10	32.85	0.81
49	0.0048	0.096	32.85	0.77
50	9.165	0.092	32.85	0.73
51	0	0.087	0	0
52	0	0.083	0	0
.	.	.	.	.
.	.	.	.	.
.	.	.	.	.
98	0	0.0088	0	0
99	0	0.0084	0	0
100	0	0.0080	0	0
	925.7	20.8	1478.3	117.0

NPV = 648.8

Present value coal savings benefits	1478.3
Present value mortality reduction benefits	117.0
Present value benefit	1595.3
Net present value	£648.8 millions.

This is on the assumption that the wilderness recreation losses cease to be operative after year 100. On this assumption, the project offers an excess of (discounted) benefit over cost and so according to the efficiency criterion it should go ahead.

Does it make any difference if it is assumed that the wilderness recreation facility is lost forever as a result of the project? Inspection of Table 8.6 suggests that the answer to this question is, due to the effects of discounting on costs and benefits arising in the distant future, likely to be 'no'. The discounted, or present, value of £1 million 100 years hence is, at $r = 0.05$, just £8,000. As we extend the time horizon over which the wilderness recreation loss continues and affects the project's NPV beyond 100 so, year by year, the increase in the present value cost attributable to the project gets smaller than £8,000. In fact, if we consider the annual sum of £x, arising at the start of each year, forever, and if the interest rate is r, the present value of the cost/benefit stream £x forever is given by

$$PV = \frac{(1+r)x}{r} \tag{8.4}$$

as shown in the mathematical note at the end of this chapter. With £x = £1 million and $r = 0.05$, equation [8.4] gives PV = £21 millions. That is to say, that if we compute the present value of the costs arising from the loss of wilderness recreation on the assumption that such loss is permanent, rather than for 100 years, we get a figure of £21 millions, rather than the £20.8 millions appearing in Table 8.6. The effect of this change on the NPV figure is negligible.

We have thus far ignored the costs attributable to the loss of wildlife habitat consequent upon going ahead with the project. We can see that such costs would have to have a present value in excess of £650 millions (in round figures) in order for their inclusion to lead to a decision against the project. This is because ignoring such costs we find the project to have an NPV of £650 millions (in round figures). We can use equation [8.4] to convert this present value figure to an annual, undiscounted, cost stream since we have noted that the habitat loss is permanent. Substituting $PV = 650$ and $r = 0.05$ in equation [8.4] we get

$$650 = (1.05/0.05)\,x = 21x$$
$$\text{i.e. } x = 650/21 = 30.95$$

so that if we were prepared to believe that people collectively were willing to pay £30 950 000 per year to preserve the habitats, we should find against the project.

Sensitivity analysis

We have at several points in our discussion noted the uncertainty attached to the figures appearing in Table 8.4. We can now examine the sensitivity of the outcome of the cost benefit analysis to such uncertainties. Such a sensitivity analysis is a crucial part of any properly conducted cost benefit analysis. It indicates the areas where the decision on the project is crucially dependent on the data input to the cost benefit analysis. In some cases it may be possible to firm up the input data by further research. In other cases the uncertainty may be unavoidable.

It is clear from Tables 8.4 and 8.6 that the outcome of the cost benefit analysis is dominated by the construction running and removal costs and the coal savings benefits, with the other costs and benefits playing a relatively minor role. Looking first at the coal savings benefits we have noted that while the appropriate basic assumption is that the price of coal increases at the same rate as the rate of interest, there are reasons why it might not so do. We can also note here that in going from the electrical output of the hydro plant to an annual quantity of coal saved, we assumed that the relationship would be constant over the life of the project. This would not be the appropriate assumption if the thermal efficiency of coal-fired power stations were to improve over time. In this case the annual coal savings attributable to the hydro plant would fall over the plant's lifetime. We can examine the sensitivity of the decision on the project to this possibility most easily by looking at the effect of different assumptions about the rate of increase in the price of coal: reducing this rate has the same effect as reducing the quantity of coal saved. The effects arising are as follows:

% increase in coal price p.a.	present value coal savings	net present value of project
4	1150.5	+321.0
3	907.2	+77.7
2	724.8	−104.7
1	586.4	−243.1
0	480.4	−349.1

The present value figures here are in £millions. We see that changes of just 1% in the assumption about the rate of growth of the undiscounted value of the coal savings (arising due to either a different price appreciation assumption and/or a different quantity assumption) exerts a large effect on the NPV result. If, for example, we assume a 4% p.a. appreciation in the value of coal savings, then with an NPV of £321 millions we find from equation [8.4] above that the annual cost attributable to habitat loss required to reject the project drops from £31 millions to £15 millions.

We now consider the construction running and shutdown costs for the project. In the central assumptions case shown in Table 8.6 these have a present value of £926 millions. We noted that at the planning stage the construction costs of large civil engineering projects are frequently underestimated. If we consider a 50% increase in construction costs, to £300 millions per year for five years, we find that the present value for construction running and removal costs increases to £1380 millions, reducing the project's NPV to £195 millions. Considering a tenfold increase in the shutdown costs, to £1000 millions, we find that this increases the present value for construction running and removal costs to £1008 millions reducing the NPV to £566 millions. The larger increase in the shutdown costs has less effect on the NPV because the shutdown costs arise at year 50 and are heavily discounted in the NPV calculation (for $t = 50$, $d_t = 0.0916$ in Table 8.5).

In discussing the environmental benefits attributable to the project, via the avoided external costs associated with coal burning, we noted (i) that in looking only at reduced human mortality we were ignoring some environmental benefits and (ii) that in estimating the size of the mortality effect and putting a unit value on it there was scope for legitimate disagreement about the appropriate numbers. Looking at the second of these points, recall first that we noted that while the mortality reduction figure used for Tables 8.4 and 8.6 was 80 per annum, figures ranging from 10 to 100 could be found in the literature. If the lower of these figures is used, the present value for the mortality reduction benefits drops to £15 millions, which change reduces the NPV to £547 millions. If we use the 100 figure for mortality reduction and double the value of an avoided premature death to £200 000, the present value of the mortality reduction benefits increases to £293 millions increasing the NPV to £825 millions.

Discounting and environmental impacts

Among those who are concerned for the natural environment, one often encounters the view that the practice of discounting all future costs and benefits in cost benefit analysis is damaging to the environment, and should be modified. There are two versions of this general position. The first is that projects with environmental impacts should, especially if the impacts are long lasting, be appraised using a lower interest rate for discounting than would normally be used. In some versions of this argument, such projects should be appraised using a zero rate of interest for discounting. The second is that, in such contexts, a cost benefit analysis should use two different rates of interest, the standard one for non-environmental costs and benefits, and a lower one for environmental costs. In some versions of this position, the lower rate should be zero. We now consider each of these arguments in turn.

The first argument is, in general, quite incorrect because it overlooks the fact that the lower weights associated with higher interest rates attach to project benefits as well as to project costs. This is not to say that there can never be projects with long run environmental costs which have positive NPVs at high interest rates and negative NPVs at lower interest rates. It is to say that there can be no general presumption that the use of lower interest rates in cost benefit analysis will reject more projects with adverse long-run environmental effects. For any project the implications of evaluation with a lower interest rate depend upon the time profiles, and sizes, of the cost and benefit streams. We shall see that for the (hypothetical) project we are considering, the effect of using a lower interest rate is, on the central assumptions behind Tables 8.4 and 8.6, to make the project more, rather than less, attractive. This is a project with long-run environmental costs. To repeat, this is to be understood as providing a counter-example to illustrate the incorrectness of the view that lower interest rates always work against projects with long-run environmental costs. It is not to be taken as suggesting that it is generally true that lower interest rates work in favour of projects with long-run environmental costs. We take up the question of the correct interest rate to use in cost benefit analysis in the next section of this chapter.

We proceed on the basis that the loss of wilderness recreation which is consequent on going ahead with the project is permanent, so that the cost stream attributable to the project on this count goes on forever. Then the present values of the cost and benefit streams and the net present value for

Table 8.7 Discount factors for $r = 0.03$

$$d_t = \left(\frac{1}{1+r}\right)^{t-1} = \left(\frac{1}{1.03}\right)^{t-1}$$

Year	d_t
1	1.0000
2	0.9709
3	0.9426
4	0.9151
5	0.8849
6	0.8626
·	·
·	·
·	·
47	0.2567
48	0.2493
49	0.2420
50	0.2350
51	0.2281
·	·
·	·
·	·
98	0.0569
99	0.0552
100	0.0536

$r = 0.05$ are shown in Table 8.8. Also shown are the same items as they are calculated, from the undiscounted cost and benefit streams which are those shown in Table 8.4 save that the £1 million for wilderness recreation loss cost goes on forever, using $r = 0.03$. We see that going from $r = 0.05$ to $r = 0.03$ means that, for everything else remaining the same, all the present values increase. The present value for construction running and removal costs increases by only 6% because this item is dominated by construction costs which arise in the early years of the project lifetime, where the interest rate change exerts relatively little leverage. The present value for the forever lasting wilderness recreation loss cost is calculated using equation [8.4]: for $x = £1$ million it goes from £21 millions with $r = 0.05$ to £34.33 millions with $r = 0.03$. The coal savings benefit stream runs from year 6 to year 50 and, undiscounted, increases year on year at 5%: the effect of going from $r = 0.05$ to $r = 0.03$ is to increase the corresponding present value by 73%, from a large base. The mortality reduction benefit present value increases by 49%. Taking costs and benefits together we see that the net present value of the project more than doubles as a result of using $r = 0.03$ rather than $r = 0.05$, notwithstanding the everlasting environmental cost. This is because that cost is small and because the interest rate reduction increases the present values of the project's benefits as well as its costs. Note finally that we have here ignored the permanent habitat loss consequent upon the project. With $r = 0.05$ we found, using equation [8.4], that this loss would have to be

Table 8.8 Effects of a lower interest rate

	Construction running removal	Wilderness recreation	Coal savings	Mortality reduction	NPV
$r = 0.05$	925.7	21.0	1478.3	117.0	648.6
$r = 0.03$	977.8	34.33	2562.8	174.3	1725.0
% increase	6	64	73	49	166

Table 8.9 Two net benefit streams

Year	Net benefit flow A	Net Benefit flow B
1	−100	−100
2	25	0
3	25	0
4	25	0
5	25	0
6	25	125

valued at at least £31 millions per year to lead to the rejection of the project. If we repeat this calculation for $r = 0.03$ we find that the corresponding figure is £50 millions. Lowering the interest rate, that is, increases by 61% the annual valuation of habitat loss that we would have to accept as the minimum which could justify project rejection.

Consider now the version of this argument which says that the discount should be reduced to zero. The basic problem with this argument is illustrated in Table 8.9. It shows the undiscounted net benefit flows for two projects, A and B. Both have lives of six years, and involve a net cost in the first year. Thereafter A shows an excess of benefit over cost in every year, whereas B shows no net benefits until the sixth year. However, that benefit is the same as the sum over years 2 to 6 for A. Both projects show an excess of undiscounted benefit over cost of £25, but in the case of B all the positive net benefit arises in the project's final year. Given that investment funds are not unlimited, neither an individual nor a society would sensibly be indifferent between these projects. However, with the interest rate for discounting set at zero, there is no way to choose between them, if it is accepted that the monetary cost and benefit flows properly capture all the relevant information about the two projects. In the context of environmental impacts, this is a very important proviso to which we return below.

We now look at the second argument, that it is only the environmental costs that should be discounted at a lower rate. There are two distinct positions from which this argument appears to be developed. The first is really a denial of the proviso just stated. It says that environmental impacts cannot, or should not, be made commensurable with other project consequences using a money metric. In this case, the argument is not really about discount rates at all. It is about cost benefit analysis itself. It is simply the argument that apples and pears cannot, or should not, be compared. The other position is based on an implicit view that the natural environment will be more valuable in the future, and that discounting environmental impact costs at the same rate as produced commodities and other inputs obscures this. Again, this is not really an argument about discounting. It is an argument about current relative prices in the future. In the hydroelectric example, we assumed that the costs associated with the lost recreation facility were constant over time. Given increasing material prosperity, and a fixed supply of wilderness recreation facilities, this may well be an inappropriate assumption. A more appropriate assumption might be that such facilities will be becoming relatively more scarce over time, and should therefore be accounted for with an increasing relative price. If the relative price assumed for the wilderness recreation loss is rising over time, this will offset the effect of discounting. If, for example, it is assumed that its price is increasing at 5% per annum against all other prices, discounting at 5% will mean that instead of the figures in Table 8.6 under Wilderness Recreation, we would have 1 for every year. This would parallel the effect of assumed increasing scarcity on the entries for coal shown in Table 8.6.

In considering these sorts of arguments two related things must be kept in mind. First, cost benefit analysis assumes that different sorts of thing can, and should, be made commensurable. Second, cost benefit analysis as project appraisal is concerned with intertemporal efficiency, not with the distribution over time of aggregate consumption, which is to be considered using the sort of analysis looked at in 7.4.

It will be apparent from our discussion in this section that at the completion of a cost benefit analysis of a large project with significant and long lasting environmental effects, there will still be scope for reasonable people to disagree on the social desirability of the project concerned. It is not the case that cost benefit analysis is a technique which can be mechanically applied to give the single correct answer on a project. It does provide a framework within which the many consequences of a project can be consistently analysed for their total effect.

8.3   The discount rate in cost benefit analysis

In discussing cost benefit analysis thus far we have referred, in the context of the discounting of future costs and benefits, to 'the interest rate' and used for this the symbol r. In previous chapters we have also used r to represent the interest rate determined in the bond market. However, it is not the case that it is possible in cost benefit analysis to simply discount future costs and benefits at the market rate of interest. There are both practical and conceptual reasons for this. Here we concentrate on the conceptual issues involved in the choice of the rate to use for discounting in cost benefit analysis.

Recall that in Chapter 6 we introduced the idea of household preferences over consumption at different dates. We begin here by looking at some of the ideas then arising in a slightly different way. Again we simplify by considering just the two periods 0 and 1, and we also assume that all households have the same preferences over consumption in these two periods, C_0 and C_1, represented by the indifference curves shown in Figure 8.3. Suppose initially that we have period 0 consumption at C'_0 and period 1 consumption at C'_1, giving the utility level corresponding to the indifference curve U_4U_4. Now consider a marginal reduction in period 0 consumption, denoted ΔC_0, with C''_0 as the new level. If utility is to remain constant, there must be a compensating increase in period 1 consumption of ΔC_1, increasing it from C'_1 to C''_1. Since we are considering marginal changes, we have

$$\Delta C_1 = (1 + s) \Delta C_0 \qquad [8.5]$$

where $1 + s$ is the slope of U_4U_4 at C'_0. In the cost benefit analysis literature, s is often referred to as the *social time preference rate*, or STPR.

Now, suppose that the reduction in C_0 from C'_0 to C''_0 is to release resources for investment in some project, which will deliver benefits in period 1 in the form of increased consumption. Let us indicate the size of the project benefits by $\Delta C'_1$. Clearly, if $\Delta C'_1$ is greater than ΔC_1 defined by equation [8.5] the project is desirable as it means that households move on to a higher indifference curve if it is adopted. If $\Delta C'_1$ is equal to DA', adopting the project raises the level of satisfaction from U_4 to U_3, for example. In terms of utility or satisfaction the C_0/C_1 combination represented by A' is equivalent to that represented by B'. Comparing B' with B we see that the former involves a higher level for C_1 than the latter, and the same level for C_0. The

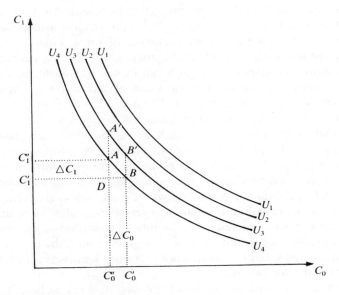

Figure 8.3 Project appraisal and the social time preference rate

project passes the efficiency improvement test in that it is equivalent to increasing C_1 without decreasing C_0.

Equation [8.5] can be written as

$$\frac{\Delta C_1}{1+s} - \Delta C_0 = 0$$

and since $\Delta C'_1 > \Delta C_1$ (> means greater than), we have

$$\frac{\Delta C_1'}{1+s} - \Delta C_0 > 0 \qquad\qquad [8.6]$$

The left-hand side here is just the net present value of the project with the future benefits discounted using s as the interest rate. Clearly, if we had considered some other project costing ΔC_0 and with benefits $\Delta C''_1 < \Delta C_1$ (< means less than) instead of equation [8.6] we would have

$$\frac{\Delta C_1''}{1+s} - \Delta C_0 < 0$$

for its net present value when discounting using s. The adoption of a project for which $\Delta C_1'' < \Delta C_1$ defined by equation [8.5] would mean a move to a lower indifference curve. What we have shown here is that if we use the social time preference rate as the interest rate for discounting, the positive net present value rule identifies projects which pass the efficiency improvement test and raise household satisfaction/utility levels.

What does all this have to do with our previous discussion of the cost benefit analysis of projects where we discounted using r the interest rate determined in the bond market? We discussed the determination of r in Chapter 6 and saw there that r was determined via the interaction of households' preferences over consumption at different times with the terms on which consumption could be shifted over time by the investment activities of firms. Figure 8.4 here now brings together the main elements of the story. The U U curves are indifference curves as above. AB gives the way in which C_0 can be transformed into C_1 by means of investment. Recall that the slope of AB is $1 + i$, where i is the marginal rate of return on investment. The line RS is drawn with slope $1 + r$. Households achieve maximum utility where RS is tangential to an indifference curve, so that we have $1 + r = 1 + s$ at X. Firms maximise their present values by investing up to the point where the rate of return equals the interest rate, so that we have $1 + i = 1 + r$ at X. The utility maximising efforts of households and the present value maximising efforts of firms are coordinated via dealings in bonds, and equilibrium in the bond market gives $s = r = i$. Given, that is, an economy with ideal conditions obtaining everywhere, equilibrium in the bond market means that the interest rate, the rate of return on investment and the social time preference rate are all equal. We observe both the rate of return on investment and the social time preference rate when we observe the interest rate determined in the bond market.

Under these conditions then to use r for discounting in cost benefit analysis is conceptually and practically equivalent to using s and/or i. In the earlier sections

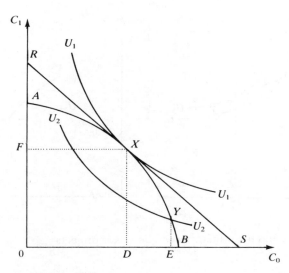

Figure 8.4 Intertemporal equilibrium

of this chapter we talked in terms of using r, with the implicit assumption that these conditions were operative. This was convenient, in order to enable us to concentrate on other issues. However, it is not generally appropriate to assume equilibrium in the bond market in actual economies where market failure prompts an interest in cost benefit analysis and consequently the question of which of i or s should be used arises. To see what the question involves, suppose that instead of the bond market equilibrium based outcome at X in Figure 8.4, the economy is at Y with $0E$ of current consumption and EB being invested. Suppose further that apart from the non-attainment of intertemporal equilibrium ideal conditions obtain in the economy, and that there is currently no government involvement in the economy. The government is now considering a project for the supply of a public good in period 1. At what rate should it discount the period 1 benefits arising? At s, given by the slope of U_2U_2 at Y, or at i given by the slope of AB at Y?

Consider first the situation where the project is to be financed by taxing households so that the resources used for the project, its cost, are at the expense of household consumption in period 0. In Figure 8.5(a) the reduction in C_0 consequent upon going ahead with the project is shown as ΔC_0. It looks as if the discussion based on Figure 8.3 applies here, and that the project's benefits in period 1 should be discounted using the rate s. If, so discounted, the net present value is positive, then we know that an indifference curve higher than U_2U_2 is attained. This does not, however, always mean that s should be used. Suppose that having secured current resources in amount ΔC_0 the government could either go for the public good supply project or use such to undertake the private sector project which would move the economy toward A along AB from Y. If it did the latter households' satisfaction would increase from the U_2U_2 level to the U_3U_3

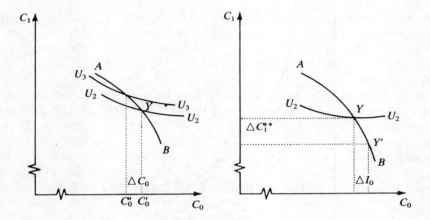

Figure 8.5   Tax and bond financed public sector projects

level. Clearly, the public good supply project should be preferred only if it does better than this. The fact that it has a positive net present value when discounting at s does not ensure that it does so do, since s is less than i. To be sure that the public good supply project does do better than the alternative private sector project it is necessary to find that it has a positive net present value when its benefit is discounted using i. If the benefit to the private sector project is $\Delta C_1{}^{**}$, then from the definition of i we have

$$1 + i = \frac{\Delta C_1{}^{**}}{\Delta C_0}$$

so that

$$\Delta C_1{}^{**} = (1 + i)\,\Delta C_0 \qquad\qquad [8.7]$$

Now let $\Delta C_1{}^{*}$ be the public sector project benefit, and its net present value using s is

(i) $\dfrac{\Delta C_1{}^{*}}{1 + s} - \Delta C_0$

and using i is

(ii) $\dfrac{\Delta C_1{}^{*}}{1 + i} - \Delta C_0$

Clearly, for $i > s$ (ii) is less than (i). If we set (ii) equal to 0, we get

$$\frac{\Delta C_1{}^{*}}{1 + i} = \Delta C_0$$

or

$$\Delta C_1{}^{*} = (1 + i)\,\Delta C_0$$

which on comparison with equation [8.7] gives $\Delta C_1{}^* = \Delta C_1{}^{**}$. For (ii) greater than 0 then we will have $\Delta C_1{}^*$ greater than $\Delta C_1{}^{**}$. If we get a positive net present value for the public sector project when discounting using i we can be sure that it will do better for household utility levels than $U_3 U_3$, the utility level attainable via the private sector project.

What we have called the rate of return, i, is often referred to in the literature as the *social opportunity cost of capital*, or SOC. We have already noted that s is known as the social time preference rate, or STPR. In this terminology the argument presented immediately above is that cost benefit analysis should use the SOC rate for discounting. The point is that the opportunity cost of the public sector project is the private sector project. The test that the former has to pass then is that it does at least as well for society as the private sector project it is alternative to. The test is effected by discounting the public sector project benefit at the SOC rate, i. This argument although developed here for a two-period analysis, with only costs in period 0 and only benefits in period 1, is quite general. It does, however, depend crucially on the public and private sector projects being real alternatives. If ΔC_0 could not alternatively be used to realise the private sector project, then, it should be clear, it would be appropriate to use the STPR to discount the public good supply project benefit.

Consider now a situation where the project for public good supply is to be financed by the government issuing bonds. In this case, we can assume there will be no effect on household consumption levels in period 0 from the government going ahead with the project. Instead, we assume that the resources input to the project will be drawn away from some private sector project. Figure 8.5(b) refers. Now what is required of the public sector project is that its adoption means that households attain a utility level greater than that indicated by $U_2 U_2$. For this to be the case, it is necessary that the project have a positive net present value when its benefits are discounted using the SOC rate i. As a result of the lost private sector project the economy moves from Y to Y', with a decrease in private sector investment equal to ΔI_0. To get back to Y by adopting the public sector project it is necessary that its benefits be at least as great as those lost on the displaced private sector project, $\Delta C_1{}^{**}$. Since $\Delta C_1{}^{**} = (1 + i)\Delta I_0$, this will be the case only if, with $\Delta C_1{}^*$ representing the public sector project benefit,

$$\Delta C_1{}^* > (1 + i)\Delta I_0$$

which in turn requires

$$\frac{\Delta C_1{}^*}{1 + i} > \Delta I_0$$

which is the same as

$$\frac{\Delta C_1{}^*}{1 + i} - \Delta I_0 > 0$$

which is the positive net present value requirement, using i for discounting.

Ignoring constraints on government behaviour, then, we see that, despite the fact that the ultimate concern is for the satisfaction levels delivered to households, we use i rather than s to discount with. This is because, in the absence of constraints, all potential projects are competitive with one another, so that a public sector project must be required to do at least as well as the marginal private sector project. In fact, it is not possible to regard all potential projects as competitive one with another, since constraints do exist and cannot be ignored. Ideally, a public sector project analysis should incorporate all the relevant constraints in such a manner as to set out the cost stream in terms of forgone consumption and the benefit stream in terms of additional consumption arising from the project. It would then be appropriate to use s for discounting. However, this is a counsel of perfection, and most economists would take the view that practical public sector project appraisal should use for discounting a rate which is some hybrid of i and s, the precise formula depending on the particular circumstances. We cannot here properly discuss, or resolve, the issues arising: references to the literature are provided in the next section. We can note the scope for reasonable people to disagree on the figure to be used in discounting the cost and benefit streams, and hence, the importance of sensitivity analysis.

8.4   Risk and uncertainty

We have referred several times to the uncertainty that attends cost benefit analysis, using the word rather imprecisely. In economics it is conventional to distinguish between risk and uncertainty. Situations involving risk are those where the possible consequences of a decision can be completely enumerated, and probabilities assigned to each possibility. There is uncertainty where probabilities cannot be attached to each possible outcome, or where the possible outcomes cannot be identified.

Risk

Individuals generally appear to be risk averse, in the sense of being unwilling to accept a fair bet. The point is most easily made with an example. Suppose that an individual is offered the choice between the gift of £2 and the gift of a ticket which is an entitlement to participate in a gamble on the toss of a fair coin. If the coin comes up heads the individual gets £4, if it comes up tails the individual gets £0. Actuarially the two gifts are equivalent, since the *expected value* of the ticket is £2 – there is a 50% chance of winning £4 and a 50% chance of winning £0. An individual indifferent between the two gifts is *risk neutral*. Most individuals would prefer the gift of £2 to the gift of the gamble ticket, and are said to be *risk averse*.

Individuals differ in their degree of risk aversion. Economists have developed a way of thinking about risk aversion on which a measure of it can be based. To see what is involved, suppose that a decision has two possible outcomes £I and £II, and that the probabilities attached to these are p_I and p_{II}. Then, the expected value associated with the decision is the probability weighted sum of the two possible outcomes:

$$E_N = p_I(II) + p_{II}(II) \qquad [8.8]$$

The subscript N here refers to a risk neutral individual. Now, suppose that the perceived value to an individual of the return to a risky outcome is less than the £ value of the outcome, so that the expected value associated with the decision is

$$E_A = p_I(I^a) + p_{II}(II^a) \qquad [8.9]$$

where a is less than one. Here the subscript A refers to a risk averse individual. E_A will be less than E_N, and the *cost of bearing risk* is defined as

$$A = E_N - E_A \qquad [8.10]$$

where A is used to indicate that the cost arises from risk aversion. If a in [8.9] were equal to one, A would be equal to zero. To illustrate, suppose that for the decision involving a gift of money and a gift of a ticket for a gamble described above, a risk averse individual has a equal to $1/2$, so that

$$E_A = 0.5(4^{0.5}) + 0.5(0^{0.5}) = 0.5(2) + 0.5(0) = £1$$

while E_N is equal to £2, as previously established. Then, in this case [8.10] gives the cost of risk bearing as £1. Values for a, and hence the cost of risk bearing, will differ across individuals. For a given individual, the value for A will vary across risky decision making situations, with variations in outcomes and their associated probabilities.

Now consider cost benefit analysis which recognises risk. Cost benefit analysis is intended to select in accordance with efficiency criteria, and therefore works with the criterion of consumer sovereignty. Consistently, if individuals are risk averse, cost benefit analysis should incorporate risk aversion. In which case, the net present value for a project is to be calculated as

$$NPV = \Sigma(B_t - C_t - A_t)/(1 + r)^t \qquad [8.11]$$

where A_t is the cost of the risk associated with the project in period t, to be calculated as sketched above. The actual use of [8.11] in CBA is rare, since it is difficult to compute A_t generally. We have noted the risk aversion would be expected to vary across individuals, so one major problem is deciding what kind of average of individuals' a values to use. Prior to this problem is the fact that the distribution of a across individuals is not known.

It is sometimes argued that risk should be handled by adjusting the discount rate so that 'riskier' projects have their NPV calculated using a higher discount rate. It should be clear that, like the other proposed *ad hoc* modifications to the discount rate discussed above, this practice has little to recommend it. Most economists would argue that it is preferable to use [8.11] with alternative guesstimates of the A_t, than to adjust the discount rate. One problem with the latter procedure is that it involves the assumption, in effect, that the cost of risk bearing is increasing over time. Clearly, this need not be the case.

In discussing the valuation of the environmental' impacts of the hydroelectric plant, we introduced option value, OV, and quasi option value, QOV. These both arise where the consequences of going ahead with the project are not known with certainty. We said that option value was willingness to pay to guarantee the availability of an area for possible future use. If an individual is risk averse and does not know for certain whether she will or will not want to use the valley for wilderness recreation in the future, option value is just another way of thinking about the cost of risk. The relevant risk is that use will be desired, but the valley is flooded and unavailable. Option value is just willingness to pay to avoid this risk. It can, if measurable, be treated in an exactly analogous manner to A_t in [8.11] above.

Option value should be included in a cost benefit analysis on the assumption that individuals are risk averse and that social decision making should reflect individual risk aversion. That individuals are risk averse is generally accepted. There is an argument that social decision making should not reflect this, since society comprises many individuals over whom risk is spread so as to become trivial for each individual. However, where the risk attaches to environmental damage this argument does not apply if the damage is in the nature of a public bad, ie non-rival in its effects. This is the typical case. It would be the case with the destruction of a wilderness recreation facility by the hydroelectric project, for example. For all potential users, the level of use goes to zero if the project goes ahead. No potential user can reduce her loss by inducing another to increase his.

Quasi option value should be incorporated in cost benefit analysis even in the absence of individual, and hence social, risk aversion. It relates to willingness to pay to avoid an irreversible commitment to action now, given that improved knowledge about the consequences of the action will be available in the future. Suppose that as part of the hydroelectric project the plant population for which the valley is the only known location is to be shifted to another location. If this exercise is successful, there will be no costs on account of the loss of the plant species. It is not known now whether or not it will be successful. The probability of success is 50%. A decision to go ahead with the project would be irreversible in that if the relocation is not successful, the plant species would be lost forever. It is understood that scientists will in the future be able to say with certainty whether or not the relocation would be successful. Then, there is a gain in delaying a decision on the project until this information is available. This gain is quasi option value. In considering whether to go ahead with the project now, while it still involves risk, the quasi option value should be treated as a cost in the calculation of NPV. Clearly, quasi option value will be difficult to estimate.

Uncertainty

Where environmental impacts are involved, the assignment of probabilities is frequently impossible. In this illustrative hydroelectric example it could be more appropriate to assume that the probability of successful relocation of the plant population is not known, and will never be known. The basis for this view would be that the attempt at relocation is an experiment of a unique nature, so that there can never be any previous experience on the basis of which to assign probabilities. In this case, we would be dealing with a situation of uncertainty rather than risk. Where uncertainty is involved there are no clearcut decision rules. Indeed, the very notion of rational behaviour becomes somewhat questionable. Decision making is considered using the ideas of *game theory*, where the outcome of a decision, or strategy, on the part of one player depends on the decisions of the other players, which decisions cannot be known in advance. For many purposes it is assumed that there is just one other player, and that this player is 'nature'. Such constructs are known as *games against nature*. The outcome consequent upon the player's decision depends upon the state of nature, but the state of nature does not depend upon the player's strategy.

To illustrate, with respect to the question of relocation of the plant population in the hydroelectric example, suppose that the NPV for the project can be reliably calculated on two different assumptions. First, it is assumed that the state of nature is favourable so that the attempt to relocate the plant species will be successful. We can use very round numbers and say that this gives an NPV for the project of £700 millions. The alternative is that nature is unfavourable so that relocation is unsuccessful, in which case the NPV is negative, say −£200 million. Two decisions or strategies are available, go ahead with the hydroelectric project or undertake the next best alternative. Assume that this is a coal fired electricity generation plant for which the NPV is £200 million, whatever the state of nature. The basic information is assembled in a *pay-off matrix*:

		State of Nature	
		F	U
	P	+700	−200
Decision			
	A	+200	+200

Here F is for favourable, U for unfavourable, P indicates the decision to undertake the hydro project, and A the decision not to. If it were possible to assign probabilities to the states F and U, a decision maker faces a risky situation and could proceed on the basis of the expected values. If the probabilities were 0.5 and 0.5 and the decision taken on the basis of risk neutrality, then for P the expected value is 250 while for A it is 200, so that the hydro project would go ahead, P would be selected.

In the case of the hydroelectric project decision, which now turns on whether or not the relocation of the plant will be successful, it may be argued that while there is no scientific basis for the assignment of objective probabilities, subjective probabilities can be assigned using the decision maker's judgement. If this is accepted, the decision can again be made on the basis of expected values. An extreme version of this is sometimes suggested on the basis of the principle of insufficient reason. According to this, if science is unable to say even which of F and U is more likely, one may as well assign subjective probabilities of 0.5 to each and make the decision on that basis. This approach is generally regarded as having little to commend it. In the hydro case, as shown above, it leads to the decision to go ahead with the project.

The three alternative approaches to be considered next here do not exhaust the possibilities. They do bring out the general nature of the problem of decision making in the face of uncertainty. According to the *maximax criterion*, the decision to be chosen is that which offers the largest best outcome. In the pay-off matrix one reads across rows and writes down an additional column showing for each possible decision the value of the best possible outcome. One then selects the decision for which the highest number appears in this new column. For the hydro project pay-off matrix, this selects P for which the best outcome is 700.

According to the *minimax* criterion, one makes the decision that gives rise to the least worst outcome. One reads across the rows of the pay-off matrix and creates a new column where the entries are the worst outcome for each decision row. One then selects the decision for which the entry in this column is least bad. In the example here this selects A.

The third criterion is *minimax regret*. The first step is to create a new pay-off matrix in which the entries are the difference between the pay-off shown in the original matrix and what the pay-off would have been had the correct decision been made. For the hydro example this *regret matrix* is:

	F	U
P	0	400
A	500	0

For F eventuating the correct decision would have been P so that if P is made there is zero regret and if A is made regret is 500. For U eventuating the correct decision would have been A so that if A is made there is zero regret, while if P is made regret is 400. One next creates a new column in which the entries are the largest regret in the corresponding row, ie 400 for P and 500 for A. The decision selected is then that for which the entry in this column is the smallest, i.e. P.

We have considered four decision making rules. Three, equal subjective probability assignment, maximax and minimax regret, say undertake the project; one, minimax, says do not. Maximax is basically an adventurous rule looking for large gains, minimax and minimax regret are cautious rules. There is no objective basis on which to choose between the rules. Further, it cannot be claimed that any one of them is rational, in the sense of doing the best that can be done in the circumstances, where the others are not. The choice of rule will depend on the decision maker's subjective feelings about the merits of the alternative rules. Three points can usefully be made here. First, setting up the pay-off matrix and using it to consider alternative rules will itself be a useful exercise in improving understanding of the nature of the decision making problem. Second, in the cost benefit analysis context, the decision maker is acting on behalf of society, where society's interests are understood to follow from the principle of consumer sovereignty. This would suggest that the rule to be adopted should reflect individuals' attitudes. The problem is that these are likely to differ across individuals, and in ways largely unknown to the decision maker. It might be argued that in acting on behalf of society, a decision maker should go for rules which are cautious in nature, in the light of the observed prevalence of risk aversion on the part of individuals. Third, it might be argued that this presumption in favour of caution is strengthened where consequences giving rise to losses involve irreversible impacts on the natural environment. This is essentially the basis for the safe minimum standard, SMS, approach to social decision making on projects with such consequences.

Safe minimum standard

This approach was originally developed in economics specifically in the context of thinking about projects possibly entailing species extinction. It can best be discussed in the context of a situation where the range of possible outcomes consequent upon a decision cannot be specified in advance. In the hydro example context we can take this to mean that if the state of nature is unfavourable, and the plant species cannot be successfully located elsewhere, we simply do not know what the cost arising will be, and cannot come up with an NPV number to put in the top right cell of the pay-off matrix. We indicate this by using a z of unknown size:

	F	U
P	+700	$-z$
A	+200	+200

SMS is based on the minimax regret criterion. The regret matrix is

	F	U
P	0	$z + 200$
A	500	0

so that the maximum regrets are $z + 200$ for P and 500 for A. SMS says presume that z is large enough to make A the preferred decision on the minimax regret criterion. The argument for this presumption is as follows. Species extinction involves an irreversible reduction in the stock of potentially useful resources which is the existing portfolio of species. There is no way of knowing how large the value to humans of any of the existing species might turn out to be in the future. Two kinds of ignorance are involved here. First, there is social ignorance about future preferences, needs and technologies.

Second, there is scientific ignorance about the characteristics of existing species as they relate to future social possibilities and needs. The extinction of any species is, therefore, to be presumed to involve future costs which may be very large, even when discounted into present value terms. The argument here is essentially that the species that may become extinct may turn out to be one for which there is no substitute.

Applying the SMS criterion to projects which could entail species extinction would mean rejecting all such projects. Note that all that is required is the possibility that going ahead with the project could involve species extinction. Further, the minimax regret criterion rejects the species threatening project however small the excess regret associated with the project is, and however much better than the alternative the project is, species loss aside. SMS is a very conservative rule. It means forgoing current gains, however large, in order to avoid future losses of unknown, but presumed large, size. In the example above, SMS means that A is selected, which means going ahead with a project with NPV equal to £200 millions rather than one with NPV £700 millions (ignoring the species loss dimension).

A *modified safe minimum standard* has been proposed according to which the option which ensures the survival of the species should be adopted, unless it entails unacceptably large costs. This is less conservative, but leaves to be determined whether any given cost is 'unacceptably large'. An answer to this question would, presumably be sought from the political process rather than economic analysis. In the example above, economic analysis is involved in establishing that the cost is a foregone NPV of £500 millions. But, if the logic of the SMS way of thinking is accepted, the acceptability of this cost is a matter of political judgement, not a matter for analysis. Indeed, the point is really more general. Once uncertainty is recognised, decision making necessarily involves judgement and cannot be reduced to a technical, and purely rational, exercise. There is no way of saying that one of the decision criteria is more rational than another.

8.5   Commentary

There are a number of textbooks on cost benefit analysis. Pearce (1971) is a relatively short treatment of the main issues. Mishan (1975) is a full length text which is primarily concerned with conceptual and methodological questions. These are also dealt with in some depth in Sugden and Williams (1978) and Pearce and Nash (1981), but these texts also give considerable attention to implementation problems and discuss some applications. Abelson (1979) is specifically concerned with the application of the cost benefit analysis methodology to environmental problems, as is Hanley and Spash (1993). Layard (1972) is a collection of some of the important early contributions to the cost benefit analysis literature, with an introductory chapter which is an excellent survey of the principles involved. All of these assume of the reader some previous knowledge of economics, but should be reasonably accessible to the reader who has persevered this far with this book.

In 8.2 above we illustrated the use of cost benefit analysis with an example where going ahead with the project, a hydroelectric facility, had adverse consequences for the amenity services provided by the natural environment. Krutilla and Fisher (1975) describe a number of applications of cost benefit analysis where the central issue is the weighing of benefits in respect of resource availability against costs in respect of losses of amenity services from undisturbed natural environments. Particularly, they report in Chapters 5 and 6 on studies of proposals to develop an area of outstanding natural beauty and interest, sections of the Snake river in the north-west of the USA, for hydroelectric power generation. The hypothetical example which we considered in 8.2 was constructed so as to bring out the major issues arising in these actual applications. Cost benefit analysis is not, of course, only applicable where projects involve developing areas otherwise supplying amenity services. Applications discussed in Pearce and Nash (1981) are: varying types of transport projects, materials recycling, and a nuclear power programme. Mishan (1975) notes its use with respect to underground railway construction, disease control, flood control, and a channel tunnel project. Abelson (1979) discusses a soil conservation project, sand mining, airport location and aircraft noise control.

The treatment of risk and uncertainty in cost benefit analysis is dealt with in Pearce and Nash (1981), where references to the original literature are provided. An introduction to game theory and some applications in economics is Weintraub (1975). The safe minimum standard was originally proposed in Ciriacy-Wantrup (1968), and the idea was developed in Bishop (1978): see Randall and Farmer (1995) for a recent discussion.

Valuing environmental services

The literature on valuing the services of natural environments, and damage to those services, for cost benefit analysis purposes is now very extensive: see the survey article of Cropper and Oates (1992). That literature focuses mainly on the use of the travel cost method, TCM, for recreational use values, and the contingent valuation method, CVM, for non-use, principally existence, values. Among the other methods used are the following. Hedonic pricing, was discussed briefly in 5.5 in connection with pollution damages: see also Ch. 4 of Hanley and Spash (1993). A variant of this approach is the *hedonic travel cost method*, which seeks to value particular attributes of recreational sites: see Ch. 5 of Hanley and Spash (1993) for an overview. Where environmental services are inputs to production, their values in such use can be estimated by a variety of methods. The *production function method* involves inferring a value from market prices for the other inputs to production and the output, using the production function to relate all inputs to output; see, for example, Ellis and Fisher (1987) for an example. A variant on this is the *substitute service method* whereby an environmental service is valued according to the costs of providing the same service by means of human production: see, for example, the approach to soil erosion adopted in Repetto *et al.* (1989), discussed further in 9.4.

In discussing the use of TCM and CVM, we shall focus on two questions:

1.   Is the method the appropriate way to incorporate environmental damage assessment into the appraisal of projects?
2.   If the answer to 1 is yes, how accurate are the methods?

In considering these questions, recall that the TCM can only look at use values. While the CVM was considered, in 8.2, in relation to non-use values, it could be applied to use value questions as well. In fact, it is not often used for that purpose, since where it is possible economists prefer to work with data on actual behaviour rather than answers to hypothetical questions.

From the perspective of neoclassical economics, the answer to the first question is obviously 'yes'. Both the TCM and the CVM are intended to ascertain willingness to pay by individuals, and consumer sovereignty is the foundational assumption of neoclassical economics. For many non-economists, the answer is obviously 'no', especially where it is existence values that are at issue. Sagoff (1988), for example, takes the view that social decisions about projects with environmental impacts should, as an ethical matter, not be based on consumer sovereignty criteria. He argues that such questions are matters for 'citizens' not 'consumers', so that they should be dealt with through political processes rather than market, or surrogate market, processes.

In relation to the second question, consider first the TCM. Economists are inclined to believe that this method is accurate. In fact, in many of the cases where the CVM has been used for use value estimation, it has been as part of an exercise also involving TCM analysis of the same environmental 'commodity', with a view to testing the reliability of the CVM by comparing its result with the TCM result. However, there are many problems associated with the implementation of the TCM: for a brief summary see Ch. 5 in Hanley and Spash (1993). At a very basic level there is the problem of measuring the travel costs. There are several ways in which this can be done in any particular case, and it is not clear that, even at the level of principle, there is one way which is unambiguously correct. In a recent paper, Randall (1994) argues that, as a result of this, the TCM is incapable of producing monetary values for recreation sites that can be used in cost benefit analysis. Bockstael (1995) is a recent survey of contributions to the theoretical basis for the TCM: it does not address the issue raised by Randall. Smith and Kaoru (1990) look at the results of 77 TCM studies conducted in the USA. They found that 43% of the variation in the results for consumer's surplus could be explained in terms of variations in the circumstances of the studies, such as the type of recreational activity involved (swimming versus hunting, for example). This leaves 56% of the variation unexplained. Further, even if most of the variation could be explained, this would not necessarily mean that the answers were very accurate.

However, the usefulness of the TCM is accepted by most economists. The CVM, on the other hand, has been quite controversial, even within the ranks of economists, and leaving aside 'philosophical' objections as exemplified by Sagoff (1988). Despite this, interest in the CVM has grown very rapidly in the two decades since the first applications: a 1995 bibliography, Carson et al. (1995), contains just over 2000 entries. The basic theory behind the CVM, and details of its application, is set out in Mitchell and Carson (1989): see also Johansson (1987), which is advanced and technically quite difficult, or Hanley and Spash (1993), for a treatment which is less mathematical. A recent survey of the main issues is Bishop et al. (1995). Basically a CVM study involves constructing a hypothetical scenario in which the environmental service/area of concern is threatened in some way, and then exposing a sample of the population to that scenario and asking them what they would be willing to pay to prevent damage, or what compensation they would need if the damage occurred. Most typically this is done using a mail survey, but face to face and telephone interviews are also used.

A basic problem in considering the accuracy of the CVM in relation to non-use values is that there is typically no data on actual behaviour that can, even indirectly, be used to check the results against. In appraising the results of any particular CVM study, the standard view is that reliability can be judged by considering the extent to which the design of the hypothetical scenario and the questioning about willingness to pay are likely to avoid several problems identified by past experience. The question of the reliability of CVM has received a great deal of attention in the USA, where its findings in relation to non-use values now have legal standing for the determination of damages payable under various pieces of legislation. These covered the case of the *Exxon Valdez* oil spill in Alaska, and legal proceedings were initiated. In the event the case was terminated as there was an out of court settlement between Exxon and the trustees representing the public interest. However, along the way Exxon had commissioned a number of research projects intended to investigate the reliability of CVM. The findings of these projects, see Hausman (1993), were generally highly critical of CVM. As a result of the controversy, a 'Nobel laureate panel' of economists was appointed by the US government to advise on the status of CVM. Its report, Arrow et al. (1992), was cautiously favourable to CVM. It said, essentially, that while there were problems, there were good prospects for overcoming them by improved survey design in regard to scenario construction and willingness to pay questioning.

As an example of the sorts of problem that has generated controversy, consider the matter of *embedding*. This term refers to the fact that some applications of CVM were showing that the willingness to pay of survey respondents was insensitive to the size of the environmental 'commodity' involved. Thus, for example, in an Australian application concerned with preservation of native forests (Blamey et al. 1995), it was found that willingness to pay did not differ significantly across three sub-samples. One was asked about preserving 10% of National Estate forests, one about 50%, and one about 100%. Similar insensitivity of willingness to pay has been found in a number of studies: see, for example, Hausman (1993). The view of the 'Nobel laureate panel' was that this kind of result could be overcome by proper survey design and administration.

Some economists are less optimistic. We noted above that Sagoff (1988), a philosopher, takes the view that where environmental damage is involved, matters should be decided by 'citizens' involved in a political process, rather than by cost benefit analysis. Sagoff (1988) also invokes a behavioural argument. He claims that many individuals considering questions about damage to the environment will, in fact, respond as 'citizens' with a vote, rather than as 'consumers' with a 'willingness to pay'. If this is correct, then when such individuals are confronted with a question about their willingness to pay in a CVM survey, their answers are likely to be such that the survey results are largely meaningless. This is a particular example of a more general, and fundamental, problem that some economists have raised about CVM for non-use values. If CVM is to produce results that can properly be used in cost benefit analysis, then it is necessary that the responding individuals have preferences such that environmental 'commodities' are commensurable with ordinary commodities and income in such a way that they have a utility function with both types of thing as arguments. If Sagoff's behavioural argument is correct, many individuals do not have the utility functions required, and the results obtained from CVM surveys do not provide useful information for input to cost benefit analysis. There is emerging some evidence that is consistent with the hypothesis that, for some individuals, the Sagoff argument, and related arguments, are valid: see, for examples, Blamey and Common (1994), Blamey et al. (1995), Spash and Hanley (1995), Stevens et al. (1991).

In sum, where it is non-use values that are at issue, the CVM is the only method available for the derivation of valuations for environmental damage to be used in cost benefit analysis, but whether it can provide accurate valuations is a matter of dispute among economists.

Mandatory deposits on beverage containers

In discussing the social assessment of the illustrative hydroelectric project, in 8.2, we did not incorporate non-use values into the calculation of net present value. Rather we calculated it without such costs, so as to see what they would have to be in order to lead to the conclusion that the project should not go ahead. Doing things this way isolates the problems associated with putting numbers on such costs from the rest of the analysis. We now consider an actual cost benefit analysis of the use of returnable beverage containers, which again shows how it can be used to highlight crucial issues and inform policy making, even when it is explicitly recognised that precise information on some project consequences is unavailable.

Porter (1978) is a study of a proposal to legislate, in the state of Michigan in the USA, for the introduction of mandatory deposits on beer and soft drinks containers. The proposed legislation was to make all beverage containers sold in Michigan subject to a returnable deposit of $0.1, whereas at the time of the proposal only 27 per cent of such were returnable. For the project which is such legislation, we have the following consequences:

(i) A reduction in the volume of solid waste for disposal by municipal authorities in Michigan.

(ii) A reduction in the amount of litter in Michigan.

(iii) A reduction in the quantity of inputs used in producing containers for beer and soft drinks.

(iv) An increase in the quantity of inputs used in putting beer and soft drinks into containers, and in distributing filled containers.

(v) An increase in the time spent by households in returning empty refillable bottles.

The consequences (i), (ii), and (iii) are social gains arising from the project adoption, while (iv) and (v) represent social losses. The implementation of the project itself, i.e. passing the law through the Michigan legislature, is assumed to be a costless activity. Hence, in cost benefit analysis terms the criterion for going ahead with the project or not is whether or not

$$\sum_{t=1}^{T} (B_{1t} + B_{2t} + B_{3t} - C_{4t} - C_{5t})/(1+r)^{t-1} \qquad [8.12]$$

is positive. This is just the project's NPV. Here we use B_{1t} to stand for the social valuation of the reduction in the volume of solid waste in year t, C_{5t} to stand for the social valuation of the increased time spent by Michigan households in year t, and similarly for (ii), (iii) and (iv) and B_{2t}, B_{3t} and C_{4t}.

Now, Porter assumes that each of the consequences identified can be directly and simply related to the number of drinks, or fillings, sold per annum. Thus, for example, if b_{1t} is the social valuation of the reduced solid waste disposal per filling in year t, and K_t is the number of fillings in year t, then $B_{1t} = K_t b_{1t}$. Then, we have

$$NPV = \sum_{t=1}^{T} (K_t b_{1t} + K_t b_{2t} + K_t b_{3t} - K_t c_{4t} - K_t c_{5t})/(1+r)^{t-1} \qquad [8.13]$$

which is, on the assumption that the number of drinks sold is constant over time at K,

$$NPV = \sum_{t=1}^{T} K(b_{1t} + b_{2t} + b_{3t} - c_{4t} - c_{5t})/(1+r)^{t-1}$$

$$= K \sum_{t=1}^{T} (b_{1t} + b_{2t} + b_{3t} - c_{4t} - c_{5t})/(1+r)^{t-1}$$

and with the further assumption that relative social valuations are constant over time, so that $b_{1t} = b_1$ for $t = 1, 2, \ldots T$ etc., this becomes

$$NPV = K(b_1 + b_2 + b_3 - c_4 - c_5) \sum_{t=1}^{T} 1/(1 + r)^{t-1} \qquad [8.14]$$

which is positive for $(b_1 + b_2 + b_3 - c_4 - c_5)$ positive, and negative for $(b_1 + b_2 + b_3 - c_4 - c_5)$ negative. Given the assumptions made, the project appraisal requires only numbers for the bs and cs.

The evaluation of b_1, b_3 and c_4 is relatively straightforward. Solid waste disposal in Michigan was costed at \$22 per ton, and Porter calculated that a switch from the pre-legislation situation to a situation of all beverages sold in returnable bottles would reduce solid waste by 121 000 tons. Hence $b_1 = \$0.0007$, given $K = 3\,950\,000\,000$ for the number of fillings (i.e. $22 \times 121\,000 = 2\,662\,000$ and $2\,662\,000 \div 3\,950\,000\,000 = 0.0007$). Similarly, Porter calculates $b_3 = \$0.0308$ and $c_4 = \$0.0277$ on the basis of data on the production and handling costs for the different kinds of container used according to whether containers are non-returnable or returnable.

It is in respect of the consequences (ii) and (v) that there are problems with the absence of market prices for valuation. With regard to b_2, there are two ways in which reduced litter generation gives rise to social benefits, i.e. cost reductions. The first is by virtue of the fact that there is a reduction in the inputs which need to be used in picking up discarded beverage containers. The second arises from the fact that with less litter lying around the citizens of Michigan will experience fewer litter-related accidents and less amenity, or 'eyesore', damage.

The reduction in litter arising from a complete switch to refillable bottles as beverage containers arises from the much lower rate at which such are dropped as litter compared with other, non deposit charged, containers. The 1974 figures for Michigan given by Porter are:

	Number (millions)	
	Fillings	Littered
Cans	2,150	140
Nonrefillable bottles	730	21
Refillable bottles	1,070	7
Total	3,950	168

Applying the littering rate for refillable bottles of 0.0065 ($= 7 \div 1,070$) to the total number of fillings gives 25 675 000 littered bottles (0.0065×3590 millions) for a situation in which all beverage fillings go into refillable bottles. This represents an 85% reduction in beverage container litter, or 142 million less containers to be picked up (in round numbers). The costs of picking up one beverage container in the USA have been estimated to be in the range \$0.01 to \$0.04, so that the litter pick up cost reduction estimated by Porter is in the range \$1 420 000 to \$5 680 000. On a per filling basis this range is

$0.0004 to $0.0014. Porter cites an alternative estimate of the total quantity of beverage container litter in Michigan in 1974 and its breakdown by container type. This is:

| | Number (millions) | |
	Fillings	Littered
Cans	2,150	317
Nonrefillable bottles	730	61
Refillable bottles	1,070	43
Total	3,950	420

Using these figures as previously gives 261 million (62%) fewer containers to be picked up. If the upper estimate of the cost per picked up container range is used, this is a cost reduction of $10 440 000 in total or $0.0026 per filling. Porter takes as his central estimate of the per filling reduction in pick up costs the mid-point of the range $0.0004 to $0.0026, i.e. $0.0015. We can note here that much of the uncertainty about litter pick up cost reduction comes from uncertainty about just how much beverage container litter there was in 1974 in Michigan. As noted in 8.1 and 8.2, the uncertainties in cost benefit analysis do not arise solely at the valuation stage.

Turning now to the second contribution to b_2, the amenity cost reduction attributable to a smaller stock of littered containers lying about, the uncertainty about how much less litter will be lying about is greatly compounded by total ignorance about the appropriate unit valuation. What is a 62% to 85% reduction in the amount of beverage container litter worth to the citizens of Michigan? How much, that is, would they be willing to pay for such a reduction? There are no market prices to refer to for an answer to this question. Litter removal is a service carried out by the municipalities, and for which no charge related to amount of service supplied is made. Indeed, service-related charging is not possible, litter removal being a public good. We discussed the problems of charging for public goods supply in section 4.5. It is possible to think of surveying a sample of Michigan citizens on litter reduction to attempt to derive a measure of willingness to pay. However, such surveys are themselves costly and are themselves attended, in terms of eliciting the true willingness to pay of households, by the problems discussed above; we discussed the problems regarding public goods in 4.5. The procedure Porter adopts is to represent the mean willingness to pay of Michiganders for a 62% to 85% reduction in beverage container litter as x dollars, and then to find critical ranges for x in terms of the effect on NPV defined by equation [8.14] above. With x so defined, the social valuation, per filling, of the litter reduction is

$$\$\frac{9\,100\,000 . x}{3\,950\,000\,000} = \$0.0023x$$

where 9 100 000 is the population of Michigan. Bringing this together with $0.0015 for the litter pick up cost reduction gives $b_2 = \$(0.0015 + 0.0023x)$.

We now come to consumer convenience, to the estimation of c_5, where according to Porter 'we move into the realm of conjecture'. That greater refillable bottle use would give rise to reduced consumer convenience to some degree cannot be doubted, since it is observed that people switched to one-ways over the past 20 years despite continued price differentials favouring consumption from refillables. The existence of such a price differential follows from the fact that, per filling, cans and nonrefillable bottles add, compared with refillable bottles, more to container production costs than they save in filling and distribution costs. Porter notes that with refillable bottles households suffer on account of 'the time, effort, and/or bother incurred by the necessity to keep, organise, and transport empty containers and then to check them in during a shopping trip' and that for the determination of c_5 we need 'knowledge of the willingness to pay to avoid this inconvenience'. Porter calls a household's willingness to pay to avoid such inconvenience its 'time of return cost'. No information is available on such costs. We have little idea how much time is involved in returning refillable bottles, and less about how to value the time. The procedure Porter adopts in the face of this ignorance is to represent by y the mean time of return cost, in cents (1 cent = \$0.01) for Michigan households per returned refillable bottle, and to find critical ranges for y in terms of the effect on NPV defined by equation [8.14] above. With y so defined the per filling cost associated with a complete switch to refillable bottles, i.e. c_5, is \$0.0068y. This figure is arrived at as follows. The extra time of return costs arising from mandatory deposits relate only to the containers which are currently cans and nonrefillable bottles and which become refillable bottles under a mandatory deposits regime. From the data given above, of the 3,950 million fillings in Michigan in 1974, 2,880 million were in cans or nonrefillable bottles. Also, it is known that 1/15th of refillable bottles are not actually returned but littered or disposed of as solid waste. Hence,

$$c_5 = \left(\frac{14}{15}\right)\left(\frac{2\,880\,000\,000}{3\,950\,000\,000}\right)\left(\frac{y}{100}\right) = \$0.0068y$$

If we now go back to equation [8.9] we have

$b_1 = 0.0007$

$b_2 = 0.0015 + 0.0023x$

$b_3 = 0.0308$

$c_4 = 0.0277$

$c_5 = 0.0068y$

so that the NPV is positive if

$$(b_1 + b_2 + b_3 - c_4 - c_5) = 0.0053 + 0.0023x - 0.0068y \qquad [8.15]$$

is positive. Of course, given the unknown x and y we do not know whether this expression is positive or not. This does not mean that the exercise has been pointless! First of all, we can see that the solid waste reduction benefits ($b_1 = 0.0007$) and the litter pick-up cost reduction benefit (the 0.0015 component of b_2) are relatively small. We can also see that the container production cost reduction benefit ($b_3 = 0.0308$) and the filling and distribution cost increase cost ($c_4 = 0.0277$) are relatively large, and of the same order of magnitude. Since they work in opposite directions in their effects on the sign of the NPV, it is clear that any uncertainties associated with the estimation of these items will be critical to the outcome of the cost benefit analysis.

Second, we can identify the way different values for x and y in equation [8.15] will affect the sign of the bracketed term on the left-hand side, and hence the sign for the NPV of the project. To do this we first find those combinations of x and y values which give $(b_1 + b_2 + b_3 - c_4 - c_5) = 0$, and hence $NPV = 0$. From equation [8.15] then we have

$$0.0053 + 0.0023x - 0.0068y = 0$$
i.e. $0.0068y = 0.0053 + 0.0023x$

so that

$$y = 0.7794 + 0.3382x \qquad [8.16]$$

identifies those combinations of y and x which are such that the NPV of the project which is legislation for mandatory deposits is exactly zero. The graph of equation [8.16] is shown in Figure 8.6(a), where the vertical axis is for y, return costs in cents per returned container, and the horizontal axis is for x,

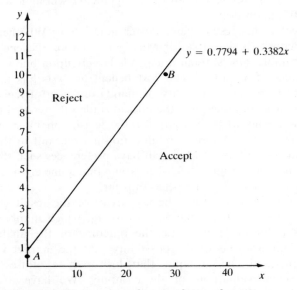

Figure 8.6 Accept and reject regions for mandatory deposits proposal

352 Environmental & Resource Economics

willingness to pay for a 62% to 85% reduction in beverage container litter in dollars per Michigan citizen. Combinations of x and y values lying above and to the left of the graph of equation [8.16] are such that $(b_1 + b_2 + b_3 - c_4 - c_5)$ is negative (try $y = 5$ and $x = 10$ in equation [8.15]). Hence this area in Figure 8.6 is labelled 'Reject', as $(b_1 + b_2 + b_3 - c_4 - c_5)$ negative means that the NPV is negative, so that for such combinations of x and y values the project should not go ahead. Combinations of x and y values lying below and to the right of the graph of equation [8.16] are such that $(b_1 + b_2 + b_3 - c_4 - c_5)$ is positive (try $y = 3$ and $x = 10$ in equation [8.15]), and the corresponding area is labelled 'Accept' as for xy values in this region the project should go ahead.

This diagram identifies the dimensions of the critical issue in deciding whether a system of mandatory deposits would be desirable, from the viewpoint of allocative efficiency, in Michigan. The critical issue is that such a system would confer benefits on households in the form of less litter, at the cost to households of greater inconvenience. We see that if the average Michigan citizen's time of return cost, y, is as low as half of a cent per returned container, then mandatory deposits would be desirable even if the average Michigan citizen were willing to pay nothing for reduced beverage container litter (point A). Given the observed shift away from returnable bottles in the recent past it is difficult to believe that y would be this low. If the average Michigan citizen's time of return cost were 10 cents per returned container (this is the deposit proposed), then in order to believe mandatory deposits desirable it would be necessary to believe that the average Michigan citizen's willingness to pay for a 62% to 85% reduction in beverage container litter was at least $27.26 (point B). With 9.1 million citizens this would imply an aggregate willingness to pay in the region of 200 million dollars!

With respect to his results here, Porter notes that: 'Whether a change to mandatory deposits is desirable for Michigan from an efficiency viewpoint is therefore debatable. One's opinion depends largely upon one's feeling for the unknown values of x and y.' The cost benefit analysis has not provided a clear cut answer on the desirability of mandatory deposit legislation. It has clarified the issues, and identified the critical trade off involved in making the decision. Those who wish to argue for the legislation must now either be prepared to argue that efficiency in allocation is irrelevant to the decision, or to believe that the citizens of Michigan have preferences such that x and y lie in the accept region of Figure 8.6, or to argue that some error has been made in the cost benefit analysis as reported thus far.

Porter does, in fact, examine the sensitivity of the result shown here as Figure 8.6 to errors in the value he uses for c_4, which number, as we have noted, exerts a lot of leverage on the outcome of the analysis. He also considers the implications of the possibility that the market valuations per unit of labour and energy input that his analysis utilises are not the appropriate social valuations of those inputs. We have in this chapter emphasised the problems which arise in cost benefit analysis where market prices do not exist. It should be clear that where market prices for consequences do exist, they are not necessarily the correct social valuations to be used in cost benefit analysis. It is conventional in the literature to call non-market observed prices used in lieu of existing market prices *shadow prices*. Shadow pricing generally is discussed in, for example, Ch. 7 of Pearce and Nash (1981). Porter uses somewhat arbitrary shadow prices for labour and energy to demonstrate the sensitivity of the outcome on mandatory deposits to the assumption that their market prices are those appropriate for social valuation.

The numbers that we have cited here from Porter's study are for a particular place and a particular time. They do not apply to a general consideration of the desirability of mandatory deposits on beverage containers. Indeed, Porter's analysis strongly suggests that no general answer to the question 'are mandatory deposits desirable' could be given. One would expect costs and benefits to vary from place to place. However, the approach adopted by Porter is generally applicable, and, we argue, useful even though not providing unique answers.

Preservation versus irreversible development

In 8.2 the illustrative example considered was the construction of a hydroelectric facility and we argued that some of the adverse consequences might reasonably be regarded as everlasting, in as much as the flooded valley would never return to exactly its original state. With respect to the loss of plant habitat particularly, we took it that a decision to go ahead with the project would be irreversible and everlasting – the species would become extinct. Now clearly this a polar case, but many would argue that a project which involves developing a wilderness area as a source of resource inputs should properly be treated as having the consequence of the everlasting loss of the amenity services of that area, and that in this respect a decision to go ahead with the project is an irreversible one. We are not here concerned to defend this view, which is discussed in Krutilla and Fisher (1975) or in Fisher (1981, Ch. 5), for example, but to look again at some of its implications for the appraisal of such projects.

Suppose that we consider a project which if undertaken will initially cost 1 of some unit of account and yield an annual flow of benefits less resource input costs of D forever, and which will also result in the loss forever of an annual flow of environmental amenity services properly valued at P, with D and P measured in the same units as the initial cost. Here we use P from preservation, as P is the flow which is a cost in the form of lost preservation benefits consequent upon the development, hence D, which is the project's purpose. This notation follows that of Porter (1982) which is an exposition and survey of contributions to the theory of cost benefit analysis of development in wilderness areas. Here we summarise some of Porter's discussion only. The present value of a stream which is x per annum forever is, with x accruing at the end of each year, shown in the mathematical note at the end of this chapter to be

$$PV = x/r$$

where r is the rate at which discounting is done. It follows that for this project

$$\text{NPV} = -1 + (D/r) - (P/r)$$

and the graph of the project's NPV against r is shown in Figure 8.7(a).

Now, the assumption thus far is that development benefits and costs, or development benefits and preservation benefits, are unchanging in relative size over time. Given this assumption, Figure 8.7(a) shows that the project is more likely to pass the NPV test the lower is the interest rate used for discounting. However, there are, as noted above, good reasons to suppose that the constancy over time of D and P in this sort of context is an inappropriate assumption. The amenity services provided by pristine natural environments are, it is argued, at best in fixed supply – no amount of capital accumulation or technical progress can increase the availability of such. More realistically, many would argue, the flow of such services must be assumed to be decreasing over future time. On the other hand, the demand for such services appears to increase as economic growth proceeds. So, it is argued, we should assume that preservation benefits are increasing over time, with

$$P_t = P(1 + a)^{t-1}$$

where P is the initial level and a the exponential growth rate. As shown in the

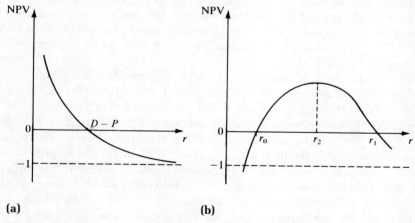

(a)   (b)

Figure 8.7 NPV and the interest rate for irreversible projects

mathematical note at the end of the chapter, the present value of such a P_t stream going on forever is

$P/(r - a)$

Now, with respect to development benefits, it is often argued that the assumption which is more appropriate than constancy is

$D_t = D(1 - b)^{t-1}$

so that such benefits decline over time, and have the present value

$D/(r + b)$

The argument here is that the material benefits of any particular development decline in relative value as economic growth proceeds.

Given these new assumptions about how the development and preservation benefit streams evolve over time, we have the project's NPV given by

$$NPV = -1 + (D/r + b) - (P/r - a)$$

and Figure 8.7(b) shows how NPV now varies with the interest rate used for discounting.[6] Now it is not true that lowering r always improves the project's NPV. For the project to pass the NPV test, r must lie in the range r_0 to r_1: to the left of r_2, reducing r reduces NPV, between r_2 and r_1 the relationship between NPV and r is as in panel (a) – lower r means higher NPV. Given the assumptions now in operation, the project can fail the NPV test on account of high (greater than r_1) or low (lower than r_0) interest rates being used. According to Porter (1982, p. 62):[7]

> The reason for this double boundary on r is easily seen. For sufficiently high rates of discount (i.e. for $r > r_1$), the development project fails for the traditional reason, that the benefits it yields (D or D_t) are too heavily discounted to offset the initial costs of the project. And for sufficiently low rates of discount (i.e. for $r < r_0$), the exponentially growing benefits of preservation (P_t) are so little discounted that their perpetual loss becomes too great a cost for the development project to shoulder.

The assumptions made in order to derive this result are, of course, rather special. However, they do make it possible to show very clearly that where projects have long lived costs and benefits, the effect of interest rate variations on NPV is, as a general matter, ambiguous. We made this point, using a numerical example, in 8.2 above. Also, the analysis here shows that what matters for irreversible projects is not just the initial sizes of the cost and benefit streams, but also the way they each evolve over time. It is not necessary, given a greater than zero so that development costs, or preservation benefits, are growing, that development benefits are declining to get the outcome shown in Figure 8.7(b). It can arise with $b = 0$ so that $D_t = D$ for all t, or for development benefits increasing over time so long as they increase at a rate less than that at which preservation benefits increase.

Cost benefit analysis and conservation

Many of those who are concerned for the natural environment oppose the use of cost benefit analysis for the appraisal of projects with environmental impacts. A number of objections are raised, some well founded, others based on misunderstandings about the nature and rôle of cost benefit analysis.

The most fundamental objection is that cost benefit analysis seeks to make commensurable things which should not be made commensurable. There are, effectively, two variants of this argument. One is that damage to the environment should never be allowed, however large the attendant benefits in terms of human economic welfare. The other is that the problem with cost benefit analysis is that it tries to make things commensurable using an inappropriate common metric, consumer preferences and willingness to pay. This could be for one or both of two reasons. First, that it is feasible but wrong to use individual's preferences as the criterion for social project appraisal. Second, that there is nothing wrong with using individual's preferences, but it is infeasible. The first of these is an ethical argument. The second is a practical one arising from the assessment that TCM and CVM, and the other methods for measuring willingness to pay, are simply not reliable enough.

If the argument against cost benefit analysis that no environmental damage should ever be allowed is accepted, matters are, in one sense, quite simple as far as social project appraisal goes. It is necessary only to establish that a project entails some environmental damage to stop it. If this cannot be established, the project can be appraised in the normal way. Most projects would fall into the first category. If the argument is that the problem is commensurability according to willingness to pay criteria, it remains to devise alternative methods for making the trade offs as between environmental damage and net project benefits. This would appear likely to involve a mixture of novel social institutions and use of technology. One suggestion that has been made (Jacobs 1991) is that decisions on projects should be appraised by a jury-like panel of members of the ordinary public, able to call on expert advice, to commission modelling studies, and to take into account the opinions of affected parties.

Cost benefit analysis is intended to select from among possible projects those that are consistent with intertemporal efficiency. In Chapter 7 we saw that intertemporal efficiency is consistent with biological extinctions. Many find the fact that intertemporal efficiency could sanction species extinction a reason for rejecting it, and cost benefit analysis, as a sensible way of deciding what is in the social interest. This is essentially the origin of the modified safe minimum standard approach. There is implicit in standard intertemporal efficiency analysis an assumption that everything has a substitute. The reason that the extinction of a species does not matter in this kind of analysis is that there is an assumption that whatever the species was doing for human interests, can be done by something else. On this view there may be particular scarcities, but there is no general scarcity in relation to the services that the natural environment performs for humankind. What disappears can always be replaced. Of course, if this view is incorrect, acting on it will give rise to future problems. It is the concern that substitution possibilities might be limited that largely underpins the recent emergence of sustainable development as a policy objective.

Notes

1. Some cost benefit analysts argue that since the distribution of income is not in fact acceptable, costs and benefits should be weighted for their distributional impacts, so that, for example, each £1 of benefit accruing to the poor would enter the final arithmetic as £$(1 + x)$, whereas £1 accruing to the rich would enter as £1. Distributional weights in cost benefit analysis are discussed in Ch. 2 of Pearce and Nash (1981).
2. GWh stands for giga watt hours. A watt is a unit of power, equal to 0.293 Btu (see 7.5 above) per hour. Giga stands for 10^9, so that one giga watt is 10^9 watts. A useful discussion of units used in energy and power measurement and analysis is Ch. 3 of Slesser (1978).
3. For references to the literature concerning the relationship between air pollution and human health see 5.4 above, and on the mortality implications of coal burning for electricity generation see also Common and Peirson (1979).
4. In Figure 8.1 the graph for equation [8.2] is a straight line which passes through all the data points plotted from Table 8.1. This is because in constructing the data we used equation [8.2]. Where actual survey data is used, things do not, of course, work out so neatly. The relationship equivalent to equation [8.2] then has to be derived from the data by the techniques of econometrics; the relationship which best fits the data will not necessarily be a straight line, and it certainly will not pass through all the data points.
5. The observant reader will have noted that in this section time starts at period 1 rather than at period 0 as in our previous discussions, and particularly in equation [8.1] for example. We have done this because it is more natural to refer to the 'first', rather than the 'zero'th', year of a project. Given our assumption that sums to be discounted accrue on the first day of each year, the formal equivalent to equation [8.1] that we are now using is

$$\text{NPV} = \sum_{t=1}^{T} \frac{B_t - C_t}{(1 + r)^{t-1}} = B_1 - C_1 + \frac{B_2 - C_2}{1 + r} + \ldots + \frac{B_T - C_T}{(1 + r)^{T-1}}$$

which lines up with the expression for d_t at the head of Table 8.5.
6. Actually the NPV profile shown in Figure 8.7(b) is not the only one which could arise given the assumptions made here. However, the other possibilities are where the NPV is never positive, and so of little interest.

7. I have changed the notation in this quote from that used by Porter in order to achieve consistency with the text here, and omitted his references to his Figure 2.

Mathematical note

1. For n years we have

(i) $$PV = x + \frac{x}{(1+r)} + \frac{x}{(1+r)^2} + \frac{x}{(1+r)^3} + \ldots + \frac{x}{(1+r)^{n-1}}$$

and if we multiply both sides of (i) by $1/(1+r)$ we get

(ii) $$\frac{PV}{(1+r)} = \frac{x}{(1+r)} + \frac{x}{(1+r)^2} + \frac{x}{(1+r)^3} + \frac{x}{(1+r)^4} + \ldots$$

$$+ \frac{x}{(1+r)^{n-1}} + \frac{x}{(1+r)^n}$$

so that subtracting (ii) from (i) gives

$$PV - \frac{PV}{(1+r)} = x - \frac{x}{(1+r)^n}$$

$$PV\left(\frac{1+r-1}{1+r}\right) = x\left(1 - \frac{1}{(1+r)^n}\right)$$

and as n goes to infinity so $1/(1+r)^n$ goes to zero, so that

$$PV\left(\frac{r}{1+r}\right) = x$$

or $$PV = \frac{(1+r)x}{r}$$

This result assumes that x accrues at the start of each year. If we assume that x accrues at the end of each year we have

(i) $$PV = \frac{x}{(1+r)} + \frac{x}{(1+r)^2} + \frac{x}{(1+r)^3} + \ldots + \frac{x}{(1+r)^n}$$

(ii) $$\frac{PV}{(1+r)} = \frac{x}{(1+r)^2} + \frac{x}{(1+r)^3} + \frac{x}{(1+r)^4} + \ldots + \frac{x}{(1+r)^{n+1}}$$

so that

$$PV - \frac{PV}{(1+r)} = \frac{x}{1+r} - \frac{x}{(1+r)^{n+1}}$$

$$PV\left(\frac{r}{1+r}\right) = x\left(\frac{1}{1+r} - \frac{1}{(1+r)^{n+1}}\right)$$

and again letting n go to infinity gives

$$PV = \frac{x}{r}.$$

This last result is that frequently used in the literature.

2. Now suppose that we are concerned with the present value of a stream of sums which grow exponentially at the rate a, so that $x_t = x(1+a)^{t-1}$. Then with x_t arising at the end of year t we have:

(i) $\quad PV = \dfrac{x}{(1+r)} + \dfrac{x(1+a)}{(1+r)^2} + \dfrac{x(1+a)^2}{(1+r)^3} + \ldots + \dfrac{x(1+a)^{n-1}}{(1+r)^n}$

(ii) $\quad \dfrac{(1+a)PV}{(1+r)} = \dfrac{x(1+a)}{(1+r)^2} + \dfrac{x(1+a)^2}{(1+r)^3} + \dfrac{x(1+a)^3}{(1+r)^4} + \ldots$

$$+ \dfrac{x(1+a)^n}{(1+r)^{n+1}}$$

so that

$$PV - \frac{(1+a)PV}{(1+r)} = \frac{x}{1+r} - \frac{x(1+a)^n}{(1+r)^{n+1}}$$

$$PV\left(\frac{1+r-1-a}{1+r}\right) = \left(\frac{x}{1+r}\right)\left(1 - \frac{(1+a)^n}{(1+r)^{n+1}}\right)$$

$$PV(r-a) = x\left(1 - \frac{(1+a)^n}{(1+r)^{n+1}}\right)$$

and letting n go to infinity gives, for $a < r$,

$$PV(r-a) = x$$

or $\quad PV = x/(r-a).$

Clearly, if we have a negative growth rate $-b$, with $x_t = 1(1-b)^{t-1}$, we will get

$$PV = x/r + b.$$

Chapter 9

Sustainable Development

In the last decade questions concerning the relationship between economic activity and the natural environment have become much more prominent in public debate and political processes, largely within the context of a concern for 'sustainable development'. This puts equity issues at the forefront, in two ways. First, there is the question of intergenerational equity. Does current economic activity impact on the natural environment in such a way as to undermine its ability to support future economic activity? Are we now acting so as to bequeath to future generations an impoverished natural environment and lower living standards? Second, there is the fact of current inequity. While some of the current human population have very high living standards, many exist in abject poverty. The fact and the question are related. The prevailing orthodoxy on poverty alleviation is that the only effective solution is economic growth. However, if the answer to the question is affirmative, the solution may not be available. Increasing the level of economic activity now and in the near future may, via its effects on the natural environment, mean that generations in the further future are made poor. The goal of sustainable development is to alleviate current poverty without creating future poverty.

Clearly, sustainable development is a global issue with many facets, to which a single chapter cannot do justice. The literature which has emerged in the last decade is enormous. This chapter will try to give an overview of some of the component and arising issues, highlight the role of economic analysis, consider its limitations, and provide useful references to the literature. It is organised as follows. In 9.1, we consider the case for economic growth as the solution to the poverty problem. Section 9.2 then looks at the emergence of the idea of sustainable development, and its impact. In 9.3 we consider the standard economic approach to the central issues, which leads naturally, in 9.4, to a discussion of proposals to modify the measurement of economic performance so as to provide an indicator of whether sustainable development is being achieved. In 9.5 we revisit the question of the nature of the interdependence between economic activity and the environment, and the implications arising for thinking about economic activity. The next two sections look briefly at two particulars of the overarching problem – the matter of biodiversity loss in 9.6, and the enhanced greenhouse effect in 9.7. The chapter concludes, 9.8, with some discussion of policy issues.

9.1 Poverty and growth

This section considers the rôle of economic growth in the alleviation of poverty. The position of most economists in the controversies which arise over the question of whether there exist environmental limits to growth can only be properly understood if one appreciates their basic understanding of this rôle. Economic growth is, of course, desired because it makes people already well off even better off. But, for many economists, the real argument for the growth objective is poverty alleviation, as follows. In the absence of growth, improving the lot of the poor requires redistribution to them from the better off. The better off are likely to resist attempts at redistribution, which will be a source of conflict. Even assuming that such resistance can be overcome, and that redistribution itself does not adversely affect overall economic performance, there are typically few well off and many poor. There will not generally be enough that can be taken from the better off to significantly improve the lot of the poor. We illustrate the argument with a simple numerical example.

Consider an economy where initially there are 10 affluent persons with incomes of £100 per head per period, and 100 poor persons with incomes of £20 per person per period. Let it be known that the poverty level is an income of £50 per period – with an income below this level a person suffers unambiguous material deprivation. Given this, the elimination of poverty requires, in the absence of growth, the transfer of £3000 per period from the affluent to the poor. This is impossible, since the total income of the rich is just £1000 per period. Even if the incomes of all of the rich were reduced to the poverty line of £50, there would not be enough money arising to raise all of the poor above the poverty line.

Now consider the impact on poverty of growth in per capita incomes, together with redistributive taxation. We will assume that the annual growth in incomes is at a constant proportional rate. If y grows at x per cent per year, this can be stated as

$$y_t = y_0 (1 + g)^t \qquad [9.1]$$

where $g = x$ divided by 100, t indicates the year and y_0 is the initial level of y. For $x = 5$ and $g = 0.05$, for example, the equation [9.1] is a shorthand way of writing

$$y_1 = y_0 \times 1.05$$
$$y_2 = y_1 \times 1.05 = y_0 \times 1.05 \times 1.05 = y_0 \times 1.05^2$$
$$y_3 = y_2 \times 1.05 = y_0 \times 1.05 \times 1.05 \times 1.05 = y_0 \times 1.05^3$$

and so on. For our numerical example, we assume that all pre-tax incomes

Table 9.1 Years to the elimination of poverty

	$g = 0.005$	$g = 0.01$	$g = 0.02$	$g = 0.03$	$g = 0.04$
$\gamma = 0$	184	93	47	31	24
$\gamma = 0.1$	174	88	44	30	23
$\gamma = 0.2$	165	83	42	28	21
$\gamma = 0.3$	156	79	40	27	20
$\gamma = 0.4$	147	74	38	25	19
$\gamma = 0.5$	139	70	36	24	18

grow at the same rate, g. In making this assumption, we abstract from the complex question of the actual evolution of pre-tax and transfer incomes with economic growth in order to focus on essentials. We assume that the incomes of the affluent are taxed at the rate γ, with the total tax revenue arising being divided equally as between the poor. The relative sizes and incomes of the two groups are as given above. Then, incomes after taxation and redistribution evolve over time according to

$$A_t = 100(1 + g)^t - \gamma[100(1 + g)^t]$$
$$P_t = 20(1 + g)^t + 10\gamma[100(1 + g)^t]/100$$

which can be written as

$$A_t = 100(1 + g)^t(1 - \gamma)$$
$$P_t = 10(1 + g)^t(2 + \gamma) \qquad [9.2]$$

where A_t is the post-tax income of an affluent person in year t, and P_t the post-transfer payment income of a poor person. Given [9.2], one can easily calculate the evolution over time of A and P for various values of g and γ. The information arising can be summarised in a variety of ways. Table 9.1 shows how long the elimination of poverty will take for combinations of values for g and γ.

There is no column for $g = 0$ in Table 9.1 because, as noted above, in the absence of economic growth, there is no level of tax and redistribution that can eliminate poverty. However, with economic growth, redistribution is not necessary for the eventual elimination of poverty. With zero taxation of the incomes of the affluent, the number of years for the incomes of the poor to rise above the poverty level decreases with the rate of economic growth. For a given rate of growth, the time to the elimination of poverty falls as the rate of taxation of the incomes of the affluent increases.

From [9.2] we get

$$P_t/A_t = (2 + \gamma)/[10(1 - \gamma)] \qquad [9.3]$$

which shows that at any date the ratio of incomes after tax and transfer payment is independent of the growth rate. The evolution over time of the ratio of the income of the poor to that of the affluent does not, that is, depend here on the rate of economic growth. It is determined solely by the rate at which the incomes of the affluent are taxed. If there is no taxation of the affluent, $\gamma = 0$, then [9.3] shows that, whatever the growth rate, the relative sizes of affluent and poor incomes remain fixed in the ratio 5:1.

Now consider a system of income taxation which does have the effect of reducing inequality as economic growth proceeds. Denote incomes for the affluent and the poor prior to taxation and transfer payments by A_t^* and P_t^* respectively. Have the affluent pay tax at the rate γ on the amount by which their income exceeds £50, the level required to avoid poverty, and the poor be paid equal shares of the receipts arising. Then

$$A_t = A_t^* - T_t = A_t^* - \gamma(A_t^* - 50)$$
$$P_t = P_t^* + (10T_t)/100 = P_t^* + (\gamma/10)(A_t^* - 50)$$
[9.4]

gives the evolution of personal incomes post tax/transfer, where T_t is the total tax paid by an affluent person. For the affluent the *marginal tax rate* is γ, the proportion paid in tax of an additional unit of income above the threshold of 50. The *average tax rate* is given by T_t/A_t^*, where

$$T_t/A_t^* = \gamma(A_t^* - 50)/A_t^*$$
$$= \gamma - (50\gamma/A_t^*)$$

so that the average tax rate increases with A_t^*. This type of tax schedule is known as *progressive taxation*. The behaviour of the ratio P_t/A_t for $A_t^* = 100(1 + g)^t$ and $P_t^* = 20(1 + g)^t$ can be tracked for given g and γ using [9.4]. Table 9.2 gives some illustrative results. The entries are for the ratio of poor to affluent post tax and transfer incomes in the 50th year.

The first row illustrates the point that, without redistribution, economic growth such that all incomes grow at equal rates has no impact on inequality. Once made this point is obvious. The first column shows that even without growth, progressive taxation reduces inequality. In this column, the numbers would be the same whatever the year chosen to consider the effects of growth and taxation. For any given growth rate, the ratio P_t/A_t is higher the larger is γ, ie the more progressive is taxation. For any given rate of taxation, except 0, the ratio is larger the higher is the rate of economic growth.

The reason for making the point that, given equal growth rates in pre-tax and transfer incomes, progressive taxation is necessary for inequality reduction is that on one view of the poverty problem, inequality reduction is necessary for its alleviation. One view of poverty is that it is the condition that exists when income is below some minimum level, £50 in the example above. This is the *absolute deprivation* view of poverty – the poor are those who lack the means to acquire subsistence defined in terms of a fixed basket of goods and services. According to the *relative deprivation* view of poverty, subsistence income is not the cost of a fixed basket of goods and services, but is what is required for access to the goods and services that are culturally determined as necessary for 'normal' life. This cultural standard will, in part, be determined by the affluent, and will increase with economic growth. On

Table 9.2 Inequality, economic growth and progressive taxation

	g = 0	g = 0.005	g = 0.01	g = 0.02	g = 0.03	g = 0.04
$\gamma = 0$	0.200	0.200	0.200	0.200	0.200	0.200
$\gamma = 0.1$	0.216	0.220	0.222	0.227	0.229	0.231
$\gamma = 0.2$	0.228	0.242	0.249	0.258	0.265	0.269
$\gamma = 0.3$	0.241	0.267	0.279	0.297	0.309	0.316
$\gamma = 0.4$	0.256	0.297	0.316	0.345	0.365	0.378
$\gamma = 0.5$	0.273	0.332	0.361	0.406	0.439	0.461

this view, the poverty level rises with economic growth, and poverty alleviation requires reduced inequality. Of course, many believe that inequality reduction is an important goal, even if it is not necessary for poverty alleviation.

The relative deprivation view of poverty is discussed in Common (1995). A classic statement of this view of poverty, with a great deal of statistical data for the UK, is Townsend (1979). Good sources of information on poverty and inequality at the global level are the annual reports on human development published by the United Nations Development Programme: see, for example, *Human Development Report 1995* (United Nations Development Programme 1995). As is made clear there, there is greater inequality as between nations than there is within nations. The nations which are now industrialised and affluent have in their recent history evolved systems of redistributive taxation and transfers, generally involving progressive income taxation. As regards global poverty and inequality, there is basic problem in that there does not exist a world government under which a similar system could be operated: see Mendez (1992). As discussed in 9.7 below, addressing some global environmental problems could be combined with international transfers that would work to reduce inequalities as between nations.

9.2   Some recent history

As noted in Chapter 1, 1972 saw the publication of *The Limits to Growth*, (*TLTG*) (Meadows *et al.* 1972). It reported results from a computer model of the world economy which included representation of the economic system's extractions from the environment, its use of natural resources of various kinds, and its insertions into it, in the form of waste discharges. Many commentators said, and some still do, that the story told in *The Limits to Growth* was simply that the world would run out of natural resources, leading to collapse of the economic system in the 21st century. *The Limits to Growth* did report that if the computer model was run on the basis of extrapolating current trends in such things as population growth using existing production technologies with stated estimates of resource reserves, then the system moved into collapse mode on account of resource exhaustion. However, the results of many other runs of the model were also reported. For example, in one run all resource reserve estimates were increased by a factor of two, but the rest of the model remained unchanged. In this run the world economic system did not experience a resource exhaustion crisis, but it did experience a pollution crisis on account of the increased waste discharges now arising because of the increased availability of resource inputs to production. This sort of outcome is, of course, entirely consistent with the materials balance principle.

On the basis of a number of variant model runs, the conclusion reached in *The Limits to Growth* was that the finite nature of the natural environment meant that, in terms of material throughput, the world economic system could not expand indefinitely. There existed environmental limits to growth. However, this was not the only major conclusion reported, and it was not asserted in *TLTG*, as was widely claimed, that global economic collapse was inevitable. In fact, a second major conclusion was that if actions were taken to modify current trends in such areas as population growth rates, the world economic system could move into a configuration that would be 'sustainable far into the future' (caption to Figure 46, page 165). A third conclusion was that the sooner such changes were effected, the greater the likelihood that sustainability would be achieved.

The Limits to Growth generated considerable debate and controversy. It was vigorously attacked from many quarters. Very few economists were prepared to see any merit at all in *TLTG*. While there is much to criticise in *TLTG* in terms both of technical matters and presentation, the nature of much of the reaction by economists was such as to suggest some deeper basis for antagonism. As discussed above, economists generally have a strong attachment to the objective of economic growth, seeing it as the only effective means for poverty alleviation. This strong commitment is not confined to economists. It is widely diffused throughout society. It is in this context that much of the reaction to *The Limits to Growth* has to be understood. It appeared to be saying that what was considered the only feasible way to eliminate poverty at the global level was, in fact, infeasible. The obvious implication of this claim, if poverty in the less developed economies was to be eliminated, was a major re-distribution of wealth and income as between rich and poor nations.

The United Nations Conference on the Human Environment was held in Stockholm in June 1972. It was attended by representatives of 113 governments, 19 intergovernmental agencies, and 400 other organisations (many of which were nongovernmental organisations, NGOs). This was not the first international conference on the natural environment. But, it was the first to explicitly relate a concern for the environment to a concern for human welfare. According to one of those active in organising the conference, before it 'people usually saw the environment ... as something totally divorced from humanity ... Stockholm recorded a fundamental shift in the emphasis of our environmental thinking' (Barbara Ward quoted in McCormick 1989). The

Stockholm Conference explicitly linked concerns for the natural environment to the problem of economic development in poor countries. Among the 26 Principles adopted were a group that stated that:

> Development and environmental concern should go together, and less developed countries should be given every assistance and incentive to promote rational environmental management.

(McCormick 1989)

This conference drew attention to the international dimensions of many environmental problems, and was responsible for the establishment of the United Nations Environment Programme, UNEP. The headquarters of this agency were established in Nairobi, with a view to giving some indication of substantive commitment to the principles cited above. Among the less developed countries there was a perception that concern for the natural environment was a luxury that they could not afford, and that in seeking to protect the global environment the rich industrial nations were likely to want things done which would impede economic development for poor nations.

The International Union for the Conservation of Nature and Natural Resources, IUCN, was established in 1948 as the International Union for the Protection of Nature, the name change taking place in 1956. As both names suggest, this organisation was originally seen by its organisers as primarily concerned with the protection and conservation of wildlife. However, over the years it came to be seen by the IUCN that this aim could not be pursued in isolation from the problem of economic development, especially since much of the wildlife of concern was located in less developed countries. In 1980 the IUCN published its *World Conservation Strategy, WCS*, the aim of which was to 'advance the achievement of sustainable development through the conservation of living resources' (International Union for the Conservation of Nature and Natural Resources 1980, p. iv). Conservation was defined as: 'the management of the human use of the biosphere so that it may yield the greatest sustainable benefit to present generations while maintaining its potential to meet the needs and aspirations of future generations'. Whereas many had previously taken the view that economic development and conservation of the natural environment were incompatible – a view read often into *The Limits to Growth* for example – the basic and essential point of *WCS* was that development which was to effectively and lastingly meet the needs of the world's poor needed to be soundly based on conservation. According to *WCS*: 'there is a close relationship between failure to achieve the objectives of conservation and failure to achieve the social and economic objectives of development – or having achieved them, to sustain that achievement'. The *WCS* did evoke some responses from governments. It had called on national governments to prepare national conservation strategies. As of 1987, eight countries has produced such documents, and a further 33 reported that they were in the process of producing conservation strategies.

The concept of sustainable development was given much greater prominence in 1987 with the publication of the so-called 'Brundtland Report', according to which:

Sustainable development seeks to meet the needs and aspirations of the present without compromising the ability to meet those of the future.
                    (World Commission on Environment and Development 1987, p. 40)

This report was produced by the World Commission on Environment and Development, WCED, set up by a resolution of the United Nations General Assembly in 1983. The report derives its popular title from the name of the Chairman of the Commission, Gro Harlem Brundtland, a former Minister for the Environment, and Prime Minister, of Norway. The official title of the report is *Our Common Future* (World Commission on Environment and Development 1987). The Brundtland Report has to be regarded as a brilliant political document. It has been widely praised and little criticised, and has evoked much more positive responses from many governments, as well as NGOs, industry and labour organisations, than did *WCS*.

The different reactions to the Brundtland Report and *The Limits to Growth* are interesting. In fact, both books tell very similar stories and reach somewhat similar conclusions. In both cases, environmental constraints on growth/development are identified and discussed. In both cases, it is argued that it is impossible to conceive that current trends can be continued far into the future. In both cases it is concluded that radical changes in the way the world economy is run are called for. The major differences are two-fold. First, *The Limits to Growth* is an exercise in quantitative modelling which illustrates its arguments with computer derived scenarios presented as graphs of the paths for major variables plotted against past and future real time. While the Brundtland Report does refer to some historical data, it does not present any numerical projections for the future paths of variables of interest. Its arguments are developed in qualitative terms.

Second, *The Limits to Growth* presents the outcome which would be consequent upon adoption of the changes that it urges as one in which the world economy is sustainable at a constant level of total material output. This is, by virtue of the quantitative approach adopted, made very explicit. What is explicitly on offer is sustainability in the sense of a constant level of total world output which can be maintained into the indefinite future. Implicit is the continuing existence of pressure for re-distribution from rich to poor nations. What is stated to be on offer in the Brundtland Report, if policy changes are adopted, is quite different. The passage in the report where the definition of sustainable development quoted above appears goes on to state:

Far from requiring the cessation of economic growth, it (i.e. sustainable development) recognises that the problems of poverty and underdevelopment cannot be solved unless we have a new era of growth in which developing countries play a large role and reap large benefits.

Further, it is made explicit that what Brundtland sees as feasible is not economic growth in the developing countries alone:

> Growth must be revived in developing countries because that is where the links between economic growth, the alleviation of poverty, and environmental conditions operate most directly. Yet developing countries are part of an interdependent world economy; their prospects also depend on the levels and patterns of growth in industrialised nations. The medium-term prospects for industrial countries are for growth of 3–4 per cent, the minimum that international financial institutions consider necessary if these countries are going to play a part in expanding the world economy. Such growth rates could be environmentally sustainable if industrialised nations can continue the recent shifts in the content of their growth towards less material- and energy-intensive activities and the improvement of their efficiency in using materials and energy (page 51)

WCED believed that an active follow-up to its report was imperative if the policy changes necessary for the attainment of sustainable development were to occur. It called for the transformation of its report into a UN Programme of Action on Sustainable Development, and recommended that:

> Within an appropriate period after the presentation of the report to the General Assembly, an international Conference could be convened to review progress made and promote follow-up arrangements that will be needed over time to set benchmarks and to maintain human progress within the guidelines of human needs and natural laws.

As a result, the United Nations Conference on Environment and Development, UNCED, took place in Rio de Janeiro in June 1992. This was the 20th anniversary of the Stockholm Conference: this timing was intentional. UNCED was preceded by over two years of preparatory international negotiations. 178 nations sent delegations, and the meeting was attended by 107 heads of government (or state). During UNCED several parallel and related conferences took place in Rio de Janeiro; the meeting for NGOs involved more participants than UNCED itself. It has been estimated that over 20,000 people were there in total.

The preparatory negotiations dealt with four main areas: draft conventions on biodiversity conservation, global climate change, forest management, and the preparation of two documents for adoption at UNCED. The main outcomes were as follows. There was complete agreement on the, non-binding, adoption of the *Rio Declaration* and *Agenda 21*. The first of these comprises 27 statements of principle in regard to global sustainable development. The second is an 800 page document covering over 100 specific programmes for the attainment of global sustainable development: many of these programmes involve resource transfers from the industrial to the developing nations. UNCED also agreed on the creation of a new United Nations agency, a Commission for Sustainable Development, to oversee the implementation of *Agenda 21*. Agreement was also reached on the, non-binding, adoption of a set of principles for forest management. The industrial nations re-affirmed their previous, non-binding, commitments to a target for development aid of 0.7% of their GNP.

Two conventions were adopted, by some 150 nations in each case, which would be binding on signatories when ratified by them. These covered global climate change and biodiversity conservation: the latter was not signed by the USA at the Rio meeting, but the USA did sign in 1993 after a change of administration. While binding, these conventions do not commit individual nations to much in the way of specific actions. The climate change convention is discussed in 9.7 below: see Barbier *et al.* (1994) on the biodiversity conservation convention. While many environmental activists, as well as many concerned to promote economic development in poor nations, regarded the actual achievements at UNCED as disappointing, it did confirm that sustainable development was, and would remain, firmly on the world political agenda. While specific commitments were not a major feature of the outcomes, there were agreements with the potential to lead to further developments. The creation of the Commission for Sustainable Development is clearly an important institutional innovation at the international level.

The convening of, and the outcomes at, UNCED suggests that the need to address the economic and environmental problems arising from economy-environment linkages is widely accepted. Equally, UNCED suggests that while the existence of a problem is widely agreed, detailed agreement on the nature of appropriate policy responses is limited. Further, there is clearly reluctance on the part of national governments to incur costs associated with policy responses, although many have issued statements concerning policy directives for national sustainable development.

In addition to this potentially major step in political and institutional evolution, 1992 also saw the publication of *Beyond the Limits* (Meadows *et al.* 1992), the sequel to *The Limits to Growth*. The 1992 book updates the analysis of the 1972 book, and states that the conclusions reached in 1972 remain valid. It seems unlikely that *Beyond the Limits* will provoke the level of controversy that resulted from the publication of *The Limits to Growth*. The climate of opinion has changed. Many economists are now working on sustainable development issues, and are heavily involved in attempts to design policies to promote its attainment. Most see the problem in terms of the use of price incentive type instruments to correct market failure, and of abandoning government policies that themselves prevent the attainment of allocative efficiency. Some, as discussed below in 9.5 and 9.8 especially, consider that the attainment of sustainability will require more fundamental changes to ways of thinking, as well as institutions.

9.3   Economic theory

We have, in discussing economic analysis, emphasised the distinction between questions of allocative efficiency and questions relating to distributional fairness. In Chapter 7, on natural resource exploitation, we first looked at the requirements for intertemporal efficiency, then, in 7.4, considered fairness in intertemporal allocation. For the latter purpose, we used a construction in which a planner considered alternative time profiles for consumption by summing the discounted value of the value of consumption at different dates, where his current marginal valuation of consumption declined with the level of consumption. We introduced natural resources issues by considering an economy in which production used inputs of capital and a non-renewable resource, according to

$$Y_t = Y_t(K_t, Q_t) \qquad\qquad\qquad [7.45]$$

with Y for output/income, K for the input of capital and Q for the resource input.

This is the basic framework within which economic analysis deals with sustainability/sustainable development issues. Given that Q is drawn from a finite stock of a non-renewable resource, it puts those issues in the sharpest possible context. As discussed in 7.4, given [7.45], the question immediately arising is whether there exists a positive level of consumption that is indefinitely sustainable. In 7.4, we saw that the answer to this question depends on the substitution possibilities as between inputs of capital and the natural resource. There are three sorts of situation, which can be distinguished according to the algebraic form for [7.45]:

1.   For $Y_t = aK_t + bQ_t$, [7.46], the resource is inessential in production, and a positive level of consumption can be sustained indefinitely, notwithstanding the non-renewable and exhaustible nature of the resource. The finite nature of the resource stock does not represent a constraint on total production and consumption. With sufficient capital, any level of consumption can be attained.
2.   For $Y_t = \min(aK_t, bQ_t)$, [7.47], the resource is essential in production, and there is no positive level of consumption that can be indefinitely sustained. Maximum output is given by bQ_t, so that with zero resource input, production and consumption are zero.
3.   For $Y_t = AK_t^\alpha Q_t^{1-\alpha}$, [7.48], the resource is essential in production. However, as shown in the numerical example, see Table 7.5, for some values of the parameter α there exists a programme of saving and capital accumulation such that there is a positive level of consumption that can be indefinitely sustained.

This is the basic framework for the economic theory of sustainability/sustainable development. It abstracts from the many complexities that attend the problem in reality, focuses on a polar case – the use in production of a non-renewable resource, and then considers the central question – is there some positive level of consumption that is indefinitely sustainable? The important answer is that 'it all depends', on the possibilities for substitution in production. If the case 1 here is operative, the answer to the question is 'yes'. If the case 2 is operative, the answer is 'no'. If the case 3 is operative, the answer is 'maybe'. Note that in this case, the analysis does not show that, if α is large enough, sustainability will be what actually occurs. It shows only that, if α is large enough, sustainability is feasible. And note further, that the analysis shows that sustainability is not feasible if α is not large enough. We now turn to the question of what will ensure that sustainability is what occurs, if α is large enough.

The Hartwick–Solow Rule

Solow (1974) showed rigorously, rather than by means of a numerical example as in 7.4 here, that given case 3 and α large enough, sustainability as constant consumption is feasible. Given case 3, the parameter α is a measure of the importance of capital, relative to the natural resource, in production. Hartwick (1977) showed that given feasibility in case 3, sustainability would be the outcome, if society followed a particular saving and investment rule. He showed that if all of the rent arising in the intertemporally efficient depletion of the natural resource were invested in capital accumulation, then consumption would be maintained constant indefinitely. We discussed rent and intertemporally efficient depletion programmes for non-renewable resources in Chapter 7. Recall that we did not claim that such resources are in fact typically depleted as required by efficiency conditions. Hence, it is important to be clear that the Hartwick Rule states that what needs to be invested is the rent that would arise if the resource were being depleted according to the intertemporally efficient programme, not the rent actually arising. Of course, if conditions in the economy were actually the ideal conditions, then the actual depletion programme and the efficient programme would coincide.

The title to this subsection is 'The Hartwick–Solow Rule'. This reflects another contribution in this area by Solow. He, in Solow (1986), showed that there is another rule which will produce sustainability, and that it is equivalent to the Hartwick Rule. The Solow Rule is to save and invest so as to keep total wealth constant, where total wealth is the value of the capital stock plus the value of the natural resource. Investing the efficiency rent arising in depleting the resource in case 3 will do this. Solow (1986) also showed that following this rule is equivalent to following the rule 'always consume an amount corresponding to the interest income on total wealth'. The Hartwick–Solow rule can be re-stated as follows. If sustainability is feasible, it can be realised by always saving and investing in man-made capital the rent arising in the efficient depletion of the natural resource. If saving and investment are as required for sustainability, total wealth will be constant, and the sustainable consumption level will be the equivalent of the interest on that constant wealth.

The Hartwick–Solow Rule and the associated analysis dominates the way economists think about sustainability issues. It is, for example, the basis for ideas about how national income accounting practice could be modified so as to better guide economic policy in the direction of actually realising sustainability/sustainable development, as discussed in the next section here. Establishing the validity of the Hartwick–Solow rule requires mathematics well beyond that assumed of readers of this book. From a verbal statement, such as that above, it is not even all that clear what the rule actually means. Actually, the rule has strong intuitive content, and we will try to bring this out in the next subsection with a numerical example.

It is important to be clear that following the Hartwick–Solow Rule would be different from following the sort of plan that we considered in Chapter 7. Planning for sustainability is different from planning for the maximisation of the discounted sum of current and future valuations of consumption. Dasgupta and Heal (1974) considered the latter kind of planning for production conditions which are case 3 above, with α large enough for constant consumption for ever to be feasible. They found that the planned time path for consumption would then have the general form shown in Figure 9.1. Consumption would initially increase, then go asymptotically to zero. Consumption would be higher in the near future than in the distant future, and would be close to zero for a very long time. Given the assumed production conditions, so that constant consumption is possible, the standard kind of planning as considered in Chapter 7 here, would not choose sustainability.

The mine owner in a competitive economy

The Hartwick–Solow Rule was developed for an economy. Here we use a numerical example concerning the owner of a mine in a competitive economy, to illustrate some of the basic ideas involved in the rule. After doing that, we will discuss how the example relates to the situation of an economy as a whole.

We consider an individual who owns a mine, and has a bank deposit. His income comes from the sale of permits to extract ore from the mine, and from interest paid on the bank deposit. The rate of interest is 5%. From Chapter 7, we know that in a fully competitive economy, this means that the price of permits to extract ore, the unit rent, will increase at 5% per year.

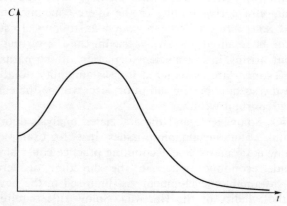

Figure 9.1 Non-sustainable consumption

This is shown in the second column of Table 9.3. Given conditions in ore extraction and the demand for ore, the rate of ore extraction from the mine we are interested in is shown in the third column, and the remaining stock of ore in the fourth. The mine is exhausted in the tenth year. The annual income from the sale of permits is given by the product of the unit rent and the amount extracted, equal to the quantity of permits sold.

Now, suppose that the mine owner decides to consume goods and services to the value of £55 000 each year. The consequent evolution of the values of his two assets, the bank deposit and the mine, is shown in the fifth and sixth columns of Table 9.3. The sum of these two values is his wealth, shown in the final column. This history arises as follows. On the first day of the first year he receives £10 900 for the sale of 10 900 one Tonne permits at £1, which he immediately adds to his bank deposit, increasing it from £1 000 000 to £1 010 900. At 5% interest this deposit increases to £1 061 445 by the last day of the year, on which £55 000 is paid for goods and services consumed during the year. Hence, as shown in the fifth column, at the start of the second year the bank balance stands at £1 006 445. The mine is valued at the stock size, 10 895 Tonnes, times the unit rent, £1.05, which is £93 555, so that the individual's wealth is £1 100 000, as it was on the first day of year 1. On the first day of year 2, receipts from permit sales are $1.05 \times 10 895 = £11 439.75$, which are added to the bank deposit to increase it to £1 017 884.8, which at 5% becomes £1 068 779 by the end of year 2. After paying for the year's consumption, there is £1 013 779 in the bank on the first day of year 3, and the mine is now worth £86 221, so that total wealth is £1 100 000 still.

Continuing like this gives the entries shown in Table 9.3. At the start of year 10 the stock remaining is 2102.66 Tonnes, all of which is extracted in that year. Permit sales realise $1.5511 \times 2102.66 = £3262$, and adding this to £1 096 738 gives £1 100 000 in the bank. At the end of year 10 this has earned £55 000 at 5%, exactly enough to pay the consumption bill, without running down the bank deposit. Thereafter, the mine is worth nothing, but annual consumption expenditure of £55 000 can be sustained as the interest arising from the bank deposit. Furthermore, at 5%, £55 000 is the interest on total wealth of £1 100 000 for years 1 to 10 also. This individual has been following the Hartwick–Solow Rule. In each year he has invested the rent arising from the depletion of the mine asset, which has kept his total wealth intact, and implied a level of consumption equal to the rate of interest times the size of his wealth.

Table 9.4 shows the results of the same calculations where the individual sets the constant level of consumption at £60 000. Given the competitively determined time profile for the unit rent, consistent with efficiency requirements, and the same conditions in extraction and ore demand, the first three columns in Table 9.4 have the same entries as those in Table 9.3, and so does the column showing the value of the mine. The result of not following the Hartwick–Solow Rule appears in the figures for the size of the bank deposit and total wealth. Given that £60 000 is initially larger than 0.05 times total wealth, the bank deposit does not grow fast enough to compensate for

Table 9.3 Sustainable consumption for a mine owner

Year	Unit rent £	Extraction tonnes	Stock tonnes	Bank £	Mine £	Wealth £
1	1	10 900.00	100 000.0	1 000 000	100 000	1 100 000
2	1.0500	10 895.00	89 100.00	1 006 445	93 555	1 100 000
3	1.1025	10 889.75	78 205.00	1 013 779	86 221	1 100 000
4	1.1576	10 884.24	67 315.25	1 022 074	77 926	1 100 000
5	1.2155	10 878.45	56 431.01	1 031 408	68 592	1 100 000
6	1.2763	10 872.37	45 552.57	1 041 862	58 138	1 100 000
7	1.3401	10 865.99	34 680.19	1 053 525	46 475	1 100 000
8	1.4071	10 859.29	23 814.20	1 066 491	33 509	1 100 000
9	1.4775	10 852.25	12 954.91	1 080 859	19 141	1 100 000
10	1.5511	2 102.66	2 102.66	1 096 738	3 262	1 100 000
11	1.6287	0.00	0.00	1 100 000	0	1 100 000
12	1.7101	0.00	0.00	1 100 000	0	1 100 000

Table 9.4 Unsustainable consumption for a mine owner

Year	Unit rent £	Extraction tonnes	Stock tonnes	Bank £	Mine £	Wealth £
1	1	10 900.00	100 000.0	1 000 000	100 000	1 100 000
2	1.0500	10 895.00	89 100.00	1 001 445	93 555	1 095 000
3	1.1025	10 889.75	78 205.00	1 003 529	86 221	1 089 750
4	1.1576	10 884.24	67 315.25	1 006 312	77 926	1 084 238
5	1.2155	10 878.45	56 431.01	1 009 857	68 592	1 078 449
6	1.2763	10 872.37	45 552.57	1 014 234	58 138	1 072 372
7	1.3401	10 865.99	34 680.19	1 019 515	46 475	1 065 990
8	1.4071	10 859.29	23 814.20	1 025 781	33 509	1 059 290
9	1.4775	10 852.25	12 954.91	1 033 114	19 141	1 052 255
10	1.5511	2 102.66	2 102.66	1 041 577	3 262	1 044 839
11	1.6287	0.00	0.00	1 033 656	0	1 033 656
12	1.7101	0.00	0.00	1 025 339	0	1 025 339

the declining value of the mine and total wealth falls. The figures in Table 9.4 for years 11 and 12 are on the basis of holding consumption at £60 000. Clearly, there is some lower constant level of consumption for year 11 and subsequently which is sustainable on the basis of the interest earned on the bank account alone. It is $0.05 \times 1\,033\,656 = £51\,682$. Clearly, if the individual had initially set a constant consumption level lower than £55 000, then his total wealth would have grown over time.

Qualifications and extensions

This consideration of an individual who has income derived from a bank deposit and ownership of a non-renewable resource deposit shows how the

Hartwick–Solow Rule would work for such an individual, and gives some insight into the essential nature of the rule in other contexts. If we consider an economy existing in a world with other economies, where there is complete capital mobility so that overseas investment is possible, the story told for the individual holds for an individual economy with a resource deposit and overseas investments. There will exist a world interest rate, and global efficiency would see the domestic economy following a depletion programme with the unit rent on the resource rising at that rate of interest. If in each period the domestic economy adds the total rent earned from the efficient depletion of its resource stock to its overseas investment portfolio, it will maintain its wealth constant, and will be able to sustain the corresponding consumption level even after it has exhausted its resource stock.

This assumes that the exhaustion of the domestic economy's resource stock has no effect on the state of the world economy, and particularly that it does not affect the global interest rate. However, if we consider a closed economy, or the world economy as a whole, where a non-renewable resource is an essential input to production we cannot simply assume that there exists a 'bank account' which pays a constant rate of interest irrespective of the amount of the resource remaining. What Hartwick (1977) showed was that for a closed economy with a production function [7.48], investing the efficiency rents could hold consumption constant as the resource was depleted. In such an economy, and following the rule, the resource stock would never actually go to zero, but would approach it asymptotically, so that eventually tiny amounts of the resource would be being used with massive amounts of capital, to produce enough output to maintain consumption and increase the capital stock. The numerical example at Table 7.5 can give some sense of what is involved here. Solow (1986) showed that, providing wealth is computed using the proper prices for man-made capital and the resource, in such circumstances, following the rule would keep wealth constant.

What requires emphasis, especially given the enthusiasm with which some have embraced these ideas in relation to, for example, green national income accounting, is that the Hartwick–Solow Rule yields sustainability only if the substitution possibilities in production are such that it is feasible. In the numerical mine owner example considered above, money is perfectly substitutable for money in the production of money, and following the rule delivers sustainability. With the production function [7.47], sustainability is not feasible, and following the Hartwick–Solow Rule cannot deliver it. The rule is necessary but not sufficient. Whether we should assume that, as a matter of fact, substitution possibilities are generally such that sustainability is feasible is a complicated question, about which there is disagreement. Economists typically assume that there is no resource for which it would be correct to assume that the production substitution possibilities are as limited as in [7.47]. Others argue that we should proceed on the assumption that this is often the operative situation: see, for example, Daly and Cobb (1989) or Daly (1995).

The question, in relation to the actual prospects for sustainability for the world economy, is complicated by virtue of many factors that we have not considered here. We have, for example, ignored the rôle of technical progress and innovation. Some argue, in effect, that human ingenuity is such that a technical solution will be found to any resource problem, effectively converting the production function from something like [7.47] to something like [7.46]. Simon (1981) advances this argument forcefully. Others argue that the laws of nature set limits to substitution possibilities: see, for example, Chapman and Roberts (1983). On the other hand, we assumed, implicitly, a constant population size. Clearly, if the population is growing, then constant total consumption implies falling per capita consumption. The operative question is then the sustainability of per capita consumption. This has been considered in the literature, for situations such as case 3 here, and the analysis indicates that in such circumstances, sustainability is feasible only if there is technical progress: see, for example, Solow (1974).

Extending the analysis to include matters such as population growth and technical progress greatly complicates it. Toman *et al.* (1995) survey the literature, and summarise the main results. They discuss recent work done on the simple problem where there is no population growth, no technical progress, and where there is just one non-renewable resource used in production. They note that even in such circumstances, matters are by no means as straightforward as economists sometimes imply. They draw attention, first, to the fact noted above, that sustainability is not guaranteed by following the Hartwick–Solow Rule. It delivers it if it is feasible, but does not itself mean that it is feasible. Second, they note that 'only by measuring resource rents *using shadow prices which reflect the sustainability constraint . . .* will Hartwick's rule provide a correct guide to sustainability' (p. 147, italics in the original). What they mean by this is that if the economy is not currently configured as required for sustainability, then even leaving aside such matters as pollution externalities, using current prices to measure wealth and hence sustainable consumption as the interest on wealth will overestimate the level of consumption that is in fact sustainable. This is clearly very important in relation to the prospects for actually measuring sustainable income, to which we now turn.

9.4   Green national income accounting

National income accounting is the means by which *Gross Domestic Product, GDP*, is measured. GDP growth is seen as a primary objective of economic policy. Since sustainable development appeared on the agenda, there has emerged a widespread view, among both economists and environmentalists, that modifications to national income accounting procedures are crucial to the pursuit of sustainability. According, for example, to Repetto *et al.* (1989):

> A country could exhaust its mineral resources, cut down its forests, erode its soils, pollute its aquifers, and hunt its wildlife to extinction, but measured income would not be affected as these assets disappeared.

Here, 'measured income' is GDP. Repetto *et al.* state that

> politicians, journalists and even sophisticated economists in official agencies
> continue to use GDP growth as the prime measure of economic performance.

and claim that

> only if the basic measures of economic performance ... are brought into
> conformity with a valid definition of income will economic policies be influenced
> toward sustainability.

The call here is for modifications to national income accounting practices
such that what is measured is sustainable income. For similar critiques see,
for examples, Daly and Cobb (1989) and Pearce *et al.* (1989).

Current accounting conventions

We begin with an overview of the current conventions for measuring
national income. These conventions are discussed in general terms in most
introductory economics texts, and in intermediate macroeconomics texts.
Beckerman (1980) provides an extended account of the conventions and the
principles underlying them. National statistical agencies publish detailed
guides to the practices followed in their official national income
publications.

Current national income accounting conventions actually produce a variety
of measures relating to national income. The most widely used are *Gross
National Product, GNP*, and *Gross Domestic Product, GDP*. We will conduct
the discussion in terms of GDP: the distinction between it and GNP is not
especially relevant to sustainability issues. The conventions now used for
GDP measurement have their origin in the information requirements for
management of the macro-economy. For this purpose, what is needed is a
measure of the total demand for the outputs of produced commodities. Given
that GDP measures total demand, it also measures the output produced to
meet that demand. GDP has come to be seen as a measure of economic
performance, or welfare. Indeed, as noted in the quotation above, for many
commentators it effectively became *the* performance indicator. Usher (1980)
discusses the welfare interpretation of national income as measured by
standard conventions.

GDP can be measured in three ways. Given the conventions for national
income accounting, each way of measuring it yields, in principle, the same
numerical result.

First, GDP is the total output sold by firms measured by value added.
Consider a bakery which buys in mixed dough and sells bread. It spends £x
on the dough, and its sales amount to £y. This bakery's contribution to GDP
is £y − £x, the value which it has added to the dough, not £y. The purchase
of the dough is the purchase of an intermediate good, or an input to its
production which has been produced elsewhere in the economy. In measuring
GDP purchases of intermediate goods are netted out.

Second, GDP is the sum of the incomes earned by persons in the economy. This is the most obvious rationale for calling GDP 'national income'. The sum of incomes is equal to the value of total output produced by firms by virtue of the convention that output is measured in terms of value added. If we subtract from a firm's sales receipts the amount that it paid to other firms for intermediate goods, what is left is both the firm's value added and the amount that it necessarily pays to the people who work for it, and to its owners.

Third, GDP is total expenditure by individuals on consumption plus expenditure by firms on items of capital equipment, ie investment. Note that firms expenditure on intermediate goods is not included here, only their expenditure on items of durable capital equipment. The distinction turns on whether or not the purchase by a firm is totally used up in current production. Thus, for the bakery the purchase of dough is not included in its expenditure for the purpose of measuring GDP. The dough is used up in current production. If, on the other hand, the bakery buys a new oven, this is an item of durable capital equipment not used up in current period production, and the expenditure involved is part of GDP.

Given these conventions, each way of measuring GDP should produce the same numerical result. The value added measure of firms' total output equals the incomes generated in firms equals total expenditure on non-intermediate goods. In actuality, the three ways of measuring GDP do not produce the same numbers due to errors arising in the collection of data from the very large number of firms and individuals in an actual economy. To preserve the principle of the conventions, published national income accounts introduce a *residual error term*, and write the final output, expenditure and income numbers as the same after adding in that term. The expenditure measure of GDP is generally regarded as the most reliable. The size of the residual error term varies from year to year, but is often in excess of 0.5% of GDP. In 1991, the UK's GDP was approximately 575 000 millions of £s, of which 0.5% is 2875 millions of £s. National income accounting is not an exact science! It is important to be clear that this is the case. Arguments which turn on differences in a nation's GDP of the order of 0.5% or less should not be taken too seriously.

It is universally agreed that the proper measure of national income for purposes of monitoring national economic performance and welfare is *Net Domestic Product, NDP*. This is GDP less that part of it required to make good the depreciation of capital equipment as it is used in production. In principle, depreciation for a period is measured as the reduction in the value of the economy's existing stock of capital equipment over that period, on account of its use in production. In fact, GDP is much more widely used than NDP. The reason for this is that it is very difficult to measure depreciation accurately. National income statisticians prefer a number which is an accurate measure of an admittedly un-satisfactory concept to an inaccurate measure of a more satisfactory concept. This needs to be kept in mind when we come to consider proposals for modifying national

income measurement so as to account for the depreciation of environmental assets.

The fact of international trade requires a modification to the above
definition of GDP. The production of goods for export generates incomes in
the domestic economy, and adds to GDP. Imports are goods consumed
domestically but produced, and generating incomes, overseas. Total
expenditure in the domestic economy needs to be reduced by the amount of
imports, if it is to correspond to domestic income and production. So, for a
trading economy, GDP is measured as total domestic expenditure plus
exports net of imports.

Consumption expenditure is by private households, investment expenditure
by private firms. Government also spends on consumption and investment,
and in so doing incomes are generated and output produced. It is, therefore,
necessary to add government to private expenditure in measuring national
income. With C for private consumption, I for private investment, G for
government expenditure, X for exports, and M for imports, the basic national
income accounting conventions define GDP in period t as

$$GDP_t = C_t + I_t + G_t + (X_t - M_t) \qquad [9.5]$$

and then, with D for depreciation, we have

$$NDP_t = GDP_t - D_t \qquad [9.6]$$

Environmental adjustment to national income measurement: theory

The central idea involved in adjusting the way that national income is defined
so that it properly measures sustainable national income is to extend the
concept of depreciation so that it covers environmental assets, as well as the
assets which are items of man made capital equipment.

For any asset, or set of assets taken together, depreciation is given by

$$D_t = V_t - V_{t-1} \qquad [9.7]$$

where V_{t-1} is its value at the start of period t and V_t its value at the end of
that period. In the previous section we considered an individual with two
assets, a bank account and a mine. We saw that if this individual managed
his affairs so that the depreciation on the mine asset was exactly offset by an
increase in the bank deposit asset, total depreciation across both assets was
zero, and wealth was maintained intact. With V_b for the bank asset and V_m
for the mine asset,

$$V_{bt} - V_{bt-1} = -(V_{mt} - V_{mt-1}) \qquad [9.8]$$

implies

$$D_t = (V_{bt} - V_{bt-1}) + (V_{mt} - V_{mt-1}) = 0$$

for the asset portfolio as a whole, so that

$$W_t - W_{t-1} = 0 \tag{9.9}$$

where W stands for wealth, the total value of the asset portfolio. We also saw that managing his affairs so that [9.8] and [9.9] held involved investing the total rent income from the mine in the bank deposit, and that given [9.9] the constant consumption level that went with doing this was equivalent to the interest on W.

Generally, for an individual we can write

$$W_t - W_{t-1} = Y_t - C_t - D_t \tag{9.10}$$

where Y is income, C is consumption, and D is the depreciation of the individual's asset portfolio. If we impose the condition that wealth must not decline over the period, this becomes

$$0 = Y_t - C_{\text{max},t} - D_t \tag{9.11}$$

where $C_{\text{max},t}$ is the maximum level of consumption consistent with non-declining wealth. Rearranging [9.11] we can write

$$C_{\text{max},t} = Y_t - D_t$$

and defining *sustainable income* as the maximum that can be consumed without reducing wealth, this gives

$$Y_{\text{sus},t} = Y_t - D_t \tag{9.12}$$

where $Y_{\text{sus},t}$ stands for sustainable income. In the mine owner example, income Y was the interest paid on the bank account plus the receipts from the sale of extraction permits. Sustainable income was what was left out of this income after making provision for depreciation such that wealth remained constant.

When we impart welfare significance to national income, we are effectively treating the nation as an individual. If we ignore environmental considerations for a moment, NDP is sustainable national income, as it is income, GDP, less the amount required to make good depreciation of the nation's wealth, the total value of its stock of capital equipment, as indicated in [9.6] and [9.7]. In an important, but mathematically difficult, paper, Weitzman (1976) showed that, assuming a perfectly competitive economy, national income as NDP could be interpreted as the equivalent of the interest payment on the nation's wealth, as the value of its stock of assets in the form of capital equipment, and that consuming NDP would keep that wealth intact. Consumption in excess of NDP would reduce wealth and the future capacity to consume. Mäler (1991), which is also mathematically difficult, adopted the same theoretical approach, and recognised the rôle in economic activity of environmental assets, as well as man made items of capital equipment. Essentially, he found that the same basic idea held, but that the concept of wealth had to be extended to include the value of environmental assets, so that

$$Y_{\text{sus},t} = Y_t - D_{kt} - D_{et} = Y_t - (V_{kt} - V_{kt-1}) - (V_{et} - V_{et-1}) \qquad [9.13]$$

where the subscript k refers to the total value of man made capital assets and e refers to the total value of environmental assets. With Y_t as GDP, [9.13] says that the proper measure of sustainable income is NDP, $Y_t - D_{kt}$, minus the depreciation of total environmental assets. The claim that in so far as current conventions for national income accounting do not allow for the depreciation of environmental assets, they overstate sustainable national income – noted at the start of this section – is supported by theoretical analysis. To the extent that this is not done, and environmental asset depreciation is ignored, measured and reported NDP will overstate the sustainable level of national income.

Consumption equal to or less than sustainable income as defined in [9.13] is sustainable, and if equal is equivalent to consuming the interest on wealth defined to include the value of environmental assets. The result [9.13] is effectively a different way of stating the Hartwick–Solow Rule. If that rule is followed consumption will be such that wealth is kept constant. Two points made in connection with the discussion of the rule in the previous section need to be repeated here, in a slightly different form. First, if [9.13] is to properly measure sustainable income, the prices used to value all assets need to be the 'right' prices. We return to this below. Second, defining sustainable income, as in [9.13], to recognise the dependence of economic activity on environmental assets does not guarantee that there is such a thing as sustainable national income. The question of the feasibility of sustainable consumption is not a matter of proper definition and measurement. It depends on the possibilities for substitution in production, as discussed in the previous section.

Environmental adjustment to national income measurement: practice

The practical possibilities for environmental modifications to national income accounting conventions have been under active consideration by a number of individuals and institutions for a number of years. Here we provide an account of the essentials of some recent developments, subsequent to the emergence of the idea of sustainable development. The United Nations Statistical Office, UNSTAT, has proposed draft guidelines for new national income accounting conventions, the System of integrated Environmental and Economic Accounting, SEEA. These guidelines involve adjusting the NDP figure for a period by the 'environmental cost' of economic activity in the period, where *environmental cost* is the difference between the opening and closing value of the stock of environmental assets. An important feature of the proposal is that it would leave intact the current conventions for the measurement of GDP and NDP, so that adoption of the proposal would mean that figures on these constructs would continue to be available on a consistent basis with past data. The balance sheets envisaged for environmental assets are, therefore, sometimes referred to as 'satellite accounts'.

Chapter 2 in Bartelmus (1994) provides a concise account of the SEEA proposals. Bartelmus *et al.* (1993) provide a somewhat more detailed account. Working through the details of the proposals is heavy going, but the essential point follows directly from the discussion of the theoretical approach to the problem above. Environmental cost, *EC*, is defined as

$$EC_t = \Sigma a_{it} v_{it} - \Sigma a_{it-1} v_{it-1} \tag{9.14}$$

where a_i represents the physical measure of the ith environmental asset and v_i the unit value assigned to that asset. EC_t is the change in the balance sheet for environmental assets over period t. It is conceptually the same as $V_{et} - V_{et-1}$ in [9.13]. Then, Environmentally Adjusted Net Domestic Product is defined as

$$EDP_t = NDP_t - EC_t \tag{9.15}$$

and *EDP* is the measure of sustainable income.

To satisfy the requirements established by the theory, the *satellite environmental accounts* should cover all the environmental assets that are involved in production and consumption. However, what appears to be actually envisaged in these proposals is that only those assets that can readily be assigned a monetary value from market data would be included. Renewable and non-renewable natural resource stocks would be included; where property rights are absent asset valuation would be inferred from market transactions based on exploitation of the assets. As well as covering natural resource depletion, it is envisaged that the degradation of the environment by way of waste discharges into it would also be covered. Here, degradation would be inferred from estimates of 'maintenance costs', i.e. the costs of action that could have prevented the degradation: 'Maintenance costs are thus potential costs of either achieving the quantity and quality levels of natural assets at the beginning of the accounting period or, if such levels cannot be 'reasonably' attained, at desirable environmental sustainability standards' (Bartelmus 1994, p. 48).

Clearly, measuring the degradation component of the environmental cost adjustment is going to involve judgement, and an element of arbitrariness. Even in the case of non-renewable natural resources where there are usually clearly defined property rights, there are differing views about how in practice asset value depreciation is to be calculated from the available data. The principle for assessing depreciation is clear and un-ambiguous – depreciation is the reduction in asset value as determined in competitive markets. The practical problem is that markets for natural resource assets are generally imperfect, and that anyway asset valuations are not directly revealed on a regular basis, so that they have to be inferred from data on the price fetched by the extracted resource and the costs of extraction. Some of those working in the area recommend the *user cost method* (see El Serafy in Ahmad *et al.* 1989), which involves making assumptions about the lifetime of the resource stock, and using price data, and interest rate assumptions to compute depreciation via a calculation of the sum that would need to be set aside from receipts so as to provide a permanent income stream equal in size to current rent. Others use the *net price method*, which simply calculates the opening and closing values of the stock as physical size multiplied by current unit rent. The various methods generally produce different results: see Hartwick and Hageman (1993) and Hartwick (1990) for a thorough discussion.

It has been argued, by Pearce *et al.* (1989) for example, that *environmental defensive expenditures* should be deducted from the measure of NDP to arrive at a figure for sustainable income. These are expenditures to prevent or remedy environmental damage. Given the current conventions, expenditure to clean up a polluted lake would, for example, actually increase national income. The argument is that this makes no sense if national income is to be regarded as a welfare measure. The SEEA proposals do not involve the subtraction of defensive expenditures from NDP. It is actually very difficult to definitively identify and measure such expenditures. More fundamentally, such subtraction might open the door to questioning the whole basis of measured national income as a welfare indicator. Leaving the natural environment aside, much of the expenditure counted in national income could be regarded as defensive – we eat and incur medical expenses to stay alive, we buy clothes to defend against the weather and social disapproval, and so on. The SEEA proposals do, however, involve identifying and reporting within the accounting system defensive environmental expenditures. Note though that the maintenance costs which form part of environmental cost are in the nature of potential, but not actual, defensive expenditures.

We now look at some exercises in green national income accounting. It appears that no governmental statistical agency has yet published official EDP data. Some, for example the Australian Bureau of Statistics, have published monetary balance sheets covering some environmental assets, and a number publish environmental asset data in physical terms (see Pearce *et al.* 1989 or Peskin with Lutz 1990). Work on the UNSTAT proposals included the preparation of illustrative accounts for a hypothetical country, see Bartelmus *et al.* (1993) and Bartelmus (1994), and of preliminary accounts for Mexico and Papua New Guinea, see chapters in Lutz (1993). The quotations from Repetto *et al.* (1989) at the start of this section are taken from the introduction to a report in which a World Resources Institute team adjusted official national income measures for Indonesia for their estimates of the depreciation of three environmental assets – oil deposits, timber, and soil. They proceeded by first constructing physical accounts, then applying unit values. In the case of oil opening stocks were valued at the current market price of the extracted oil less estimated average extraction cost. Closing stocks were computed by subtracting extraction during the year and adding new discoveries, and valued in the same way as the opening stocks using the

Table 9.5 GDP and an EDP estimate for Indonesia 1971–84

Year	GDP	EDP	EDP/GDP
1971	1	1	1.20
1972	1.09	0.90	0.99
1973	1.22	0.97	0.96
1974	1.32	1.48	1.36
1975	1.38	0.98	0.85
1976	1.47	1.12	0.92
1977	1.60	1.08	0.81
1978	1.73	1.19	0.78
1979	1.83	1.19	0.78
1980	2.01	1.28	0.76
1981	2.17	1.48	0.82
1982	2.22	1.58	0.86
1983	2.32	1.49	0.78
1984	2.44	1.68	0.83

price ruling at the end of the period. This is an application of the net price method. The procedure followed with timber is the same except that it allows for natural growth over the year. The physical data here is recognised as being less firmly based than in the case of oil. For soil erosion, estimated physical losses over the year were valued using estimates of the loss of agricultural output entailed. It is recognised that the results here are not firm.

Table 9.5 here reports the results obtained by Repetto *et al.* in index number form, where EDP is GDP minus the depreciation of the three environmental assets considered. The average per annum growth rates are 7.1% for GDP and 4.1% for EDP. EDP grows more slowly than GDP over the period 1971 to 1984. The fourth column shows the ratio of the EDP estimate to GDP, and shows that the former behaves more erratically than the latter. This is principally due to the effect on the former of changes in the price of extracted oil, and of new discoveries of oil. The EDP figures for 1973 and 1974 show the effects of the increase in the world price of oil. If EDP is understood as sustainable income, these figures show sustainable income increasing by 51% in one year! This potential for wide year on year change in EDP, due to new discoveries and/or market price changes, is one of the reasons why some official statistical agencies favour keeping the asset balance sheets as satellite accounts, and not using changes in them to adjust the national income figures.

Young (1990) undertook a similar exercise for Australia, with the results shown in Table 9.6. Young treated all mineral resources in the way that Repetto *et al.* treated just oil, and also followed them in considering from among the renewable resources only timber. However, Young's valuation of the depreciation of this asset is based only on an estimate of its implications for wildlife habitat loss. As regards soil degradation, Young used estimates of the value of agricultural productivity losses. Unlike Repetto *et al.*, Young incorporates an estimate of the degradation of environmental assets by pollution. This is done by subtracting from GDP an estimate of expenditure by households and government to offset the effects of pollution. We noted above that the deduction of such defensive expenditures is not part of the SEEA proposals. Young describes his calculations as 'back of the envelope', and claims to have been 'environmentally generous' in producing his figures.

In Table 9.6, Young's results are reported in index number form for GDP, EDP_1 and EDP_2, where

$EDP_1 = $ GDP $-$ depreciation on account of land degradation

$-$ depreciation on account of timber production

$-$ defensive expenditures

and

$EDP_2 = EDP_1 - $ depreciation on account of mineral depletion

'Pop' stands for population, and the last two columns give the index numbers for GDP per capita and EDP_2 per capita. Shown at the bottom of each column is the average annual growth rate implied by the index numbers above. Several points are worth noting. First, the behaviour of GDP and EDP_1 is quite similar. Second, as with the Repetto *et al.* figures, EDP_2 is quite erratic over time. This is, again, due to the effects of price changes and new discoveries. Third, the average growth rate for EDP_2 is actually substantially greater than that for GDP. In 1980 the EDP_2 to GDP ratio was 0.84: in 1988 the ratio was 0.97. The fourth point concerns the adjustment for population growth. Clearly, if we wish to give national income a welfare interpretation, it needs to be measured per capita. Official national statistical publications do not generally report on a per capita basis, and commentary is frequently based on those unadjusted figures. The Repetto *et al.* results are for Indonesia's total national income, not per capita national income. For Australia, Table 9.6 shows that adjusting for population growth reduces GDP growth by 2% per annum, whereas adjusting GDP for environmental depreciation actually increases national income growth. Fifth, on these figures, per capita sustainable income after allowing for environmental depreciation, is growing at 3.3% per annum.

It should be noted that Young, and Repetto *et al.*, do not subtract from GDP the depreciation of man made capital. If this were done, it would reduce their EDP figures in terms of levels, but it is unlikely that it would much affect the growth rate results.

The prospects for measuring sustainable national income

The results of Repetto *et al.* (1989) and Young (1990) are subject to a number of recognised omissions and deficiencies. The question that we wish to consider here is whether it is reasonable to expect that with more effort, sustainable national income could be accurately measured. If this is to be

Table 9.6 GDP and EDP estimates for Australia 1980–8

Year	GDP	EDP$_1$	EDP$_2$	GDP/Pop	EDP$_2$/Pop
1980	1	1	1	1	1
1981	1.03	1.03	1.16	1.01	1.13
1982	1.07	1.07	1.14	1.03	1.10
1983	1.04	1.03	1.15	0.98	1.09
1984	1.09	1.09	1.04	1.00	0.96
1985	1.17	1.17	1.34	1.06	1.22
1986	1.22	1.22	1.62	1.08	1.44
1987	1.25	1.26	1.09	1.09	0.95
1988	1.31	1.32	1.52	1.12	1.30
Growth rate	3.4%	3.5%	5.4%	1.4%	3.3%

done, all of the environmental assets relevant to economic activity need to be accounted for in measuring environmental cost. This is an impossible task. As will become clear in the next section, where we re-visit the question of the dependence of economic activity on the natural environment (looked at previously in 1.2), we cannot definitively list such assets, never mind measure changes in their physical magnitudes. Even if we could do this, there would remain the valuation problem. The SEEA, and related, proposals envisage that valuation would be based on market prices as much as possible. Existing market prices, and hence valuations derived from them, reflect market failures of various kinds. The SEEA literature recognises that for many of the environmental assets of concern, there are no market prices (on account of the absence of private property rights). As a long run objective, it is apparently envisaged that valuations for such assets will be obtained by the techniques, such as contingent valuation, for non-market valuation discussed in Chapter 8. We noted there that economists disagree about whether such techniques can be expected, even with further refinement, to produce accurate estimates of willingness to pay. We also noted the view that consumer willingness to pay is not the proper way to value environmental assets.

The valuation question is important, because if the wrong values are used to calculate wealth and sustainable income, using those values would send the wrong signals, even if there were available all the necessary physical information about environmental assets. Some commentators seem to take the view that precise valuation is not really necessary, that so long as national income is measured giving environmental assets some positive value, where current conventions give them zero value, matters will be improved from the point of view of achieving sustainable development. The numerical example in Table 9.7 is constructed to show the dangers that may be involved in adopting such a view.

We suppose that there are just two environmental assets, R_1 and R_2 and just one type of man-made capital equipment, K. The numbers refer to quantities

Table 9.7 Valuation and EDP measurement

Quantities	K	R_1	R_2	
t	100	100	100	
$t+1$	100	110	80	
Conventional prices				
	p_K	p_1	p_2	W
t	1	0	0	100
$t+1$	1	0	0	100
Correct prices				
	p_K	p_1	p_2	W
t	1	1	2	400
$t+1$	1	0.9	2.1	367
Incorrect prices				
	p_K	p_1	p_2	W
t	1	3	1	500
$t+1$	1	2.9	1.1	507

and prices at the start of some period, t, and at the end of that period, $t+1$. Over the period, depreciation of K is made good, and there are 100 units of K at the start and end of the period. The physical stock of R_1 increases by 10 units, that of R_2 decreases by 20 units. The prices shown as 'Conventional' are those used for wealth measurement when no account is taken of environmental assets, so that p_1 and p_2 are both zero, and p_K is set at 1 to make the arithmetic simple. The 'Correct' prices are the relative prices which properly reflect the relative scarcities of these two environmental assets in relation to the sustainability objective. Using these prices with the physical changes given, wealth is reduced over the period. If these correct prices are not known, and wrongly estimated as shown under 'Incorrect Prices', using the estimated prices will indicate that wealth has increased over the period. The conclusion would be that the level of consumption during the period was sustainable, whereas in fact it was not. The size of the misleading signal with these incorrect prices is larger than with the conventional, zero, prices for the environmental assets.

The point being made here is not that this sort of outcome is inevitable. It is that it is possible, and that if it occurs, the signals sent by measurements of total wealth and environmentally adjusted national income will be misleading. To illustrate the potential for this kind of problem, suppose that R_2 is a termite species and R_1 is some charismatic mammal species. Ecologists appear to understand that termites are generally much more important in ecosystem function than charismatic mammals, in the sense that extinction of one of the former species would have major effects on ecosystem function whereas extinction of one of the latter would not. If, in the absence of property rights and markets, these two species were valued by asking people what they were willing to pay to save them from extinction, one can be reasonably sure that R_1 would be assigned a higher value than R_2. Of course, if all individuals were aware of the rôles of the two species in ecosystem functioning, cared about ecosystem functioning, and if the contingent valuation could be relied upon to reveal their true relative valuations, R_2 would come out with a higher value than R_1. To list these conditions is to make the point about the possible outcome in practice.

In fact, as noted above, over and above this, we do not know the complete list of all relevant environmental assets, and for those that are known to be relevant, accurate physical measurement is typically impossible. It seems clear that there is no real prospect of accurately measuring sustainable income. The operative question is then whether the implementation of proposals such as the SEEA would actually promote the cause of sustainability. There appears to be a view that, notwithstanding that EDP or some variant thereof is going to be an imperfect measure of sustainable income, publishing data on it will protect the environment and promote sustainability. The argument is roughly as follows. If we make any adjustment to national income for the environmental effects of economic activity, that adjustment will be negative. Lowering the national income figure will make people see the error of their ways, and cause them to do less damage to environmental assets. In fact, as shown above in Table 9.6, this is not always what happens. However, even if it could be granted that the adjustments would always be downwards, it would not necessarily follow that this would modify national policy and individual behaviour in the intended direction. A government simply informed that national income had been lower, and growing more slowly, than previously thought, could as likely respond with policies in pursuit of higher income and faster growth, resulting in increased environmental damage, as with policies to protect the environment. Of course, the response here by those favouring attempts at EDP measurement would be that this would be temporary. Any such inappropriate response would further reduce measured EDP, and eventually the government would see the error of its ways. While this may be true, there is a lot to be said for a more direct approach, which is to argue for policies to promote sustainability, such as imposing taxes on environmentally damaging activities.

Finally here we should note that although GDP/NDP is widely used as a welfare indicator, there are a number of long recognised problems with its use in this way, which have nothing to do with environmental considerations: see, for example, Beckerman (1980) or Usher (1980). Some of the more important are as follows. First, there are the problems associated with defensive expenditure noted above. Second, if increasing NDP is to be interpreted as increasing welfare for the representative household, it is necessary to assume that that preferences are unchanging. While this may be a reasonable assumption for comparisons spanning a few years, it clearly is not when comparing situations decades apart. Third, NDP completely ignores a wide range of economic activity, such as that taking place within households, except in so far as it entails market purchases. If a man paints his house it does not show up in NDP except via bought tools and paint, whereas if he pays somebody else to do it the payment is an addition to

NDP. Fourth, changes in NDP take no account of changes in leisure, except in so far as they have implications for commodity purchases. If the average working week fell by one hour, with no follow on effects, NDP would not change. Fifth, there is the question of the distribution of incomes across households, on which NDP gives no information.

Alternative approaches

Given these sorts of problems, some economists interested in sustainability have taken the view that NDP is not the place to start. Daly and Cobb (1989) make a number of adjustments to private consumption in order to derive, for the USA 1950–86, an Index of Sustainable Economic Welfare, ISEW. Subsequently, ISEW series have been constructed for a number of other countries. Daly and Cobb make adjustments for: changes in the distribution of incomes; extra-market household labour; some defensive expenditures; resource depletion; environmental degradation. Not everybody would agree with the welfare judgements embedded in Daly and Cobb's calculations. Leisure is not accounted for, and an increase in unpaid household labour, other things equal, increases the level of the ISEW. Where ISEWs have been produced for other countries, they do not necessarily have the same arguments as the original.

Some economists argue that it is pointless to try to reduce everything of interest to a single index number, and that the cause of promoting economic management for sustainable economic welfare would be better served by reporting movements in a small number of environmental and economic indicators: see, for examples, Anderson (1991) and Young (1992).

The view that sustainable income, or sustainable economic welfare, cannot be properly measured does not imply the view that there is no point in collecting and publishing data on environmental assets. On the contrary, regularly available comprehensive physical environmental balance sheet data, on the a_{it} and a_{it-1} in [9.14], is precisely what is needed for the improved understanding of economy–environment interdependencies that is necessary for management for sustainability. As noted above, some countries have already instituted this kind of physical natural resource accounting. A number of countries publish 'state of the environment reports', where the data is in biophysical terms, and where it is organised according to environmental classifications rather than economic categories. Parker and Hope (1992) provide a brief survey of state of the environment reporting around the world. These reports are intended to promote informed public debate about the natural environment and its protection, rather than to be of direct use in environmental management. They generally focus on flora and fauna, rather than non-renewable resources.

One sustainability relevant indicator follows fairly directly from the Hartwick–Solow Rule. Recall that this rule says that it is necessary, but not sufficient, for constant consumption that the rents arising in the intertemporally efficient exploitation of natural resources be invested in man-made capital. A sustainability relevant indicator would be the ratio of net investment in capital equipment, i.e. total investment minus depreciation as reported in the existing national income accounts, to total natural resource rents. It should not be difficult for most national statistical agencies to compute the ratio required, but currently they do not. Natural resource rents as such are not generally reported in national income accounts. However, they could be approximated by deducting from profits, or gross operating surplus, in the resource exploiting industries, an estimate of payments for capital and entrepreneurial services. Pearce and Atkinson (1993) report the results of an exercise of this nature: see also Pearce and Atkinson (1995). They compare total investment with a figure for the total of depreciation on made capital and the estimated depreciation of 'natural capital', which is a term now widely used to refer to generally environmental assets. If investment is greater than the sum of the two depreciations, it could be said that a necessary condition for sustainability is likely being approximately satisfied, subject to caveats about the accuracy of the depreciation of natural capital, and of man made capital. It is necessary to say 'likely' and 'approximately' because the Hartwick–Solow Rule requires a fully competitive economy and the investment of the efficiency rents, rather than the rents actually arising in economies that are not fully competitive. Of the 18 countries considered in Pearce and Atkinson (1993), 10 have net investment equal to or greater than total depreciation. The eight for which a necessary condition for sustainability is not apparently being satisfied are all developing countries.

Proops and Atkinson (1996) consider the implications for this sort of sustainability indicator of the fact that national economies are open to trade. Given trade, an economy's inputs to its production and consumption may involve the depreciation of overseas, rather than domestic, environmental assets. This is sometimes referred to as 'exporting unsustainability'. Japan, for example, imports most of its raw materials, while having a high level of domestic saving and investment. The measure used by Pearce and Atkinson would, for Japan, ignore the depreciation of overseas environmental assets, but count the domestic investment in man made capital. Using input–output analysis methods, Proops and Atkinson develop a measure which can account for the depreciation of overseas environmental assets. They report results for a variant of the measure used by Pearce and Atkinson both on the assumption of a closed economy and when accounting for international trade and overseas resource depletion, for several regional groupings of national economies. They find that the conclusion on whether such economies are satisfying the necessary condition for sustainability varies as to whether the closed or open economy measure is used.

Actually, given international trade in goods and services and international capital mobility, it is questionable whether it makes a great deal of sense to think about sustainability in national terms. It is also the case, as will be discussed in the next three sections, that for many environmental problems, it is the global environment, rather than the environment of a particular nation, that it is the appropriate unit of analysis. Given this, a Proops and Atkinson open economy type measure might be interpreted as showing contributions, positive or negative, to global sustainability rather than whether a particular economy is behaving consistently with the requirements for its own sustainability.

9.5   Economy–environment interdependence

We considered the relationship between economic activity and the environment in 1.2. In the light of the literature that has emerged in relation to sustainable development, we now re-visit that topic.

Economic activity takes place within, and is part of, the system which is the earth and its atmosphere. This system itself has an environment, the rest of the universe. The biosphere is:

> The region of the earth and its atmosphere in which life exists. It is an envelope extending from up to 6000 metres above to 10 000 metres below sea level and embraces alpine plant life and the ocean deeps. The special conditions which exist in the biosphere to support life are: a supply of water; a supply of usable energy; the existence of interfaces, ie areas where the liquid, solid and gaseous states meet; the presence of nitrogen, phosphorous, potassium and other essential nutrients and trace elements; a suitable temperature range; and a supply of air.
>
> (Holister and Porteous 1976).

Figure 9.2 is a schematic representation of economy–environment interdependence.

The heavy black lined box represents the biosphere, which is a thermodynamically closed system, in that it exchanges energy but not matter with its environment. The biosphere receives inputs of solar radiation. Some of that radiation is absorbed and drives biospheric processes. Some is reflected back into space. This is represented by the arrows crossing the heavy black line at the top of Figure 9.2. Matter does not cross the heavy black line at all, meteorites and space craft aside. The balance between energy absorption and reflection determines the way the global climate system functions. The energy in and out arrows are shown passing through three boxes, which represent three of the functions that the environment performs in relation to economic activity. This is to indicate that it is the energetic openness of the biosphere which drives these three functions. It also drives the fourth function, represented by the heavy black lined box itself, which is the provision of the life support services which hold the whole system together. Note that the three boxes intersect one with another and that the heavy black line passes through them. This is to indicate that the four functions interact with one another.

As compared with the representation in Figure 1.4, Figure 9.2 does three important things:

1. It makes it explicit that economic activity takes place *within* the natural environment, which is a thermodynamically closed system.
2. It introduces a fourth function for the environment in relation to economic activity, the provision of life support services.

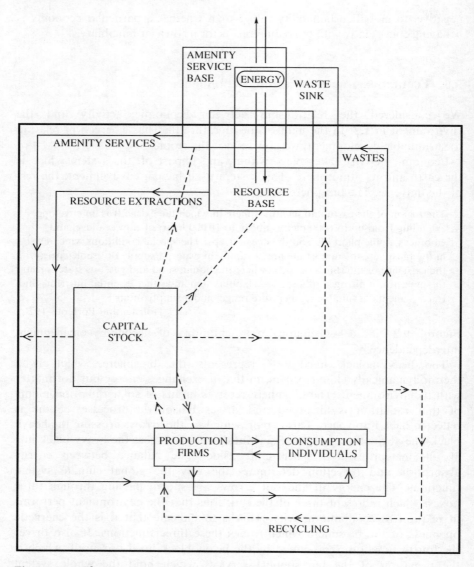

Figure 9.2   The economy in the environment

3.   It introduces possibilities for substituting the services of capital
     equipment for environmental services.

The discussion of economy–environment interdependence in terms of
Figure 9.2 which follows is neither rigorous nor comprehensive. Readers
interested in a proper account of the way the biosphere functions should
consult an environmental science text, such as Watt (1973) for example, and/
or an ecology text, such as Krebs (1972) for example. Bowler (1992) is a

history of the environmental sciences. Thermodynamics, in relation to sustainability issues, is covered in Peet (1992). Perrings (1987) provides a mathematical model of the relationship of economic activity to the natural environment.

Life support functions

Over and above serving as resource base, waste sink and amenity base, as discussed in 1.2, the biosphere currently provides the basic life support functions for humans. While the range of environmental conditions that humans are biologically equipped to cope with is greater than for most other species, there are limits to the tolerable. We have, for example, quite specific requirements in terms of breathable air. The range of temperatures that we can exist in is wide in relation to conditions on earth, but narrow in relation to the range on other planets in the solar system. Humans have minimum requirements for water input. And so on and so on. The biosphere functions now in such manner that humans can exist in it. Rather than try to provide an exhaustive account of the life support functions of the biosphere, we will consider two aspects of the matter, which illustrate the differentiation of this function from the three discussed in 1.2 and subsequently, and the interconnections involved.

Consider first solar radiation. This is relevant to the resource base, in so far as it is solar radiation which drives photosynthesis, and hence is the basis for the existence of most species of flora and fauna, some of which are exploited as renewable natural resources. For some people at least, sunbathing, ie exposing the skin to solar radiation, is an environmental amenity service. In fact, solar radiation as it arrives at the earth's atmosphere is harmful to humans. There it includes the ultraviolet wavelength UV-B, which causes skin cancer, adversely affects the immune system, and can cause eye cataracts. UV-B radiation adversely affects other living things as well. Solar radiation arriving at the surface of the earth has much less UV-B than it does arriving at the atmosphere. Ozone in the stratosphere absorbs UV-B, performing a life support function by filtering solar radiation. In the absence of stratospheric ozone, it is questionable whether human life could exist. Currently, stratospheric ozone is being depleted by the release into the atmosphere of Chlorofluorocarbons, CFCs, which are compounds which exist only by virtue of human economic activity. They were invented for their useful properties in a variety of production and consumption contexts, and have been in use since the 1940s. Their ozone depleting properties were recognised in the 1980s, and policy to reduce this form of pollution is now in place. Notwithstanding this, it is anticipated that human skin cancer rates will increase substantially, and adverse effects on the growth of organisms at the base of many food chains are possible. For further discussion of ozone depletion see Meadows et al. (1992).

Consider next biodiversity. Many species of flora and fauna are exploited as renewable resource inputs to production. Many species are involved in the transformation of the wastes that are discharged into the environment, and contribute to its assimilative capacities. The amenity services that individuals derive from the environment are dependant on the existence in it of flora and fauna. In each of these cases, the environmental function of interest can typically be identified as being based upon particular species. The number of species currently existing is unknown, but is certainly much larger than the number of species that can be identified as being directly involved in resource base, waste assimilation and amenity service provision. This does not mean that the species not thus identifiable as of direct concern to humans are, from the human perspective, redundant.

The current functioning of the biosphere involves all extant species. Some may be more important than others, but rather little is known about this. It should be presumed that the extinction of any species will change the way the biosphere functions. Such changes may, considered separately, be beneficial or harmful to human interests, in terms of the environmental functions which are resource base, wastes assimilation and amenity service provision. Again, very little is known about this. What is clear is that the extinction of any species reduces the pool of genetic material in existence. Such reduction can be presumed deleterious to human interests on two counts. First, a species not currently regarded as directly useful may turn out to be regarded as directly useful in the future. Second, genetic diversity is the basis on which natural selection works to produce evolution. Evolutionary processes can be regarded as part of the life support function of biosphere. We can be reasonably certain that the environment will change over time. To keep it functioning in human interests may require the emergence of new species. The potential for such emergence is reduced to the extent that the size of the currently existing gene pool is reduced.

Function interactions

The relationships between economic activity and the natural environment are pervasive and complex. The complexity is enhanced when we recognise that the four classes of function that we have distinguished each interact one with another. In Figure 9.2 this is indicated by having the three boxes intersect one with another, and jointly with the heavy black line representing the life support function. What is involved can be illustrated by considering the global climate system and the rôle of the so-called greenhouse gases. The presence of these gases in the atmosphere affects the balance between energy flows into and out of the earth system, making the earth's atmosphere warmer than it would otherwise be. Without the presence in the atmosphere of these gases, the mean surface temperature would be some 33°C lower, and life on earth would almost certainly not exist. The basic physics of the climate system and the rôle of the greenhouse gases are explained in a reasonably non-technical way in, for example, Leggett (1990): Houghton et al. (1990) is more authoritative, but more difficult to read. Common (1995), in Ch. 10, provides a brief overview and further references.

The major greenhouse gas is carbon dioxide. It, like the other greenhouse gases, is a natural constituent of the earth's atmosphere. However, in the last two centuries carbon dioxide concentrations in the atmosphere have been increasing as a result of human activities, notably fossil fuel combustion. The majority view amongst competent scientific commentators is that it should be assumed that this will lead to increasing global average temperatures, with the rate of increase greater than anything that the global system has experienced in the last 10,000 years, and rapid by the standards of the last 1,000,000 years.

The anticipated consequences of global climate change are a matter of uncertainty, and some dispute. However, if global warming does occur at the rate envisaged by majority scientific opinion, some of the broad features of responses in terms of the functions of the biosphere in relation to human interests are reasonably clear. In terms of resource availability, there would, first, be losses in low lying coastal areas due to sea level rise. Changes in regional climates would mean changes in the crops that could be grown there. Some crops and wild species in some areas would grow faster with higher temperatures and carbon dioxide concentrations. Others would grow more slowly. The interactive effects of increased ultra violet radiation with higher temperatures and carbon dioxide concentrations on species are largely unknown. Matters are further complicated by the fact that global warming would likely be accompanied by increased cloud cover. About all that can reliably be said is that the geographical patterns of availability of renewable resources and agricultural crops would change.

In terms of waste assimilative functions there is also little definitive that can be said beyond that changes would occur. To take just one example, the assimilative capacity of a river for organic sewage decreases as water temperature increases. On the other hand, it is expected that high temperatures would generally be accompanied by increased rainfall, which would suggest greater rates of stream flow and hence increased assimilative capacity in river systems. But again, it is expected that while average rainfall would increase this would in many areas be accompanied by greater variability over time. Increased average rainfall is not inconsistent with increased incidence of periods without rain. To the extent that this occurred there would be an increased temporal variability in the assimilative capacity of a river.

As regards amenity services, the direct implications of global warming might be thought to depend fairly closely on where one lives. Whereas the inhabitants of Siberia might welcome warmer winters, the inhabitants of, say, Athens might not welcome warmer summers. Assessment of the overall impact would also be expected to depend on one's inclinations. In Australia, for example, it would be expected that opportunities for skiing would diminish, which would trouble some Australians, while others would welcome the reduction in the impact of skiing on the natural environment.

For some commentators, it is in the area of what are here called life support services that the possible implications of global warming are seen as most worrying. This worry arises via the prospects for biodiversity in relation to the anticipated rate of climate change. As noted above this anticipated rate is greater than is thought to have occurred in the last 10,000 years. Most species of flora have quite narrow ranges of climatic tolerance. Adaptation to climate change would involve genetic evolution and/or migration. The rates at which either of these processes can occur is slow relative to that anticipated for climate change, and the prospect envisaged is of the extinction of many species of flora. This would, in turn, have implications for species of fauna which have evolved to be dependent on particular species of flora. Reductions in biodiversity resulting from climate change would have implications for amenity services as well as life support functions. The natural recreational facilities available in particular areas would change.

All of this is very inconclusive. This in itself is a particular example of an important general feature of the interconnections between the natural environment and economic activity. They are characterised by uncertainty. We shall return to the matter of global climate change in 9.7 below.

Substituting for biospheric services

Figure 9.2 shows some dashed lines, as well as the solid ones discussed thus far here, and in connection with Figure 1.4. The dashed lines represent possibilities for the substitution of economic activities and products for biospheric services.

Consider first recycling. This involves interception of the waste stream prior to it reaching the natural environment, and the return of some part of it to production. Recycling substitutes for environmental functions in two ways. First, it reduces the demands made upon the waste sink function. Second, it reduces the demands made upon the resource base function, in so far as recycled materials are substituted for extractions from the environment. The extent to which recycling is possible varies across resource types, and with the nature of the transformation involved in the production process. Fossil fuel combustion is an irreversible process such that no recycling at all is possible. The recycling of other natural resources is a process which itself requires inputs of energy and labour. Generally, the complete recycling of any mineral resource extracted from the environment is impossible. This follows from the second law of thermodynamics: see Peet (1992).

Also shown in Figure 9.2 are four dashed lines from the box for capital running to the three boxes and the heavy black line representing environmental functions. These lines are to represent possibilities for substituting the services of capital for environmental services. As discussed in the previous two sections, modern economics sees the problem of sustainability largely in terms of substituting the services of capital equipment for the services of environmental assets.

Consider the waste sink function. The possibility of recycling as a means of reducing demands for this function was noted above. Also, capital equipment can be used to augment assimilative capacity. To illustrate, consider again the discharge of sewage into a river estuary. Various levels of treatment of the sewage prior to its discharge into the river are possible. According to the level of treatment, the demand made upon the assimilative capacity of the estuary is reduced for a given level of sewage. The sewage treatment plant substitutes for the natural environmental function of waste sink to an extent dependent on the level of treatment that the plant provides. The higher the level of treatment the more capital equipment is needed. The operation of the capital equipment would require inputs of labour, and, if mechanised, of energy. Note also that the construction of the capital equipment itself requires the extraction of resources from the environment.

An example from the field of energy conservation illustrates the substitution of capital for resource base functions. For a given level of human comfort, the energy use of a house can be reduced by the installation of insulation and control systems. These add to that part of the total stock of capital equipment which is the house and all of its fittings, and thus to the total capital stock. Note again, however, that the insulation and control systems are themselves material structures the production of which involves extractions, including energy, from the environment. Similar fuel saving substitution possibilities exist in productive activities.

Consider next some examples in the context of amenity services, involving the ways in which individuals spend their leisure time. An individual who likes swimming can either do this in a river or lake, or from an ocean beach, or in a man-made swimming pool. The experiences involved are not identical, of course, but given the existence of swimming pools, recreational swimming is still a possibility for individuals without access to natural facilities. Similarly, it is not now necessary to actually go into a natural environment to derive aesthetic benefit from seeing it. The capital equipment in the entertainment industry means that it is possible to see wild flora and fauna without leaving an urban environment, and in the case of television and video equipment without leaving one's place of residence. Apparently, it is envisaged that computer technology will, via virtual reality devices, make it possible to experience most of the sensations of actual use of the natural environment without actual use of it.

It appears that in the context of the life support function many regard the substitution possibilities as severely limited. However, from a technical point of view, it is not clear that this is the case. Artificial environments capable of supporting human life have already been created, and in the form of space vehicles and associated equipment have already enabled humans to live outside the biosphere, albeit for limited periods. It would apparently be possible, if expensive, to create conditions capable of sustaining human life on the moon, given some suitable energy source. Equally, human life could apparently survive on a biologically dead planet earth. In both examples, what is involved is the substitution for environmental services of the services of man made machines and buildings. The life support services provided by the biosphere in its current state are not absolutely irreplaceable. But, as these examples indicate, they are irreplaceable on the scale that they operate.

Creating an artificial life supporting environment for some 5 billion humans is very different from doing it for 5.

As shown in Figure 9.2, capital is accumulated when output from current production is not used for current consumption. Current production is not solely of material structures, and capital does not only comprise equipment – machines, buildings, roads etc. Economists recognise *human capital* as well as material capital. Human capital is increased when current production is used to add to the stock of knowledge, and is what forms the basis for technological innovation, which can open up substitution possibilities not formerly available. It is now possible, for example, to substitute uranium for fossil fuel as a source of electrical energy. However, in order for technical change to impact on economic activity, it generally requires embodiment in new equipment. Knowledge that could reduce the demands made upon environmental functions does not actually do so until it is incorporated into equipment that substitutes for environmental functions.

In Figure 9.2 environment–economy flows are shown as single lines. These single lines each represent many different physical flows. Thus, for example, the resource input flow comprises flows of stock and flow resources, where the former comprises flows of renewable and non-renewable resources, which comprise oil, iron ore, copper ore etc. With respect to each of the flows shown in Figure 9.2, substitutions as between components of the flow are possible and affect the demands made upon environmental functions. The implications of any given substitution may extend beyond the environmental function directly affected. For example, a switch from fossil fuel use to hydroelectric power reduces fossil fuel depletion and also waste generation in fossil fuel combustion, and also impacts on the amenity service flow in so far as a natural recreation area is flooded.

Ecological sustainability

An ecosystem is 'the biotic community and its abiotic environment' (Krebs 1972). The biosphere could alternatively be referred to as the global ecosystem. Ecologists are individuals working in the discipline of ecology, and study the functioning of ecosystems. Ecologists have a concept of sustainability, which is rather different to that of economists.

Resilience is the ability of an ecosystem to maintain its structure and patterns of behaviour in the face of disturbance: see Holling (1986). A resilient system is one that stays in existence, functioning in the same essential way, in the face of a major shock to it. An ecosystem that is not resilient collapses in the face of a major shock to it. 'Functioning in the same essential way' would be indicated, for example, by the total amount of incident solar radiation captured by the system's photosynthetic processes remaining constant. A system is sustainable in the ecological sense if it is resilient.

In this sense, sustainability is a system property the presence or absence of which can only be determined with hindsight by observation of its behaviour in the face of disturbance. An important research topic in ecology is the question of whether there are indicators of resilience, such that by looking at such it would be possible to say prior to a disturbance whether or not the system would prove to be resilient. A related matter is the existence and identification of *keystone species*, ie species the loss of which would cause the system to loose structure and function differently. At the present time, it would appear that there are no agreed resilience indicators available. Further, a system that has proved resilient to one type/size of disturbance may not prove resilient in the face of a shock of a different size/type. While it is clear that the concept of resilience is what characterises an ecological approach to sustainability, there are no precise definitions of sustainability arising. The idea of resilience has been used, and explicitly related to a definition of sustainability defined in terms of human interests, in the analysis of agricultural systems. Conway (1985) defines agricultural productivity in an agricultural system as 'the yield or net income per unit of resource'. Sustainability is then defined as: 'the ability of the system to maintain productivity in spite of a major disturbance', the incidence of which is essentially unpredictable, such as a rare drought or a new pest. This sustainability concept is a resilience concept. Note that on Conway's definition of yield, it is not necessary that exactly the same crops are produced after the shock as prior to it. What matters is the ability to produce comparable yield, in physical and/or financial terms. No simple prescription for the avoidance of a lack of sustainability is offered. In line with our remarks above on the non-availability of sustainability indicators for ecosystems, Conway notes that:

> Satisfactory methods of measuring sustainability still need to be found, however. Lack of sustainability may be indicated by declining productivity but, equally, collapse may come suddenly and without warning.

It is not that there are no indicators that are relevant to sustainability: in relation to agricultural systems, Conway notes several. Rather, there is no indicator, or group of indicators, performance against which guarantees sustainability in the face of all conceivable shocks to the system.

Ecological sustainability is, then, not a well defined state to be attained by following some simple rules defined in terms of indicator(s) performance. We can say that it is the requirement that the resilience of the system be maintained through time. But, there is not a set of indicators such that performance against them can be said to demonstrate that resilience is, or is not, being maintained. The economic approach to sustainability yields a precise definition, constant consumption, and, at the theoretical level, a rule that is necessary, but not sufficient, for its realisation. The attainment of that kind of sustainability could be consistent with massive environmental degradation as normally understood. This does not, on the economics approach, matter so long as consumption is constant. Economics tends to assume that the degree of possible substitution between environmental services and economic services which would permit consumption to remain constant, if the Hartwick–Solow Rule were followed, does actually exist.

The concept of ecological sustainability is imprecise beyond the injunction to maintain the functioning of the ecosystems, the biosphere in total, that support life. The notion of functioning itself is imprecise and not identifiable from a set of indicators in any well defined way. One could, though apparently ecologists have not, extend Conway's definition for agroecosystems to the biospheric level, and define global ecological sustainability as constant total biomass. *Biomass* is simply the total mass of living tissue. From a human perspective this might not be an appealing definition, since it does not differentiate between types of tissue. It does not accord privileged status to human tissue: biomass could remain constant with plant tissue substituting for human tissue. Further, it is not clear what rules for human conduct it would imply, since the functioning of ecosystems are poorly understood.

In thinking about sustainability, economists emphasise human management in human interests, and neglect considerations relating to the functioning of the biosphere and its constituent systems. Ecologists emphasise system function considerations, but cannot readily and unambiguously relate those to human interests in any direct and simple way. The question which arises is whether there can exist a synthetic approach, which can inform the debate over how human society should behave.

Ecological economics

Ecological economics is an emerging discipline, which is motivated by the desire for synthesis. The Greek word oikos is the root for eco in both ecology and economics. Oikos means household, and we can say that ecology is the study of nature's housekeeping, while economics is the study of housekeeping in human societies. Ecological economics can be said to be the study of how these two housekeepings are related to one another. It is anthropocentric, ie looks at matters from the perspective of human interests, and seeks to inform human housekeeping by an understanding of the implications for it of nature's housekeeping.

In Chapter 1 we cited a definition of economics as:

> the study of how people make their living, how they acquire the food, shelter, clothing and other material necessities and comforts of this world. It is a study of the problems they encounter, and of the ways in which these problems can be reduced.

> (Wonnacott and Wonnacott 1979)

Ecology has been defined as:

> the study of the total relations of the animal to both its organic and inorganic environment.

This definition is attributed to the man who coined the term 'ecology', Haeckel, in 1869. A more modern definition is

> Ecology is the scientific study of the interactions that determine the distribution and abundance of organisms.

> (Krebs 1972)

The basic motivation for ecological economics is the idea that the proper study of how 'people make their living' has to be located within an understanding of the relations of people to their 'organic and inorganic environment'. Those relations are set out schematically in Figure 9.2. Ecological economics involves the idea that neither economics alone nor ecology alone are capable of dealing satisfactorily with the problems arising from the interdependence of economic and ecological systems. It is interdisciplinary. In the first article in the first issue of the journal *Ecological Economics*, the President of the newly established International Society for Ecological Economics, ISEE, stated that:

> Ecological economics addresses the relationships between ecosystems and economic systems in the broadest sense. These relationships are the locus of many of our most pressing current problems ... but they are not well covered by any existing discipline ... (ecological economics) will include neoclassical environmental economics and ecological impact studies as subsets, but it will also encourage new ways of thinking about the linkages between ecological and economic systems.
>
> (Costanza 1989)

The first ISEE conference was held in Washington DC in 1990, and was attended by about 300 people, suggesting that Costanza's perception of a need for 'new ways of thinking' about 'our most pressing current problems' was quite widely shared. The second conference, in Stockholm in 1992, attracted about 500 people, and the third, in 1994 in Costa Rica, about 900. The disciplinary backgrounds of those attending these conferences have included: economics, ecology (Costanza is an ecologist), physics, chemistry, biology, philosophy, geography, sociology, and mathematics. The varied nature of what ecological economists do can be seen in the pages of the journal *Ecological Economics*, and in three volumes based upon the papers presented at the 1990 and 1992 conferences: Costanza (1991), van den Bergh and van der Straaten (1994), and Jansson *et al.* (1994). For discussion of the historical roots of ecological economics see Martinez-Alier (1987) and Christensen (1989). Important contributions pre-dating the establishment of ISEE include: Ayres and Kneese (1969), Boulding (1966), Daly (1968, 1973), Erhlich and Ehrlich (1970), Georgescu-Roegen (1971, 1979) and Meadows *et al.* (1972).

The first issue of the journal *Ecological Economics* contains several papers addressing the question: what is ecological economics to be about? Here we will summarise the answers given by saying that it is about sustainability. The study of the natural environment suggests that there might be limits to the expansion of human economic activity. This has implications dealing with human economic problems:

> Issues of sustainability are ultimately issues about limits. If economic growth is sustainable indefinitely by technology then all environmental problems can (in theory at least) be fixed technologically. Issues of equity and distribution (between subgroups and generations of our species and between our species and others) are also issues of limits. We do not have to worry so much about how an expanding pie is divided, but a constant or shrinking pie presents real problems.
>
> (Costanza 1989)

We discussed the way economists see economic growth as *the* solution to the problem of human poverty in 9.1 above. Consideration of the interdependence of economic and ecological systems calls into question the feasibility of that solution. It also makes clear the pervasive uncertainty involved in considering future prospects for economic and ecological systems, which arises because the feedbacks between economic activity and the state of natural systems are complex and poorly understood. Thinking about how to cope with uncertainty is a fundamental characteristic of ecological economics. It cannot be said that it has yet come up with any simple solutions to this problem. We consider some emerging ideas in relation to policy in the final section of this chapter. In the next two sections we look at two particular aspects of the global sustainability problem, which illustrate the problem of uncertainty in relation to it.

9.6   Biodiversity loss

Biodiversity loss is usually understood to occur when a species becomes extinct. Species extinction is a normal evolutionary event, which predates the emergence of human beings. The normal, or background, rate at which species extinction occurs has been estimated from the fossil record. Many biologists take the view that the rate at which species are now going extinct, due to the impacts of human activity, is above the background or normal rate. They argue that there is now occurring an extinction 'crisis' or 'spasm' of the same order of magnitude as that which occurred some 65 million years ago, and involved the extinction of the dinosaurs and many other life forms.

It is not known how many species exist. Some 1.6 million species have been identified (Myers 1979). Myers (1979) gives an estimate for the total number of species of 10 million. Simon and Wildavsky (1993) cite a 1980 estimate of a range from 3 to 10 million. Ehrlich and Ehrlich (1992) give an estimate of 10 million, from a range of 2 to 50 million. Vitousek *et al.* (1986) give a range of 5 to 30 million for the number of animal species.

Given uncertainty over the number of species in existence, estimates of rates of species loss are also clearly speculative in nature, and again a wide range can be found in the literature. Myers (1979) gives one per day for 1979, one per hour for the late 1980s, and a total of 1 million in the last quarter of the twentieth century. Simon and Wildavsky (1993) cite a 1980 estimate of 500,000 to 600,000 species losses for the last two decades of the century. Erhlich and Ehrlich (1992) cite the following estimates. Their own, from Ehrlich and Ehrlich (1981) of 40 to 400 times the normal rate for birds and mammals. A 1989 estimate of an annual extinction rate of '4000 to 6000 species, some 10 000 times the background rate before *Homo sapiens* started practising agriculture'. Based on 1988 estimates, they note that it is 'conceivable that the rate is actually 60 000 to 90 000 species annually: 150 000 times background'. Barbier *et al.* (1994) provide further information on rates of species loss, and references to the literature: WRI (1994) provides data for the geographical distribution of habitat losses, protected areas, and threatened species.

Clearly, in regard to biodiversity loss, there is uncertainty about the current situation and future prospects. Many biologists argue that notwithstanding this, it is clear that action to protect biodiversity is an urgent necessity. While some argue that it is in terms of the interests of non-human species, most would claim that action to reduce the rate of species loss is in human interests. There are basically four reasons why biodiversity loss is held to adversely affect human interests. First, many species of plants and animals are directly useful to human productive activity, providing inputs to the manufacture of drugs, and genetic material for crop breeding, for example. If a species becomes extinct, its usefulness is irreversibly lost. Second, there is the idea that biodiversity is a form of amenity service, so that humans would generally find an environment characterised by less biodiversity less enjoyable than one characterised by more. Third, plant and animal species play rôles in the functioning of ecosystems, and of the biosphere as a whole. The exact rôle that most species play is unknown. Fourth, to the extent that the diversity of genetic material in existence is reduced, it must be assumed that evolutionary potential is reduced. The argument for maintaining evolutionary potential is that this is what will, through the emergence of new life forms, promote the ability of the biosphere to cope with stresses, including those originating in human activity. New life forms may also form the basis for directly useful inputs to production. Note that since many of the species going extinct are unknown to science, there is complete uncertainty about their, actual (in relation to ecosystem function) and potential (as inputs to production), usefulness to human beings.

Many economists have accepted these arguments, and are actively engaged in addressing the problem of biodiversity loss. However, the seriousness of the situation and the need for action are not universally accepted. Simon and Wildavsky (1993), for example, argue that there is 'now no prima facie case for any expensive species-safeguarding policy without more extensive analysis'. They note the paucity of reliable historical data on species extinctions, and comment that:

> It is clear that without bringing into consideration some additional force, one could extrapolate almost any rate (of extinction) one chooses for the year 2000 ... many forecasters would be likely to project a rate much closer to the past ... on the basis of the common wisdom that in the absence of additional information, the best first approximation for a variable tomorrow is its value today .... (parenthesis added)

Simon and Wildavsky are also sceptical about the benefits from species preservation, on the grounds that past extinctions have not involved much cost to humans:

> Perhaps we should look back and wonder: Which species were extinguished when the settlers clear-cut the Middle West of the United States? Are we the poorer now for their loss? Obviously we do not know the answers. But can we even imagine that we would be enormously better off with the persistence of any hypothetical species? It does not seem likely. This casts some doubt on the economic value of species that might be lost elsewhere.

Simon and Wildavsky appear to overlook the rôle of biodiversity in ecosystem function, seeing species as relevant to human interests only in so far as they are a source of direct inputs to production, or the source of amenity value. Even on this basis, their extrapolation concerning the costs of species extinction is highly dubious if an accelerated rate of species extinction is accepted. However, it would be unwise to accept their extrapolation argument, as there is 'some additional force' to be taken into consideration in assessing likely rates of species extinction. This is the human appropriation of solar radiation.

The appropriation of solar radiation

We now consider estimates concerning the current situation in terms of the human appropriation of *net primary production*, NPP, which is the amount of living tissue created by photosynthesis. As discussed briefly in 7.5, photosynthesis is the process by which plants convert the solar radiation into living tissue: see also an ecology text such as Krebs (1972). NPP is the basis for the maintenance, growth and reproduction of all of the species that feed off plant life: it is the total food resource of the biosphere. Here we are concerned with the share of this food resource appropriated by the human species.

Table 9.8 shows that per unit area, the land surface of the earth produces more of this food than does the part of the surface covered by water. Although the aquatic zone accounts for 71% of the total surface area, it accounts for only 31% of total NPP. Table 9.9 shows three alternative estimates of the share of Terrestrial, Aquatic and total NPP appropriated by the human species. These tables are based on data taken from Vitousek *et al.* (1986). For the low estimate what is counted is only the actual use by humans and their domesticated animals as food, fuel, fibre and timber. The intermediate estimate adds to this what 'is used in human-dominated ecosystems by communities of organisms different from those in corresponding natural ecosystems' (Vitousek *et al.* 1986). Thus, for example, whereas the low estimate uses the food actually eaten by humans, the intermediate estimate uses the NPP of the agricultural land on which the food is produced – the amount of wheat grown rather than of wheat based products consumed. Finally, the high estimate also accounts for 'potential NPP lost as a consequence of human activities'. In regard to agriculture, for example, this estimate includes NPP lost as a result of turning forest into pasture for domestic animals. This estimate also allows for NPP losses on account of desertification and on account of the covering of land with materials which prevent photosynthetic capture, such as roads and buildings. Note that the estimate for aquatic NPP appropriation is the same on the low, intermediate and high bases, reflecting the fact that human exploitation of marine ecosystems is still dominantly in the nature of hunting and gathering rather than farming, notwithstanding the use of technologically sophisticated methods. Note also that these estimates are necessarily somewhat imprecise.

Table 9.8 Proportions of total surface area and net primary production

	Surface area	NPP
Terrestial	29%	59%
Aquatic	71%	41%

Table 9.9 NPP proportions appropriated by humans

	Low	Intermediate	High
Terrestial	4%	31%	39%
Aquatic	2%	2%	2%
Total	3%	19%	25%

For this reason, they have been reported here as rounded numbers. In relation to their high terrestrial estimate, Vitousek *et al.* (1986) make the observation that

> An equivalent concentration of resources into one species and its satellites has probably not occurred since land plants first diversified.

and state the view that the share of NPP appropriation now achieved by humans threatens the functioning of the biosphere, given its implications for the availability of NPP to other species. They express the opinion that:

> Observers who believe that limits to growth are so distant as to be of no consequence for today's decision makers ... appear unaware of these biological realities.

Policy issues

As noted in 9.2, an international convention on biodiversity conservation was one of the outcomes of the 1992 UNCED meeting in Rio de Janeiro. This indicates that, at the level of international diplomacy anyway, the sceptical position of Simon and Wildavsky, noted above, is a minority view. However, many would argue that while there is much pro-conservation political rhetoric, in relation to the scale of the problem, effective action is currently totally inadequate. In the last few years economists have produced a large literature on biodiversity conservation, in regard to both the determination of policy targets, and the design of suitable policy instruments. Here we provide only an overview of some of the main topics: for a more comprehensive discussion, and references to the literature on the issues raised here, see Barbier *et al.* (1994).

Effective action on biodiversity loss requires an understanding of its causes. The major causes can be listed as follows:

1. The appropriation of net primary production, discussed above, as manifest primarily in the denial of habitat to non-human species by the use of land for agriculture, timber production and urban development. The process of habitat loss is driven by the growth of human numbers, and increasing levels of material consumption per human individual.

2. The appropriation of net primary production through the harvesting of renewable resources, frequently at rates that are in excess of the maximum sustainable yield. In some cases, such as fishing, problems arise not only in relation to the taking of the target species, but also in relation to the 'by-catch' of species that are not of commercial interest.

3. Pollution, which may kill individual species members, affect reproduction, and/or mean that habitat is effectively denied. Global climate change will affect habitats, and species which cannot adapt or move fast enough will be adversely affected.

4. The introduction of exotic species, which out compete native species, leading to their extinction.

The most direct response to the major causes of species extinction is the reduction of human numbers, and/or consumption levels. Policies intended to protect biodiversity in this way are not discussed very much in the literature, for obvious reasons. Policies aimed at reducing human population growth, especially in developing countries, are discussed a lot, but in the context of raising consumption levels rather than protecting biodiversity. The latter may be a welcome byproduct of such policies, or, if their actual objective is realised, it may not be as rising levels of per capita material consumption offset the effects of lower population growth.

The favoured policy response to habitat loss is the creation of various types of 'nature reserve'. The first question arising is: how much land, and which land, should be set aside for biodiversity conservation? Most economists would want to see this question answered in terms of cost benefit analysis, of the type discussed in Chapter 8. Some argue that these questions should be addressed using the safe minimum standard approach, also discussed in Chapter 8. With either approach, a problem that arises for biodiversity conservation is that it is often the case that the land which is richest in biodiversity is also most suitable for human activities such as agriculture or timber production. In any case, the cost of setting land aside from such activities is clearly higher the larger the human population and the higher its material living standards. In many cases, taking land into nature reserves involves the financial compensation of private owners, or of individuals who had use rights over publicly owned land, which is a further call on public expenditures generally regarded as already involving excessive tax burdens. Some economists favour policies to make it easier for individuals to acquire land to be used as nature reserves, such as offering matching funding to trusts that raise money from private donations for this purpose.

Recent work on policy instruments for the control of the free-access exploitation of renewable resources was briefly discussed in 7.5. This is relevant to biodiversity conservation. The problem remains, of course, of setting the target levels of harvest so that they are consistent with biodiversity conservation requirements, and the political pressures here, given growing human numbers and consumption aspirations, are clear. Instruments for the control of environmental pollution were discussed in Chapter 5, and the next section will look at some of the issues arising in relation to global climate change. The control of the introduction of exotic species has received relatively little attention in the literature, but the issues are generically related to those discussed in connection with pollution control – dependability, cost, enforcement, etc.

From an economic point of view, species are environmental assets. In 9.4, on accounting for sustainable income, we noted the difficulties arising from the problems of identifying and measuring stocks of such in physical terms, and in coming up with valuations. As noted at the beginning of this section, these problems are especially acute in regard to the assets that are species. Hence, it is widely recognised that research into the state, and values, of biological diversity is an important input to policy for its conservation. In so far as such research produces results which increase public awareness of the state and value of biodiversity, it could function as an instrument for conservation of the moral suasion class discussed in 5.5.

Recently, some economists have taken a property rights approach to biodiversity conservation. The basic argument is essentially the same as in the pollution context. It is that biodiversity is threatened because private economic agents lack the incentives to conserve it to the 'optimal' levels because of the absence of private property rights in non-domesticated species, and/or the services that they do provide, or could provide. The solution is, it is argued, clear. Create the private property rights that would support the incentive structure for conservation. Clearly, there are some technical and legal problems in creating the kinds of property rights required here, but technology is changing and economists have come up with some interesting ideas. Barbier *et al.* (1994) discuss some of these ideas, and provide references. Barbier *et al.* (1990) consider the relationship between the trade in ivory and the prospects for the African elephant. Vogel (1994) argues for the creation of private property rights in genetic material.

The biodiversity conservation problem has a number of important international dimensions. First, note that it follows from the reasons given above as to why it is in human interests to protect biodiversity, that biodiversity loss in one country is a problem for citizens of other countries. In the terminology of 5.4, where we considered the international dimensions of pollution problems, it is a variant of a Type II or a Type III situation. The damage that crosses national boundaries is not a material flow, but it is damage nonetheless, and much of the analysis set out there applies. Consider, for example, forest clearing in tropical countries, which causes habitat loss there, and reductions in global biodiversity. This has lead to calls for bans on the imports of timber from such countries. Economists argue that this would be a second best approach, forgoing gains from trade. Bribery, having the victim pay, could in principle be tailored to secure gains from trade while minimising environmental damage – payment could be made conditional on the observance of certain logging practices, such as no clearfelling.

The countries which are particularly rich in biodiversity are typically tropical developing countries, ie they are poor in terms of human living standards. The IUCN has identified 12 'megadiversity' countries, of which only one, Australia, is not a developing country. The pressure on non-human habitat, from human population growth and economic development aspirations, is particularly strong in developing countries. This suggests that victim-pays type approaches, with rich industrial countries as 'victims', could be seen as desirable on equity as well as efficiency grounds. In fact, since the UNCED meeting in 1992, there have been some developments in this direction, with industrial nations financing nature reserves and related measures in developing countries in various ways, such as through the multilateral agency of the Global Environmental Facility: see Barbier *et al.* (1994). The Australian situation in regard to biodiversity loss, which has been very rapid since the European invasion just 200 years ago, its causes, and conservation policy is discussed in Common and Norton (1992).

9.7   The enhanced greenhouse effect

As noted in 9.5, there is no question but that there exists a 'greenhouse effect' – the presence in the earth's atmosphere of greenhouse gases makes the earth warmer than it would otherwise be. This section is called 'The enhanced greenhouse effect' because the policy relevant problem is global climate change due to increasing concentrations of the greenhouse gases, due to human activity, in the atmosphere. It is the policy dimensions of the problem that are the focus of this section. References to the scientific background were given in 9.5. The policy literature itself is now extensive, and we can do no more than provide an overview, highlighting the main issues. We treat the enhanced greenhouse effect as a pollution problem, and draw upon earlier discussions of such problems, in Chapter 5 especially.

It is useful (following Schelling 1986) to distinguish three types of policy response:

1.   Abatement policies would be intended to slow or halt the rate of increase in atmospheric concentrations of greenhouse gases. The concentration in the atmosphere of any given greenhouse gas depends upon the balance between the rate of emission and the rate at which the sinks for the gas absorb it. In the carbon dioxide case, emissions are mainly from fossil fuel and biomass combustion, and the main sinks are growing vegetation and the oceans. Thus, abatement policy could target emissions rates and/or absorption rates.

2.   Mitigation policies would be intended to offset or ameliorate the climatic effects of increased concentrations of greenhouse gases.

3.   Adaptation policies would be intended to facilitate human adjustment to the impacts of climatic change consequent upon increased greenhouse gas concentrations.

These are not mutually exclusive classes of policy response, of course. Given that actually halting the rate of increase is effectively impossible within the next 50 years, for example, it might be argued that while 1 is the obvious way to go, policies of types 2 and 3 should also be put in place. We now provide illustrative examples of each type of response. In regard to 1, this is in relation to carbon dioxide, which is the most important of the greenhouse gases in that it is the one with the largest potential to contribute to climate change.

1.   Reductions in the use of fossil fuels. Switching as between different fossil fuels with different carbon contents. Removal of carbon dioxide from power plant smokestacks, its sequestration as carbon, and disposal in such manner that there is no leakage to the atmosphere. Switching from fossil fuel combustion to biomass combustion, with the biomass harvested on a sustainable basis. Sink enhancement, especially reforestation, with the timber eventually harvested to be used so as to prevent carbon dioxide release to the atmosphere, such as by encasement in plastic.

2.   Release particulates into the atmosphere. Release into the atmosphere gases that offset the effects of the greenhouse gases. Promote cloud formation. Steer hurricanes and tornadoes away from populated areas.

3.   Facilitate outward migration from adversely affected areas. Compensate those who are adversely affected. Build defences against rising sea levels. Stop new development in low lying coastal areas. Change agricultural practices, use different plant and animal varieties. Research new plant and animal varieties.

While there is debate over the relative merits of policies from each of these categories, most attention focuses on abatement policies, and those in relation to carbon dioxide. In the interests of brevity we shall follow this practice, beyond making two points. First, that responses of type 2 all appear to involve further anthropogenic, ie originating in human activity, impacts on a poorly understood climatic system. Second, that the attractiveness of adaptation policies, type 3, will generally be greater, the slower the rate of change which is to be adapted to. This might reasonably be taken to imply that even if the appropriate primary response were thought to be adaptation, there would remain a rôle for abatement policies.

The key characteristic of abatement policies is that their effectiveness depends upon international agreement and cooperation. Whatever one nation does to reduce emissions or enhance sinks will have little effect on global atmospheric concentrations, and therefore on climate change prospects, unless at least the majority of other nations take similar action. The enhanced greenhouse problem is an example of a reciprocal spillover, Type III, problem, as discussed in 5.4. In this particular example, regional variations in the nature and extent of damage are expected: some nations may anticipate some beneficial impacts, making the free rider problem more complex as such nations could perceive that the avoidance of global climate change is not in their national interest. Given the internationalisation of the global human system, it actually seems unlikely that any country could isolate itself from the adverse effects of global climate change elsewhere. Large numbers of 'environmental refugees' are anticipated, for example. However, the incorrectness of the perception does not reduce the problem that it raises for securing international cooperation.

Abatement: target setting

Here we assume away the problems of securing international cooperation, and consider the question of setting an abatement target as if there were a world government. The assumption enables us to focus on the central issue attending target setting, which is uncertainty. Given that we place a lot of emphasis on uncertainty, it is important to be clear about what is known, what is not in dispute. It is known that the greenhouse gases warm the earth, and that their concentrations in the atmosphere have been increasing in the last two hundred years. The Intergovernmental Panel on Climate Change, IPCC, was established in 1988 to provide authoritative assessments, and its reports give the view of the majority of the relevant scientific community. According to the 1992 IPCC report (Houghton *et al.* 1992): 'global mean surface air temperature has increased by 0.3 to 0.6°C over the last 100 years'. The IPCC 1992 report noted that:

> the size of this warming is broadly consistent with predictions of climate models, but it is also of the same magnitude as natural climate variability. Thus the observed increase could be largely due to this natural variability; alternatively this variability and other human factors could have offset a still larger human-induced greenhouse warming ... the unequivocal detection of the enhanced greenhouse effect from observations is not likely for a decade or more.

According to press reports late in 1995, the availability of additional data since the 1992 report had lead the IPCC to the conclusion that the observed global warming could be attributed to an enhanced greenhouse effect. These press reports were based on a draft version of an IPCC report which had not been finalised and published at the time of this writing.

In Chapter 5 we discussed the economic approach to determining the appropriate target for the abatement of environmentally damaging activities. On this approach, the costs and benefits involved are to be equated at the margin. Applying this to the enhanced greenhouse effect, emissions should be abated up to the point where the marginal benefits of so doing are equal to the marginal costs involved. Benefits are the damages from climate change that are avoided by the reduction of greenhouse gas emissions. Using this approach to determine the optimal level of global greenhouse gas abatement faces a number of difficulties. The two most obvious are the assessment of the damage avoided by emissions reduction, and the fact that whereas costs would be incurred now the benefits thereby secured lie in the future. We now look at the problems of benefit assessment and discounting, and come back later to cost assessment.

The first of these problems is in part a question for scientific inquiry: if emissions are reduced by $x\%$ now, by how much will future climate change impacts be reduced? This is a very complex problem, involving massive uncertainties. It is not solely a matter for the natural sciences. Given estimates of physical damage reductions of various kinds, it remains to put them in terms that are comparable with the cost estimates. This involves valuation and aggregation. The second problem is all about valuation. How do we compare, assuming that the first problem has been entirely solved, current costs with future benefits? This raises the vexed question of discounting.

Before looking at some results which illustrate these problems, a word on terminology is necessary. Although this approach to determining the greenhouse gas emissions abatement target involves weighing costs and benefits, it would be wrong to call it cost benefit analysis, as that term was used in Chapter 8. There we used cost benefit analysis to refer to project appraisal according to social, as opposed to financial or commercial, criteria. Further, social criteria are interpreted as contributing to the goal of intertemporal efficiency in allocation.

The greenhouse gas abatement target determination case is different. Here we are not dealing with a problem in allocative efficiency. We are dealing with a problem about the distribution over time of aggregate consumption. It is not a question of allocating inputs to this project rather than that one. It is a question of the costs in terms of aggregate consumption to be incurred now in order to protect future consumption levels. This does involve discounting future benefits, but the issues involved are different to those which arise in the context of cost benefit analysis as project appraisal. The issues involved are those of fairness in intertemporal distribution, and are to be considered in the optimal planning framework discussed in 7.4.

In order to illustrate these issues we look at the analysis of the abatement target question in Nordhaus (1991): Nordhaus (1994) provides a more extended and detailed analysis along similar lines. The principal conclusion that emerges from this analysis is that:

> the appropriate level of control depends critically upon three central parameters of the climate-economic system: the cost of control of GHGs, the damage from greenhouse warming, and the time dynamics as reflected in the rate of discount of future goods and services along with the time lags in the reaction of the climate to emissions.

> (Nordhaus 1991)

'GHGs' means greenhouse gases. The model used is recognised as a gross simplification of the climate-economic system, and it is noted that

> estimates of both costs and damages are highly uncertain and incomplete, and our estimates are therefore highly tentative.
>
> Nordhaus (1991)

The uncertainty is highlighted by presenting the results for the appropriate target arising under three different sets of assumptions:

1.   Using 'identified' damages from climate change, to be discussed below, and a 'middle' assumption about the discount rate, also to be discussed below, the target is a 2% abatement of emissions from current levels. This would involve 'very little' reduction in carbon dioxide emissions, and come mostly from the CFC phase out which the industrial nations are already committed to on the basis of acting on the ozone depletion problem (see 9.4). The CFCs are greenhouse gases.

2.   Using 'medium' damages and a 'middle' assumption about the discount rate produces an abatement target of 11%. This would involve a 2% reduction in carbon dioxide emissions from fossil fuel combustion, with the rest of the abatement coming from the CFC phase out.

3.   Using 'high' damages and a zero rate of discount gives a target of 33% abatement for greenhouse gas emissions. This would involve a substantial reduction in carbon dioxide emissions from fossil fuel combustion. Inspection of a Figure in the paper indicates a reduction in these emissions of approximately 20%.

While 'medium' and 'middle' might be suggestive of capturing the best estimates/assumptions about the crucial parameters, Nordhaus (1991) does not commit himself to any one of these targets. This reflects the uncertainties involved, especially in regard to abatement benefits. Note that this study assumes that there is an enhanced greenhouse effect driving climate change.

The discount rate used for making future consumption benefits commensurable with current consumption costs depends upon: society's pure rate of time preference for current over future consumption, the social discount rate in 7.4; a parameter which describes how the current marginal social valuation of consumption declines as consumption increases; and the growth rate assumed for the economy. This discount rate will be higher the higher the pure time preference rate is, and lower the higher the rate of growth assumed. This makes a good deal of sense. For any given rate of pure time preference, future benefits will now count for less the better off we assume the future to be. If a positive growth rate is assumed and a zero rate of pure time preference used, the discount rate will be negative. If zero growth is assumed, then the discount rate to be used is just the pure rate of time preference, and is zero if that is zero. This is the case for 3 above. For 1 and 2 the 'middle' discount rate used is 1%, corresponding to a positive rate

Table 9.10 Estimates of 'identified' climate damage costs for the US

Sector	Impact estimate
Farms – impact of greenhouse warming and carbon dioxide fertilisation	−10.6 to +9.7
Forestry, fisheries, other	small + or −
Construction	positive
Water transportation	?
Energy and utilities –	
electricity demand	−1.65
non-electric space heat	+1.16
water and sanitary	negative ?
Real estate (land rent component of sea level rise) –	
loss of land	−1.55
protection of coast	−3.74
Hotels, lodging, recreation	?
Total (central estimate)	−6.23

Units are US$ billions, at 1981 prices.
A minus sign indicates a cost, a plus sign a gain.
Source: Nordhaus (1991)

of pure time preference and a positive assumed growth rate, with the former exceeding the latter.

Table 9.10 shows the estimates used by Nordhaus of the damage arising in the US consequent upon a doubling the carbon dioxide equivalent greenhouse gas concentration in the earth's atmosphere. These are the basis for the 'identified' damages used in the case 1 for which results are reported above. The assumption made is that the estimated US loss of one quarter of one percent of national income, GNP, is the appropriate estimate for the world as a whole. Nordhaus recognises that some economies may be more vulnerable to climate change impacts than the US, so that his 'medium' damage estimate, case 2, is double this – one half of one percent of world income. Finally, the 'high' damage estimate, case 3, arises by multiplying identified US damage as a percentage of national income by a factor of four, to get one percent of world income. This is intended to take some account of the impacts omitted from the accounting in Table 9.10.

The first point to note about the estimates in Table 9.10 concerns the derivation of the total from the components. The items for which no figure appears are treated as giving rise to zero $ cost. The total is then calculated taking as the damage cost for the impact on farms the mid-point of the range shown for it, which is 0.45 US$ billions. The range is from a cost of 10.6 to a gain of 9.7 US$ billions. If these range end-points are used the total is either −16.38 or +3.92 US$ billions, which correspond to −0.68% and +0.16% of

US national income. The total damages could, that is, be almost three times as large as the estimate used, or they could be gains rather than damages. This leaves out of account the items for which no number appears.

The second point is that these 'identified' items are all costs based on impacts which affect economic activities with outputs sold in markets. Nordhaus explicitly notes omissions in respect 'non-marketed goods and services' such as 'human health, biological diversity, amenity values of everyday life and leisure, and environmental quality'. There are a number of other omissions which may have been determined as inoperative in the case of the USA, but which cannot be ruled out globally, such as storm damage and salt water intrusion into coastal freshwater aquifers. It is clear that the total for impact damage derived from the summing of identified costs should be regarded as a lower bound.

So, we have a lower bound, which could be higher than 0.68% of US national income, to a range which is totally unknown, for the effects of a carbon dioxide equivalent doubling on the USA. We have already noted that for many commentators, it is the rate of change of climate that is seen as the major problem, especially in regard to species loss. These calculations ignore this dimension of the problem. We can also note that the significance of US based estimates for other countries, even after multiplication by a factor of four (which for 0.68% in the US would make the high world damage estimate 2.72% of world income), is questionable. However, the main point to be drawn from this, and the other aspects of the Nordhaus study is that the whole problem is characterised by massive ignorance and uncertainty.

Since 1991 a great deal of work has been done on the biophysical consequences of climate change, and on the economic costs involved, which become the benefits of abatement. The IPCC had a group of experts, Working Group III, review the literature arising. At the time of writing this Working Group III's report was not published, so direct quotation is not possible. However, drafts of the report have been circulated, and based on those one can indicate the nature of the findings. The report will emphasise that abatement benefit estimates show a wide range of variation because of: limited knowledge of biophysical impacts; difficulties attending the valuation of non-market impacts; future technological developments; the possibility of catastrophic events. For example, in the literature estimates of the value of the damage per tonne of carbon dioxide emitted now range from 5 to 125 US $1990. The report will also review estimates of the costs of abatement, to which we return below.

While analysis of the optimal level of abatement can illuminate some issues, it not clear that it corresponds at all closely to the situation confronting our notional world government. The problem it faces is one of decision making in the face of uncertainty, where the decision is whether or not to adopt an arbitrary standard for emissions abatement. We now draw on the discussion in 8.4 to provide a short and simple illustration of what is involved.

Table 9.11 is a pay-off matrix for a game against nature as it arises in the

Table 9.11 A pay-off matrix for a greenhouse emissions abatement target

| | | State of Nature | |
		No EGE	EGE
Decision	Bau	0	$-a$
	Abate	$-b$	$\pm z$

climate change context. The question at issue is whether the notional world government should or should not adopt a proposed arbitrary standard for abating greenhouse gas emissions by $x\%$. The possible responses are yes and no. We can imagine iteration on a final target whereby if the answer on $x\%$ is 'yes' a tighter standard, cut by more than $x\%$, is considered, and if the answer is 'no' a smaller level of reduction is considered. In Table 9.11 EGE stands for enhanced greenhouse effect, Bau for the decision to continue with business as usual, ie not to adopt the $x\%$ cut standard, and Abate indicates that the $x\%$ standard is adopted. The entries are normalised on business as usual in the event that there is no enhanced greenhouse effect giving rise to zero cost, in the top left cell. No greenhouse effect means that the state of nature is favourable in the sense that increasing greenhouse gas concentrations will not lead to climate change. If the decision is not to abate and nature is unfavourable, there is an enhanced greenhouse effect, damage costs arise in amount a. If the decision is to cut emissions by $x\%$ and there is no enhanced greenhouse effect, costs in amount b arise, where b is the costs of unnecessary abatement.

The bottom right hand cell refers to the outcome where there is an enhanced greenhouse effect and abatement action is taken. If it were known that a cut of $x\%$ would completely avoid climate change, the entry here would be equal to $a - b$, where benefits a are obtained at the cost of b. Note that this could be a positive or a negative number, in principle. The costs of preventing climate change could exceed the damage avoided. However, generally for a cut of $x\%$ it is not known that it will completely eliminate climate change. Hence, this entry is shown as z, which may be positive or negative.

Supposing that numerical values for a, b and z were known, what should the decision be? As discussed in 8.4, there is no technical answer to this question. There is no rule for decision making in the face of uncertainty which can be argued to be the correct rule. It is a matter of judgement for the decision maker. There are a variety of rules that have been suggested. The minimax rule would indicate selecting the decision for which the worst outcome is the smallest of the worst outcomes that might arise. It is a cautious rule.

However, in the case of the climate change problem, it is unrealistic to assume that the numerical values for a, b and z would be known. So, the minimax rule does not help very much. In 8.4, we discussed the Safe

416 Environmental & Resource Economics

Minimum Standard approach, which can be applied here. It says essentially that in the face of all the uncertainties, and given that the no abatement outcome when there is an enhanced greenhouse effect could be catastrophic (which possibly cannot, according to the IPCC, be completely ruled out), it should be assumed that a is the largest negative entry in Table 9.11. Then minimax says go for the abatement decision. The modified Safe Minimum Standard approach says do this if the costs are not unacceptably large. As we noted in 8.4, this is an interesting way of reformulating the decision making problem, rather than a solution to it. It remains to determine what is unacceptably large.

So, the notional world government would have to exercise its judgement, rather than look for a simple technical rule for dealing with the uncertainties confronting it. Its situation would actually be considerably more complex and uncertain than Table 9.11 suggests. First, it assumes that a, the damage costs associated with an enhanced greenhouse effect, and b, the costs of abatement to the arbitrary standard, are known, whereas in fact they are not. Second, it assumes that there are just two possible states of nature to consider. Any actual deliberation using the pay-off matrix approach would involve multiple states of nature. Third, it is not the case that the only options are do nothing or cut emissions. Currently, prospective climate change is being used as the basis for calls for more funding for research into climate change science and fossil fuel and energy conservation, as alternatives, or complements, to emissions abatement. The former research is intended to reduce uncertainty at some future date, the latter to provide less costly means of emissions abatement. Finally, there is in fact no world government to deal with the decision making problem. What exists in fact is a situation involving many sovereign nations considering their national interests in relation to international cooperation to abate greenhouse gas emissions. The additional problem dimensions that this introduces can be discussed in the context of the question of the choice of instrument for the control of greenhouse gas emissions.

Abatement: instrument choice

In the absence of world government, the enhanced greenhouse effect/global climate change problem is in the nature of a trade and the environment Type III situation as discussed in 5.4. To simplify the discussion here we shall consider just the abatement of carbon dioxide emissions from fossil fuel combustion. As already noted, carbon dioxide is the most important greenhouse gas: fossil fuel combustion is the dominant source of carbon dioxide emissions, accounting for over 90%. When a fossil fuel is burned, the carbon contained in it is released into the atmosphere as carbon dioxide. Given that the carbon content of the various fossil fuels is known, the emissions arising when a given quantity is burned are known, to a close approximation. The fossil fuel with the lowest carbon content is natural gas, next is oil, and coal has the highest carbon content. If the carbon content of natural gas is set to 1, that for oil is approximately 1.3, and that for coal 1.9.

In discussing alternative policy instruments for the attainment of an arbitrary standard for global carbon dioxide emissions abatement, we draw on the analysis of Chapter 5. However, given the reciprocal international spillover nature of the carbon dioxide problem, and the absence of a world government, there is an additional criterion for instrument evaluation here – how does it affect the incentives for participation in an international agreement to reduce emissions? Given reciprocal spillovers, unilateral action on carbon dioxide emissions would be ineffective.

To appreciate this, and the different circumstances of nations as relevant to participation in an international agreement, it is useful to consider some data. Table 9.12 gives data on carbon dioxide emissions from fossil fuel combustion, per capita incomes and population sizes for five nations plus the European Community, the EC. These six economies account for over 70% of the total of world emissions.

The US is the largest national contributor to carbon dioxide emissions. Its per capita emissions are more than 20 times as large as India's, and more than twice those for the EC. It accounts for approximately a quarter of total world emissions. From one perspective this is a very large share. However, it means that even the US acting alone to cut emissions would have a limited impact on total emissions, and hence concentrations. This is even more the case than Table 9.12 suggests, since over the next 50 years it is reasonably certain that the US share of the total will substantially decline, as the developing countries increase their use of fossil fuels with economic growth. The current per capita fossil fuel and carbon dioxide emissions in countries such as India and China are low by the standards of the industrial countries. If, as they plan to do, they follow the development path previously

Table 9.12 Emissions, income and population: selected nations 1988

	Carbon dioxide per capita[a]	Carbon dioxide per unit GDP[b]	GDP per capita[c]	Population[d]	Carbon dioxide total	Share of world total[f]
US	21.39	1.09	19.59	248.2	5310	23.7
USSR	13.01	1.50	8.66	288.7	3756	16.7
EC	8.47	0.61	13.89	325	2753	12.3
Japan	8.68	0.58	14.96	123.2	1069	4.8
China	2.37	7.54	3.12	1112.3	2638	11.8
India	0.84	3.03	0.28	833.4	699	3.1

Source: Based on Grubb (1990)
[a] Tonnes
[b] Tonnes per thousand $US
[c] Thousands $US
[d] Millions
[e] Tonnes $\times 10^6$ (Megatonnes)
[f] %

experienced in the industrial world, these per capita levels will grow substantially. Countries such as India and China currently do not see their national interest as involving the abandoning of the pursuit of economic growth in the interest of slowing prospective global warming. This perception depends, in part, on the uncertainties attending the enhanced greenhouse effect.

Table 9.12 shows that nations differ in the efficiency with which they turn fossil fuel combustion, and hence carbon dioxide emissions, into national income. The USSR emitted more than twice as much carbon dioxide per dollar of national income as the EC and Japan, and the US 40% more. This suggests that there is in the US considerable scope for greater efficiency in energy use, and reduced emissions per unit income. In India and China, emissions per unit income are much higher than in the industrial nations. However, given the low income levels and the technologies employed, the scope for increased efficiency in energy use in such countries is seen as relatively limited for the foreseeable future. At the stage of development that they are at, significant reductions in energy, ie fossil fuel, use would be seen as prohibitively costly in terms of material living standard improvements foregone.

In terms of the incentives for participation in collective action to reduce carbon dioxide emissions, the situation is broadly as follows. The bulk of future growth in emissions is expected to occur in developing countries. They see curtailing that growth as impairing their prospects for improving now the material living standards of their citizens. Problems associated with global warming are in the future, and anyway uncertain. The industrial countries could be more inclined to act, they are better able to afford the costs involved, but see that if they alone act the impact on the enhanced greenhouse effect could be limited, as the developing countries to some extent replace, as it were, their foregone emissions. This refers to the industrial nations collectively. If they are considered separately, then any one considering action to reduce emissions faces the prospect of reduced competitiveness in international trade. Whatever the true extent of this problem in any particular case, industrial interests will argue that it is a serious problem.

Following the discussion in Chapter 5, three broad classes of instrument are considered here – quantity regulation (otherwise command and control), taxation, and tradeable permits. Given that we are considering carbon dioxide emissions from fossil fuel combustion, in each of these cases the instrument could be applied to fossil fuel use rather than actual emissions. This is, in fact, what most of the literature assumes. Much of the literature on alternative instruments is in the form of reports by governmental, or intergovernmental agencies, and is not very accessible. Tietenberg (1995) deals mainly with tradeable permits, and provides useful references: see also Grubb (1990).

Quantity regulation would involve each nation being required to cut back on emissions by a given proportional amount from some base year level, or to emit only up to a certain absolute amount. The analysis from Chapter 5 indicates that there is a presumption that choice of this class of instrument would not lead to standard attainment at least cost. It would, that is, be a choice implying inefficiency for the world economy as a whole. That analysis also indicated, however, that, leaving aside enforcement problems, this choice would have the property of dependability – the global target would be realised.

If national targets were internationally agreed, there remains the question of the means by which a nation would seek to realise its own particular target. This question could itself be decided as part of the international agreement, or left for decision by the individual participating nations. The latter option would involve nations in a smaller perceived sacrifice of national sovereignty than the former. Under this arrangement individual nations could adopt quantity regulation or price incentive systems, and the discussion of Chapter 5 applies straightforwardly to each nation.

The central question in negotiating this type of international agreement would be the determination of the national targets. It seems likely that perceptions of equity as between nations would dominate consideration of this question. The simple approach of equal proportional cutbacks across all nations would penalise nations already fossil fuel efficient and the less developed nations. An alternative suggestion that has been made is that the initial standard should relate to allowable global emissions which would then be shared equally on a per capita basis. This would generally favour less developed as opposed to industrial nations. Obviously, many variants on these simple allocations are conceivable. It seems likely that it would be difficult to reach agreement on differentiated national targets.

Given the restriction to carbon dioxide emissions arising in fossil fuel combustion, monitoring of compliance would be relatively simple and inexpensive via monitoring of combustion of the fossil fuels. Enforcement of compliance raises more difficult problems. A system of fines for non-compliance would be the obvious approach. They would have to be administered by an international agency, so that some loss of national sovereignty would be involved. The proceeds could, it has been suggested, used to finance greenhouse research and/or technology transfer. Alternatively, it has been suggested that trade sanctions could be used against non-complying nations.

Taxation would involve an international agreement to tax carbon dioxide emissions at a uniform rate across all sources in all nations. It could take two forms. The first would involve the tax being levied by an international agency, the second would involve it being levied by nation states. In both cases taxation would be globally efficient, ie least cost, but not dependable. The common global tax rate would, that is, realise some emissions reduction at the least possible cost in resource terms, but it would not guarantee the attainment of the global arbitrary standard for emissions reduction.

Taxation by an international agency would mean revenues accruing to it, and if the tax were set at rates intended to realise significant global emissions reductions these revenues would be substantial. In 1990 global carbon dioxide emissions were approximately 20,000 megatonnes. Taxation at the rate of US$20 per tonne would then yield of the order of US$400 billions per annum. The global carbon tax revenue potential is larger than the size of all but the largest national economies. This gives rise to problems and possibilities. The problems concern the perceived loss of sovereignty by nation states which would be involved in the creation of an international body with significant spending power outside of their influence. The possibilities concern the related questions of equity and inducement to participate in an international agreement. While taxation is efficient it is not necessarily equitable. Rules could be negotiated according to which the international agency would disburse its revenues which would promote equity. A rule could involve, for example, countries receiving a share of total revenue dependent, positively, on population size and, negatively, on per capita national income. This would favour large less developed nations, such as India and China, and might be expected to encourage their participation. Of course, such a revenue sharing rule would work against the interests of nations such as the USA, and to that extent discourage their participation.

The tax base would actually be fossil fuels, with the rate differing across the fossil fuels according to their carbon content. This input taxation, in the terminology of Chapter 5, would greatly facilitate, and reduce the costs of, monitoring. Given monitoring, compliance enforcement with taxation is a problem only in so far as nations refuse to pay their tax assessments. This would be tantamount to openly leaving the international consensus, and could presumably be dealt with through trade and/or political sanctions.

The problems of perceived national sovereignty losses and revenue disbursement could be avoided by a form of agreement which had the common tax rate across nations levied by nation states, which would retain the revenue arising. This would also involve the loss of the possibility of promoting equity and encouraging participation by some key players. An additional consideration arises with this form of international agreement where fossil fuels are the tax base. This is that the distributional implications across nations then differ according to whether production or consumption is used as the tax base. In the former case the revenue accrues to the governments of fossil fuel producing nations and is spent there, while the prices paid by fossil fuel importing nations rise. In the latter case, the revenue arises, and is spent, where the fossil fuel is used. Fossil fuel exporting nations would face lower export prices and volumes.

Tradeable emissions permits were shown in Chapter 5 to be both efficient and dependable. This carries over, in principle, into the international context, where it would seem to make them preferable to either quantity regulations or taxation. The first point to note is that the carry over is assured only if permits are freely tradeable globally between individual emissions sources, so that the world context is the exact analogue of the nation state. The carry over is not assured if permits are tradeable only between nation states, since a nation state could choose to meet the emissions quantity it holds permits for by quantity regulation within its borders. In this case, dependability at the global level holds, but full efficiency does not. It would seem intuitive that permits tradeable between nation states would offer efficiency advantages over international quantity controls whatever form of control nation states adopted within their borders. However, this does not appear to have been demonstrated in the published literature.

It would appear that tradeable permits would be seen, in whatever form, to involve less sacrifice of national sovereignty than would internationally administered taxation. The international equity implications would depend primarily on the initial allocation of permits. It is difficult to see how this could be negotiated by nation states except on the basis that permits attached to nation states rather than to individual emissions sources. As with internationally administered taxation, there are problems and possibilities here. The initial allocation would be contentious, but would offer opportunities for addressing existing inequities as between states and for creating incentives for some states to participate. Initial national allocations based on equal per capita shares of total allowable emissions would serve the cause of international equity, and generate incentives for participation by developing nations.

There does appear to be a problem about tradeable permits, not discussed in the literature. We have noted the advantages in terms of monitoring and administration from using fossil fuels, rather than carbon dioxide emissions, as the base for taxation or quantity regulation. It is not clear that such an advantage attaches to tradeable permits. Its realisation would depend on permits relating to fossil fuels use rather than emissions. This would require that permits be defined in carbon dioxide equivalent fuel units, with one coal unit exchanging for 1.9 natural gas units, for example. Clearly, administering a system with permits so defined would involve higher costs than a system of emissions permits.

It is clear that the choice of instrument for arbitrary standard attainment for global carbon dioxide emissions abatement is a complex matter to which there is no simple answer. The weights to be attached to the various criteria are a matter of judgement. The alternative instruments score differently against each criterion.

Abatement: the size and incidence of costs

Economists have done a lot of work estimating the costs of carbon dioxide emissions abatement. They generally take a 'top-down' approach which involves using economy-wide models, and conclude that costs are substantial. Others, such as engineers, tend to follow a 'bottom-up' approach, which looks at individual production processes and methods for supplying domestic energy services, and find that there are opportunities for energy conservation and fuel switching such that substantial emissions reductions could be achieved at very low cost. Here our concern is with global abatement costs and their distribution across nations, so that we consider the modelling work of economists. A recent survey of much of this work finds that:

> estimates centre on a global loss of around 2 to 4 per cent in order to reduce emissions by about 40 to 60 per cent relative to what they otherwise would be.
>
> (Winter 1992)

In relation to these estimates, the survey notes that they 'depend on various parameters of economic behaviour' and that in the modelling studies 'there are wide variances in the assumptions used concerning some of these parameters'. Comparison of the results from different studies is also made difficult by the fact that they generally consider different standards for the global level of abatement. The draft report of the IPCC Working Group III noted above also surveys abatement cost studies. It urges caution in interpreting study results on account of differing methodologies and assumptions. For the western industrial economies it cites a range of from 1 to 2% of GDP for estimates of the national cost of stabilising carbon dioxide emissions at 1990 levels beyond the year 2000. It draws attention to the possibilities and problems in developing countries, and notes that measures to reduce atmospheric concentrations by sink enhancement, rather than emissions abatement, have considerable potential, and may involve costs similar to those for abatement: see also Read (1993).

Here we will consider the modelling work of Whalley and Wigle (1991). In terms of the global costs of carbon dioxide emissions reductions, their results lie at the higher end of the range revealed in the survey cited above. The purpose here is not to endorse these particular estimates, but rather to use them to illustrate some of the issues raised in the previous sub-section. In this model the world is divided into six regional economies, as shown in Table 9.13. Two types of energy source are distinguished, the fossil fuel and other, non-carbon, sources such as nuclear power. These are substitutable for one another in production, and energy and other inputs are also substitutes in production. International trade involves fossil fuels but not non-fossil energy, and commodities produced using both energy sources. The costs of reducing carbon dioxide emissions are measured as percentage reductions in GDP.

The results shown in Table 9.13 refer to three alternative routes to the achievement in the model of a global 50% reduction in emissions on what would otherwise have been the case. In options 1 and 2 each economy acts to cut its emissions by 50%. In 1 this is done by the imposition of the required rate of tax on the production of fossil fuels. In 2 it is the consumption of fossil fuels that is taxed. It should be noted that in terms of the discussion of alternative instruments above, both of these are, at the global level, quantity control type instruments. Each economy is required to cut by 50%, so we are dealing, from the global perspective, with uniform emissions reductions across all sources. Each source in this case is a regional economy, which uses taxation to achieve the emissions cutback required of it. Hence, at the global level neither of these is an efficient way to achieve an overall 50% cut in emissions.

Table 9.13 Costs associated with alternative instruments for emissions reductions

Region	Option 1	Option 2	Option 3
EC	−4.0	−1.0	−3.8
N. America	−4.3	−3.6	−9.8
Japan	−3.7	+0.5	−0.9
Other OECD	−2.3	−2.1	−4.4
Oil Exporters	+4.5	−18.7	−13.0
Rest of World	−7.1	−6.8	1.8
World	−4.4	−4.4	−4.2

Source: Whalley and Wigle (1991)

This is shown in Table 9.13, where world costs are higher with both 1 and 2 than with option 3. This, 3, does involve the use of the taxation instrument as discussed above. In the model, the tax is levied and collected by an international agency. Note, however, that according to these results, the cost saving in adopting the least cost instrument, as compared with quantity control and equal percentage reductions, is not great −0.2% of world GDP. This would, of course, be a large number if translated into a monetary sum. However, given the qualifications that have to be attached to the output from this kind of model, and the sensitivity of the output to plausible variations in parameter values input, we can say that the model does not demonstrate that the cost savings from following the theoretically preferred route are very great. It suggests, that is, that if an international agreement were reached which chose to ignore the theoretical case for taxation as opposed to quantity control, the costs incurred for the world as a whole would not be very great.

The results for the individual economies show how the distribution of costs varies with instrument choice. In options 1 and 2, tax revenues accrue to the individual economies, and are spent there. Option 1 then benefits carbon energy exporters at the expense of importers, especially the rest of the world which includes the developing nations together with the formerly centrally planned economies. The developing nations do slightly less badly where 50% reductions in each economy are achieved by a fossil fuel consumption tax. In this case, the oil exporters suffer heavily in GDP terms, and Japan actually gains. The costs to the fossil fuel importers are reduced because the world price of fossil fuel before tax falls, and the tax revenues are recycled within those economies.

From a sustainability perspective, it is option 3 that is interesting. Here a uniform global tax is levied and collected by an international agency. This is what gives rise to the minimised world cost. The agency disposes of the revenues by grants to each economy based on their population size. The per capita grant is the same throughout the world. In this case, not only do we have minimised cost to the global economy, but we also have a distributional impact that works to reduce inequity, by, generally, transferring funds to the developing economies. As we have noted, in the case of the enhanced greenhouse effect, equity is important not only for itself, but also for the incentives for participation that arise, in the light of the need to induce participation from large developing economies such as India and China. The distributional impact of the use of tax revenue accruing to an international agency could be made even stronger by, for example, adjusting the per capita payments such that they increased as per capita income decreased. Of course, to the extent that the industrial countries are not convinced that they can afford to have income re-distributed in this way, the incentives for them to participate would be reduced by this kind of modification.

While these results are interesting, it should be kept in mind that they are attended by numerous qualifications and uncertainties. They should not be regarded as predictions. It should be kept in mind that they refer only to costs, no benefits from carbon dioxide abatement being accounted for. These could vary across the economies distinguished in Table 9.13. Note that a tradeable permits regime should have effects similar to those shown for option 3, if the initial allocation of the permits was arranged so as to favour developing countries, as discussed above.

The Global Convention on Climate Change

As noted in 9.2, an international agreement on dealing with climate change was signed by some 150 nations in 1992. Having subsequently been ratified, this convention is now binding on its signatories. How does this convention align with the forgoing discussion?

The stated objective is the achievement of:

> stabilisation of greenhouse gas concentrations in the atmosphere at a level that would prevent dangerous anthropogenic interference with the climate system. Such a level should be achieved within a timeframe sufficient to allow ecosystems to adapt naturally to climate change, to ensure that food production is not threatened and to enable economic development to proceed in a sustainable manner.

Neither the target level for stabilisation nor the timeframe for its achievement are quantified. It should, however, be noted that it is implied, by the reference to the adaptation of ecosystems, that these are not such as to completely avoid climate change. It was agreed that during the following decade there would be two further meetings of the parties to the agreement, to review progress, and the possibility was left open for amendments in the light of new information. All the parties agreed to provide regular information on their greenhouse gas emissions, and on their efforts to prevent climate change, and mitigate its effects. This global target is in the nature of a provisional arbitrary standard, of a non-specific nature.

The industrial nations agreed to take steps to limit their emissions of greenhouse gases, with the aim of returning them to their 1990 levels by the year 2000. The convention does not say this in so many words. For the 'developed country Parties', Commitment 2a refers to 'the return by the end of the present decade to earlier levels', and Commitment 2b refers to 'their 1990 levels'. This has, to date, generally been interpreted as meaning a commitment to return to 1990 levels by 2000. Within this group of nations, the agreement is on equal proportional emissions reductions. The convention does not establish an international monitoring authority, and does not specify any penalities for non-compliance. The convention does not specify any specific targets for the developing nations.

The convention does not say anything about the instruments to be used in industrial nations. In fact, most industrial nations have not introduced any of: quantity controls, emissions taxation, tradeable permits. Most appear to be relying on moral suasion type instruments, and voluntary agreements with large fossil fuel users such as the electricity supply industry. Most already tax fossil fuels for reasons un-related to the enhanced greenhouse effect – given a relatively inelastic demand with respect to price (see 4.6) they are a good revenue base – and many are considering raising the rates for such taxation. Fossil fuel combustion is a major source of many forms of environmental pollution.

Clearly, the economic analysis of choice of instrument for pollution control has to date had little impact on the design of the 1992 international agreement concerning greenhouse gas emissions. Given the experience within nations looked at in 5.5, this should not be surprising. Nor, given the discussion generally of reciprocal spillovers in 5.4 and of the particular circumstances of the enhanced greenhouse problem here, should the non-specific nature of the global target and lack of obligations placed on developing nations be surprising.

9.8   Sustainability and policy

Clearly, the sustainability/sustainable development problem raises a very wide range of policy issues, as reflected in the extensive and rapidly growing literature. In this final section, we briefly consider just two of these issues. The first is the idea that economic growth itself is the solution to environmental problems. The second is the question of the appropriate response to the uncertainty that we have argued is a central feature of economy–environment interdependence.

Growth and the environment

The World Bank's *World Development Report 1992* (IBRD 1992) was sub-titled 'Development and the Environment'. It noted that: 'The view that greater economic activity inevitably hurts the environment is based on static assumptions about technology, tastes and environmental investments' (p. 38). If we consider, for example, the per capita emissions of some pollutant into the environment, e, and per capita income, y, then the view that is being referred to can be represented as

$$e = \alpha y \qquad\qquad [9.16]$$

so that e increases linearly with y, as shown in panel (a) of Figure 9.3. Suppose, alternatively, that the coefficient α is itself a linear function of y:

$$\alpha = \beta_0 - \beta_1 y \qquad\qquad [9.17]$$

Then, substituting [9.17] into [9.16] gives the relationship between e and y as:

$$e = \beta_0 y - \beta_1 y^2 \qquad\qquad [9.18]$$

For β_1 sufficiently small in relation to β_0, the e/y relationship takes the form of an inverted U, as shown in (b) of Figure 9.3. With this form of

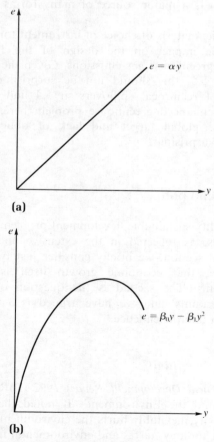

(a)

(b)

Figure 9.3   Environmental impact and income

relationship, economic growth means higher emissions per capita until per capita income reaches the turning point, y^*, and thereafter actually reduces emissions per capita.

It has been hypothesised that a relationship like that shown in 9(b) of Figure 9.3 holds for many forms of environmental degradation. Such a relationship is sometimes called an 'Environmental Kuznets Curve', EKC, after Kuznets (1955) who hypothesised an inverted U for the relationship between a measure of inequality in the distribution of income and the level of income. If the EKC hypothesis held generally, it could imply that instead of being a threat to the environment as argued in, for example, *The Limits to Growth* (Meadows *et al.* 1972), economic growth is the means to environmental improvement. That is, as countries develop economically, moving from lower to higher levels of per capita income, overall levels of environmental degradation will eventually fall.

The argument for the EKC hypothesis has been succinctly put as follows:

> At low levels of development both the quantity and intensity of environmental degradation is limited to the impacts of subsistence economic activity on the resource base and to limited quantities of biodegradable wastes. As economic development accelerates with the intensification of agriculture and other resource extraction and the take off of industrialisation, the rates of resource depletion begin to exceed the rates of resource regneration, and waste generation increases in quantity and toxicity. At higher levels of development, structural change towards information-intensive industries and services, coupled with increased environmental awareness, enforcement of environmental regulations, better technology and higher environmental expenditures, result in leveling off and gradual decline of environmental degradation.
>
> (Panayotou 1993)

Clearly, in the context of a concern for sustainable development, the empirical status of the EKC hypothesis is a matter of great importance. If economic growth is actually and generally good for the environment, there is no need to curtail growth in the world economy in order to protect the global environment. In recent years there have been a number of attempts to use econometric techniques to test the EKC hypothesis against the data. Some of the results arising are discussed below. According to one economist, the results support the conclusion that:

> there is clear evidence that, although economic growth usually leads to environmental degradation in the early stages of the process, in the end the best – and probably the only – way to attain a decent environment in most countries is to become rich.
>
> (Beckerman 1992)

With respect to the global sustainability problem, two questions arise. First, are the data generally consistent with the EKC hypothesis? Second, if the EKC hypothesis holds, does the implication that growth is good for the global environment follow? We now consider each of these questions.

Stern *et al.* (1996) critically review several investigations of the first question. Shafik and Bandyopadhyay (1992) estimated the coefficients of relationships between environmental degradation and per capita income for ten different environmental indicators as part of a background study for the *World Development Report 1992* (IBRD 1992). The indicators are: lack of clean water, lack of urban sanitation, ambient levels of suspended particulate matter, ambient sulfur oxides, change in forest area between 1961 and 1986, the annual rate of deforestation between 1961 and 1986, dissolved oxygen in rivers, faecal coliforms in rivers, municipal waste per capita, and carbon emissions per capita. Lack of clean water and lack of urban sanitation were found to decline uniformly with increasing income. Both measures of deforestation were found not to depend on income. River quality tends to worsen with increasing income. The two air pollutants, however, conform to the EKC hypothesis. Both municipal waste and carbon emissions per capita unambiguously increase with rising income. Shafik and Bandyopadhyay summarise the implications of their results by stating:

> It is possible to 'grow out of' some environmental problems, but there is nothing automatic about doing so. Action tends to be taken where there are generalised local costs and substantial private and social benefits.

Panayotou (1993) investigated the EKC hypothesis for: sulfur dioxide, SO_2; nitrous oxide, NO_x; suspended particulate matter, SPM; and deforestation. The three pollutants are measured in terms of emissions per capita on a national basis. Deforestation is measured as the mean annual rate of deforestation in the mid 1980's. All the fitted relationships are inverted U's, consistent with the EKC hypothesis. The result for SO_2 is shown in Figure 9.4: the turning point is around $3000 per capita.

Relationships such as that shown in Figure 9.4 might lead one to believe that, given likely future levels of income per capita, the global environmental impact concerned would decline in the medium term future. The turning point is near world mean income. In fact, because of the highly skewed distribution for per capita incomes, with many more countries – including some with very large populations – below rather than above the mean, this may not be what such a relationship implies.

Sterm *et al.* (1996) illustrated this, using the projections of world economic growth and world population growth published in the *World Development Report 1992* (IBRD, 1992), together with Panayotou's EKC estimates for deforestation and SO_2 emissions to produce global projections of these variables for the period 1990–2025. These are important cases from a sustainable development perspective. SO_2 emissions are a factor in the acid rain problem: deforestation, especially in the tropics, is considered a major source of biodiversity loss. They projected population and economic growth for every country in the World with a population greater than 1 million in 1990. The aggregated projections give world population growing from 5265 million in 1990 to 8322 million in 2025, and mean world per capita income rising from £3957 in 1990 to $7127 in 2025. They then forecast deforestation and SO_2 emissions for each country individually using the coefficients for

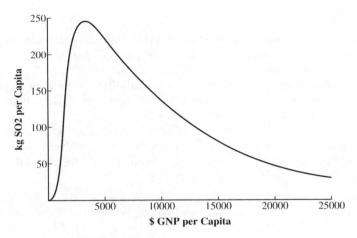

Source: Panayotou (1993)

Figure 9.4 An EKC for SO_2

Panayotou's fitted ECKs. These forecasts were aggregated to give global projections for forest cover and SO_2 emissions. Total global SO_2 emissions rise from 383 million tonnes in 1990 to 1181 million tonnes in 2025; emissions of SO_2 per capita rise from 73 kg to 142 kg from 1990 to 2025. Forest cover declines from 40.4 million km^2 in 1990 to a minimum of 37.2 million km^2 in 2016, and then increases to 37.6 million km^2 in 2025. Biodiversity loss on account of deforestation is an irreversible environmental impact, except on evolutionary timescales, so that even in this case the implications of the fitted EKC are not reassuring.

Generally, the work of Stern *et al.* shows that the answer to the second question is that even if the data appear to confirm that the EKC fits the experience of individual countries, it does not follow that further growth is good for the global environment. Arrow *et al.* (1995) reach a similar position on the relevance of the EKC hypothesis for policy in relation to sustainability. They note that:

> The general proposition that economic growth is good for the environment has been justified by the claim that there exists an empirical relation between per capita income and some measures of environmental quality.

They then note that the EKC relationship has been 'shown to apply to a selected set of pollutants only', but that some economists 'have conjectured that the curve applies to environmental quality generally'. Arrow *et al.* conclude that

> Economic growth is not a panacea for environmental quality; indeed it is not even the main issue

and that

> policies that promote gross national product growth are not substitutes for environmental policy.

Responding to uncertainty

We have laid some stress on the uncertainties attending sustainability issues. In Chapter 8 we discussed some aspects of the way risk and uncertainty are handled in economics, and, particularly in cost benefit analysis. In recent years the increasing prominence of sustainability on political agenda has given rise to the emergence of some new ideas about dealing with risk and uncertainty. These are now briefly reviewed.

The *precautionary principle* is gaining widespread acceptance, at the governmental and intergovernmental levels, as a concept which should inform policy toward the natural environment. Thus, for example, Principle 15 of the June 1992 Rio Declaration is that:

> In order to protect the environment, the precautionary approach shall be widely applied by States according to their capabilities. Where there are threats of serious or irreversible damage, lack of full scientific certainty shall not be used as a reason for postponing cost-effective measures to prevent environmental degradation.

The principle addresses a problem central to sustainability – an inability to predict all of the future consequences for human interests of current actions with environmental impacts. However, it does not offer much in the way of guidance as to how the problem should be dealt with. To say that a lack of certainty should not be a reason for not taking measures to protect the environment from serious and irreversible damage, does not say anything about what should be done and how much should be done. Nor does the principle as enunciated in such statements as that cited above suggest how one might set about answering such questions.

The status of the precautionary principle is similar to that of the modified safe minimum standard discussed in Chapter 8. That says that a project with irreversible consequences which are unknown but could be serious should not be undertaken, unless the social costs of not undertaking the project are unacceptably high. As noted in Chapter 8, it remains in any particular case to determine what 'unacceptably high' means. However, as compared with the standard cost benefit analysis approach, the question to be answered has been changed. A wholehearted adoption of the precautionary principle would appear to imply a similar re-orientation. Currently, the situation generally is that there is a presumption in favour of going ahead with commercially viable projects. The presumption may be overturned in any particular case if it can be established that serious or irreversible environmental damage is entailed. According to a strong interpretation of the precautionary principle, the presumption is reversed. Since all projects have some environmental impact, it is necessary that any particular project be shown not to have serious or irreversible consequences before it can be approved. A loose analogy is a shift from the judicial assumption of the accused person's innocence unless guilt can be proved, to an assumption of guilt unless innocence can be proved.

Clearly, such a shift could have profound consequences for economic activity, given that many prospective projects involve genuine innovation and novelty, so that there is no previous experience upon which to base an assessment of their consequences. The question which arises is whether there are any policy instruments which are consistent with the precautionary principle, and which could constitute a feasible means for its implementation in such a way as to avoid an outcome which simply prohibits projects with uncertain environmental consequences from being undertaken.

Environmental performance bonds have recently been advocated as policy instruments consistent with the precautionary principle, but which avoid simply prohibiting projects attended by major environmental uncertainties: see Perrings (1989) and Costanza and Perrings (1990). The basic ideas involved can be discussed by considering some firm which wishes to undertake a project involving technological innovation, so that there is not past experience according to which probabilities can be assigned to all possible outcomes. An example of such a project would have been the construction of the first nuclear power plant.

We assume that there is in existence an Environmental Protection Agency, EPA, without permission from which the firm cannot go ahead with the project. The EPA takes independent expert advice on the project, and comes to a view about the worst conceivable environmental outcome of the project going ahead. Approval of the project is then conditional on the firm depositing with the EPA a bond of £x, where this is the estimate of the social cost of the worst conceivable outcome. The bond is fully or partially returned to the firm at the end of the project's lifetime, according to the damage actually occurring over the lifetime. Thus, if there is no damage the firm gets back £x, plus some proportion of the interest. The withheld proportion of the interest is to cover EPA administration costs and to finance EPA research. If the damage actually occurring is £y, the firm gets back £x − £y, with appropriate interest adjustment. For £x equal to £y, the firm gets nothing back, forfeiting the full value of the bond. It is, of course, possible that £y will turn out to be greater than £x, in which case also the firm gets back £0.

The advantages claimed for such an instrument are in terms of the incentives it creates for the firm to undertake research to investigate environmental impact and means to reduce it, as well as in terms of stopping projects. Taking the latter point first, suppose that the EPA decides on £x as the size of the bond, and that the firm assesses lifetime project net returns to it as £$(x − 1)$, and accepts that £x is the appropriate estimate of actual damage to arise. Then it will not wish to go ahead with the project. If, however, the firm took the view that actual damage would be less than £x, it would wish to go ahead with the project. The firm has, then, an incentive to itself assess the damage that the project could cause, and to research means to reduce that damage. Further, if it does undertake the project it has an ongoing incentive to seek damage minimising methods of operation, so as to increase the eventual size of the sum returned to it, £x − £y. This incentive effect could be enhanced by having the size of the bond posted periodically adjustable. Thus, if the firm could at any point in time in the life of the project, on the basis of its research, convince the EPA that the worst conceivable lifetime damage was less than £x, the original bond could be returned and a new one for an amount less than £x be posted.

Environmental performance bonds would entail the shift in the basic presumption about projects that a strong interpretation of the precautionary principle implies. At the end of the project lifetime, the burden of proof as to the magnitude of actual damage would rest with the firm, not the EPA. The presumption would be, that is, that the bond was not returnable. It would be up to the firm to convince the EPA that actual damage was less than £x if it wished to get any of its money back. This would generate incentives for the firm to monitor damage in convincing ways, as well as to research means to minimise damage. In the event that damage up to the amount of the bond, £x, occurred, society, as represented by the EPA, would have received compensation. If damage in excess of £x had occurred, society would not receive full compensation. Recall that £x is to be set at the largest amount of damage seen as conceivable by the EPA at the outset, on the basis of expert advice. A socially responsible EPA would have an incentive to take a cautious view of the available evidence, implying a high figure for £x, so that society would not find itself un-compensated. This, it could be argued, would coincide with the selfish motivations of EPA staff, since a higher £x would mean more funding available for EPA administration and research.

Environmental performance bonds are clearly an interesting idea as an addition to the range of instruments for environmental protection, given the pervasiveness of uncertainty and the need for research addressed at reducing it. In the form discussed here, they do not appear to be in use anywhere. Their usefulness would appear, as with other environmental policy instruments, to vary with particular circumstances, and clearly further consideration of the details of their possible implementation is warranted.

The precautionary principle entails a largely different way of thinking about project appraisal in relation to social goals from that embodied in the standard economics approach via allocative efficiency and cost benefit analysis. On the other hand, given recognition of pervasive uncertainty and acceptance of the precautionary principle, economists should have no problems with the idea of environmental performance bonds. They are an example of the class of price incentive type policy instruments. This exemplifies a more general point. Sustainability as a policy objective makes questionable the standard economics of determining policy goals, while leaving largely intact the standard economic analysis of policy instruments. This general point is developed in Common (1995).

References

Abelson, P. 1979. *Cost Benefit Analysis and Environmental Problems*. Farnborough: Saxon House.

Ahmad, Y., El Serafy, S. and Lutz, E. (eds) 1989. *Environmental Accounting for Sustainable Development: A UNDP-World Bank Symposium*. Washington: World Bank.

Anderson, E.J. 1985. *Natural Resources in Canada: economic theory and policy*. Agincourt, Ontario: Methuen.

Anderson, K. 1992a. The standard welfare economics of policies affecting trade and the environment. In: Anderson, K. and Blackhurst, R. (eds) *The Greening of World Trade Issues*. Hemel Hempstead: Harvester Wheatsheaf.

Anderson, K. 1992b. Effects on the environment and welfare of liberalising world trade: the cases of coal and food. In: Anderson, K. and Blackhurst, R. (eds) *The Greening of World Trade Issues*. Hemel Hempstead: Harvester Wheatsheaf.

Anderson, L.G. (ed). 1977. *Economic Impacts of Extended Fisheries Jurisdiction*. Anne Arbor, Michigan: Science Publishers.

Anderson, L.G. 1995. Privatising open access fisheries: individual transferable quotas. In: Bromley, D.W. (ed) *The Handbook of Environmental Economics*. Oxford: Blackwell.

Anderson, V. 1991. *Alternative Economic Indicators*. London: Routledge.

Arndt, H.W. 1978. *The Rise and Fall of Economic Growth: a study in contemporary thought*. Sydney: Longman Cheshire.

Arrow, K., Solow, R., Leamer, E., Portney, P., Radner, R. and Schuman, H. 1992. *Report of the NOAA Panel on Contingent Valuation*. Federal Register, 58, 10, p. 4601–14, Washington D.C..

Arrow, K., Bolin, B., Costanza, R., Dasgupta, P., Folke, C., Holling, C.S., Jansson, B.-O., Levin, S., Miler, K-G., Perrings, C. and Pimental, D. 1995. Economic growth carrying capacity and the environment, *Science*, **268**, 520–1.

Ashley, H., Rudman, R. and Whipple, C. 1976. *Energy and the Environment: a risk-benefit approach*. New York: Pergamon.

Ayres, R.U. and Kneese, A.V. 1969. Production consumption and externalities, *American Economic Review*, **59**, 282–97.

Barbier, E.B., Burgess, J.C., Swanson, T.M. and Pearce, D.W. 1990. *Elephants, Economics and Ivory*. London: Earthscan.

Barbier, E.B., Burgess, J.C. and Folke, C. 1994. *Paradise Lost?: the ecological economics of biodiversity*. London: Earthscan.

Barbour, I.G. 1980. *Technology Environment and Human Values*. New York: Praeger.

Barnett, H.J. and Morse, C. 1963. *Scarcity and Growth: the economics of natural resources availability*. Baltimore: Johns Hopkins University Press.

Bartelmus, P. 1994. *Environment Growth and Development: the concepts and strategies of sustainability*. London: Routledge.

Bartelmus, P., Stahmer, C. and van Tongeren, J. 1993. Integrated environmental and economic accounting – a framework for an SNA satellite system. In: Lutz, E. (ed.) *Toward Improved Accounting for the Environment*. An UNSTAT – World Bank Symposium, The World Bank, Washington DC.

Baumol, W.J. and Oates, W.E. 1971. The use of standards and prices for the protection of the environment. *Swedish Journal of Economics*, **73**, 42–54.

Baumol, W.J. and Oates, W.E. 1979. *Economics Environmental Policy and the Quality of Life*. Englewood Cliffs, New Jersey: Prentice-Hall.

Baumol, W.J. and Oates, W.E. 1988. *The Theory of Environmental Policy: externalities public outlays and the quality of life* (2nd edn). Englewood Cliffs, New Jersey: Prentice Hall.

Bayliss-Smith, T.P. 1982. *The Ecology of Agricultural Systems*. Cambridge: Cambridge University Press.

Beckerman, W. 1974. *In Defence of Economic Growth*. London: Jonathan Cape.

Beckerman, W. 1980. *Introduction to National Income Analysis* (3rd edn). London: Weidenfeld & Nicolson.

Beckerman, W. 1992. Economic growth and the environment: whose growth? whose environment?, *World Development*, **20**, 481–96.

Berck, P. 1995. Empirical consequences of the hotelling principle. In: Bromley, D.W. (ed.) *The Handbook of Environmental Economics*. Oxford: Blackwell.

Bernstam, M.S. 1991. *The Wealth of Nations and the Environment*. London: Institute of Economic Affairs.

Bishop, R.C. 1978. Endangered species and uncertainty: the economics of a safe minimum standard, *American Journal of Agricultural Economics*, **60**, 10–18.

Bishop, R.C., Champ, P.A., and Mullarky, D.J. 1995. Contingent valuation. In: Bromley, D.W. (ed.) *The Handbook of Environmental Economics*. Oxford: Blackwell.

Bisset, R. 1983. A critical survey of methods for environmental impact assessment. In: O'Riordan, T. and Turner, R.K. (eds). *An Annotated Reader in Environmental Planning and Management*. Oxford: Pergamon.

Blackman, S.A.B. and Baumol, W.J. 1980. Modified fiscal incentives in environmental policy. *Land Economics*, **56**, 417–43.

Blamey, R. and Common, M. 1994. Sustainability and the limits to pseudo market valuation. In: van den Bergh, J. and van der Straaten, J. (eds) *Concepts, Methods and Policy for Sustainable Development: critique and new approaches*. Washington D.C.: Island Press.

Blamey, R., Common, M. and Quiggin, J. 1995. Respondents to contingent valuation: consumers or citizens?, *Australian Journal of Agricultural Economics*, **39**, 263–88.

Blaug, M. 1985. *Economic Theory in Retrospect* (4th edn). Cambridge: Cambridge University Press.

Bliss, M. 1975. *Capital Theory and the Distribution of Income*. Amsterdam: North Holland.

Bockstael, N.E. 1995. Travel cost models. In: Bromley, D.W. (ed) *The Handbook of Environmental Economics*. Oxford: Blackwell.

Böhm, P. 1974. *Social Efficiency: a concise introduction to welfare economics*. London: Macmillan.

Böhm, P. and Russell, C.C. 1985. Comparative analysis of alternative policy instruments. In: Kneese, A.V. and Sweeney, J.L. (eds) *Handbook of Natural Resource and Energy Economics Volume I*. Amsterdam: North-Holland.

Boulding, K.E. 1966. The economics of the coming spaceship earth. In: Jarrett, H. (ed.) *Environmental Quality in a Growing Economy*. Baltimore: Johns Hopkins University Press.

Boulding, K.E. 1981. *Evolutionary Economics*. Beverly Hills: Sage.

Bowes, M. and Krutilla, J.V. 1989. *Multiple Use Management: the economics of public forest-lands*. Washington D.C.: Resources for the Future.

Bowler, P.J. 1992. *The Fontana History of the Environmental Sciences*. London: Fontana.

Brown, G.M. and Field, B.C. 1978. Implications of alternative measures of resource scarcity, *Journal of Political Economy*, **86**, 229–43.

Buchanan, J.M. and Tullock, G. 1980. *Toward a Theory of the Rent Seeking Society*. Texas: A & M Press.

Burmeister, E. 1980. *Capital Theory and Dynamics*. Cambridge: Cambridge University Press.

Burrows, P. 1979. *The Economic Theory of Pollution Control*. London: Martin Robertson.

Bussey, L.E. 1978. *The Economic Analysis of Industrial Projects*. Englewood Cliffs, New Jersey: Prentice-Hall.

Cairncross, F. 1992. *Costing the Earth: the challenge for governments, the opportunities for business*. Boston: Harvard Business School.

Carraro, C. and Siniscalco, D. (eds) 1993. *The European Carbon Tax: an economic assessment*. Dordrecht: Kluwer.

Carson, R. 1962. *Silent Spring*. Harmondsworth: Penguin.

Carson, R., Wright, J., Carson, N., Aberni, A. and Flores, N. 1995. *A Bibliography of Contingent Valuation Studies and Papers*. La Jolla: Natural Resource Damage Assessment Inc.

Central Statistical Office. 1991. *Annual Abstract of Statistics*. London: HMSO.

Central Statistical Office. 1993. *Economic Trends Annual Supplement: 1992 edition*. London: HMSO.

Chapman, P. 1975. *Fuel's Paradise: energy options for Britain*. Harmondsworth: Penguin.

Chapman, P. and Roberts, F. 1983. *Metal Resources and Energy*. London: Butterworth.

Christensen, P. 1989. Historical roots for ecological economics: biophysical versus allocative approaches, *Ecological Economics*, **1**, 17–36.

Christoff, P. 1995. Market-based instruments: the Australian experience. In: Eckersley, R. (ed) *Markets, the State and the Environment*. Melbourne: Macmillan.

Cipolla, C. 1962. *The Economic History of World Population*. Harmondsworth: Penguin.

Ciriacy-Wantrup, S.V. 1968. *Resource Conservation: economics and politics*. Los Angeles: University of California.

Clark, C.W. 1976. *Mathematical Bioeconomics*. New York: John Wiley & Sons.

Cleveland, C.J. 1993. An exploration of alternative measures of resource scarcity: the case of petroleum resources, *Ecological Economics*, **7**, 123–57.

Coase, R. 1960. The problem of social cost. *Journal of Law and Economics*, **3**, 1–44.

Common, M.S. 1977. A note on the use of taxes to control pollution. *Scandinavian Journal of Economics*, **79**, 346–9.

Common, M.S. 1981. Implied elasticities in some UK energy projections. *Energy Economics*, **3**, 154–9.

Common, M.S. 1985. The distributional implications of higher energy prices in the UK. *Applied Economics*, **17**, 421–36.

Common, M.S. 1989. The choice of pollution control instruments: why is so little notice taken of economists' recommendations? *Environment and Planning A*, **21**, 1297–314.

Common, M.S. 1995. *Sustainability and Policy: Limits to Economics*. Melbourne: Cambridge University Press.

Common, M.S. and Peirson, J. 1979. Environmental benefits and the economics of UK solar energy schemes. *Energy Economics*, **1**, 134–8.

Common, M.S. and McPherson, P. 1982. A note on energy requirements calculations using the 1968 and 1974 input output tables. *Energy Policy*, **10**, 42–9.

Common, M. and Norton, T.W. 1992. Biodiversity: its conservation in Australia, *Ambio*, **XXI**, 258–65.

Common, M. and Salma, U. 1992. Accounting for Australian carbon dioxide emissions. *The Economic Record*, **68**, 31–42.

Commoner, B. 1963. *Science and Survival*. New York: Ballantine.

Commoner, B. 1972. *The Closing Circle*. London: Jonathan Cape.

CONEAS. 1980. *Energy in Transition 1985–2010.* Final report of the Committee on Nuclear and Alternative Energy Systems. San Francisco: W.H. Freeman.

Conway, G.R. 1985. Agroecosystem analysis, *Agricultural Administration,* **20**, 31–55.

Conrad, J.M. and Clark, C.W. 1987. *Natural Resource Economics: notes and problems.* Cambridge: Cambridge University Press.

Costanza, R. 1989. What is ecological economics?, *Ecological Economics,* **1** 1–17.

Costanza, R. (ed.) 1991. *Ecological Economics: the science and management of sustainability.* New York: Columbia University Press.

Costanza, R. and Perrings, C. 1990. A flexible assurance bonding system for improved environmental management, *Ecological Economics,* **2**, 57–75.

Cropper, M.L. and Oates, W.E. 1992. Environmental economics: a survey. *Journal of Economic Literature,* **XXX**, 675–740.

Dales, J.H. 1968. *Pollution, Property and Prices.* Toronto: Toronto University Press.

Daly, H.E. 1973. The steady state economy: toward a political economy of biophysical equilibrium and moral growth. In: Daly, H.E. (ed.) *Toward a Steady State Economy.* San Francisco: W.H. Freeman.

Daly, H.E. 1968. On economics as a life science. *Journal of Political Economy,* **76**, 392–406.

Daly, H.E. 1995. On Wilfred Beckerman's critique of sustainable development. *Environmental Values,* **4**, 49–55.

Daly, H.E. and Cobb, J.B. 1989. *For the Common Good: redirecting the economy toward community, the environment and a sustainable future.* Boston: Beacon.

Darnell, R.M. 1973. *Ecology and Man.* New York: W.C. Brown.

Dasgupta, P. 1982. *The Control of Resources.* Oxford: Basil Blackwell.

Dasgupta, P.S. and Heal, G.M. 1974. The optimal depletion of exhaustible resources. *Review of Economic Studies,* Symposium, 3–28.

Dasgupta, P. and Heal, G.M. 1979. *Economic Theory and Exhaustible Resources.* Cambridge: Cambridge University Press.

Department of Employment. 1992. *Family Expenditure Survey 1980.* London: HMSO.

Department of Energy. 1984. *Digest of United Kingdom Energy Statistics 1983.* London: HMSO.

Dorfman, R., Samuelson, P.A. and Solow, R.T. 1958. *Linear Programming and Economic Analysis.* New York: McGraw-Hill.

Dovers, S. 1994. Historical and current patterns of energy use. In: Dovers, S. (ed.) *Sustainable Energy Systems: pathways for Australian energy reform.* Cambridge: Cambridge University Press.

Eden, R., Posner, M., Bending, R., Crouch, E. and Stanislaw, J. 1981. *Energy Economics: growth resources and policies.* Cambridge: Cambridge University Press.

Ehrlich, P.R. and Ehrlich, A.H. 1970. *Population Resources Environment.* San Francisco: W.H. Freeman.

Ehrlich, P.R. and Ehrlich, A.E. 1981. *Extinction: the causes and consequences of the disappearance of species.* New York: Random House.

Ehrlich, P.R. and Ehrlich, A.E. 1992. The value of biodiversity. *Ambio,* **XXI**, 219–26.

Ellis, G.M. and Fisher, A.C. 1987. Valuing the environment as input. *Journal of Environmental Economics and Management,* **25**, 149–56.

Esty, D.C. 1994. *Greening the GATT: trade environment and the future.* Washington D.C.: Institute for International Economics.

Fernie, J. and Pitkethly, A.S. 1985. *Resources, Environment and Policy.* New York: Harper & Row.

Fisher, A.C. 1981. *Resource and Environmental Economics.* Cambridge: Cambridge University Press.

Forster, B.A. 1975. Optimal pollution control with a non-constant exponential decay rate, *Journal of Environmental Economics and Management,* **2**, 1–6.

Freeman, A.M. 1979. *The Benefits of Environmental Improvement: theory and practice.* Baltimore: Johns Hopkins University Press.

Freeman, A.M. 1982. Benefits of air pollution control. In: Tolley, G.S., Graves, P.E.

and Cohen, A.S. (eds) *Environmental Policy: air quality*. Cambridge, Massachusetts: Ballinger.

Freeman, A.M. 1985. Methods for assessing the benefits of environmental programs. In: Kneese, A.V. and Sweeney, J.L. (eds) *Handbook of Natural Resource and Energy Economics Volume I*. Amsterdam: North-Holland.

Freeman, A.M. 1995. Hedonic pricing methods. In: Bromley, D.W. (ed.) *The Handbook of Environmental Economics*. Oxford: Blackwell.

Frey, B.S., Schneider, F. and Pommerehne, W.W. 1985. Economists' opinions on environmental policy instruments: analysis of a survey, *Journal of Environmental Economics and Management*, **12**, 62–71.

Georgescu-Roegen, N. 1971. *The Entropy Law and the Economic Process*. Cambridge, M.A.: Harvard University Press.

Georgescu-Roegen, N. 1976. Energy and economic myths. In: Georgescu-Roegen, N.E. *Energy and Economic Myths: institutional and analytical economic essays*. New York: Pergamon.

Georgescu-Roegen, N. 1979. Energy analysis and economic valuation. *Southern Economic Journal*, **45**, 1023–58.

Gilpin, A. 1995. *Environmental Impact Assessment: a cutting edge for the twenty-first century*. Cambridge: Cambridge University Press.

Goldsmith, E., Allen, R., Allaby, M., Davoll, J. and Lawrence, S. 1973. *A Blueprint for Survival*. London: Tom Stacey.

Gravelle, H. and Rees, R. 1981. *Microeconomics*. London: Longman.

Griffin, J.M. and Steele, H.B. 1980. *Energy Economics and Policy*. New York: Academic Press.

Grubb, M. 1990. *Energy Policies and the Greenhouse Effect: Volume 1 policy appraisal*. Aldershot: Royal Institute of Economic Affairs.

Gujarati, D.N. 1995. *Basic Econometrics* (3rd edn). New York: McGraw-Hill.

Hahn, R.W. 1993. Getting more environmental protection for less money: a practitioner's guide. *Oxford Review of Economic Policy*, **9**, 112–23.

Hahn, R.W. 1995. Economic prescriptions for environmental problems: lessons from the United States and continental Europe. In: Eckersley, R. (ed.) *Markets, the State and the Environment*. Melbourne: Macmillan.

Hahn, R.W. and Hester, G. 1989a. Marketable permits: lessons for theory and practice. *Ecology Law Quarterly*, **16**, 361–406.

Hahn, R.W. and Hester, G. 1989b. Where did all the markets go?: an analysis of EPA's emission trading program. *Yale Journal on Regulation*, **6**, 109–53.

Hall, C.A.S., Cleveland, C.J. and Kaufman, R. 1992. *Energy and Resource Quality: the ecology of the economic process*. Niwot: University of Colarado Press.

Hall, D.C. and Hall, J.V. 1984. Concepts and measures of natural resource scarcity with a summary of recent trends. *Journal of Environmental Economics and Management*, **11**, 363–79.

Halm, G.N. 1968. *Economic Systems: a comparative analysis (3rd edn)*. New York: Holt Rinehart & Winston.

Hanley, N. and Spash, C. 1993. *Cost-benefit Analysis and the Environment*. Aldershot: Edward Elgar.

Hardin, G. 1968. The tragedy of the commons, *Science*, **162**, 1243–8.

Hardin, G. 1993. *Living within Limits: ecology economics and population taboos*. New York: Oxford University Press.

Hardin, G. and Baden, J. 1977. *Managing the Commons*. San Francisco: W.H. Freeman.

Hartwick, J.M. 1977. Intergenerational equity and the investing of rents from exhaustible resources. *American Economic Review*, **66**, 972–4.

Hartwick, J.M. 1989. *Non-renewable Resource Extraction Programs and Markets*. Chur: Harwood Academic.

Hartwick, J.M. 1990. National accounting and economic depreciation. *Journal of Public Economics*, **43**, 291–304.

Hartwick, J.M. and Hageman, A.P. 1993. Economic depreciation of mineral stocks and the contribution of El Serafy. In: Lutz, E. (ed.) *Toward Improved Accounting for the Environment: an UNSTAT-World Bank Symposium*. Washington: World Bank.

Hartwick, J.M. and Olewiler, N.D. 1986. *The Economics of Natural Resource Use*. New York: Harper & Row.

Hausman, J. (ed.) 1993. *Contingent Valuation: a critical assessment*. Amsterdam: North Holland.

Hawkins, C.J. and Pearce, D.W. 1971. *Capital Investment Appraisal*. London: Macmillan.

Henderson, J.V. and Tugwell, M. 1979. Exploitation of the lobster fishery: some empirical results. *Journal of Environmental Economics and Management*, **6**, 287–96.

Herfindahl, O.C. and Kneese, A.V. 1974. *Economic Theory of Natural Resources*. Columbus, Ohio: C.E. Merrill.

Hirsch, F. 1977. *Social Limits to Growth*. London: Routledge & Kegan Paul.

Hirshleifer, J. 1980. *Price Theory and Applications* (2nd edn). Englewood Cliffs, New Jersey: Prentice-Hall.

Holister, G. and Porteous, A. 1976. *The Environment: a dictionary of the world around us*. London: Arrow.

Holling, C.S. 1986. The resilience of terrestial ecosystems: local surprise and global change. In: Clark, W.C. and Munn, R.E. (eds) *Sustainable Development in the Biosphere*. Cambridge: Cambridge University Press.

Houghton, J.T., Jenkins, G.J. and Ephrams, J.J. 1990. *Climate Change: the IPCC scientific assessment*. Cambridge: Cambridge University Press.

Houghton, J.T., Callander, B.A., and Varney, S.K. (eds) 1992. *Climate Change 1992: The Supplementary Report to the IPCC Scientific Assessment*. Cambridge: Cambridge University Press.

Howe, C.W. 1979. *Natural Resource Economics: issues analysis and policy*. New York: John Wiley & Sons.

Hunt, E.K. and Sherman, H.J. 1981. *Economics: an introduction to traditional and radical views*. New York: Harper & Row.

IBRD. 1992. *World Development Report 1992*. New York: Oxford University Press.

Inhaber, H. 1979. Risk with energy from conventional and nonconventional sources. *Science*, **203**, 718–23.

International Union for Conservation of Nature and Natural Resources 1980. *World Conservation Strategy*. Gland: IUCN/UNEP/WWF.

Jacobs, M. 1991. *The Green Economy: environment sustainable development and the politics of the future*. London: Pluto.

Jacobs, M. 1995. Financial incentives: the British experience, in Eckersley, R. (ed.) *Markets, the State and the Environment*. Melbourne: Macmillan.

Jansson, A.M., Hammer, M., Folke, C. and Costanza, R. (eds) 1994. *Investing in Natural Capital: the ecological economics approach to sustainability*. Washington D.C.: Island Press.

Jevons, W.S. 1865. *The Coal Question: An inquiry concerning the progress of the nation and the probable exhaustion of our coal mines*. Flux, A.W. (ed). (rev. 3rd edn 1965). New York: A.M. Kelly.

Johansson, P.-O. 1987. *The Economic Theory and Measurement of Environmental Benefits*. Cambridge: Cambridge University Press.

Johansson, P. and Löfgren, K. 1985. *The Economics of Forestry and Natural Resources*. Oxford: Basil Blackwell.

Johnson, R.W. and Brown Jnr, G.M. 1976. *Cleaning up Europe's Waters: economics management and policies*. New York: Praeger.

Jorgenson, D.W. and Wilcoxen, P.J. 1990. Environmental regulation and U.S. economic growth, *Rand Journal of Economics*, **2**, 314–41.

Kapp, K.W. 1950. *The Social Costs of Private Enterprise*. Cambridge, Mass.: Harvard University Press.

Keynes, J.M. 1936. *The General Theory of Employment, Interest and Money*. London: Macmillan.

Kneese, A.V. and Bower, B.T. 1968. *Managing Water Quality: economics technology and institutions*. Baltimore: Johns Hopkins University Press.

Kneese, A.V., Ayres, R.V. and D'Arge, R.C. 1970. *Economics and the Environment: a materials balance approach*. Baltimore: Johns Hopkins University Press.

Kneese, A.V. 1977. *Economics and the Environment*. Harmondsworth: Penguin.

Krebs, C.J. 1972. *Ecology: the experimental analysis of distribution and abundance*. New York: Harper & Row.

Krutilla, J.V. and Fisher, A.C. 1975. *The Economics of Natural Environments: studies in the valuation of commodity and amenity resources*. Baltimore: Johns Hopkins University Press.

Kuznets, S. 1955. Economic growth and income inequality. *American Economic Review*, **49**, 1–28.

Landsberg, H.H. (chairman) 1979. *Energy: the next twenty years*. Report sponsored by the Ford Foundation and administered by Resources for the Future. Massachusetts: Ballinger.

Lave, L. and Seskin, E. 1977. *Air Pollution and Human Health. Resources for the Future*. Baltimore: Johns Hopkins University Press.

Layard, P.R.G. (ed) 1972. *Cost Benefit Analysis*. Harmondsworth: Penguin.

Layard, P.R.G. and Walters, A.A. 1978. *Microeconomic Theory*. New York: McGraw-Hill.

Leach, G. 1975. *Energy and Food Production*. London: International Institute for Environment and Development.

Leach, G., Lewis, C., Romig, F., Van Buren, A. and Foley, G. 1977. *A Low Energy Strategy for the UK*. London: International Institute for Environment and Development.

Lecomber, R. 1975. *Economic Growth versus the Environment*. London: Macmillan.

Leeman, W.A. 1977. *Centralized and Decentralized Economic Systems: the Soviet-type economy market socialism and capitalism*. Chicago: Rand McNally.

Leggett, J. (ed.) *Global Warming: the Greenpeace report*. Oxford: Oxford University Press.

Leontief, W. 1966. *Input–output Economics*. Oxford: Oxford University Press.

Leontief, W. 1970. Environmental repercussions and economic structure. *Review of Economics and Statistics*, **52**, 262–71.

Leontief, W. and Ford, D. 1972. Air pollution and economic structure: empirical results of input output computations. In: Brody, A. and Carter, A. (eds). *Input Output Techniques*. Amsterdam: North-Holland.

Lovins, A.B. 1975. *World Energy Strategies*. New York: Friends of the Earth.

Lowe, J. and Lewis, D. 1980. *The Economics of Environmental Management*. Oxford: Philip Allan.

Lutz, E. (ed.) 1993. *Toward Improved Accounting for the Environment: an UNSTAT-World Bank Symposium*. Washington: World Bank.

McCormick, J. 1989. *The Global Environmental Movement; Reclaiming Paradise*. London: Bellhaven Press.

McGartland, A.E. and Oates, W.E. 1985. Marketable permits for the prevention of environmental deterioration. *Journal of Environmental Economics and Management*, **12**, 207–28.

McInerney, J. 1976. The simple analytics of natural resource economics. *Journal of Agricultural Economics*, **27**, 31–52.

Maddox, J. 1972. *The Doomsday Syndrome*. New York: McGraw-Hill.

Mäler, K.-G. 1990. International environmental problems. *Oxford Review of Economic Policy*, **6**, 80–107.

Mäler, K.-G. 1991. National accounts and environmental resources. *Environmental and Resource Economics*, **1**, 1–15.

Malthus, T. 1798. *An Essay on the Principle of Population.* Flew, A. (ed. 1970). London: Pelican.

Mandell, E. 1968. *Marxist Economic Theory.* London: Merlin Press.

Marshall, A. 1890. *Principles of Economics.* London: Macmillan.

Martinez-Alier, J. 1987. *Ecological Economics.* Oxford: Basil Blackwell.

Marx, K. 1960 edition. *Capital* (3 vols). Moscow: Foreign Languages Publishing House.

Meadows, D.H., Meadows, D.L., Randers, J. and Behrens, W.W. 1972. *The Limits to Growth.* New York: Earth Island.

Meadows, D.H., Meadows, D.L., and Randers, J. 1992. *Beyond the Limits: global collapse or a sustainable future.* London; Earthscan.

Mendez, R.P. 1992. *International Public Finance: a new perspective on global relations.* New York: Oxford University Press.

Merrett, A.J. and Sykes, A. 1973. *The Finance and Analysis of Capital Projects* (2nd edn). London: Longman.

Midgley, K. and Burns, R. 1977. *The Capital Market: its nature and significance.* London: Macmillan.

Mill, J.S. 1857. *Principles of Political Economy.* London: J.W. Parker & Son.

Mills, E.S. 1978. *The Economics of Environmental Quality.* New York: Norton.

Mishan, E.J. 1975. *Cost Benefit Analysis* (2nd edn). London: George Allen & Unwin.

Mishan, E.J. 1977. *The Economic Growth Debate: an assessment.* London: George Allen & Unwin.

Mitchell, R. and Carson, R. 1989. *Using Surveys to Value Public Goods: the contingent valuation method.* Washington D.C.: Resources for the Future.

Montgomery, D.W. 1972. Markets in licences and efficient pollution control programs. *Journal of Economic Theory,* **5**, 395–418.

Montgomery, C.A. and Adams, D.M. 1995. Optimal timber management policies. In: Bromley, D.W. (ed.) *The Handbook of Environmental Economics.* Oxford: Blackwell.

Moran, A., Chisholm, A. and Porter, M. 1991. *Markets Resources and the Environment.* Sydney: Allen & Unwin.

Myers, N. 1979. *The Sinking Ark.* New York: Pergamon.

National Economic Development Office. 1975. *Price Propagation in an Input–output Model – determining the implications of higher energy prices for industrial costs.* London: HMSO.

Nelson, R.H. 1987. The economics profession and the making of public policy. *Journal of Economic Literature,* **XXV**, 49–91.

Neuberger, E. and Duffy, W. 1976. *Comparative Economic Systems: a decision-making approach.* Boston: Allyn & Bacon.

Nijkamp, P. 1980. *Environmental Policy Analysis: operational methods and models.* New York: John Wiley & Sons.

Nordhaus, W.D. 1977. The demand for energy: an international perspective. In: Nordhaus, W.D. (ed.) *International Studies in the Demand for Energy.* Amsterdam: North Holland.

Nordhaus, W.D. 1973. The allocation of energy resources. *Brookings Papers on Economic Activity,* **3**, 529–76.

Nordhaus, W.D. 1991. To slow or not to slow: the economics of the greenhouse effect, *The Economic Journal,* **XXV**, 49–91.

Nordhaus, W.D. 1994. *Managing the Global Commons: the economics of climate change.* Cambridge, M.A., MIT Press.

Norton, G.A. 1984. *Resource Economics.* London: Edward Arnold.

O'Connor, R. and Henry, E.W. 1975. *Input–output Analysis and its Applications.* London: Charles Griffin & Co.

OECD. 1980. *Pollution Charges in Practice.* Paris: OECD.

OECD. 1989. *Economic Instruments for Environmental Protection.* Paris: OECD.

Page, T. 1977. *Conservation and Economic Efficiency: an approach to materials policy.* Baltimore: Johns Hopkins University Press.

Panayotou, T. 1993. *Empirical Tests and Policy Analysis of Environmental Degradation at Different Stages of Economic Development,* Working Paper WP238, Technology and Employment Programme, International Labor Office, Geneva.

Parker, J. and Hope, C. 1992. The state of the environment: a survey of reports from around the world. *Environment,* **34**, 19–21 and 39–44.

Patterson, W.C. 1976. *Nuclear Power.* Harmondsworth: Penguin.

Pearce, D.W. 1971. *Cost Benefit Analysis.* London: Macmillan.

Pearce, D.W. 1976. The limits to cost benefit analysis as a guide to environmental policy. *Kyklos,* **29**, 97–112.

Pearce, D.W. 1991. The role of carbon taxes in adjusting to global warming. *Economic Journal,* **101**, 938–48.

Pearce, D.W. and Walter, I. (eds). 1977. *Resource Conservation: social and economic dimensions of recycling.* London: Longman.

Pearce, D.W. and Edwards, L. and Beuret, G. 1979. *Decision Making for Energy Futures.* London: Macmillan.

Pearce, D.W. and Nash, C.A. 1981. *The Social Appraisal of Projects: a text in cost benefit analysis.* London: Macmillan.

Pearce, D.W. and Atkinson, G.D. 1993. Capital theory and the measurement of sustainable development: an indicator of 'weak' sustainability. *Ecological Economics,* **8**, 103–8.

Pearce, D. and Atkinson, G. 1995. Measuring sustainable development. In: D.W. Bromley (ed.) *The Handbook of Environmental Economics.* Oxford: Blackwell.

Pearce, D.W., Markandya, A. and Barbier, E.B. 1989. *Blueprint for a Green Economy.* London: Earthscan.

Pearce, F. 1987. *Acid Rain.* London: Penguin.

Peet, J. 1992 *Energy and the Ecological Economics of Sustainability.* Washington D.C.: Island Press.

Peirce, W.S. 1986. *Economics of the Energy Industries.* Belmont, California: Wadsworth.

Perman, R., Yue, M. and McGilvray, J. 1996. *Natural Resource and Environmental Economics.* Harlow: Longman.

Perrings, C. 1987. *Economy and Environment: a theoretical essay on the interdependence of economic and environmental systems.* Cambridge: Cambridge University Press.

Perrings, C. 1989. Environmental bonds and environmental research in innovative activities. *Ecological Economics,* **1**, 95–115.

Peskin, H. with Lutz, E. 1990. *A Survey of Resource and Environmental Accounting in Industrialised Countries.* Washington D.C.: World Bank, Environmental Working Paper 37.

Pigou, A.C. 1920. *The Economics of Welfare.* London: Macmillan.

Pindyck, R.S. 1978. *The Structure of World Energy Demand.* Cambridge, Massachusetts: MIT Press.

Plourde, C.G. 1972. A model of waste accumulation and disposal. *Canadian Journal of Economics,* **5**, 199–225.

Poindexter, J.C. and Jones, C.P. 1980. *Money Financial Markets and the Economy.* St Paul, Minnesota: West Publishing.

Porter, M 1990. *The Comparative Advantage of Nations.* New York: Free Press.

Porter, R.C. 1978. A social cost benefit analysis of mandatory deposits on beverage containers. *Journal of Environmental Economics and Management,* **5**, 351–75.

Porter, R.C. 1982. The new approach to wilderness preservation through cost benefit analysis. *Journal of Environmental Economics and Management,* **9**, 59–80.

Proops, J.L.R. and Atkinson, G. 1995. A practical sustainability criterion when there is international trade. In: Fauchaux, S., O'Connor, M. and van der Straeten, J. (eds), *Sustainable Development: analysis and public policy*. Amsterdam: Kluwer.

Proops, J., Faber, M. and Wagenhals, G. 1993. *Reducing CO_2 Emissions: a comparative input-output study for Germany and the UK*. Berlin: Springer-Verlag.

Read, P. 1993. *Responding to Global Warming: the technology economics and politics of sustainable energy*. London: Zed Books.

Rees, J. 1985. *Natural Resources: allocation economics and policy*. London: Methuen.

Repetto, R., Magrath, W., Wells, M., Beer, C. and Rossini, F. 1989. *Wasting Assets: natural resources in the national income accounts*. Washington D.C.: World Resources Institute.

Rettig, R.B. 1995. Management regimes in ocean fisheries. In: Bromley, D.W. (ed.) *The Handbook of Environmental Economics*. Oxford: Blackwell.

Randall, A. 1994. A difficulty with the travel cost method. *Land Economics*, **70**, 88–96.

Randall, A. and Farmer, M.C. 1995. Benefits costs and the safe minimum standard of conservation. In: Bromley, D.W. (ed.) *The Handbook of Environmental Economics*. Oxford: Blackwell.

Ricardo, D. 1817. *Principles of Political Economy and Taxation*. Reprint, 1926, London: Everyman.

Ridker, R.G. (ed). 1972. *Population Resources and the Environment*. Washington: US Government Printing Office.

Roberts, R.D. and Roberts, T.M. 1984. *Planning and Ecology*. London: Chapman & Hall.

Royal Commission on Environmental Pollution. 1984. *Tackling Pollution: experience and prospects*. Tenth Report, Command 9149, London.

Runge, C.F. 1995. Trade pollution and environmental protection. In: Bromley, D.W. (ed.) *The Handbook of Environmental Economics*. Oxford: Blackwell.

Sagoff, M. 1988. *The Economy of the Earth*. Cambridge: Cambridge University Press.

Samuelson, P. and Nordhaus, W. 1985. *Economics* (12th edn). New York: McGraw-Hill.

Sandbach, F. 1982. *Principles of Pollution Control*. London: Longman.

Sardar, M.H. 1994. *Environmental Impact Assessment*. Ottawa: Carleton University Press.

SCEP. 1970. *Man's Impact on The Global Environment: assessment and recommendations for action*. Report of the study of critical environmental problems. Cambridge, Massachusetts: MIT Press.

Schelling, T. 1986. Implications for welfare and policy: anticipating climate change. *Environment*, **26**, 6–35.

Scott, A. 1955. *Natural Resources: the economics of conservation*. Toronto: University of Toronto Press.

Shafik, N. and S. Bandyopadhyay 1992. Economic Growth and Environmental Quality: Time Series and Cross-Country Evidence, Background Paper for the World Development Report 1992, The World Bank, Washington D.C.

Simmons, I.G. 1984. *The Ecology of Natural Resources*. London: Edward Arnold.

Simon, J.L. 1981. *The Ultimate Resource*. Princeton: Princeton University Press.

Simon, J.L. and Wildavsky, A. 1993. *Assessing the Empirical Basis of the 'Biodiversity Crisis'*. Washington D.C.: Competitive Enterprise Foundation.

Slesser, M. 1978. *Energy in the Economy*. London: Macmillan.

Smith, A. 1776. *The Wealth of Nations*. (Cannan, E. ed., 1961). London: Methuen.

Smith, S. 1993. Distributional implications of a European carbon tax. In: Carraro, C. and Siniscalco, D. (eds), *The European Carbon Tax: an economic assessment*. Dordrecht: Kluwer.

Smith, V.K. and Kaoru, Y. 1990. Signals or noise? Explaining the variation in recreation benefit estimates. *American Journal of Agricultural Economics*, **May**, 419–33.

Smith, V.K. (ed). 1979. *Scarcity and Growth Reconsidered*. Baltimore: Johns Hopkins University Press.

Solow, R. 1974. Intergenerational equity and exhaustible resources. *Review of Economic Studies*, Symposium, 29–45.

Solow, R. 1986. On the intergenerational allocation of natural resources. *Scandinavian Journal of Economics*, **88**, 141–9.

Spash, C.L. and Hanley, N.D. 1995. Preferences information and biodiversity preservation. *Ecological Economics*, **12**, 191–208.

Spiegel, H.W. 1971. *The Growth of Economic Thought*. Durham, North Carolina: Duke University Press.

Stern, D.I., Common, M. and Barbier, E.B. 1996. Economic growth and environmental degradation: the environmental Kuznets curve and sustainable development. *World Development*, **24**, 1–10.

Stevens, T.H., Echeverria, J., Glass, R.J., Hager, T. and More, T.A. 1991. Measuring the existence value of wildlife; what do CVM estimates really show? *Land Economics*, **67**, 390–400.

Stobaugh, R. 1983. World Energy to the year 2000. In: Yergin, D. and Hillenbrand, M. (eds). *Global Insecurity: a strategy for energy and economic research*. Atlantic Institute for International Affairs, Penguin.

Stone, R. 1972. The evaluation of pollution: balancing gains and losses. *Minerva, X*, 412–25.

Sugden, R. and Williams, A. 1978. *The Principles of Cost Benefit Analysis*. Oxford: Oxford University Press.

Supplementary Benefits Commission 1979. *Supplementary Benefits Commission Annual Report 1978*. London: HMSO.

Symons, E.J., Proops, J. and Gay, P.W. 1991. Carbon taxes consumer demand and carbon dioxide emissions: a simulation analysis for the UK. *Fiscal Studies*, **15**, 19–43.

Thirring, H. 1958. *Energy for Man*. Bloomington: Greenwood.

Thomas, R.L. 1993. *Introductory Econometrics: theory and applications* (2nd edn). London: Longman.

Tietenberg, T.H. 1980. Transferable discharge permits and the control of stationary source air pollution: a survey and synthesis. *Land Economics*, **56**, 391–415.

Tietenberg, T.H. 1992. *Environmental and Natural Resource Economics* (3rd edn). New York: Harper Collins.

Tietenberg, T.H. 1995. Transferable discharge permits and global warming. In: Bromley, D.W. (ed.) *The Handbook of Environmental Economics*. Oxford: Blackwell.

Tolley, G.S., Graves, P.E. and Cohen, A.S. (eds). 1982. *Environmental Policy: air quality*. Cambridge, Massachusetts: Ballinger.

Toman, M.A., Pezzey, J. and Krautkraemer, J. 1995. Neoclassical economic growth theory and 'sustainability'. In: D.W. Bromley (ed.) *The Handbook of Environmental Economics*. Oxford: Blackwell.

Townsend, P. 1979. *Poverty in the United Kingdom: a survey of household resources and standards of living*. Harmondsworth: Penguin.

United Nations Development Programme. 1995. *Human Development Report 1995*. New York: Oxford University Press.

Usher, D. 1980. *The Measurement of Economic Growth*. Oxford: Basil Blackwell.

van den Bergh, J.C.J.M. and van der Straaten, J. (eds) 1994. *Concepts, Methods and Policy for Sustainable Development: critique and new approaches*. Washington D.C.: Island Press.

Victor, P. 1972. *Pollution: economy and environment*. Toronto: Toronto University Press.

Vitousek, P.M., Ehrlich, P.R., Ehrlich, A.H. and Matson, P.A. 1986. Human appropriation of the products of photosynthesis. *Bioscience*, **36**, 368–73.

Vogel, J.H. 1994. *Genes for Sale: privatization as a conservation policy*. New York: Oxford University Press.

Watt, K.E.F. 1973. *Principles of Environmental Science*. New York: McGraw-Hill.

Watt, K.E.F. 1982. *Understanding the Environment*. Boston: Allyn & Bacon.

Webb, M.G. and Ricketts, M.J. 1980. *The Economics of Energy*. London: Macmillan.

Weintraub, E.R. 1975. *Conflict and Cooperation in Economics*. London: Macmillan.

Weitzman, M.L. 1976. On the welfare significance of national product in a dynamic economy. *Quarterly Journal of Economics,* **90**, 156–62.

Weyman-Jones, T. 1986. *The Economics of Energy Policy*. Aldershot: Gower.

Whalley, J. and Wigle, R. 1991. The international incidence of carbon taxes. In: Dornbusch, R. and Poterba, J. (eds) *Economic Policy Responses to Global Warming*. Cambridge, Mass.: MIT Press.

Willrich, M. 1975. *Energy and World Politics*. New York: The Free Press.

Wilson, R. and Jones, W. 1974. *Energy Ecology and the Environment*. New York: Academic Press.

Winter, I.A. 1992. The trade and welfare effects of greenhouse gas abatement: a survey of empirical estimates, in Anderson, K. and Blackhurst, R. (eds) *The Greening of World Trade Issues*. New York: Harvester Wheatsheaf.

Wonnacott, P. and Wonnacott, R. 1979. *Economics*. New York: McGraw-Hill.

World Commission on Environment and Development 1987. *Our Common Future*. Oxford: Oxford University Press.

WRI 1994. *World Resources 1994–5: A Report by the World Resources Institute*. New York: Oxford University Press.

Young, M.D. 1990. Natural resource accounting. In: Common, M.S. and Dovers, S. (eds.) *Moving Toward Global Sustainability: policies and implications for Australia*. Canberra: Centre for Continuing Education, Australian National University.

Young, M.D. 1992. *Sustainable Investment and Natural Resource Use: equity environmental integrity and economic efficiency*. Paris: United Nations Scientific and Cultural Organisation.

Index